MICROECONOMICS
A SYNTHESIS OF MODERN AND NEOCLASSICAL THEORY

MICROECONOMICS
A SYNTHESIS OF MODERN AND NEOCLASSICAL THEORY

R. ROBERT RUSSELL
University of California, San Diego

MAURICE WILKINSON
Columbia University

JOHN WILEY & SONS

New York • Chichester • Brisbane • Toronto • Singapore

Library of Congress Cataloging in Publication Data

Russell, R Robert.
Microeconomic theory.

Includes bibliographies.
1. Microeconomics. I. Wilkinson, Maurice,
joint author. II. Title.
HB171.5.R85 330.1 78-17175
ISBN 0-471-94652-4

Printed in the United States of America

10

TO JUDY AND INGE

ABOUT THE AUTHORS

R. Robert Russell is a Professor of Economics at the University of California, San Diego. He has taught graduate and undergraduate courses in microeconomic and macroeconomic theory, mathematical economics, and growth theory.

Professor Russell earned his Ph.D. in economics from Harvard University in 1965. He is a coauthor of an advanced theoretical treatise, *Duality, Separability, and Functional Structure*: *Theory and Economic Applications*, published in 1978. He has also published extensively in many leading economic journals, including *Econometrica, The Journal of Economic Theory, The Review of Economic Studies, The American Economic Review, The International Economic Review, The Journal of Econometrics*, and *The Review of Economics and Statistics*.

Dr. Russell spent one year on the professional staff of the president's Council of Economic Advisors and he has served as a consultant to several government agencies (including the U.S. Departments of Labor; Health, Education, and Welfare; and Housing and Urban Development) and to both profit and nonprofit organizations. He is currently on a one-year leave from the University of California, serving as deputy director of the president's Council on Wage and Price Stability.

Maurice Wilkinson is a professor at the Graduate School of Business, Columbia University. Dr. Wilkinson has taught undergraduate and graduate courses in microeconomic and macroeconomic theory, growth theory, and econometrics.

Professor Wilkinson earned his Ph.D. in economics from Harvard University in 1965. His articles have appeared in *Econometrica, The International Economic Review, The American Economic Review, The Review of Economics and Statistics, The Journal of the American Statistical Association*, and *Management Science*. He has received research grants from the National Science Foundation, Ford Foundation, and Rockefeller Foundation. He is the editor for the North Holland series in *Dynamic Economics*: *Theory and Applications* and an associate editor for the *Journal of Economic Dynamics and Control*.

Professor Wilkinson has consulted with the Bureau of Labor Statistics, the National Oceanographic and Atmospheric Administration, the United States Department of Agriculture, and a number of profit and nonprofit organizations.

PREFACE

As the title of this book suggests, current microeconomic analysis can be dichotomized into two approaches: the neoclassical approach and the modern approach. The former approach has its intellectual roots in the late nineteenth-century writings of the "marginalist" school of economists led by Jevons, Menger, Walras, von Thünen, and Gossen, and it reached maturity in the treatises of Hicks [1939] and Samuelson [1947a]. The modern approach is so called because it was pioneered as recently as the early 1950s by Arrow and Debreu. Since this time, many economists have made substantial contributions to this body of theory (see the suggested readings following each part of this book).

The two approaches to microeconomic theory coexist today. They are distinguished primarily by style (the modern approach tends to be more axiomatic and less discursive), the mathematical tools employed (the neoclassical approach exploits the calculus whereas the modern approach makes more use of set-theoretical and topological mathematical tools), and the fundamental assumptions (the neoclassical theory invokes sufficient smoothness assumptions to facilitate use of the calculus whereas the modern approach typically requires weaker assumptions, primarily convexity).

The dichotomization of microeconomic theory is reflected in the array of microeconomic textbooks; most adopt the neoclassical approach, perhaps with a token reference to modern microeconomic theory. A few books employ the modern approach. The important fact about the extant stock of microeconomic textbooks, however, is that virtually all of them adopt one of these two approaches to the virtual exclusion of the other. It is as if students (or, more accurately, their teachers) must decide whether they wish to join the ranks of neoclassical or of modern economists. Less dramatically, introducing students exclusively to one of these approaches to microeconomic theory can leave them with a distorted view of the subject.

Both approaches are commonly employed in economic analysis. Because of the convenience of the calculus for solving optimization problems, most studies in applied microeconomics still employ the neoclassical approach. This is especially true of econometric studies that employ specific functional forms in order to formulate and test economic hypotheses. On the other hand, many important theoretical problems (such as the existence and optimality of equilibrium) yield more readily to the techniques of the modern approach. Indeed, most theoretical results in economics are more readily (and elegantly) derived by means of the Arrow–Debreu approach. Furthermore, the purpose and the economic interpretation of assumptions are frequently better appreciated in modern microeconomic theory (for example, constraints on consumer preferences are more easily understood than differentiability conditions on utility functions). In addition, entire areas of economic analysis (such as the theory of choice and the theory of social choice in particular) rely extensively on the concepts and results of the Arrow–Debreu approach to microeconomic theory. Finally, a significant potential exists for applying modern economic theory to economic problems with the use of nonparametric statistical techniques.

The foregoing remarks provide the motivation for the following themes of this book: (1) There are pedagogically sound reasons for introducing students to both the modern and the neoclassical approaches to microeconomic theory. (2) Although the development of modern microeconomic theory has relied on the use of sophisticated mathematical tools, the flavor and essence of this theory can be conveyed to students with a minimal background in mathematics. (3) The teaching of modern and neoclassical microeconomic theory are not mutually exclusive activities; indeed, it is fruitful to view the neoclassical theory as a special case of the modern theory in which the assumptions are strengthened to guarantee smoothness (differentiability) of mathematical functions and interior solutions to constrained optimization problems. Thus, this book attempts to integrate the two approaches to microeconomic theory.

A concomitant of the incorporation of the modern approach is the inclusion of topics that are not typically treated in microeconomic textbooks. For example, chapter 2 contains an elementary introduction to preference theory. Chapter 18 contains a fairly thorough discussion of economic externalities and Pareto optimality, including a comparison of the proposed solutions to the externality problem (tax-transfer schemes and artificial markets) and a discussion of fundamental nonconvexities in externalities. Also treated in chapter 18 is the theory of public commodities. Chapter 19 introduces the student to the theory of social choice, including Arrow's impossibility theorem and the subsequent literature on collective rationality.

Of course, it would be imprudent, if not infeasible, to attempt to treat every important microeconomic topic in a textbook. We have therefore been forced to make (sometimes painful) decisions to exclude some topics from the text. We apologize to those whose favorite topic is not treated. We have, however, made an attempt to draw the reader's attention to omitted topics. The historical notes and suggested reading sections provide brief descriptions of these topics and direct the reader to the appropriate literature. In addition, some topics that are not explicitly discussed in the text are introduced through the exercises that follow each chapter (for example, consumer surplus is introduced in exercise 4.3). An instructor who wishes to emphasize such topics can do so by elaborating on the appropriate exercises.

We have grappled at length with the problem of balancing rigor on the one hand and simplicity and clarity on the other. The compromise that we have adopted is as follows. We have attempted to be very precise and consistent about definitions and notations. In addition, we have attempted to be careful about explicitly identifying the assumptions that are required for our results to hold. On the other hand, we have provided proofs of propositions only if the proof is sufficiently short, comprehensible to a student with little mathematical background (one year of calculus), and illuminating. We do, however, attempt to convey the intuition underlying each result; in particular, we attempt to explain why each assumption is necessary (or, in the case of sufficiency conditions, conditionally nonexcludable) for a result to hold. In addition, the suggested readings at the end of each part direct the reader to the literature where formal proofs can be found. Our approach thus reflects our view that, while a theorem is thoroughly understood only when the proof is comprehended, a great deal about a result can be learned by intuitive discussion, graphical illustrations, and examination of special cases and counter examples.

We have also made every effort to integrate the mathematical and graphical approaches to the exposition of microeconomic theory. In particular, each topic is typically first treated mathematically, then verbally (providing the intuition for the mathematical result), and then graphically (illustrating the result for special two-variable cases).

With the exception of the optional sections 5.3, 5.4, and 7.5 dealing with comparative-static analysis of the consumer and producer (which can be skipped without loss of continuity), the mathematics employed is limited to elementary differential calculus. The optional sections noted above require elementary linear algebra and the mathematical results on constrained optimization. Many of the mathematical concepts employed are explained when they are first introduced. We have also provided explicit references in which proofs of all mathematical results can be found. These references are provided at those points where the results are used. We have thus resisted the temptation of many economics textbook writers to teach mathematics.

It is our opinion that microeconomic theory should be learned with pencil in hand. We have therefore provided a number of exercises at the end of each chapter. Some of these exercises are essentially examples of abstract concepts treated in the text. Others ask the student to provide simple proofs of results that are not proved in the text. Some are essentially applications of the theory; many of these test the students' ingenuity in extending the theoretical concepts or in applying them to a new type of problem.

The book is appropriate for use in an undergraduate microeconomic theory course with a calculus prerequisite or a first-year graduate course in microeconomic theory. To facilitate the use of the book, in the table of contents we have designated with asterisks those chapters or sections that contain mathematically advanced or conceptually difficult material that can be skipped without loss of continuity. Chapter 1 is a brief introduction to economic methodology. As this subject is best appreciated after some familiarity with economic theory, Chapter 1 should be skimmed at first and then reread following the reading of Parts 1 and/or 2 (the theory of the consumer and producer). A basic *one-semester undergraduate course* could be constituted from the following chapters and sections:

Chapter 1
Sections 2.1–2.3
Sections 3.1–3.5
Sections 4.1–4.2, 4.4–4.5
Sections 6.1–6.3
Sections 7.1–7.4
Chapter 8
Chapter 9

Chapter 11
Sections 13.1–13.5
Sections 15.1–15.3
Sections 17.1–17.2

A *two-semester undergraduate course* could add the following to the above list:

Section 6.4
Chapter 10
Chapter 12
Sections 13.6–13.8
Chapter 14
Section 15.4
Sections 16.1–16.4
Sections 17.3, 17.5
Chapter 18
Sections 19.1–19.3
Chapter 20

A first-year graduate course would include the remaining sections employing more advanced mathematics, conceptually difficult material, and advanced topics. The suggested-reading sections should also be helpful in providing the additional journal articles typically included in a graduate course.

We have received valuable comments and advice from a large number of our colleagues and students and several anonymous reviewers. We are especially grateful to Enrique Arzac, Chuck Blackorby, Vince Crawford, Jean Pierre Danthine, David Donaldson, Rick Emmerson, Walter Heller, Judy Mann, Vikram Pandit, Andy Postlewaite, Dick Ruppert, Ross Starr, and Brett Trueman. Finally, generous logistical support was provided by the Department of Economics, University of California, San Diego, and the Graduate School of Business, Columbia University.

R. Robert Russell
Maurice Wilkinson

CONTENTS

1 INTRODUCTION TO ECONOMIC SCIENCE

1.1 Economics and Economic Theory 1
1.2 The Economic Environment 6
1.3 Suggestions for Further Reading 8

PART I THEORY OF THE CONSUMER

2 PREFERENCE THEORY

2.1 Introduction 11
2.2 The Consumption Space and the Preference Relation 12
2.3 Budget Set and Consumer Choice 15
*2.4 The Existence of an Optimal Consumption Bundle 18
Exercises 24

3 UTILITY THEORY

3.1 Introduction 26
3.2 The Utility Function 26
3.3 Nonsatiation and Convexity 29
3.4 The Marginal Rate of Substitution 32
3.5 Utility Maximization 36
*3.6 The Measurability of Utility: An Historical Digression 45
Exercises 49

4 DEMAND THEORY

4.1 Introduction 51
4.2 Demand Functions 52
*4.3 The Composite Commodity Theorem 55
4.4 The Effect of a Change in Income Upon Demand: Graphical Analysis 59
4.5 The Effect of a Change in Price Upon Demand: Graphical Analysis 62
Exercises 70

*5 ADVANCED DEMAND THEORY

5.1 Introduction 73
5.2 Duality and Consumer Theory 73
5.3 Mathematical Analysis of the Effect of Income and Price Changes Upon Demand 86
5.4 Substitutes and Complements 92
Exercises 95

6 TOPICS IN DEMAND THEORY
6.1 Introduction 96
6.2 Elasticities of Demand 96
6.3 Labor Supply 101
6.4 The Theory of Revealed Preference 108
Exercises 114

PART I HISTORICAL NOTES AND SUGGESTED READING 117

PART II THE THEORY OF THE PRODUCER

7 THE THEORY OF PRODUCTION
7.1 Introduction 123
7.2 The Technology Set and Profit Maximization 124
7.3 Technological Efficiency and The Net Production Function 129
7.4 Profit Maximization Subject to the Net-Production-Function Constraint 131
*7.5 Mathematical Analysis of The Effect of Price Changes Upon Net Supply 134
Exercises 138

8 THE PRODUCTION FUNCTION, DERIVED DEMAND, AND SUPPLY
8.1 Introduction 140
8.2 The Production Function 140
8.3 Total-, Average-, and Marginal-Product Curves 145
8.4 Profit Maximization 151
8.5 Graphical Illustration of Profit Maximization 153
Exercises 156

9 THE THEORY OF COST
9.1 Introduction 159
9.2 Constrained Outlay Minimization and The Cost Function 159
9.3 Graphical Derivation of the Expansion Path, Returns to Outlay, and The Cost Function 162
9.4 Homogeneous Production Functions and Returns to Scale 167
9.5 Profit Maximization and the Cost Function 169
9.6 The Cost Function and Profit Maximization With Fixed Inputs 172
Exercises 180

***10** LINEAR PRODUCTION TECHNOLOGIES, ACTIVITY ANALYSIS, AND LINEAR PROGRAMMING
10.1 Introduction 182

10.2 Activity Analysis 183
10.3 Linear Production Processes With One Output 186
10.4 Linear Programming 193
10.5 Duality and Linear Programming 196
10.6 An Example of a Linear Programming Problem 203
Exercises 208

PART II HISTORICAL NOTES AND SUGGESTED READING 213

PART III THE THEORY OF MARKET STRUCTURES

11 EQUILIBRIUM OF PERFECTLY COMPETITIVE MARKETS

11.1 Introduction 217
11.2 The Assumptions of Perfect Competition 217
11.3 Short-Run Market Equilibrium 219
11.4 Long-Run Market Equilibrium 225
11.5 Summary and Conclusion 229
Exercises 230

12 COMPARATIVE STATICS AND THE STABILITY OF EQUILIBRIUM

12.1 Introduction 231
12.2 The Method of Comparative Statics 232
12.3 Dynamics and The Stability of Equilibrium 234
12.4 A Price-Adjustment Model 237
12.5 A Quantity-Adjustment Model 242
12.6 The Cobweb Model 245
Exercises 249

13 THE THEORIES OF MONOPOLY AND MONOPOLISTIC COMPETITION

13.1 Introduction 251
13.2 The Assumptions of Classical Monopoly Theory 253
13.3 Monopoly Demand and Revenue Functions 254
13.4 Monopoly Equilibrium 256
13.5 Input Demand of The Monopolist 260
13.6 Monopsony 262
13.7 Monopoly Regulation 265
13.8 The Price-Discriminating Monopoly 268
13.9 The Theory of Monopolistic Competition 272
13.10 Concluding Remarks 276
Exercises 276

14 GAME THEORY AND MODELS OF OLIGOPOLISTIC INTERDEPENDENCE

14.1 Introduction 279
14.2 The Cournot Duopoly Problem 280
14.3 Quantity and Price Leadership and Collusion 283
14.4 Game Theory 291
14.5 Conclusion 299
Exercises 299

Part III HISTORICAL NOTES AND SUGGESTED READING 302

PART IV THE THEORY OF GENERAL EQUILIBRIUM AND ECONOMIC WELFARE

15 GENERAL COMPETITIVE EQUILIBRIUM IN AN EXCHANGE ECONOMY

15.1 Introduction 305
15.2 Bilateral Exchange 306
15.3 Bilateral Exchange: A Graphical Exposition 310
15.4 General Exchange Equilibrium 317
Exercises 322

16 GENERAL COMPETITIVE EQUILIBRIUM IN A PRODUCTION ECONOMY

16.1 Introduction 323
16.2 General Equilibrium for a Production and Exchange Economy 324
16.3 Graphical Illustration of Competitive Equilibrium With One Consumer, One Producer, and Two Commodities 329
16.4 Graphical Illustration of Competitive Equilibrium With Two Consumers, Two Producers, Two Inputs, and Two Outputs 333
*16.5 Competitive Equilibrium and The Core 342
*16.6 Concluding Remarks: Existence, Uniqueness, and Stability 347
Exercises 349

17 PARETO OPTIMALITY AND COMPETITIVE EQUILIBRIUM

17.1 Introduction 350
17.2 Pareto Optimality and Competitive Equilibrium in an Exchange Economy 352

17.3 Pareto Optimality and Competitive Equilibrium in a Production Economy 358
*17.4 The Fundamental Optimality Principles Reexamined 362
17.5 Concluding Remarks 371
Exercises 372

18 THE THEORY OF ECONOMIC EXTERNALITIES AND PUBLIC COMMODITIES
18.1 Introduction 373
18.2 Economic Externalities 375
18.3 The Theory of Public Commodities 387
18.4 Decentralized Planning and Incentive Compatibility 395
18.5 Uncertainty and The Pareto Optimality of Competitive Equilibrium 397
Exercises 398

19 THE THEORY OF SOCIAL CHOICE
19.1 Introduction 400
19.2 Social Orderings and Social Choice 402
19.3 The Impossibility Theorem 404
*19.4 Proof of the Impossibility Theorem 411
*19.5 Collective Rationality 413
19.6 Conclusions 419
Exercises 420

20 INTERPERSONAL COMPARABILITY AND SOCIAL OPTIMALITY
20.1 Introduction 421
20.2 Measurability and Comparability 422
20.3 Social Orderings and Quasiorderings 424
20.4 Social Optimality 432
20.5 Concluding Remarks 437
Exercises 439

PART IV HISTORICAL NOTES AND SUGGESTED READING 440

REFERENCES 443

INDEX 455

CHAPTER 1
INTRODUCTION TO ECONOMIC SCIENCE

1.1 ECONOMICS AND ECONOMIC THEORY

Economics and Scarcity

Most of the problems with which economics is concerned can be traced to the fact that a society's resources—land, labor, capital, etc.—are limited, or scarce, relative to the uses to which these resources can be put. Given this fundamental situation of scarcity, the allocation of the available resources to the multitude of potential uses becomes the central problem of economics. Indeed, a long-standing definition of economics is "the study of the allocation of scarce resources."

The problem of allocating scarce resources to alternative uses confronts us with the necessity of choice. Given the resources available to an economic system or society, a choice must be made among the many alternative combinations of commodities that can be produced. Much of economics is concerned with how this choice is made by the interaction of the decision-making units—consumers, producers, and public agencies—in an economic system.

A large part of economics is confined to analyzing and describing the ways in which an economic system combines the decisions of consumers, producers, and public agencies to arrive at particular allocations of commodities. No attempt is made to evaluate or compare one such allocation with another. This approach is referred to as *positive* economics. Another branch of economics (which is closely related to the disciplines of political science and philosophy) goes beyond this type of analysis and evaluates the criteria by which alternative allocations are made. This branch of economics is called *normative economics* or *welfare economics*. It compares the implications of alternative rules, or methods, of making choices among the alternative uses of the scarce resources.

In summary, the problems with which economics is concerned and the methods by which these problems are analyzed are largely based upon the realization that society must make a choice in allocating scarce resources among alternative uses. The processes by which economic systems or societies arrive at the choices and the need to compare one choice or allocation with another impart to the field of economics its particular focus.

Microeconomics vs. Macroeconomics

One aspect of the allocation problem is the rate at which scarce resources are employed and thus the level of output that can be produced. *Macroeconomics* is concerned with how the actions of consumers, producers, and public agencies determine the rate of employment (and unemployment) of labor and capital and the total output of an economic system. In order to deal with this difficult problem, macroeconomics utilizes highly aggregated concepts such as total or aggregate consumption, investment, output, etc.

In contrast, *microeconomics*—the subject matter of this book—deals with individual consumers, producers, etc., and is concerned with the allocation of resources among these economic agents. Since there are many possible allocations, each involving a different composition of commodities and a different distribution of the commodities among consumers, the choice of a particular allocation is a fundamental social problem. Indeed, the questions with which microeconomics deals are basic to an understanding of macroeconomics. Much of the latter utilizes the results of microeconomic analysis. An understanding of such problems as unemployment and inflation requires knowledge of the manner in which individual economic units respond to varying economic conditions.

Economic Theory

There are a number of approaches that could be employed in studying and attempting to solve the problems with which economics is concerned. We might begin by gathering data or observations on the economic decisions of consumers, producers, and public agencies and seek patterns or regularities in these data. For example, by collecting budget data for consumers, we might establish patterns in the proportions of consumer income that are allocated to various types of commodities. If repeated observation indicates that certain regular proportions of a consumer's budget are spent upon rent, clothing, or food, we could utilize this empirical relationship to predict consumer demand for commodities. The research strategy of inferring general relationships from individual observations, referred to as the *inductive* approach, is typical of many of the social and physical sciences.

An alternative approach to prediction is to develop a body of *theory* which purports to explain behavior of the relevant subjects. The theory can be used to predict individual phenomena. This research strategy, referred to as the *deductive* approach, is perhaps more typical of physical than of social sciences, but is nevertheless commonly employed in economic research.

A theory can be defined as *a body of deductive thought erected on a few premises that seem to be well-chosen first approximations of a complicated reality*. *Economic theory* is the core of economic science and is the foundation for the study of the allocation of scarce resources and of the numerous problems that are derived from this central concern of economics. Economic theory can be defined as *deriving the implications of purposive behavior of consumers, producers, and other economic agents from the interaction of the tastes and the constraints facing them*. This definition recognizes three fundamental characteristics of economic theory. First, economic agents are assumed to be seeking to achieve some goal that depends upon tastes or preferences. Second, the goal is pursued in a purposive or consistent manner. Finally, economic agents are not free to make *any* choice in the pursuit of their goals—the choices are subject to constraints. This relates to the fundamental fact of scarcity, to which we earlier referred. For example, consumers are viewed as seeking a particular combination of commodities in accordance with their tastes or preferences. The choice of goods and services available to consumers is limited by the fact that they must purchase them in the marketplace and they do not have unlimited money income. In the same manner, public agencies are viewed as seeking highways, school systems, defensive systems, etc., with limited tax revenues.

The Role of Economic Theory

The goal of positive economics is the derivation, testing, and implementation of predictions, or hypotheses, about economic behavior. Thus, the goal of positive economic theory is the derivation of predictions, or hypotheses, that are, at least in principle, testable. Provided that the positive economic theory provides a "good enough" explanation of economic phenomena (i.e., the theory is "confirmed" by the empirical test), the predictions are usable by public and private decision makers in the formation of economic policy. Consumer theory is concerned with understanding the effects that changes in consumers' incomes and prices of commodities have upon demands for these commodities. Such knowledge concerning the factors determining consumer demand can be used by producers to forecast sales and thus plan production, the purchase of new capital goods, the hiring of labor, etc. In the same way, the theory of the producer may enable public agencies to better understand the effects that taxation and other policies toward business have upon the decisions of producers. Our increased understanding of the impact of public policies toward business may be utilized to improve economic policy.

A secondary, but nonetheless important, function of economic theory in positive economics is to economize on the information required to explain and predict economic phenomena. In contrast to the inductive approach to the study of social and economic problems, economic theory attempts to deduce or derive conclusions from a few well-chosen premises or postulates. The choice of these premises or postulates requires far less information concerning actual economic phenomena than does the determination of empirical generalizations or laws. Furthermore, the conclusions or predictions of economic theory help to focus our attention on the fundamental factors explaining the economic phenomena in question. In this manner, the information required to make accurate predictions or forecasts concerning economic problems is minimized.

Economic theory plays an equally important role in normative economic analysis. Fundamentally, the goal of normative economics is to compare the properties and implications of alternative social decision rules. A property that is normally desired in social decision rules is that they be responsive to individual preferences. Therefore, the theory of individual preferences plays an important role in normative economics. Moreover, social decision rules must take into account the behavior of producers and the constraints imposed by resource scarcity. Consequently, the theory of microeconomic behavior plays an important role in the formulation of normative economic policies.

The Structure of Economic Theory: Abstraction and Simplification

Economic theory involves generalizing or *abstracting* from experience and observations on economic phenomena. In dealing with a particular problem, economic theory seeks to simplify the analysis by abstracting from much of the complex nature of reality. There are a number of reasons for this procedure. First, economic phenomena are far too complex to be described in detail. Moreover, many of the details concerning these phenomena are of minor importance in explaining the question at hand. Economic theory seeks to embody in the analysis only the most fundamental factors influencing the economic agents involved. Second, the data—the observations on economic activity with which economists must work—are incomplete and measured with error. By abstracting and simplifying, we economize on the scarce information available. The cost of gathering data is not insignificant.

The first step in the construction of a theory is to select the postulates (sometimes termed premises or assumptions) from which the conclusions or predictions of the theory are derived. The postulates are basic statements about the economic phenomena under analysis that are not themselves conclusions from earlier parts of the reasoning in the same piece of analysis. It is these postulates that embody the generalization or abstraction from the phenomena under investigation.

Two types of postulates are usually distinguished. Psychological postulates contain statements about the motivations or preferences of the economic decision makers. Thus, consumers are assumed to be able to rank consistently the choices available to them. Producers are assumed to be motivated by the objective of profit maximization. Such psychological postulates as these abstract from a good deal of the details concerning the motivation or goals of consumers and producers. Nevertheless the mark of a good theory is that the postulates are sufficiently good approximations of the complicated reality to enable the theory to explain and predict adequately the decisions of the consumers and producers.

Technological postulates are statements concerning the institutional and physical setting in which economic actors make decisions. For example, consumers' expenditures are assumed to be constrained by their income or by their wealth, and quantities produced are assumed to be constrained by the state of technology.

Once the postulates have been formalized, the appropriate body of logic is applied to derive conclusions or predictions. Should the logic reveal a contradiction among the postulates, or show that the postulates are inadequate for unambiguous conclusions or predictions, one or more of the postulates must be changed.

Maximum Principles and Economic Theory

The conclusions or predictions of economic theory are most often derived with a body of logic known as the maximum principles of mathematics. This follows from the central concern of economics with the optimal allocation of scarce resources, together with the deductive approach of economic theory.

Much of economic theory can be formulated as a constrained maximization problem:

$$\begin{aligned} \underset{x_1, \ldots, x_n}{\text{Maximize}} \quad & F(x_1, \ldots, x_n) \\ \text{subject to} \quad & G^1(x_1, \ldots, x_n) = 0, \\ & G^2(x_1, \ldots, x_n) = 0, \\ & \vdots \qquad\quad \vdots \\ & G^m(x_1, \ldots, x_n) = 0, \end{aligned}$$

where $x_1, \ldots, x_n$ are the variables that the decision maker controls, $F(x_1, \ldots, x_n)$ is the objective or goal of the decision maker and the last m equalities represent the system of constraints facing the decision maker. The objective function F might represent the preferences of the consumer or the profits of a producer. The system of constraint functions, $G^1, \ldots, G^m$, could represent the budget constraint of a consumer or the production technology and input prices facing a producer. The properties or characteristics of these functions are specified by the postulates of economic theory. For example, if we postulate that the consumer always prefers more of each commodity, the first partial derivatives of the objective function are positive if F is the preference index and $x_1, \ldots, x_n$ are the quantities consumed of n commodities.

The maximizing model described above might be solved by one of the maximum principles of mathematics. Some of the principles most commonly employed in economic theory are discussed in subsequent chapters.

Evaluation and Testing of Economic Theory

One method of evaluating or testing economic theory is to derive empirically refutable conclusions and confront them with evidence from the real world. The accuracy of the forecasts or predictions is thus a measure of the value of the theory in explaining economic phenomena. An extreme interpretation of this position is that the validity of economic theory is only to be tested by the accuracy of its conclusions and not by the descriptive "realism" of its assumptions. That is, we should never concern ourselves with the realism of the postulates of economic theory but only with the accuracy of the predictions generated by these assumptions. The test of the predictions of the theory constitutes an indirect evaluation of the postulates since all conclusions of theory are derived from the postulates.

Since economics is a social rather than a laboratory science, however, the opportunities to test the predictions of economic theory are limited by the experiments performed by history. It is not possible in most cases to repeat an experiment and thus generate sufficient new observations to constitute a new test of the predictions. Thus it has been argued that we should not only seek to test the predictions of theory but also to evaluate the plausibility of the postulates. Furthermore, since the conclusions derived from any model are only a subset of all possible conclusions that could be derived, testing of the predictions of a model is never a complete test of the postulates. Both of these arguments suggest that in view of the difficulty of testing the implications of economic theory we should be concerned with the "realism" of the postulates; i.e., whether in fact the postulates are "well-chosen first approximations of a complicated reality." Of course, many postulates utilized in economic theory, particularly psychological postulates, are very difficult to test directly (e.g., profit maximization by producers).

1.2 THE ECONOMIC ENVIRONMENT

As the preceding discussion of economic science might suggest, the salient components of an economic theory are the fundamental economic decision makers (consumers and producers) and the objects of their consumption and production activities (commodities). A less obvious—but equally important—component is the set of commodity prices. Although the real-world counterparts of these components of an abstract theory are familiar to the reader, some discussion of them as theoretical concepts is helpful at the outset. Before discussing them, however, we first characterize briefly another facet of the economic environment that is implicit in the theoretical development that follows, namely the nature of the time period.

The Time Period

The state of a real-world economy is the outcome of a long history of decisions and events. Economic decision makers repeatedly revise their decisions, reacting to changes in variables which they do not control. A "realistic" theory of economic behavior would attempt to model the dynamics of sequential decision making. It is, however, prudent and efficient to begin the study of economic theory by examining decision making at an instant in time. Hence, most of the theory developed in this book is static. In static (as opposed to dynamic) theories, time does not enter into the analysis in any essential way.[1] Most important economic problems can be adequately examined in the context of a static model.

The fact that we examine the problem of scarce-resource allocation at a given instant in time does not mean that the decisions which we analyze are only about the present. The decision variables of the consumer or the producer may involve the consumption or production of future goods; the decision is nevertheless a static one because we only consider a once-and-for-all decision on the part of the consumer or producer. We do not examine a sequence of decisions or the way in which these decisions get revised over time.[2]

We assume that time is divided into periods of elementary intervals of equal lengths. These intervals must be short enough for all instants of an

[1] The first part of chapter 12 contains a discussion of the nature of dynamic and static reasoning.

[2] There is a large literature on intertemporal, or dynamic, decision making—most of it hard going. The interested reader is referred to the suggested-reading sections of parts I, II, and IV.

interval to be indistinguishable from the point of view of the analysis. That is, the periods are short enough so that the economic decision maker does not, for example, distinguish the first half of the period from the second half. The first of these periods will be called the present and all others will be called the future. Thus, at an instant of time the consumer or producer is assumed to be making a choice about the consumption or production of goods in every time period.[3]

Commodities and Prices

The basic object of consumption or production is called a commodity. A commodity is characterized, or identified, by three properties: (a) its physical characteristics, (b) the date at which it is available, and (c) the location at which it is available.

For example, following the excellent example of Debreu [1959], consider the class of commodities called wheat. There are actually many different commodities called "wheat," each differentiated from the other by its physical properties and the dates and locations of delivery. The physical properties of wheat are carefully classified by such categorizations as "number 2 red winter wheat." Moreover, the same type of wheat available at two different points in time is considered to be two different commodities. Similarly, one physical type of wheat available at the same point of time is classified as different commodities depending upon whether it is available in, say, Chicago or Minneapolis.

Associated with each commodity is a price, expressed in dollars per unit of that commodity. The price is the amount which has to be paid now for the (possibly future) availability of one unit of that commodity at a particular location.

It is sometimes convenient to dichotomize commodities into two types: goods and services. Goods are tangible commodities which are measured in natural physical units. Services, on the other hand, are less tangible and are usually measured in time units. The most obvious example is labor services, but durable goods such as lawn mowers and automobiles also provide a flow of services.

Producers and Consumers

The producer is defined abstractly as a decision-making entity which, through the process of production, converts bundles of inputs into bundles of outputs. The commodities produced by a producer might be final goods and services—for consumption by consumers—or intermediate commodities to be used as inputs by other producers.[4] In addition to consuming the commodities produced by producers, the consumer might supply "primary" inputs—principally labor—to producers.

The producer or consumer might be a collection of individuals—a multiple-person household or a committee of production managers—but we treat these

[3] Section 18.5 introduces the problem of uncertainty concerning the conditions under which commodities will be delivered in the future.

[4] "Capital goods" are also classified as "final goods."

agents as though they were single individuals. The decision making of a group of individuals—a family, a corporate board, etc.—may be exceedingly more complex than is the decision-making process of a single, independent individual. We therefore abstract from these complications in the analysis that follows. The interested reader is referred, however, to the analysis of group decision making in chapter 19 (which is as applicable to a multiperson household as it is to an entire society).

1.3 HISTORICAL NOTES AND SUGGESTED READING

The serious study of economic methodology should begin with **J. N. Keynes** [1891]. **Robbins** [1932] raises the distinction between "positive" and "normative" economics. **Hutchinson** [1938] considers the question of how economic propositions are to be verified.

Friedman [1953] states the case for testing economic theory by evaluating the accuracy of the predictions rather than considering the appropriateness of the postulates. **Koopmans** [1957] discusses the axiomatic approach to the construction of economic theory and states the arguments for evaluating the postulates of theory.

The issue of the deductive versus inductive approach to economic analysis is discussed by **Koopmans** [1947], and there is a reply by **Vining** [1949] and a rejoinder by **Koopmans** [1949].

The question of what constitutes an operational or useful economic theory is discussed in **Archibald** [1961, 1963], **Friedman** [1963], and **Stigler** [1963].

The methodological issue of testing predictions versus postulates of economic theory has been revisited by **Samuelson** [1963] and **Nagel** [1963]. This question also occupies a good part of **Machlup** [1967].

The role of mathematics in economic theory has recently been discussed in **Samuelson's** [1972] Nobel Prize address, in **Hurwicz** [1963], and in **Morgenstern** [1963].

Leontief [1971] has recently "lectured" the economics profession on the dangers of forgetting that economics is essentially an "empirical science" while **Morgenstern** [1972] raises a number of challenging issues for economic theorists.

A good introduction to basic calculus is **Courant** and **Robbins** [1941]. **Taylor** and **Mann** [1972] and **Apostle** [1974] are advanced texts. For matrix algebra, **Hadley** [1961] is an introductory text while **Yaari** [1971] is more advanced but has the advantage of being written for social scientists.

PART I
THEORY OF THE CONSUMER

The theory of consumer behavior, developed in this first part of the book, begins with the fundamental ("primitive") notion of "consumer preference," examined in chapter 2. By imposing certain "rationality" assumptions on consumer preferences, a complete theory of consumer choice is constructed. Consumers choose that bundle which is preferred to (more exactly, "no worse than") all other bundles that can be purchased with their income.

Given certain assumptions about consumer preferences, these preferences can be represented by a "utility function," which associates a level of "utility" or "satisfaction" with each conceivable consumption bundle. The consumer-choice problem can then be formulated in terms of (expenditure-constrained) utility maximization. The theory of utility is developed in chapter 3.

Consumer choice generates demands for commodities. The theory of demand, focusing upon the effects that changes in prices and income have upon quantities demanded, is developed in chapters 4 and 5. Chapter 4 examines these concepts using graphical (or diagrammatic) tools and chapter 5 contains a more mathematically advanced treatment of the theory of demand (including the application of duality to consumer theory). Chapter 6 completes part I with some additional topics in demand theory: (1) the use of ("unit-free") demand elasticities to measure the responsiveness of demand to changes in income or prices, (2) the work-leisure choice of the consumer (which determines the supply of labor and hence, given the wage rate, the consumer's income), and (3) the theory of "revealed preference," in which consumer preferences are revealed by actual choices in different price-income situations.

CHAPTER 2
PREFERENCE THEORY

2.1 INTRODUCTION

The central purpose of the theory of consumer choice is to explain the allocation of a consumer's income, or wealth, among the myriad commodities which may be purchased in an advanced economy. In this chapter, the theory is developed in its most fundamental form, i.e., the assumptions which are made about consumer behavior are, given the state of the science, very close to the weakest that can be made and still permit an explanation of consumer choice. It is primarily in the area of consumer theory that economists have been most zealous in their application of the principle of Occam's razor. Most of the assumptions which are required in order to explain consistent consumer choice are fairly weak (although, as are all assumptions, they are unrealistic in the sense that they are abstractions rather than an attempted description of a very complex set of real phenomena).

In section 2.2, we define the consumption space and introduce the notion of consumer preference. This is the most primitive concept in the modern theory of the consumer. By primitive we mean that we simply assume that consumers are able to say *whether* they prefer one bundle of commodities to another without attempting to ascertain why. That is, the notion of individual preference is not derived from any previous analysis. We then invoke some assumptions about consumer preferences which allow us to infer that consumers are able to rank bundles of goods.

In section 2.3, we describe the constraints under which consumers are assumed to operate. The fact that consumers cannot spend more income than they have (ignoring borrowing) means that they are restricted in their choice of consumption bundles. It is assumed that consumers choose to consume the bundle of commodities that is "optimal" (as defined in section 2.3). A mathematical problem regarding the existence of an optimal consumption bundle is discussed in the optional section 2.4 (which can be skipped without loss of continuity). Section 2.5 concludes with a diagrammatic illustration of the consumer-choice problem.

2.2 THE CONSUMPTION SPACE AND THE PREFERENCE RELATION

The Consumption Space

In the interest of simplicity and convenience, we assume that each of the n commodities[1] available in the economy is continuously divisible. That is, the quantity of any commodity available for consumption can be any nonnegative real number.

This assumption of perfect divisibility means that there is no lumpiness in the consumption of the commodities. Thus, for example, it is possible to consume π automobiles. This lumpiness is not, however, as serious as it appears at first glance. The reason is that in the case of very lumpy commodities what is consumed within one time period is not the commodity itself but the services of the commodity. Most commodities, such as beer and bread, can be consumed in very small units.

Nevertheless, it is clearly true that there is a smallest unit in which every commodity can be purchased and this is true for fairly divisible commodities such as water as well as more lumpy types of commodities. Hence, we must recognize that this assumption is a restrictive one which we posit primarily for convenience in much of what follows. It is possible to construct a theory of the consumer if the assumption of perfect divisibility is dropped, and most of the results which we derive hold (though perhaps in a slightly modified form) in a world in which commodities are not perfectly divisible.[2]

With the introduction of the above assumptions regarding the way in which commodities can be consumed, we can now define more rigorously the field of choice of the consumer. First, define a commodity bundle as a collection of amounts of all goods and services. Denote this commodity bundle by x. Obviously, goods and services can only be consumed in real-valued amounts so that, if there are n commodities in the economy, x is a vector of real numbers $[x_1, \ldots, x_i, \ldots, x_n]$, where x_i, $i = 1, \ldots, n$, is the amount consumed of the ith commodity. Equivalently, x is a point in Euclidian n-space.

The consumption space, or field of choice, of the consumer is the set of all consumption bundles among which the consumer could conceivably choose and is denoted X. Under our assumption, X is equivalent to the nonnegative Euclidian n-orthant so that the consumer conceivably can consume any finite nonnegative amount of each commodity.[3] We summarize the above discussion with the following assumption.

Assumption 2.1 (Consumption Space) The consumption space, X, is the nonnegative Euclidian n-orthant.

[1] Of course, n is a finite integer. One can imagine an economy in which at least one commodity is available in a continuum of "qualities." In principle, then, there would be an infinite number of commodities.

[2] A notable exception is the first optimality principle of welfare economics (see section 17.4).

[3] See Apostle [1974, pp. 32, 47] and Klein [1973, pp. 3–4, 24–25] for an elementary discussion of sets and Euclidean space.

The Preference Relation

The theory of consumer choice begins with the primitive notion of preference. That is, we take the statement "the consumer prefers commodity bundle x to commodity bundle $\hat{x}$" to be self-evident and to require no explanation. Put differently, we don't care why the consumer prefers x to $\hat{x}$. As we shall see below, our only concern is that the consumer be able to say whether or not he prefers x to $\hat{x}$ and to be consistent in his preferences.[4]

A convenient shorthand is to write $x \succ \hat{x}$ whenever x is preferred to $\hat{x}$. Thus, the symbol $\succ$ should be read "is preferred to." $\succ$ is called the *preference relation*.

What if a consumer cannot state a preference between two commodity bundles? In other words, suppose that neither $x \succ \hat{x}$ nor $\hat{x} \succ x$ holds. In this case we say that the consumer is indifferent. This suggests the notion of an *indifference relation*, $\sim$, defined as follows: $x \sim \hat{x}$ if (not $x \succ \hat{x}$) and (not $\hat{x} \succ x$) where "(not $x \succ \hat{x}$)" is the negation of $x \succ \hat{x}$; i.e., x is not preferred to $\hat{x}$.

The preference relation and the indifference relation together suggest the *weak preference relation* $\succcurlyeq$. Thus, $x \succcurlyeq \hat{x}$ means either $x \succ \hat{x}$ or $x \sim \hat{x}$, but not $\hat{x} \succ x$; i.e., x is no worse than $\hat{x}$. To distinguish it from the weak preference relation, $\succ$ is often referred to as the *strict preference relation*.

It is worth noting, at this point, that the definition of indifference as the absence of preference guarantees that all pairs of commodity bundles are comparable; i.e., given any two commodity bundles in X, the consumer is either indifferent between the two or prefers one to the other. In other words, the weak preference relation is *complete*: given any two commodity bundles, say $\bar{x}$ and x', in X, either $\bar{x} \succcurlyeq x'$ or $x' \succcurlyeq \bar{x}$.

The completeness of $\succcurlyeq$ might be interpreted as precluding ignorance on the part of the consumer if ignorance is equivalent to an inability to express either preference or indifference between two commodity bundles. For example, if a consumer who had never been to Paris were offered a choice between two consumption bundles which were identical except that one contained dinner at La Tour d'Argent and the other contained dinner at Le Beaujolais, he might be unable to express indifference or a preference of one over the other.

On the other hand, rather than precluding areas of ignorance in the consumer's preferences, the completeness of $\succcurlyeq$ might be interpreted as saying that the consumer is actually indifferent between two bundles about which he is ignorant; that is, whenever he is ignorant about two alternative consumption bundles the consumer treats them as equally desirable.

Asymmetry and Transitivity

A useful theory of consumer choice cannot be constructed without placing some constraints on one or more of the above preference relations. There

[4] The reader should keep in mind the fact that x and $\hat{x}$ are commodity *bundles*, i.e., amounts consumed of a collection of commodities. For example, in a particular case, the statement "the consumer prefers x to $\hat{x}$" might read "the consumer prefers two bottles of beer and one loaf of bread to one bottle of beer and two loaves of bread." It will *never* mean "the consumer prefers beer to bread," a comment which, per se, is not operational.

are alternative ways of stating these assumptions, depending upon which preference relation we wish to work with, but for our purposes it is most convenient to work with the strict preference relation $\succ$ and the indifference relation $\sim$.[5] Two of the assumptions which we need in order to develop a theory of consumer choice are as follows:

Assumption 2.2 (Asymmetry) Given any two commodity bundles, say x' and $\bar{x}$, contained in the consumption space, X, $x' \succ \bar{x}$ implies (not $\bar{x} \succ x'$).

Assumption 2.3 (Transitivity) Given any three consumption bundles, say $\bar{x}$, $\hat{x}$, and x', contained in the consumption space, X, $\bar{x} \succ \hat{x}$ and $\hat{x} \succ x'$ implies that $\bar{x} \succ x'$. Moreover, $\bar{x} \sim \hat{x}$ and $\hat{x} \sim x'$ implies $\bar{x} \sim x'$.

These two assumptions together comprise the notion of *consistency*. The first, asymmetry, might be referred to as "two-term consistency" whereas the second might be referred to as "three-term consistency."[6] Without these assumptions, the consumer's preferences could go around in circles, reflecting a type of inconsistency which would make the problem of predicting the consumer's behavior extremely problematical.[7]

A violation of the transitivity assumption may be generated by the so-called "threshold" effect. This effect is perhaps best illustrated by the following analogy. Suppose that a consumer cannot tell the difference between two temperatures that are only one degree apart but can tell the difference and can express a preference between two temperatures that are two degrees apart. Then the consumer might be indifferent between, say, 69° and 70° and also between 70° and 71°, but might prefer 71° to 69° so that $71° \succ 69°$, contradicting the transitivity assumption.

Although this threshold effect does not seem unreasonable, it has some perverse implications regarding consumer behavior. An intransitive consumer could be duped into a sequence of trades which would make him worse off. For example, suppose that there are only two goods, beer and bread, and that the consumer has a threshold effect in both bread and beer, in that he is indifferent between a given bundle of the two goods and an alternative bundle which contains only one ounce more of beer and only one slice more of bread. This means that we could induce him to trade his existing bundle for an alternative bundle with one slice less of bread and one ounce less of beer (since he is indifferent). We could continue to induce him into such trades until we had extracted all of his beer and bread, making him much worse off than he was to begin with.

[5] Thus, we treat $\succ$ and $\sim$ as "primitives." For an alternative approach in which $\succcurlyeq$ is treated as the primitive, see exercise 2.2.

[6] In fact, three-term consistency implies "*n*-term consistency"; see exercise 2.4.

[7] In fact, a weaker assumption than transitivity ("acyclicity") is sufficient for consumer choice to be well defined, but it is not convenient to weaken assumption 2.3 in the development of the theory of the consumer primarily because the utility function, extensively utilized in the subsequent chapters of part I, would then not necessarily exist. See section 19.5 for a discussion of the acyclicity condition. Exercise 2.6 is also relevant.

The principal justification for assumptions 2.2 and 2.3 is that without them the problem of formulating a useful theory of consumer choice would be more difficult. These assumptions are important because, in principal, they permit the consumer to order bundles of goods according to the preference relation. That is, if assumptions 2.2 and 2.3 are satisfied, the bundles can be ordered such that x precedes $\bar{x}$ in the ordering if and only if $\bar{x} \succ x$. Similarly x does not precede $\bar{x}$ in the ordering if and only if $x \succcurlyeq \bar{x}$ and x neither precedes nor follows $\bar{x}$ in the ordering if and only if $x \sim \bar{x}$. This ordering is referred to as the consumer's *preference ordering*.[8] It is on the basis of the preference ordering that the consumer is assumed to make his choice of a commodity bundle.

2.3 THE BUDGET SET AND CONSUMER CHOICE

The Budget Set

In our initial examination of the problem of consumer choice, the following assumption is made:

Assumption 2.4 (Positive Prices and Income) The consumer is endowed with a given (positive) amount of income, y, and can purchase any (nonnegative) amount of the n commodities at fixed positive prices, $p = [p_1, \ldots, p_n]$.

Total expenditure on the ith commodity is given by the amount of the ith commodity multiplied by its price, $p_i x_i$. Thus, the total expenditure of the consumer is

$$p_1 x_1 + \cdots + p_i x_i + \cdots + p_n x_n = \sum_{i=1}^{n} p_i x_i, \tag{2.1}$$

where Σ is the summation operator.

The consumer's expenditures are constrained by his income. That is, the consumer cannot spend more income then he has. This constraint can be expressed algebraically as follows:

$$\sum_{i=1}^{n} p_i x_i \leq y. \tag{2.2}$$

This constraint, referred to as the *budget constraint*, restricts the consumer's consumption to a subset of the consumption space. This subset is called the

[8] Mathematically speaking, a binary relation such as $\succ$, which satisfies assumptions 2.2 and 2.3, is called a *strict ordering*. The reflexive, symmetric, and transitive relation, $\sim$, is called an *equivalence*, and the complete, reflexive, transitive relation, $\succcurlyeq$, is called a *complete ordering* (see exercise 2.1.) See Klein [1973, pp. 27–31, 35–39], Sen [1970, pp. 7–12] and Yaari [1971, pp. 8–15] for discussions of the different types of mathematical relations and orderings.

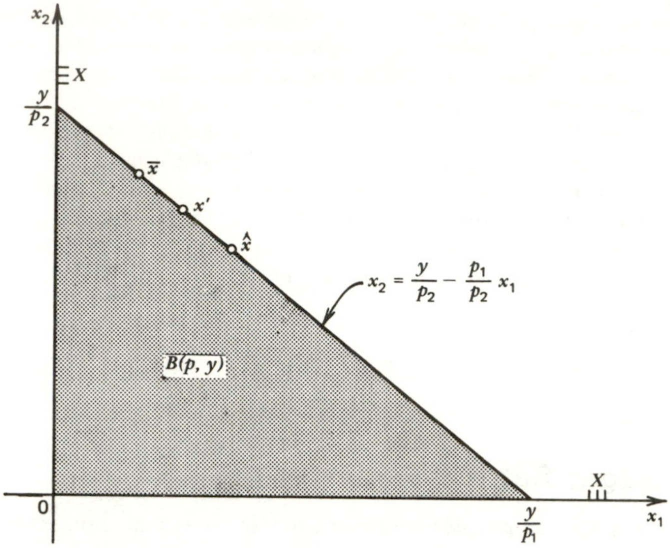

Figure 2.1

budget set, denoted $B(p, y)$, and is defined as the set of all commodity bundles in the consumption space which satisfy the budget constraint (2.2), given income and prices.

For the purpose of illustration, consider the case where there are only two commodities so that the budget constraint is

$$p_1 x_1 + p_2 x_2 \leq y. \tag{2.3}$$

In figure 2.1, we measure units of commodity 1 along the horizontal axis and units of commodity 2 along the vertical axis. As negative consumption is not permitted, the consumption set is the nonnegative quadrant of this diagram. To illustrate the budget set, consider the equality,

$$p_1 x_1 + p_2 x_2 = y, \tag{2.4}$$

which defines those commodity bundles which exactly exhaust the consumer's income, y, given the prices, p_1 and p_2. Solving this equation for x_2 yields a linear function of x_1,

$$x_2 = \frac{y}{p_2} - \frac{p_1}{p_2} x_1 = \zeta(x_1) \tag{2.5}$$

where y/p_2 is the vertical intercept and $-p_1/p_2$ is the slope of the linear function. This line, referred to as the *budget line*, is drawn in figure 2.1 for nonnegative values of x_1 and x_2. By setting x_2 equal to zero and solving equation (2.4) for x_1, it is easy to see that the intercept of this budget line with the horizontal axis is y/p_1. The intercepts make sense. For example, if the consumer were to expend his entire income on commodity 1, it is clear that he could purchase y/p_1 units of this commodity. If commodity 1 is bread, the price of bread is 50¢, and income is $100 per period, then by expending his entire income on bread the consumer would be able to purchase 100/.5 = 200 loaves of bread.

The slope of the budget line,

$$\frac{d\zeta(x_1)}{dx_1} = -\frac{p_1}{p_2}, \tag{2.6}$$

also has an intuitive interpretation. The slope tells us how much the consumption of commodity 2 changes when the consumption of commodity 1 is increased by one unit and total expenditure is held constant (equal to y). The negative sign of the slope (assuming positive prices) reflects the fact that, as the consumption of commodity 1 is increased, the consumption of commodity 2 must be decreased in order to keep total expenditure constant. By way of example, suppose that commodity 2 is bread, priced at 50¢ a loaf, and commodity 2 is beer, priced at 25¢ a bottle. If the consumer is spending all of his income and wishes to increase his consumption of bread by one loaf, it is clear that he must reduce his consumption of beer by 2 bottles. This figure is, in fact, equal to the price ratio, $p_1/p_2 = .50/.25 = 2$.

All commodity bundles on the budget line exactly exhaust the consumer's money income and are therefore part of the budget set. However, the consumer does not have to spend all of his income; hence all commodity bundles represented by points below this line but contained in the nonnegative quadrant also belong to the budget set. This set is identified as the shaded area in figure 2.1.

Consumer Choice

The consumer-choice problem can now be defined as the problem of choosing a commodity bundle from the budget set. Define the *preferred subset* of the budget set as the set of all commodity bundles in the budget set which are no worse, in the consumer's preference ordering, than any other consumption bundle in the budget set. That is, the preferred subset $\overset{*}{X}(p, y)$ of the budget set $B(p, y)$ is the set of all bundles x contained in $B(p, y)$ that satisfy $x \succcurlyeq \bar{x}$ for all $\bar{x}$ contained in $B(p, y)$. This is the set of commodity bundles which are the consumer's "most preferred" bundles, given the budget constraint.

The fundamental notion of consumer rationality is embodied in the following postulate:

Assumption 2.5 (Consumer Choice) Given any set of positive prices and income, the consumer chooses a consumption bundle—called the *optimal consumption bundle*—in the preferred subset $\overset{*}{X}(p, y)$ of the budget set, $B(p, y)$.

This assumption is so reasonable that it needs little discussion. There is, however, a mathematical problem which arises because, under our assumptions, the preferred subset might be empty—that is, there might not be a "most preferred consumption bundle." This problem is a mathematical curiosity which is entirely attributable to our assumption that commodities are continuously divisible. If there were a smallest unit in which goods could be consumed, this mathematical problem would not arise; an optimal bundle would exist so long as all prices were positive (assumption 2.4).[9] It is therefore fair to say that this problem is a matter of mathematical but not economic interest, and need not detain us. It can be resolved by a very technical assumption with no easy intuitive economic interpretation. We therefore relegate the discussion of the nonexistence problem and its resolution to the optional section 2.4 (which may be skipped without loss of continuity).

2.4 THE EXISTENCE OF AN OPTIMAL CONSUMPTION BUNDLE*

The existence issue has to do with whether or not the preferred subset contains any consumption bundles. If this set is empty, assumption 2.5 is vacuous and consumer choice is impossible.

It might seem obvious that, since assumptions 2.2 and 2.3 are equivalent to the existence of a preference ordering, there exists at least one most preferred point in the budget set (so long as prices are strictly positive), but this unfortunately is not the case. There do exist cases (albeit pathological) where these two assumptions do not guarantee the existence of an optimum. To see this, consider a dipsomaniac with an almost ungovernable passion for beer which is, however, mitigated by the nutritional concern that he should drink some milk—no matter how little—every day. Thus, given any two bundles with some positive amount of milk, he prefers the bundle with the greatest amount of beer, regardless of the relative amount of milk in the two bundles. If the two bundles have the same amount of beer, he prefers the one with the most milk. Finally, his concern for his health leads him to prefer any bundle with some milk to a bundle with no milk at all.

Letting x_b and x_m be the consumption of beer and milk, respectively, the preference ordering can be formally described as follows: $\bar{x} = [\bar{x}_b, \bar{x}_m] \succ [x'_b, x'_m] = x'$ if

$$\text{(i)} \qquad \bar{x}_m > 0 \quad \text{and} \quad x'_m = 0,$$

or

$$\text{(ii)} \qquad \bar{x}_m > 0 \quad \text{and} \quad \bar{x}_b > x'_b,$$

or

$$\text{(iii)} \qquad \bar{x}_m = x'_m = 0 \quad \text{and} \quad \bar{x}_b > x'_b,$$

or

$$\text{(iv)} \qquad \bar{x}_b = x'_b \quad \text{and} \quad \bar{x}_m > x'_m.$$

[9] To assume that indivisibilities exist for all commodities would bail us out of this quagmire but would only cause problems later on. We would be deprived of all of neoclassical economics which is based upon differential calculus and the underlying smoothness assumptions.

* Starred sections represent relatively difficult material which can be skipped without loss of continuity.

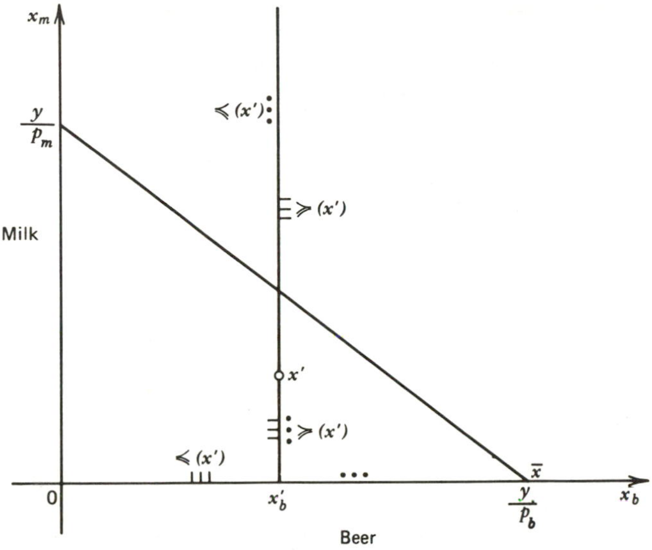

Figure 2.2

The reader should verify that this preference relation satisfies assumptions 2.2 and 2.3.

The preference ordering of this dipsomaniac is illustrated in figure 2.2. Along any vertical line, such as the one shown in figure 2.2, points higher on the line represent more preferred bundles. All points on the line except the point of intersection with the x_b-axis represent bundles that are preferred to all bundles represented by points to the left of the line. Finally, all points to the right of the line except points on the x_b-axis represent bundles that are preferred to bundles corresponding to points on the line.

Also drawn in figure 2.2 is a representative budget line. The preference ordering of the dipsomaniac implies that all points below the budget line are inferior in the preference ordering to some points on the budget line. Hence no point off the budget line can be in the preferred subset. Moreover, as we move to the right along the budget line, we move to more preferred consumption bundles except for the fact that all points on the budget line are preferred to $\bar{x} = [y/p_b, 0]$. As a result, there is no most preferred point in the feasible consumption set. Given any point on the budget line except $\bar{x}$, we can move to a more preferred point by moving closer to $\bar{x}$. But $\bar{x}$ is inferior in the preference ordering to all points on the budget line. Hence, it is impossible to find an optimal consumption bundle; the preferred subset is empty. Moreover, the preferences of the disomaniac clearly satisfy assumptions 2.2 and 2.3, i.e., a preference ordering is defined on the consumption space X. Hence, we must posit an additional assumption in order to assure the possibility of consumer choice defined by assumption 2.5. The additional assumption requires the introduction of some new concepts.

Define the no-worse-than-x set, $\succcurlyeq(x)$, as the set of all bundles, $\bar{x}$, in X satisfying $\bar{x} \succcurlyeq x$. Similarly, define the no-better-than-x set, $\preccurlyeq(x)$, as the set of all bundles, $\bar{x}$, in X satisfying $x \succcurlyeq \bar{x}$. Finally, define the x-indifference set, $I(x)$, as the set of bundles, $\bar{x}$, in X satisfying $x \sim \bar{x}$.

The sets, $\succcurlyeq(x')$ and $\preccurlyeq(x')$, induced by the preference ordering of the dipsomaniac are delineated in figure 2.2. The set $I(x')$ is composed of the single point x'; i.e., there does not exist a consumption bundle $x \neq x'$ such that $x \sim x'$. Note that the sets, $\succcurlyeq(x')$ and $\preccurlyeq(x')$, do not contain their boundaries. $\succcurlyeq(x')$ does not contain the x_b-axis boundary or the vertical boundary below x' and $\preccurlyeq(x')$ does not contain its vertical boundary above x'. This suggests a way out of our difficulty.

Assumption 2.6 (Regularity) For all consumption bundles x in X, the no-worse-than-x set, $\succcurlyeq(x)$, and the no-better-than-x set, $\preccurlyeq(x)$, contain their boundaries.

This assumption unfortunately has no obvious behavioral interpretation other than that it precludes preference orderings such as that illustrated in figure 2.2 where the indifference classes, $I(x)$, degenerate to single points. The fact that the dipsomaniac example is bizarre is a good thing from the standpoint of the theory of consumer choice. It hints (but only hints) that assumption 2.6, designed specifically to rule out such bizarre preferences, is easy to accept (i.e., not very restrictive).

We are now prepared to state a major proposition of the theory of consumer choice:

If assumptions 2.2 (*asymmetry*), 2.3 (*transitivity*), 2.4 (*positive income and prices*), *and* 2.6 (*regularity*) *hold, the preferred subset of the budget set is nonempty.*

Proof of this proposition is beyond the scope of this book, but we attempt to provide some intuitive feeling for the proposition by discussing why we need each of the four conditions. The role of the regularity condition, assumption 2.6, has already been discussed.

If the asymmetry or transitivity assumption were not satisfied, a most preferred subset might not exist because the consumer's preferences might end up going around in circles. For example, suppose that $\bar{x}$, x', and $\hat{x}$ in figure 2.1 are preferred to all other commodity bundles in $B(p, y)$. Suppose further that $\bar{x} \succ x'$, $x' \succ \hat{x}$, and $\hat{x} \succ \bar{x}$, in which case the transitivity axiom is violated. Clearly, under these circumstances, there is no preferred subset of $B(p, y)$ since each of the three commodity bundles is inferior, according to the preferences of the consumer, to at least one other.

Finally, if the prices which the consumer faces are not all strictly positive (assumption 2.4), there might be no most preferred subset of $B(p, y)$. For example, suppose that, in our two-commodity example, bread is free; i.e., $p_1 = 0$. The budget equation, (2.4) or (2.5), becomes the constant function,

$$x_2 = \frac{y}{p_2}. \tag{2.7}$$

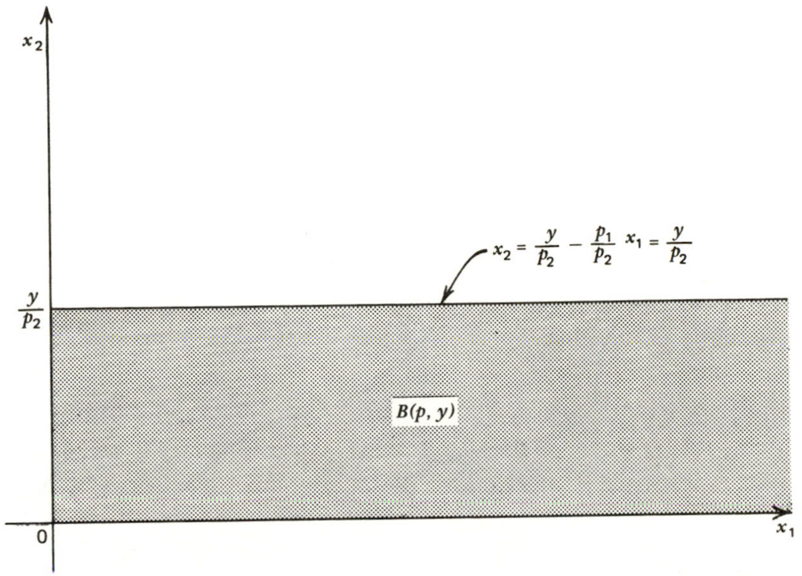

Figure 2.3

This budget equation is illustrated as the horizontal line with intercept y/p_2 in figure 2.3. In this case, the budget set $B(p, y)$ is not bounded. That is, unlike the budget set in figure 2.1, it is not possible to enclose the budget set in figure 2.2 in a square with finite dimensions. The upshot of this is that there is no limit to the amount of bread which the consumer can consume even though his income is finite.

As long as he would rather have more bread than less, there is no commodity bundle in $B(p, y)$ which is not inferior in the consumer's preference ordering to some other commodity bundle—namely, a commodity bundle with more bread. In this case, then, the preferred subset is empty.

2.5 DIAGRAMMATIC ILLUSTRATION OF CONSUMER CHOICE

Consumer choice is best illustrated by exploiting the notion of the x-indifference set, $I(x)$. An $\bar{x}$-indifference set, $I(\bar{x})$, is defined as the set of all bundles x in X that satisfy $x \sim \bar{x}$. Note that $I(\bar{x})$ is clearly nonempty for all x in X since, trivially, $\bar{x} \sim \bar{x}$ (see exercise 2.5).

In the two-commodity case, an indifference set might be represented by a curve, such as those illustrated in figure 2.4. All of the commodity bundles, x, on the curve labeled $I(\bar{x})$ satisfy the condition, $\bar{x} \sim x$. Analagous conditions hold for $I(x')$, $I(\overset{*}{x})$, and all other indifference sets (not shown in figure 2.4).

In three-space, indifference sets would be represented by three-dimensional surfaces. More generally, in Euclidean n-space, indifference sets are represented by n-dimensional (hyper) surfaces.

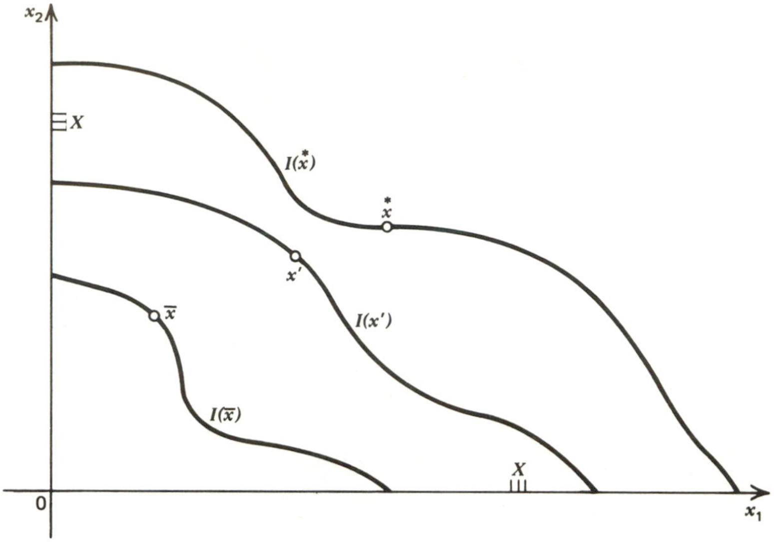

Figure 2.4

So long as the indifference sets can be represented by curves in the two-commodity case and surfaces in the n-commodity case, there are an infinite number of indifference sets because of the assumption of perfect divisibility. The complete set of indifference curves, or surfaces, is referred to as the consumer's *indifference map*.

As $\bar{x}$, x', and $\overset{*}{x}$ lie on different indifference curves, it is apparent that the consumer is not indifferent between any two of these three bundles. Thus, either $\bar{x} \succ x'$ or $x' \succ \bar{x}$, etc. Merely for the purpose of illustration (although this is posited as a formal assumption later on), assume that one commodity bundle is preferred to another if it lies on a higher indifference curve.[10]

If higher indifference curves contain commodity bundles which are strictly preferred to bundles on lower indifference curves, the problem of consumer choice can be described as the problem of choosing a commodity bundle which is on the highest indifference curve that can be attained given the consumer's budget constraint. Given the set of indifference curves and the budget set in figure 2.5, the choice axiom indicates that the consumer will choose commodity bundle $\overset{*}{x}$. Any other consumption bundle in the budget set lies on a lower indifference curve and is therefore worse than $\overset{*}{x}$, given the consumer's preference ordering. For example, the choice of x' in the interior of the budget set or $\bar{x}$ on the boundary of the budget set would place the consumer on an indifference curve which is lower than $I(\overset{*}{x})$, violating assumption 2.5.

Two additional observations should be made regarding the choice of $\overset{*}{x}$ as the most preferred bundle. First, this bundle lies on the upper boundary of the budget set. This is because of the fact that higher indifference curves contain

[10] Note that, given assumption 2.3 (transitivity), indifference curves cannot intersect (see exercise 2.3).

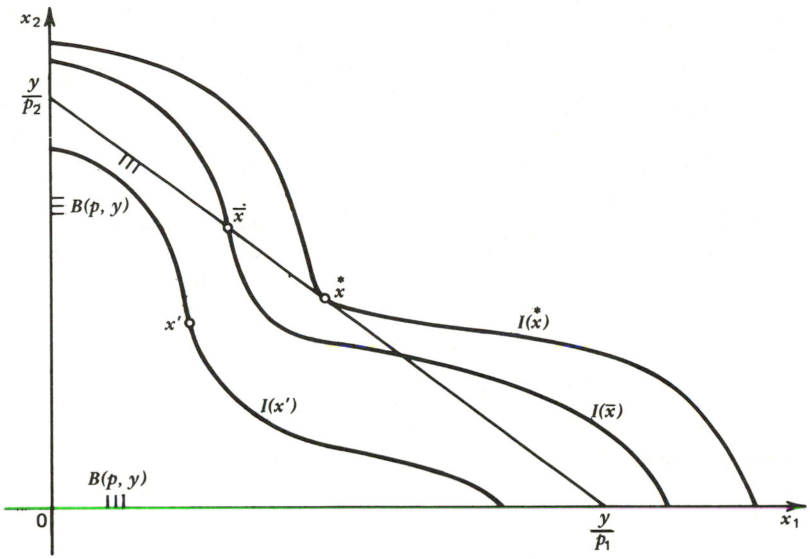

Figure 2.5

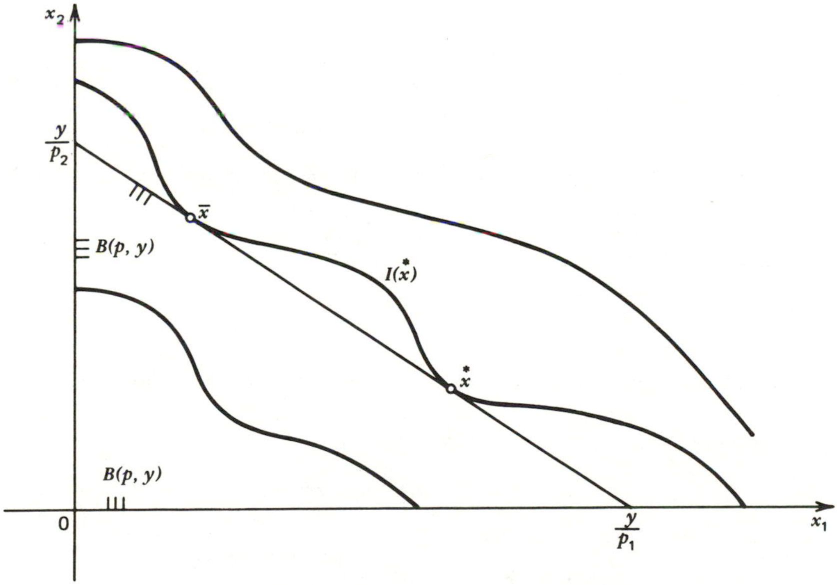

Figure 2.6

commodity bundles which are preferred to all commodity bundles on lower indifference curves. If this were not true, the optimal consumption bundle might lie in the interior of the budget set. We will say more about this in chapter 3.

We might also note that, given the preference ordering illustrated in figure 2.5, the preferred subset $\overset{*}{X}(p, y)$, is composed of the single point $\overset{*}{x}$. Figure 2.6 illustrates a preference ordering in which the most preferred subset does not degenerate to a single point. In this case, $X(p, y)$ consists of the two points, $\overset{*}{x}$ and $\bar{x}$. Thus, the choice axiom (2.5) indicates that the consumer will choose either $\overset{*}{x}$ or $\bar{x}$ but the theory does not indicate which of the two. For many purposes, this type of indecision is not a problem, but for other purposes, such as those of chapter 3 below, this indecisiveness is problematical and has to be assumed away.

EXERCISES*

2.1* Assuming that $\succ$ is asymmetric and transitive and that $\sim$ is transitive, prove the following:

a. $\sim$ is symmetric: for all $(\bar{x}, x)$ in X, $\bar{x} \sim \hat{x}$ implies $\hat{x} \sim \bar{x}$.
b. $\sim$ is reflexive: for all x in X, $x \sim x$.
c. $\succcurlyeq$ is reflexive.
d. $\succcurlyeq$ is transitive.
e. if $\bar{x} \succ \hat{x}$ and $\hat{x} \sim x'$, then $\bar{x} \succ x'$.
f. if $\bar{x} \sim \hat{x}$ and $\hat{x} \succ x'$, then $\bar{x} \succ x'$.

2.2* Let the weak preference relation, $\succcurlyeq$, be the "primitive" and define the strict preference and indifference relations as follows:

$$\bar{x} \succ x \text{ if and only if } \bar{x} \succcurlyeq \hat{x} \text{ and (not } \hat{x} \succcurlyeq \bar{x})$$

and

$$\bar{x} \sim \hat{x} \text{ if and only if } \bar{x} \succcurlyeq \hat{x} \text{ and } \hat{x} \succcurlyeq \bar{x}.$$

Assuming that $\succcurlyeq$ is transitive and complete (hence reflexive), prove the following:

a. $\sim$ is reflexive.
b. $\sim$ is symmetric.
c. $\sim$ is transitive.
d. $\succ$ is asymmetric.
e. $\succ$ is transitive.

2.3 Use assumption 2.3 to prove that indifference curves cannot intersect.

2.4* Prove that assumption 2.3 (transitivity) implies "n-term consistency": for all "chains," $\{x^1, \ldots, x^k\}$, in X,

$$x^1 \succ x^2,\ x^2 \succ x^3,\ \ldots,\ x^{k-1} \succ x^k \text{ implies } x^1 \succ x^k.$$

* Starred exercises are relatively more difficult.

2.5* Prove that the set of indifference sets, $\{I(x)\}$, is a "partition" of X: (a) for all x in X, $I(x)$ is nonempty and (b) each x in X is in one and only one indifference set.

2.6* Acyclicity of $\succ$ is defined as follows: For all chains $\{x^1, \ldots, x^k\}$ in X,

$$x^1 \succ x^2,\ x^2 \succ x^3, \ldots, x^{k-1} \succ x^k \text{ implies (not } x^k \succ x^1).$$

Prove that acyclicity of $\succ$ is weaker than transitivity of $\succ$ (i.e., transitivity implies acyclicity but acyclicity does not imply transitivity).

CHAPTER 3
UTILITY THEORY

3.1 INTRODUCTION

The classical consumer theory of the nineteenth century was built on the assumption that each consumer associates with any given consumption bundle the degree of satisfaction, or utility, which results from the consumption of that bundle. The problem of consumer choice may then be interpreted as the maximization of the consumers' utilities subject to the constraint that they not spend more income than they possess. In section 3.2, we discuss the representation of a preference ordering by a real-valued utility function. In section 3.3, some additional assumptions are placed upon the preferences, and hence upon the utility function, of the consumer. The notion of the marginal rate of substitution is introduced in section 3.4, and in section 3.5 the utility maximization problem is examined. An interesting result of this discussion is that a complete theory of consumer choice can be constructed without the existence of a utility function. Preference theory, rather than utility theory, constitutes the foundation of consumer choice. Finally, in section 3.6, the relationship between the utility function and the consumer choice problem is explored further, particularly with respect to the notion of measurability of utility.

3.2 THE UTILITY FUNCTION

Representation of the Preference Ordering

Suppose that we were to associate with every indifference set a unique real number.[1] This association would define a function, mapping from the set of all indifference classes to the set of real numbers. Moreover, this induces a mapping from the entire consumption space to the real line. That is, if we associate with every commodity bundle the unique real number associated with the indifference set to which that bundle belongs, the result is a function mapping from X to the set of real numbers. Each commodity bundle maps into a unique real number because each bundle belongs to one and only one indifference set. (But, of course, any number of commodity bundles may map into a given real number.) Let us call this mapping U so that the real number associated with any commodity bundle x (i.e., the image of x by U) is denoted $U(x)$.

Clearly, by construction, whenever any two commodity bundles in the consumption space, say $\bar{x}$ and x', satisfy $\bar{x} \sim x'$, $U(\bar{x}) = U(x')$. If, in addition, we number the indifference classes so that for any two consumption bundles,

[1] This is not always possible.

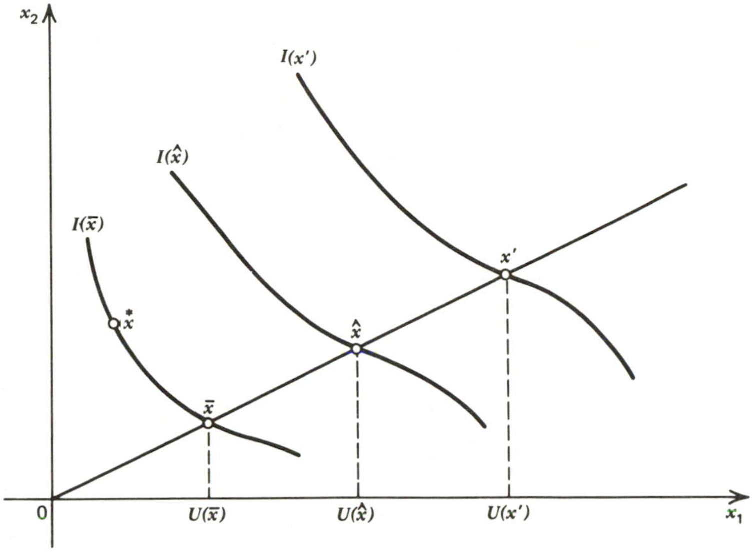

Figure 3.1

say $\bar{x}$ and x', $\bar{x} \succ x'$ implies $U(\bar{x}) > U(x')$, we say that the function U is *order preserving*. That is, the function preserves the ordering on the consumption space induced by the preference relation $\succcurlyeq$. Another way of saying this is that the function U *represents* the consumer's preference ordering.[2]

The construction of a function U in the two-commodity case is illustrated in figure 3.1. Superimposed on the indifference map in figure 3.1 is an arbitrary ray from the origin. To construct the function U, we must associate a real number with every indifference curve. Moreover, the correspondence between indifference curves and real numbers must preserve the preference ordering. Consider, for example, the indifference curve $I(\bar{x})$. The ray intersects $I(\bar{x})$ at $\bar{x}$. Project a straight line to the horizontal axis and let the real number at this point of the axis be $U(\bar{x})$. Of course, if $\overset{*}{x}$ is on the same indifference curve as $\bar{x}$, then $U(\overset{*}{x}) = U(\bar{x})$. The real numbers attached to other indifference curves are analogously constructed. It is clear that, so long as indifference curves are negatively sloped everywhere,[3] this construction associates with each indifference curve one and only one real number. Moreover, these real numbers satisfy $U(\hat{x}) > U(\bar{x})$ if and only if $\hat{x} \succ \bar{x}$.

Nonuniqueness of the Representation

The fact that the function U represents, or preserves, the preference ordering is a very appealing property. Intuitively, we might think of the image

[2] See Apostle [1974, pp. 32–35] and Yaari [1971, pp. 16–21] for a discussion of mathematical functions and related concepts.

[3] If this assumption is not satisfied, some modest alterations must be made in the construction.

value, $U(x)$, as the level of satisfaction or the level of "utility" which the consumer derives from the consumption of the bundle x. It is true that the numbering system—i.e., the utility level—is arbitrary except for the fact that it preserves the preference ordering. That is, the function, or "utility index," U, is arbitrary except for the fact that the value is higher for preferred bundles. However, given our state of knowledge, this is probably a proper reflection of the notion of "utility." That is, the "measurement" of utility is itself an arbitrary procedure, much as the volume of a certain amount of mercury constitutes measurement of the elusive concept of "temperature."[4]

If the consumer's preference ordering is represented by an order-preserving, real-valued (utility) function,[5] the problem of consumer choice may be represented as that of maximizing the utility function subject to the budget constraint (2.2). That is, the problem of choosing the most preferred point in the budget set, which is equivalent to attaining the highest indifference curve in figure 2.5 or 2.6, is also equivalent to maximizing the utility index subject to the budget constraint.

Because of a mathematical problem, bizarre types of preference orderings exist which satisfy assumptions 2.2 and 2.3 yet cannot be represented by an order-preserving, real-valued function.[6] As it turns out, the technical assumption (2.6) which suffices to show that an optimal consumption bundle exists so long as all prices are strictly positive also suffices to prove the existence of an order-preserving, real-valued utility function.[7]

As mentioned earlier, we refer to the function U as the consumer's utility function but it should be kept in mind that the consumer theory which we shall develop in no way depends upon the existence of any measurable physiological or psychological entity called *utility* nor does it even require that the consumer be cognizant of any such notion. All that is required is that the consumer's preference ordering satisfy assumptions 2.2 and 2.3 (and the technical assumption 2.6, which precludes the bizarre class of preference orderings that are not representable).

We also need to emphasize that the utility function representing the preference ordering is arbitrary in the sense that it is not unique. Any order-preserving function will do. Put differently, if U is a representation then so is $\tilde{U}$, defined by $\tilde{U}(x) = F(U(x))$ for all x in X where F is an increasing (strictly monotonic) function, or transformation, of its one variable; i.e., $U(\bar{x}) > U(x')$ if and only if $F(U(\bar{x})) > F(U(x'))$ for all $\bar{x}$, x' in X. Examples of strictly monotonic transformations are $F(U(x)) = a + bU(x)$ where $b > 0$ and a is an arbitrary real number, and $F(U(x)) = (U(x))^2$ so long as $U(x)$ is everywhere positive.

The critical aspect of a strictly monotonic transformation is that it does not change the ordering of utility levels attached to consumption bundles. In other

[4] We will have more to say about the measurement of utility in section 3.6 below.

[5] Apostle [1974, pp. 94–95] and Klein [1973, pp. 92–93] briefly review real-valued and increasing (strictly monotonic) functions.

[6] Proof of this fact is beyond the scope of this book, but the dispomaniac's preference ordering illustrated in figure 2.2 is an example of the class of preference orderings which are not representable. The mathematically sophisticated student is referred to a clever proof by Debreu [1959, pp. 72–73] that this preference ordering is not representable.

[7] See Debreu [1959, pp. 56–59].

words, in numbering the indifference classes, only the order counts. For example, in figure 3.1, we could associate with $I(\bar{x})$, $I(\hat{x})$, and $I(x')$ the values 1, 2, and 3, respectively. The ordering would be unaffected, however, if we were to associate with these three indifference curves the values 1, 1.1, and 1000, respectively (see exercise 3.1).

3.3 NONSATIATION AND CONVEXITY

If the consumer's preference ordering can be represented by a utility function, the consumer choice problem may be characterized as maximizing the utility function subject to the budget constraint; i.e.,

$$\max_x U(x) = U(x_1, \ldots, x_n) \qquad \text{s.t.} \sum_{i=1}^{n} p_i x_i \leq y. \tag{3.1}$$

In order to exploit this fact, we have to make additional assumptions about the utility function.[8] To be consistent with our view of preference theory as the foundation of the theory of demand, we shall state the next two assumptions in the context of preference theory and interpret them in terms of the utility function.

Nonsatiation

Assumption 3.1 (Nonsatiation) There is some j such that $\bar{x} \succ x'$ if $\bar{x}_j > x'_j$ and $\bar{x}_i = x'_i$ for all $i \neq j$.

That is, there is some commodity—say the jth—of which the consumer would always prefer to consume more, i.e., with which he is never sated.

If the preference ordering is representable, the nonsatiation assumption is equivalent to the assumption that, for some j, $U(\bar{x}) > U(x')$ if $\bar{x}_j > x'_j$ and $\bar{x}_i = x'_i$ for all $i \neq j$. Thus, if the consumption of the jth commodity is increased and the consumption of the other $n - 1$ commodities is held constant, the consumer's utility is increased (similarly, a reduction in the consumption of the jth commodity reduces the consumer's utility level).

The nonsatiation assumption guarantees that all bundles in the preferred subset exhaust the consumer's income. That is, preferred consumption bundles are represented by points on, and not below, the budget plane. This follows from the fact that any bundle that does not exhaust the consumer's income is inferior, in the preference ordering, to a bundle which uses up the remaining income on the commodity with which the consumer is not sated.

[8] The utility function discussed thus far is nothing more than a one-to-one, order-preserving mapping from X to a set of real numbers and it is entirely possible that a particular mapping cannot be written in any analytical form. It is true, however, that any continuous function can be represented arbitrarily closely by a polynomial of some degree.

Strict Convexity

The next assumption requires the introduction of a new concept. The *convex combination* (weighted average) of consumption bundles, $\bar{x}$ and $\hat{x}$, is given by $\alpha\bar{x} + (1 - \alpha)\hat{x}$ for all values of α satisfying $0 < \alpha < 1$. The notion of a convex combination is best understood by a simple numerical example. Suppose that $\bar{x} = [6, 4]$ and $\hat{x} = [2, 8]$. These two vectors correspond to the points, $\bar{x}$ and $\hat{x}$, in figure 3.2. The points represented by $\alpha\bar{x} + (1 - \alpha)\hat{x}$ all lie on the straight line connecting $\bar{x}$ and $\hat{x}$. For example, suppose that $\alpha = .5$, in which case $\alpha\bar{x} + (1 - \alpha)\hat{x} = .5\bar{x} + .5\hat{x} = .5[6, 4] + .5[2, 8] = [4, 6]$. This convex combination is represented by the point x', with coordinates 4 and 6, in figure 3.2. It will be noted that this point lies on the straight line drawn from $\bar{x}$ to $\hat{x}$, exactly halfway between the two points, reflecting the fact that the two vectors $\bar{x}$ and $\hat{x}$ receive equal weights in the convex combination, x'. As the value of α moves closer to 1 (in which case the value of $1 - \alpha$ moves closer to 0), the convex combination approaches the point $\bar{x}$. For example, suppose that $\alpha = .9$, in which case $\alpha\bar{x} + (1 - \alpha)\hat{x} = .9\bar{x} + .1\hat{x} = [5.4, 3.6] + [0.2, .8] = [5.6, 4.4]$. This convex combination is represented by the point $\overset{*}{x}$ in figure 3.2. The last thing to notice is that since α is not allowed to take on the value of 0 or 1, $\alpha\bar{x} + (1 - \alpha)\hat{x}$ can be made arbitrarily close to either $\hat{x}$ or $\bar{x}$ by appropriate choice of the value of α, but this convex combination cannot be made equal to either of these two vectors. That is, the convex combination lies on the interior of the line drawn between $\bar{x}$ and $\hat{x}$.

Assumption 3.2 (Strict Convexity) If $\bar{x}$ and $\hat{x}$ are two consumption bundles in the consumption space satisfying $\bar{x} \succcurlyeq \hat{x}$, then $\alpha\bar{x} + (1 - \alpha)\hat{x} \succ \hat{x}$ for all values of α satisfying $0 < \alpha < 1$.

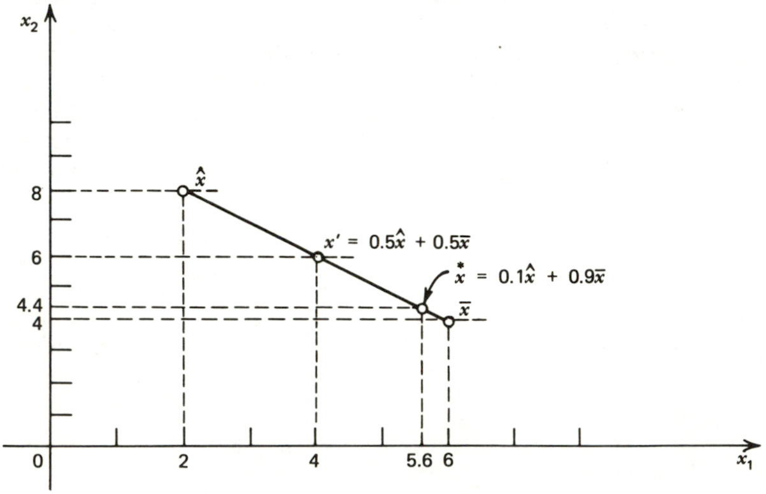

Figure 3.2

This assumption states that, if the bundle $\bar{x}$ is no worse than the bundle $\hat{x}$, then all commodity bundles represented by points on the interior of the straight line drawn between $\bar{x}$ and $\hat{x}$ are strictly preferred to $\hat{x}$. This assumption imposes strong restrictions on the form of the consumer's indifference surfaces. This is easy to demonstrate in two-space. For example, consider the indifference curve in figure 3.3. This indifference curve may be divided into two segments: that to the left of $\bar{x}$ and that to the right of $\bar{x}$. The first of these segments is strictly "convex to the origin" whereas the second is strictly "concave to the origin."

The essential feature of assumption 3.2 is that it precludes indifference curves which take the shape illustrated in the second segment. To see this, consider the straight line drawn between the consumption bundles $\bar{x}$ and x'. As $\bar{x} \sim x'$ and therefore $\bar{x} \succcurlyeq x'$, assumption 3.2 implies that all of the commodity bundles represented by points on the interior of the straight line drawn between $\bar{x}$ and x' are strictly preferred to x'. As all of these points lie below the indifference curve, $I(x')$, the nonsatiation assumption 3.1 implies that x' is strictly preferred to all of these commodity bundles, arriving at a contradiction. Therefore, assumptions 3.1 and 3.2 are inconsistent with an indifference curve which assumes the shape exhibited to the right of point $\bar{x}$ in figure 3.3. On the other hand, it is easy to see that an indifference curve with the shape exhibited to the left of point $\bar{x}$ satisfies assumption 3.2, since all points on the interior of the line drawn between $\bar{x}$ and $\hat{x}$ lie above the indifference curve through $\hat{x}$ and hence are strictly preferred to this commodity bundle. In conclusion, assumption 3.2 implies that all indifference curves are strictly convex to the origin.

Assumption 3.2 precludes not only indifference curves that are concave to the origin, but also indifference curves with flat segments such as that displayed in figure 3.4. The flat segment between points $\bar{x}$ and $\hat{x}$ is precluded by assumption

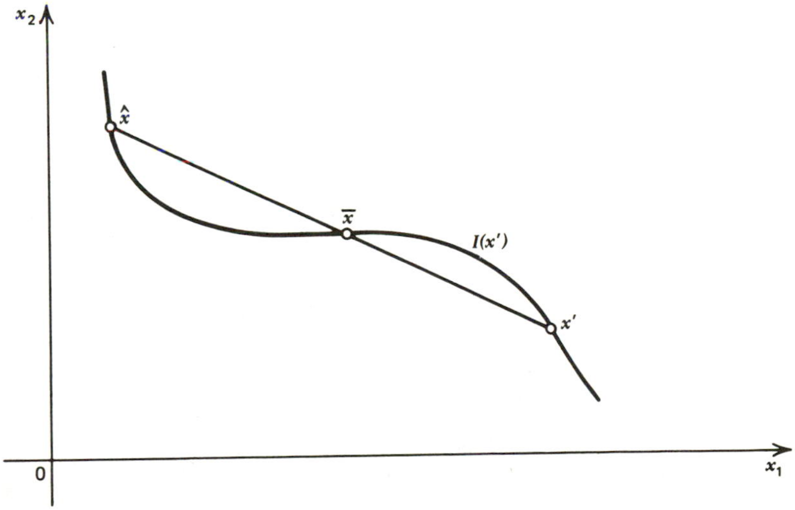

Figure 3.3

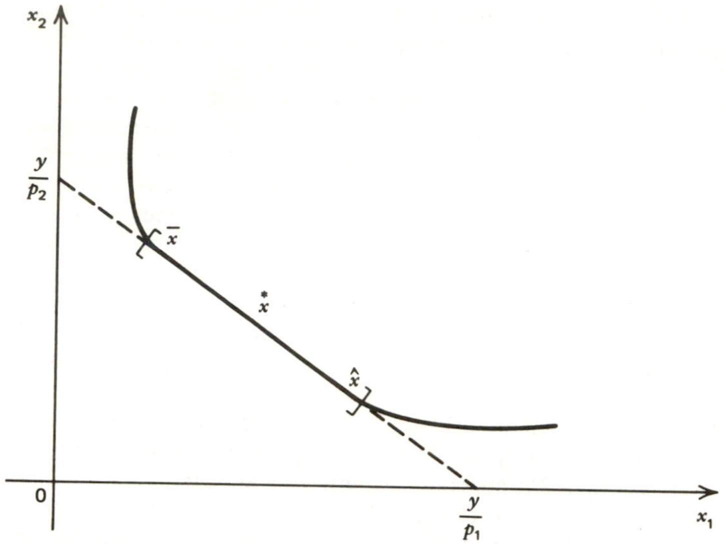

Figure 3.4

3.2 since all of the points on this flat segment are themselves convex combinations of $\bar{x}$ and $\hat{x}$. As $\bar{x} \sim \hat{x}$, hence $\bar{x} \succsim \hat{x}$, assumption 3.2 implies that all commodity bundles represented by points on the interior of this line are strictly preferred to $\hat{x}$. However, as these points are on the same indifference curve as $\hat{x}$, it is clear that the consumer is indifferent between any commodity bundle on this line and the bundle $\hat{x}$, arriving at a contradiction. Thus, assumption 3.2 precludes flat segments as well as strictly concave segments in indifference curves.

The principal implication of the strict convexity assumption is that the set of preferred bundles, $\overset{*}{X}(p, y)$, contains only one bundle for all positive (p, y); that is the optimal consumption bundle is necessarily unique for all positive prices and incomes. The multiple optima in figures 2.6 and 3.4 are ruled out by strict convexity.[9]

3.4 THE MARGINAL RATE OF SUBSTITUTION

Differentiability and Marginal Utilities

If the utility function is differentiable, the strict convexity assumption can be clarified by the introduction of a new concept. The following assumption will be useful both now and later:

[9] Assumption 3.2 would also allow us to weaken assumption 3.1 without undermining the implication that consumers spend their entire income. In particular, assumption 3.1 can be weakened to "global nonsatiation": given any x in X, there is some other $\overset{*}{x}$ in X such that $\overset{*}{x} \succ x$ (see exercise 3.2).

Assumption 3.3 (Differentiability) The utility function, U, is differentiable for all strictly positive consumption bundles.

This assumption guarantees, so long as $x_i > 0$ for all i, that the derivative, $\partial U(x)/\partial x_i$, exists. This derivative has an intuitive interpretation in terms of the notion of "utility." It tells us by how much utility is increased when the consumption of the ith commodity is increased at the rate of one unit per time period. This notion is commonly referred to as the *marginal utility* of the ith commodity, denoted $MU_i(x)$.

Two things should be noted about the marginal utility of a commodity. First, the marginal utility of the ith commodity depends in general on the consumption of *all n* commodities. Second, marginal utility is not unique; i.e., it is not invariant under strictly monotonic transformations of the utility function. Put differently, only the sign, but not the magnitude, of the marginal utility is meaningful in the modern theory of the consumer (see exercise 3.3).

The Marginal Rate of Substitution Defined

Define the *marginal rate of substitution* of the ith for the jth commodity, $MRS_{ij}(x)$, as the maximal rate at which the consumer's consumption of commodity j can be reduced, without reducing his utility, when the consumption of the ith commodity is increased at the rate of one additional unit per time period. Clearly, the value of $MRS_{ij}(x)$ generally depends upon the consumption level of the two commodities and indeed of all other commodities.

The concept of the marginal rate of substitution can be clarified by reference to the indifference curve in figure 3.5. In the two-commondity case,

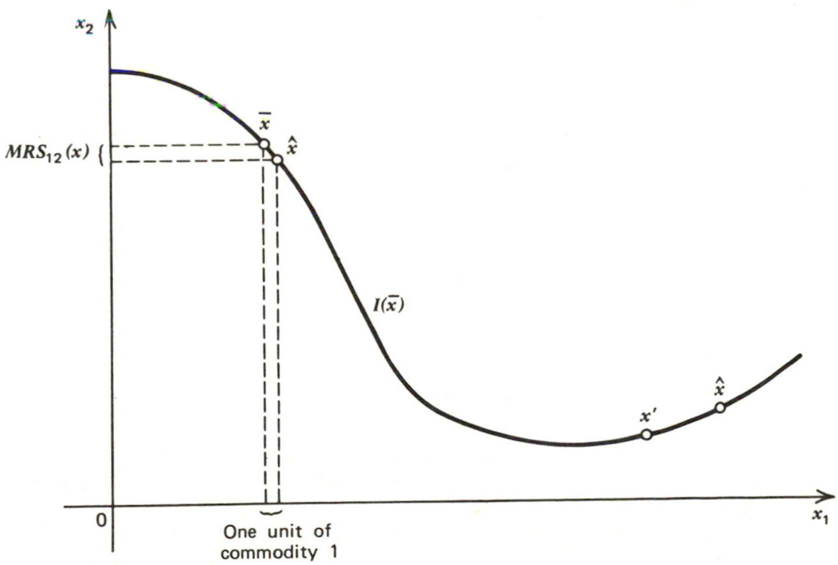

Figure 3.5

the *marginal rate of substitution of the first for the second commodity is simply the negative of the slope of the indifference curve.* To see why this is so, note that the slope of the indifference curves indicates the rate at which the consumption of commodity 2 is changed when the consumption of commodity 1 is increased at the rate of one unit per time period, holding the consumer on the same indifference curve. Thus, if the slope is negative, it clearly indicates the rate at which commodity 2 may be decreased under those circumstances. If the slope of the indifference curve is positive, the consumption of commodity 2 must be *increased* when the consumption of commodity 1 is increased in order to keep the consumer on the same indifference curve. In this case, the amount by which the consumer is willing to "reduce" the consumption of commodity 2 when the consumption of commodity 1 is increased by one unit is a negative amount (an awkward way of saying that the consumption of this commodity is increased). Thus, a negatively sloped indifference curve indicates a positive marginal rate of substitution and a positively sloped indifference curve reflects a negative marginal rate of substitution.[10] We might also note that the slope of the indifference curve referred to the vertical axis (i.e., the inverse of the slope referred to the horizontal axis) is nothing other than the marginal rate of substitution of commodity 2 for commodity 1, since it indicates the amount by which the consumption of commodity 1 must be reduced in order to compensate the consumer for a one-unit increase in the consumption of commodity 2.

Relation Between the Marginal Rate of Substitution and Marginal Utilities

The notion of the marginal rate of substitution can be clarified by a slightly more rigorous examination. When there are only two commodities, the utility of the consumer may be expressed as

$$u \doteq U(x_1, x_2). \tag{3.2}$$

Suppose that both partial derivatives of U (both marginal utilities) are positive.[11] Then the indifference curves would necessarily be negatively sloped. This means that an indifference curve, corresponding to utility level u, can be represented by an equation

$$x_2 = \phi_u(x_1) \tag{3.3}$$

where ϕ_u is a decreasing function. Thus, $\phi_u(x_1)$ is the quantity of commodity 2 that yields utility level u if the quantity of commodity 1 is x_1. Setting the utility function image equal to u, $U(x_1, x_2) = u$, we can substitute for x_2 using (3.3):

$$U(x_1, \phi_u(x_1)) = u. \tag{3.4}$$

[10] If the slope is zero, the marginal rate of substitution is zero and if the indifference curve is vertical (the slope is "infinite" or "undefined") the marginal rate of substitution is infinite ("undefined").

[11] If we divided the consumption space into regions such that the partial derivatives of U would not change sign within each region, the following analysis would go through for each region.

As (3.4) is an identity, we can partially differentiate with respect to x_1:

$$\frac{\partial U(x_1, \phi_u(x_1))}{\partial x_1} + \frac{\partial U(x_1, \phi_u(x_1))}{\partial \phi_u(x_1)} \frac{d\phi_u(x_1)}{dx_1} = 0.$$

Rearranging yields

$$-\frac{d\phi_u(x_1)}{dx_1} = \frac{\partial U(x_1, \phi_u(x_1))/\partial x_1}{\partial U(x_1, \phi_u(x_1))/\partial \phi_u(x_1)}$$

Substituting for $\phi_u(x_1)$ from (3.3) in the right-hand side,

$$-\frac{d\phi_u(x_1)}{dx_1} = \frac{\partial U(x_1, x_2)/\partial x_1}{\partial U(x_1, x_2)/\partial x_2}$$

Each side of this identity has an economic interpretation. The left-hand side is the negative of the slope of the u-indifference curve; from above, we know that this is the marginal rate of substitution of commodity 1 for commodity 2. The right-hand side is the ratio of marginal utilities. Thus,

$$MRS_{12}(x_1, x_2) = \frac{\partial U(x_1, x_2)/\partial x_1}{\partial U(x_1, x_2)/\partial x_2} = \frac{MU_1(x_1, x_2)}{MU_2(x_1, x_2)}; \tag{3.5}$$

that is, the marginal rate of substitution is equal to the ratio of marginal utilities. This condition generalizes to

$$MRS_{ij}(x) = \frac{\partial U(x)/\partial x_i}{\partial U(x)/\partial x_j}, \qquad i = 1, \ldots, n, \quad j = 1, \ldots, n, \tag{3.6}$$

so long as $\partial U(x)/\partial x_j \neq 0$ for all j.*

***NOTE** An indifference surface can be represented by

$$x_j = \phi_u^j(x_1, \ldots, x_{j-1}, x_{j+1}, \ldots, x_n) = \phi_u^j(x^{-j}).$$

Hence

$$U(x_1, \ldots, x_{j-1}, \phi_u^j(x^{-j}), x_{j+1}, \ldots, x_n) = u.$$

Differentiating with respect to x_i $(i \neq j)$, say, yields

$$\frac{\partial U(x_1, \ldots, x_{j-1}, \phi_u^j(x^{-j}), x_{j+1}, \ldots, x_n)}{\partial x_i} + \frac{\partial U(x_1, \ldots, x_{j-1}, \phi_u^j(x^{-j}), x_{j+1}, \ldots, x_n)}{\partial \phi_u^j(x^{-j})} \cdot \frac{\partial \phi_u^j(x^{-j})}{\partial x_i} = 0.$$

Rearranging terms and substituting x_j for $\phi_u^j(x^{-j})$, we obtain

$$MRS_{ij}(x) = -\frac{\partial \phi_u^j(x^{-j})}{\partial x_i} = \frac{\partial U(x)/\partial x_i}{\partial U(x)/\partial x_j}.$$

The Law of Diminishing Marginal Rate of Substitution

The strict convexity assumption (3.2) can be reinterpreted in terms of the concept of the marginal rate of substitution. Strict convexity of the preference ordering implies that the indifference curves are strictly convex with respect to the origin. Hence the rate of change of the marginal rate of substitution of commodity 1 for commodity 2 with respect to a change in the consumption of commodity 1, holding utility constant, is strictly negative; i.e.,

$$\frac{\partial MRS_{12}(x_1, \phi_u(x_1))}{\partial x_1} < 0.$$

This formulation explains why assumption 3.2 is sometimes called the assumption of *diminishing marginal rate of substitution.*

The strict convexity assumption is fairly reasonable. Suppose that commodity 1 is bread and commodity 2 is beer. This assumption says that as the consumer acquires more and more bread, the amount of beer he is willing to give up for one more unit of bread diminishes. That is, if the consumer has a lot of beer and very little bread, he may be willing to give up quite a bit of beer to get another loaf of bread. On the other hand, if he has a large amount of bread and very little beer, he is willing to give up very little beer to secure an additional unit of bread.[12]

3.5 UTILITY MAXIMIZATION

First-Order Conditions for Interior Solutions

The nonsatiation and strict convexity assumptions (3.1 and 3.2) guarantee that the optimal consumption bundle is unique and is represented by a point on (rather than below) the budget plane. It remains possible that the consumer's optimal commodity bundle is generated by a "corner solution" such as that illustrated in figure 3.6. In order to exploit the calculus, corner solutions must be precluded. Hence we posit another assumption.

Assumption 3.4 (Interior Solution) The (unique) optimal consumption bundle, $\overset{*}{x} = [\overset{*}{x}_1, \ldots, \overset{*}{x}_n]$, satisfies $\overset{*}{x}_i > 0$, $i = 1, \ldots, n$.

As we have seen, the problem of consumer choice can be represented as the problem of maximizing the utility function subject to the budget constraint (see 3.1 above). However, by assumption 3.1 (nonsatiation), we know that the

[12] For additional interpretation of the assumption of diminishing marginal rate of substitution, see exercise 3.4.

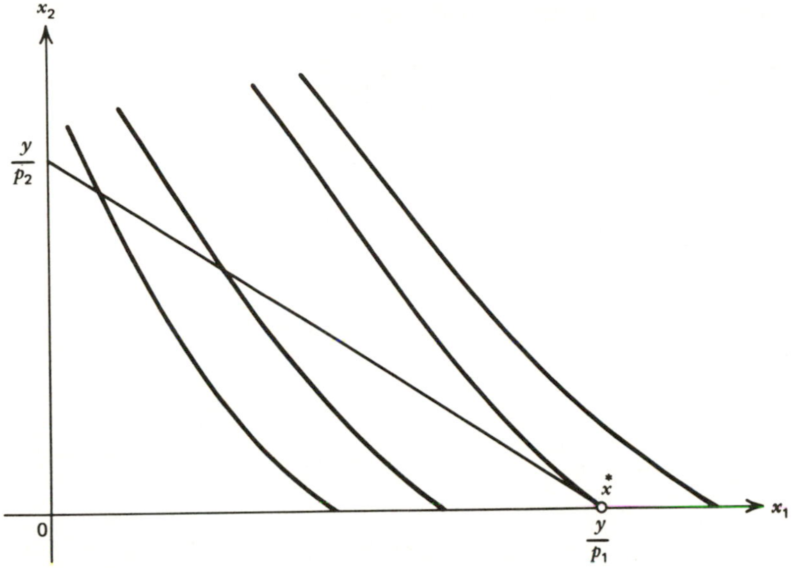

Figure 3.6

utility-maximizing consumer will expend all of his income. Hence, by assumption 3.1, we may express the utility-maximization problem as

$$\operatorname*{Max}_{x} U(x) = U(x_1, \ldots, x_n) \qquad \text{s.t. } y = \sum_{i=1}^{n} p_i x_i. \tag{3.7}$$

One method of solving a constrained maximization problem such as (3.7) is to substitute the constraint into the objective function. Solving the budget equation for x_1, we obtain

$$x_1 = \frac{y - \sum_{i=2}^{n} p_i x_i}{p_1} = \frac{y}{p_1} - \sum_{i=2}^{n} \frac{p_i}{p_1} x_i = \psi(y, p, x_2, \ldots, x_n). \tag{3.8}$$

If we substitute (3.8) into the utility function, the maximization problem becomes

$$\operatorname*{Max}_{x} U(\psi(y, p, x_2, \ldots, x_n), x_2, \ldots, x_n). \tag{3.9}$$

The first-order conditions for the utility function to be maximized are that all of the partial derivatives be equated to zero.[13] Thus, we must differentiate the objective function (3.8) with respect to $x_2, \ldots, x_n$. Using the chain rule,[14] we

[13] See Apostle [1974, pp. 376–379] and Hadley [1964, pp. 53–60] for necessary (first-order) conditions for unconstrained optimization.

[14] Apostle [1974, pp. 106, 352] discusses the chain, or composite function, rule of differential calculus.

find that the first-order conditions for solving (3.9) are

$$\frac{\partial U(\psi(p, y, x_2, \ldots, x_n), x_2, \ldots, x_n)}{\partial \psi(y, p, x_2, \ldots, x_n)} \frac{\partial \psi(p, y, x_2, \ldots, x_n)}{\partial x_2} + \frac{\partial U(\psi(p, y, x_2, \ldots, x_n), x_2, \ldots, x_n)}{\partial x_2} = 0,$$

$$\frac{\partial U(\psi(p, y, x_2, \ldots, x_n), x_2, \ldots, x_n)}{\partial \psi(p, y, x_2, \ldots, x_n)} \frac{\partial \psi(p, y, x_2, \ldots, x_n)}{\partial x_3} + \frac{\partial U(\psi(p, y, x_2, \ldots, x_n), x_2, \ldots, x_n)}{\partial x_3} = 0,$$

$$\frac{\partial U(\psi(p, y, x_2, \ldots, x_n), x_2, \ldots, x_n)}{\partial \psi(p, y, x_2, \ldots, x_n)} \frac{\partial \psi(p, y, x_2, \ldots, x_n)}{\partial x_n} + \frac{\partial U(\psi(p, y, x_2, \ldots, x_n), x_2, \ldots, x_n)}{\partial x_n} = 0.$$

Evaluation of the derivatives of ψ in this system using equation (3.8) and substitution from (3.8) yields

$$\frac{\partial U(x)}{\partial x_1}\left(-\frac{p_2}{p_1}\right) + \frac{\partial U(x)}{\partial x_2} = 0$$

$$\frac{\partial U(x)}{\partial x_1}\left(-\frac{p_3}{p_1}\right) + \frac{\partial U(x)}{\partial x_3} = 0$$

$$\vdots$$

$$\frac{\partial U(x)}{\partial x_1}\left(-\frac{p_n}{p_1}\right) + \frac{\partial U(x)}{\partial x_n} = 0.$$

Straightforward algebraic manipulation of this system yields

$$\frac{\partial U(x)/\partial x_2}{\partial U(x)/\partial x_1} = \frac{p_2}{p_1}$$

$$\frac{\partial U(x)/\partial x_3}{\partial U(x)/\partial x_1} = \frac{p_3}{p_1} \tag{3.10}$$

$$\vdots$$

$$\frac{\partial U(x)/\partial x_n}{\partial U(x)/\partial x_1} = \frac{p_n}{p_1}.$$

But, because the marginal rate of substitution between the ith and the jth commodity is simply the ratio of partial derivatives of the utility function with respect to these two commodities, the first-order conditions are expressed as

$$MRS_{21}(x) = \frac{p_2}{p_1}$$

$$MRS_{31}(x) = \frac{p_3}{p_1}$$

$$\vdots$$

$$MRS_{n1}(x) = \frac{p_n}{p_1}.$$

Finally, as the choice of the variable to substitute out of the utility function is arbitrary, this system of first-order conditions may be expressed succinctly as follows:

$$MRS_{ij}(x) = \frac{p_i}{p_j}, \qquad i, j = 1, \ldots, n. \tag{3.11}$$

This condition makes sense. Recall that the marginal rate of substitution of the ith for the jth commodity is defined as the rate at which the consumer is *willing* to give up commodity j in order to increase his consumption of the ith commodity at the rate of one unit per time period. Moreover, from section 2.3, we know that the price ratio, p_i/p_j, is the negative of the derivative of the budget equation and thus reflects the rate at which the consumer *must* give up commodity j in order to secure additional consumption of the ith commodity at the rate of one unit per time period. Condition (3.11) therefore states that, at the margin, the rate at which the consumer is *willing* to give up commodity j in order to increase his consumption of the ith commodity at the rate of one unit per period must be equal to the rate at which he *must* give it up. Moreover, this condition holds for all pairs of commodities.

To further our conviction that the set of first-order conditions (3.11) makes sense, suppose that the equality does not hold; in particular, suppose that

$$MRS_{ij}(x) > \frac{p_i}{p_j} \tag{3.12}$$

for some i and j. In this case, the consumer is willing to give up more of the jth commodity to obtain additional amounts of the ith than he has to, given the prices of these two commodities. That is, to hold his utility level constant the consumer could give up more of the jth commodity than he has to. This means that if he engages in an exchange of the jth for the ith commodity at the rate given by the price ratio, he will give up less of the jth commodity than he is willing to, and will therefore increase his welfare; i.e., he will move to a higher indifference curve. Thus, if the inequality (3.12) holds, the associated bundle of commodities cannot be an optimum.

It is left to the reader to establish that, if the inequality in (3.12) is reversed, the consumer can move to more preferred bundles of commodities by exchanging the ith for the jth commodity. Thus, only when the marginal rate of substitution

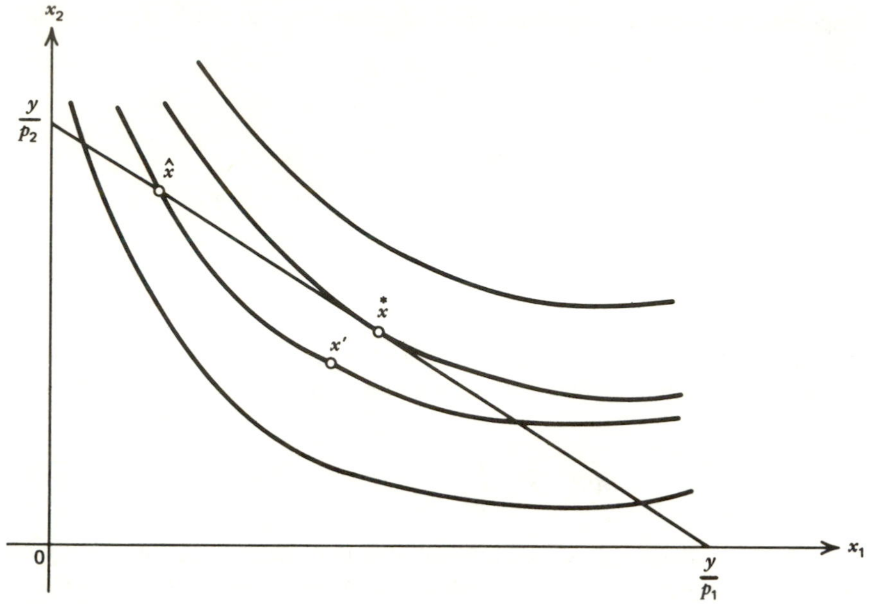

Figure 3.7

is equal to the price ratio is the consumer unable to increase his utility by exchanging one commodity for the other.

The optimality conditions in the two-commodity case are illustrated in figure 3.7. We have already noted above that the consumer's optimum is attained at a point of tangency between an indifference curve and the budget line. But at this point of tangency the slopes of the two curves are equal. As the slope of the indifference curve is simply the negative of the marginal rate of substitution between the first and the second good, $-MRS_{12}(x)$, and as the slope of the budget line is simply the negative of the ratio of the price of the first to the second commodity $-p_1/p_2$, this equilibrium is identical to condition (3.11).

As further justification of the equilibrium condition, consider the commodity bundle $\hat{x}$ in figure 3.7. This commodity bundle lies on an indifference curve lower than that which passes through $\overset{*}{x}$ and hence is inferior to $\overset{*}{x}$ in the consumer's preference ordering. Moreover, at $\hat{x}$ *the slope of the budget line* is greater than *the slope of the indifference curve* and therefore the marginal rate of substitution (the negative of the slope of the indifference curve) is greater than the price ratio (the negative of the slope of the budget line). Consequently, the consumer's utility is increased by the exchange of commodity 2 for commodity 1. The exchange of the second for the first commodity moves the consumer down the budget line. As the commodity bundle shifts down the budget line, higher and higher indifference curves are intersected until the commodity bundle $\overset{*}{x}$ is reached. Beyond that point, further movement down the budget line would intersect lower and lower indifference curves, thus lowering the consumer's utility level.

The Method of Lagrange

It is instructive at this point to consider an alternative technique for carrying out the optimization problem. Whenever an objective function is to be maximized subject to a constraint which takes the form of an equality, such as the budget equality, the method of Lagrange may be used.[15] To illustrate this method, note that the budget equation may be rewritten as

$$\sum_{i=1}^{n} p_i x_i - y = 0.$$

Form the Lagrange function,

$$L(x, \lambda) = U(x) - \lambda\left(\sum_{i=1}^{n} p_i x_i - y\right),$$

where λ is a new variable which is called the *Lagrange multiplier*. The constrained utility-maximization problem is solved by finding the critical point of this function (i.e., the point where the partial derivatives of $L(x, \lambda)$ vanish).[16] To convince the reader of this fact, let us derive the first-order utility-maximization conditions using this approach to see that they are identical to those developed by the method of substituting the constraint into the objective function. This is worth the trouble now because we are going to use the method of Lagrange to solve constrained-optimization problems throughout this book. It is more convenient than the alternative method of substituting the constraint into the objective function.

The critical point of the Lagrange function is found by solving the following set of equations:

$$\begin{aligned}
\frac{\partial L(x, \lambda)}{\partial x_1} &= \frac{\partial U(x)}{\partial x_1} - \lambda p_1 = 0 \\
&\vdots \\
\frac{\partial L(x, \lambda)}{\partial x_i} &= \frac{\partial U(x)}{\partial x_i} - \lambda p_i = 0 \\
&\vdots \\
\frac{\partial L(x, \lambda)}{\partial x_n} &= \frac{\partial U(x)}{\partial x_n} - \lambda p_n = 0 \\
\frac{\partial L(x, \lambda)}{\partial \lambda} &= -\sum_{i=1}^{n} p_i x_i + y = 0.
\end{aligned} \tag{3.13}$$

[15] See Hadley [1964, pp. 61–68] and Apostle [1974, pp. 380–384] on the method of Lagrange.

[16] Note that the critical point of $L(x, \lambda)$ is neither a maximum nor a minimum. In fact, in the above problem, $L(x, \lambda)$ has neither a maximum nor a minimum. Rather, the critical point is a *saddle point* of $L(x, \lambda)$. That is, the critical point $(\bar{x}, \bar{\lambda})$ satisfies $L(x, \bar{\lambda}) \leq L(\bar{x}, \bar{\lambda}) \leq L(\bar{x}, \lambda)$ for all values of (x, λ).

This is a system of $n + 1$ equations in the $n + 1$ unknowns, $x_1, \ldots, x_n$, and λ. The optimization problem is completed by the solution of the $n + 1$ equations for the $n + 1$ unknowns. System (3.13) may be simplified by rewriting the first n equations as

$$\frac{\partial U(x)}{\partial x_1} = \lambda p_1$$

$$\vdots$$

$$\frac{\partial U(x)}{\partial x_i} = \lambda p_i$$

$$\vdots$$

$$\frac{\partial U(x)}{\partial x_n} = \lambda p_n.$$

Dividing the last $n - 1$ of these equations by the first, we have

$$\frac{\partial U(x)/\partial x_2}{\partial U(x)/\partial x_1} = \frac{p_2}{p_1}$$

$$\vdots$$

$$\frac{\partial U(x)/\partial x_i}{\partial U(x)/\partial x_1} = \frac{p_i}{p_1} \tag{3.14}$$

$$\vdots$$

$$\frac{\partial U(x)/\partial x_n}{\partial U(x)/\partial x_1} = \frac{p_n}{p_1}$$

or, recalling equation (3.6), we obtain

$$MRS_{21}(x) = \frac{p_2}{p_1}$$

$$\vdots$$

$$MRS_{i1}(x) = \frac{p_i}{p_1} \tag{3.15}$$

$$\vdots$$

$$MRS_{n1}(x) = \frac{p_n}{p_1}.$$

Thus, the partial derivatives of $L(x, \lambda)$ vanish where the marginal rates of substitution are equated to respective price ratios. This set of conditions is, of course, equivalent to the set of first-order maximization conditions obtained by substituting the budget constraint into the objective function.

The Roles of the Assumptions

Assumptions 3.2–3.4 imply that the set of first-order conditions (3.15) are satisfied by a unique bundle of commodities in the consumer's budget set. In the absence of differentiability (assumption 3.3), the optimal commodity bundle might be given by $\overset{*}{x}$ in figure 3.8 but as this point, the derivative of the indifference curve, hence the marginal rate of substitution, is undefined.

Assumption 3.1 (nonsatiation) provides assurance that the optimal commodity bundle lies on the budget line. If this assumption is not satisfied, the optimal commodity bundle might be a bliss point, such as $\overset{*}{x}$ in figure 3.9. In this case, again, the marginal rate of substitution is not defined.

Assumption 3.2 (strict convexity) guarantees us that the optimal commodity bundle is unique. In the absence of this assumption we may have multiple equilibria such as those shown in figure 2.6 and figure 3.4.

The assumption of strict convexity also guarantees that second-order maximization conditions are satisfed. If the indifference curves were concave to the origin, as displayed in figure 3.10, the commodity bundle $\bar{x}$ would satisfy the first-order conditions for maximizing utility subject to the budget constraint, but would be characterized by minimum utility along the budget line rather than by maximum utility. This can be seen by the fact that moving in either direction

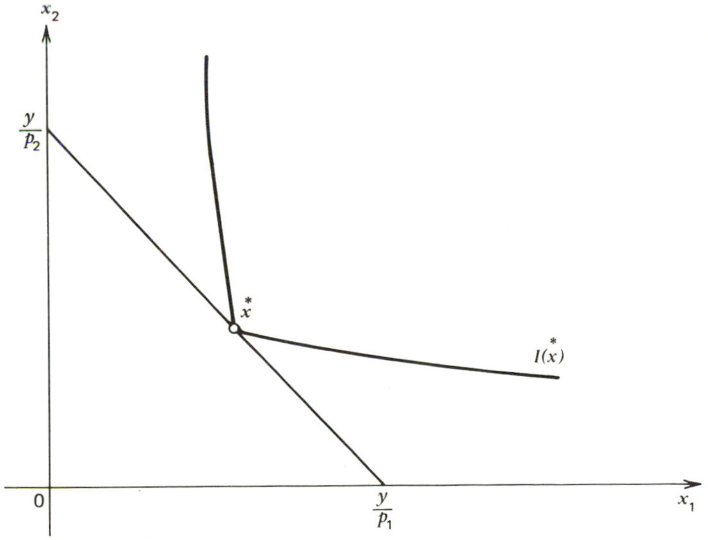

Figure 3.8

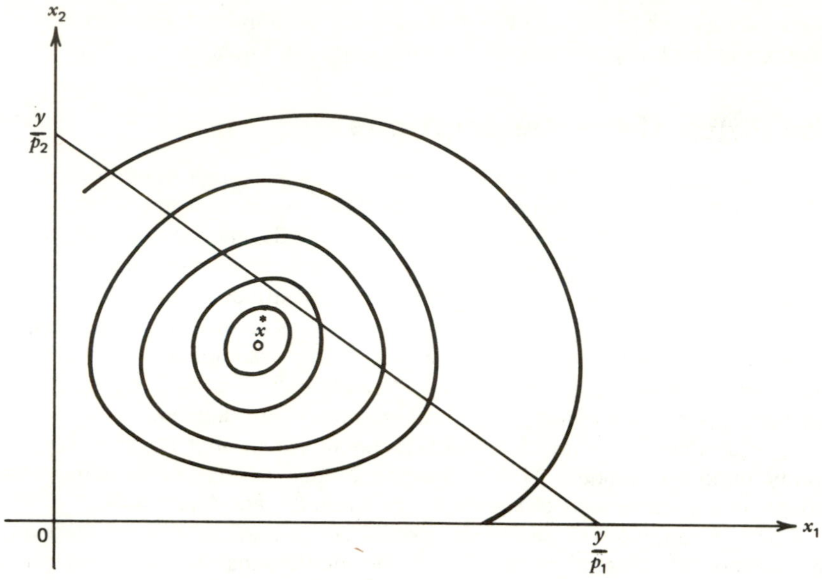

Figure 3.9

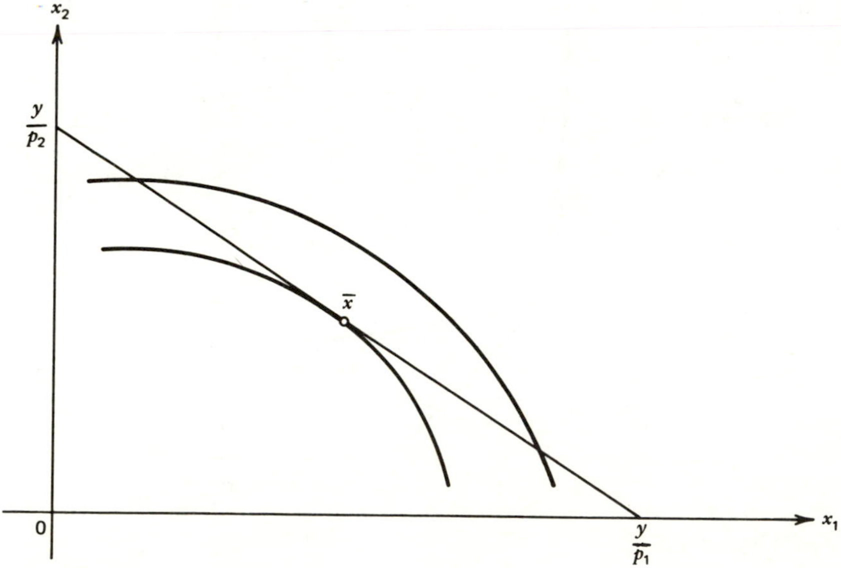

Figure 3.10

on the budget line would increase the consumer's utility since higher indifference curves would be attained.*

**NOTE* The second-order conditions for the maximization of utility subject to the budget equality are that the bordered principal minors,

$$\begin{vmatrix} U_{11}(\overset{*}{x}) & U_{12}(\overset{*}{x}) & -p_1 \\ U_{21}(\overset{*}{x}) & U_{22}(\overset{*}{x}) & -p_2 \\ -p_1 & -p_2 & 0 \end{vmatrix}, \ldots, \begin{vmatrix} U_{11}(\overset{*}{x}) & U_{12}(\overset{*}{x}) & \cdots & U_{1n}(\overset{*}{x}) & -p_1 \\ U_{21}(\overset{*}{x}) & & \cdots & U_{2n}(\overset{*}{x}) & -p_2 \\ \vdots & & & \vdots & \\ U_{n1}(\overset{*}{x}) & & \cdots & U_{nn}(\overset{*}{x}) & -p_n \\ -p_1 & & \cdots & -p_n & 0 \end{vmatrix}$$

where $U_{ij}(x) = \partial^2 U(x)/\partial x_i \partial x_j$, alternate in sign beginning with a positive sign. See Apostle [1974, pp. 380–84] and Intriligator [1978] on sufficient conditions for constrained optimization.

We have already noted that assumption 3.4 (interior solution) precludes corner solutions such as that illustrated in figure 3.6. Note that at $\overset{*}{x}$ in figure 3.6 the marginal rate of substitution is undefined. Moreover, if the definition were altered to admit a definition of $MRS_{12}(x)$ at $\overset{*}{x}$, the conditions (3.15) would not be satisfied.

Finally, note that system (3.15) contains $n - 1$ equations which, when combined with the budget equation, provide a system of n equations in the n unknown quantities, $x_1, \ldots, x_n$. The solution of this system of n equations for the n quantities solves the optimization problem for the consumer.

3.6 THE MEASURABILITY OF UTILITY: AN HISTORICAL DIGRESSION*

Strictly Monotonic Transformations and the First-Order Conditions

The analysis carried out in section 2.3 (and especially in the optional section 2.4) indicates that the problem of consumer choice can be analyzed independently of any notion of consumer utility. (Indeed, consumer choice may be possible even if the consumer has a preference ordering that *cannot* be represented by a utility function.) It is primarily because it is convenient for the theory of demand, to be studied in chapters 4 through 6, that we have gone on to examine the problem of consumer choice when the preference ordering is represented by a well-behaved utility function. We should keep in mind, however, that we do not assume that the consumer is at all cognizant of any such concept as utility. We only assume that the consumer chooses the most preferred bundle in his feasible consumption set. If the appropriate set of assumptions (2.1–2.6) are satisfied (so that the consumer's preference ordering is representable) he acts *as if* he maximizes a well-behaved utility function image subject to the budget constraint.

Recall, however, that the utility function representing the preference ordering of the consumer is not unique. Any utility function which preserves the consumer's preference ordering may be used in the utility analysis. Put differently, if U is a representation of the consumer's ordering, then $\tilde{U}$, defined by $\tilde{U}(x) = F(U(x))$ for all x in X where F is a strictly monotonic transform, is also a representation. If we assume that the transformation F is differentiable, then we may say that F is a strictly monotonic transform if and only if $F'(U(x)) > 0$ (where F' is the derivative of F) for all values of $U(x)$. That is, if and only if F is a strictly monotonic transform, the value of the utility index $\tilde{U}(x) = F(U(x))$ goes up (down) whenever the utility index $U(x)$ goes up (down).

In order to show that the consumer's optimum is unaffected by a monotonic transformation of the utility function which represents his preference ordering, let us consider the problem of maximizing a monotonic transform of the original utility index, $U(x)$, subject to the budget equality. The critical conditions of the Lagrange function,

$$F(U(x)) - \lambda\left(\sum_{i=1}^{n} p_i y_i - y\right)$$

are

$$F'(U(x))\,\frac{\partial U(x)}{\partial x_1} - \lambda p_1 = 0$$

$$\vdots$$

$$F'(U(x))\,\frac{\partial U(x)}{\partial x_n} - \lambda p_n = 0$$

$$-\sum_{i=1}^{n} p_i x_i + y = 0.$$

Adding λp_i to the ith equation for $i = 1, \ldots, n$, we have

$$\begin{aligned} F'(U(x))\,\frac{\partial U(x)}{\partial x_1} &= \lambda p_1 \\ &\vdots \\ F'(U(x))\,\frac{\partial U(x)}{\partial x_n} &= \lambda p_n. \end{aligned} \tag{3.16}$$

Dividing the last $n - 1$ of these equations by the first, we are left with

$$\begin{aligned} \frac{F'(U(x))(\partial U(x)/\partial x_2)}{F'(U(x))(\partial U(x)/\partial x_1)} &= \frac{p_2}{p_1} \\ &\vdots \\ \frac{F'(U(x))(\partial U(x)/\partial x_n)}{F'(U(x))(\partial U(x)/\partial x_1)} &= \frac{p_n}{p_1}. \end{aligned} \tag{3.17}$$

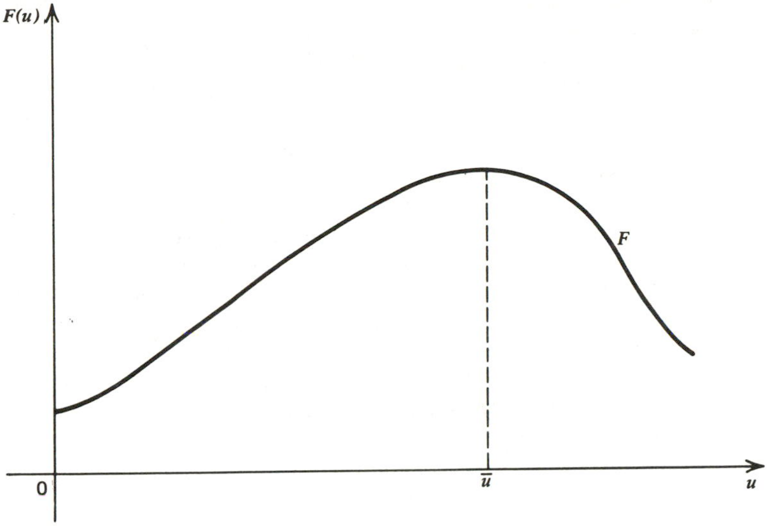

Figure 3.11

As $F'(U(x))$ cancels out of each of the ratios on the left-hand side, this system is identical to the system of equations (3.10) so that the first-order conditions for maximizing the utility function image, $U(x)$, subject to the budget equality, are identical to the first-order conditions for maximizing a strictly monotonic transform, $F(U(x))$, subject to the budget constraint.

The important thing to notice about this exercise is that it is legitimate if F is a strictly monotonic transform. If F is not a strictly monotonic transform, in which case $F'(U(x))$ is not everywhere strictly positive, the step which gets us from system (3.16) to system (3.17) is illegitimate. To see this, consider figure 3.11 which depicts a nonmonotonic differentiable transformation of the utility index, $U(x)$. At utility level $\bar{u}$, $F'(\bar{u}) = 0$, in which case the attempt to derive system (3.17) would entail dividing by zero, an illegitimate operation.

Measurability of Utility

The fact that consumer choice does not rely on the existence of a utility function, let alone consumer cognizance of such a concept, is the culminating discovery in a long history of refinements of consumer theory. Early consumer theory assumed that consumers are able to measure subjectively the number of "utiles" which they enjoy by the consumption of any given bundle of commodities. As in the more modern theory, the consumers were assumed to maximize this utility function subject to a budget constraint. It was not until the turn of the twentieth century that the Italian economist Vilfredo Pareto discovered that the formal utility-maximization problem does not require consumer ability to measure the amount of satisfaction experienced in the consumption of a particular commodity bundle. As Pareto pointed out, all that is necessary in order to develop the theory of the consumer is consumer ability to *rank* bundles of commodities. The observable results of a demand theory based upon an ordinal ranking of commodity bundles are not different from those of a theory based upon consumer measurement of the utility of the consumption of alternative commodity bundles. The logical principal of Occam's razor dictates, then, that the assumption of measurable utility should be jettisoned from consumer theory.

The pre-Paretian consumer theory was predicated upon the notion of a *cardinal* utility index, whereas the Paretian theory of utility is based on an *ordinal* utility index. Roughly speaking, a cardinally measurable index implies that consumers are able to say by how much they prefer one commodity bundle to another and to say that the increased utility from consuming two additional bottles of beer is, say, twice as large as the added utility from the consumption of one additional bottle. Ordinal utility theory, on the other hand, presumes only that consumers are able to say that they prefer one bundle to another, but the statement that one bundle is "twice as good as another" has no meaning in the context of ordinal utility theory.

More rigorously, there are several notions of measurability. This is because all types of measurement allow some degrees of freedom for the choice of a measurement index. In the most restrictive form of measurement, the only degree of freedom is in the choice of the unit of measurement. For example, weight may be measured in grams, pounds, ounces, tons, or any of a potentially infinite number of units. There is, however, a natural origin in the measurement of weight; that is, the notion of zero weight is not an arbitrary one. When only the unit of measurement is arbitrary, we say that the entity is measurable up to a *linear* transformation. That is, if I is a measurement index then so is aI, where a is an arbitrary positive scalar. The scalar, a, simply transforms the unit of measurement.

If the choice of the origin, as well as the unit of measurement, is arbitrary, we say that the entity is measurable up to an *affine* transformation. That is, if I is an index, so is $a + bI$, where a is an arbitrary scalar and b is an arbitrary positive scalar. The scalar, b, transforms the unit of measurement and the scalar, a, transforms the origin. An example of measurability up to an affine transformation is the way in which temperature is measured. The two common indices of temperature measurement are the Farenheit and Centrigrade indices. To convert the Centigrade measure into the Farenheit measure, the formula is $F = 32 + 1.8C$. Thus, the Farenheit measure is an affine transformation of the Centigrade measure in which the origin is increased by 32 units and the unit of measurement is multiplied by 1.8.

Both of the above measures are cardinal. The classical utility theory of the nineteenth century assumed that utility was measurable up to an affine transformation. That is, pre-Paretian utility theory assumed that the consumer could measure the utility attached to any commodity bundle although the choice of an origin and a unit of measurement is arbitrary. What this means is that in numbering the indifference curves, two of them may be numbered arbitrarily since there are two degrees of freedom in the measurement index. Once these are numbered, however, the number of all other indifference curves in the consumer's preference map are determined. Paretian utility theory, on the other hand, assumes that utility is measurable only up to a strictly monotonic transformation. That is, if

$U(x)$ is a utility index so is $F(x)$, where F is a strictly monotonic transform. This means that the numbering of the indifference curve of the consumer is arbitrary except for order. That is, it is only necessary that the number attached to any indifference curve be greater than the number attached to all indifference curves with inferior commodity bundles.

The Paretian revolution, then, divested consumer theory of the notion of cardinally measurable utility without any damage whatever to the robustness of the theory. Similarly, the theory of preferences as developed by Debreu and others in the post-World War II era has divested many aspects of consumer theory of the notion of utility itself. The modern theory of the consumer is founded on the notion of consumers' preference orderings. It is not necessary that the consumers be cognizant of any notion such as a utility function nor even that their preference ordering be representable by a utility function. Thus, the history of the development of consumer theory has been one of continual refinement and weakening of the basic assumptions needed to deal with consumer choice. This refinement has increased the generality of the theory. We should note, however, that these refinements have not enhanced the predictive, or positive, content of consumer theory. The set of implications remains unchanged; only the assumptions have been weakened. While this constitutes considerable improvement in the theory, particularly from a logical point of view, much of the research which has gone in the other direction—toward *less* generality or more specialization—has been just as valuable. That is, in order to extract useful predictive content from consumer theory, it has been necessary to strengthen the assumptions underlying consumer choice (by, for example, specifying a particular form of a utility function). Some of these developments are discussed briefly in the suggested reading section following part I.

This chapter has laid the basic foundation for the theory of the consumer. We have not yet, however, derived any empirically refutable implications of the theory. We have only discussed the nature of consumer choice. In the next chapter, we shall examine the effect that changes in commodity prices and income have upon the consumer's optimal commodity bundle. It is this comparative-static analysis which yields the predictive, or positive, content of the modern theory of the consumer.

EXERCISES*

3.1 Consider the utility functions defined by

$$U(x) = x_1 \cdot x_2,$$

$$\hat{U}(x) = \log x_1 + \log x_2,$$

and

$$\tilde{U}(x) = (x_1)^2 \cdot (x_2)^2.$$

Do they imply different consumer preference orderings? Demonstrate.

*Starred exercises are relatively more difficult.

3.2* *Global nonsatiation* is defined as follows: for all x in X, there exists an $\overset{*}{x}$ in X such that $\overset{*}{x} \succ x$.

a. Show that global nonsatiation, together with strict convexity (assumption 3.2), implies *local nonsatiation*: for all x in X, there is no neighborhood of x such that $x \succcurlyeq \bar{x}$ for all $\bar{x}$ in the neighborhood.[17] (Note: local nonsatiation rules out "thick" indifference surfaces—i.e., "indifference bands" in two-space. See figure 17.8.)

b. Show that local nonsatiation implies that the consumer spends all of his income (so that the budget constraint is satisfied as an equality).

3.3 Show that the sign but not the magnitude of $\partial u(x)/\partial x_i$ is invariant under a monotonic transformation of U.

3.4* Prove that the assumption of diminishing and independent marginal utilities,

$$\frac{\partial U^2(x)}{\partial x_i^2} < 0, \qquad i = 1, \ldots, n,$$

and

$$\frac{\partial^2 u(x)}{\partial x_i\, \partial x_j} = 0, \qquad i \neq j, \quad i, j = 1, \ldots, n,$$

is stronger than the assumption of diminishing marginal rates of substitution.

3.5 Draw the general shape of the indifference curves associated with each of the following situations. Also, put in a budget constraint and identify the optimum.

a. Nickels and dimes are the two commodities.

b. Right and left shoes are the two commodities.

c. The more salted peanuts you eat the more you want (use money as the other commodity).

d. You would have to be paid to eat jalapeño peppers (use money as the other commodity).

e. You can't tell the difference between margarine and "the high-priced spread."

3.6 Derive the first-order conditions for maximizing

$$U(x) = \sum_{i=1}^{n} \beta_i \cdot \log(x_i - \gamma_i),$$

where β_i and γ_i, $i = 1, \ldots, n$, respectively, are positive and nonpositive parameters, subject to a budget constraint.

3.7* What is the reason for the restrictions on the parameters, β_i and γ_i, $i = 1, \ldots, n$, in exercise 3.6? (This one is tricky.)

[17] An ε-neighborhood of x is defined as the set of $\bar{x}$ in X such that $|\bar{x} - x| < \varepsilon$. Thus in two-space, an ε neighborhood of x is the set of points in X that are also in (the interior of) a circle with center x and radius ε.

CHAPTER 4
DEMAND THEORY

4.1 INTRODUCTION

The theory of consumer choice developed in the previous two chapters provides the behavioral foundation for the analysis of consumer demand. The empirical content of consumer theory is embodied in the theory of demand since prices, income, and consumer purchases are observable phenomena. Facts about consumer preferences can only be inferred from observed data on prices, income, and consumer purchases. Conversely, assumptions about consumer preferences and behavior impose constraints on the relationships between prices, income, and consumer purchases which are subject to empirical testing. The purpose of this chapter is to derive empirically testable implications of consumer theory. For the most part, these empirical implications are concerned with the effect that changes in the exogenous variables (prices and income) have upon consumer demand.

It should be pointed out that the implications which we derive in this chapter are those that can be extracted from the very general and abstract theory of the consumer. Additional, more specific (stronger) predictions can be derived if a specific form of the consumer's utility function is assumed, in which case the demand functions also have specific forms and hence specific empirically testable implications.[1] The models of consumer demand generated by positing specific utility functions may form the basis for forecasting models to be used by firms and government agencies for planning purposes.

Section 4.2 discusses the derivation of consumer demand functions, which generate quantities demanded at different prices and income levels. Section 4.3 proves a result—attributable to John R. Hicks—which rationalizes the drawing of indifference curves with the consumption of one commodity on one axis and money spent on all other commodities on the other axis. This construction is then used in sections 4.4 and 4.5 to examine the effect of a change in income and a change in price, respectively, upon demand for this one commodity.

[1] Imposing "structure" on the utility function (which is weaker than assuming a particular form) also imposes structure on demand functions (see the suggested reading at the end of part I).

4.2 DEMAND FUNCTIONS

Derivation of Demand Functions

If the consumer's preference and indifference relations satisfy the asymmetry, transitivity, and regularity conditions (assumptions 2.2, 2.3, and 2.6), the preference ordering may be represented by a utility function. In this case, the consumer choice problem may be characterized as that of maximizing utility subject to the budget constraint:

$$\max_{x} U(x) \qquad \text{s.t.} \sum_{i=1}^{n} p_i x_i \leq y. \tag{4.1}$$

Moreover, if the assumptions of nonsatiation and strict convexity are satisfied, there exists a unique solution to the utility maximization problem and the optimal consumption bundle lies on the upper boundary of the feasible consumption set (all income is expended). Finally, if the unique optimal commodity bundle is in the interior of the consumption space (the consumer consumes a strictly positive amount of every commodity), this optimum is determined by solving the set of $n + 1$ equations obtained by setting the derivatives of the Lagrange expression,

$$L(x, \lambda) = U(x) - \lambda\left(\sum_{i=1}^{n} p_i x_i - y\right), \tag{4.2}$$

where λ is the Lagrange multiplier, equal to zero:

$$\frac{\partial U(x)}{\partial x_i} - \lambda p_i = 0, \qquad i = 1, \ldots, n, \tag{4.3}$$

$$\sum_{i=1}^{n} p_i x_i - y = 0,$$

or

$$\frac{\partial U(x)/\partial x_i}{\partial U(x)/\partial x_n} = \frac{p_i}{p_n}, \qquad i = 1, \ldots, n-1, \tag{4.4}$$

$$\sum_{i=1}^{n} p_i x_i - y = 0.$$

The solution value of each of the amounts consumed, x_i, $i = 1, \ldots, n$, depends of course upon the values of the exogenous variables, p_i, $i = 1, \ldots, n$, and y. Hence, the optimal amount consumed of each commodity can be expressed as a function of all prices and income,

$$x_i = D_i(p, y), \qquad i = 1, \ldots, n. \tag{4.5}$$

The functions D_i, $i = 1, \ldots, n$ are the consumer's *demand functions*.

Homogeneity

The purpose of the general theory of demand is to derive constraints which are imposed upon these demand functions by the underlying assumptions regarding the preferences and behavior of the consumer. (Additional constraints can be derived by positing more specific assumptions about the consumer's preferences.) The first restriction that will be derived requires the introduction of a mathematical concept which may be new to the reader. Consider a function f with image $f(x) = f(x_1, \ldots, x_n)$. We say that f is homogeneous of degree α if the multiplication of each of the variables, x_i, $i = 1, \ldots, n$, by a given positive scalar, κ, multiplies the image by this same scalar raised to the power α. That is, f is homogeneous of degree α in x if

$$f(\kappa x_1, \ldots, \kappa x_n) = \kappa^\alpha f(x_1, \ldots, x_n). \tag{4.6}$$

The important characteristic of this property of the function is that when each of the variables is multiplied by a scalar it is possible to factor this scalar out of the function. For example, suppose that

$$f(x) \equiv f(x_1, x_2) = bx_1 + cx_2, \tag{4.7}$$

where b and c are constants. Multiplication of the variables by κ yields

$$f(\kappa x_1, \kappa x_2) = b\kappa x_1 + c\kappa x_2 = \kappa(bx_1 + cx_2) = \kappa f(x_1, x_2). \tag{4.8}$$

Thus, this specific function is homogeneous of degree one in x_1 and x_2. As a further example, a function defined by

$$f(x_1, x_2) = bx_1^2 + cx_2^2 \tag{4.9}$$

is homogeneous of degree two since

$$f(\kappa x_1, \kappa x_2) = b(\kappa x_1)^2 + c(\kappa x_2)^2 = \kappa^2(bx_1^2 + cx_1^2) = \kappa^2 f(x_1, x_2). \tag{4.10}$$

On the other hand, f defined by

$$f(x_1, x_2) = a + bx_1 + cx_2 \tag{4.11}$$

is not homogeneous since it is not possible to separate

$$f(\kappa x_1, \kappa x_2) = a + b\kappa x_1 + c\kappa x_2 \tag{4.12}$$

into two terms: $(a + bx_1 + cx_2)$ and κ raised to some power. This example illustrates the fact that the graphs of homogeneous functions necessarily intersect the origin; that is, if f is homogeneous, $f(\underset{\sim}{0}) = 0$ (where $\underset{\sim}{0}$ is a vector of zeros). On the other hand, functions whose graphs intersect the origin are not necessarily homogeneous, as illustrated by the function defined by

$$f(x_1, x_2) \equiv bx_1 + cx_2^2. \tag{4.13}$$

Homogeneity of Degree Zero in Prices and Income

The first restriction on the demand functions generated by a preference ordering satisfying the assumptions of the previous chapters is:

Homogeneity *The demand functions are homogeneous of degree zero in prices and income; i.e.,*

$$D_i(\kappa p, \kappa y) = \kappa^0 D_i(p, y) = D_i(p, y), i = 1, \ldots, n. \tag{4.14}$$

To demonstrate that this proposition is true, we only have to multiply all prices and income by some arbitrary scalar and show that the first-order conditions for constrained utility maximization are unaffected. Multiplication of p_i, $i = 1, \ldots, n$, and y in system (4.4) by κ yields

$$\frac{\partial U(x)/\partial x_i}{\partial U(x)/\partial x_n} = \frac{\kappa p_i}{\kappa p_n}, \qquad i = 1, \ldots, n, \tag{4.15}$$

$$\sum_{i=1}^{n} \kappa p_i x_i - \kappa y = 0.$$

Clearly, the factor κ cancels out of each of these equations so that the first-order conditions are unaffected by proportionate changes in income and all prices.[2]

This restriction on the form of the demand functions is not at all surprising. Multiplying all prices and income by the same factor (e.g., doubling all prices and doubling income) leaves the consumer no better off or worse off than before and facing the same set of relative prices. Hence, we would not expect the consumer's choice to be altered by proportionate changes in income and prices. Put differently, the budget set of the consumer is unaffected by proportionate changes in all prices and income since the budget equality is not affected. This is illustrated graphically in figure 4.1. The budget set in two-space is determined by the location of the intercepts on the two axes, y/p_1 and y/p_2. Obviously, the values of these intercepts are unchanged by the multiplication of p_1, p_2, and y by a common positive factor. Hence, the budget line is unaffected by the proportionate change in prices and income. Consequently, the budget set is unaffected and the consumer's optimum is unchanged.

If price and income changes are not proportional, the optimal consumption bundle is generally changed. The most instructive approach to ascertaining the effect of nonproportional price and income changes is to consider first the effect of an income change, holding all prices constant, and then the effect of a change in one price, holding all other prices and income constant. In sections 4.4 and 4.5, we carry out these partial analyses graphically, leaving the mathematical analysis for chapter 5. (Chapter 5 may be skipped without loss of continuity.)

Using a construct attributable to John R. Hicks [1939], it is possible to analyze the effect of income (and price) changes in a two-dimensional diagram. If the prices of $n - 1$ of the n commodities are held constant,[3] it is possible to

[2] It is possible to demonstrate that the second-order conditions are also unaffected.

[3] Actually, it is only necessary that the ratios of these $n - 1$ prices remain constant.

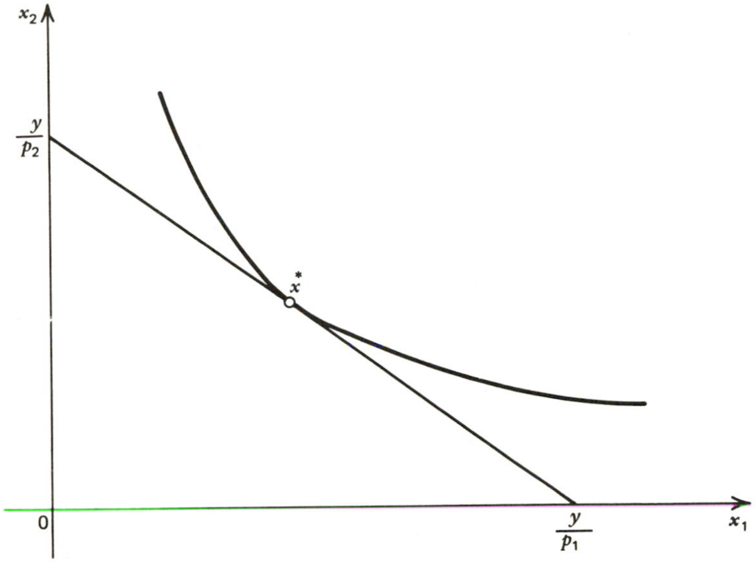

Figure 4.1

treat the expenditure on these $n - 1$ commodities as a "composite commodity." The consumer's preference ordering induces a preference ordering over this composite commodity and the omitted commodity. Denoting the expenditure on the $n - 1$ commodities with constant prices by m and the amount consumed of the other commodity by x_i, indifference curves can be drawn in $m - x_i$ space. The optimal quantity of the ith commodity can be obtained by maximizing utility with respect to x_i and m (attaining the highest indifference curve in $x_i - m$ space). This result is proved in section 4.3 but no loss in continuity results if the reader skips this analysis and goes on to section 4.4.

4.3 THE COMPOSITE COMMODITY THEOREM*

To demonstrate Hicks' result, let p_j be fixed for all $j \neq i$ and define

$$m = \sum_{\substack{j=1 \\ j \neq i}}^{n} p_j x_j. \tag{4.16}$$

Next, consider the maximization problem

$$\max_{x^{-i}} U(x_1, \ldots, x_n) \qquad \text{s.t.} \sum_{\substack{j=1 \\ j \neq i}}^{n} p_j x_j = m, \tag{4.17}$$

where $x^{-i} = (x_1, \ldots, x_{i-1}, x_{i+1}, \ldots, x_n)$. The first-order conditions for this constrained optimization problem can be solved for the $x_j (j \neq i)$ as functions of m, $p_j (j \neq i)$, and x_i:

$$x_j = \phi_j(m, p^{-i}, x_i), \qquad j = 1, \ldots, n (j \neq i), \tag{4.18}$$

where

$$p^{-i} = [p_1, \ldots, p_{i-1}, p_{i+1}, \ldots, p]. \tag{4.19}$$

The functions ϕ_j, $j = 1, \ldots, n (j \neq i)$ determine the optimal consumption of all commodities except the ith, given the consumption of the ith commodity and given expenditure on and prices of all except the ith commodity. Substituting $\phi_j(m, p^{-i}, x_i)$ for x_j, $j = 1, \ldots, n (j \neq i)$, in the utility-function image, utility is expressed as a function of the two variables, x_i and m (for fixed p^{-i}):

$$\hat{U}(x_i, m) = U(\phi_1(m, p^{-i}, x_i), \ldots, x_i, \ldots, \phi_n(m, p^{-i}, x_i)). \tag{4.20}$$

The function $\hat{U}$ yields the *maximum* utility, given x_i, that can be achieved with expenditure, m, on all other commodities.

Setting the utility level equal to some value and tracing out the relationship between x_i and m in $x_i - m$ space identifies an indifference curve in this space. These indifference curves are continuous and strictly convex to the origin.[4] Moreover, maximization of $\hat{U}(x_i, m)$ with respect to x_i and m subject to the expenditure constraint,

$$p_i x_i + m = y, \tag{4.21}$$

yields the optimal values of x_i and m. That is, if $(\hat{x}_i, \hat{m})$ is a solution to

$$\max_{x_i, m} U(x_i, m) \qquad \text{s.t. } p_i x_i + m = y, \tag{4.22}$$

then

$$\hat{x}_i = \overset{*}{x}_i \tag{4.23}$$

and

$$\hat{m} = \sum_{\substack{j=1 \\ j \neq i}}^{n} p_j \overset{*}{x}_j \tag{4.24}$$

where $\overset{*}{x}_k$, $k = 1, \ldots, n$, is the solution to the conventional utility maximization problem,

$$\max_{x} U(x) \qquad \text{s.t. } \sum_{k=1}^{n} p_k x_k = y. \tag{4.25}$$

Moreover, substitution of $\hat{m}$ into the functions ϕ_j yields the optimal consumption of x_j, $j = 1, \ldots, n (j \neq i)$, i.e.,

$$\overset{*}{x}_j = \phi_j(\hat{m}, p^{-i}, \overset{*}{x}_i), \qquad j = 1, \ldots, n (j \neq i). \tag{4.26}$$

[4] See Gorman [1953] or Diewert [1974] for proof of this assertion.

To see that the solution to (4.22) does in fact yield the overall optimum, note that the first-order conditions for (4.22) can be written as

$$\frac{\partial \hat{U}(\hat{x}_i, \hat{m})}{\partial x_i} - \delta p_i = 0, \tag{4.27}$$

$$\frac{\partial \hat{U}(\hat{x}_i, \hat{m})}{\partial m} - \delta = 0, \tag{4.28}$$

and

$$p_i \hat{x}_i + \hat{m} - y = 0, \tag{4.29}$$

where δ is the Lagrange multiplier. The first-order conditions for solving (4.17) are

$$\frac{\partial U(\hat{x})}{\partial x_j} - \lambda p_j = 0, \qquad j = 1, \ldots, n (j \neq i), \tag{4.30}$$

and

$$\sum_{\substack{j=1 \\ j \neq i}}^{n} p_j \hat{x}_j - m = 0 \tag{4.31}$$

where λ is the Lagrange multiplier for this problem and, of course, $\hat{x}$ is the solution value of x in problems (4.17) and (4.22).

Our task now is to show that the first-order conditions (4.27)–(4.31) for the two-stage optimization procedure, (4.17) and then (4.22), imply the first-order conditions for the overall optimization problem (4.25). To show this, we first evaluate the derivatives in (4.27) and (4.28) using the identity (4.20):

$$\frac{\partial \hat{U}(x_i, m)}{\partial x_i} = \sum_{\substack{j=1 \\ j \neq i}}^{n} \frac{\partial U(x)}{\partial x_j} \frac{\partial \phi_j(m, p^{-i}, x_i)}{\partial x_i} + \frac{\partial U(x)}{\partial x_i}$$

and

$$\frac{\partial \hat{U}(x_i, m)}{\partial m} = \sum_{\substack{j=1 \\ j \neq i}}^{n} \frac{\partial U(x)}{\partial x_j} \frac{\partial \phi_j(m, p^{-i}, x_i)}{\partial m}.$$

Substitution of (4.30) into these expressions yields

$$\frac{\partial \hat{U}(x_i, m)}{\partial x_i} = \lambda \sum_{\substack{j=1 \\ j \neq i}}^{n} p_j \frac{\partial \phi_j(m, p^{-i}, x_i)}{\partial x_i} + \frac{\partial U(x)}{\partial x_i} \tag{4.32}$$

and

$$\frac{\partial \hat{U}(x_i, m)}{\partial m} = \lambda \sum_{\substack{j=1 \\ j \neq i}}^{n} p_j \frac{\partial \phi_j(m, p^{-i}, x_i)}{\partial m}, \tag{4.33}$$

respectively.

Next substitute $\phi_j(m, p^{-i}, x_i)$ for $x_j, j = 1, \ldots, n (j \neq 1)$, in the constraint (4.31),

$$\sum_{\substack{j=1 \\ j \neq i}}^{n} p_j \phi_j(m, p^{-i}, x_i) - m = 0,$$

and differentiate with respect to x_i and m, respectively:

$$\sum_{\substack{j=1 \\ j \neq i}}^{n} p_j \frac{\partial \phi_j(m, p^{-i}, x_i)}{\partial x_i} = 0 \tag{4.34}$$

and

$$\sum_{\substack{j=1 \\ j \neq i}}^{n} p_j \frac{\partial \phi_j(m, p^{-i}, x_i)}{\partial m} - 1 = 0. \tag{4.35}$$

Because of (4.34) and (4.35), the partial derivatives (4.32) and (4.33) become

$$\frac{\partial \hat{U}(x_i, m)}{\partial x_i} = \frac{\partial U(x)}{\partial x_i} \tag{4.36}$$

and

$$\frac{\partial \hat{U}(x_i, m)}{\partial m} = \lambda. \tag{4.37}$$

The first-order conditions (4.27) and (4.30) imply that

$$\frac{\partial U(\hat{x})/\partial x_j}{\partial \hat{U}(\hat{x}_i, \hat{m})/\partial x_i} = \frac{\lambda p_j}{\delta p_i}, \qquad j = 1, \ldots, n (j \neq i). \tag{4.38}$$

However, because of (4.36) the denominator of the left-hand side of (4.38) is $\partial U(\hat{x})/\partial x_i$. Also, (4.28) and (4.37) imply that $\delta = \lambda$. Hence

$$\frac{\partial U(\hat{x})/\partial x_j}{\partial U(\hat{x})/\partial x_i} = \frac{p_j}{p_i}, \qquad j = 1, \ldots, n (j \neq i). \tag{4.39}$$

Finally, addition of (4.29) and (4.31) yields

$$\sum_{j=1}^{n} p_j \hat{x}_j - y = 0. \tag{4.40}$$

But (4.39) and (4.40) are the first-order conditions for solving the overall optimization problem (4.25); hence, $\hat{x}$ is optimal. These results are summarized as follows:

Hicks' Composite Commodity Theorem *If the prices of all but the ith commodity are fixed, utility can be expressed as a differentiable function of the consumption of the ith commodity, x_i, and expenditure on all other commodities, m; i.e.,*

$$\hat{u} = \hat{U}(x_i, m). \tag{4.41}$$

Moreover, the indifference curves in $x_i - m$ space representing $\hat{U}$ are continuous and strictly convex to the origin. Finally, maximizing this utility function subject to $y = m + p_i x_i$ yields the optimal consumption of the ith commodity and optimal expenditure on all other commodities.

The indifference map in $x_i - m$ space is illustrated in figure 4.2. This construct will be used to analyze the effects of a change in income and a change in one of the prices in the next two sections.

4.4 THE EFFECT OF A CHANGE IN INCOME UPON DEMAND: GRAPHICAL ANALYSIS

As the price of a dollar is trivially one dollar, the budget line in $x_i - m$ space (figure 4.2) intersects the m-axis at y, the level of total income. (By definition, if the consumer expends his total income on the $n - 1$ commodities with constant prices, $m = y$.) At the optimum, the consumer spends $\overset{*}{m}$ on all commodities other than the ith; hence, expenditure on the ith commodity is given by $y - \overset{*}{m}$.

A change in the income level of the consumer obviously shifts the budget line and therefore changes the budget set. If prices are unchanged, however, the slope of the budget line is unaffected by the income change. Put differently, a change in income shifts the intercepts with two axes by proportionate amounts and therefore leaves the slope of the budget line unchanged. Moreover, a rise in income clearly shifts the budget line outward, whereas a fall in income moves the budget line closer to the origin. Thus, increasing income expands the budget

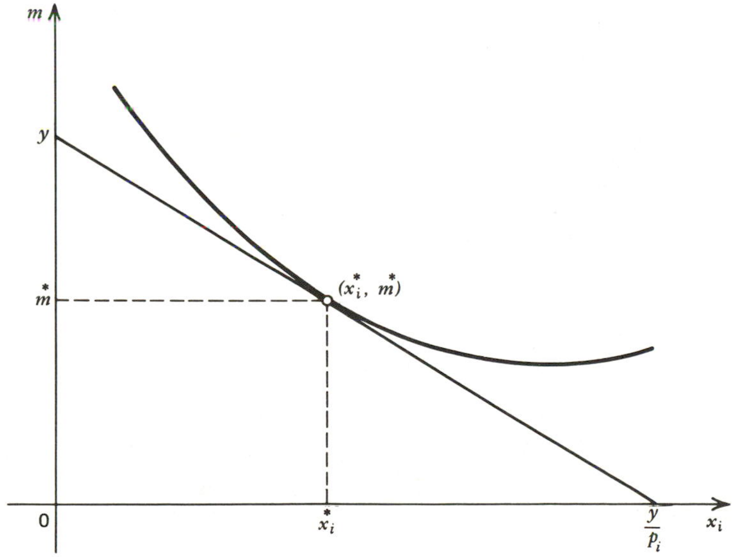

Figure 4.2

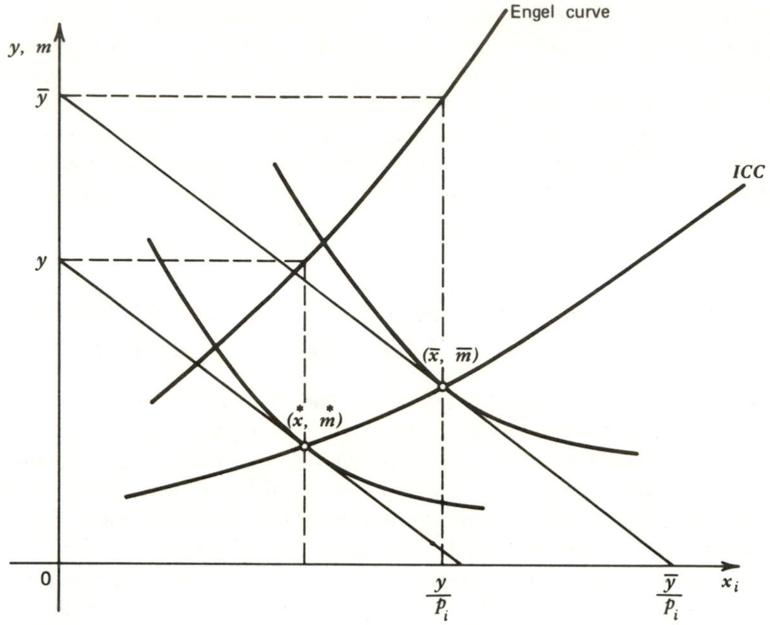

Figure 4.3

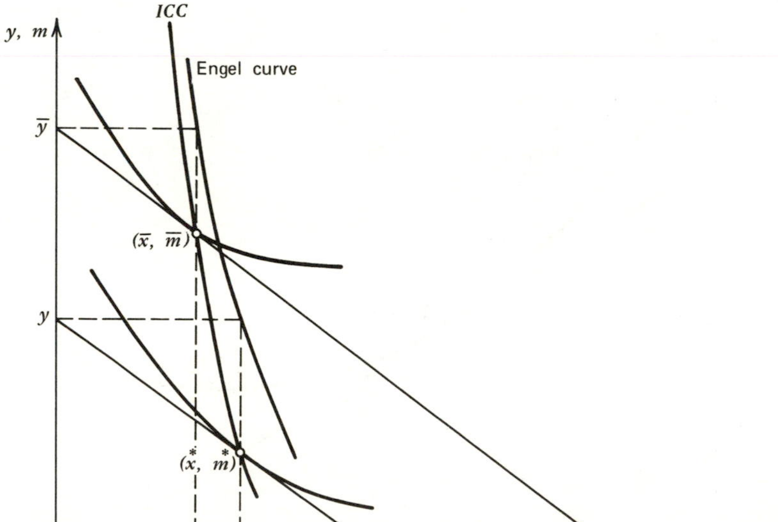

Figure 4.4

set whereas decreasing income contracts the budget set. A rise in income from y to $\bar{y}$ is illustrated in figure 4.3. The optimum at income y is given by ($\overset{*}{x}$, $\overset{*}{m}$). At the higher income level, $\bar{y}$, the budget set is expanded and the consumer chooses "commodity bundle" ($\bar{x}$, $\bar{m}$).

In the case illustrated in figure 4.3, the increase in the consumer's income induces him to buy more of the ith commodity. It is, however, possible to construct indifference curves which satisfy all of our assumptions but which, at least over a range of income, result in less consumption of the ith commodity when income is increased. This case is illustrated in figure 4.4. If a consumer purchases less of a commodity as his income grows, that commodity is called an *inferior commodity*. If more is purchased as income rises, the commodity is called *normal*.

The locus of all points of tangency between indifference curves and budget lines with unchanged slopes but representing different levels of income is defined as an *income-consumption curve* (ICC). Thus, the income-consumption curve in figure 4.3 defines a relationship between the amount of the ith commodity purchased by the consumer and the amount expended upon all other commodities as income changes. If the consumer expends his entire income on only two commodities, as illustrated in figure 4.5, the ICC curve in $x_1 - x_2$ space represents the relationship between the amounts consumed of these two commodities as income changes.

The ICC curves in figures 4.3 and 4.4 can be converted into a direct relationship between income and the amount consumed of the ith commodity.

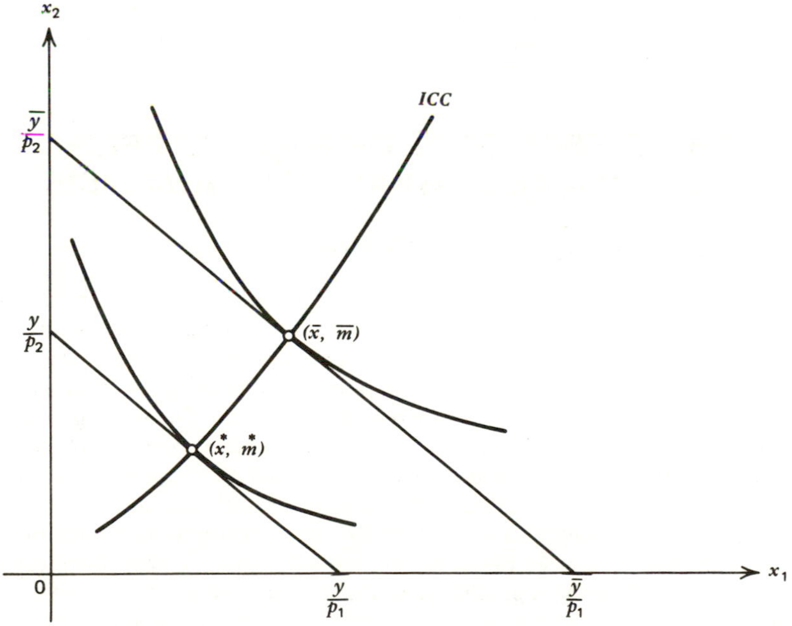

Figure 4.5

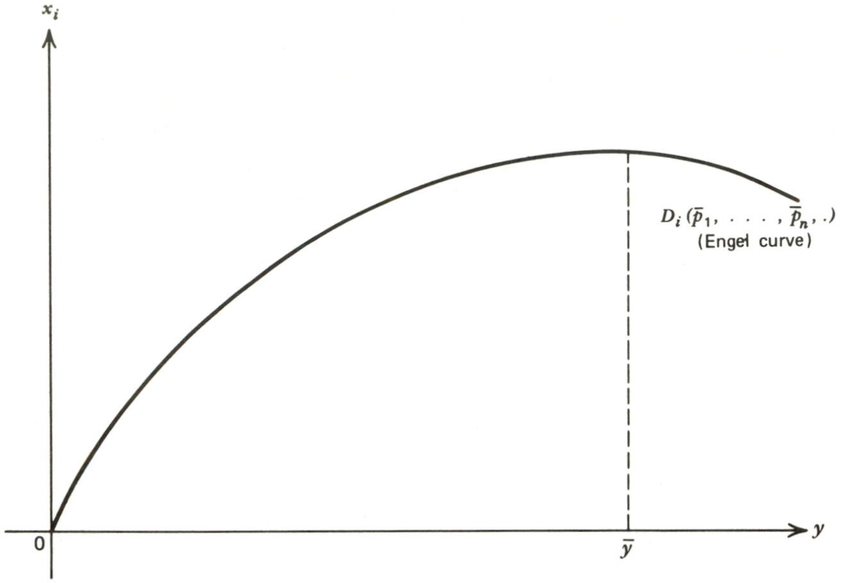

Figure 4.6

This relationship, which is called an *Engel curve*, is illustrated in figures 4.3 and 4.4. Conventionally, in the graphing of Engel curves, income is measured along the horizontal axis, as in figure 4.6. In this figure, the ith commodity is a normal commodity up to income level $\bar{y}$ and an inferior commodity thereafter.

4.5 THE EFFECT OF A CHANGE IN PRICE UPON DEMAND: GRAPHICAL ANALYSIS

The Price-Consumption Curve

Using the indifference map in $m - x_i$ space, it is also possible to assess the effect that a change in the price of the ith commodity has on the demand for that commodity when all other prices and income are held constant. Decreasing the price of the ith commodity from p_i to $\bar{p}_i$ clearly increases the intercept, y/p_i, of the budget line in figure 4.7. As income and all of the prices are unchanged, the vertical intercept is unchanged. The result of the price decrease is to increase the size of the budget set, allowing the consumer to move from $(\overset{*}{x}_i, \overset{*}{m})$ to $(\bar{x}_i, \bar{m})$ at a higher level of utility. While the illustrated price decrease in figure 4.7 increases the amount consumed of the ith commodity, it cannot be concluded that this is always the case. Figure 4.8 shows a price decrease that results in a smaller amount purchased of the ith commodity. Hence, the analysis of the effect of a price change leads to the same indeterminacy that was encountered in the analysis of the effect of an income change.

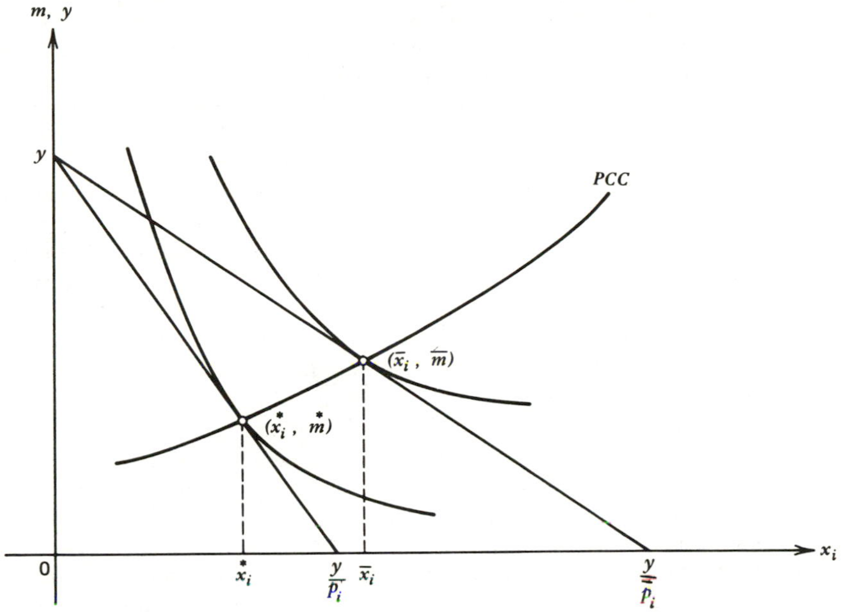

Figure 4.7

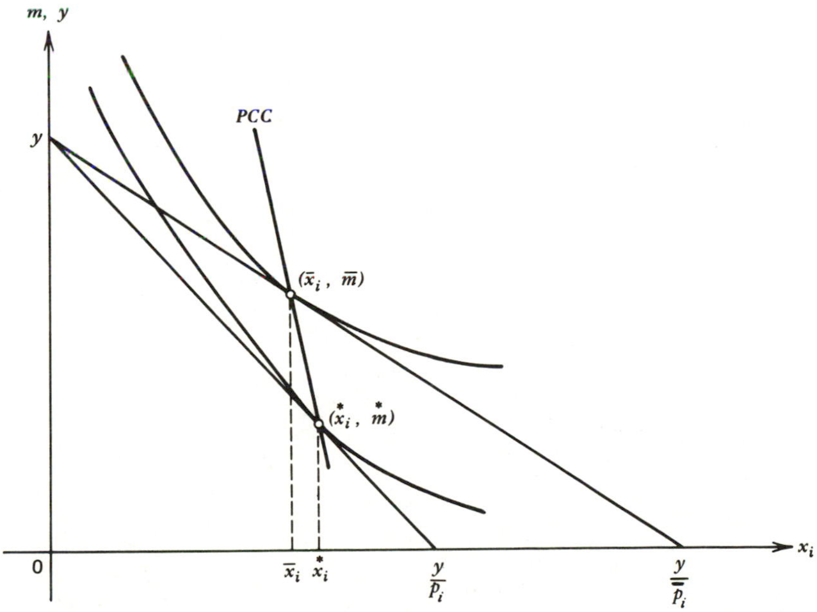

Figure 4.8

A decline in price resulting in a reduction in quantity demanded (or equivalently a rise in price resulting in increased quantity demanded) is referred to as the *Giffen paradox,* and the commodity in question is called a *Giffen commodity*. Possible real-world examples of Giffen commodities will be given below after we have examined more carefully the effect of a change in price.

The locus of all points of tangency between indifference curves and budget lines representing different prices of the ith commodity but a constant level of income and constant values of all other prices is called the *price-consumption curve* (PCC) and is illustrated in figures 4.7 and 4.8. The price-consumption curve is therefore a relationship between the amount consumed of the ith commodity and the expenditure on all other commodities. When there are only two commodities, as illustrated in figure 4.9, the locus of tangencies of indifference curves and budget lines representing different prices of one of the two commodities but a constant price of the other commodity and constant income is also referred to as a price-consumption curve.

Although a graphical description of the derivation is not practical, it is possible to derive from the price-consumption curves in figure 4.7 and 4.8 a relationship between the price and quantity demanded of the ith commodity. We simply plot against each price level in figures 4.10 and 4.11 the optimal amount of the ith commodity associated with the corresponding budget line in figures 4.7 and 4.8. That is, each point on the vertical axis in figure 4.10 corresponds to the slope of a budget line in figure 4.7. For example, the price level $\bar{p}_i$ in figure 4.10 corresponds to the budget line with intercept $y/\bar{p}_i$ in figure 4.7. The shape of the PCC curve in figure 4.7 yields the downward-sloping demand curve in

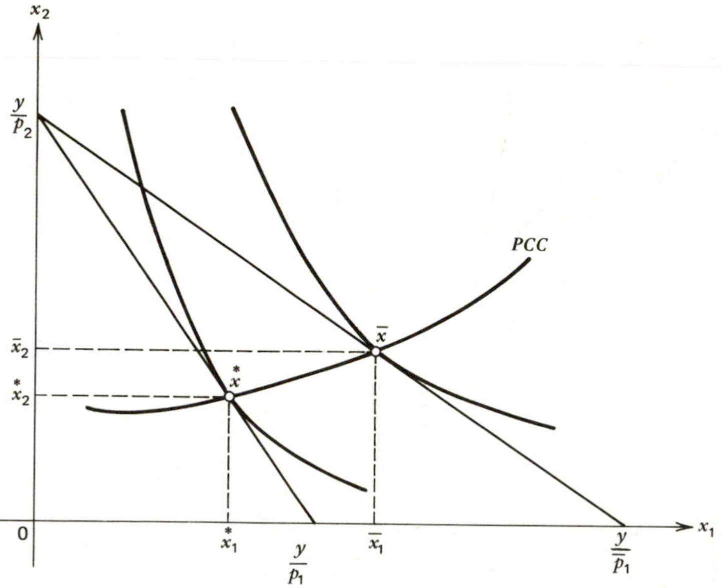

Figure 4.9

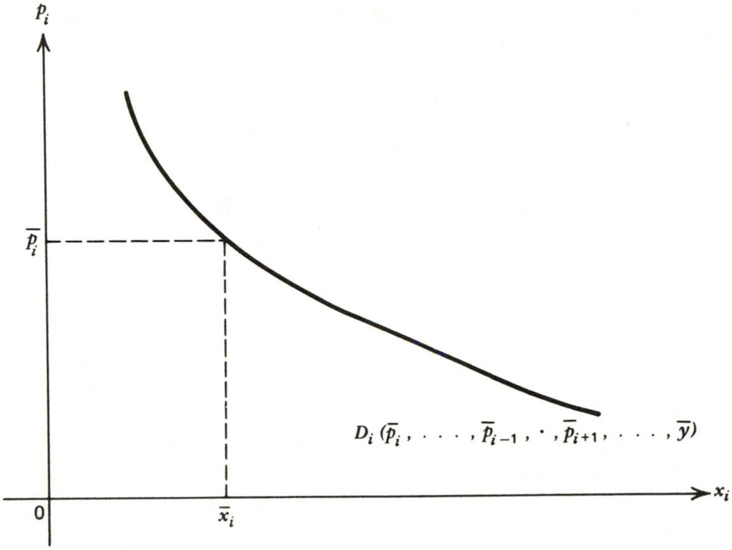

Figure 4.10

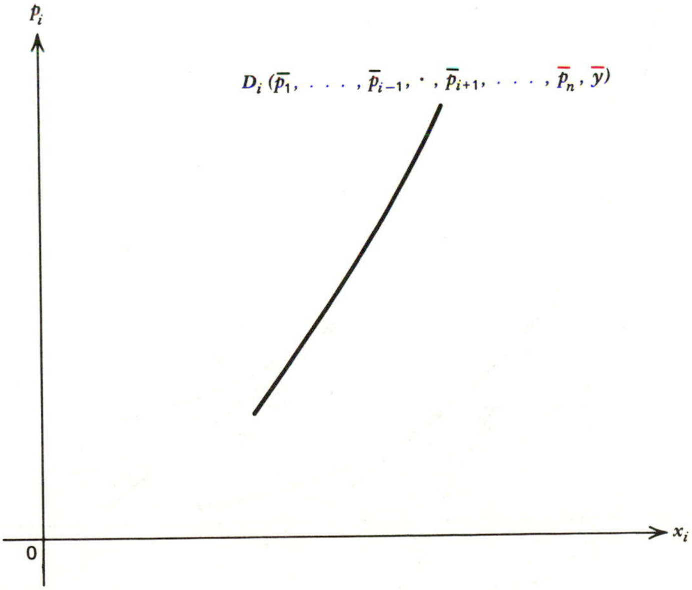

Figure 4.11

figure 4.10 whereas the PCC curve in figure 4.8 yields the upward-sloping demand curve in figure 4.11.

Income and Substitution Effects

A change in price of one of the commodities consumed has two distinguishable effects on the consumer's optimum. In the first place, a reduction in the price of one commodity (that is purchased by the consumer) makes the consumer better off since it expands his budget set and allows him to attain a more preferred consumption bundle. Similarly, a rise in the price of one commodity contracts the budget set and forces the consumer onto a lower indifference curve. Put differently, a fall in one price raises the consumer's real income in the sense that he is able to purchase more of every commodity because of the decrease in this one price. This effect of a price change is therefore referred to as the *income effect*.

If we were to compensate a consumer for a price increase by giving him enough additional (money) income to maintain his standard of living (i.e., to remain on the same indifference curve as before the price increase), the consumer still would generally alter his consumption bundle. Thus, there is an additional effect of a price increase, brought about by the fact that a price increase of one commodity makes it more expensive relative to other commodities. Hence, even

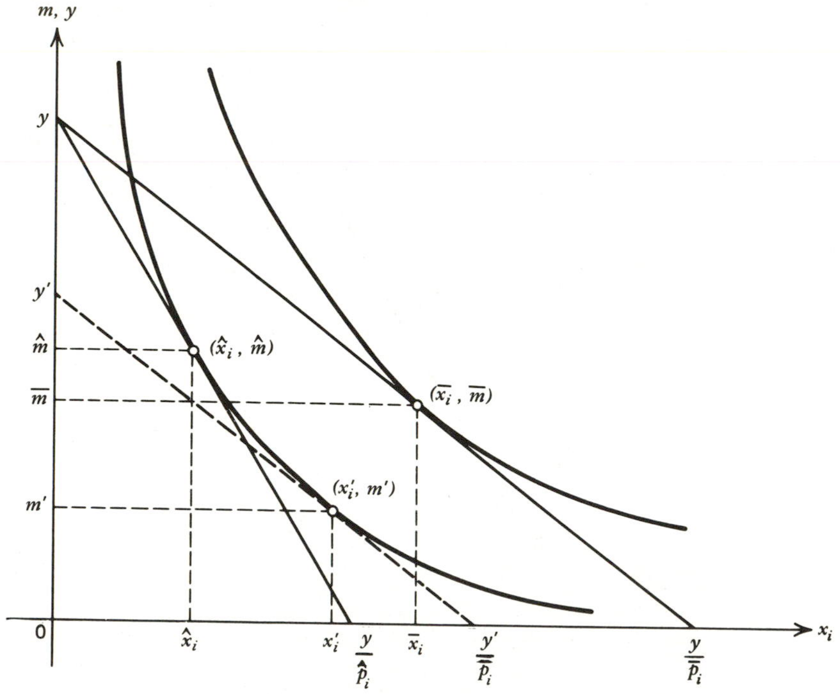

Figure 4.12

if the consumer's utility level is maintained by an income compensation, he might still wish to substitute consumption of the commodities which have become relatively cheaper for the commodity which has become relatively more expensive. This effect is therefore referred to as the *substitution effect* of a price increase.

The income and substitution effects of a price change are illustrated in figure 4.12. A fall in the price of the ith commodity from $\hat{p}_i$ to $\bar{p}_i$ shifts the consumer's optimum from $(\hat{x}_i, \hat{m})$ to $(\bar{x}_i, \bar{m})$. Because of the price decrease, the consumer's real income is higher; he can achieve a preferred consumption bundle on a higher indifference curve. If we were to compensate the consumer for this change in his well-being by taking away $y - y'$ income, holding the price of the ith commodity equal to the new price $\bar{p}_i$, he could just achieve his old utility level by choosing the commodity bundle represented by (x_i', m') in figure 4.12. As the bogus optimum (x_i', m') is on the same indifference curve as the old optimum $(\hat{x}_i, \hat{m})$, the shift from $(\hat{x}_i, \hat{m})$ to (x_i', m') is a pure substitution effect; that is, there is no change in utility, or "real income," in the move from $(\hat{x}_i, \hat{m})$ to (x_i', m'). The entire effect is therefore a substitution effect. Similarly, the shift from (x_i', m') to $(\bar{x}_i, \bar{m})$ as income is increased to its old level, holding the price of the ith commodity at the new level, $\bar{p}_i$, represents a pure income effect of the price change since the two optima (x_i', m') and $(\bar{x}_i, \bar{m})$ are generated by identical prices but different levels of income. In summary, the total effect of a decrease in the price of the ith commodity from $\hat{p}_i$ to $\bar{p}_i$ is equal to $\bar{x}_i - \hat{x}_i$ and this total effect can be dichotomized into the substitution effect, $x_i' - \hat{x}_i$, and the income effect, $\bar{x}_i - x_i'$.

Note that, because of the strict convexity of the indifference curves, the substitution effect is always negative. That is, the income-compensated effect of a change in the ith price on the demand for the ith commodity is necessarily inverse—an income-compensated fall in the ith price necessarily results in a rise in the demand for the ith commodity, and an income-compensated rise in the ith price necessarily results in a fall in the demand for the ith commodity. This is because the new budget constraint with a lower slope can be tangent to the old indifference curve only at a point to the right of $(\hat{x}_i, \hat{m})$ because of the assumption of diminishing marginal rate of substitution. The slope of the indifference curve at all points to the left of $(\hat{x}_i, \hat{m})$ is greater (in absolute value) than the slope of the new budget line.

Although the substitution effect is necessarily negative, the income effect can be either positive or negative. In the case illustrated in figure 4.12, the income effect reinforces the substitution effect. That is, the income effect in figure 4.12 is negative in the sense that a *decline* in price results in a higher income which generates a *higher* demand for the ith commodity. The income effect reinforces the substitution effect only if the commodity is a normal commodity. If the ith commodity is inferior, the income effect of a price change is positive in the sense that the *reduction* in price (which raises real income) tends to *reduce* the demand for the ith commodity. This case is illustrated in figure 4.13, where the total effect of a price decrease from $\hat{p}_i$ to $\bar{p}_i$ is to increase the demand for the ith commodity by $\bar{x}_i - \hat{x}_i$ even though the substitution effect, $x_i' - \hat{x}_i$, is larger. This is because the income effect, $\bar{x}_i - x_i'$, partially cancels out the substitution effect rather than reinforcing it as in figure 4.12.

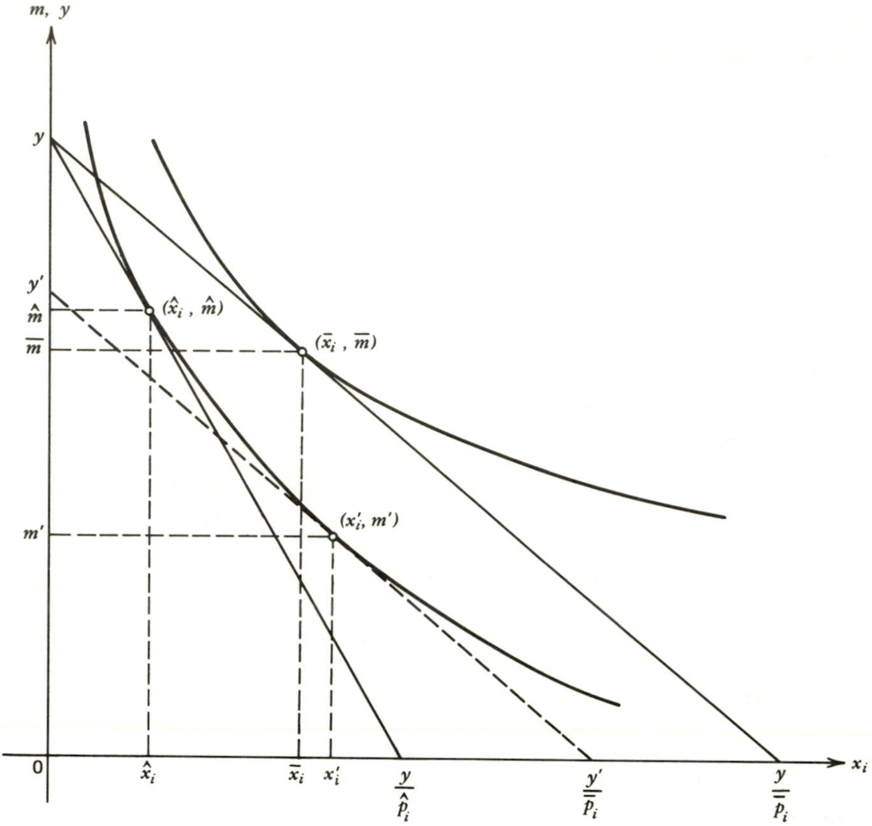

Figure 4.13

Giffen Commodities and the Law of Demand

If the commodity is inferior and if the income effect is large enough, it can dominate the substitution effect, in which case the total effect of a price decrease can be negative (price and quantity demanded are directly rather than inversely related). Thus, a commodity is a Giffen commodity only if it is an inferior commodity *and* the income effect is so large that it more than cancels out the substitution effect of a price change. This case of the Giffen paradox is illustrated in figure 4.14.

In summary, the substitution effect of an increase in the *i*th price on the demand for the *i*th commodity is necessarily negative but the income effect is ambiguous and consequently the total effect is indeterminant. If, however, the income effect reinforces the substitution effect of a price change, the relationship between price and demand for any commodity is necessarily inverse. Such a relationship is formalized in the following proposition:

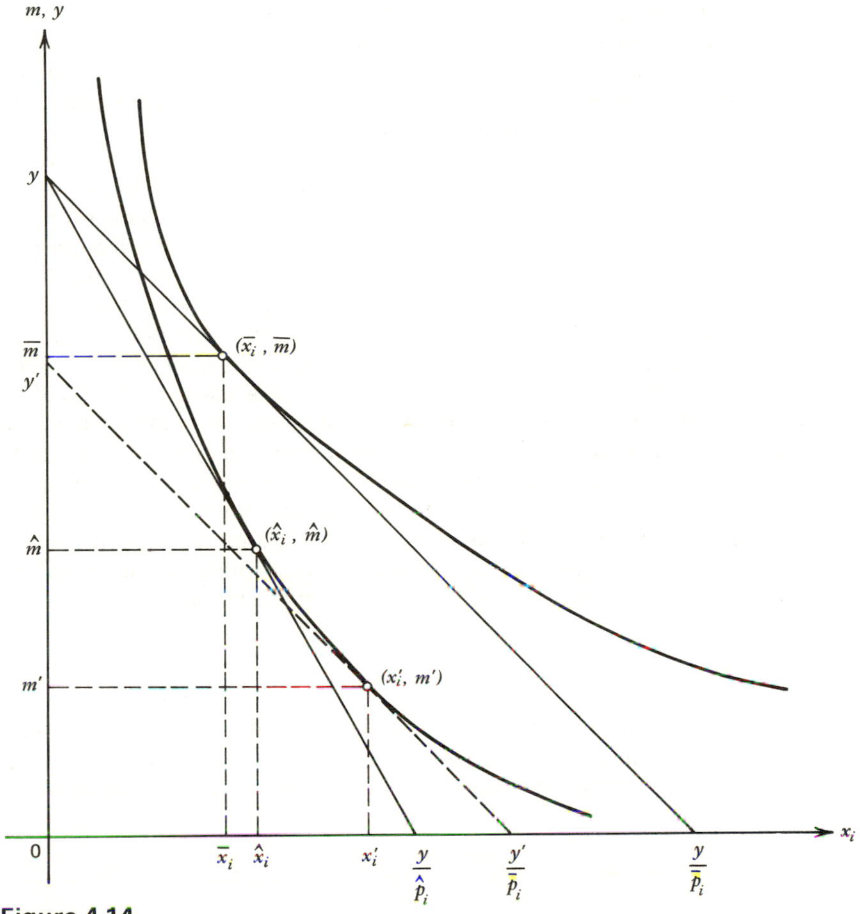

Figure 4.14

The "Law" of Demand *If the amount demanded of a commodity increases (decreases) when income increases (decreases), the amount demanded of that commodity decreases (increases) when its price is increased (decreased).*

How likely is it that Giffen commodities will be found in the real world? The most likely possibility (apart from the price of a commodity actually affecting the consumer's preferences because of the snob appeal of higher priced goods) is when a commodity is an essential staple in a relatively primitive economy.[5] In this case, the consumer may be spending a very large proportion of his income on this staple and therefore the income effect of a change in the price of that commodity may be very large. Consider, for example, a primitive society in which the typical consumption bundle is composed very largely of rice. A fall in the price of rice would therefore cause a fairly large increase in the consumer's

[5] A "primitive economy" is one in which there are very few commodities available for consumption; no value judgment is implied.

real income. The result may be that he is able to consume a more balanced diet of foods, in which case his consumption of rice actually decreases. We should point out that while this is a distinct possibility and cannot be precluded on the basis of our assumptions regarding consumer behavior, the actual evidence on the existence of Giffen goods is inconclusive at best.

The implication for demand functions contained in the above proposition is not particularly dramatic. It would appear that the general theory of the consumer does not have a great deal of empirical content. Because of the ambiguity of the income effect, it is simply not possible to predict the direction of change in demand when price changes without making more specific assumptions about the consumer's preferences. Therefore, in empirical applications, there is a tendency to assume that the consumer's preferences do not admit inferior commodities. Moreover, in many applications specific functional forms for the utility function are posited, in which case the exact forms of the demand functions are determined and exact quantitative as well as qualitative predictions regarding the effect of price and income changes can be made. Thus, the theory developed thus far provides a basic foundation which can be used in empirical demand studies if more specific assumptions are made about the consumer's preferences. Moreover, for many purposes, particularly those of normative economics discussed in the final four chapters of this book, the general theory of the consumer yields interesting implications.

EXERCISES

4.1 In the following diagram, x_i is consumption of the ith commodity, m is expenditure on all commodities except the ith, and y is income. The "circles" are indifference curves and $\overset{*}{x}$ is a point of (global) satiation.

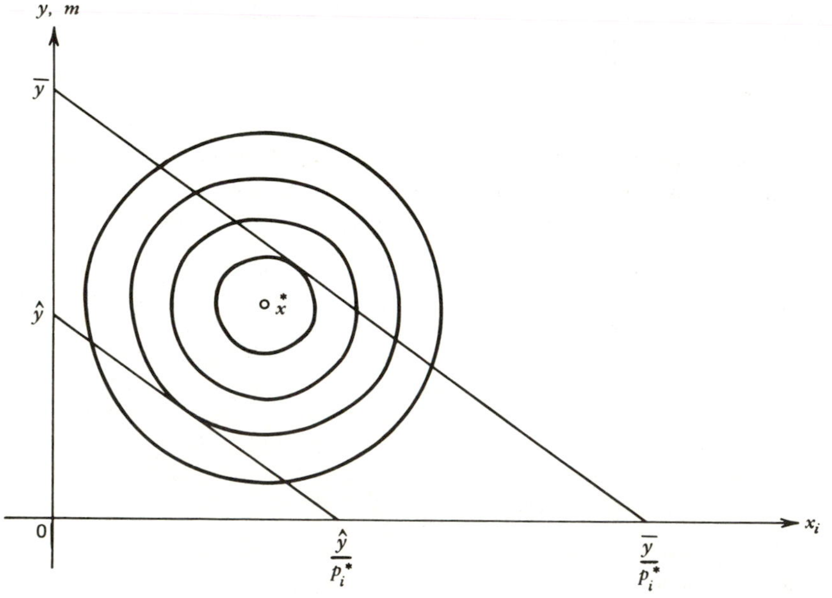

a. Identify the optimal consumption bundles at income levels $\hat{y}$ and $\bar{y}$, respectively.
b. What is the relationship between the marginal rate of substitution, $MRS_{im}(x_i, m)$, and the price of the ith commodity at each of these two optima?
c. Draw an income consumption curve that is consistent with the diagram for $p_i = p_i^*$.
d. Draw an Engel curve that is consistent with the diagram for $p_i = p_i^*$.

4.2 Characterize the indifference map in $x_i - m$ space on the assumption that $MRS_{im}(x_i, m)$ is constant (invariant with respect to m) for any given value of x_i. Identify income and substitution effects. Can the ith commodity be inferior? Can it be subject to the Giffen paradox?

4.3 Draw an indifference map in $x_i - m$ space in which the indifference curves are conventionally shaped and are allowed to intersect the axes. Draw in a budget line and identify the optimal bundle. Indicate
a. the amount of money which the consumer spends on commodity i;
b. the (lump sum) amount of money which the consumer would be willing to pay in order to *retain* the privilege of purchasing the ith commodity *at the market price*;
c. the (lump sum) amount of money which the consumer must be paid in order to induce him to *relinquish* the privilege of purchasing the ith commodity *at the market price*; and
d. the (lump sum) amount of money which the consumer would be willing to pay for the *optimal* quantity of ith commodity.

4.4 Consider again (see exercises 3.6 and 3.7) the utility function defined by

$$U(x) = \sum_{i=1}^{n} \beta_i \log(x_i - \gamma_i)$$

where β_i and γ_i, $i = 1, \ldots, m$, are, respectively, positive and nonpositive parameters.
a. Derive the demand functions.
b. Show that the demand functions are homogeneous of degree zero in p and y.
c. Derive the Engel curves.
d. Can any commodities be inferior?

4.5 Assume that two commodities are characterized by diminishing and independent marginal utilities; i.e.,

$$\frac{\partial^2 U(x_1, x_2)}{\partial x_1\, \partial x_2} = \frac{\partial^2 U(x_1, x_2)}{\partial x_2\, \partial x_1} = 0$$

and

$$\frac{\partial^2 U(x_1, x_2)}{\partial x_i^2} < 0, \qquad i = 1, 2.$$

a. Prove the following relationship regarding the ratios of the slopes of the indifference curves: slope at a/slope at b = slope at c/slope at d.

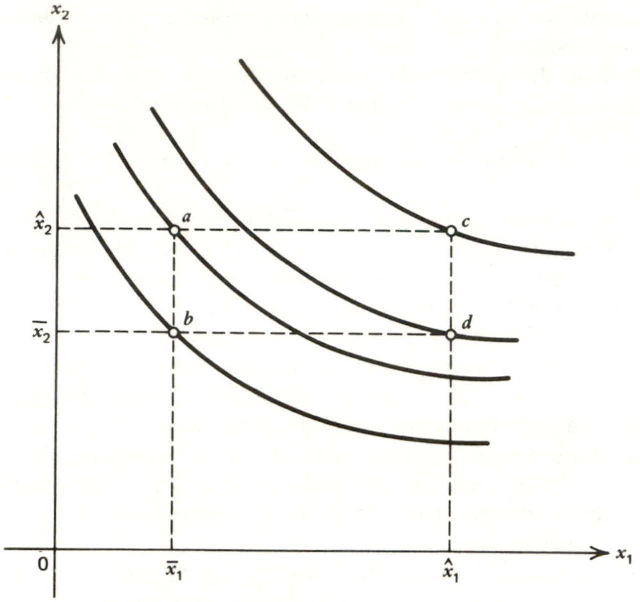

b. If commodity 2 is money spent on all commodities other than commodity 1, prove that 1 cannot be an inferior commodity.

4.6 Prove that homogeneity of degree zero of the demand functions, D_i, $i = 1, \ldots, n$, allows us to express optimal quantities as a function of "normalized" prices, $p_1/y, \ldots, p_n/y$: $x_i = D_i(p_1/y, \ldots, p_n/y, 1) = d_i(p_1/y, \ldots, p_n/y)$, $i = 1, \ldots, n$.

CHAPTER 5 ADVANCED DEMAND THEORY*

5.1 INTRODUCTION

In this chapter, we extend the results of chapter 4 in several directions. Section 5.2 provides an introduction to consumer duality theory. This theory, which develops the ideas of an indirect utility function (yielding maximum utility as a function of prices and income) and the consumer expenditure function (showing the minimum cost of attaining a given utility level for a given set of prices), has proved in recent years to be a very important development for the purposes of applying consumer theory to demand analysis. In particular, this theory turns out to be very important for the econometric estimation of demand systems that could be generated by utility maximization.

Section 5.3 contains a comparative-static analysis of the theory of demand. This section examines the (differential) effects that changes in price and/or income have on quantities demanded. In other words, section 5.3 provides the mathematical foundation for the diagrammatic results developed in chapter 4. These comparative static results constitute the empirically testable content of the abstract theory of the consumer developed in the preceding chapters.

Finally, section 5.4 utilizes the results obtained in section 5.3 to examine the concepts of substitutability and complementarity between commodities consumed by the consumer.

5.2 DUALITY AND CONSUMER THEORY

In an incredibly prescient paper in 1932, Harold Hotelling introduced the theory of duality to economics. For a regrettably long period, this classic work was virtually neglected by economists, but in recent years the theory of duality has become increasingly important in both theoretical and empirical economic analysis. This section contains a very brief introduction to the use of duality in consumer theory. Readers interested in pursuing the subject beyond this short introduction are referred to the suggested-reading section following part I.

Duality is a logical concept which, as it turns out, is best understood in the context of specific examples. Nevertheless, as a prelude to the discussion of duality in the context of consumer theory, we attempt to provide a general verbal definition of duality. Essentially, duality is defined as the existence of two logical systems characterized by certain interrelationships. The essence of a dual system is a correspondence between concepts in one logical system and concepts in the other which allows us to derive a correspondence between results in one system and results in the other. For example, there is generally a correspondence between variables in one system and variables in the other, between functions in one system and functions in the other, and between operations in one system and operations in the other. Duality theorems, then, say that if a certain proposition can be proved and if we can show that a proposition in the alternative system is dual to that one, then we know that the dual proposition holds as well. This is important because it often makes it easier to prove the proposition that is dual to the first one. This notion, abstract as it is, has proved to be exceptionally useful in applied (econometric) economic research as well as in the development of economic theory. The notion will hopefully become clear as we develop the particular dual structure of consumer theory.

The Indirect Utility Function

It will be recalled from chapter 4 that demand functions are derived by solving the utility-maximization problem,

$$\operatorname*{Max}_{x} U(x) \qquad \text{s.t.} \sum_i p_i x_i \leq y.$$

Note that, letting $\xi_i = p_i/y$, this problem can be formulated equivalently as

$$\operatorname*{Max}_{x} U(x) \qquad \text{s.t.} \sum_i \xi_i x_i \leq 1. \tag{5.1}$$

In this form, the utility-maximization problem has two sets of n variables: consumption quantities, with values x, and normalized prices, with values $\xi = [\xi_1, \ldots, \xi_n]$. The optimal consumption bundle is given by the system of demand functions, with images

$$x_i = d_i(\xi), \qquad i = 1, \ldots, n. \tag{5.2}$$

Note that this system of demand functions with *normalized* prices as arguments is obtained directly by a simple reformulation of the utility-maximization problem. The system (5.2) can alternatively be derived by exploiting the demand function property of homogeneity of degree zero in prices and income (see exercise 4.6).

The maximum utility level is obtained by substituting the optimal bundle into the utility function. Of course, this optimal bundle depends on the income level and the vector of prices, as reflected in the above system of demand functions. Substituting these demand-function images into the utility function yields a function of normalized prices with image,

$$V(\xi) = U(d_1(\xi), \ldots, d_n(\xi)). \tag{5.3}$$

The function V yields the maximum value of utility for any set of normalized prices (i.e., for any price vector and any level of income). In a sense, then, this function reflects the fact that the utility level depends indirectly on prices and income. For this reason, V is called the *indirect utility function*. Note that implicit in the construction of this function is the optimization principle (5.1). That is, the indirect utility function implicitly reflects an optimization procedure.

What are the properties of the indirect utility function? First, given that U is continuous, V is continuous at all positive (normalized) prices. Second, V

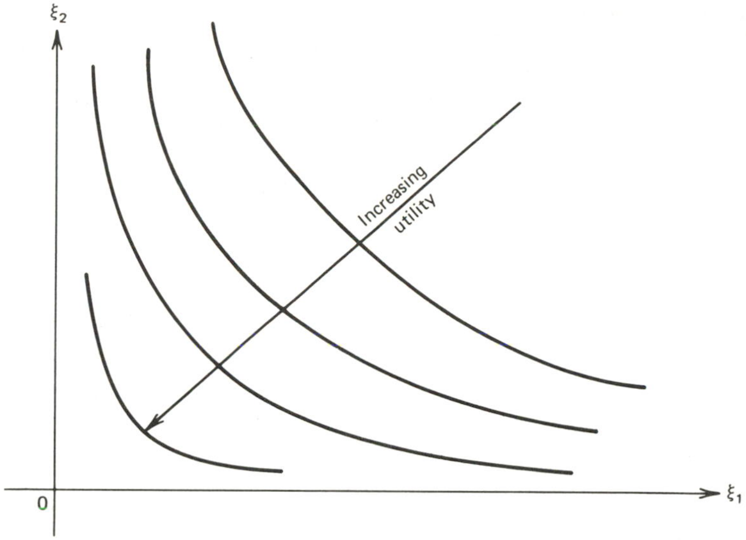

Figure 5.1

is nonincreasing in its arguments; increasing a price (or lowering income) cannot increase maximal utility.[1] However, V is not necessarily decreasing in the ith normalized price even if U is increasing in the ith consumption quantity; if $\overset{*}{x}_i = 0$ (i.e., $\overset{*}{x}$ is a corner solution), increasing p_i (and hence ξ_i) does not affect the consumer's utility (raising the price of Rolls Royces has no effect on most consumers' utility levels).

To examine the other properties of the indirect utility function, it is instructive to note that it is possible to construct indifference sets in the space of normalized prices. In order to employ two-dimensional diagrams, let us consider the case in which there are only two commodities, as shown in figure 5.1, where normalized prices are plotted on the two axes. If the consumer is not sated with either commodity, then any movement in the northeast direction of this diagram (i.e., an increase in *all* prices) reduces utility and any movement in the southwest direction (decreasing all prices) increases utility. An indifference curve in this space shows those combinations of normalized prices which leave the maximum utility level unchanged. In order to avoid ambiguities, we refer to indifference curves in normalized price space as *indirect indifference curves*.

A tough question is now posed: Under our assumption about the utility function, are these indifference curves convex or concave to the origin? The answer is that these indifference curves are convex to the origin so that they might be represented, for example, by the indifference curves in figure 5.1. This indirect indifference map looks exactly like a typical indifference map for the

[1] This is true even if U is not nondecreasing; i.e., even if a bliss point exists. See Diewert [1974] for formal proofs of the properties of V.

direct utility function. There is, however, one important difference: *higher* indirect indifference curves in figure 5.1 are associated with *lower* utility levels.

Why are these indirect indifference curves convex to the origin? The proof of this property proceeds by contradiction and therefore sheds little light on the reason.* This convexity obviously reflects the fact that, at relatively high values of the normalized price of commodity 2, ξ_2, relatively small changes in the normalized price of commodity 1, ξ_1, are required to compensate for large changes in ξ_2. The opposite is true at low levels of ξ_2.

● ●

**NOTE* Proof of convexity: Convexity to the origin of indirect indifference curves is equivalent to convexity of "no-better-than-ξ" sets $W(\xi) = \{\bar{\xi}$ such that $V(\xi) \geq V(\bar{\xi})\}$. Letting $V(\xi') = V(\xi'')$, it suffices to show that convex combinations of ξ' and ξ'', $\bar{\xi} = \theta\xi' + (1-\theta)\xi''$, $0 < \theta < 1$, are contained in $W(\xi') = W(\xi'')$. This situation is depicted in the diagram, Let x', x'', and $\bar{x}$ be the optimal

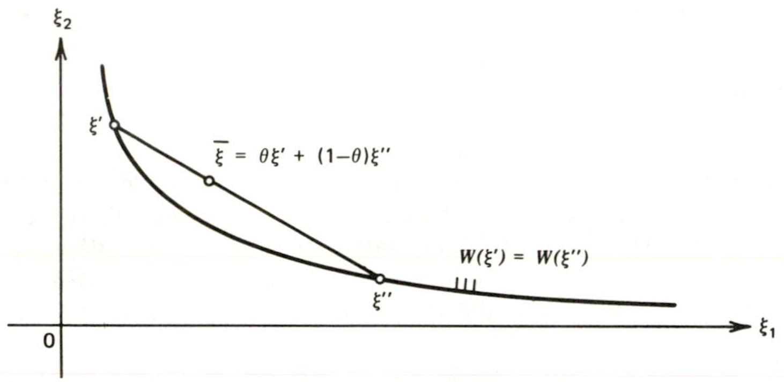

consumption bundles corresponding to ξ', ξ'', and $\bar{\xi}$ respectively. Note that

$$\sum_i \xi_i' x_i' \geq \sum_i \xi_i' \bar{x}_i \qquad \text{(a)}$$

or, equivalently,

$$\sum_i p_i' x_i' \geq \sum_i p_i' \bar{x}_i$$

implies that $U(x') \geq U(\bar{x})$ since x' is chosen at normalized prices ξ' although $\bar{x}$ could be purchased at those prices (see section 6.4 below). It follows that

$$V(\xi') \geq V(\bar{\xi}). \qquad \text{(a')}$$

Similarly,

$$\sum_i \xi_i'' x_i'' \geq \sum_i \xi_i'' \bar{x}_i \qquad \text{(b)}$$

implies

$$V(\xi'') \geq V(\bar{\xi}). \qquad \text{(b')}$$

As either inequality (a′) or (b′) is equivalent to the convex combination $\bar{\xi}$ being in the set $W(\xi') = W(\xi'')$, it suffices to show that either (a) or (b) must hold. The remainder of the proof proceeds by way of contradiction. Thus, suppose that neither (a) nor (b) holds. Then

$$\sum_i \xi_i' \bar{x}_i > \sum_i \xi_i' x_i' = 1 \tag{c}$$

and

$$\sum_i \xi_i'' \bar{x}_i > \sum_i \xi_i'' x_i'' = 1. \tag{d}$$

Now, since

$$\bar{\xi}_i = \theta\xi_i' + (1 - \theta)\xi_i'', \qquad i = 1, \ldots, n,$$

we can write

$$\sum_i \bar{\xi}_i \bar{x}_i = \theta \sum_i \xi_i' \bar{x}_i + (1 - \theta) \sum_i \xi_i'' \bar{x}_i.$$

But since the right-hand side is a convex combination of two terms which are greater than unity [from (c) and (d)], it follows that

$$\sum_i \bar{\xi}_i \bar{x}_i > 1$$

or

$$\sum_i \bar{p}_i \bar{x}_i > \bar{y},$$

violating the budget identity. Hence (a) and (b) cannot both be valid.

Note that this proof does not exploit convexity (to the origin) of the direct indifference curves. In fact, convexity of the indirect indifference curves does not require that preferences be convex.

• •

The principal use of indirect utility functions stems from the implications of the following (rather "nonbehavioral") minimization problem:

$$\underset{\xi}{\text{Min}}\ V(\xi) \qquad \text{s.t.} \sum_i \xi_i x_i \leq 1. \tag{5.4}$$

Unlike the utility-maximization problem, this problem takes the consumption bundle, x, as fixed and chooses a normalized price vector, ξ, to minimize the level of utility. Represent the solution of this minimization problem by the following set of n equations:

$$\xi_i = g_i(x), \qquad i = 1, \ldots, n. \tag{5.5}$$

Figure 5.2 illustrates this optimization problem for the case in which there are only two commodities. In the two-commodity case, the (budget) equality of the minimization problem is $\xi_1 x_1 + \xi_2 x_2 = 1$. Solving this equation for ξ_2, $\xi_2 = (1/x_2) - (x_1/x_2)\xi_1$, we see that the constraint can be represented in figure 5.2 by a straight line with intercept $1/x_2$ and slope $-x_1/x_2$. It is similarly easy to show that the horizontal intercept is $1/x_1$. Recalling that *lower*

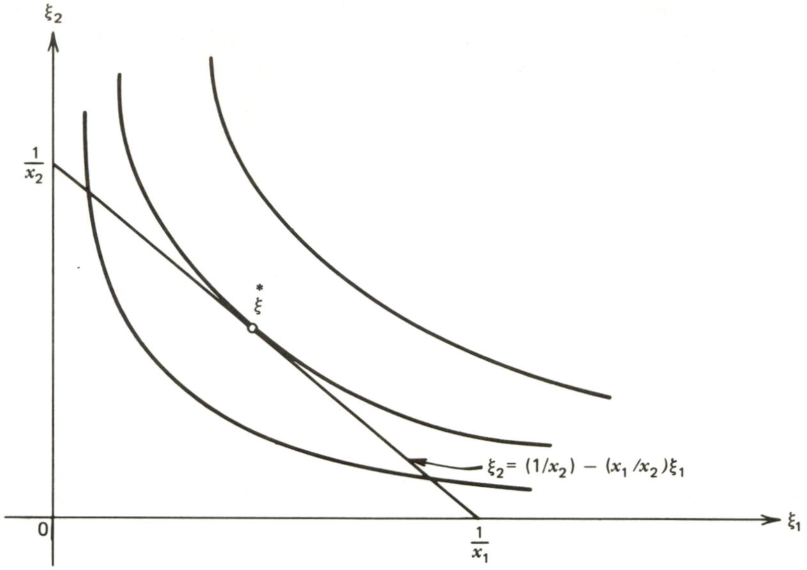

Figure 5.2

indirect indifference curves correspond to *higher* utility levels, it is clear that utility is *minimized* subject to the budget constraint at $\overset{*}{\xi}$ where the *highest* possible indirect indifference curve (the *lowest* utility level) is attained.

This minimization problem is important because of the following fundamental duality result: if $\overset{*}{x}$ solves the direct utility-maximization problem (5.1) when normalized prices are $\overset{*}{\xi}$, then $\overset{*}{\xi}$ solves the indirect utility-minimization problem when the consumption bundle is fixed at $\overset{*}{x}$. Since the two systems of functions (5.2) and (5.5) represent the solutions to these two maximization problems, this duality theorem can be restated as follows: if $\overset{*}{x}_i = d_i(\overset{*}{\xi}), i = 1, \ldots, n$, then $\overset{*}{\xi}_i = g_i(\overset{*}{x}), i = 1, \ldots, n$. What this means is that the relationship between normalized prices and optimal consumption bundles is reflected either in the system of direct demand functions (5.2) or in the system of functions (5.5) obtained by the dual minimization problem.[2]

The important thing is that the relationship between normalized prices and optimal consumption bundles can be obtained either from the direct utility function or the indirect utility function. The two optimization problems, (5.1) and (5.4), are therefore dual problems in the following sense. If we substitute the variables ξ for the variables x, the indirect utility function V for the direct utility function U, and the minimization operation for the maximization operation, the same set of demand functions are obtained. Thus, in these dual optimization problems, x is dual to ξ, U is dual to V, and "max" is dual to "min." In a word,

[2] The system of functions (5.5) is simply the inverse of the system of direct demand functions (5.2).

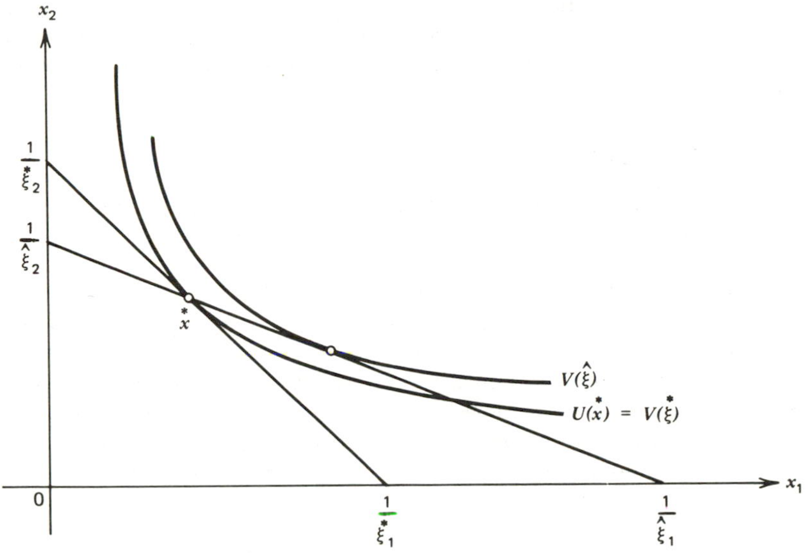

Figure 5.3

the two optimization problems are dual to one another and either can generate the consumer's demand system.

This dual structure is of more than passing theoretical interest. In carrying out empirical work with systems of demand functions that can be generated by utility maximization, the investigator can specify either a direct utility function or an indirect utility function with the appropriate monotonicity and convexity properties. A consumer's preferences can be represented by either a direct or an indirect utility function. That is, it is just as appropriate to specify the form of an indirect utility function and derive the demand functions by the above minimization problem as to specify a direct utility function and derive the demand functions by the utility-maximization procedure.

We can sketch a proof of the above duality theorem as follows: Suppose that the consumption bundle $\overset{*}{x}$ is picked at given normalized prices $\overset{*}{\xi}$. Consider any alternative set of normalized prices, say $\hat{\xi}$, such that

$$\sum_i \hat{\xi}_i \overset{*}{x}_i = \sum_i \overset{*}{\xi}_i \overset{*}{x}_i = 1. \tag{5.6}$$

This equality indicates that $\overset{*}{x}$ satisfies the budget equality at the alternative normalized prices $\hat{\xi}$ and hence could be chosen given those normalized prices. Hence at normalized prices $\hat{\xi}$, the maximum level of utility would be at least as great as $U(\overset{*}{x})$. That is, $V(\hat{\xi}) \geq V(\overset{*}{\xi})$ for all $\hat{\xi}$ satisfying the constraint (5.6). But this means that $\overset{*}{\xi}$ minimizes utility subject to the constraint, $\sum_i \xi_i \overset{*}{x}_i = 1$.

This proof is illustrated in (two-) commodity space in figure 5.3, where $\overset{*}{x}$ is picked, given normalized prices $\overset{*}{\xi}$. The set of consumption bundles satisfying the constraint (5.6) at normalized prices $\hat{\xi}$ is given by the points on the line with slope $-\hat{\xi}_1/\hat{\xi}_2$ passing through the point $\overset{*}{x}$. It is clear that the maximum utility level along this new budget line, $U(\xi)$, is greater than $V(\overset{*}{\xi}) = U(\overset{*}{x})$. This, in fact, is clearly true for any price vector other than $\overset{*}{\xi}$. Thus, the budget line corresponding to $\overset{*}{\xi}$ yields the lowest level of (maximum) utility of all budget lines passing through the point $\overset{*}{x}$.

Roy's Theorem

It turns out that being able to represent consumer preferences by an indirect utility function is especially instrumental in the derivation of ordinary consumer demand functions. Conceptually, demand functions are usually derived by solving the $n + 1$ first-order conditions of the maximization problem (5.1). Anyone who has attempted to solve a large system of nonlinear equations can appreciate the enormity of this problem. Indeed, for "flexible" specifications of U, solution of the first-order maximization condition is usually impossible.[3] If, however, the form of the consumer's *indirect* utility function is specified, a result known as Roy's theorem allows us to derive the system of ordinary demand functions by straightforward differentiation (without solving a system of simultaneous equations).

Roy's Theorem *Define $\hat{V}$ by $\hat{V}(p, y) \equiv V(\xi)$. If the indirect utility function is differentiable, the demand functions are given by*

$$x_i = d_i(\xi) = -\frac{\partial \hat{V}(p, y)/\partial p_i}{\partial \hat{V}(p, y)/\partial y}, \qquad i = 1, \ldots, n.$$

PROOF The first-order conditions for the minimization problem (5.4) are

$$\frac{\partial V(\xi)}{\partial \xi_i} - \kappa x_i = 0, \qquad i = 1, \ldots, n,$$
$$\sum_i \xi_i x_i = 1, \tag{5.7}$$

where κ is the Lagrange multiplier. Multiplying both sides of (5.7) by ξ_i and summing over all i yields

$$\sum_i \frac{\partial V(\xi)}{\partial \xi_i} \xi_i - \kappa \sum_i \xi_i x_i = 0,$$

or, since

$$\sum_i \xi_i x_i = 1,$$

$$\kappa = \sum_i \frac{\partial V(\xi)}{\partial \xi_i} \xi_i .$$

[3] Examples are translog (Christensen, Jorgensen, and Lau [1975]) and generalized Leontief (Diewert [1971]) functions.

Substituting for κ in (5.7) and solving for x_i, we obtain

$$x_i = \frac{\partial V(\xi)/\partial \xi_i}{\sum_j (\partial V(\xi)/\partial \xi_j)\xi_j}, \qquad i = 1, \ldots, n. \tag{5.8}$$

Next note that, applying the chain rule, we obtain

$$\frac{\partial \hat{V}(p, y)}{\partial y} = \sum_j \frac{\partial V(\xi)}{\partial \xi_j}\left(-\frac{p_j}{y^2}\right)$$

so that (since $p_j/y^2 = \xi_j/y$),

$$\sum_j \frac{\partial V(\xi)}{\partial \xi_j}\xi_j = -y\frac{\partial \hat{V}(p, y)}{\partial y}. \tag{5.9}$$

Similarly,

$$\frac{\partial \hat{V}(p, y)}{\partial p_i} = \frac{\partial V(\xi)}{\partial \xi_i}\frac{1}{y}$$

so that

$$\frac{\partial V(\xi)}{\partial \xi_i} = y\frac{\partial \hat{V}(p, y)}{\partial p_i}. \tag{5.10}$$

Substitution of (5.9) and (5.10) for the denominator and numerator, respectively, of (5.8) yields the formula of Roy's theorem.

The Expenditure Function and Hotelling's Theorem

Closely related to the dual structure outlined in the previous subsection is the derivation of the consumer expenditure function. The solution to the problem,

$$\min_x \sum_i p_i x_i \qquad \text{s.t. } U(x) \geq u, \tag{5.11}$$

determines the consumption bundle which minimizes expenditure subject to the constraint that the utility level be at least as great as u. That is, this problem determines the cheapest way of achieving a given utility level, given a set of prices. The solution to (5.11) depends on the values of prices and utility. Denote this solution by the system of equations,

$$x_i = h_i(p, u), \qquad i = 1, \ldots, n. \tag{5.12}$$

It is easy to see that the solution to this minimization problem, $\overset{*}{x}$, at prices $\overset{*}{p}$ and utility level $U(\overset{*}{x})$, is also the solution to the ordinary utility-maximization problem (5.1) when the price vector is given by $\overset{*}{p}$ and total expenditure is $\sum_i \overset{*}{p}_i \overset{*}{x}_i$. To see this in the two-commodity case, refer to figure 5.4. The consumption bundle $\overset{*}{x}$ clearly maximizes utility at income $\overset{*}{y}$ and prices $(\overset{*}{p}_1, \overset{*}{p}_2)$. Alternative expenditure levels, given prices $\overset{*}{p}$, are depicted by alternative budget lines parallel to the budget lines tangent to the indifference curve corresponding to $\overset{*}{u}$. The minimization problem (5.11) is equivalent to searching for the lowest

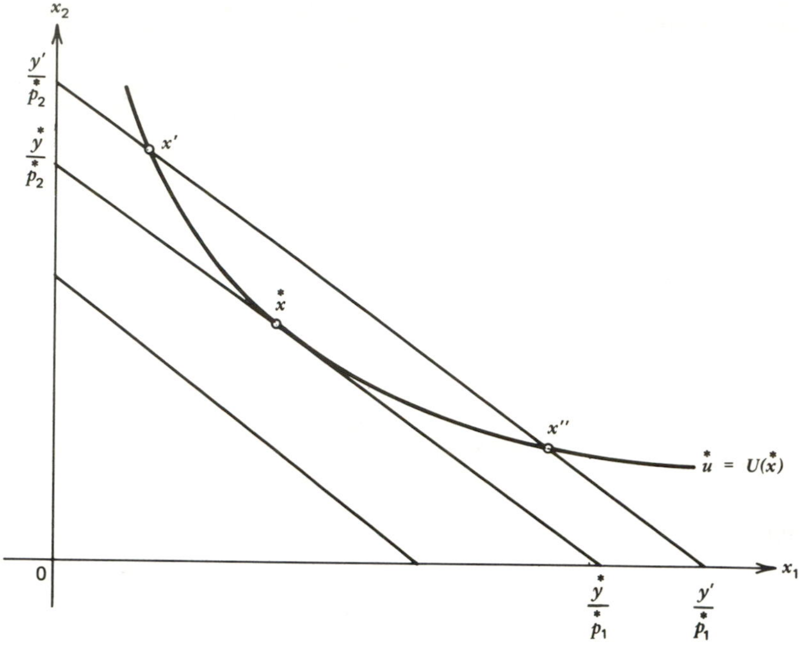

Figure 5.4

of these parallel budget lines which allow the consumer to attain utility level $\overset{*}{u} = U(\overset{*}{x})$. It is clear that budget lines above that tangent to the $\overset{*}{u}$ indifference curve allow the consumer to attain utility level $\overset{*}{u}$. For example, the budget line corresponding to income y' is sufficient to achieve utility level $\overset{*}{u}$ at either x' or x''. However, budget lines below the budget line through $\overset{*}{x}$ in figure 5.4 place the $\overset{*}{u}$ indifference curve entirely outside the budget set. Thus, it is clear that the lowest possible budget line consistent with attaining utility level $\overset{*}{u}$ is that which passes through $\overset{*}{x}$, the optimal consumption bundle.*

• •

******NOTE* If U is differentiable and satisfies the nonsatiation assumption (3.1), the first-order conditions for solving (5.11) can be used to show that, if $\overset{*}{x}$ is an interior solution of (5.1), the solution to

$$\operatorname*{Min}_{x} \sum_{i=1}^{n} p_i x_i \qquad \text{s.t. } U(x) = U(\overset{*}{x})$$

is $\overset{*}{x}$. The first-order conditions are

$$p_i - \kappa \frac{\partial U(x)}{\partial x_i} = 0, \qquad i = 1, \ldots, n, \tag{a}$$

and

$$U(x) - U(\overset{*}{x}) = 0, \tag{b}$$

where κ is a Lagrange multiplier. Dividing the first $n-1$ equations of (a) by the nth, we obtain

$$\frac{p_i}{p_n} = \frac{\partial U(x)/\partial x_i}{\partial U(x)/\partial x_n}, \qquad i = 1, \ldots, n-1. \tag{c}$$

But (c) is equivalent to the first $n-1$ of the first-order conditions for solving (5.1) (see equation 3.14). Hence $\overset{*}{x}$ satisfies (c). Moreover, $\overset{*}{x}$ by assumption satisfies (b). Hence, $\overset{*}{x}$ satisfies the first-order conditions for solving the cost-minimization problem (5.11).

• •

The diagrammatic construction of figure 5.4 makes it clear that the functions h_i are homogeneous of degree zero in prices: $h_i(\delta p, u) = h_i(p, u)$, $i = 1, \ldots, n$, for all $\delta > 0$. That is, multiplying all prices by the same (positive) scalar leaves the slope of the budget line unchanged; hence, the consumption bundle which minimizes expenditure to attain a given utility level is unaffected by an equiproportionate change in all prices.[4]

The solution to the minimization problem (5.11) depends, of course, upon the given price vector and utility level, as reflected in the system (5.12). Substituting these functions into the objective function in (5.11) yields a function which represents the minimal level of expenditure that can attain utility level $\overset{*}{u}$, given prices $\overset{*}{p}$:

$$\overset{*}{y} = H(\overset{*}{p}, \overset{*}{u}) = \sum_i p_i h_i(\overset{*}{p}, \overset{*}{u}). \tag{5.13}$$

This function is referred to as the consumer's *expenditure function.*[5]

A very interesting and important property of the expenditure function is given by Hotelling's theorem.

Hotelling's Theorem *If the expenditure function is differentiable, the optimal consumption bundle is given by*

$$\overset{*}{x}_i = h_i(p, u) = \frac{\partial H(p, u)}{\partial p_i}, \qquad i = 1, \ldots, n. \tag{5.14}$$

That is, the optimal consumption of the ith commodity is obtained by straightforward partial differentiation of the expenditure function with respect to the ith price. To prove Hotelling's Theorem, let $\overset{*}{x}$ be chosen at prices $\overset{*}{p}$ and utility level $\overset{*}{u}$—i.e., $\overset{*}{x}_i = h_i(\overset{*}{p}, \overset{*}{u})$, 1, . . . , n. Then $H(\overset{*}{p}, \overset{*}{u}) = \sum_i \overset{*}{p}_i \overset{*}{x}_i$ is an identity, and we can differentiate totally to arrive at

$$\sum_i H_i(\overset{*}{p}, \overset{*}{u})dp_i + H_u(\overset{*}{p}, \overset{*}{u})du = \sum_i \overset{*}{x}_i dp_i + \sum_i \overset{*}{p}_i dx_i,$$

[4] Note that multiplying all prices in (b) and (c) in the note above by a positive scalar leaves these first-order conditions unchanged.

[5] The expenditure function is continuous in u and p, concave, homogeneous of degree zero, and nondecreasing in prices, and increasing in u (see theorem A.3 of Blackorby, Primont, and Russell [1978]).

where $H_i(\overset{*}{p}, \overset{*}{u}) = \partial H(\overset{*}{p}, \overset{*}{u})/\partial p_i$ and $H_u(\overset{*}{p}, \overset{*}{u}) = \partial H(\overset{*}{p}, \overset{*}{u})/\partial u$. At the optimum, equations (a) of the foregoing note hold:

$$\overset{*}{p}_i = \kappa \frac{\partial U(\overset{*}{x})}{\partial x_i}. \tag{a}$$

Using (a) and setting $du = 0$ (i.e., holding utility constant at $\overset{*}{u}$), and substituting into the total differential above, we obtain

$$\sum_i H_i(\overset{*}{p}, \overset{*}{u})\, dp_i = \sum_i \overset{*}{x}_i\, dp_i + \kappa \sum_i U_i(\overset{*}{x})\, dx_i.$$

Letting $dp_i = 0$ for all $i \neq j$ (so that only p_j is varied), we obtain $H_j(\overset{*}{p}, \overset{*}{u}) = \overset{*}{x}_j$.

Cost-of-Living Indices

As noted above, the duality between direct and indirect utility functions has proved especially useful in empirical demand analysis. Duality between the utility function and the expenditure function turns out to be useful for, among other things, the study of cost-of-living indices. These indices purport to compare the cost of living at two different points in time (or in different markets). Clearly, the notion of the cost of living is not to be taken too literally, for the cost of "living" depends upon the standard of well-being—i.e., upon the utility level—of the consumer.

The consumer expenditure function is ideally suited for the study of the cost of living because it is defined as the cost of attaining a given utility level (i.e., a given standard of living). Let $p(t)$ and $p(t')$ be two sets of prices in the alternative situations, t and t'. The situations might refer to two different time periods in the same location or to two different locations. The cost of attaining utility level $\bar{u}$ in situation t relative to situation t' is given by

$$\Pi(\bar{u}, p(t), p(t')) = \frac{H(\bar{u}, p(\mathrm{t}))}{H(\bar{u}, p(t'))}, \tag{5.15}$$

where, as above, H is the consumer's expenditure function.

It is apparent that the cost of living in one situation relative to another depends upon the level of well-being (the utility level) that is used as a basis for comparison. It is common in the construction of cost-of-living indices to adopt the (maximal) utility level in one of the two situations as a benchmark. Thus, if t' is the benchmark situation or period, the cost of living in situation t (relative to situation t') is given by

$$\Pi(\hat{V}(y(t'), \mathrm{p}(t')), p(t), p(t')) = \frac{H(\hat{V}(y(t'), p(t')), p(t))}{H(\hat{V}(y(t'), p(t')), p(t'))}. \tag{5.16}$$

It is also apparent that the cost-of-living index depends critically upon the form of the utility function, which in turn determines the form of the expenditure function. Not all conceivable cost-of-living indexes are consistent with an underlying utility function. Some cost-of-living indices are consistent with the theory of the cost of living only if the utility function assumes a particular form.

We close this section by examining the implications regarding consumer preferences of the form of a commonly applied cost-of-living index.

It is common in many countries to construct cost-of-living indexes that are ratios of linear functions of prices:

$$\Pi(u, p(t), p(t)) = \frac{\sum_{i=1}^{n} b_i p_i(t)}{\sum_{i=1}^{n} b_i p_i(t')}. \tag{5.17}$$

It is apparent that this cost-of-living index is consistent with the underlying theory of utility maximization if and only if the expenditure function has the following form:

$$H(u, p) = u \sum_{i=1}^{n} b_i p_i.^{6} \tag{5.18}$$

It can be shown that this particular expenditure function is rationalized by a utility function in which the indifference curves are right angles with the cusps on a ray emanating from the origin. That is, a fixed-proportions utility function with image,

$$U(x) = \min\left(\frac{x_1}{b_1}, \ldots, \frac{x_n}{b_n}\right), \; b_i > 0, \qquad i = 1, \ldots, n, \tag{5.19}$$

generates the expenditure function (5.18). Figure 5.5 draws the indifference curves corresponding to this utility function for the case in which there are only two commodities.

To see that the expenditure function that is dual to (5.19) is given by (5.18), consider the problem,

$$\operatorname*{Min}_{x} \sum_{i=1}^{n} p_i x_i \qquad \text{s.t. } \min\left(\frac{x_1}{b_1}, \ldots, \frac{x_n}{b_n}\right) \geq u. \tag{5.20}$$

It is apparent that the solution to this optimization problem must occur on the ray through the cusps of the right-angle indifference curves. Thus, the cost-minimizing consumption bundles satisfy $x_1/b_1 = x_2/b_2 = \cdots = x_n/b_n = u$. Hence, the optimal consumption quantities are given by $x_i = b_i u$, $i = 1, \ldots, n$. Note that, as is apparent from the diagram, the optimal consumption bundle is independent of prices and depends only on the given utility level. Substituting these optimal consumption quantities into the objective function in the minimization problem (5.20) yields the consumer expenditure function image:

$$H(u, p) = \sum_{i=1}^{n} p_i b_i u = u \sum_{i=1}^{n} b_i p_i,$$

which is identical to (5.18) above.

Thus, the commonly employed cost-of-living index based on a linear expenditure function is consistent with consumer theory if the underlying

[6] More generally, $H(u, p) = \phi(u) \cdot \sum_{i=1}^{n} b_i p_i$ where ϕ is an increasing function, but this expenditure function can be converted into the form (5.18) by a monotonic transformation (in particular ϕ^{-1}) of the utility function.

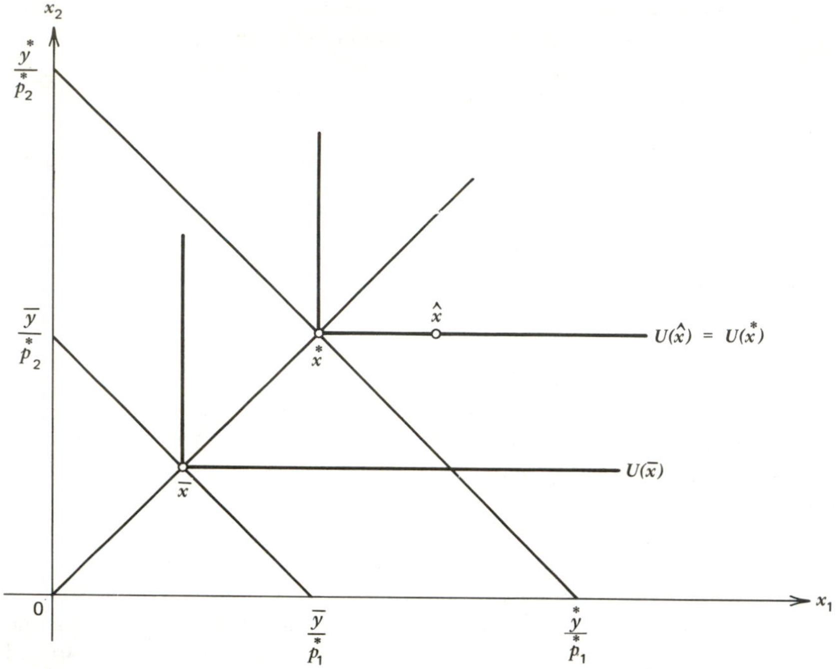

Figure 5.5

utility function is of the fixed-proportions type.[7] This means that there is absolutely no scope for substitution between commodities; i.e., all commodities are "perfect complements"). This is clearly a very restrictive assumption regarding consumer preferences.

Students wishing to explore the implications for the cost-of-living index of alternative specifications of the utility function are referred to exercise 5.1 at the end of this chapter.

5.3 MATHEMATICAL ANALYSIS OF THE EFFECT OF INCOME AND PRICE CHANGES UPON DEMAND

In order to examine mathematically the comparative statics of consumer demand, we will maintain all of the assumptions of chapters 2 and 3. In fact, we

[7] It can also be shown that the linear expenditure function (5.18) implies a fixed-proportions utility function (5.19) (see Blackorby, Primont and Russell [1978, pp. 37–38]); hence, this form of the utility function is necessary and sufficient for the cost-of-living index with linear weights to be rationalized by an underlying preference ordering.

must strengthen the differentiability assumption (3.3) to *twice* differentiability of the utility function U.

The utility-maximizing consumer's demand functions are obtained by solving

$$\operatorname*{Max}_{x} U(x) \qquad \text{s.t.} \sum_{i=1}^{n} p_i x_i - y = 0.$$

The first-order conditions for $\overset{*}{x}$ to solve this problem are

$$U_i(\overset{*}{x}) - \lambda p_i = 0, \qquad i = 1, \ldots, n, \tag{5.21}$$

and

$$y - \sum_{i=1}^{n} p_i \overset{*}{x}_i = 0, \tag{5.22}$$

where λ is the Lagrange multiplier and $U_i(\overset{*}{x}) = \partial U(\overset{*}{x})/\partial x_i$. The second-order conditions[8] are that the bordered principal minors,

$$\begin{vmatrix} U_{11}(x) & U_{12}(x) & -p_1 \\ U_{21}(x) & U_{22}(x) & -p_2 \\ -p_1 & -p_2 & 0 \end{vmatrix}, \ldots, \begin{vmatrix} U_{11}(x) & U_{12}(x) & \cdots & U_{1n}(x) & -p_1 \\ U_{21}(x) & U_{22}(x) & \cdots & U_{2n}(x) & -p_2 \\ \vdots \\ U_{n1}(x) & U_{n2}(x) & \cdots & U_{nn}(x) & -p_n \\ -p_1 & -p_2 & \cdots & -p_n & 0 \end{vmatrix}$$

where $U_{ij}(\overset{*}{x}) = \partial^2 U(\overset{*}{x})/\partial x_i\, \partial x_j$, alternate in sign beginning with a positive sign.

The demand functions are obtained by solving (5.21)–(5.22) for $\overset{*}{x}$: $\overset{*}{x}_i = d_i(p, y)$, $i = 1, \ldots, n$. Therefore, from (5.21) and (5.22),

$$U_i(d_1(p, y), \ldots, d_n(p, y)) - \lambda(p, y) \cdot p_i = 0, \quad i = 1, \ldots, n, \tag{5.23}$$

and

$$y - \sum_{i=1}^{n} p_i d_i(p, y) = 0, \tag{5.24}$$

where $\lambda(p, y)$ signifies that λ depends upon p and y. Moreover, these conditions hold identically (for all price and income values that generate interior solutions) because of the definition of the demand functions. We can therefore differentiate

[8] See Apostle [1974, pp. 380–84] and Intriligator [1978] on second-order conditions for constrained optimization.

(5.23) and (5.24) with respect to prices and income. Using the composite-function rule[9] and letting $d(p, y) = (d_1(p, y), \ldots, d_n(p, y))$, we can write

$$\sum_{k=1}^{n} U_{ik}(d(p, y)) \frac{\partial d_k(p, y)}{\partial p_j} - \frac{\partial \lambda(p, y)}{\partial p_j} p_i - \delta_{ij}\lambda(p, y) = 0, \qquad i = 1, \ldots, n, \quad j = 1, \ldots, n,$$

$$\sum_{k=1}^{n} U_{ik}(d(p, y)) \frac{\partial d_k(p, y)}{\partial y} - \frac{\partial \lambda(p, y)}{\partial y} p_i = 0, \qquad i = 1, \ldots, n,$$

$$-\sum_{k=1}^{n} p_k \frac{\partial d_k(p, y)}{\partial p_j} - d_j(p, y) = 0, \qquad j = 1, \ldots, n,$$

$$1 - \sum_{k=1}^{n} p_k \frac{\partial d_k(p, y)}{\partial y} = 0,$$

where $\delta_{ij} = 1$ if $j = i$ and $\delta_{ij} = 0$ if $j \neq i$.

This system of equations can be written in matrix form[10] as follows:

$$\begin{bmatrix} U_{11}(d(p, y)), \ldots, U_{1n}(d(p, y)), -p_1 \\ U_{21}(d(p, y)), \ldots, U_{2n}(d(p, y)), -p_2 \\ \vdots \qquad\qquad \vdots \qquad\qquad \vdots \\ U_{n1}(d(p, y)), \ldots, U_{nn}(d(p, y)), -p_n \\ -p_1, \ldots\ldots\ldots\ldots, -p_n, \quad 0 \end{bmatrix}$$

$$\times \begin{bmatrix} \dfrac{\partial d_1(p, y)}{\partial p_1}, \ldots, \dfrac{\partial d_1(p, y)}{\partial p_n}, \dfrac{\partial d_1(p, y)}{\partial y} \\ \vdots \qquad\qquad\qquad \vdots \\ \dfrac{\partial d_n(p, y)}{\partial p_1}, \ldots\ldots\ldots, \dfrac{\partial d_n(p, y)}{\partial y} \\ \dfrac{\partial \lambda(p, y)}{\partial p_1}, \ldots\ldots\ldots, \dfrac{\partial \lambda(p, y)}{\partial y} \end{bmatrix}$$

$$= \begin{bmatrix} \lambda(p, y), 0, \ldots\ldots\ldots, 0 \\ 0, \lambda(p, y), \ldots\ldots\ldots, 0 \\ \vdots \qquad\qquad\qquad \vdots \\ 0, \ldots\ldots, 0, \lambda(p, y), \; 0 \\ d_1(p, y), \ldots, d_n(p, y), -1 \end{bmatrix}$$

or

$$B(p, y) \times D(p, y) = C(p, y) \tag{5.25}$$

where $B(p, y)$ is the bordered Hessian matrix, $D(p, y)$ is the matrix of demand (and Lagrange multiplier) derivatives (with respect to prices and income), and

[9] Apostle [1974, pp. 106, 352] discusses the chain or composite-function rule of differential calculus.

[10] See Hadley [1961, p. 60] for an elementary discussion of a matrix.

$C(p, y)$ is a matrix with nondifferential components, all evaluated at the point (p, y). The "differential" comparative statics of demand are then summarized by solving for $D(p, y) = B(p, y)^{-1}C(p, y)$, where $B(p, y)^{-1}$ is the inverse of $B(p, y)$.[11] This solution provides the entire matrix of differential effects of changes in prices and income on demand at the point (p, y).

In order to examine these derivatives more carefully, let us use Cramer's rule to solve for $\partial d_i(p, y)/\partial p_j$:

$$\frac{\partial d_i(p, y)}{\partial p_j} = \frac{|B^{ji}(p, y)|}{|B(p, y)|}$$

where $B^{ji}(p, y)$ is the matrix $B(p, y)$ with the ith column replaced by the jth column of $C(p, y)$—viz., $[0, \ldots, 0, \lambda(p, y), 0, \ldots, 0, d_j(p, y)]$ where $\lambda(p, y)$ is the jth component—and $|B^{ji}(p, y)|$ and $|B(p, y)|$ are determinants of the indicated matrices.[12] Expanding $|B^{ji}(p, y)|$ along the jth column, we have

$$\frac{\partial d_i(p, y)}{\partial p_j} = \frac{\lambda(p, y)B_{ij}(p, y)}{|B(p, y)|} + \frac{d_j(p, y)B_{n+1,i}(p, y)}{|B(p, y)|} \tag{5.26}$$

where $B_{ij}(p, y)$ is the i, j cofactor of $B(p, y)$.[13]

Similarly, using Cramer's rule, we find that the income derivative of the ith demand function is

$$\frac{\partial d_i(p, y)}{\partial y} = -\frac{B_{n+1,i}(p, y)}{|B(p, y)|}. \tag{5.27}$$

In order to interpret these derivatives, we exploit the duality theory developed in section 5.2. In particular, recall that minimizing expenditure subject to a utility constraint yields the same optimal consumption bundle as maximizing utility subject to a budget constraint. More precisely, if $\overset{*}{x}$ solves

$$\operatorname*{Max}_x U(x) \qquad \text{s.t.} \sum_{i=1}^{n} p_i x_i = y, \tag{5.28}$$

it also solves

$$\operatorname*{Min}_x \sum_{i=1}^{n} p_i x_i \qquad \text{s.t. } U(x) = U(\overset{*}{x}) = \overset{*}{u}. \tag{5.29}$$

The first-order conditions for solving (5.29) can be written as

$$p_i + \kappa(p, \overset{*}{u}) \frac{\partial U(h(p, \overset{*}{u}))}{\partial h_i(p, \overset{*}{u})} = 0, \qquad i = 1, \ldots, n, \tag{5.30}$$

and

$$U(h(p, \overset{*}{u})) - \overset{*}{u} = 0, \tag{5.31}$$

[11] This inverse exists if the determinant of $B(y, p)$ is nonzero; but this is implied by the second-order conditions for $d(p, y)$ to be a constrained maximum.

[12] Cramer's rule is discussed in Hadley [1961, p. 166] and Yaari [1971, p. 141]. The determinant of a matrix is discussed in Hadley [1961, p. 85].

[13] See Hadley [1961, p. 90] or Yaari [1971, p. 136] for the concept of a cofactor.

where $\kappa(p, \overset{*}{u})$ is the Lagrange multiplier. The first-order utility-maximization condition (5.21) implies that

$$\lambda(p, y) = \frac{\partial U(d(p, y))/\partial d_i(p, y)}{p_i}, \qquad i = 1, \ldots, n,$$

whereas (5.30) implies that

$$\frac{1}{\kappa(p, \overset{*}{u})} = -\frac{\partial U(h(p, \overset{*}{u}))/\partial h_i(p, y)}{p_i}, \qquad i = 1, \ldots, n.$$

However, as $d(p, y) = h(p, \overset{*}{u})$, it must be that $\kappa(p, \overset{*}{u}) = -1/\lambda(p, y)$. The conditions (5.30) can therefore be written as

$$\frac{\partial U(h(p, \overset{*}{u}))}{\partial h_i(p, \overset{*}{u})} - \lambda(p, y)p_i = 0, \qquad i = 1, \ldots, n. \tag{5.30a}$$

Differentiation of the indentities (5.30a) and (5.31) with respect to prices yields

$$\sum_{k=1}^{n} U_{ik}(h(p, \overset{*}{u})) \frac{\partial h_k(p, \overset{*}{u})}{\partial p_j} - \frac{\partial \lambda(p, y)}{\partial p_j} p_i - \delta_{ij}\lambda(p, y) = 0, \qquad \begin{matrix} i = 1, \ldots, n, \\ j = 1, \ldots, n, \end{matrix} \tag{5.32}$$

and

$$-\sum_{k=1}^{n} U_k(h(p, \overset{*}{u})) \frac{\partial h_k(p, \overset{*}{u})}{\partial p_j} = 0, \qquad j = 1, \ldots, n. \tag{5.33}$$

In matrix notation the system (5.32)–(5.33) is

$$\begin{bmatrix} U_{11}(h(p, \overset{*}{u})), \ldots, U_{1n}(h(p, \overset{*}{u})), -p_1 \\ \vdots \qquad\qquad \vdots \qquad\qquad \vdots \\ U_{n1}(h(p, \overset{*}{u})), \ldots, U_{nn}(h(p, \overset{*}{u})), -p_n \\ -U_1(h(p, \overset{*}{u})), \ldots, -U_n(h(p, \overset{*}{u})), \quad 0 \end{bmatrix} \times \begin{bmatrix} \frac{\partial h_1(p, \overset{*}{u})}{\partial p_1}, \ldots, \frac{\partial h_1(p, \overset{*}{u})}{\partial p_n} \\ \vdots \qquad\qquad \vdots \\ \frac{\partial h_n(p, \overset{*}{u})}{\partial p_1}, \ldots, \frac{\partial h_n(p, \overset{*}{u})}{\partial p_n} \\ \frac{\partial \lambda(p, y)}{\partial p_1}, \ldots, \frac{\partial \lambda(p, y)}{\partial p_n} \end{bmatrix}$$

$$= \begin{bmatrix} \lambda(p, y), & 0, \ldots\ldots, 0 \\ 0, & \lambda(p, y), \ldots, 0 \\ \vdots & \ddots \quad \vdots \\ 0 \ldots\ldots 0, & \lambda(p, y), 0 \\ 0 \ldots\ldots & \ldots\ldots 0 \end{bmatrix}$$

or

$$A(p, \overset{*}{u}) \times H(p, \overset{*}{u}) = \Lambda(p, y), \tag{5.34}$$

where $A(p, \overset{*}{u})$ is the appropriate bordered Hessian, $H(p, \overset{*}{u})$ is the matrix of derivatives of constant-utility, or income-compensated, demand functions, and $\Lambda(p, y)$ is a matrix with the Lagrange multiplier values (for the utility-maximization problem) along the first n elements of the diagonal and zeros elsewhere.

The important thing to note about the system (5.34) is that the matrix $A(p, \overset{*}{u})$ is very similar to the matrix $B(p, y)$ in the system (5.25). The only difference is in the last rows of the two matrices. Recalling, however, that

$$U_i(h(p, \overset{*}{u})) = \lambda(p, y)p_i, \qquad i = 1, \ldots, n, \tag{5.35}$$

we can relate the two matrices more closely. Substituting (5.35) into $A(p, \overset{*}{u})$, we see that this matrix is equivalent to $B(p, y)$ apart from the multiplication of the last row by the positive scalar $\lambda(p, y)$. It follows that

$$|A(p, \overset{*}{u})| = \lambda(p, y)|B(p, y)|; \tag{5.36}$$

i.e., the determinant of $A(p, \overset{*}{u})$ is equal to the determinant of $B(p, y)$ multiplied by the positive scalar $\lambda(p, y)$.[14] Similarly,

$$A_{ij}(p, \overset{*}{u}) = \lambda(p, y)B_{ij}(p, y) \tag{5.37}$$

where $A_{ij}(p, \overset{*}{u})$ and $B_{ij}(p, y)$ are i, j cofactors of $A(p, \overset{*}{u})$ and $B(p, y)$, respectively.

The constant-utility, or income-compensated, demand derivatives with respect to prices at the point $(p, \overset{*}{u})$ are obtained by solving (5.34): $H(p, \overset{*}{u}) = A(p, \overset{*}{u})^{-1}\Lambda(p, y)$. Employing Cramer's rule, we obtain

$$\frac{\partial h_i(p, \overset{*}{u})}{\partial p_j} = \frac{|A^{ji}(p, \overset{*}{u})|}{|A(p, \overset{*}{u})|},$$

where $A^{ji}(p, \overset{*}{u})$ is the matrix $A(p, \overset{*}{u})$ with the ith column replaced by the jth column of $\Lambda(p, y)$—viz., $(0, \ldots, 0, \lambda(p, y), 0, \ldots, 0)$ where $\lambda(p, y)$ is the jth component. Expanding $A^{ji}(p, \overset{*}{u})$ along the ith column, we have

$$\frac{\partial h_i(p, \overset{*}{u})}{\partial p_j} = \frac{\lambda(p, y)A_{ij}(p, \overset{*}{u})}{|A(p, \overset{*}{u})|} = \frac{\lambda(p, y)B_{ij}(p, y)}{|B(p, y)|}, \tag{5.38}$$

where the last equality follows by substitution from (5.36) and (5.37) and cancellation of $\lambda(p, y)$ from the numerator and denominator.

We can now interpret the derivative of $d_i(p, y)$ with respect to p_j. Substituting (5.27) and (5.38) into (5.26), we have

$$\frac{\partial d_i(p, y)}{\partial p_j} = \frac{\partial h_i(p, \overset{*}{u})}{\partial p_j} - d_j(p, y)\frac{\partial d_i(p, y)}{\partial y}. \tag{5.39}$$

That is, the rate of change of demand for the ith commodity with respect to a change in the jth price is dichotomized into two parts. The first is the rate of change of demand holding utility constant, or, as the story goes, compensating

[14] Multiplying a row or column of a determinant by a scalar multiplies the value of the determinant by that scalar value. This is easily seen by expanding the determinant along the row or column that is multiplied by the scalar.

the consumer for the real-income effects of the price change. The second term is the negative of the rate of change of demand for the ith commodity as income changes weighted by the level of consumption of the jth commodity. Of course, the first of these terms represents the substitution effect and the second represents the income effect of the change in the jth price, both analyzed diagrammatically in chapter 4. The dichotomization of the effect of change in the jth price on the rate of change of demand for the ith commodity was developed by Slutsky [1915] and (5.39) is commonly referred to as the *Slutsky equation*.

The term reflecting the income effect deserves further discussion. The derivative $\partial d_i(p, y)/\partial y$ reflects, of course, the (differential) effect of income changes on the demand for the ith commodity. It is multiplied by $d_j(p, y)$, which reflects the change in real income due to a change in the jth price; the more of the jth commodity that the consumer is consuming, the larger is the change in real income induced by a change in the jth price. Finally, this term enters (5.39) with a negative sign because a *rise* in the jth price *lowers* real income.

What can be said about the qualitative content of the basic model of consumer demand—that is, the signs of the demand derivatives? Unfortunately, very little. As the ratio of determinants, $B_{i,n+1}(p, y)/|B(p, y)|$, cannot be signed without additional information, the signs of the income derivatives $\partial d_i(p, y)/\partial y$, $i = 1, \ldots, n$, are not determined. Following the terminology of chapter 4, we refer to the ith commodity as normal if $\partial d(p, y)/\partial y > 0$ and inferior if $\partial d_i(p, u)/\partial y < 0$.

The income-compensated price derivative $\partial h_i(p, \overset{*}{u})/\partial p_j$ is also unsigned since the sign of $B_{ij}(p, y)/|B(p, y)|$ is not determined. On the other hand, the income-compensated *own*-price derivative $\partial h_i(p, \overset{*}{u})/\partial p_i$ is necessarily negative since $B_{ii}(p, y)$ and $|B(p, y)|$ have opposite signs. The latter follows from the second-order utility-maximization conditions since $D_{ii}(p, y)$ is an n-dimensional principal minor of the $n + 1$-dimensional determinant $|B(p, y)|$ and $B_{ii}(p, y)$ and $|B(p, y)|$ are therefore of opposite sign (since these principal minors must alternate in sign).

The above discussion indicates that both terms of the *cross*-price derivative (5.39) are of ambiguous sign. The first term of the *own*-price derivative (being the income-compensated own price derivative) is necessarily negative. The second term (the weighted income derivative) is of ambiguous sign. If, however, the ith commodity is normal ($\partial d_i(p, y)/\partial y > 0$), the second term (because of the negative sign) is necessarily negative, thus reinforcing the negative substitution effect. Thus, for all normal commodities, $\partial d_i(p, y)/\partial p_i$ is negative.

5.4 SUBSTITUTES AND COMPLEMENTS

Pairs of commodities are often classified as substitutes or complements, according to the way in which the demand for one of the commodities responds to changes in the price of the other. Two commodities are largely substitutable for one another if a rise in the price of either of the commodities increases the amount demanded of the other as it is substituted for the commodity whose price has increased. Similarly, two commodities are considered to be complementary to one another if a rise in the price of one of the commodities decreases the amount purchased of both that commodity and of the other as well.

For example, if the price of bacon increases, we might expect the demand for sausage to increase, in which case bacon and sausage are substitutable in the consumer's preference ordering. On the other hand, a rise in the price of automobiles might decrease the demand for automobile tires, in which case these two commodities are complements in the consumer's preference ordering. In summary, two commodities, say the ith and the jth, are defined as *gross substitutes* if $\partial d_i(p, y)/\partial p_j > 0$ and *gross complements* if $\partial d_i(p, y)/\partial p_j < 0$.

Pairs of commodities which satisfy these constraints are called *gross* substitutes and complements because the classification is induced by the signs of the gross, or total, cross derivatives of demand with respect to price. This classification criterion is unsatisfactory for many purposes because the total effect that a change in the jth price has on the demand for the ith commodity includes an income effect which has little relationship to the notion of intrinsic substitutability and complementarity. That is, a pair of commodities may be classified as complements under the above criterion even if they are totally unrelated to one another in basic use simply because the income effect of a rise in the price of the jth commodity results in a decline in the amount purchased of the ith commodity.

A more serious deficiency with the gross, or total, derivative criterion for classifying pairs of commodities as substitutes or complements is that it is not necessarily consistent. That is, because the income effects are not symmetrical, the gross price derivatives are not symmetrical. Consequently, it may be that $\partial d_i(p, y)/\partial p_j < 0$ and $\partial d_j(p, y)/\partial p_i > 0$, in which case the ith and jth commodities are classified as both complements and substitutes, depending upon which of the two prices is changed. Although for some purposes this internal inconsistency is not a devastating weakness, it is clearly an unsatisfactory characteristic of the classification scheme.[15] An alternative classification criterion which does not suffer from this internal inconsistency makes use of the income-compensated price derivative, or substitution term,

$$S_{ij}(p, \overset{*}{u}) = \frac{\partial h_i(p, \overset{*}{u})}{\partial p_j} = \frac{A^{ji}(p, \overset{*}{u})}{|A(p, \overset{*}{u})|}.$$

It will be recalled from the previous section that $A(p, \overset{*}{u})$ is symmetric and thus $S_{ij}(p, \overset{*}{u}) = S_{ji}(p, \overset{*}{u})$. The ith and the jth commodities are defined as *net substitutes* if $S_{ij}(p, \overset{*}{u}) = S_{ji}(p, \overset{*}{u}) > 0$ and *net complements* if $S_{ij}(p, \overset{*}{u}) = S_{ji}(p, \overset{*}{u}) < 0$. Pairs of commodities satisfying either of these restrictions are referred to as *net* substitutes or complements because the cross-price derivatives are net of the income effects.

Although in general any pair of commodities can be either net substitutes or net complements for one another, there is a sense in which substitutability between commodities dominates complementarity. To formalize this notion,

[15] The notion of gross substitutability plays an important role in the analysis of the stability of general equilibrium systems. See the suggestions for further reading following part IV.

expand the determinant of the matrix $B(p, y)$ by alien cofactors along the last column.[16] This expansion must equal zero:

$$-p_1 B_{1j}(p, y) - p_2 B_{2j}(p, y) - \cdots - p_n B_{nj}(p, y) = 0 \quad (j \neq n+1).$$

Multiplication through this equation by $-\lambda / |B(y, p)|$ yields

$$\sum_{i=1}^{n} p_i \frac{\lambda B_{ij}(y, p)}{|B(y, p)|} = 0.$$

Recalling the definition of $S_{ij}(p, \overset{*}{u})$ and substituting from (5.38), we obtain

$$\sum_{i=1}^{n} p_i S_{ij}(p, \overset{*}{u}) = 0.$$

Subtraction of $p_j S_{jj}(p, \overset{*}{u})$ from both sides of this equation yields

$$\sum_{\substack{i=1 \\ i \neq j}}^{n} p_i S_{ij}(p, \overset{*}{u}) = -p_j S_{jj}(p, \overset{*}{u}).$$

But the strict positivity of prices and strict negativity of the own substitution term, $S_{jj}(p, \overset{*}{u})$, implies that

$$\sum_{\substack{i=1 \\ i \neq j}}^{n} p_i S_{ij}(p, \overset{*}{u}) > 0. \qquad (5.40)$$

Thus, net substitutability dominates net complementarity in the sense that the sum of the price-weighted substitution terms is strictly positive. It follows that a commodity can be a net substitute for all other commodities (in which case every term of equation (5.40) is strictly positive), but no commodity can be a net complement to every other commodity since $S_{ij}(p, \overset{*}{u}) < 0$ for all $i \neq j$ would violate condition (5.40).

The dominance of the substitutability between pairs of commodities is reflected in figure 4.13 in the previous chapter. The substitution effect, which is measured from the original optimum $(\hat{x}, \hat{m})$ to the bogus optimum (x_i', m'), must reduce m (from $\hat{m}$ to m') just as inexorably as it must increase x_i (from $\hat{x}_i$ to x_i'). Thus, when the price of the ith commodity is decreased from $\hat{p}_i$ to $\bar{p}_i$, and the consumer is compensated for the price change with a reduction in nominal income, the amount spent on all other commodities *must* decrease. Thus, the income-compensated effect of a decrease in the price of the ith commodity is to decrease the amount expended on all other commodities and the income-compensated effect of an increase in the price of the ith commodity is to increase the amount expended on all other commodities. This reflects the dominance of the substitution effect.

Moreover, in the special case where there are only two commodities, condition (5.40) becomes $p_1 S_{12}(p, \overset{*}{u}) > 0$ so that the two commodities must be net substitutes for one another.

[16] See Yaari [1971, p. 139] for a discussion of expansion by cofactors.

EXERCISES

5.1 Consider again (see exercises 3.6, 3.7, and 4.4) the direct utility function defined by

$$U(x) = \sum_{i=1}^{n} \beta_i \cdot \log(x_i - \gamma_i),$$

where β_i and γ_i, $i = 1, \ldots, n$, are, respectively, positive and nonpositive parameters.

a. Derive the indirect utility function and show that it is decreasing in its arguments.

b. Verify Roy's theorem.

c. Derive the expenditure function and show that it is homogeneous of degree one and nondecreasing in prices.

d. Verify Hotelling's theorem.

e. Derive the cost-of-living index from the expenditure function derived in (c).

5.2 For the utility function defined in exercise 5.1,

a. derive the Slutsky equation, and

b. determine whether the commodities are (gross) complements or substitutes.

CHAPTER 6
TOPICS IN DEMAND THEORY

6.1 INTRODUCTION

In this chapter we consider three additional topics in demand theory. Section 6.2 introduces and analyzes unit-free measures (namely, elasticities) of the effects of income and price changes on demand. Those measures are widely applied in empirical demand studies. Section 6.3 relaxes the assumption that consumer income is given and examines the decision regarding the division of the consumer's time into work and leisure. This problem determines jointly the consumer's income, expenditure on each commodity, and supply of labor.

Finally, section 6.4 describes the theory of revealed preference. This theory, which was originally developed by Nobel Laureate Paul Samuelson as an attempt to purge consumer theory of the concept of utility, is based on the notion that consumers reveal their preferences by the choices that they make when faced with different price-income situations. The objective of revealed preference theory is to derive the restrictions on consumer demand functions without exploiting the notion of utility maximization.

6.2 ELASTICITIES OF DEMAND

It is interesting for many purposes to compare the responsiveness of the demand for two alternative commodities to changes in a price or income. Consider for example the responsiveness of the demand for two commodities to changes in their own prices. If the demand curves for the two commodities are illustrated in figure 6.1, it is tempting to say that commodity 1 is much more responsive to changes in its own price than is commodity 2. Such a conclusion, however, may be overly hasty. Suppose, for example, that the units of commodity 1 are apples and the units of commodity 2 are boxcar loads of oranges. Or suppose that commodity 1 is apples and commodity 2 is refrigerators. In either case, any conclusion about the responsiveness of demand to own-price changes would be meaningless because of the fact that the units on the two diagrams are not commensurate. Thus, any measure of the responsiveness of demand to price or income changes should be independent of the units in which we measure the commodity in question.

One obvious way around this problem is to measure everything in terms of proportionate rates of change since such changes are independent of the units of measurement. The proportionate rate of change in demand for the ith commodity resulting from a proportionate rate of change in its price is called

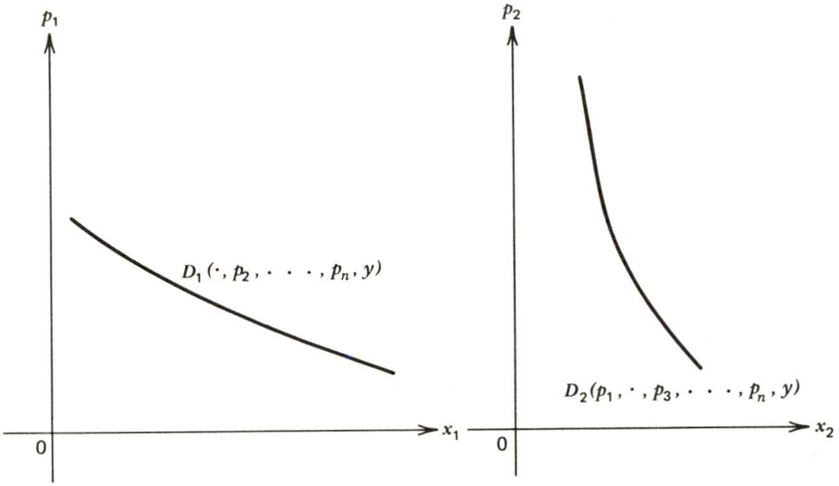

Figure 6.1

the *own-price elasticity of demand* and is denoted as follows:

$$e_{ii}(p, y) = \frac{\partial D_i(p, y)}{\partial p_i} \frac{p_i}{D_i(p, y)}. \tag{6.1}$$

Similarly, the *cross-price elasticity of demand* for the ith commodity with respect to the jth price is defined as the proportionate rate of change of demand for the ith commodity in response to proportionate rates of change in the jth price,

$$e_{ij}(p, y) = \frac{\partial D_i(p, y)}{\partial p_j} \frac{p_j}{D_i(p, y)}. \tag{6.2}$$

Finally, we define the *income elasticity of demand* for the ith commodity as the proportionate rate of change of demand for the ith commodity resulting from a proportionate rate of change in income,

$$e_{iy}(p, y) = \frac{\partial D_i(p, y)}{\partial y} \frac{y}{D_i(p, y)}. \tag{6.3}$$

Commodities are commonly classified according to the values of certain elasticities. From our previous analysis, we know that the ith commodity is normal at (p, y) if $e_{iy}(p, y) > 0$ and inferior if $e_{iy}(p, y) < 0$. Another interesting dividing line in classifying commodities according to the values of their income elasticities of demand is the number one. If $e_{iy}(p, y) = 1$, a given change in income induces an equal proportionate change in the amount demanded of the commodity. Thus, if income goes up by 1 percent and all prices are held constant, the demand for the ith commodity goes up by 1 percent. As a result, unitary income elasticity of demand implies that the percentage of the income expended on the ith commodity is invariant with respect to changes in income. If

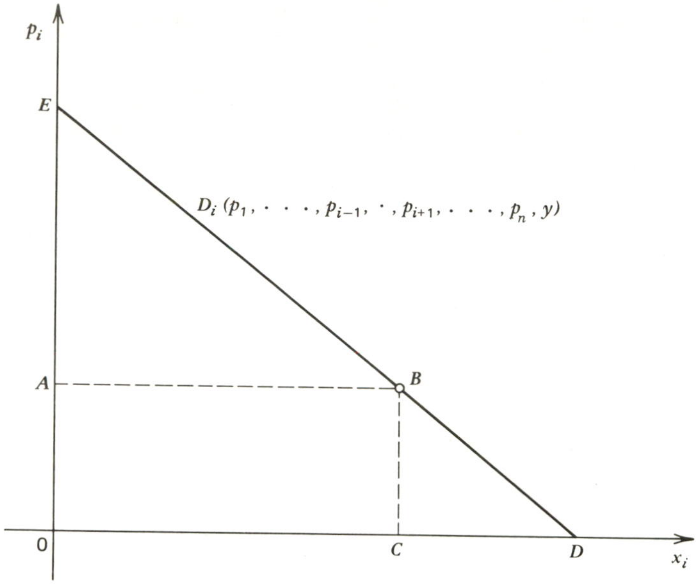

Figure 6.2

$e_{iy}(p, y) > 1$, an increase in income induces a more-than-proportionate increase in the demand for the ith commodity. Thus, as income goes up, a greater proportion of income is allocated to the ith commodity. On the other hand, if $e_{iy}(p, y) < 1$, the ith commodity commands a decreasing share of the consumer's budget as income grows. Because of these relationships, a commodity is commonly classified as a *luxury* if $e_{iy}(p, y) > 1$ and as a *necessity* if $e_{iy}(p, y) < 1$.

From previous analysis we also know that a commodity is a Giffen commodity if and only if the own-price elasticity of demand, $e_{ii}(p, y)$, is positive. Unity is also an interesting dividing line in the classification of commodities according to their responsiveness of change in demand to own prices. If $e_{ii}(p, y) = -1$, increasing the ith price results in an equal proportionate decrease in the demand for the ith commodity. In this case, the total expenditure on the ith commodity is invariant with respect to changes in its own price, since x_i increases (decreases) at the same rate as p_i decreases (increases). Similarly, if $e_{ii}(p, y) < -1$, in which case the absolute value of the own-price elasticity of demand is greater than 1, increasing the price results in a more than proportionate decrease in the amount demanded. Hence, increasing the price reduces total expenditure on the commodity and decreasing price increases total expenditure on the commodity. Finally, if $e_{ii}(p, y) > -1$, the absolute value of the own-price elasticity of demand is less than 1 and quantity demanded is relatively unresponsive to changes in the price of the commodity. In this case, increasing (decreasing) the price increases (decreases) total expenditure on the commodity. If the own-price elasticity of demand is less than -1 (absolutely greater than 1) we say that demand is *elastic,* and if the own-price elasticity of demand is greater than -1 (absolutely less than 1) we say that demand is *inelastic*.

It is important to note that elasticities generally vary over the domain of a function. Only in very special cases are the elasticities constant over the entire range of the function (see exercises 6.1, 6.2, and 6.4). To illustrate this point, consider the linear demand curve plotted in figure 6.2. The slope of this demand curve does not vary with respect to changes in price but, as is easily demonstrated, the elasticity does vary. At the arbitrary point B, the slope of the demand curve is equal to the ratio of two line segments, BC/CD. Hence, $\partial d_i(p, y)/\partial p_i$, the *inverse* of the slope of this demand function (since x_i is on the horizontal axis), is CD/BC. At the point B, the price is represented by the line segment BC and quantity demanded is represented by line segment OC. Thus, the absolute value of the own-price elasticity of demand is given by

$$|e_{ii}(p, y)| = \frac{CD}{BC}\frac{BC}{OC} = \frac{CD}{OC}. \tag{6.4}$$

But since two parallel lines divide the two arms of an angle into proportional parts, $CD/OC = BD/EB$. This formula provides a simple rule for evaluating the own-price elasticity of demand at any point on a linear demand curve. Clearly, as the point B moves toward D, the own-price elasticity of demand goes to 0 and as the point B moves to the point E, the price elasticity of demand explodes to $-\infty$. (At the point E on the vertical axis, the own-price elasticity of demand is, of course, undefined since we cannot divide by 0.) Finally, at a point exactly

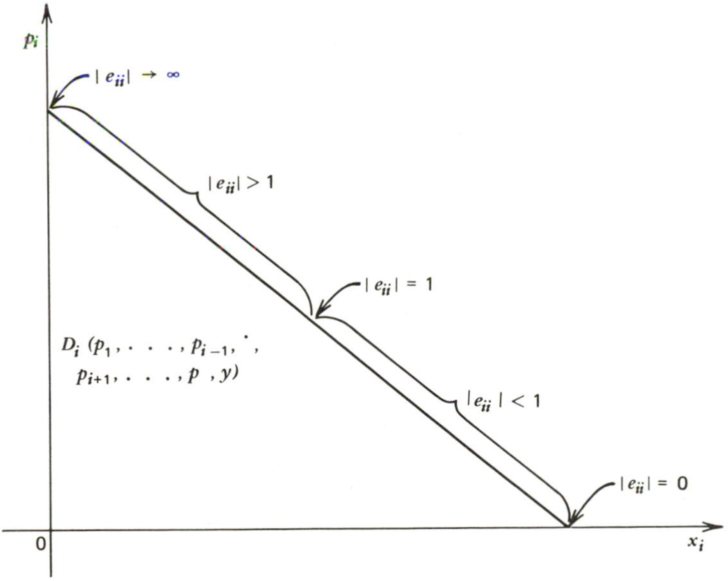

Figure 6.3

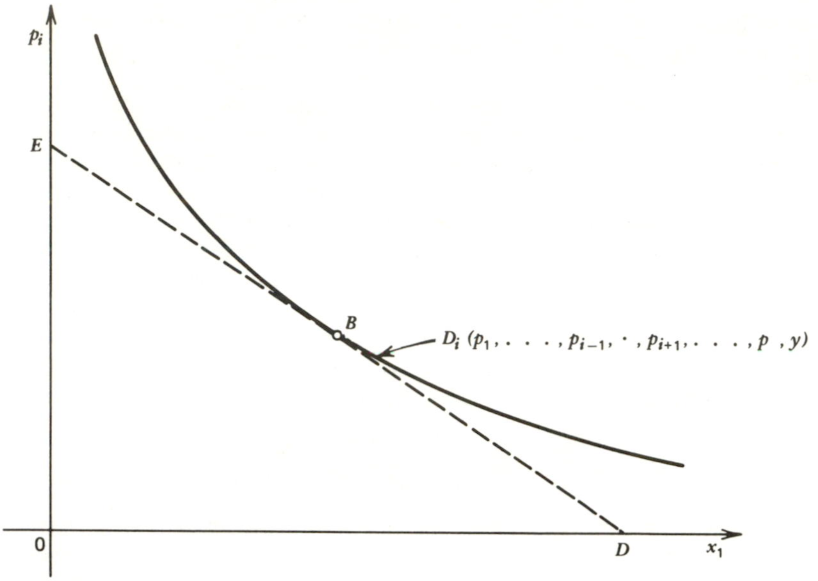

Figure 6.4

halfway down the demand curve the own-price elasticity of demand is equal to −1. These relationships are summarized in figure 6.3.

The above method of evaluating the own-price elasticity of demand can also be applied to nonlinear demand curves such as that illustrated in figure 6.4. For example, to evaluate the own-price elasticity of demand at the point *B*, simply draw a line tangent to the demand curve at *B*. The absolute value of the own-price elasticity of demand at *B* is equal to *BD*/*EB*.

Finally, given the definitions of gross substitutes and complements, it is obvious that two commodities are gross complements if the cross-price elasticities of demand are negative and gross substitutes if the cross-price elasticities of demand are positive.

The restriction on demand functions that they be homogeneous of degree zero in prices and income (see section 4.2) imposes a restriction on the set of price and income elasticities. In order to derive this restriction, we must first develop an important property of homogeneous functions. Recall that a function f is homogeneous of degree α in the vector x if

$$f(\kappa x) = \kappa^{\alpha} f(x) \quad \text{for all } \kappa > 0, \qquad \text{for all } x. \tag{6.5}$$

Since this relationship is an identity, the partial derivatives of both sides of the identity with respect to κ are also identically equal to one another. Differentiating with respect to κ, we obtain

$$\sum_{i=1}^{n} \frac{\partial f(x)}{\partial \kappa x_i} x_i = \alpha \kappa^{\alpha-1} f(x). \tag{6.6}$$

As this identity must hold for all positive values of κ, it must, for example, hold when $\kappa = 1$; hence,

$$\sum_{i=1}^{n} \frac{\partial f(x)}{\partial x_i} x_i = \alpha f(x). \tag{6.7}$$

Hence, if the function f is homogeneous of degree α, the sum of the values of the first partial derivatives weighted by the appropriate variables is equal to the value of the function multiplied by α, the degree of homogeneity. In particular, if f is homogeneous of degree one,

$$\sum_{i=1}^{n} \frac{\partial f(x)}{\partial x_i} x_i = f(x), \tag{6.8}$$

so that the value of the function image, $f(x)$, can be expressed as the sum of the first partial derivatives weighted by the corresponding variables. Similarly, if f is homogeneous of degree zero in x,

$$\sum_{i=1}^{n} \frac{\partial f(x)}{\partial x_i} x_i = 0. \tag{6.9}$$

This property of functions that are homogeneous of degree zero is used in order to impose restrictions on the set of income and price elasticities.

As the demand functions are homogeneous of degree zero in prices and income, the sum of the derivatives of the demand function with respect to all prices and income, appropriately weighted, is equal to 0:

$$\sum_{j=1}^{n} \frac{\partial D_i(p, y)}{\partial p_j} p_j + \frac{\partial D_i(p, y)}{\partial y} y = 0. \tag{6.10}$$

Dividing through by $D_i(p, y)$, we have

$$\sum_{j=1}^{n} \frac{\partial D_i(p, y)}{\partial p_j} \frac{p_j}{D_i(p, y)} + \frac{\partial D_i(p, y)}{\partial y} \frac{y}{D_i(p, y)} = 0. \tag{6.11}$$

Recalling the definitions of price and income elasticities of demand, note that this identity becomes

$$\sum_{i=1}^{n} e_{ij}(p, y) + e_{iy}(p, y) = 0. \tag{6.12}$$

Thus, the price and income elasticities of demand sum to zero.

6.3 LABOR SUPPLY

Throughout part I, the consumer's income has been assumed to be fixed. Typically, however, a consumer has some choice about how much to work and hence about his level of income (and therefore total expenditure). The examination of this problem begins with the observation that the consumer is endowed with a fixed amount of time (e.g., 24 hours per day) which can be consumed in the form of leisure or devoted to income-earning labors. This formulation entails the introduction of a new commodity in the consumer's utility function: leisure. Hence, denoting by ℓ the hours of leisure enjoyed by the consumer, we can express the utility function image as

$$u = U(x, \ell). \tag{6.13}$$

Letting w represent the fixed hourly wage rate which the consumer can earn by selling his time to firms (or other consumers) in the form of labor, and letting γ be the number of hours per time period, the consumer's income is $y = w(\gamma - \ell) = wL$, where, of course, $\gamma - \ell = L$ is the labor supply. As ℓ (and hence L) is a choice variable of the consumer, it is apparent that y is also a choice variable (subject to a fixed wage rate and a fixed endowment of time).

As before, the consumer's expenditure on marketed goods and services is constrained to be less than or equal to his income; that is,

$$\sum_{i=1}^{n} p_i x_i \leq y = w(\gamma - \ell). \tag{6.14}$$

The consumer's choice problem can now be formulated as that of jointly choosing a consumption bundle x and a level of leisure ℓ which maximizes his utility subject to the constraints that his expenditure not exceed his income and his leisure time not exceed the time allotment γ:

$$\operatorname*{Max}_{x,\ell} U(x, \ell) \qquad \text{s.t.} \sum_{i=1}^{n} p_i x_i \leq w(\gamma - \ell) \text{ and } \ell \leq \gamma. \tag{6.15}$$

If we assume, as before, that the consumer is not sated with at least one commodity, that the utility function is differentiable, and that the solution to (6.15) is interior ($x_i > 0$ for all i and $0 < \ell < \gamma$), we can use the calculus to characterize the optimum. As the nonsatiation assumption guarantees that the consumer spends his entire income, the first-order conditions for (6.15) are given by the critical-value conditions for the Lagrange expression,

$$L(x, \ell, \lambda) = U(x, \ell) - \lambda\left(\sum_{i=1}^{n} p_i x_i - w(\gamma - \ell)\right),$$

where λ is the Lagrange multiplier. The critical values of x, ℓ, and λ are given by the solution to

$$\frac{\partial L(x, \ell, \lambda)}{\partial x_i} = \frac{\partial U(x, \ell)}{\partial x_i} - \lambda p_i = 0, \qquad i = 1, \ldots, n, \tag{6.16a}$$

$$\frac{\partial L(x, \ell, \lambda)}{\partial \ell} = \frac{\partial U(x, \ell)}{\partial \ell} - \lambda w = 0, \tag{6.16b}$$

and

$$\frac{\partial L(x, \ell, \lambda)}{\partial \lambda} = -\sum_{i=1}^{n} p_i x_i + w(\gamma - \ell) = 0. \tag{6.16c}$$

Adding λp_i to both sides of the ith equation, $i = 1, \ldots, n$, and taking ratios, we obtain

$$\frac{\partial U(x, \ell)/\partial x_i}{\partial U(x, \ell)/\partial x_j} = \frac{p_i}{p_j}, \qquad i, j = 1, \ldots, n.$$

That is, as in the fixed-income case, utility maximization requires that marginal rates of substitution be equated to corresponding price ratios. In fact, the same fundamental condition is obtained for the added commodity, leisure, since dividing the ith equation ($i \leq n$) by the $(n + 1)$th yields

$$\frac{\partial U(x, \ell)/\partial x_i}{\partial U(x, \ell)/\partial \ell} = \frac{p_i}{w}, \qquad i = 1, \ldots, n. \tag{6.17}$$

That is, the marginal rate of substitution between the ith commodity and leisure must be equated to the price-wage ratio, p_i/w. However, as w is what is given up by consuming an hour of time in the form of leisure rather than employing that hour to earn income, it is the "price," or "opportunity cost," of leisure. In other words, the leisure-consumption trade-off condition (6.17) is formally equivalent to the ordinary utility-maximization condition which requires that marginal rates of substitution be equated to respective price ratios.

As w is simply the price of leisure, the "budget constraint," which can be rewritten as

$$\sum_{i=1}^{n} p_i x_i + w\ell \leq w\gamma, \tag{6.18}$$

is seen to be exactly analogous to the fixed-income budget constraint since $w\gamma$, the value of the time endowment, is analogous to income. In other words, the consumer is endowed with $w\gamma$ which can be "spent" on marketed commodities (supplied by producers) and leisure.

The solution of the $n + 2$ equations for the x_i, $i = 1, \ldots, n$, ℓ, and λ yields the consumer's *modified* demand functions, with images

$$x_i = \delta_i(p, w, \gamma), \qquad i = 1, \ldots, n, \tag{6.19}$$

and

$$\ell = \ell(p, w, \gamma). \tag{6.20}$$

The labor supply function is given by

$$L_s = \gamma - \ell(p, w, \gamma) = L_s(p, w, \gamma). \tag{6.21}$$

The first-order utility-maximization conditions and the derivation of the labor supply function can be illustrated graphically by holding constant the commodity price ratios, p_i/p_j, $i, j = 1, \ldots, n$, so that, invoking Hick's composite-commodity theorem, we can draw indifference curves in leisure-income space. Thus, hours of leisure are plotted on the horizontal axis and income, or expenditure on all other commodities,

$$y = \sum_{i=1}^{n} p_i x_i,$$

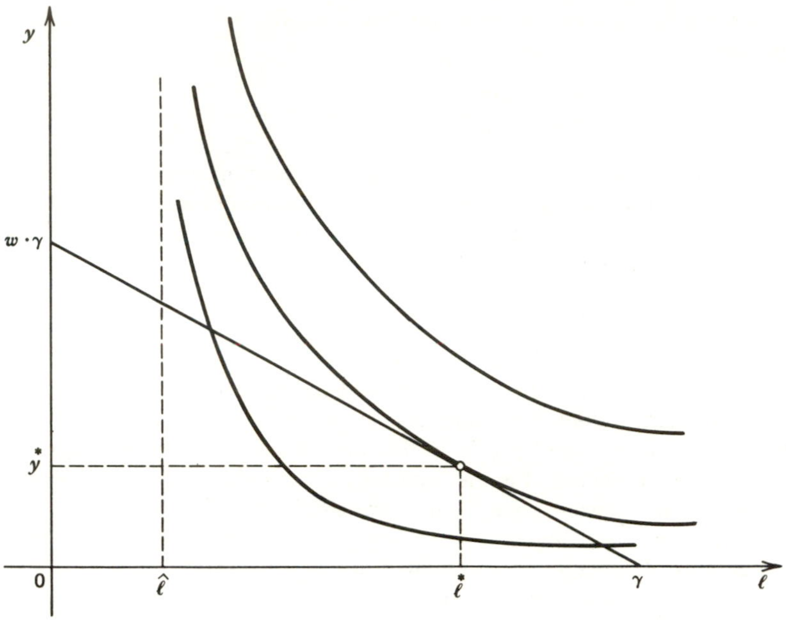

Figure 6.5

is plotted on the vertical axis of figure 6.5. As an added note of realism, the indifference map is restricted to the subset of the nonnegative quadrant corresponding to the interval on the horizontal axis above a physiologically essential number of leisure hours, $\hat{\ell}$.[1]

The downward-sloping characteristic of the indifference curves in figure 6.5 reflects an implicit assumption that the consumer would rather consume leisure than work. In other words, he must be paid to work. Convexity of the indifference curves reflects an implicit assumption that the less leisure a consumer is enjoying, the more he is willing to pay in the form of forgone income for an additional hour of leisure. Put differently, the more hours a consumer is working, the more he must be paid to induce him to work an additional hour.

The budget set for the optimization problem (6.15) is determined by equation (6.14). This budget set can be characterized by plotting the equality,

$$y = w(\gamma - \ell). \tag{6.22}$$

When $y = 0$, $\ell = \gamma$ and when $\ell = 0$, $y = w\gamma$. The set of points satisfying the equality (6.22) is therefore represented by the straight line with horizontal and

[1] One might also wish to restrict the indifference map to (y, ℓ) pairs such that $\ell \leq \gamma$, the time endowment, since it doesn't make sense to posit preferences over consumption bundles with more than 24 hours of leisure per day. On the other hand, who has not heard the expression, "What I wouldn't give for a 25-hour day?"

vertical intercepts of γ and $w\gamma$, respectively. The budget set is therefore given by the nonnegative points on or below this straight line, which will be referred to as the *wage line*.

The wage line representing equation (6.22) is easy to interpret. Note first that the absolute slope of this line is clearly equal to the wage rate, w. The consumer is endowed with γ hours of time which he can consume entirely in the form of leisure, in which case he earns no income; or he can reduce his leisure, earning w for each hour that he works. A reduction in hours of leisure consumed is equivalent therefore to an increase in the supply of labor and is represented on the diagram by a movement up the wage line from γ toward the vertical intercept. For example, if the consumer were to work the maximum amount that is physiologically possible, $\gamma - \hat{\ell}$, he would earn income equal to $w(\gamma - \hat{\ell})$.

Given the indifference map in figure 6.5, the maximum utility is obtained at the point of tangency where $\overset{*}{\ell}$ hours of leisure are consumed and $\gamma - \overset{*}{\ell}$ hours are worked, and earned income equals $\overset{*}{y} = w(\gamma - \overset{*}{\ell})$. Of course, at this point of tangency, the marginal rate of substitution between leisure and income is equal to the wage rate.

The effect on the demand for leisure, and hence on labor supply, of a change in the wage rate is illustrated in figure 6.6. At the wage rate $\overset{*}{w}$, the

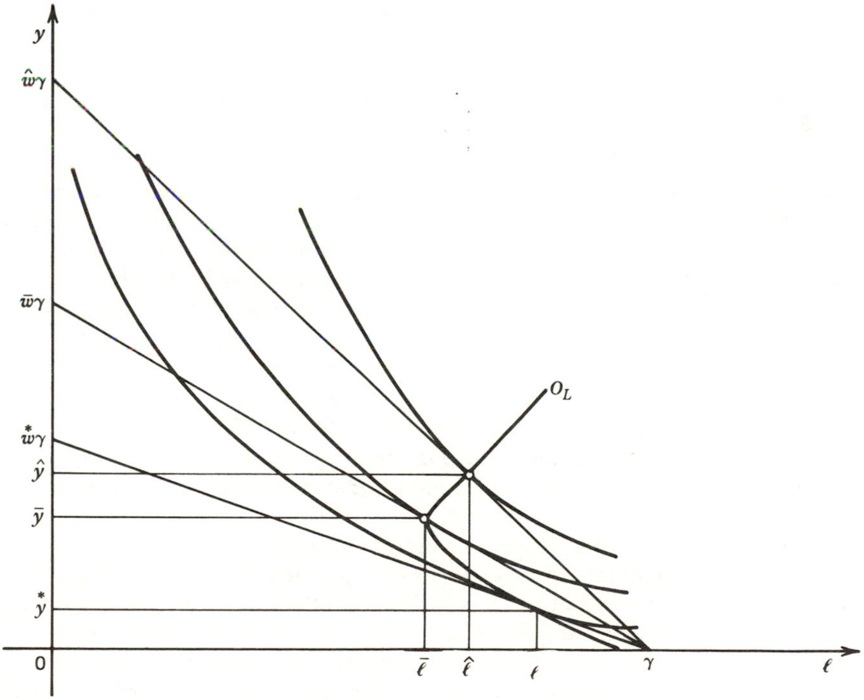

Figure 6.6

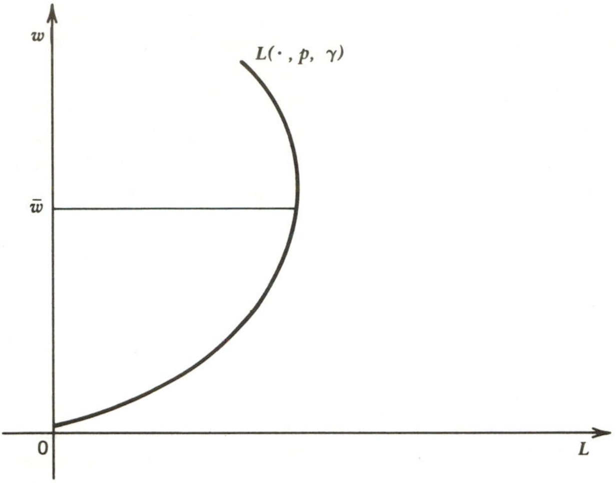

Figure 6.7

consumer supplies $\gamma - \overset{*}{\ell}$ hours of labor to earn an income equal to $\overset{*}{y}$. A rise in the wage rate, say from $\overset{*}{w}$ to $\bar{w}$, raises the vertical intercept from $\overset{*}{w}\gamma$ to $\bar{w}\gamma$, as depicted in figure 6.6. The rise in the wage rate from $\overset{*}{w}$ to $\bar{w}$ in this case increases the supply of labor from $\gamma - \ell$ to $\gamma - \bar{\ell}$. Corresponding to any arbitrary (positive) wage rate, we can evaluate the supply of labor by identifying the point of tangency between the "wage line" with slope equal to the positive wage rate, and an indifference curve. The locus of all such tangencies is referred to as the offer curve of labor and is denoted O_L in figure 6.6.

It will be noted that the offer curve, as drawn, has a negative slope at low wage rates and a positive slope when the wage rate is high. This shape of the offer curve is fairly characteristic of what would be obtained with an arbitrarily drawn set of indifference curves and requires no deliberate contortion of the indifference curves. In fact, this shape is exactly analogous to the typical shape of the price consumption curve derived in section 4.5. Note that wage-rate changes which generate tangencies in the upward-sloping portion of the offer curve are characterized by the fact that a *rise* in the wage rate *lowers* the supply of labor. Consequently, the labor-supply curve (in which the wage rate is plotted against the labor supply) corresponding to the offer curve in figure 6.6. is upward sloping at low wage rates and negatively sloped—"backward bending"—at high wage rates. This labor-supply curve, denoted $L(\cdot, p, \gamma)$, is drawn in figure 6.7.

In order to clarify the relationship between the wage rate and labor supply, it is instructive to dichotomize the effect of a wage-rate change into a substitution effect (essentially equivalent to the substitution effect analyzed in sections 4.5 and 5.3 above) and an "income effect" (analogous to the income effect of sections 4.5 and 5.3). It is important, however, to define these concepts—particularly the income effect—carefully. The income effect of a price change in sections 4.5 and 5.3 was derived under the supposition that income is parametric

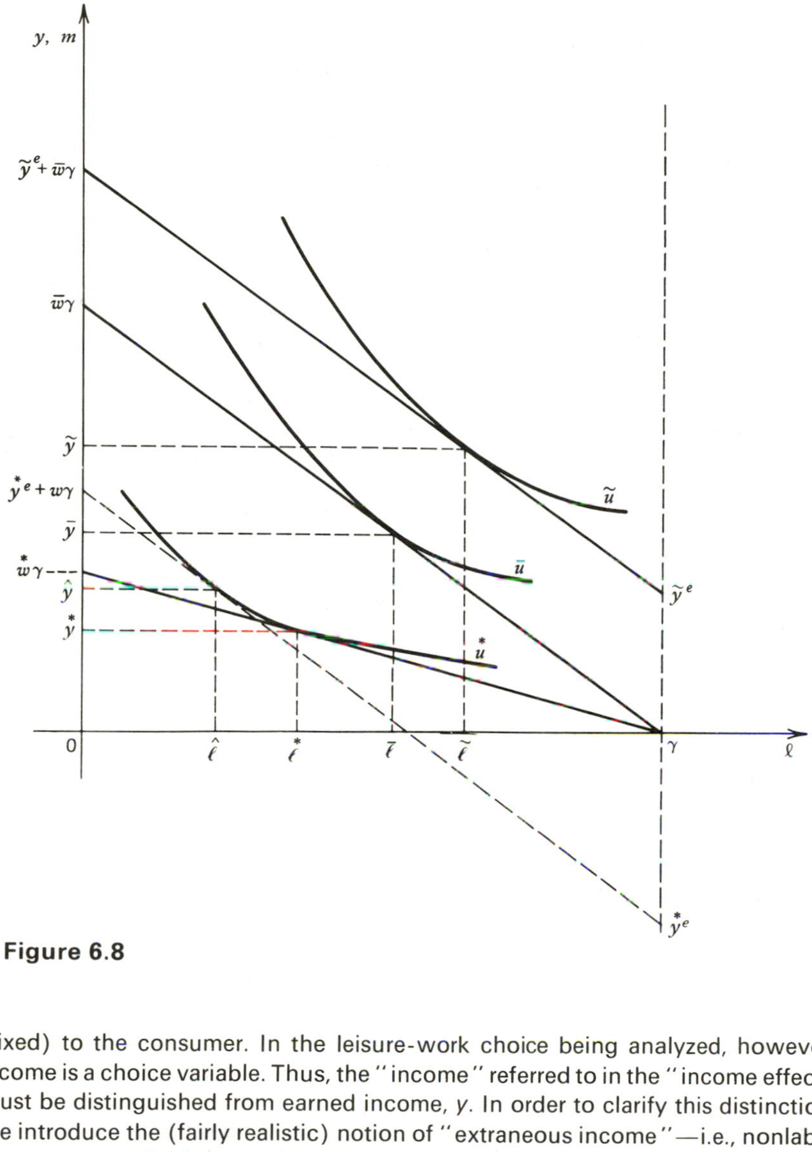

Figure 6.8

(fixed) to the consumer. In the leisure-work choice being analyzed, however, income is a choice variable. Thus, the "income" referred to in the "income effect" must be distinguished from earned income, y. In order to clarify this distinction, we introduce the (fairly realistic) notion of "extraneous income"—i.e., nonlabor income—denoted y^e. In principle, y^e can be positive or negative; $y^e < 0$ can be interpreted, for example, as a lump-sum tax (see exercises 6.5 and 6.6). Thus, if the consumer has positive extraneous income equal to $\tilde{y}^e$ in figure 6.8, he can attain utility level $\tilde{u}$ by working $\gamma - \tilde{\ell}$ hours to increase his income to $\hat{y}^e + w(\gamma - \hat{\ell}) = \hat{y}$.

The constructive dichotomization of the effect of a wage-rate change into a substitution effect and an "income effect" is illustrated in figure 6.8. Assume that the consumer has zero extraneous income and consider a rise in the wage rate from $\overset{*}{w}$ to $\bar{w}$. The consumer takes advantage of the rise in the wage rate to increase his utility from $\overset{*}{u}$ to $\bar{u}$ by reducing his hours of work from $\gamma - \overset{*}{\ell}$ to $\gamma - \bar{\ell}$ (increasing his consumption of leisure from $\overset{*}{\ell}$ to $\bar{\ell}$), while nevertheless increasing his income (expenditure on all other commodities) from $\overset{*}{y}$ to $\bar{y}$ because of the increase in the hourly wage rate. The wage-rate change has two effects. First, the increase in the wage rate, which is the opportunity cost of leisure, makes leisure more expensive relative to other commodities and induces the consumer to substitute other commodities for leisure. The wage-rate increase also has the effect, however, of increasing the consumer's "real income" since the value of this time endowment increases from $\overset{*}{w}\gamma$ to $\bar{w}\gamma$. If leisure is a normal commodity, this tends to induce the consumer to consume more leisure (reduce his labor supply). In the construction of figure 6.8, the substitution effect is generated by lowering the wage line back to the old indifference curve so that the consumer can just obtain the utility level which he enjoyed at the wage rate $\overset{*}{w}$. This is equivalent to a (negative) extraneous-income compensation of $\overset{*}{y}^e$. The change in leisure consumed from $\overset{*}{\ell}$ to $\hat{\ell}$ therefore represents the substitution effect. The income effect is given by the movement from $\hat{\ell}$ to $\bar{\ell}$.

An interesting feature of the work-leisure choice is that the substitution and income effects work in *opposite* directions when leisure is a normal good. It will be recalled from sections 4.5 and 5.3 that the opposite is true in the case of the allocation of a fixed income among marketed commodities; if a commodity is normal, the income effect and the substitution effect work in the same direction. It is because of this distinction between the work-leisure choice problem and the fixed-income allocation problem that the backward-bending supply function is not the anomaly that the Giffen commodity is in the case of fixed income.It is apparent that the labor-supply curve cannot be backward bending if leisure is an inferior commodity (see exercise 6.8).

6.4 THE THEORY OF REVEALED PREFERENCE

The theory of revealed preference was originally developed by Paul Samuelson [1938, 1947a, 1948, 1953a] as an alternative to the theory of demand that is predicted on the hypothesis of utility maximization. Samuelson's announced purpose was to develop the theory of consumer behavior freed from any vestigial traces of the utility concept. Put differently, Samuelson's goal was to derive the basic restrictions on demand functions from assumptions regarding observable price-quantity data. The basic approach is founded on the notion that the consumption-bundle choice, given a set of prices, reveals a consumer's preferences for that bundle over all of the alternative consumption bundles that could have been purchased at the existing price-income situation.

Although revealed-preference theory was originally conceived as a substitute for utility theory, subsequent research has shown that, once certain technical details (primarily regarding continuity conditions) are taken into account, revealed-preference theory and utility theory are logically equivalent. That is, each implies the other and there is no more content in one than in the other. In this respect, there is no basis for choosing between the two theories; revealed-preference theory is now viewed as complementary to the traditional approach to consumer choice.

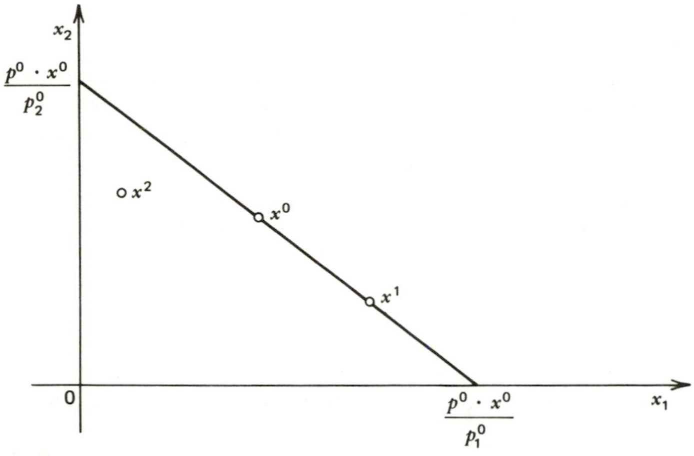

Figure 6.9

The Weak Axiom of Revealed Preference

In what follows, p_i^t and x_i^t represent, respectively, the price and quantity purchased of the ith commodity in situation t. A situation is formally defined as a set of prices and (implicitly) an expenditure level, $\sum_i p_i^t x_i^t$. Different situations might correspond to different times, places, etc. The vectors of prices and commodity quantities are designated by p^t and x^t, respectively. Total expenditure in situation t—assumed to equal total income[2]—is represented by $p^t \cdot x^t$.

Figure 6.9. illustrates the observed price-quantity data for a given situation. At the prevailing set of prices, p^0, the consumer is observed to purchase the commodity bundle x^0. The income (or at least expenditure) available to the consumer in this situation is therefore given by $p^0 \cdot x^0$. The choices that are available to the consumer in situation 0 (the budget set) are represented in figure 6.9 by the nonnegative bundles on or below the budget constraint passing through x^0 with a slope equal to the negative of the relative prices of the two commodities.

The fundamental relationship of revealed-preference theory is the comparison of the commodity bundle x^0 purchased by the consumer at prices p^0 and income $p^0 \cdot x^0$ and all other commodity bundles that could have been purchased given these prices and income. These commodity bundles are given by x^j, $j \neq 0$, such that $p^0 \cdot x^j \leq p^0 \cdot x^0$ and are represented in figure 6.9 by all commodity bundles other than x^0 in the budget set. Thus, the commodity bundle x^1 could have been purchased by the consumer since it costs the same as x^0 and commodity bundle x^2 could have been purchased since it costs less than x^0. The consumer's choice of x^0 in this particular price-income situation is

[2] This is obviously not critical. If the consumer saves, everything that follows goes through if we interpret $p^t \cdot x^t$ as total expenditure in situation t.

said to *reveal* his preference for this commodity bundle over all of the alternative bundles that cost no more.

The derivation of meaningful propositions from this notion of revealed preference requires assumptions that guarantee the consistency of consumer choice. That is, if the consumer reveals a preference for x^0 in situation 0 over an alternative bundle, say x^1, then x^1 must not in turn be revealed preferred to x^0 in another situation. Thus, if the consumer reveals a preference for x^0 over x^1, when he is observed to purchase x^1 it must be because the new price-income situation does not allow him to purchase x^0. That is, $p^1 \cdot x^0 > p^1 \cdot x^1$.

The notion of consistency outlined in the preceding paragraph is formally stated in Samuelson's *weak axiom of revealed preference*: $p^0 \cdot x^0 \geq p^0 \cdot x^1$ and $x^0 \neq x^1$ implies $p^1 \cdot x^0 > p^1 \cdot x^1$. It should be noted that this statement of the weak axiom implicitly assumes that a unique commodity bundle is chosen for each price-income situation (i.e., the demand functions are single-valued).[3]

Homogeneity of Degree Zero in Income and Prices

We now show that the weak axiom of revealed preference implies that demands are invariant with respect to proportionate changes in all prices and income. To see this, consider an initial price-income situation, p^0 and $p^0 \cdot x^0$, where, of course, x^0 is the commodity bundle that is purchased. Consider next an alternative situation in which all commodity prices and income are multiplied by a positive scalar, λ; i.e.,

$$p^1 = \lambda p^0 \tag{6.23}$$

and

$$p^1 \cdot x^1 = \lambda p^0 \cdot x^0 \tag{6.24}$$

where x^1 is the commodity bundle chosen in the new situation.

To prove that demand functions are homogeneous of degree zero in income and all prices, it suffices to show that $x^0 = x^1$. Let us proceed by way of contradiction. Thus, assume $x^1 \neq x^0$.

Note that (6.23) can be rewritten as $(1/\lambda)p^1 = p^0$. Substitution into (6.24) yields $p^1 \cdot x^1 = \lambda(1/\lambda)p^1 \cdot x^0 = p^1 \cdot x^0$, which implies[4]

$$p^1 \cdot x^1 \geq p^1 \cdot x^0. \tag{6.25}$$

Similarly, substitution from (6.23) into (6.24) yields $\lambda p^0 \cdot x^1 = \lambda p^0 \cdot x^0$, which implies

$$p^0 \cdot x^0 \geq p^0 \cdot x^1. \tag{6.26}$$

But (6.25) and (6.26) violate the weak axiom of revealed preference if x^0 and x^1 are distinct. Therefore, $x^0 = x^1$.

[3] For some purposes, it is convenient to work with a weak axiom in a weaker form which does not require that demand functions be single-valued. See Samuelson [1947a, p.111] and Katzner [1970, pp. 106–7, 114].

[4] Note that $a \geq b$ means (i) $a > b$ *or* (ii) $a = b$; hence, if a and b satisfy *either* (i) *or* (ii), they satisfy $a \geq b$.

The homogeneity property can be described in the context of figure 6.9, where, in the initial price-income situation (p^0 and $p^0 \cdot x^0$), x^0 is revealed preferred to all other commodity bundles in the budget set. Multiplication of p^0 and $p^0 \cdot x^0$ by $\lambda > 0$ obviously leaves the budget line unchanged. Since the budget set remains the same, x^0 must be chosen at prices λp^0 and income $\lambda p^0 \cdot x^0$ since it has been revealed preferred to all other bundles in the budget set. Any other choice would violate the weak axiom.

Negativity of the Compensated Price Effect

One of the important implications of utility theory is that the own, income-compensated, price derivative is necessarily negative. That is, own substitution terms ($S_{ii}(p, \overset{*}{u})$) are necessarily negative. (See section 5.3). It will be recalled that this compensated price effect is calculated by compensating the consumer for the price change in such a way as to keep him on the same indifference surface. Indifference surfaces, however, play no role in the theory of revealed preference. All we have to work with are observed prices and quantities. Consequently, the compensation to eliminate the income effect must be characterized in terms of observable data. An appropriate approach therefore is to compensate the consumer for a price change by adjusting his money income to make it just possible for the consumer to purchase the initial-situation commodity bundle at the new prices.[5] Thus, let p^0 and x^0 be the observed price vector and consumption bundle in situation 0 and let p^1 and x^1 be the comparable prices and quantities in situation 1, where $p^1 \cdot x^1$ just allows the consumer to purchase x^0; that is,

$$p^1 \cdot x^1 = p^1 \cdot x^0. \tag{6.27}$$

As this trivially implies $p^1 \cdot x^1 \geq p^1 \cdot x^0$, it follows that x^1 is revealed preferred to x^0. Hence, by the weak axiom of revealed preference,

$$p^0 \cdot x^1 > p^0 \cdot x^0. \tag{6.28}$$

Next note that (6.27) and (6.28) can be rewritten as follows:

$$\sum_{i=1}^{n} p_i^1 (x_i^1 - x_i^0) = 0 \tag{6.29}$$

and

$$\sum_{i=1}^{n} p_i^0 (x_i^1 - x_i^0) > 0. \tag{6.30}$$

Multiplying through (6.30) by -1 reverses the inequality:

$$\sum_{i=1}^{n} (-p_i^0)(x_i^1 - x_i^0) < 0. \tag{6.31}$$

[5] This approach was called "overcompensation" by Samuelson [1953a] because the adjustment in income required to make the consumer as well off as before the price change might be less than the adjustment that allows him to buy the old commodity bundle.

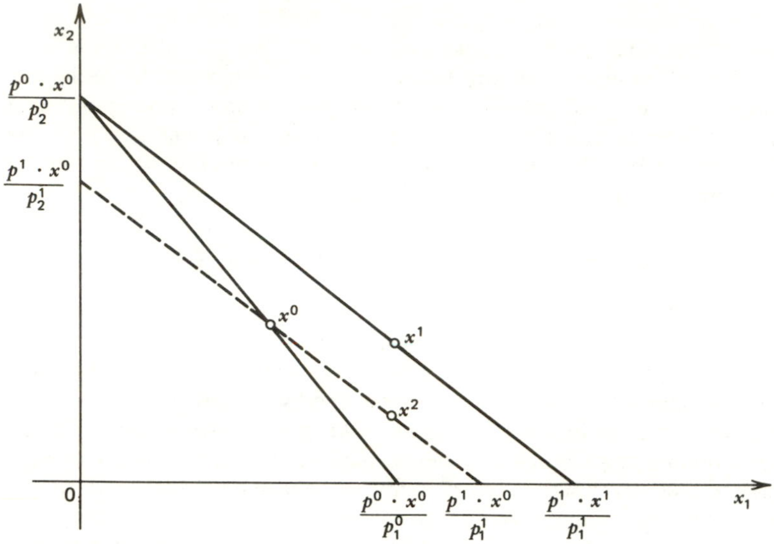

Figure 6.10

Adding (6.29) and (6.31) and collecting terms, we obtain

$$\sum_{i=1}^{n} (p_i^1 - p_i^0)(x_i^1 - x_i^0) < 0. \tag{6.32}$$

Consider now the (relevant) case where only one price, say the kth, changes. Then all but the kth term of (6.32) vanishes and

$$(p_k^1 - p_k^0)(x_k^1 - x_k^0) < 0$$

or

$$\Delta p_k \cdot \Delta x_k < 0.$$

Thus, Δp_k and Δx_k are of opposite signs, implying that, as the price of the kth commodity increases, all other prices held constant, less will be purchased of the kth commodity. Thus, the compensated own-price effect is negative.

Figure 6.10 illustrates the above analysis for a case in which only two commodities are consumed. The budget line for the price-income situation, p^0 and $p^0 \cdot x^0$, is shown with vertical intercept $p^0 \cdot x^0/p_2^0$ and horizontal intercept $p^0 \cdot x^0/p_1^0$. Commodity bundle x^0 is purchased in this situation and is thus revealed preferred to all commodity bundles on or below the budget line. A fall in the price of commodity 1 generates a new price situation as reflected by the new solid budget line in figure 6.10. Suppose that the chosen bundle in situation 1 is given by x^1 in figure 6.10. We are, however, interested in isolating the compensated price effect. Thus, shift the new budget line in a downward direction, maintaining the new slope, until it intersects the old budget line at x^0. This means that, at the new prices, the consumer is just able to buy the old commodity bundle. The consumer has therefore been compensated for the increase in real income caused by the fall in the price of commodity 1.

The above result says that the chosen commodity bundle at prices p^1 and expenditure $p^1 \cdot x^0$—say x^2—must lie to the right of x^0 on the bogus budget line. If x^2 were to lie to the left of x^0, then x^0 would be revealed preferred to x^2 in situation 0 and x^2 would be revealed preferred to x^0 in situation 1, violating the weak axiom of revealed preference.

The Strong Axiom of Revealed Preference

Although the weak axiom is both necessary and sufficient for the homogeneity property of demand functions and for the negativity of own compensated price effects, there are additional implications of utility theory (viz., symmetry of the substitution terms) which are not implied by the weak axiom. Put differently, the weak axiom of revealed preference is not sufficient to demonstrate that revealed consumer preferences can be represented by a utility function.

In an important paper, Houthakker [1950] completed the theory of demand derived from the notion of revealed preference by introducing the *strong axiom of revealed preference*: Let $x^0, x^1, \ldots, x^k$ be a sequence (or chain) of $k + 1$ ($k \geq 1$) bundles satisfying $x^0 R x^1, x^1 R x^2, \ldots, x^{k-1} R x^k$ where $x^i R x^j$ reads "x^i is revealed preferred to x^j." Thus, $x^0 R x^k$.

The strong axiom of revealed preference clearly generalizes the weak axiom. The weak axiom amounts to two-term (or more descriptively, two-bundle) consistency whereas the strong axiom is a formalization of n-term ($n > 1$) consistency. The strong axiom thus plays a role in the theory of revealed preference that is similar to the role played by the assumption of transitivity in the preference-theory approach to consumer choice developed in chapter 2.

Houthakker demonstrated that the strong axiom of revealed preference (together with a continuity condition) implies the existence of a utility function which rationalizes the consumer's revealed preferences. It is this important theorem which establishes the fundamental equivalence of the two approaches to consumer choice, much as the theory of utility and preference theory are unified by the representation theorem discussed in chapter 3.

Applications of Revealed Preference Theory

Although traditional consumer theory and the theory of revealed preference are logically equivalent to one another, since the latter is stated in terms of observed price-quantity relationships it might be more suitable for empirical application. The principal uses to which revealed preference theory has been applied are the evaluation of economic index numbers and empirical tests of the consistency of consumer choice. An economic index number is an attempt to utilize price and quantity data to make statements about the preferences of consumers for one price-income situation versus another. The weak axiom of revealed preference can be used to evaluate directly a given index number. More specifically, the results of the economic theory of index numbers can be derived directly from the theory of revealed preference (Samuelson [1947a, pp. 156–63]).

The second empirical application of revealed preference theory has been empirical tests based upon consumer budget data of the consistency of (usually aggregate) consumer choice (Houthakker [1963]). These tests utilize direct observations on consumer purchases in order to ascertain whether or not consumers (collectively) violate the weak or strong axiom of revealed preference.

EXERCISES

Elasticities

6.1 Draw an ICC on an indifference map (in $x_i - m$ space) which yields Engel curves with unitary income elasticity of demand everywhere.

6.2 Draw a PCC on an indifference map (in $x_i - m$ space) which yields unitary own-price elasticity of demand everywhere.

6.3 The three straight lines in the diagram represent three demand curves.

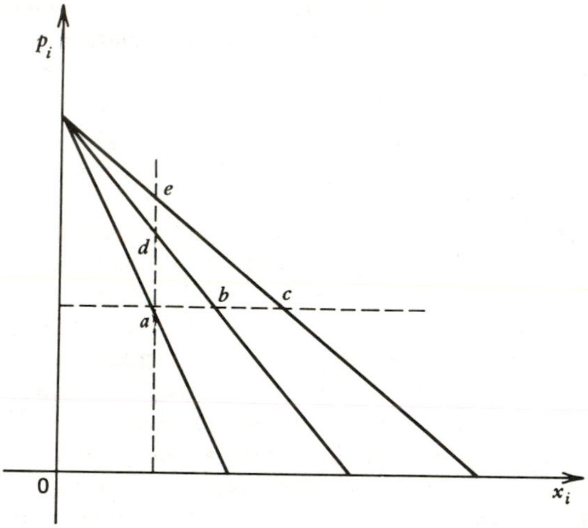

Compare the own-price elasticities of demand

i. at points *a*, *b*, and *c*.

ii. at points *a*, *d*, and *e*.

6.4* Prove that, if the demand elasticity is everywhere unitary, expenditure on commodity *i* is insensitive to price changes. (Hint: Unitary elasticity is equivalent to $\partial \log D_i(p, y)/\partial p_i = -1$. Integrate over $\log p_i$, take antilogs, and multiply by p_i. Note that the same technique can be employed to show that, if $\partial \log D_i(p, y)/\partial p_i = -b$, expenditure on commodity *i* is directly [inversely] related to price if $b < 1$ [$b > 1$].)

Labor Supply

6.5 Draw the "effective" wage line (i.e., identify the feasible income-leisure combinations) for a worker facing

a. a lump-sum tax,

b. a proportional income tax ($T = ty$ where $t > 0$ and T is the total tax payment), and

c. a progressive income tax ($T = t(y) \cdot y$ where $t'(y) > 0$).

6.6 Show that a worker is generally better off (and certainly no worse off) paying a lump-sum tax than an equivalent amount of proportional taxes.

6.7 Dichotomize the effect of a *decrease* in the wage rate from $\bar{w}$ to $\overset{*}{w}$ in figure 6.8 into the substitution effect and the (extraneous) income effect.

6.8 Show that the labor-supply curve cannot be backward bending if leisure is an inferior commodity.

6.9 Prove that a worker with strictly convex indifference curves in leisure-income space can always be induced to work longer hours by means of an overtime pay rather than by any straight hourly wage rate.

6.10 Suppose that the indifference curves in leisure-income space are vertical translates. Can the labor-supply curve be backward bending?

Revealed Preference

6.11 Show that strict convexity of indifference curves implies that the weak axiom of revealed preference is satisfied. What modified form of the weak axiom of revealed preference is implied by nonsatiation (without strict convexity)?

6.12 The following table lists prices faced and quantities chosen of tnree commodities in three different situations (over which the consumer's preference are invariant). Is it possible to provide an unambiguous ranking of the consumer's utility in the three situations?

Situation	p_1	p_2	p_3	x_1	x_2	x_3
1	1	2	3	3	5	3
2	2	1	3	2	8	5
3	1	1	4	4	7	3

6.13 The following table lists prices faced and quantities chosen of the only two commodities consumed by a consumer in two successive periods. Have the consumer's tastes (preferences) changed?

Period	p_1	p_2	x_1	x_2
1	2	4	20	10
2	3	2	30	5

6.14 Suppose that the information on prices faced and quantities consumed by a consumer in two situations is insufficient to infer the relative levels of utility in the two situations. Can additional information on prices and quantities in a third situation enable us to rank the consumer's utility in the first two periods (as well as the third)?

6.15 Laspeyres and Paasche (price-weighted) quantity indices are defined respectively as $p^0 \cdot x^1 / p^0 \cdot x^0$ and $p^1 \cdot x^1 / p^1 \cdot x^0$, where the superscripts denote two situations (usually a current period, 1, and a base period, 0). Which of the following combinations are consistent with the weak axiom of revealed preference?

a. Both indices are less than 1.

b. Both are greater than 1.

c. The Laspeyres is less than 1 and the Paasche is greater than 1.

d. The Paasche is less than 1 and the Laspeyres is greater than 1.

PART I
HISTORICAL NOTES AND SUGGESTED READING

Modern *preference and utility theory* was developed essentially as a by-product of the theories of welfare economics (**Arrow** [1951a], **Arrow** and **Debreu** [1954], and **Debreu** [1954]) and social choice (**Arrow** [1951b]), and reached maturity in **Arrow** [1959] and chapter 3 of **Debreu** [1959]. Many of the ideas were anticipated, however, in a classic series of papers by **Wold** [1943–44]. For an elementary textbook treatment, see chapter 2 of **Newman** [1965], and, for more advanced treatments, see chapter 1* of **Sen** [1970a] and chapter 2 of **Katzner** [1970].

The neoclassical *theory of demand* was developed independently by **Slutsky** [1915] (translated in 1952) and **Hicks** and **Allen** [1934], and incorporated into the treatises of **Hicks** [1939, Part 1], **Samuelson** [1947a, chapter 5], and **Wold** and **Jureen** [1953]. For a modern textbook treatment, see **Katzner** [1970].

As noted in the text, the theory of *duality* goes all the way back to **Hotelling** [1932], although many of the same ideas were conceived independently by **Roy** [1942]. The modern approach was developed independently by **Malmquist** [1953], **Samuelson** [1953b], and **Shephard** [1953], and honed into a powerful tool for demand analysis by, among others, **Uzawa** [1964], **Gorman** [1968], **Shephard** [1970], **McFadden** [1970], and **Diewert** [1971, 1974]. For a synthesis of this literature, see chapter 2 of **Blackorby, Primont, and Russell** [1978].

The theory of *revealed preference* was developed in a series of papers by **Samuelson** [1938, 1948, 1953a]. The unification with utility theory is due to **Houthakker** [1950]. For modern treatments, see **Richter** [1966] and **Uzawa** [1960].

The *composite-commodity theorem* was developed independently by **Hicks** [1939] and **Leontief** [1936]. An alternative approach to the aggregation of commodities and prices is attributable to **Leontief** [1947a, 1947b] and **Sono** [1961] (originally published in Japanese in 1945), who independently conceived the notion of *separability*. This concept was used to study *consumer budgeting* and *price and quantity aggregation* by **Strotz** [1957] and **Gorman** [1959]. For a comprehensive treatment of this subject, see **Blackorby, Primont**, and **Russell** [1978].

The problem of *aggregation across agents* was first examined by **Gorman** [1953], who showed that (if consumers consume positive amounts of all commodities) consistent aggregation of demand functions across consumers is possible if and only if Engel curves are linear (not necessarily intersecting the origin) and have identical slopes for all consumers. A simpler examination of this problem can be found in **Samuelson** [1956].

Empirical demand analysis has been greatly influenced by the pioneering work of **Stone** [1954], who investigated the *linear expenditure system*, and of **Houthakker** [1960], who specified the direct and indirect *addilog functions*. The linear expenditure system was first formulated by **Klein** and **Rubin** [1947] in the context of the theory of cost-of-living indexes. The form of the utility function that generates the linear expenditure system was derived by **Samuelson** [1947b]. Generalizations of the linear expenditures system have been investigated recently by **Brown** and **Heien** [1972], **Wales** [1972], and **Blackorby, Boyce**, and **Russell** [1978].

Many recent demand studies employ functional forms that satisfy **Diewert's** [1971] notion of *flexibility*—i.e., functions that can provide a second-order approximation to an arbitrary, twice-differentiable function. The most widely employed of these specifications are the *generalized Leontief* (**Diewert** [1971]), the *translog* (**Christensen, Jorgenson**, and **Lau** [1975]), and the *quadratic mean of order r* (**Denny** [1974]).

Surveys of the literature on empirical demand analysis—which, however, do not cover the recent work on flexible functional forms—can be found in **Phlips** [1974] and **Theil** [1975–76].

A thorough diagramatic analysis of *consumer surplus* (see exercise 4.3), which has been widely applied in normative market studies (see the part III suggested readings), can be found in **Hicks** [1943]. A mathematical analysis can be found in section 7.5 of **Katzner** [1970]. Because of certain theoretical difficulties regarding its measurement, the concept was in a state of some disrepute until its use was rationalized in a recent paper by **Willig** [1977].

The *labor-leisure model* of section 6.3 has been elaborated into a model of household production and the allocation of time by **Becker** [1965] and others. Closely related to these notions is the *consumption-characteristics model*, in which utility depends directly on characteristics such as "entertainment," "meals," and "travel," that are "produced" by the consumption of commodities. This approach has been popularized by **Lancaster** [1966]. The literature on *hedonic indices* is an outgrowth of the characteristics theory (see **Muellbauer** [1974] for a recent synthesis). A penetrating critique of this literature can be found in **Pollak** and **Wachter** [1975].

The *intertemporal theory of the consumer* (utility maximization over time) has its intellectual origin in another prescient piece by **Hotelling** [1931]. **Arrow** and **Kurz** [1970] is a modern treatise on this topic. The issue of *intertemporal consistency* (whether an intertemporal consumption plan will be followed or revised in subsequent time periods) was investigated by **Strotz** [1955]. (An error regarding Strotz's "sophisticated planning strategy" was corrected by **Pollak** [1968].)

The theory of the consumer under conditions of *uncertainty* dates back (at least) to **von Neuman** and **Morgenstern** [1944]. Chapter 2 of **Luce** and **Raiffa** [1957] contains a simplified exposition of this theory. An explanation of the paradox of simultaneously gambling and buying insurance, in terms of the von Newmann–Morgenstern theory, can be found in **Friedman** and **Savage** [1948]. The modern *state-preference approach* to modeling uncertainty, in which the "state of nature" (e.g., whether or not it rains) is a variable, was introduced in some papers that appeared in French in 1953. See **Hirschleifer** [1966] for an elementary exposition of this approach or **Arrow** [1964a, 1970] for a more advanced exposition. **Drèze** [1974] and **Sandmo** [1974] are good survey articles.

The theory of decision making under uncertainty has spawned a vast literature on *portfolio choice* and other aspects of financial economics. Much of the research in this area stems from the classic papers of **Tobin** [1958] and **Markowitz** [1952]. For a systematic exposition, see **Arrow** [1965].

PART II
THE THEORY OF THE PRODUCER

The consumer and the producer constitute the principal decision-making units in microeconomic theory. A theory of consumer behavior was constructed in the previous five chapters. The next four chapters develop the theory of the profit-maximizing producer. The theory of the consumer underlies demand and the theory of the producer underlies supply.

The treatment of producer theory is somewhat analogous to the treatment of the theory of the consumer. We begin with a description of the production technology. The technological relationships between commodities plays a role in the theory of the producer which is similar to the role played by the preference relation in the theory of the consumer. The production technology is characterized by the specification of a technology set. Much as the consumer preference ordering could, under certain conditions, be represented by a utility function, the technology of a producer can be represented by a production function.

The goal of the consumer is to maximize utility subject to a budget constraint (or, in the case of the labor-leisure model of section 6.3, a time-endowment constraint), the goal of the producer is assumed to be that of maximizing profit subject to the technological constraints embodied in the technology set. No attempt is made in this book to consider alternative theories of the producer based upon alternative objectives (e.g., sales maximization, "satisficing," etc.). These alternative theories are very accessible in the literature (see the suggested reading for part II). The theory developed in this book is, however, fundamental to any model which attempts to consider the formation of objectives and resource allocation within a firm or organization.

Chapter 7 develops the foundations of production theory in terms of the technology set and the implications of the assumptions of profit maximization for the net production function. This chapter concludes with a comparative-static analysis of the effect that a change in prices has on the net output decisions of the producer. Chapter 8 utilizes an explicit production function (with a single output) to analyze the implications of profit maximization for the producer's demand for inputs and supply of output. Chapter 9 introduces the notion of a cost function, relating the output of the producer to the (minimal) cost of producing that output, and develops the dual relationships between cost and production functions. The cost functions are then used to analyze the problem of profit maximization. In chapter 10, a special production technology characterized by linear production processes is introduced. This particular technology is especially useful for applied problems because of its relationship to a widely used optimization algorithm—linear programming—also discussed in chapter 10.

CHAPTER 7
THE THEORY OF PRODUCTION

7.1 INTRODUCTION

A *producer* is defined abstractly as a decision-making entity which, through the process of production, converts bundles of commodities (inputs) into alternative bundles of commodities (outputs). In deciding upon the exact mix of inputs nd outputs, the producer is assumed to be motivated by the goal of profit maximization, where profit is defined as the difference between gross revenue and gross expenditure.[1] The maximal profit of the producer is assumed to be constrained by a technological relationship between inputs and outputs which reflects the fact that not all conceivable combinations are technologically feasible.

As in the theory of the consumer, we assume, for simplicity of exposition, that each of the n commodities (where n is finite) is continuously divisible. Thus, the quantity produced or used of any commodity can be any nonnegative real number.

It is a matter of casual observation that many producers produce more than one—indeed elaborate arrays—of commodities. It is, moreover, feasible for a producer to be both a supplier and a user of any particular commodity. Whether a producer is a net supplier or a net user of a commodity or service may depend upon relative prices. Many steel companies, for example, operate their own coal mines. In most cases, the steel companies use all of the gross output of coal as an input in the production of steel and, in fact, purchase additional coal from other (coal-mining) companies. If, however, the price of coal were high enough relative to the price of steel, steel companies which also produce coal might well become net suppliers of coal as well as steel.

The theory of production developed in this chapter does not restrict the producer, a priori, to be a net supplier or a net user of any particular commodity. Rather, the analysis begins with an underlying technology set (the set of feasible production bundles) from which a production function can be derived. Thus, the technology set is analogous to the preference ordering of the consumer described in some detail in chapter 2. Much as the preference ordering constitutes the foundation of utility theory, the technology set provides a foundation for production theory. Moreover, just as a theory of consumer choice could be developed without the introduction of a utility function, the theory of the profit-maximizing producer can be developed without introducing the notion of a

[1] The theory of cost minimization developed in chapter 9 is equally applicable to "nonprofit institutions."

production function. Thus, the theory of profit maximization, supply, and derived demand is first carried out in the context of the more fundamental concept of a technology set.

Section 7.2 develops the notion of a technology set and describes the maximization of profit subject to this technology set. Section 7.3 examines the notion of technological efficiency in the context of the technology set and describes how technologically efficient points can be represented by a net production function. Section 7.4 examines the problem of profit maximization subject to the constraint implied by the net production function. Finally, Section 7.5 works out mathematically the (differential) comparative statics of output supply and input demand; this analysis is analogous to the comparative statics of consumer demand developed in section 5.3.

7.2 THE TECHNOLOGY SET AND PROFIT MAXIMIZATION

The Technology Set

Let q_i be the *gross* amount produced of the ith commodity and let v_i represent the *gross* amount of the ith commodity used in the production process. The *net* amount produced of the ith commodity is $z_i = q_i - v_i$. Thus, in the context of the steel-coal example described in section 7.1, if the ith commodity is coal, $z_i < 0$ for the typical steel producer even though $q_i > 0$.

If $q_i < v_i$, the producer is, on balance, a net user of the ith commodity and we say that the ith commodity is a net input in the production process of the producer. If $q_i > v_i$, we say that the ith commodity is a net output. Whether a particular commodity is a net input or a net output may depend upon the production choice of the producer and, therefore, as we shall see, may depend upon the relative prices.

A *production bundle* of the producer is a list of n real numbers, $z = [z_1, \ldots, z_n]$, representing the net amounts produced of each commodity. The production possibilities of the producer are not unlimited. The producer cannot, for example, produce infinite amounts of all commodities without using any inputs. The constraints on the production possibilities of the producer are embodied in the *technology set* of the producer, defined as the set of all *feasible* production bundles.

As a very simple-minded example of a technology set which can be illustrated in a two-dimensional diagram, consider an ancient farm in the captive Greek territory of the Roman Empire. Suppose, further, that Greek slaves can be bought and sold in a marketplace. The farm can use Greek slave labor to produce food or it can use food to raise and sell Greek slaves. The production possibilities are illustrated in the technology set in figure 7.1. The set of production possiblities for the slave labor farm are defined by the set of points Z. For example, the technology set includes the origin. This reflects the feasibility of complete inactivity; that is, the farm can engage in no activity at all, in which case it uses and produces neither food nor slave labor. Another possibility is given by

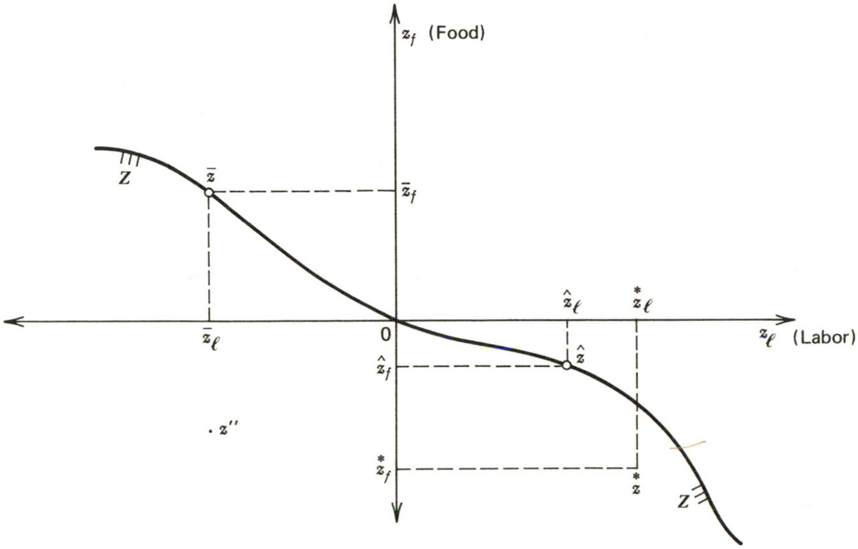

Figure 7.1

the point $\bar{z}$. At this point, the farm is using $-\bar{z}_\ell$ units of labor to produce $\bar{z}_f$ units of food. On the other hand, at point $\overset{*}{z}$, the farm is purchasing $-\overset{*}{z}_f$ units of food to raise $\overset{*}{z}_\ell$ units of slave labor. Finally, the point z'' in the technology set indicates the feasibility of being a net user of both food and labor. On the other hand, as drawn, the technology set precludes the possibility of a positive net output of *both* food and labor. Thus, this technology set incorporates a common assumption regarding technology sets, colorfully referred to as the "no-free-lunch" or "impossibility-of-the-land-of-Cockaigne" assumption.[2] Unless there is a hidden third input, this restriction surely makes sense (and is consistent with the laws of physics).

Profit Maximization

The profit, or net revenue, of the producer is defined as the difference between gross revenue from the sale of produced commodities and the gross cost of commodities used in production:

$$\pi = \sum_{i=1}^{n} p_i q_i - \sum_{i=1}^{n} p_i v_i = \sum_{i=1}^{n} p_i z_i . \tag{7.1}$$

Assumption 7.1 (Profit Maximization) The producer chooses a production bundle, z, in the technology set, Z, at fixed positive prices, $p_1 = [p_1, \ldots, p_n]$, which yields the maximal level of profits, π.

[2] Cockaigne is a mythical land of plenty.

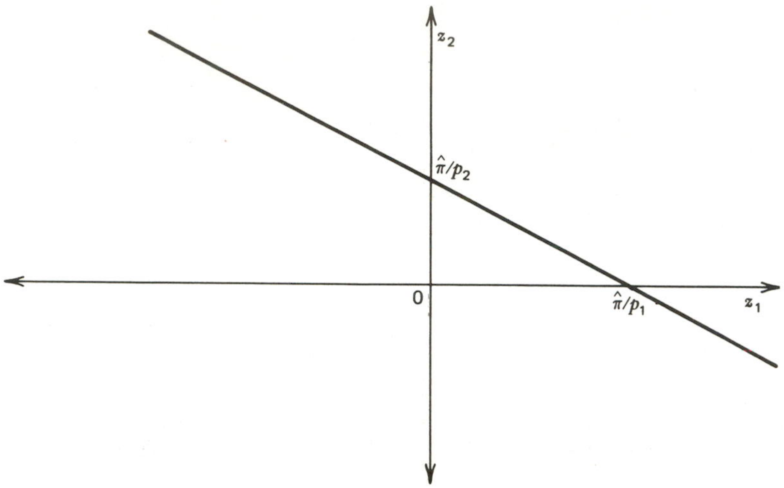

Figure 7.2

Profit maximization on the technology set can be illustrated graphically if we restrict the number of commodities to two. In this case,

$$\pi = p_1 z_1 + p_2 z_2. \tag{7.2}$$

Given fixed prices, this equation contains three unknowns, π, z_1, and z_2. To represent it in two-space, we can arbitrarily fix profits at say $\hat{\pi}$ and solve for z_2:

$$z_2 = \frac{\hat{\pi}}{p_2} - \frac{p_1}{p_2} z_1. \tag{7.3}$$

This equation is a relationship between z_1 and z_2 representing all combinations of these two net output values which yield profits of $\hat{\pi}$.

Equation (7.3), with fixed p_1, p_2, and $\hat{\pi}$, is plotted in figure 7.2. The vertical intercept is $\hat{\pi}/p_2$ and the slope is $-p_1/p_2$. Note also that the solution of equation (7.3) for z_1 in terms of z_2 yields a horizontal intercept of $\hat{\pi}/p_1$, as indicated in figure 7.2. The line plotted in figure 7.2 is referred to as an *equal-profit line* since, at the given prices, p_1 and p_2, all combinations of z_1 and z_2 on this line yield profit $\hat{\pi}$. Given an arbitrary equal-profit line, the corresponding profits are indicated by the vertical or horizontal intercept. The vertical intercept gives the value of profit in units of commodity 2 whereas the horizontal intercept gives the value of profits in units of commodity 1. Multiplying by p_2 in the former case and p_1 in the latter case converts the profit figure to dollar units. Finally, note that the profit level associated with any production bundle can be determined by drawing a line with slope $-p_1/p_2$ through the point representing this production bundle and taking note of the value of the intercept. For example, in figure 7.3 the choice of the production bundle represented by the point z' yields the (positive) profit level π', as indicated by the vertical and horizontal intercepts. An alternative bundle represented by the point $\hat{z}$ generates (negative) profits, $\hat{\pi}$.

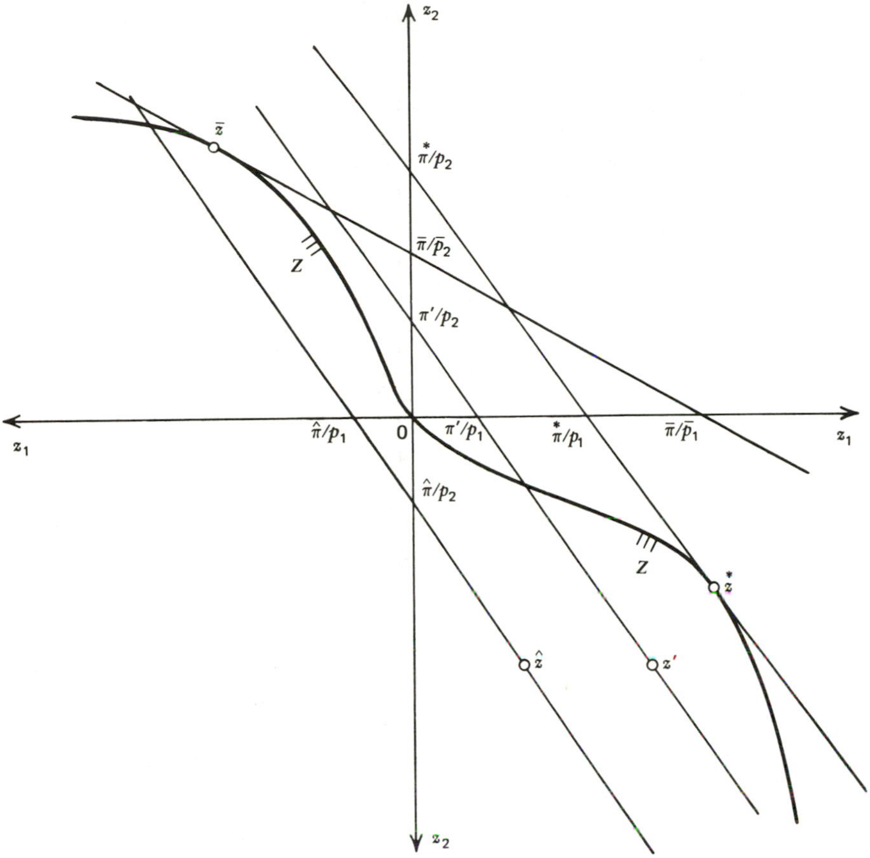

Figure 7.3

The profit-maximization objective can be represented graphically as choosing a point in the technology set which generates an equal-profit line with an intercept no lower than that generated by any alternative point in the technology set of the producer. Thus, the profit-maximizing production bundle, at prices (p_1, p_2), in figure 7.3 is $\overset{*}{z}$. This production choice results in an equal-profit line which is tangent to the boundary of the technology set and yields maximum profits $\overset{*}{\pi}$. Any other choice of a net output vector in the technology set would, at the prevailing prices, result in a lower profit for the producer.

Note that the profit-maximizing vector entails a negative net output of food (commodity 2) and a positive net output of labor services (commodity 1). This choice reflects the prevailing prices. If the price ratio is reduced to $\bar{p}_1/\bar{p}_2$, generating the new equal-profit line in figure 7.3, the resultant optimal net output vector $\bar{z}$ implies that labor is a net input and food is a net output.

To guarantee that a profit maximum exists, and therefore that producer choice is possible, it is necessary to restrict the form of the technology set. This is analogous to the fact that it is necessary to impose restrictions on the preference

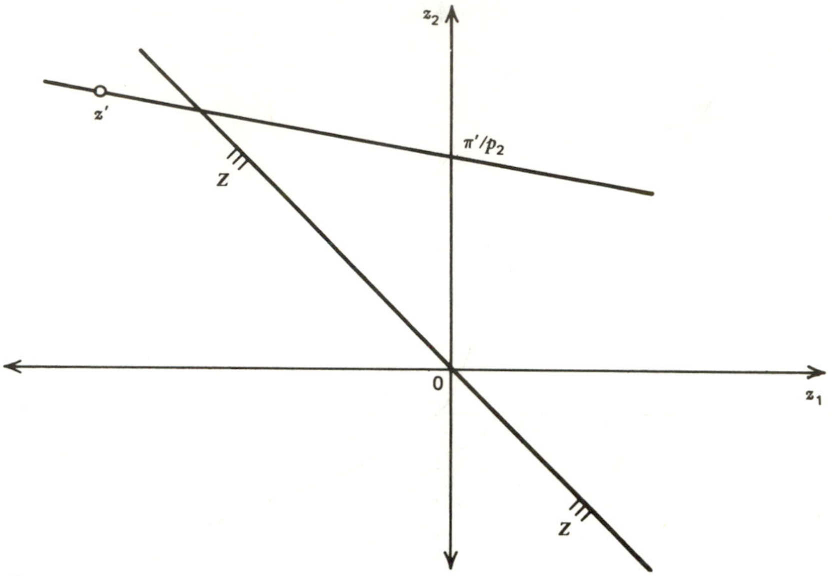

Figure 7.4

relation of the consumer in order to guarantee that an optimum to the consumer choice problem exists. The two assumptions that we make are as follows:

Assumption 7.2 (Boundedness) There exists a production bundle $\bar{z} = (\bar{z}_1, \ldots, \bar{z}_n)$ such that $\bar{z}_i \geq z_i$, $i = 1, \ldots, n$, for all $z = (z_1, \ldots, z_n)$ in the technology set, Z.

Assumption 7.3 (Regularity) The technology set includes its boundaries.

The first of these two assumptions has the following interpretation in two-space. There exists some point in the production space such that the set formed by drawing a horizontal line through and to the left of that point and a vertical line down from that point includes the technology set. Clearly, this is not possible in the case of the technology set illustrated in figure 7.4. What this assumption does, then, is place an upper bound on the amount that can be produced of any commodity. This guarantees us that, so long as prices are strictly positive, profit cannot be pushed to unboundedly large values.[3]

[3] Assumption 7.2 is actually stronger than needed since it implies bounded net positive output. The mathematically trained reader will note that a necessary and sufficient condition for a profit maximum to exist for all positive prices is that the recession cone of the technology set be contained in the nonpositive orthant (and that assumption 7.3 is satisfied). The assumption does not bound net production and is therefore more realistic than assumption 7.2; for the purposes of this book, however, little would be gained by an attempt to posit and explain the recession-cone assumption (see Rockafellar [1970] on recession cones).

The second assumption is a technical one which does not place severe restrictions on the production technology in the real world. Suppose that the technology set in figure 7.3 included all points below the boundary but did not include the points on the boundary itself. In this case, the optimum represented by the point $\overset{*}{z}$ would not be feasible. Moreover, the closer we move the choice of a production bundle to the point $\overset{*}{z}$ the higher profits would become (at price ratio, p_1/p_2). Hence, we can make profit increase by moving closer to $\overset{*}{z}$ but $\overset{*}{z}$ is not itself a feasible choice. Consequently, there does not exist a maximum profit in this case in which the technology set does not include its boundaries.

Thus, we have the following proposition regarding the theory of the producer:

Profit Maximization *If assumptions 7.2 and 7.3 are satisfied and if all prices are strictly positive, a profit maximum exists.*[4]

7.3 TECHNOLOGICAL EFFICIENCY AND THE NET PRODUCTION FUNCTION

Technological Efficiency

A production bundle $\hat{z} = [\hat{z}_1, \ldots, \hat{z}_n]$ in the technology set Z is (technologically) *efficient* if there does not exist an alternative bundle $z = [z_1, \ldots, z_n]$ in Z such that $z_i \geq \hat{z}_i$, $i = 1, \ldots, n$, and $z_j > \hat{z}_j$ for some (at least one) j. That is, a production bundle is technologically efficient if there is no alternative bundle in the technology set with more net output of some commodity and no less net output of any commodity.[5] A production bundle is technologically inefficient if it is not technologically efficient. For example, all points in the interior of the technology set are technologically inefficient. Moreover, some bundles on the boundary of Z, such as $\hat{z}$ in figure 7.5, may be technologically inefficient. The set of technologically efficient production bundles is represented by the points on the heavy portion of the boundary of the technology set in figure 7.5.

Obviously, a profit-maximizing producer will never choose a technologically inefficient production bundle so long as all prices are strictly positive. In developing the theory of the profit-maximizing producer, we can therefore ignore all technologically inefficient production bundles. Economic decisions are made among technologically efficient production bundles. Technologically inefficient bundles can be eliminated from consideration without looking at prices (so long as they are strictly positive). The (economic) choice among technologically efficient bundles depends upon relative prices.

[4] Strictly speaking, it is also necessary to assume that the technology set is nonempty. That is, there must exist at least one feasible production bundle. Our exposition makes this assumption implicit in the definition of the producer. At the least, the process of inactivity, $z = 0$, should be available to the producer.

[5] Equivalently, a production bundle is technologically efficient if there is no alternative bundle in the technology set with *less* net *input* of some commodity and no more net input of any other commodity.

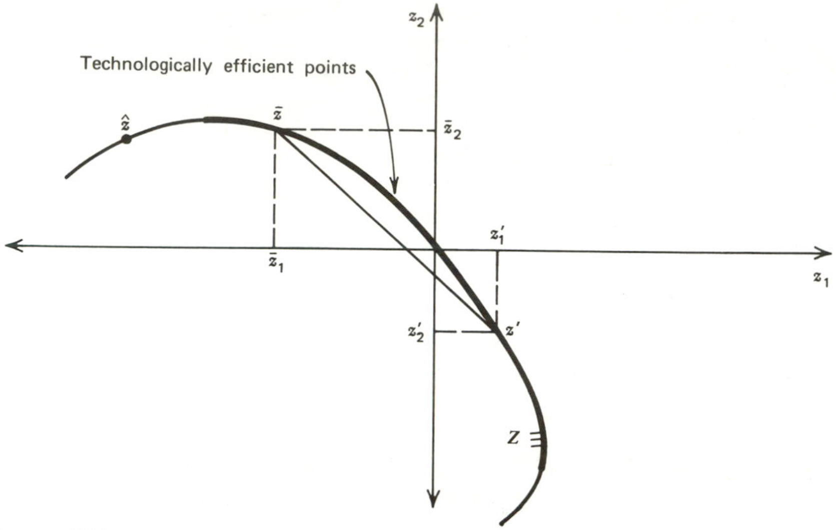

Figure 7.5

The Net Production Function

An important fact about the set of technologically efficient production bundles is that, for any set of values of all but one of the net outputs, there corresponds at most one value of the remaining net-output variable which makes the resulting production bundle technologically efficient. For example, in figure 7.5, given $z_1 = \bar{z}_1$, $\bar{z}_2$ is the only value of z_2 which, in combination with $\bar{z}_1$, is technologically efficient. Conversely, given $z_2 = \bar{z}_2$, $\bar{z}_1$ is the only technologically efficient value of z_1. This means that the set of technologically efficient bundles—the darkened portion of the boundary of Z in figure 7.5—is characterized by a one-to-one correspondence between z_1 and z_2. Thus, the efficient bundles in figure 7.5 are characterized by a function, f^2, with image $z_2 = f^2(z_1)$. In other words, $(\bar{z}_1, \bar{z}_2)$ is technologically efficient if and only if $\bar{z}_2 = f^2(\bar{z}_1)$. The darkened portion of the boundary of Z in figure 7.5 is the graph of f^2.

The same characterization of technologically efficient net output bundles is possible (and instructive) in the general n-commodity case. Given values of all but one, say the jth, of the net outputs, $\hat{z}^{-j} = [\hat{z}_1, \ldots, \hat{z}_{j-1}, \hat{z}_{j+1}, \ldots, \hat{z}_n]$, there is (at most) only one value of z_j that, combined with $\hat{z}^{-j}$, constitutes a technologically efficient bundle. Thus there is a one-to-one correspondence between the $n - 1$ dimensional vector z^{-j} and the scalar z_j. Consequently, the set of technologically efficient bundles can be represented by a function, f^j, with image,

$$z_j = f^j(z^{-j}).^6 \tag{7.4}$$

[6] Of course, the domain of f^j must be restricted to those values of z^{-j} such that there exists a technologically efficient value of z_j. Apostle [1974, pp. 32–35] discusses the domain of a function.

This function—referred to as the *efficiency function*—relates the values of net outputs which are technologically efficient. That is, $\bar{z}$ is technologically efficient if and only if $\bar{z}_j = f^j(\bar{z}^{-j})$.

Equation (7.4) can be written equivalently as

$$F(z) = z_j - f^j(z^{-j}) = 0. \tag{7.5}$$

Equation (7.5) implicitly defines the efficiency function in the sense that $\hat{z}_j = f^j(\hat{z}^{-j})$ if and only if $F(\hat{z}) = 0$. The choice of j in (7.4) and (7.5) is arbitrary; we could have normalized on any other input. Hence the function F and the identity $F(z) = 0$ constitute a perfectly symmetrical representation of the efficient points of the technology set; $\bar{z}$ is technologically efficient if and only if $F(\bar{z}) = 0$.

We refer to F as the *net production function*.

7.4 PROFIT MAXIMIZATION SUBJECT TO THE NET-PRODUCTION-FUNCTION CONSTRAINT

Profit Maximization and Strict Convexity

As economic decision making is restricted to choice among technologically efficient production bundles, the theory of the producer can be carried out with the concept of the net production function as well as with the concept of the technology set. For many purposes, the former approach is more convenient. In this section, we examine the problem of profit maximization subject to the net-production-function constraint (equation (7.5)).

The profit-maximization problem which incorporates the implicit production function can be formulated as

$$\max_z \sum_{i=1}^{n} p_i z_i \qquad \text{s.t. } F(z) = 0. \tag{7.6}$$

In order to exploit the calculus in carrying out this maximization problem, we posit the following assumptions:

Assumption 7.4 (Differentiability) The function F is twice differentiable.

Assumption 7.5 (Strict Convexity) If $\bar{z}$ and z' are two points on the boundary of the technology set, Z, $\kappa\bar{z} + (1 - \kappa)z'$ is in the interior[7] of Z for all values of κ satisfying $0 < \kappa < 1$.

To illustrate this assumption, consider the two points, $\bar{z}$ and z', on the boundary of Z in figure 7.5. The points $\kappa\bar{z} + (1 - \kappa)z'$, $0 < \kappa < 1$, are represented by all points on the line drawn from $\bar{z}$ to z', excluding the two end points (since $\kappa \neq 0$ and $\kappa \neq 1$). Clearly, all of these points lie in the interior of Z. As this is true for all pairs of points on the boundary of Z, this technology set satisfies assumption 7.5. On the other hand, the technology sets in figures 7.3

[7] Intuitively, the interior of Z is the set of points in Z that are not on the boundary of Z

and 7.4 do not satisfy assumption 7.5. This may be demonstrated by noting that a line drawn between $\bar{z}$ and $\bar{\bar{z}}$ in figure 7.3 lies partly outside of Z and a line drawn between any two points on the boundary of Z in figure 7.4 lies entirely on the (linear) boundary.

It is easy to see that for appropriately specified price ratios, multiple optima are generated in figures 7.3 and 7.4. Assumption 7.5 precludes such multiple optima. Moreover, as will be seen below, assumption 7.5 guarantees that second-order optimization conditions are satisfied.

First-Order Conditions and the Rate of Commodity Transformation

The solution to (7.6) is yielded by the critical values of the Lagrange function, with image

$$L(z, \lambda) = \sum_{i=1}^{n} p_i z_i + \lambda F(z). \tag{7.7}$$

Differentiation yields

$$\frac{\partial L(z, \lambda)}{\partial z_i} = p_i + \lambda \frac{\partial F(z)}{\partial z_i} = 0, \qquad i = 1, \ldots, n, \tag{7.8}$$

and

$$\frac{\partial L(z, \lambda)}{\partial \lambda} = F(z) = 0. \tag{7.9}$$

Division of the ith equation of (7.8) by the jth yields

$$\frac{p_i}{p_j} = \frac{\partial F(z)/\partial z_i}{\partial F(z)/\partial z_j}. \tag{7.10}$$

Thus, profit maximization requires that price ratios be equated to corresponding ratios of partial derivatives of F. To interpret this condition, recall that equation (7.5) implicitly defines the efficiency function f^j in the sense that $\hat{z}_j = f^j(\hat{z}^{-j})$ if and only if $F(\hat{z}) = 0$. We can therefore substitute for z_j in (7.5) using (7.4):

$$F(z_1, \ldots, z_{j-1}, f^j(z^{-j}), z_{j+1}, \ldots, z_n) = 0. \tag{7.11}$$

Differentiation with respect to z_i $(i \neq j)$ yields

$$\frac{\partial F(z_1, \ldots, z_{j-1}, f^j(z^{-j}), z_{j+1}, \ldots, z_n)}{\partial f^j(z^{-j})} \frac{\partial f^j(z^{-j})}{\partial z_i} + \frac{\partial F(z_1, \ldots, z_{j-1}, f^j(z^{-j}), z_{j+1}, \ldots, z_n)}{\partial z_i} = 0.$$

Solving for $-\partial f^j(z^{-j})/\partial z_i$ and substituting for $f^j(z^{-j})$ from (7.4), we find that

$$-\frac{\partial f^j(z^{-j})}{\partial z_i} = \frac{\partial F(z)/\partial z_i}{\partial F(z)/\partial z_j}. \tag{7.12}$$

Thus, the ratio of values of partial derivatives of the net production function F with respect to commodities i and j is the rate at which z_j must be reduced if z_i is increased at the rate of one unit per time period (and all other net output values are, of course, held constant). We refer to this concept as the rate of commodity transformation of i for j, denoted $RCT_{ij}(z)$.[8] Clearly the value of $RCT_{ij}(z)$ depends in general upon the values of all net outputs. The technological efficiency characterized by f^j (and by F) implies that $RCT_{ij}(z)$ is positive for all technologically efficient z and for all i and j.

Using (7.12), we see that the profit-maximization condition (7.10) says that price ratios must be equated to respective rates of commodity transformation:

$$\frac{p_i}{p_j} = -\frac{\partial f^j(z^{-j})}{\partial z_i} = RCT_{ij}(z), \qquad i, j = 1, \ldots, n. \tag{7.13}$$

To see that this condition makes sense, rewrite it as follows:

$$\frac{p_j}{p_i}\frac{\partial f^j(z^{-j})}{\partial z_i} = -1, \qquad i, j = 1, \ldots, n.$$

But it is easily seen that (holding prices constant, of course) this is equivalent to

$$\frac{\partial(p_j f^j(z^{-j}))}{\partial(p_i z_i)} = -1, \qquad i, j = 1, \ldots, n.^9 \tag{7.14}$$

The term on the left is the differential rate of change of $p_j z_j$ which results from increasing $p_i z_i$ at the rate of one unit per time period and adjusting z_j (hence $p_j z_j$) in order to stay on the boundary of the technology set (while holding all other net outputs constant). Thus, profit maximization requires that, at the margin, substituting the ith commodity for the jth lowers $p_j z_j$ at the same rate at which $p_i z_i$ is increased. Hence, at the margin, substituting the ith for the jth commodity in the production process leaves profit unchanged. If, on the other hand,

$$RCT_{ij}(z) = -\frac{\partial f^j(z^{-j})}{\partial z_i} < \frac{p_i}{p_j},$$

in which case

$$\frac{p_j}{p_i}\frac{\partial f^j(z^{-j})}{\partial z_i} > -1,$$

substitution of the ith for the jth commodity lowers $p_j z_j$ by less than it raises $p_i z_i$, thus increasing profit. Similarly, if $RCT_{ij}(z) > (p_i/p_j)$, substitution of the jth for the ith commodity raises profit.

Finally, note that the optimality condition (7.10) corresponds to the tangency condition illustrated in figure 7.3. At the point of tangency the slope of

[8] The analogy between the $RCT_{ij}(z)$ and the above analysis leading up to it and the marginal rate of substitution in consumption $MRS_{ij}(x)$ and the analysis leading up to it in section 3.4 should be obvious.

[9] In general, if a is a nonzero constant, $\partial af(x)/\partial z_i = a\partial f(x)/\partial z_i$ and $\partial f(z)/\partial az = (\partial f(z)/\partial z)/a$.

the equal-profit line, $-p_1/p_2$, is equal to the slope of the graph of f^2. But, by construction, this slope is the rate of commodity transformation.

Net Supply Functions

The first-order profit-maximization conditions (7.8–9) constitute a set of $n + 1$ equations, which, given our assumptions, can be solved for the optimal values of z_i, $i = 1, \ldots, n$, (and λ) as functions of the exogenous prices:

$$z_i = \phi_i(p), \qquad i = 1, \ldots, n. \tag{7.15}$$

The solution functions, ϕ_i, $i = 1, \ldots, n$, are the net supply functions (equivalently, the net input demand functions) of the producer. These functions generate optimal values of z given any set of positive prices, p. Substitution of (7.15) for the z_i in the profit function yields the maximal level of profit as a function of all prices,[10]

$$\Pi(p) = \sum_{i=1}^{n} p_i \cdot \phi_i(p). \tag{7.16}$$

The empirically testable implications of the theory of the producer are embodied in the form of the choice functions—the net output functions (7.15). Section 7.5 develops mathematically the qualitative content of the general theory of a profit-maximizing producer.

7.5 MATHEMATICAL ANALYSIS OF THE EFFECT OF PRICE CHANGES UPON NET SUPPLY*

Comparative Statics

The differential effects of a change in a price upon the net supplies of a profit-maximizing producer can be analyzed in a manner similar to the mathematical analysis of the effect of a price change on the demands of a consumer in the optional section 5.3.

First substitute the net supply function images into the first-order constrained-profit-maximization conditions (7.8–9):

$$\lambda(p)F_i(\phi(p)) + p_i = 0, \qquad i = 1, \ldots, n \tag{7.17a}$$

[10] Although we do not take the space to go into it in this book, it is perhaps worth noting that there exists a dual structure based upon the duality between the technology set Z (equivalently, the net production function F) and the profit function Π (see the part II suggested readings for references). This theory is similar to the duality between the utility function U and the consumer expenditure function H developed in section 5.2 above and the duality between the production function and the cost function developed in section 9.2 below. In particular, analogously to Hotelling's theorem ($\partial H(u, p)/\partial p_i = h_i(u, p)$ for all i) we have "Gorman's theorem:" $\partial \Pi(p)/\partial p_i = \phi_i(p)$, $i = 1, \ldots, n$. (see exercise 7.4).

and

$$F(\phi(p)) = 0, \tag{7.17b}$$

where $\phi(p) = [\phi_1(p), \ldots, \phi_n(p)]$ and $F_i(\phi(p)) = \partial F(\phi(p))/\partial \phi_i(p)$, and $\lambda(p)$ signifies that the Lagrange multiplier value depends on p. As these conditions hold identically (for all positive prices), we can differentiate with respect to prices. Using the composite function rule, we obtain

$$\sum_{k=1}^{n} \lambda(p) F_{ik}(\phi(p)) \frac{\partial \phi_k(p)}{\partial p_j} + F_i(\phi(p)) \frac{\partial \lambda(p)}{\partial p_j} + \delta_{ij} = 0, \qquad \begin{array}{l} i = 1, \ldots, n, \\ j = 1, \ldots, n, \end{array} \tag{7.18a}$$

and

$$\sum_{k=1}^{n} F_k(\phi(p)) \frac{\partial \phi_k(p)}{\partial p_j} = 0, \qquad j = 1, \ldots, n, \tag{7.18b}$$

where

$$F_{ik}(\phi(p)) = \frac{\partial^2 F(\phi(p))}{\partial \phi_i(p) \partial \phi_k(p)},$$

$\delta_{ij} = 1$ if $i = j$, and $\delta_{ij} = 0$ if $i \neq j$. This system of equations can be written in matrix form as follows:

$$\begin{bmatrix} \lambda(p)F_{11}(\phi(p)), \ldots, \lambda(p)F_{1n}(\phi(p)), & F_1(\phi(p)) \\ \vdots & \vdots \\ \lambda(p)F_{n1}(\phi(p)), \ldots, \lambda(p)F_{nn}(\phi(p)), & F_n(\phi(p)) \\ F_1(\phi(p)), \ldots, F_n(\phi(p)) & 0 \end{bmatrix}$$

$$\times \begin{bmatrix} \dfrac{\partial \phi_1(p)}{\partial p_1}, \ldots, \dfrac{\partial \phi_1(p)}{\partial p_n} \\ \vdots \qquad \vdots \\ \dfrac{\partial \phi_n(p)}{\partial p_1}, \ldots, \dfrac{\partial \phi_n(p)}{\partial p_n} \\ \dfrac{\partial \lambda(p)}{\partial p_1}, \ldots, \dfrac{\partial \lambda(p)}{\partial p_n} \end{bmatrix}$$

$$= \begin{bmatrix} -1 & 0 & \cdots & 0 \\ 0 & -1 & & \vdots \\ \vdots & & & \\ & & -1 & 0 \\ 0 & \cdots & 0 & 0 \end{bmatrix}$$

or

$$B(p) \times S(p) = C \tag{7.19}$$

where $B(p)$ is the bordered Hessian matrix, $S(p)$ is the matrix of net supply (and Lagrange multiplier) derivatives with respect to prices, and C is a matrix with -1 on the first n elements of the diagonal and zero elsewhere. The differential comparative statics of net supply are summarized by solving for $S(p) = B(p)^{-1} \times C$. (The second-order maximization condition guarantees that $|B(p)| \neq 0$ so that the inverse $B(p)^{-1}$ exists.)

In order to examine the components of $S(p)$ more carefully, use Cramer's rule[11] to solve for $\partial\phi_i(p)/\partial p_j$:

$$\frac{\partial\phi_i(p)}{\partial p_j} = \frac{|B^{ji}(p)|}{|B(p)|}$$

where $B^{ji}(p)$ is the matrix $B(p)$ with the ith column replaced by the jth column of C (a vector of zeros except for the jth component which is -1). Expansion of $|B^{ji}(p)|$ along the jth column yields

$$\frac{\partial\phi_i(p)}{\partial p_j} = -\frac{B_{ij}(p)}{|B(p)|} \tag{7.20}$$

where $B_{ij}(p)$ is the i, j cofactor of $B(p)$.

If $i \neq j$, then $B_{ij}(p)/|B(p)|$ is unsigned so that the differential effect that a change in the jth price has upon net supply of the ith commodity is generally indeterminate. Because of the symmetry of $B(p)$, however, these derivatives are symmetric:

$$\frac{\partial\phi_i(p)}{\partial p_j} = \frac{\partial\phi_j(p)}{\partial p_i}. \tag{7.21}$$

This result contrasts with the nonsymmetric cross-price effects in the theory of consumer demand (section 5.3).

Setting $j = i$ in (7.20) generates the own-price change result:

$$\frac{\partial\phi_i(p)}{\partial p_i} = -\frac{B_{ii}(p)}{|B(p)|}. \tag{7.22}$$

The second-order conditions imply that $B_{ii}(p)$ and $|B(p)|$ must have opposite signs. Hence,

$$\frac{\partial\phi_i(p)}{\partial p_i} > 0, \qquad i = 1, \ldots, n. \tag{7.23}$$

Thus, a rise in the ith price necessarily increases the net supply of the ith commodity (equivalently, decreases the producer's net demand for the ith commodity). This result also contrasts with the comparative statics of consumer demand, in which it was found that the differential own-price effect is of ambiguous sign.

[11] Cramer's rule is discussed in Hadley [1961, p. 166] and Yaari [1971, p. 141]. The determinant of a matrix is discussed in Hadley [1961, p. 85].

Substitutes and Complements in Production*

The rather striking contrasts between the comparative-static results for producers and consumers is attributable to the fact that the expression (7.21) includes nothing that is comparable to the income effect of consumer demand. It is this income effect which makes cross-price derivatives nonsymmetric and own-price derivatives of ambiguous sign in the theory of consumer demand. Because there is nothing in the theory of production that is analogous to the income effect in the theory of consumer demand, there is no distinction between net and gross price effects.[12] The determinantal expression in (7.20) is analogous to the substitution effect in the comparative statics of consumer demand. Because of this fact, there is no distinction between net and gross substitutes in the theory of production. The ith and jth commodities are called *substitutes* if

$$\frac{\partial \phi_i(p)}{\partial p_j} = \frac{\partial \phi_j(p)}{\partial p_i} < 0$$

and *complements* if

$$\frac{\partial \phi_i(p)}{\partial p_j} = \frac{\partial \phi_j(p)}{\partial p_i} > 0.$$

To interpret these definitions, recall that if a producer is a net user of the ith commodity, $\phi_i(p) < 0$, and $\partial \phi_i(p)/\partial p_j < 0$ implies that the *gross* use of the ith commodity *increases* if p_j increases. That is, $\partial \phi_i(p)/\partial p_j < 0$ means that the ith commodity is substituted for the jth as the price of the jth commodity increases.

Although the individual cross-price effects are unsigned, it can be shown that substitutability dominates complementarity in the same sense that net substitutability dominates net complementarity in consumer theory. Expansion by alien cofactors of the determinant of $B(p)$ along the last row (or column) yields

$$\sum_{i=1}^{n} F_i(\phi(p))B_{ji}(p) = 0.$$

Division by $|B(p)|$ and substitution from (7.20) yields

$$-\sum_{i=1}^{n} F_i(\phi(p)) \frac{\partial \phi_j(p)}{\partial p_i} = 0.$$

Substituting for $F_i(\phi(p))$, $i = 1, \ldots, n$, from the first-order conditions, and recalling that $\partial \phi_j(p)/\partial p_i = \partial \phi_i(p)/\partial p_j$, we have

$$\sum_{i=1}^{n} \frac{p_i}{\lambda(p)} \frac{\partial \phi_i(p)}{\partial p_j} = 0.$$

[12] If we were to introduce a financial constraint into the theory of the producer, the disparity between the theories of the consumer and the firm is reduced. See the suggestions for further reading following part II.

Multiplying through by $\lambda(p)$ and subtracting $p_j(\partial\phi_j(p)/\partial p_j)$ from both sides, we obtain

$$\sum_{\substack{i=1\\ i\neq j}}^{n} p_i \frac{\partial\phi_i(p)}{\partial p_j} = -p_j \frac{\partial\phi_j(p)}{\partial p_j} < 0, \tag{7.24}$$

where the inequality comes from (7.23). This inequality indicates that the sum of the cross-price effects weighted by prices must be negative. Hence, substitutability must dominate complementarity. In particular, if there are only two commodities, (7.24) becomes

$$p_1 \frac{\partial\phi_1(p)}{\partial p_2} < 0;$$

hence, the two commodities must be substitutes in production.

EXERCISES

7.1. **a.** Identify in the diagram below the set of technologically efficient production bundles.

b. For a fixed value of p_2, plot the net supply function for commodity 1 corresponding to the technology set below (i.e., plot $z_1 = \phi_1(p_1, \bar{p}_2)$ against p_1. (Hint: the function is discontinuous.)

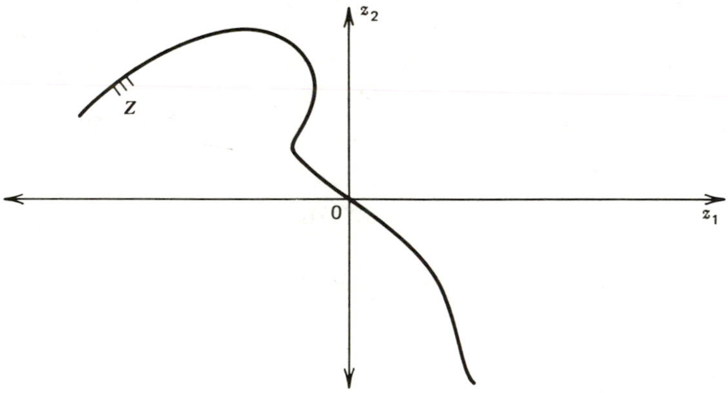

7.2. Show that the net supply functions are homogeneous of degree zero and the profit function is homogeneous of degree one.

7.3. Let the net production function be defined by the Cobb-Douglas function:

$$F(z) = \alpha \cdot z_1^{\alpha_1} \cdot z_2^{\alpha_2} \cdots z_n^{\alpha_n} - 1 = 0$$

a. Derive the first-order conditions for profit maximization.

b. Derive the net supply functions

c. Verify that a rise in the ith price necessarily increases the net supply of the ith commodity (equivalently decreases the producer's net demand for the ith commodity).

7.4. a. Derive the profit function Π (see equation (7.16)).

b. Verify "Gorman's theorem:"

$$\frac{\partial \Pi(p)}{\partial p_i} = \phi_i(p), \qquad i = 1, \ldots, n.$$

CHAPTER 8
THE PRODUCTION FUNCTION, DERIVED DEMAND, AND SUPPLY

8.1 INTRODUCTION

This chapter particularizes the production technology of chapter 7 in order to develop the theory of production in a more traditional context. The production technology of this chapter is characterized by the assumption that one commodity is necessarily an output (net supply is necessarily nonnegative) and the others are necessarily inputs (net supply is nonpositive). In this case, the production technology can be represented by a production function that maps input quantities into the quantity of output. This production function is analyzed in section 8.2. Section 8.3 describes a production process in which there is only one variable input (perhaps because all but one of the inputs are contractually fixed). Section 8.4 formulates the profit-maximization problem of the producer and derives optimal input demands and output supply. This optimization problem is illustrated graphically in section 8.5.

8.2 THE PRODUCTION FUNCTION

The Single-Output Production Function

A single-output, m-input production function can be derived from the more general production function generated by the technology set discussed in section 7.2 by imposing the following restrictions: $z_i \leq 0$, $i = 1, \ldots, n-1 = m$, say, and $z_n \geq 0$ for all $z = [z_1, \ldots, z_n]$ in the technology set. That is, the technology of the firm permits a positive net output of only one commodity, say the nth, and the other $n - 1 = m$ commodities can only be used as net inputs in the production process. As the signs of z_i are predetermined by the production technology, there is no ambiguity if we let

$$v_i = -z_i, \qquad i = 1, \ldots, m, \tag{8.1}$$

and

$$q = z_n. \tag{8.2}$$

Also let $w_i = p_i$, $i = 1, \ldots, m$, and $p = p_n$. That is, represent prices of inputs by w_i, $i = 1, \ldots, m$, and the output price by p.

The solution of equation (7.5) for the nth variable yields $z_n = f^n(z^{-n})$ (recall that $z^{-n} = [z_1, \ldots, z_{n-1}]$), and substitution from (8.1) and (8.2) yields the single-output production function, with image

$$q = f^n(-v) = f(v), \text{ say.} \tag{8.3}$$

Because of the technological efficiency property of f (see the discussion of the net production function in section 7.3), the image of v by f is not just any output that can be produced by this input level. Thus, the production function does not include combinations of inputs and output which are dominated in the sense that more output could be produced with no more of any input. Clearly, so long as all input and output prices are strictly positive, no profit-maximizing producer would choose an input-output combination which is dominated in this way. Nor would a profit-maximizing producer choose an input bundle for which the utilization of one of the inputs could be decreased, holding output constant, without increasing the required use of at least one other input.

Technological efficiency is to be distinguished from *economic efficiency*, which entails a choice between alternative input bundles, one of which contains more of at least one input and less of at least one other input than the alternative bundle. Another economic problem is the choice between two alternative combinations of inputs and output, one of which contains more output but also more of at least one input. These latter choices clearly depend upon the relative prices of the inputs and output. Technological efficiency is independent of prices (so long as they are positive), whereas an economically efficient choice clearly depends upon relative prices.

Marginal Product and Technological Efficiency

The production function (8.3) is assumed to be differentiable (assumption 7.4) and the derivative $\partial f(v)/\partial v_i$ has a useful interpretation. It tells us by how much output is increased (differentially) when the utilization of the ith input is increased at the rate of one unit per time period. This notion is referred to as the *marginal product* of the ith input, denoted $MP_i(v)$. Two things should be noted about the marginal product of an input. First, the marginal product of the ith input depends in general on the utilization of *all m* inputs. Second, the technological efficiency property of the production function requires that all marginal products be positive.

Isoquants

The production function can be represented graphically if we let $m = 2$ (i.e., restrict the technology to include only two inputs). In figure 8.1, the amounts used of the two inputs are graphed along the vertical and horizontal axes. The locus of all (technologically efficient) combinations of inputs that produce a given output is defined as an *isoquant*. The isoquant is analogous to an indifference curve, which graphs all combinations of amounts consumed that yield

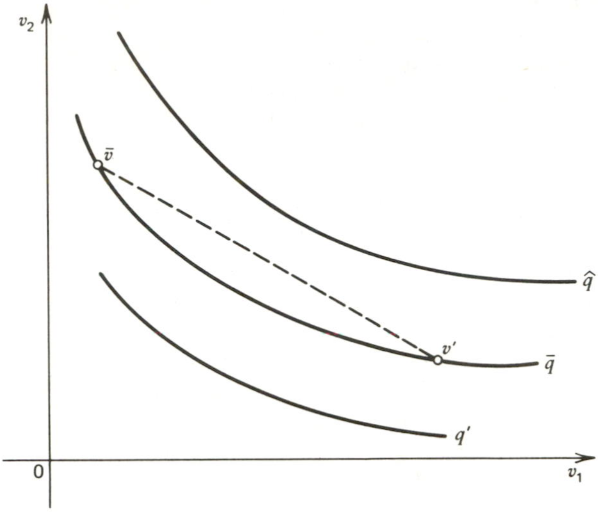

Figure 8.1

a given level of utility to the consumer. Note that the isoquants measure inputs and not outputs, and that output is only represented by the symbol attached to the isoquant (e.g., $\bar{q}$ in figure 8.1). A three-dimensional diagram would be required to measure both output and the two inputs on the diagram. Finally, note that a three-input isoquant is a three-dimensional surface and an m-dimensional isoquant is an m-dimensional (hyper) surface.

The complete representation of the two-input production function consists of an infinite family of isoquants. The property of technological efficiency guarantees that the isoquants are nonintersecting and downward sloping (see exercise 8.2).

Strict convexity of the technology set (assumption 7.5) guarantees that the isoquants of the single-output production function are strictly convex to the origin. To see this, consider the two input combinations, $\bar{v}$ and v', yielding output level $\bar{q}$ in figure 8.1. Strict convexity of Z implies that the convex combination, $\kappa(-\bar{v}, \bar{q}) + (1 - \kappa)(-v', \bar{q})$, is inefficient for all κ satisfying $0 < \kappa < 1$. The level of output $\bar{q}$ can be produced with less of one or both inputs. Inefficiency of this linear combination in turn implies that $\kappa\bar{q} + (1 - \kappa)\bar{q} = \bar{q} < f(\kappa\bar{v} + (1 - \kappa)v')$. That is, the convex combination of the output level in the two production bundles is less than the efficient output produced with a convex combination of the inputs. But this inequality says that the output level corresponding to a convex combination of two input combinations on the same isoquant is greater than the output associated with that isoquant. Graphically, a straight line drawn between two points on the same isoquant lies everywhere above that isoquant (except, of course, for the end points of the line). This, however, is equivalent to strict convexity (relative to the origin) of the isoquants.

Rate of Technological Substitution Defined

The *rate of technological substitution* of the *i*th for the *j*th input, $RTS_{ij}(v)$, is defined as the rate at which input *j* must be substituted for input *i* in order to maintain a given level of output with all remaining inputs fixed. This concept can be clarified by reference to the isoquant map in figure 8.1. In the two-input case, *the rate of technological substitution is simply the negative of the slope of the isoquant curve*. The slope of the isoquant curves indicates the rate at which the utilization of input 2 is changed when the use of input 1 is increased at the rate of one unit per time period, holding the producer on the same isoquant. The negative slope of the isoquant indicates a positive rate of technological substitution. That is, as the utilization of input 2 is reduced, in order to maintain the same level of output, the utilization of input 1 must be increased.

The concept of the rate of technological substitution can be clarified by a slightly more rigorous examination. With only two inputs, output can be expressed as

$$q = f(v_1, v_2). \tag{8.4}$$

Since the isoquants are negatively sloped, an isoquant, corresponding to output level $\bar{q}$, can be represented by an equation

$$v_2 = \theta_{\bar{q}}(v_1) \tag{8.5}$$

where $\theta_{\bar{q}}$ is a decreasing function. Thus $\theta_{\bar{q}}(v_1)$ is the rate of utilization of input 2 that yields the output level $\bar{q}$ if the rate of utilization of input 1 is v_1. Setting the production-function image equal to $\bar{q}$, $f(v_1, v_2) = \bar{q}$, we can substitute for v_2 using (8.5):

$$f(v_1, \theta_{\bar{q}}(v_1)) = \bar{q}. \tag{8.6}$$

Since (8.6) is an identity, we can partially differentiate with respect to v_1:

$$\frac{\partial f(v_1, \theta_{\bar{q}}(v_1))}{\partial v_1} + \frac{\partial f(v_1, \theta_{\bar{q}}(v_1))}{\partial \theta_q(v_1)} \cdot \frac{d\theta_{\bar{q}}(v_1)}{dv_1} = 0.$$

Rearrangement yields

$$-\frac{d\theta_{\bar{q}}(v_1)}{dv_1} = \frac{\partial f(v_1, \theta_{\bar{q}}(v_1))/\partial v_1}{\partial f(v_1, \theta_{\bar{q}}(v_1))/\partial \theta_{\bar{q}}(v_1)}.$$

Substituting for $\theta_{\bar{q}}(v_1)$ from (8.5) on the right-hand side, we obtain

$$-\frac{d\theta_{\bar{q}}(v_1)}{dv_1} = \frac{\partial f(v_1, v_2)/\partial v_1}{\partial f(v_1, v_2)/\partial v_2}.$$

The left-hand side of this expression is the negative of the slope of the $\bar{q}$ isoquant; from above, we know that this is the rate of technological substitution of input 1 for input 2. The right-hand side is the ratio of marginal products. Thus,

$$RTS_{1,2}(v_1, v_2) = \frac{\partial f(v_1, v_2)/\partial v_1}{\partial f(v_1, v_2)/\partial v_2} = \frac{MP_1(v_1, v_2)}{MP_2(v_1, v_2)}. \tag{8.7}$$

That is, the rate of technological substitution is equal to the ratio of marginal products. This condition generalizes to

$$RTS_{i,j}(v) = \frac{\partial f(v)/\partial v_i}{\partial f(v)/\partial v_j}, \qquad i = 1, \ldots, n, \quad j = 1, \ldots, n. \tag{8.8}$$

Law of Diminishing Rate of Technological Substitution

The assumption of strict convexity (7.5) can be reinterpreted in terms of the concept of the rate of technological substitution. Strict convexity of the technology set implies strict convexity of the isoquants with respect to the origin. Hence the rate of technological substitution diminishes as input 1 is substituted for input 2, holding output constant. Letting $\overline{RTS}_{1,2}(v_1, \bar{q}) = RTS_{1,2}(v_1, \theta_{\bar{q}}(v_1))$, we can express the strict-convexity assumption as follows:

$$\frac{\partial \overline{RTS}_{1,2}(v_1, \bar{q})}{\partial v_1} < 0.$$

This formulation explains why assumption 7.5 is sometimes called the assumption of diminishing rate of technological substitution.

Thus, the strict-convexity assumption says that, as the utilization of the jth input is reduced, in order to maintain the level of output unchanged, the utilization of the ith input must not only be increased but must be increased at an increasing rate.

The Elasticity of Substitution

The degree of convexity of the isoquant is an indication of the "ease" with which one input can be substituted for another in the production process. The "more convex" the isoquant, the greater is the effect that a change in the input ratio along the isoquant has upon the rate of technological substitution. Consequently, the "more convex" the isoquant, the faster will the required substitution of one input for another rise as the amount of the latter input utilized is decreased. This is what is meant by "difficulty" in substitution. Conversely, the "less convex" is the isoquant, the smaller is the effect of changes in input ratios upon the rate of technological substitution. Consequently, one input can be substituted for another without a rapid increase required in one input to hold the output level constant when the amount of the other input is diminished.

The *elasticity of substitution*, σ, is defined as the percentage rate of change in the input ratio when the rate of technological substitution is increased at the rate of 1 percent, holding output constant. Thus, the elasticity of substitution is independent of units and increases monotonically with the scope for substitution between the two inputs. The elasticity of substitution generally varies over the isoquant map; i.e., it is a function of the amounts of the two inputs employed (see, however, exercises 8.6 and 8.7).

In the range of efficient input combinations, the elasticity of substitution is bounded from below by zero and is unbounded from above. It is instructive to illustrate the isoquant maps for these two limiting cases. Figure 8.2a illustrates

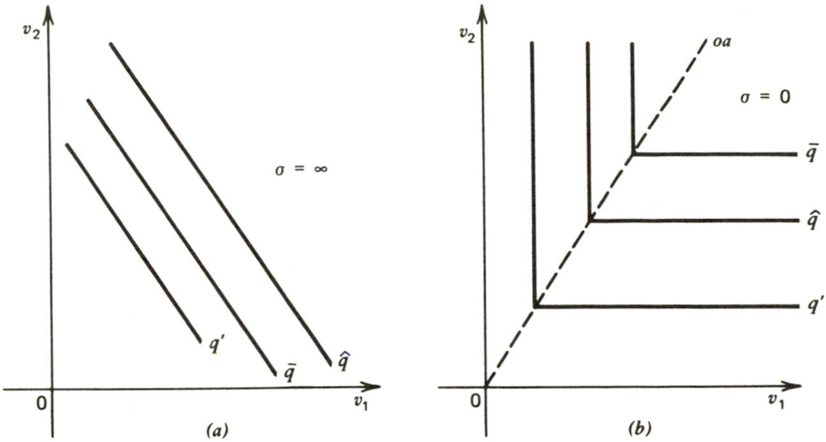

Figure 8.2

the case in which the elasticity of substitution is infinite. In this case, there is no change in the rate of technological substitution as the input ratio is varied, and the inputs are called perfect substitutes. Figure 8.2b illustrates the case in which the elasticity of substitution is zero, i.e., there is no possibility of substitution between the two inputs. In this case, the change in the rate of technological substitution at an efficient point (on the ray *oa*) is "infinitely large" for any change in the input ratio. The class of production functions characterized by zero elasticity of substitution plays an important role in operations research. The ray *oa* in figure 8.2b is a linear process. The theory which deals with linear processes of this type is called linear programming and is discussed in chapter 10.

The actual degree of substitution which is possible in a production process, and hence the value of the elasticity of substitution, is a purely technological concept. Nevertheless, it is an extremely useful concept in discussing particular economic problems—especially the problem of the distribution of income among the factors of production (see exercises 8.6c and 8.8).

8.3 TOTAL-, AVERAGE-, AND MARGINAL-PRODUCT CURVES

The Total-Product Curve

Fixing the quantity of all inputs except one, say the *i*th, at some set of values $\bar{v}^{-i} = [\bar{v}_1, \ldots \bar{v}_{i-1}, \bar{v}_{i+1}, \ldots \bar{v}_m]$ yields a relationship between output and this one variable input, $q = f(\bar{v}_1, \ldots, \bar{v}_{i-1}, v_i, \bar{v}_{i+1}, \ldots, \bar{v}_m) = f_i(v_i, \bar{v}^{-i})$. The graph of this relationship, illustrated in the lower panel of figure 8.3, is usually called a *total-product curve.* The graphical derivation of this total-product curve from a production function with two variable inputs is illustrated

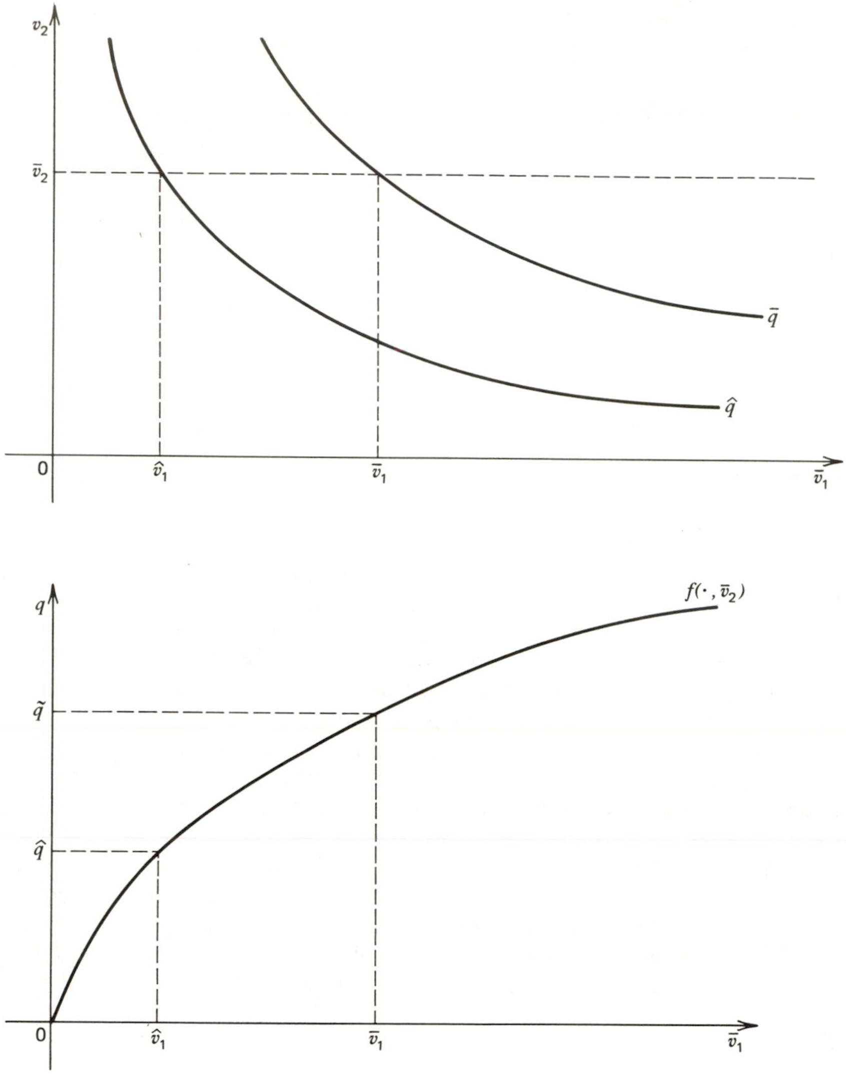

Figure 8.3

in figure 8.3. The isoquant map in the top panel represents the production function. Fixing v_2 at $\bar{v}_2$ reduces the relevant portion of the isoquant map to the horizontal line through $\bar{v}_2$ on the vertical axis. The (maximal) output corresponding to any value of v_1, given $v_2 = \bar{v}_2$, is given by the output corresponding to the isoquant which intersects the horizontal line at $(v_1, \bar{v}_2)$. For example, if $v_1 = \hat{v}_1$, the maximal output is $\hat{q}$. The graph defined by this relationship between v_1 and q, given $v_2 = \bar{v}_2$, is drawn in the lower panel of figure 8.3. Of course, a different fixed value of v_2 would generate a new total-product curve in the lower panel of the figure. Indeed, there is an (infinite) family of total-product curves, each corresponding to a different quantity of the fixed inputs.

The Marginal- and Average-Product Curves

The marginal product of the ith variable was defined above as the ith partial derivative of the production function f. It is apparent that this derivative is given by the slope of the total-product curve (or, of course, by the slope of a tangent line at the appropriate point).

The average product of the ith variable, denoted $AP_i(v)$, is defined by

$$AP_i(v) = \frac{f(v)}{v_i}. \tag{8.9}$$

At $v^{-i} = \bar{v}^{-i}$, the average product of input i at a point $\hat{v}_i$, say, is equal to the slope of a ray through the point on the total product curve where $v_i = \hat{v}_i$. Thus, in the top panel of figure 8.4, $\hat{q} = f_i(\hat{v}_i, \bar{v}^{-i})$ is the output when $\hat{v}_i$ is the quantity of input i (and, of course, $v^{-i} = \bar{v}^{-i}$). The slope of the ray oa ($\tan \theta$) is equal to $f_i(\hat{v}_i, \bar{v}^{-i})/\hat{v}_i = \hat{q}/\hat{v}_i$, the average product of input i at $(\hat{v}_i, \bar{v}^{-i})$.

The graphs of the marginal- and average-product functions, for fixed values of all but the one input, are called marginal- and average-product curves. The marginal- and average-product curves corresponding to the total-product curve in the top panel of figure 8.4 are drawn in the lower panel of this figure. It is important to keep in mind that there is an infinite family of these curves, each corresponding to a different value of v^{-i}, the quantities of all inputs except the ith.

The Law of Variable Proportions

The total-product curve in figure 8.4 generates average- and marginal-product curves that are everywhere decreasing. The particular shapes of the total-, average-, and marginal-product curves, however, depend upon the underlying technology set and therefore the form of the production function.

A rising marginal product of an input, given fixed quantities of other inputs, is certainly plausible and perhaps realistic for at least some interval of values of the variable.[1] This is especially plausible for ranges of v in which very little of the variable input is employed relative to the quantities of the fixed inputs. However, an assumption which has adorned production theory for more than a century is that every production function is characterized by a range of diminishing marginal product of a variable input, holding quantities of other inputs fixed. This time-honored assumption is referred to as the *law of variable proportions*: if the quantities of all of the inputs except one are fixed at a given level and the remaining variable input is increased, the resulting increments in output eventually decline.

The law of variable proportions, or, as it is sometimes called, "the law of eventually diminishing returns," reflects the effect of combining increasing amounts of the variable input with a set of fixed inputs. Consider the case of a

[1] This property of a production function would, of course, violate the assumption of strict convexity of the technology set (assumption 7.5).

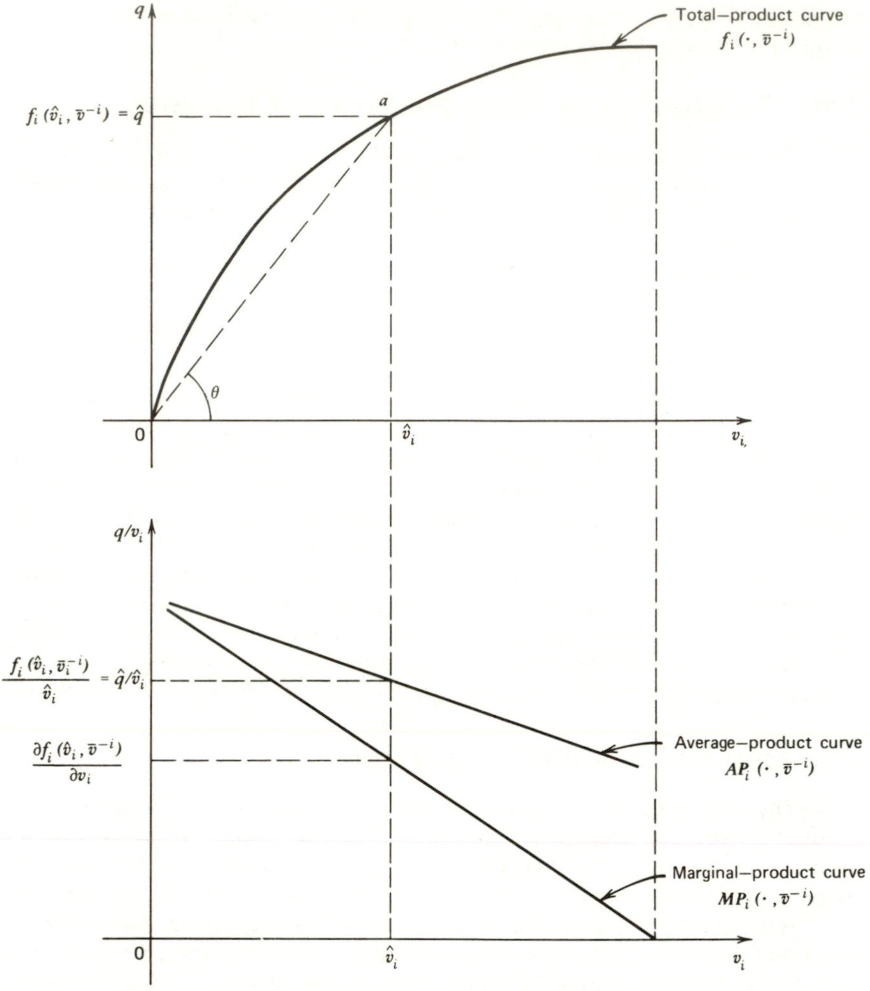

Figure 8.4

farm which employs fixed amounts of land, fertilizer, etc., and variable amounts of labor. Adding additional units of labor to the farm increases output but eventually the stage of diminishing returns is reached and the increases in output take place at a decreasing rate. If enough units of labor are added to the farm the output may fail to increase with additional labor input. That is, the fixed inputs (land, fertilizer, etc.), may reach the physical limits of their productive capacity and the marginal product of the variable input (labor) vanishes. Should enough units of labor be added to the land, the marginal product of labor could become negative.[2] Such input combinations are clearly technologically inefficient.

[2] This is clearly true of fertilizer; too much fertilizer (on a fixed amount of land) damages crop yields.

Relationships Between Total, Average, and Marginal Products

In figure 8.5, a more complicated production function with an initial stage of increasing marginal product for the variable input is exhibited. The total-product curve in the top panel of figure 8.5 is characterized by an increasing slope up to the point of inflection, C. At point C, where $v_i = \bar{v}_i$, the slope of the

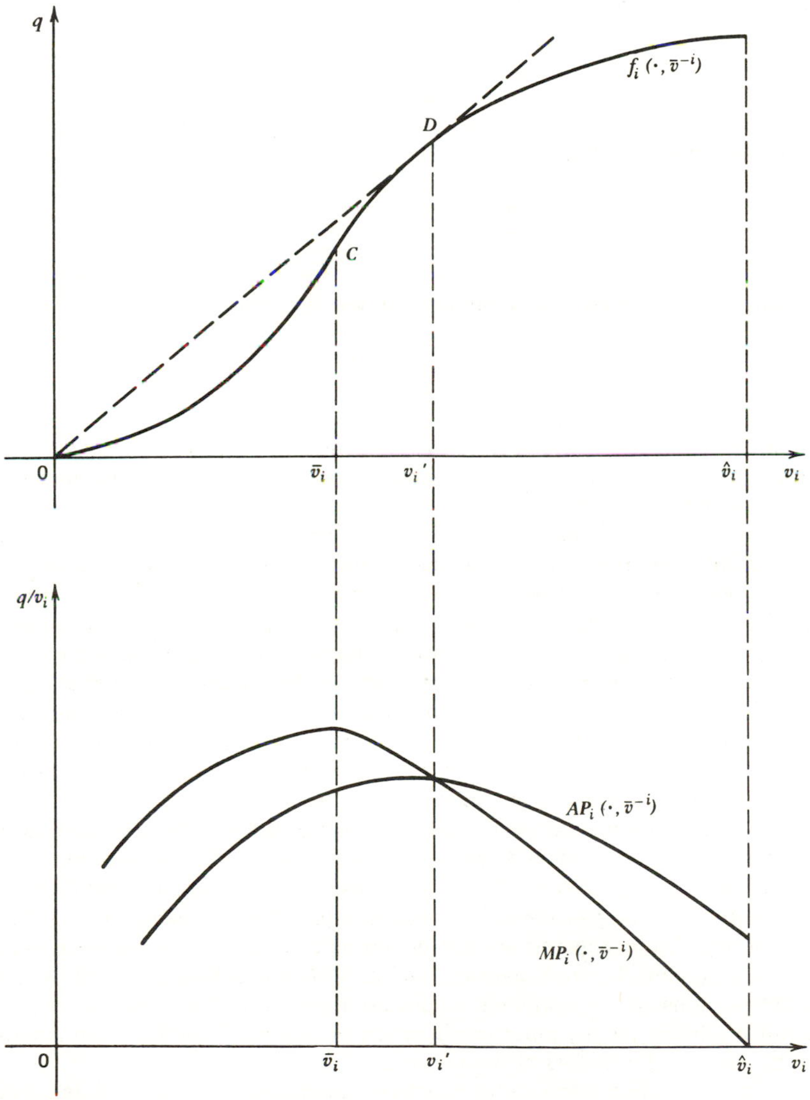

Figure 8.5

total-product curve reaches a maximum and begins to decline. The marginal-product curve corresponding to this total-product curve therefore reaches a maximum at $v_i = \bar{v}_i$ (bottom panel of figure 8.5).

The average-product curve can be derived from the top panel of figure 8.5 by calculating the slope of a ray drawn from the origin to the total-product curve. The average-product curve, also exhibited in the lower panel of figure 8.5, reaches a maximum at $v_i = v_i'$ where the slope of the ray is maximized. The marginal-product curve intersects the average-product curve at the maximum point of the latter. To demonstrate the validity of this relationship, note that $AP_i(v)$ is maximized where the value of the first derivative of the average-product function (8.9) is equated to zero:

$$\frac{\partial(f(v)/v_i)}{\partial v_i} = 0.$$

Evaluating this derivative, we obtain

$$\frac{\partial f(v)/\partial v_i}{v_i} - \frac{f(v)}{v_i^2} = 0.$$

Multiplying through by v_i and rearranging, we find that

$$\frac{\partial f(v)}{\partial v_i} = \frac{f(v)}{v_i};$$

hence, recalling the definitions of marginal and average products, we obtain $MP_i(v) = AP_i(v)$. Thus, when the average product is at a maximum, it is equal to the marginal product.

This relationship between the average- and marginal-product curves can also be inferred from the diagrammatic construction in figure 8.5. Average product is maximized at output v_i' where the ray from the origin to the appropriate point on the total-product curve is tangent to the latter curve (at point D). But the slope of this ray (the average product at v_i') is equivalent to the slope of the total-product curve at point D (the marginal product at v_i').

Whether or not the production function exhibits the more complicated shape that is illustrated in figure 8.5 depends, of course, upon the underlying technology set. Obviously, the production functions depicted in figures 8.4 and 8.5 do not exhaust the possibilities.

The total-product curves illustrated in figures 8.4 and 8.5 are characterized by the existence of a global output maximum. That is, the marginal product of the variable input falls to zero. An isoquant map which generates a total-product curve with this characteristic is illustrated in figure 8.6. The isoquants are drawn only for technologically efficient combinations of v_1 and v_2. If we were to map out the isoquants for inefficient as well as efficient values of v_1 and v_2, the dotted portions of the isoquants would be included in the isoquant map. The output produced by any input combination on a dotted portion of an isoquant can be produced with *less* of both inputs.

The two-input production function illustrated in figure 8.6 reaches a

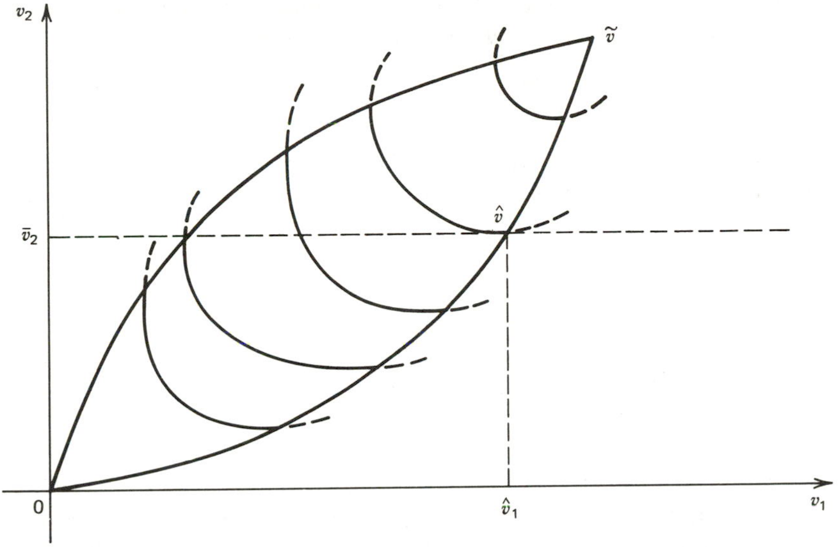

Figure 8.6

global maximum at the point $\tilde{v}$ in input space.[3] The two curves drawn from the origin to $\tilde{v}$ through points where the isoquants are vertical and horizontal, respectively, map out efficient input combinations; all points outside these two curves, referred to as *ridge lines*, are technologically inefficient.

Along the horizontal line that intersects the vertical axis at $\bar{v}_2$, the first input is variable and the second is fixed (at $\bar{v}_2$). An increase in v_1 beyond $\hat{v}_1$ would lower output. The value $\hat{v}_1$ in figure 8.6 corresponds to $\hat{v}_i$ in the total- and marginal-product curves in figure 8.5. Total product is maximal and the marginal product equals zero.

8.4 PROFIT MAXIMIZATION

As in chapter 7, profit is defined as the difference between gross revenue

$$R(p, v) = p \cdot q = p \cdot f(v) \tag{8.10}$$

and gross outlay

$$O(w, v) = \sum_{i=1}^{m} w_i v_i . \tag{8.11}$$

The profit-maximization problem is therefore given by $\text{Max}_v\ (R(p, v) - O(w, v))$.

[3] This point corresponds to a "bliss point" in an indifference map (see figure 3.9).

In order to exploit the calculus in analyzing this profit-maximization problem, we must assume that the solution is in the interior of the input space:

Assumption 8.1 The profit-maximizing input bundle $\overset{*}{v}$ is positive; i.e., $\overset{*}{v}_i > 0$, $i = 1, \ldots, m$.

The first-order maximization conditions are obtained by setting the partial derivatives of the profit function with respect to input quantities equal to zero:

$$\frac{\partial R(p, v)}{\partial v_i} - \frac{\partial O(w, v)}{\partial v_i} = 0, \qquad i = 1, \ldots, m,$$

or

$$\frac{\partial R(p, v)}{\partial v_i} = \frac{\partial O(w, v)}{\partial v_i}, \qquad i = 1, \ldots, m. \tag{8.12}$$

Thus, to maximize profit, the producer utilizes all inputs up to the point at which the rates of change of revenue and of outlay with respect to changes in the variable inputs are equal. This makes sense. If

$$\frac{\partial R(p, v)}{\partial v_i} > \frac{\partial O(w, v)}{\partial v_i}$$

for some i, increasing v_i would add more to revenue than to outlay, thus raising the producer's profit. Conversely, if

$$\frac{\partial R(p, v)}{\partial v_i} < \frac{\partial O(w, v)}{\partial v_i},$$

reducing the rate of utilization of the ith input would reduce outlay by more than it would reduce revenue, thus increasing profit.

Evaluating the derivatives in (8.12) using (8.10) and (8.11), we can express the first-order profit maximization conditions as follows:

$$p \frac{\partial f(v)}{\partial v_i} = w_i, \qquad i = 1, \ldots, m,$$

or

$$p \cdot MP_i(v) = w_i, \qquad i = 1, \ldots, m. \tag{8.13}$$

Thus, profit maximization requires that the price of each input (the effect upon cost of changing v_i) be equated to the marginal product of the input multiplied by (evaluated by) the output price. This latter concept indicates the rate at which revenue changes when v_i changes and is termed the *value of the marginal product* of the ith input, $VMP_i(v, p)$. Thus, (8.13) can be written as

$$VMP_i(v, p) = w_i, \qquad i = 1, \ldots, m.^4 \tag{8.14}$$

The quantities demanded of the m inputs are obtained by solving the system of m equations (8.13) or (8.14) for v as a function of the given prices:

$$v_i = \delta_i(p, w_1, \ldots, w_m), \qquad i = 1, \ldots, m. \tag{8.15}$$

The functions δ_i, $i = 1, \ldots, m$, are *input demand functions*. They are commonly called derived demand functions because the demand for the m inputs "derives from" the demand for the producer's output.

Finally, substitution of the input demand function into the production function yields the optimal output as a function of input and output prices; i.e., the producer's supply function, denoted s:

$$q = f(\delta_1(p, w), \ldots, \delta_m(p, w)) = s(p, w). \tag{8.16}$$

Fixing $w = [\bar{w}_1, \ldots, \bar{w}_m]$ and plotting q against p generates the *supply curve*, examined in more detail below in chapter 9.[5]

8.5 GRAPHICAL ILLUSTRATION OF PROFIT MAXIMIZATION

The principles of profit maximization, derived demand, and output supply examined in section 8.4 can be illustrated diagrammatically if we restrict ourselves to the special case in which there is only one variable input. To make the story somewhat realistic, suppose that the quantities of all but one input, say the ith, are contractually fixed during the period of analysis, i.e., $v^{-i} = \bar{v}^{-i}$. Gross revenue is given by

$$R(p, v_i, \bar{v}^{-i}) = p \cdot f_i(v_i, \bar{v}^{-i}) \tag{8.17}$$

and gross outlay is given by

$$O(w, v_i, \bar{v}^{-i}) = w_i v_i + \sum_{\substack{j=1 \\ j \neq i}}^{m} w_j \bar{v}_j. \tag{8.18}$$

[4] Second-order conditions require that the $m \times m$ Hessian matrix, with components $p\partial^2 f(v)/\partial v_i \partial v_j$ be negative definite, i.e., that the principal minors of this matrix alternate in sign beginning with a negative 2×2 determinant. It is worth noting that negative definiteness requires that all diagonal elements be negative, i.e., that $\partial^2 f(v)/\partial v_i^2 < 0$ or $\partial MP_i(v)/\partial v_i < 0$, $i = 1, \ldots, m$. Thus the ith marginal product—hence the ith value of marginal product—must be decreasing with respect to increases in v_i, for all i.

[5] The mathematical analysis of the optional section 7.5 above establishes that the input demand functions satisfy $\partial\delta_i(p, w)/\partial w_i < 0$, $i = 1, \ldots, m$, and that the supply function satisfies $\partial s(p, w)/\partial p > 0$. These qualitative results are clarified by graphical illustration in section 8.5 and section 9.5.

Thus, outlay decomposes into two parts: variable, $w_i v_i$, and fixed,

$$\sum_{\substack{j=1 \\ j \neq i}}^{m} w_j \bar{v}_j .$$

Maximizing profit,

$$\Pi(p, w, v_i, \bar{v}^{-i}) = p \cdot f_i(v_i, \bar{v}^{-i}) - w_i v_i - \sum_{\substack{j=1 \\ j \neq i}}^{m} w_j \bar{v}_j ,$$

with respect to the single choice variable, v_i, yields the first-order condition,

$$p \frac{\partial f_i(v_i, \bar{v}^{-i})}{\partial v_i} - w_i = 0$$

or

$$VMP_i(v_i, \bar{v}^{-i}) = w_i .$$

The second-order condition is

$$\frac{\partial^2 \Pi(p, w, v_i, \bar{v}^{-i})}{\partial v_i^2} = p \frac{\partial^2 f(v_i, \bar{v}^{-i})}{\partial v_i^2} < 0,$$

or

$$\frac{\partial MP_i(v_i, \bar{v}^{-i})}{\partial v_i^2} < 0,$$

or

$$\frac{\partial VMP_i(v, p)}{\partial v_i} < 0.$$

Thus, profits are maximized when the variable input is utilized up to the point at which the value of its marginal product is equated to its price and is decreasing with respect to changes in the rate of utilization of the variable input.

The solution to the profit-maximization problem is illustrated in figure 8.7. The revenue curve is obtained by shifting the total-product curve by the factor p. As p is constant, this revenue curve, plotted in figure 8.7, has the same basic shape as the total-product curve. The outlay curve is a straight line with intercept

$$\sum_{\substack{j=1 \\ j \neq i}}^{m} w_i \bar{v}_i$$

and slope w_i.

Profit (or loss) is represented by the vertical distance between the revenue curve and the outlay curve. This difference is plotted as the graph of the profit function, Π, in figure 8.7. Profit is negative for low values of v_i, positive for values of v_i between $\bar{v}_i$ and $\tilde{v}_i$, and negative for values greater than $\tilde{v}_i$. The optimal value of v_i is $\overset{*}{v}_i$ where the profit function peaks. At this value of v_i, the slopes of the outlay and revenue curves are equal. Over the range $[\bar{v}_i, \overset{*}{v}_i]$, the

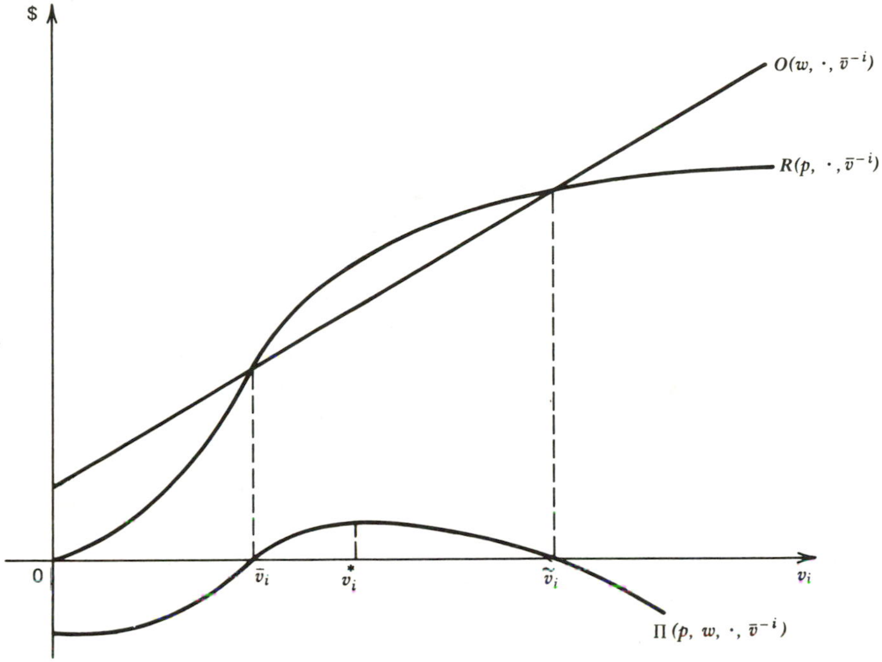

Figure 8.7

two curves move further apart with increases in v_i since the slope of the revenue curve is greater than that of the cost curve. Over the range $[\overset{*}{v}_i, \tilde{v}_i]$ the two curves move closer together since the slope of the revenue curve is smaller. Note that the slope of the revenue curve is the value of the marginal product of the variable input and the slope of the cost curve is the input price. Thus, at $\overset{*}{v}_i$, $VMP_i(p, \overset{*}{v}_i, \bar{v}^{-i}) = w_i$, confirming the mathematical analysis.

The profit-maximization conditions are illustrated with the value-of-marginal-product curve in figure 8.8. As $VMP_i(p, v_i, \bar{v}^{-i}) = p \cdot MP_i(v_i, \bar{v}^{-i})$ the value-of-marginal-product curve is obtained by shifting the marginal-product curve (figure 8.5) by the output price, p. As p is constant, the value-of-marginal-product curve has the same basic shape as the marginal-product curve. The variable-input price, w_i, is represented by the horizontal line (the "wage line") which intersects the vertical axis at the prevailing price, $\overset{*}{w}_i$.

The first-order profit-maximization condition, $VMP_i(p, v_i, \bar{v}^{-i}) = w_i$, is represented by the intersection of the wage line and the value-of-marginal-product curve. There are two such intersection points in figure 8.8—at $\bar{v}_i$ and $\overset{*}{v}_i$. At the first of the intersection points, however, the second-order condition is not satisfied. Thus, profits are maximized at $\overset{*}{v}_i$ and minimized at $\bar{v}_i$.

For the case of a single variable input, the declining portion of the value-of-marginal-product curve is the (derived) demand function for that variable input. The optimal rate of utilization of the single variable input can be found at the intersection point of the horizontal wage line, depicting the per-unit cost of

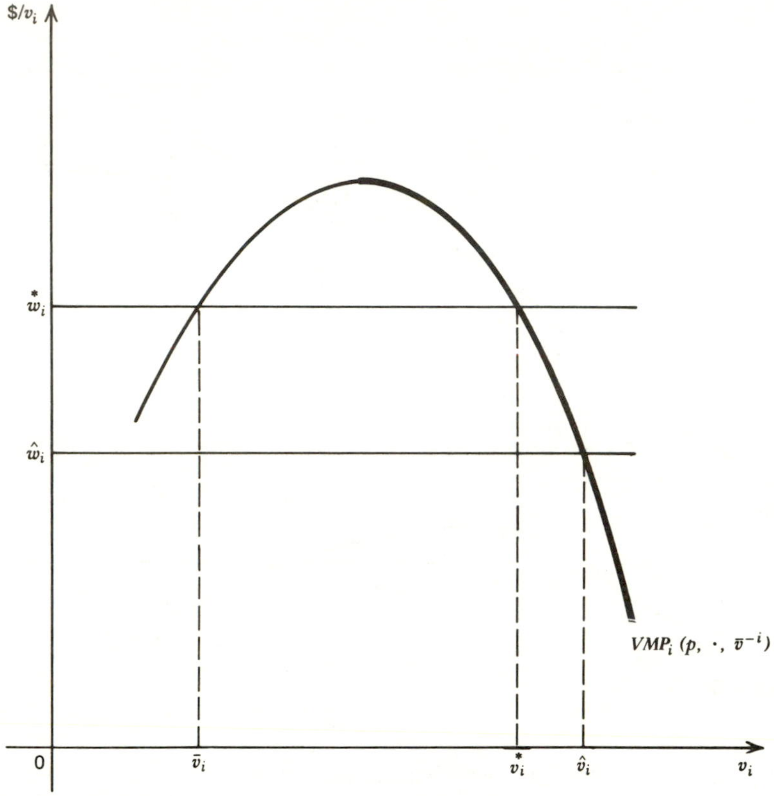

Figure 8.8

the variable input, and the downward-sloping portion of the value-of-marginal-product curve. If the price of the variable input were to be changed to $\hat{w}_i$ the new optimum would require a higher utilization of the variable input, viz., $\hat{v}_i$.

Finally, note that, if there is more than one variable input, the *VMP* curve for each input shifts when other input quantities are changed. Hence, the derived input demand function is not equivalent to the *VMP* curve.

EXERCISES

8.1 Consider a profit-maximizing producer employing only one variable input which must be purchased in integer amounts. Suppose that the output, q, for each level of v_i is given by the following schedule:

v_i:	0	1	2	3	4	5	6	7	8
q:	0	2	7	10	12	13	13	12	10

a. Compute the arithmetic schedules for average and marginal product.

b. Assuming that the output price and input price are \$2/unit and \$4/unit, respectively, compute the total-revenue schedule and the VMP_j schedule.

c. How much of the input is purchased by the producer?

8.2 Show that the technological efficiency of a production function, $q = f(v_1, v_2)$, implies that isoquants (in $v_1 - v_2$ space) are nonintersecting and negatively sloped.

8.3 Suppose that a variable input in a production process is free (e.g., air). At the optimum, what is the numerical magnitude of the marginal product of that input?

8.4 Suppose that the output of a producer is also an input in that producer's production process (e.g., an agricultural crop that can be harvested and sold or used to reseed). At the optimum, what is the numerical magnitude of the marginal product of that commodity?

8.5 The Cobb–Douglas production function, defined by

$$q = \alpha v_1^{\beta_1} v_2^{\beta_2}, \tag{8.19}$$

where α, β_1, and β_2 are positive parameters, is commonly employed in empirical economics.

a. Show that this function is homogeneous. What is the degree of homogeneity?

b. What constraints on the parameters would make the production function homogeneous of degree one?

c. Show that the expansion path is a straight line.

d. Show that, if the function is homogeneous of degree one, the shares of the two inputs in total revenue, $w_1 v_1/pq$ and $w_2 v_2/pq$, are β_1 and β_2, respectively.

8.6 In working the following problems, assume that the production function is Cobb–Douglas (exercise 8.5) and homogeneous of degree one.

a. Show that the rate of technological substitution can be written as a function of the input ratio:

$$RTS_{12}(v_1, v_2) = g\left(\frac{v_1}{v_2}\right)$$

(Note, in particular, that the rate of technological substitution is independent of the output level for a given input ratio [Relate this to exercise 8.5].)

b. Calculate the elasticity of substitution, which, because of the result in (a), can be written as

$$\sigma\left(\frac{v_1}{v_2}\right) = -\left(\frac{d \log g(v_1/v_2)}{d \log(v_1/v_2)}\right)^{-1}$$

c. Why is the result in part (b) related to the property of the Cobb–Douglas production function illustrated by exercise 8.5d?

8.7 Another production function that is commonly employed in empirical studies is defined by

$$q = \gamma[\alpha v_1^\rho + (1 - \alpha)v_2^\rho]^{1/\rho}, \qquad (8.20)$$

where γ and α are positive parameters, $\rho \leq 1$, and $\rho \neq 0$.

a. Show that this function is homogeneous of degree one.

b. Show that the expansion path is a straight line.

c. Show that, as in the case of the Cobb–Douglas production function (8.19), $RTS_{12}(v_1, v_2) = g(v_1/v_2)$ (exercise 8.6a).

d. Show that the elasticity of substitution (exercise 8.6b) is constant (in fact, equal to $1/(1 - \rho)$). (The production function (8.20), together with the Cobb–Douglas production function (8.19) are the only two-variable production functions with constant elasticity of substitution. Moreover, (8.19) can be obtained as the limit of (8.20) as $\rho \to 0$—as $1/(1 - \rho) \to 1$. For this reason, (8.20) is called the constant-elasticity-of-substitution production function. See the part II suggested readings for further discussion.)

8.8 Analyze the relationship between the elasticity of substitution and the effect that changes in the input ratio, v_1/v_2, have upon relative income shares (see exercise 8.5d).

8.9* A production function f is *homothetic* if there exists a homogeneous-of-degree-one function g and an increasing function (a strictly monotonic transformation) h such that $f(v) = h(g(v))$.

a. Show that the expansion path is a straight line if the production function is homothetic.

b. Show that the Cobb–Douglas production function (8.19) is homothetic (for any positive values of the parameters).

c. The CES function (8.20) is homogeneous of degree one (hence trivially homothetic). Can you think of a way of modifying this function so that it is homothetic but not necessarily homogeneous of degree one? (Hint: add a parameter.)

CHAPTER 9
THE THEORY OF COST

9.1 INTRODUCTION

In this chapter we retain the assumption of chapter 8 that restricts the technology set to include one output and m inputs, and we consider the problem of choosing an input bundle to minimize the cost of producing any (technologically) feasible output, given fixed input prices. The solution to this cost-minimization problem, which determines minimum cost as a function of input prices and output, is defined as the cost function of the firm. The cost function bears a fundamental dual relationship to the production function. This duality between cost and production functions is a powerful analytical tool in economics, particularly in econometric applications.

Section 9.2 derives the cost function of the producer from a constrained cost-minimization problem. Section 9.3 provides a graphical analysis of the cost-minimization problem and derivation of the cost function, together with the associated average- and marginal-cost functions. Section 9.4 introduces the particular class of homogeneous production functions and considers the accompanying form of the cost function. Section 9.5 examines the conditions for profit maximization, utilizing the cost function and its related analytical concepts. In this section we again analyze the supply function of the producer and demonstrate that it is upward sloping. This graphical exposition confirms the mathematical analysis undertaken in section 7.5. Finally, Section 9.6 examines the family of cost functions for a producer with one fixed and one variable input and their relationship to cost functions for a producer for which all inputs are variable.

Throughout the chapter, we retain assumptions 7.1–7.5 and assumption 8.1. As usual, many of the following results would be true under a weaker set of assumptions.

9.2 CONSTRAINED OUTLAY MINIMIZATION AND THE COST FUNCTION

Dual Constrained-Optimization Problems

The problem that we address in this section is the derivation of the cost function of the producer—a relationship which gives the minimum cost of producing a given output. Recall that the outlay on an input bundle, v, is defined as

$$o = \sum_{i=1}^{m} w_i v_i, \tag{9.1}$$

where the input price vector is given. The choice of the profit-maximizing output and input bundle for the producer may be analyzed by means of either of two constrained-optimization problems. One is that of maximizing output subject to an outlay constraint:

$$\operatorname*{Max}_{v} f(v) \qquad \text{s.t.} \sum_{i=1}^{m} w_i v_i = 0. \tag{9.2}$$

The other is that of minimizing outlay subject to an output constraint:

$$\operatorname*{Min}_{v} \sum_{i=1}^{m} w_i v_i \qquad \text{s.t. } f(v) = q. \tag{9.3}$$

The Lagrange expression for the second of these problems is

$$L(v, \lambda) = \sum_{i=1}^{m} w_i v_i - \lambda(f(v) - q), \tag{9.4}$$

where, of course, λ is the Lagrange multiplier. The critical values of λ and v are generated by the conditions,

$$w_i - \lambda \frac{\partial f(v)}{\partial v_i} = 0, \qquad i = 1, \ldots, m, \tag{9.5}$$

and

$$f(v) - q = 0. \tag{9.6}$$

Division of the ith equation in (9.5) by the jth yields

$$\frac{\partial f(v)/\partial v_i}{\partial f(v)/\partial v_j} = \frac{w_i}{w_j}. \tag{9.7}$$

Recalling the definition of the rate of technological substitution ($RTS_{ij}(v)$), we obtain

$$RTS_{ij}(v) = \frac{w_i}{w_j}. \tag{9.8}$$

Thus, the cost-minimizing values of the inputs, given output, are determined by equating the rates of technological substitution to input-price ratios. $RTS_{ij}(v)$ indicates the rate at which one input can be substituted for another while holding output constant. On the other hand, the input-price ratio indicates the rate at which one input can be substituted for another while holding outlay constant. If (9.8) is not satisfied, it is possible to decrease outlay by substituting one input for another in such a way as to hold output constant. If $RTS_{ij}(v) > w_i/w_j$, the ith input should be substituted for the jth to reduce outlay, and vice versa if the opposite inequality holds.

The reader can verify that the first-order conditions of the constrained-maximization problem (9.2) yields the same relationship between $RTS_{ij}(v)$ and w_i/w_j. Moreover, if the minimum outlay from the output-constrained minimization problem (9.3) is used in the outlay constraint in the constrained-maximization problem (9.2), the optimal inputs are identical for the two problems. Consequently, these two problems are said to be "dual" to one another.

The Cost Function

We are now in a position to derive the relationship between the least-cost combination of inputs (minimum cost of production) and output (that is, the *cost function* of the producer). The outlay-minimizing bundle of inputs—the solution values for the problem (9.3)— depend upon the "givens," q and w; hence

$$\overset{*}{v}_i = g_i(q, w), \qquad i = 1, \ldots, m. \tag{9.9}$$

The functions g_i, $i = 1, \ldots, m$, are output-constrained input demand functions.[1] Under the differentiability and interior-solution assumptions (assumptions 7.4 and 8.1), these functions can be obtained by solving the system of $m + 1$ equations (9.5) and (9.6) for λ and v_i in terms of q and w.

Substitution of (9.9) into the outlay equation (9.1) yields the cost function, with image

$$C(q, w) = \sum_{i=1}^{m} w_i g_i(q, w). \tag{9.10}$$

The cost function specifies the minimum cost of producing q, with given input prices w, when the producer is free to choose the optimal (cost-minimizing) rate of input utilization that is technologically feasible. Since the cost function is derived from an outlay-minimization problem subject to the production-function constraint, it incorporates or embodies the constraints upon production represented by the production function. In this way, the cost and production functions are "dual" to one another. Thus, the cost function contains all of the necessary information required for the solution of the profit-maximization problem of the producer.[2]

[1] The analogy to the consumer's utility-constrained (income-compensated) demand functions will be apparent to those who read the optional section 5.2. Each g_i is homogeneous of degree zero in w.

[2] Hotelling's theorem, presented in section 5.2, is equally applicable to the theory of the producer; that is, the output-constrained input demand functions can be derived from the cost function by straightforward differentiation: $g_i(q, w) = \partial C(q, w)/\partial w_i$, $i = 1, \ldots, m$. See exercise 9.4b.

9.3 GRAPHICAL DERIVATION OF THE EXPANSION PATH, RETURNS TO OUTLAY, AND THE COST FUNCTION

The Expansion Path

The constrained-optimization problems and the derivation of the cost function of the producer can be illustrated graphically if we restrict the technology of the producer to include only two imputs ($m = 2$). The production function is represented by the isoquant map in figure 9.1. For only two inputs, the outlay equation (9.1) is $o = w_1 v_1 + w_2 v_2$. This equation is represented in figure 9.1 by the linear function,

$$v_2 = \frac{o}{w_2} - \frac{w_1}{w_2} v_1, \tag{9.11}$$

with vertical intercept, o/w_2 and slope $-(w_1/w_2)$. Similarly, the horizontal intercept is o/w_1. This linear function, which is termed the *equal-outlay line*, graphs the combinations of the two input quantities which can be purchased with an outlay equal to o.

Alternative levels of outlay on the two inputs generate alternative equal-outlay lines with the same slopes (given the input prices). For example, the higher level of outlay o' yields the higher equal-outlay line in figure 9.1. Outlay minimization subject to the constraint that output be equal to $\overset{*}{q}$ can be characterized as finding the lowest equal-outlay line with slope, $-w_1/w_2$, that intersects (or touches) the isoquant corresponding to output level $\overset{*}{q}$. Clearly, the unique equal-outlay line satisfying this property is the one which is tangent to the $\overset{*}{q}$-isoquant at $\overset{*}{v}$. At the point of tangency, the slope of the isoquant $(-RTS_{ij}(v))$ is equal to the slope of the equal-outlay line $(-w_1/w_2)$. Thus, the graphical solution to the output-constrained outlay-minimization problem yields the same optimality conditions as the mathematical analysis (equation 9.8).

The dual problem of outlay-constrained output maximization can be described as that of finding the highest isoquant along the equal-outlay line. Clearly, the isoquant which is tangent to the equal-outlay line is the one isoquant with this property. The tangency occurs at the input combination $\overset{*}{v} = (\overset{*}{v}_1, \overset{*}{v}_2)$ which produces output $\overset{*}{q}$. Thus, the dual output-constrained outlay-minimization and outlay-constrained output-maximization problems are solved by the same input combination for consistent output and outlay levels.

Of course, the outlay on the inputs by the producer is not fixed. Alternative levels of outlay yield different optimal input quantities, determined by the points of tangency between the corresponding equal-outlay lines and isoquants.

The locus of all points of tangency between a family of equal-outlay lines (for given prices) and a family of isoquants is defined as an *expansion path*. In figure 9.2 an expansion path ($EP(w)$) is shown with three members of the family of equal-outlay lines and isoquants. The expansion path shows the optimal combination of the two inputs, v_1 and v_2, for any given level of outlay on these two inputs. Alternatively, it shows the optimum combination of inputs

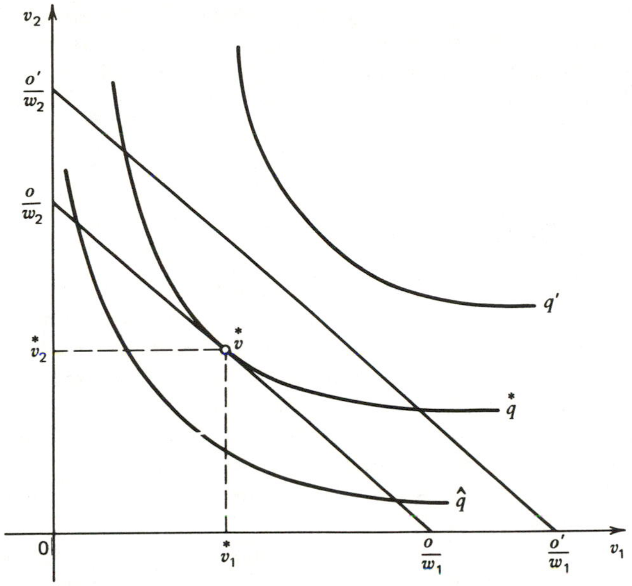

Figure 9.1

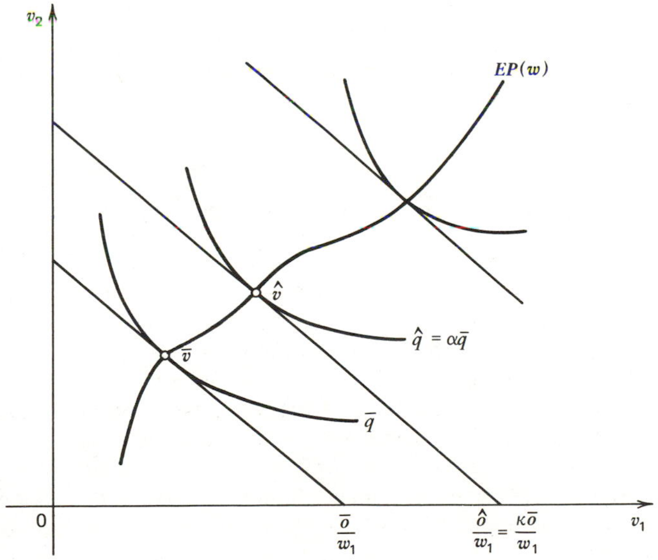

Figure 9.2

and the necessary outlay, given the prices of these inputs, for any level of output. It is therefore obvious that the expansion path is the set of all input combinations satisfying the optimality condition, $RTS_{12}(v) = w_1/w_2$. The expansion path can therefore be more generally defined (even if $m > 2$) as the set of points satisfying (9.8) or (9.7) for all pairs, i, j.

Returns to Outlay

An expansion path can be characterized by increasing, constant, or decreasing *returns to outlay*. The returns-to-outlay concept refers to the relationship between a given change in outlay on the inputs and the corresponding change in output. If the outlay is increased by a given proportion, say κ, and the output of the producer increases proportionately more than κ, then the production function is said to be characterized by increasing returns to outlay. If output increases less than proportionately to outlay, returns to outlay are decreasing; if output increases in the same proportion as outlay, the expansion path is characterized by constant returns to outlay.

To illustrate the returns-to-outlay concept, let us refer again to figure 9.2. At the outlay $\bar{o}$, $\bar{q}$ is produced with input combination $\bar{v}$. If the outlay is increased by the proportional factor κ to $\hat{o} = \kappa\bar{o}$, the producer utilizes input combination $\hat{v}$ to produce $\hat{q} = \alpha\bar{q}$. If $\alpha > \kappa$, the expansion path is characterized by increasing returns to outlay. Decreasing and constant returns to outlay are characterized by $\alpha < \kappa$ and $\alpha = \kappa$, respectively.

It is not necessary, or even likely, that returns to outlay remain unchanged over the whole range of the expansion path. Depending upon the existing technology, the expansion path might initially show a range of increasing returns and eventually a range of decreasing returns to outlay. In addition, even with a given technology, alternative expansion paths (corresponding to alternative input-price vectors) are generally characterized by different returns-to-outlay characteristics.

Total-, Average-, and Marginal-Cost Curves

Figure 9.3 illustrates three alternative shapes of the graph of the cost function in cost-output space with a fixed set of input prices. This graph is referred to as the (total) *cost curve*. The shape of the cost curve clearly depends upon the returns to outlay. If the expansion path is characterized by increasing returns to outlay, the cost of the optimal input bundle increases proportionately less than output, and the total cost curve has the shape shown in figure 9.3a. Figure 9.3b illustrates the total cost curve for an expansion path characterized by decreasing returns to outlay; the cost of the optimal input bundle increases proportionately more than output. Finally, figure 9.3c illustrates an expansion path characterized by an initial range of increasing returns to outlay (for output less than q'), followed by decreasing returns to outlay (for output greater than q').

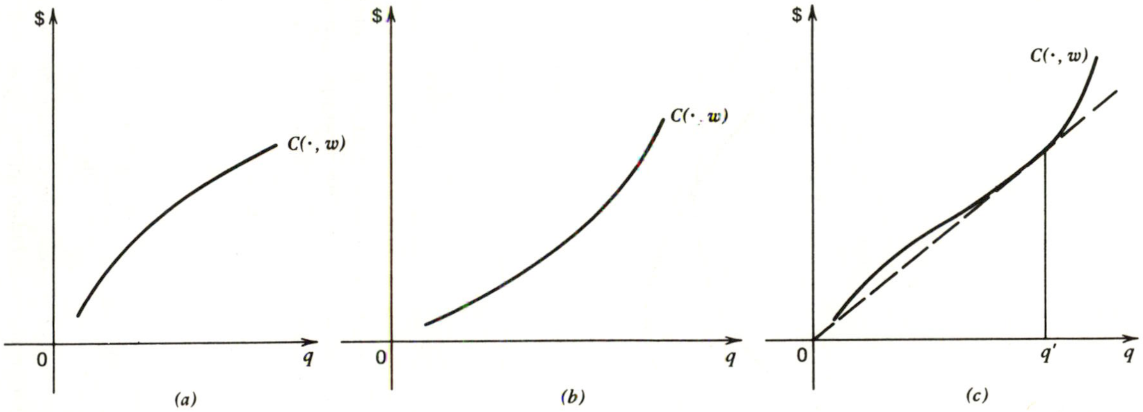

Figure 9.3

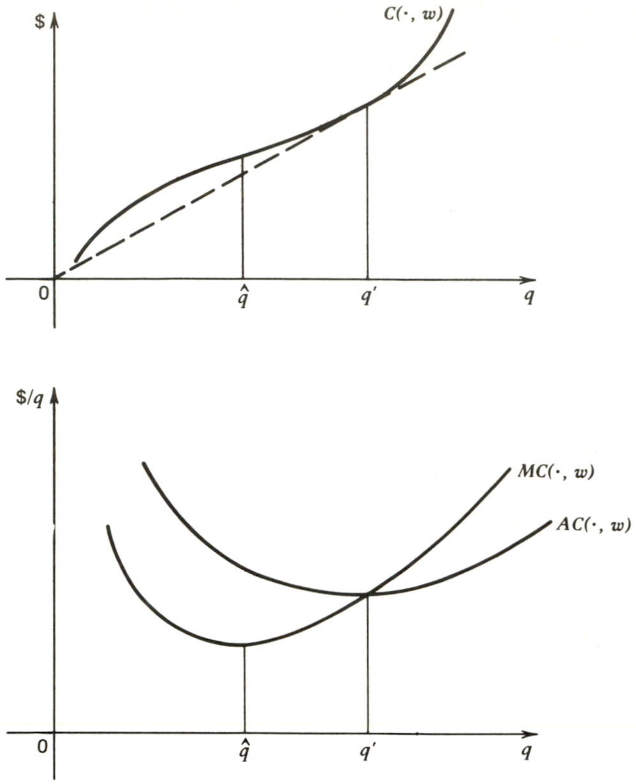

Figure 9.4

Corresponding to the (total) cost curve that is depicted in figure 9.3 are the usual average and marginal curves. The average-cost and marginal-cost functions are defined as follows:

$$AC(q, w) = \frac{C(q, w)}{q}, \tag{9.12}$$

and

$$MC(q, w) = \frac{\partial C(q, w)}{\partial q}. \tag{9.13}$$

The average- and marginal-cost curves can be derived geometrically from the (total) cost curve in the usual manner. In figure 9.4, the marginal-cost curve reaches a minimum at the point of inflection of the total-cost curve (at output level $\hat{q}$). The average-cost curve reaches a minimum at output level q' where it is intersected by the marginal-cost curve. The reader can associate the returns to outlay with the different ranges of the average-cost curve.

9.4 HOMOGENEOUS PRODUCTION FUNCTIONS AND RETURNS TO SCALE

A commonly encountered concept that is related to, but generally different from, returns to outlay is that of *returns to scale*. The latter concept refers to the relationship between proportional changes in output and *equiproportionate* changes in input quantities. Thus, returns to scale refers to the proportionate increase in output when the input quantities are increased along a ray such as that labeled S, for "scale line," in figure 9.5.

It is clear that only when the expansion path for the producer is linear and passes through the origin are returns to scale and returns to outlay the same. If the expansion path is nonlinear, returns to scale are generally lower than returns to outlay. This follows from the derivation of the expansion path as the locus of optimal combinations of inputs. For example, consider the optimal input bundle v' in figure 9.5 and suppose that both of the inputs, and therefore outlay, are increased by the factor λ. The new input combination is $\lambda v'$ on the "scale line," S. On the other hand, the new least-cost combination of inputs corresponding to the increased outlay $\lambda o'$ is represented by the point $\overset{*}{v}$ on the expansion path. The output obtained from employing input combination $\overset{*}{v}$ exceeds that from $\lambda v'$, and thus returns to outlay exceed returns to scale.

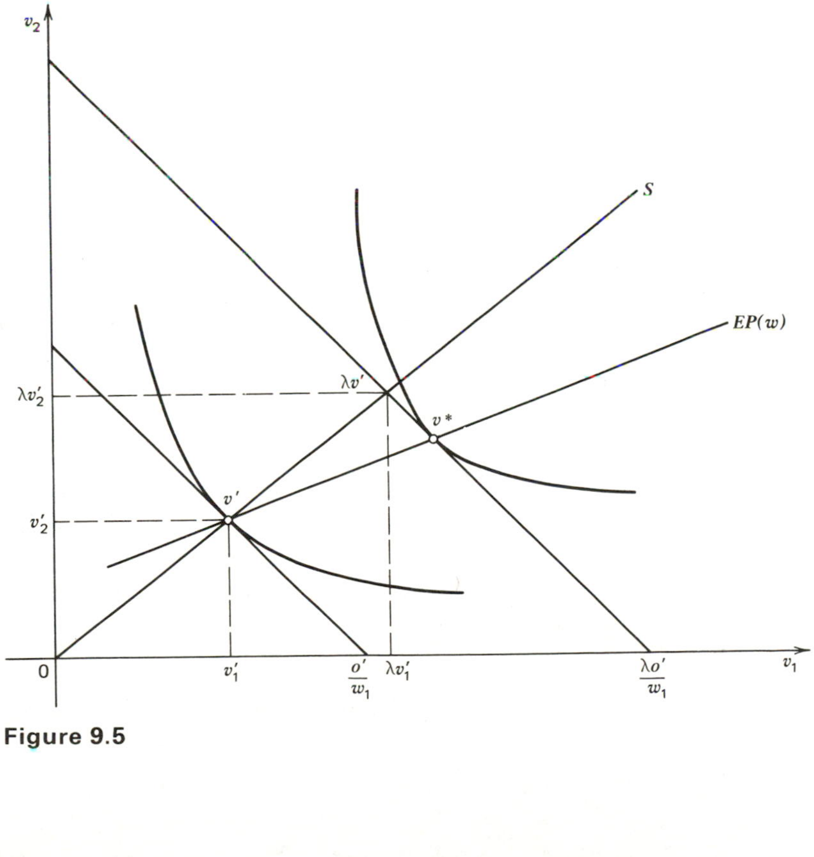

Figure 9.5

It is apparent that the class of production functions for which returns to scale and returns to outlay are identical is the class with expansion paths that are linear and intersect the origin. Production functions with this property are called *homothetic* (see exercise 8.9). An important subset of this class of production functions is the class of *homogeneous production functions*. It will be recalled (see section 4.2) that a (production) function f is homogeneous of degree κ if

$$f(\lambda v) = \lambda^{\kappa} f(v), \qquad \text{for all } \lambda > 0, \quad \text{for all } v. \tag{9.14}$$

Thus, if all input quantities are multiplied by a common (positive) factor λ, output is increased by the factor λ^{κ}. It is therefore apparent that if the production function is homogeneous, returns to scale are (everywhere) increasing, constant, or decreasing according to whether $\kappa > 1$, $\kappa = 1$, or $\kappa < 1$. Thus, a production function that is homogeneous of degree one is sometimes referred to as a "constant-returns-to-scale production function."

To see that returns to scale and returns to outlay are identical for a production technology characterized by a homogeneous production function, we must show that the expansion paths are all linear and intersect the origin for this class of functions. To see this, we first show that each partial derivative of a function that is homogeneous of degree κ is in turn homogeneous of degree $\kappa - 1$. Differentiate both sides of (9.14) with respect to v_i,[3]

$$\lambda \cdot \frac{\partial f(\lambda v_1, \ldots, \lambda v_m)}{\partial \lambda v_i} = \lambda^{\kappa} \cdot \frac{\partial f(v_1, \ldots, v_m)}{\partial v_i}, \tag{9.15}$$

and divide through by λ,

$$\frac{\partial f(\lambda v_1, \ldots, \lambda v_m)}{\partial \lambda v_i} = \lambda^{\kappa - 1} \cdot \frac{\partial f(v_1, \ldots, v_m)}{\partial v_i}. \tag{9.16}$$

To see that this property of marginal-product functions implies that the expansion path is a ray from the origin, recall that the expansion path (given a set of input prices) is the set of points satisfying equation (9.7). It suffices, therefore, for our purposes to show that if v satisfies (9.7), so does λv, for all $\lambda > 0$. But, as homogeneity of degree κ of the production function implies homogeneity of degree $\kappa - 1$ of the marginal-product function,

$$\frac{\partial f(\lambda v)/\partial v_i}{\partial f(\lambda v)/\partial v_j} = \frac{\lambda^{\kappa-1} \partial f(v)/\partial v_i}{\lambda^{\kappa-1} \partial f(v)/\partial v_j} = \frac{\partial f(v)/\partial v_i}{\partial f(v)/\partial v_j} = \frac{w_i}{w_j}, \qquad i = 1, \ldots, n, \quad j = 1, \ldots, n. \tag{9.17}$$

Thus, the expansion path is a ray from the origin, and returns to outlay are identical to returns to scale (see exercise 9.4c).

[3] Note that this is legitimate because (9.14) is an identity (i.e., it holds for all values of v).

9.5 PROFIT MAXIMIZATION AND THE COST FUNCTION

Profit Maximization

The output-constrained cost-minimization problem examined in section 9.2 determines the cheapest means of producing any given output, but it does not solve the profit-maximization problem; it remains to choose the profit-maximizing output. Using the cost function, which embodies the information on cost-minimizing input bundles, the profit-maximization problem can be written

$$\max_{q}(R(p, q) - C(q, w)) \tag{9.18}$$

where

$$R(p, q) = p \cdot q. \tag{9.19}$$

The first-order condition for this problem is

$$\frac{\partial R(p, q)}{\partial q} - \frac{\partial C(q, w)}{\partial q} = 0. \tag{9.20}$$

Taking the indicated derivatives and recalling the definition of marginal cost, we find that

$$p = MC(q, w). \tag{9.21}$$

The first-order condition for profit maximization thus requires that a level of output be chosen which equates the output price to the marginal cost of production. If this condition is not fulfilled, the profit of the producer can be increased by either reducing or increasing the level of output. For example, if

$$p > MC(q, w), \tag{9.22}$$

profits could be increased by raising the level of output, since the price of the output indicates the contribution to revenue of additional output while the marginal cost of production indicates the contribution to cost of increasing output.

The second-order condition for (9.18) is

$$\frac{\partial^2 R(p, q)}{\partial q^2} - \frac{\partial^2 C(q, w)}{\partial q^2} < 0 \tag{9.23}$$

or

$$\frac{\partial^2 C(q, w)}{\partial q^2} > 0. \tag{9.24}$$

The second-order condition for profit maximization thus requires that marginal cost increase with respect to output in the neighborhood of the profit-maximizing level of output.

Graphical Illustration

Figure 9.6 is a graphical illustration of the profit-maximizing output for the producer. The revenue curve is a straight line from the origin with a slope equal to the price of the output. The cost curve shown in figure 9.6 is similar to those discussed above with an initial range of increasing returns to outlay followed by a range of decreasing returns to outlay. The level of profit corresponding to any level of output is the dotted line which graphs the distance between the revenue and cost curves. The vertical distance between the two curves—profit—is greatest at output $\overset{*}{q}$ where the slopes of the revenue and cost curves are the same. Recalling that these slopes are equal to output price and marginal cost, respectively, we see that the graphical analysis confirms the first-order profit-maximization condition that price be equated to marginal cost.

The choice of the profit-maximizing output for the producer can also be illustrated by means of the average-cost and marginal-cost curves corresponding to the (total) cost curve in figure 9.6. The average-cost and marginal-cost curves are shown in figure 9.7. The price of output is illustrated by means of the horizontal line with intercept p. Note that the first-order condition for profit maximization (9.21) is satisfied at two levels of output, q' and $\overset{*}{q}$. However, only output $\overset{*}{q}$ fulfills the second-order condition for a *maximum* (increasing marginal cost); thus q' *minimizes* profit while $\overset{*}{q}$ maximizes profit.

The Supply Function

The effect that changes in the output price have upon the optimal level of output can be examined by allowing the horizontal line in figure 9.7 to shift. First note that, should the price of the output decline sufficiently so that the price line falls below the minimum point of the average-cost curve $\underline{AC}$, the producer would cease production; in this circumstance, there is no level of output at which the producer can cover the cost of production. The second point to consider is that the portion of the marginal-cost curve above the average-cost curve indicates the profit-maximizing output of the producer for any output price. That is, this portion of the marginal-cost curve is the *supply curve*.

Mathematically, for interior solutions (i.e., for values of the output price greater than or equal to $\underline{AC}$), the supply function is obtained by inverting the first-order condition (9.21) in q to obtain

$$q = s(p, w). \qquad (9.25)$$

The supply function of the producer derived from (9.21) is the same as that derived from the problem of optimal input demand in section 8.4. This follows from the duality between cost and production functions and the dual nature of the output-constrained outlay-minimization problem and the outlay-constrained output-maximization problem that was discussed earlier in this chapter. Note also that, as proved in section 7.5, the supply curve has a positive slope, implying that price and quantity supplied are necessarily directly related.

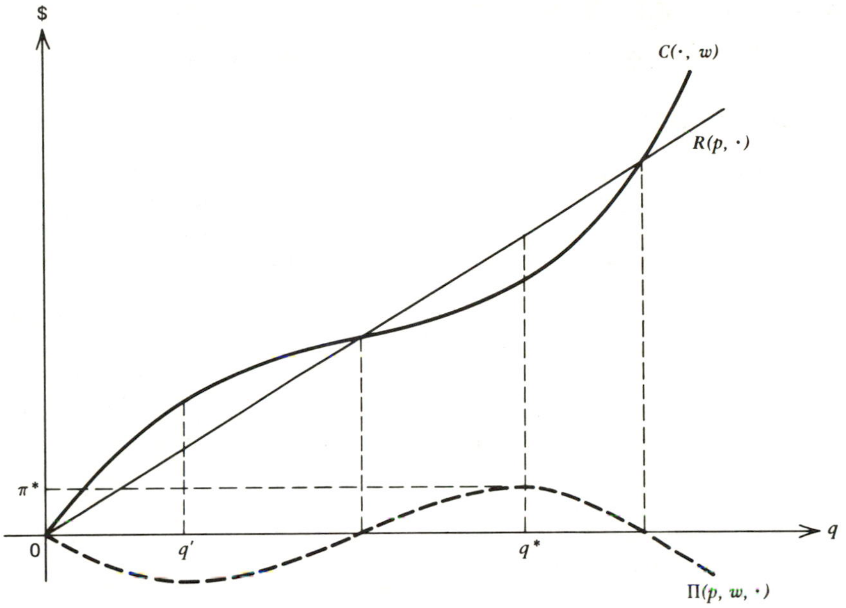

Figure 9.6

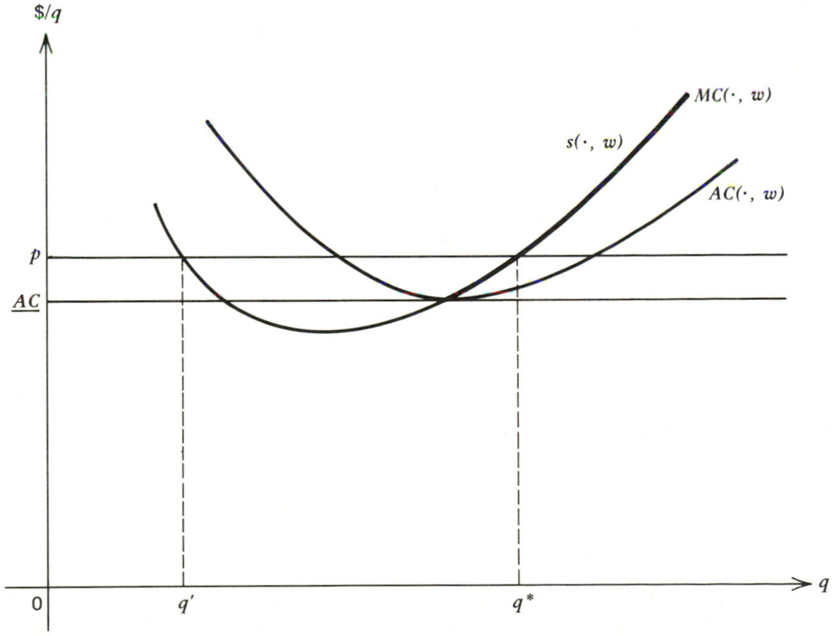

Figure 9.7

9.6 THE COST FUNCTION AND PROFIT MAXIMIZATION WITH FIXED INPUTS

Cost Function with Fixed Inputs

Because of contractual obligations or other business arrangements, it may be that not all inputs can be varied instantaneously. Hence, it may be that in the short run some inputs are fixed. In order to examine the nature of the cost function with fixed inputs, let us therefore assume that of the m input quantities, $v = [v_1, \ldots, v_m]$, the first m', denoted $v^v = [v_1, \ldots, v_{m'}]$ are variable and the remaining are fixed at some set of values, $\bar{v}^f = [\bar{v}_{m'+1}, \ldots, \bar{v}_m]$. Thus, we have the following relationship between output and the variable inputs:

$$q = f(v_1, \ldots, v_{m'}, \bar{v}_{m'+1}, \ldots, \bar{v}_m) = f(v^v, \bar{v}^f). \tag{9.26}$$

In this case, the cost function is generated by the following minimization problem:

$$\underset{v_1, \ldots, v_{m'}}{\text{Min}} \sum_{i=1}^{m'} w_i v_i \qquad \text{s.t. } q = f(v^v, \bar{v}^f). \tag{9.27}$$

As the last $m - m'$ inputs are fixed, the minimization takes place over only the first m' inputs. The optimal values of these variable inputs depend upon the specified output level, the set of input prices,[4] and the fixed levels of the last $m - m'$ inputs:

$$v_i = \bar{h}_i(q, w, \bar{v}^f). \tag{9.28}$$

The cost-function image, constrained by the existence of fixed inputs, can now be written as follows:

$$TC(q, w, \bar{v}^f) = \sum_{i=1}^{m'} w_i \bar{h}_i(q, w, \bar{v}^f) + \sum_{i=m'+1}^{m} w_i \bar{v}_i. \tag{9.29}$$

The cost function thus decomposes into two parts: outlay on variable inputs and outlay on fixed inputs. Only the first of these two components is a function of output. It is therefore instructive to rewrite the cost function as follows:

$$TC(q, w, \bar{v}^f) = VC(q, w, \bar{v}^f) + FC(w_{m'+1}, \ldots, w_m, \bar{v}^f), \tag{9.30}$$

where VC is referred to as the variable-cost function and FC is the fixed-cost function.

Average-Cost Curves

The relationship between the total-, variable-, and fixed-cost curves can be clarified by diagrammatic illustration. Suppose that, in Figure 9.8 the second input is fixed at $\bar{v}_2$. The producer is constrained to utilize the input combination

[4] Actually, the optimal level of the ith variable input does not depend upon the prices of the fixed inputs. However, as the above exposition remains formally correct and would be complicated by taking this fact into account, we choose to ignore it.

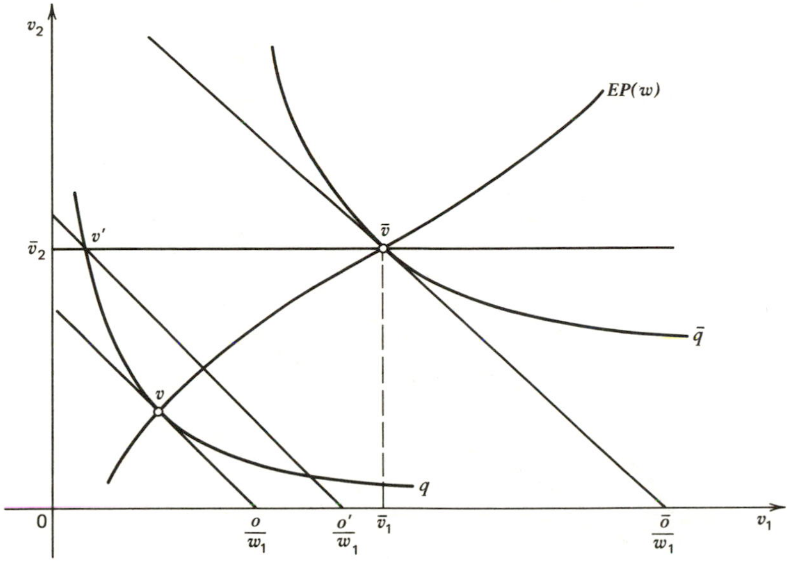

Figure 9.8

represented by the point of intersection of the relevant isoquant and the horizontal line with vertical intercept $\bar{v}_2$ (the constraint line). Note that for only one output, $\bar{q}$, does the unconstrained optimal input combination, $\bar{v}$, coincide with the input combination that must be used when the producer is constrained by $v_2 = \bar{v}_2$.

In order to derive the cost curves of a producer with one fixed and one variable input, note that each point on the horizontal constraint line has associated with it a level of output and outlay on the two inputs. These can be read from the isoquant and equal-outlay line that intersect the constraint line at any particular point. The cost of $\bar{v}_2$ units of input is the *fixed cost* of the producer; it cannot be avoided even by discontinuing production.[5] Since the fixed costs do not vary with output, they appear in the cost-output space in figure 9.9a as a horizontal line with intercept $w_2\bar{v}_2$:

$$FC(w_2, \bar{v}_2) = w_2\bar{v}_2. \tag{9.31}$$

The *variable-cost curve* is obtained by mapping the points on the horizontal line in figure 9.8 into the cost-output space (figure 9.9a). The properties of this variable-cost curve depend upon the relationship between the changes in outlay on the variable input and corresponding changes in output. In figure 9.9a the variable-cost curve is drawn assuming an initial stage of increasing returns to outlay on the variable input, followed by a stage of decreasing returns to

[5] This implies that the origin is not contained in the underlying technology set and thus complete inactivity is not possible. See section 7.2.

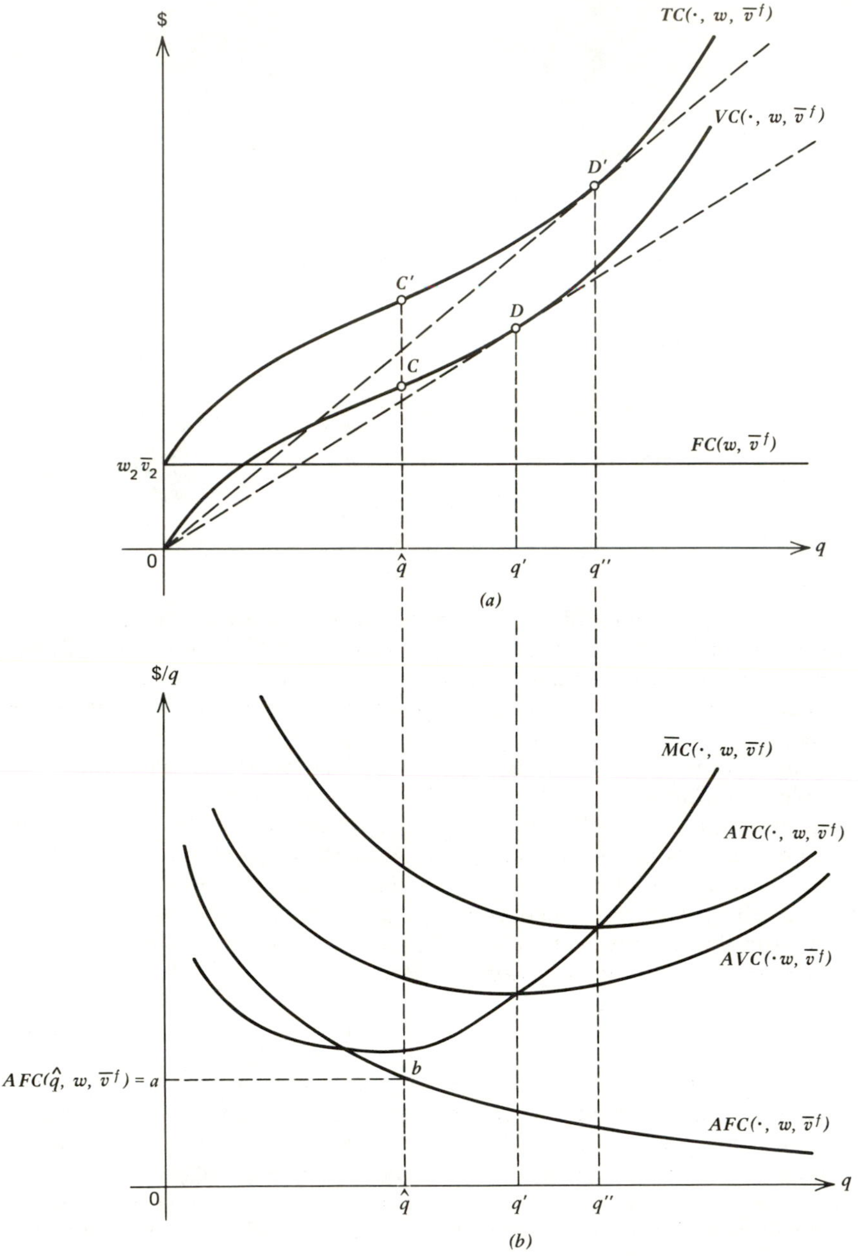
$
TC(·, w, v̄ᶠ)
VC(·, w, v̄ᶠ)
D′
C′
D
C
FC(w, v̄ᶠ)
w₂v̄₂
0
q̂
q′
q″
q
(a)
$/q
M̄C(·, w, v̄ᶠ)
ATC(·, w, v̄ᶠ)
AVC(·w, v̄ᶠ)
AFC(q̂, w, v̄ᶠ) = a
b
AFC(·, w, v̄ᶠ)
0
q̂
q′
q″
q
(b)

Figure 9.9

outlay. The particular shape of this cost curve depends upon the underlying technology set.

The (total-) cost curve exhibited in figure 9.9a is the sum of the fixed-cost and variable-cost curves. It can be mapped directly from figure 9.8 or calculated as the sum of the fixed-cost and variable-cost curves. Note that at all levels of output it has the same slope as the variable-cost curve, since adding a constant to a function does not change its slope.

Marginal- and average-cost functions in the presence of fixed inputs are defined analogously to the definitions in section 9.3. The marginal-cost function is defined by

$$\overline{MC}(q, w, \bar{v}^f) = \frac{\partial TC(q, w, \bar{v}^f)}{\partial q} = \frac{\partial VC(q, w, \bar{v}^f)}{\partial q}, \tag{9.32}$$

where the last equality follows from equation (9.30) and the fact that fixed cost is independent of q. If some inputs are fixed, there are three different average-cost concepts: average variable cost, average fixed cost, and average total cost. The respective functions are defined as follows:

$$AVC(q, w, \bar{v}^f) = \frac{VC(q, w, \bar{v}^f)}{q}, \tag{9.33}$$

$$AFC(q, w, \bar{v}^f) = \frac{FC(w, \bar{v}^f)}{q}, \tag{9.34}$$

and

$$ATC(q, w, \bar{v}^f) = \frac{TC(q, w, \bar{v}^f)}{q} = AVC(q, w, \bar{v}^f) + AFC(q, w, \bar{v}^f). \tag{9.35}$$

The marginal-cost and average-cost curves corresponding to the total-cost curve in figure 9.9a are shown in figure 9.9b. Two features of these curves should be noted. First, the marginal-cost curve intersects both the average-total-cost curve and the average-variable-cost curve at the output levels at which each is minimized. This property can easily be shown by setting the partial derivatives of $AVC(q, w, \bar{v}^f)$ and $ATC(q, w, \bar{v}^f)$ equal to zero.

Second, note that the average-fixed-cost curve is a rectangular hyperbola; i.e., the area of any rectangle such as $ab\hat{q}o$ in figure 9.9b equals fixed cost $FC(q, w, \bar{v}^f)$, which is, of course, independent of q (the area of $abqo = AFC(\hat{q}, w, \bar{v}^f) \cdot \hat{q} = FC(w, \bar{v}^f)$).

We now turn to an examination of the relationship between the cost curves with and without fixed input quantities. As previously noted, at only one level of output, $\bar{q}$, does the optimal input bundle for two variable inputs coincide with the input combination that must be employed with one fixed input. At all other levels of output, not only do the input combinations differ, but the cost of production with the fixed input is higher. This follows from the fact that the expansion path, $EP(w)$, in figure 9.8 is defined as the locus of optimal or least-cost combination of inputs for the production of any level of output, given the input prices.

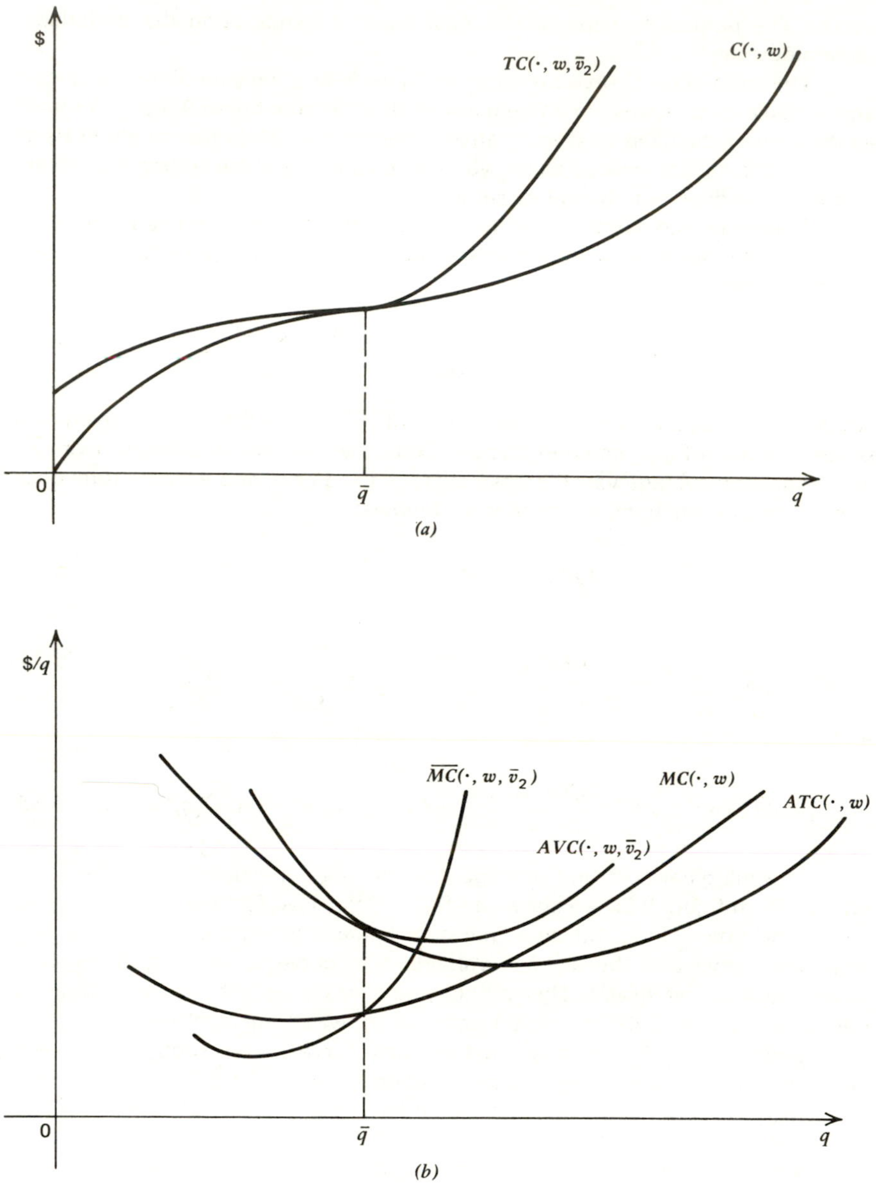

Figure 9.10

Figure 9.10a exhibits the cost curve with two variable inputs and the cost curve with one fixed and one variable input. At the level of output $\bar{q}$, corresponding to the input combination $\bar{v}$ in figure 9.8, the two cost curves are tangent. At all other levels of output the cost curve with a fixed input lies above the cost curve with both inputs variable. The two sets of average-cost and marginal-cost curves are shown in figure 9.10b. The marginal-cost curves corresponding to the constrained and unconstrained production technologies intersect at the level of output $\bar{q}$, since the corresponding total-cost curves are tangent at this level of output.

Of course, corresponding to any arbitrary level of the fixed input, there is a constrained total-cost curve that is tangent to the unconstrained cost curve at that output where the quantity of the fixed input is optimal (given input prices). Similarly, corresponding to any fixed input quantity is a constrained average-cost curve that is tangent to the average-cost curve corresponding to the unconstrained cost function. In other words, the unconstrained average-cost curve is the "envelope" of the family of constrained average-cost curves.

Profit Maximization with Fixed Inputs

The profit-maximization problem with fixed inputs is as follows:

$$\operatorname*{Max}_{q}(R(p, q) - TC(q, w, \bar{v}^f)). \tag{9.36}$$

The first-order condition for this problem is

$$\frac{\partial R(p, q)}{\partial q} - \frac{\partial TC(q, w, \bar{v}^f)}{\partial q} = 0. \tag{9.37}$$

Evaluation of the derivatives in (9.37) using (9.19) yields

$$p - \frac{\partial TC(q, w, \bar{v}^f)}{\partial q} = 0. \tag{9.38}$$

Substituting from (9.32), we have the following:

$$p = \overline{MC}(q, w, \bar{v}^f). \tag{9.39}$$

The second-order condition for (9.36) is

$$\frac{\partial^2 R(p, q)}{\partial q^2} - \frac{\partial^2 TC(q, w, \bar{v}^f)}{\partial q^2} < 0, \tag{9.40}$$

which implies

$$\frac{\partial^2 TC(q, w, \bar{v}^f)}{\partial q^2} > 0, \tag{9.41}$$

or, because of (9.32),

$$\frac{\partial \overline{MC}(q, w, \bar{v}^f)}{\partial q} > 0.$$

The second-order condition requires that marginal cost rise with respect to output in the neighborhood of the profit-maximizing level of output (see exercises 9.1b and 9.2).

Graphical Illustration of Profit Maximization with Fixed Inputs

We conclude this chapter by illustrating graphically the maximization of profit with fixed inputs and hence fixed costs. Illustrated in the top panel of figure 9.11 are the total-cost, variable-cost, and fixed-cost curves; and illustrated in the bottom panel are the corresponding marginal and average curves. Total revenue of the producer, $p \cdot q$, is represented in the top panel of figure 9.11 by a ray from the origin with slope equal to p. The profit of the producer is, as before, given by the vertical distance between this revenue line and the total-cost curve. The profit curve, thus constructed, is also drawn in the top panel of figure 9.11. Note that, in contrast to the case where there are no fixed inputs, at zero output the producer incurs losses (equal to fixed costs).

Profits are maximized at output $\overset{*}{q}$ where the slope of the total-cost curve is equal to the slope of the revenue line. This means, of course, that $MC(q, w, \bar{v}^f) = p$, as has already been shown above. Note that marginal cost and price are also equated at output $\bar{q}$ where profits are minimized (losses are maximized). Note also that maximal profits can also be obtained by finding that output where the vertical distance between the revenue line and the *variable*-cost curve is maximized. At this point the slopes of both curves are equal and the first-order conditions for profit maximization are satisfied.

The profit-maximization condition is also illustrated in the lower panel of figure 9.11. The market price in this diagram is reflected by the horizontal line intersecting the vertical axis at p. As profit maximization requires that price be equated to marginal cost, the indicated profit-maximization output is $\overset{*}{q}$. At price p and output $\overset{*}{q}$ the total revenue of the producer, $p \cdot \overset{*}{q}$, is equal to the area of the rectangle $opa\overset{*}{q}$. Total cost is equal to $\overset{*}{q} \cdot ATC(\overset{*}{q}, w, \bar{v}^f)$, which is represented by the area of the rectangle $ocb\overset{*}{q}$. It is clear, therefore, that total profit, $p \cdot \overset{*}{q} - \overset{*}{q} \cdot ATC(\overset{*}{q}, w, \bar{v}^f)$, is reflected by the area of the rectangle $cpab$. Total variable cost at output $\overset{*}{q}$ is given by the area of the rectangle $oed\overset{*}{q}$, and total fixed cost is given by the area of the rectangle $ogf\overset{*}{q}$ (see exercise 9.1).

The Supply Function with Fixed Inputs

If there are no fixed costs, the profit-maximizing producer discontinues operation whenever the price falls below minimal average cost, since maximal profits are then equal to zero. This principle does not hold in the case where there are fixed inputs. The reason, of course, is that the producer cannot earn zero profits by discontinuing operation since he must incur the fixed costs whether or not he produces any output. Consequently, when output is equal to zero, profit is equal to the negative of fixed costs. Thus, so long as the profit-maximizing producer can at least cover his variable costs by operating, he will not choose to discontinue operation when the price falls below total cost. Any excess of revenue over total variable costs can be used to finance part of the fixed costs.

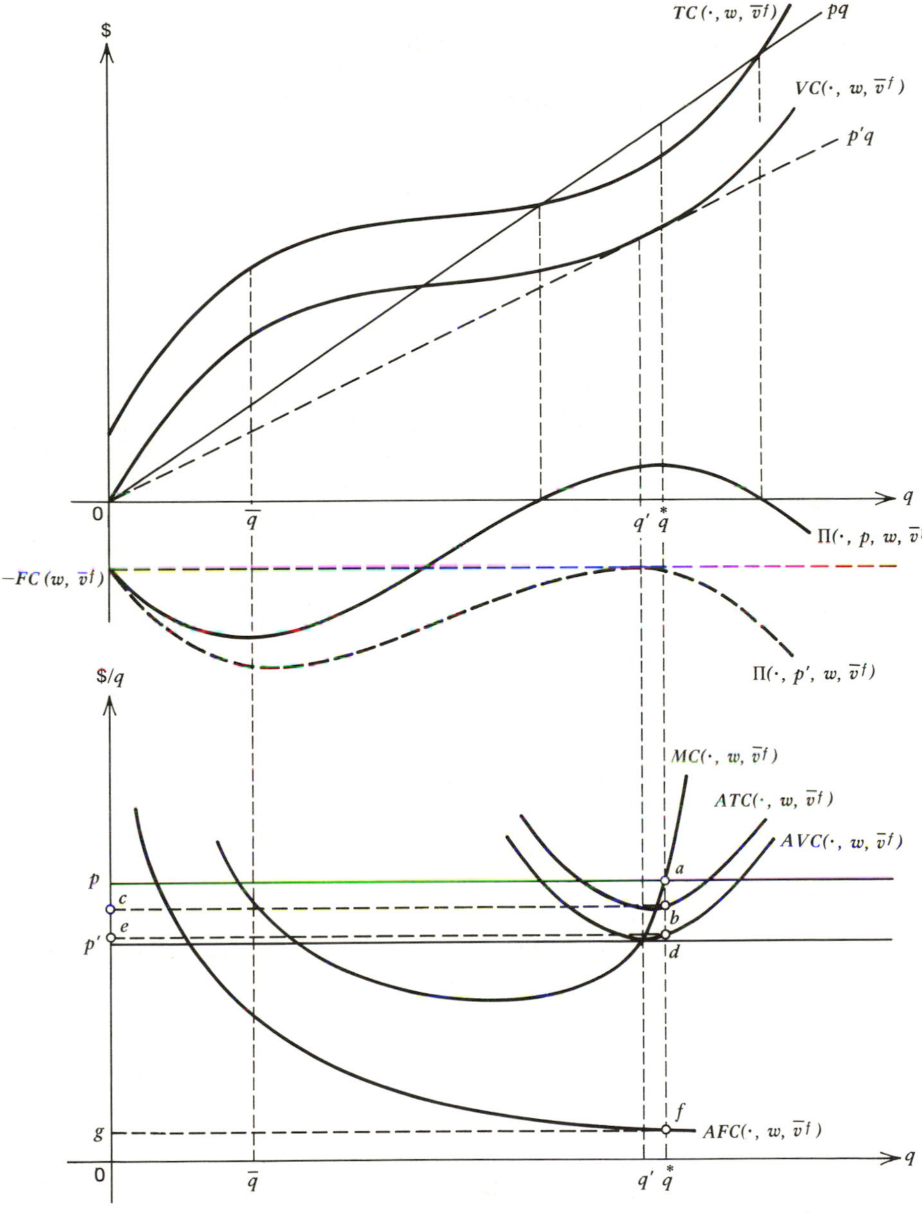

$
TC(·, w, v̄f)
pq
VC(·, w, v̄f)
p'q
q
0
q̄
q'
q*
Π(·, p, w, v̄f)
−FC(w, v̄f)
Π(·, p', w, v̄f)
$/q
MC(·, w, v̄f)
ATC(·, w, v̄f)
AVC(·, w, v̄f)
p
a
c
b
e
p'
d
f
g
AFC(·, w, v̄f)

Figure 9.11

Thus, so long as the price exceeds average variable cost, the producer will continue operation.

The critical price at which the producer is indifferent between continuing and discontinuing operation is therefore given by the minimum point of the average-variable-cost curve. This critical price is p' in figure 9.11. The dotted revenue line in the top panel has a slope equal to p'. At the price p' there are two maximal profit levels, at zero output and at output q'. In each case the producer incurs losses equal to fixed costs (i.e., the vertical distance between the total-cost curve and the variable-cost curve). If $p < p'$, losses are minimized by discontinuing operation.

The above analysis indicates that the supply curve of the profit-maximizing producer with fixed inputs is given by the marginal-cost curve truncated at the minimum point of the average-variable-cost curve. An implication of this characterization of the supply curve is that if there are no fixed costs, in which case the average-cost and average-variable-cost curves coincide, the supply curve of the producer is coincident with the marginal-cost curve truncated at the minimum point of the average-total-cost curve. Thus, the supply curve derived in section 9.5 under the assumption of no fixed costs is generated as a special case of the above characterization of the supply curve.

EXERCISES

9.1 The total cost schedule for a profit-maximizing producer is as follows:

Output:	0	1	2	3	4	5	6	7	8	9	10	11
Total Cost:	10	19	26	32	37	41	45	50	56	63	72	83

a. Calculate the following schedules:
  1. average total cost.
  2. total variable cost.
  3. average variable cost.
  4. average fixed cost.
  5. marginal cost.

b. Assuming that the price of the output is \$7, determine the level of output which will be produced.

9.2 Consider a producer facing the following cost functions: $MC(q, w) = 10 + q$ and $AVC(q, w) = 10 + 1/2q$.

a. Assuming that fixed costs are 5000 and that the output price is 100, find the maximum profit.

b. Would this producer continue to operate in the short run? In the long run?

9.3 A producer owns two plants. Both have constant marginal costs; however, the fixed cost and the marginal cost of one plant differ from those of the other. Will the producer ever operate both plants simultaneously?

9.4 Suppose that the production technology is described by the Cobb–Douglas production function defined in exercise 8.5 (equation (8.19)).

a. Show that the expansion path is a straight line.

b. Derive the cost function (assuming that $\alpha + \beta < 1$).

c. Derive the output-constrained input demand functions.
d. What constraints on the parameters result in returns to scale being equal to returns to outlay?

9.5 For the cost function derived in 9.4a,
a. derive the first-order conditions for profit maximization and
b. derive the supply curve.

CHAPTER 10*
LINEAR PRODUCTION TECHNOLOGIES, ACTIVITY ANALYSIS, AND LINEAR PROGRAMMING

10.1 INTRODUCTION

This chapter examines a particular class of production technologies that is characterized primarily by the assumption that each commodity can be produced by a finite number of "methods" (also called "processes" and "techniques") which require that the output and inputs be combined in fixed proportions. That is, output generated by any one of these techniques can be doubled only by doubling the quantity of every input. Because of this property, these techniques are called "linear processes" and the set of such processes constitutes a "linear production technology."

The class of linear production technologies is neither more nor less general than the class of neoclassical production technologies examined in chapters 8 and 9. Each includes technologies that the other excludes. The neoclassical model requires and exploits differentiability, which is ruled out by the assumptions of a linear production technology. On the other hand, linear production technologies require constant returns to scale, whereas the neoclassical model does not. The principal characteristic of the neoclassical technology is "smoothness," whereas the principal characteristic of the linear production technology is "linearity."

Of course, both the neoclassical and the linear production technologies are special cases of the convex technology set described in section 7.2. Each is based upon a simplification of the general technology set and each has achieved widespread application.

Employing linear production technologies, German and Austrian mathematical economists made important contributions to the theory of general equilibrium (see chapters 15–16). Abraham Wald's pioneering analysis of the existence of competitive equilibrium assumed that each commodity could only be produced with given proportional amounts of primary inputs—i.e., by a single linear process. John von Neumann generalized Wald's model of production to allow for the possibility of producing commodities with multiple linear processes (see the suggested reading following part IV). Finally, Nobel Laureate Wassily Leontief employed a linear production technology in his construction of the input-output model to be used in studies of complicated interindustry relationships. These studies document the wide applicability of linear production technologies.

Finally, the formulation of efficient computational algorithms—such as simplex techniques—for solving optimization problems with linear objective functions and constraints has greatly enhanced the applicability of linear production theory. These techniques, referred to as "linear programming," have been widely applied to the solution of allocation problems of individual economic units and economic systems.

The next two sections introduce the basic concepts and assumptions of a linear production technology. Section 10.2 develops axiomatically the general activity-analysis model, which is analogous to the general theory of production developed in section 7.2. Section 10.3 restricts this technology by requiring given commodities to be inputs or outputs in the production process. Section 10.4 discusses linear programming, while section 10.5 examines the dual structure of linear programming. Section 10.6 closes the chapter with a simple numerical example of an application of linear programming to a multiple-commodity production problem.

10.2 ACTIVITY ANALYSIS

Activities

The linear technology set—a special case of the technology set examined in section 7.2—can be built up from the notion of a production "activity" and a set of axioms regarding activities. Formally, an *activity* is simply a net production bundle $z = [z_1, \ldots, z_n]$. More fundamental is a *basic activity*, defined as a vector of n (real-valued) coefficients (constants) denoted $a = [a_1, \ldots, a_n]$. Thus, a_1 can be positive (a net output in the basic activity), zero (not involved in the basic activity), or negative (a net input in the basic activity). Figure 10.1 illustrates two basic activities in the two-commodity (food and labor) case discussed in section 7.2. Basic activity $\bar{a}$ is characterized by net output of food and net input of labor and a' is characterized by net output of labor and net input of food.

Axioms

Three axioms regarding activities and basic activities constitute the foundation of activity analysis.

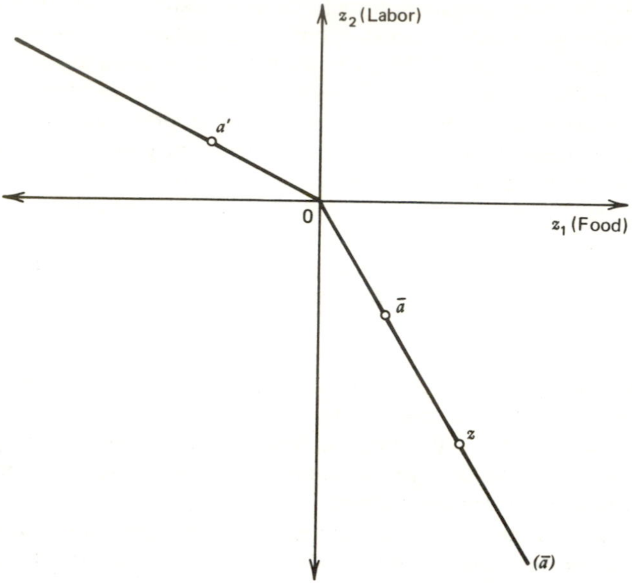

Figure 10.1

Assumption 10.1 (Basic Activities) There exists a finite number of basic activities. Each basic activity is characterized by a vector of real numbers representing the net output of each commodity.

The crux of this assumption is that the existing technology allows for only a finite number of methods of production.

The next two assumptions specify how the basic activities can be combined in order to derive additional production possibilities.

Assumption 10.2 (Homogeneity) If $a = (a_1, \ldots, a_n)$ is a basic activity, then the activity $\lambda a = (\lambda a_1, \ldots, \lambda a_n)$ is feasible for $\lambda \geq 0$.

Assumption 10.2 says that, if $\bar{a}$ in figure 10.1 is a basic activity, then all points on the halfline passing through $\bar{a}$ and ending in the origin (i.e., the ray through $\bar{a}$), denoted $(\bar{a})$, represent feasible net production bundles. Clearly, this assumption implies that if the net production bundle z in figure 10.1 is feasible, so are all bundles on the ray through z. The ray through a basic activity is called a *basic process*.

Assumption 10.3 (Additivity) Any number of feasible activities can be engaged in simultaneously and the joint net output of any commodity is the sum of the net outputs of that commodity from all the individual activities.

Assumption 10.3 allows for the joint operation of activities without any interaction between them. Two or more activities can be engaged in at the

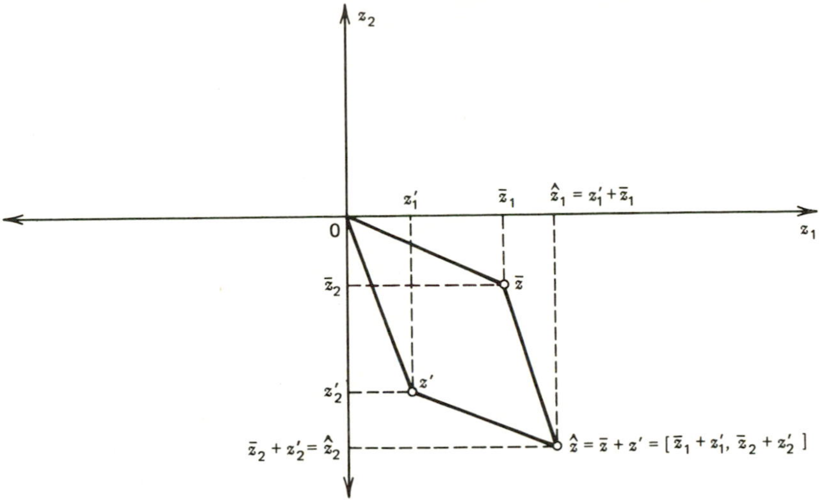

Figure 10.2

same time without any one affecting the outcome of the others. Figure 10.2 illustrates the implications of the additivity postulate. If z' and $\bar{z}$ are two feasible activities, then their vector sum, $\hat{z} = z' + \bar{z}$, also represents a feasible activity.

Linear Processes and the Technology Set

To characterize the technology set implied by assumptions 10.1–10.3, first note that setting $\lambda = 0$ in assumption 10.2 for all basic processes generates the zero vector as a feasible net production bundle—complete inactivity is feasible. Next note that assumption 10.2 is equivalent to constant returns to scale along any basic process ray (e.g., $(\bar{a})$ in figure 10.1). To see that this property holds everywhere, consider any feasible activity z. There must exist a set of basic activities $\{a^1, \ldots, a^k\}$ such that $z = \sum_{j=1}^{k} a^j$. By assumption 10.2 λa^j is feasible for all j so that, by assumption 10.3, $\lambda z = \sum_{j=1}^{k} \lambda a^j$ is feasible. Hence, if z is a feasible activity, so is λz for all $\lambda \geq 0$.

In figure 10.3, for example, the feasibility of $\hat{z}$ means that all activities on the ray through $\hat{z}$ are feasible. This ray is called a *feasible process*, or sometimes simply a *process*. Clearly, basic processes are special cases of feasible processes. The technology set is given by the set of all feasible processes. This set is a *cone* (a set Z is a cone if z in Z implies that all points on the ray through z belong to Z). Because of assumption 10.3, it is in fact a *convex cone* (any point on a straight line between two feasible activities, say $\bar{z}$ and $\hat{z}$, is feasible since it can be produced by combining the two activities, $\bar{z}$ and $\hat{z}$; or, more accurately, by combining the processes that produce $\bar{z}$ and $\hat{z}$). Finally, Z is a *convex polyhedral cone*—a cone with many "flat sides" (or "faces" or "facets") with edges given by basic processes that are not redundant (i.e., that cannot be generated by combining other basic processes).

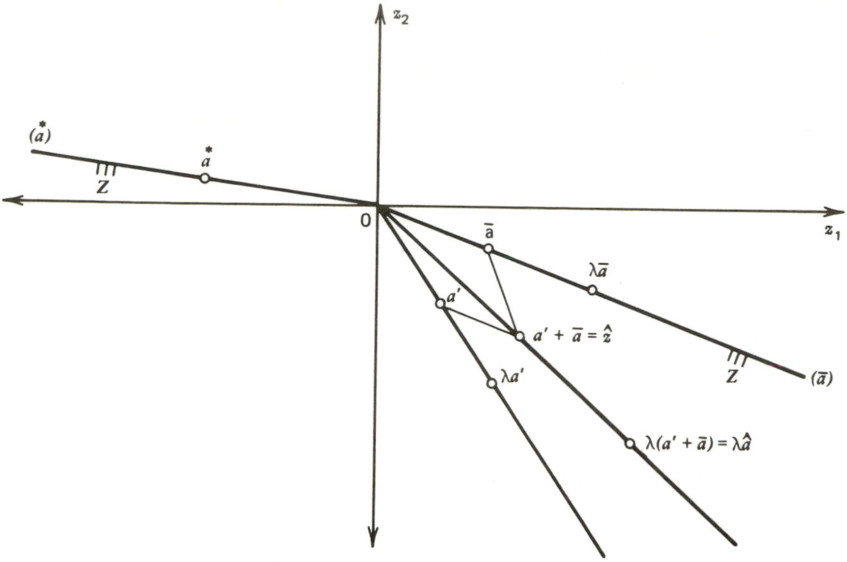

Figure 10.3

Of course, in two-space, redundant basic processes and nonbasic processes are technologically inefficient. In fact, as is apparent from figure 10.3, only two basic processes are efficient: viz., $(\overset{*}{a})$ and $(\bar{a})$. The technology set is the convex polyhedral cone with $(\overset{*}{a})$ and $(\bar{a})$ as boundaries.[1]

The activity-analysis model of production sketched in this section has been applied to the study of general equilibrium and welfare economics (part IV). For the purposes of this chapter on production theory, it is useful to restrict the linear technology set analogously to the restrictions imposed on the neoclassical production technology in chapter 8. We turn to this discussion in the next section.

10.3 LINEAR PRODUCTION PROCESSES WITH ONE OUTPUT

Isoquant Map for a Linear Production Technology

Consider the restricted linear production technology defined by $z_i \leq 0$, $i = 1, \ldots, n - 1 = m$, and $z_n \geq 0$, for all $z = [z_1, \ldots, z_n]$ in the technology set. That is, the technology allows for positive net output of one commodity, say the

[1] Note that the angle formed by $(\bar{a})$ and $(\overset{*}{a})$ should be acute; otherwise, $(\bar{a})$ and $(\overset{*}{a})$ could be combined to generate processes in the positive quadrant, thus allowing us to produce positive amounts of both commodities, violating the no-free-lunch restriction (see section 7.2).

nth, and the remaining $n - 1 = m$ commodities may only be used as inputs. As in chapter 8, let $v_i = -z_i$, $i = 1, \ldots, m$, and $q = z_n$.

Assumption 10.1 implies that the nth commodity can be produced by a finite number, say k, of basic processes, each defined by an activity $a^i = (a_{1i}, \ldots, a_{ni})$ that specifies the (nonnegative) amounts of all inputs, $a_{1i}, \ldots, a_{mi}$, required to produce a given quantity, a_{ni}, of output. Because of assumption 10.2, there is no loss in generality in normalizing the basic processes so that $a_{ni} = 1$, $i = 1, \ldots, k$. Thus, $(a_{1i}, \ldots, a_{mi})$ is the vector of input quantities required to produce one unit of output using the ith basic process. As $a_{ni} = 1$ for all i, no confusion should result if we let $(a_{1i}, \ldots, a_{mi})$ represent a basic process. Let λ_i, $i = 1, \ldots, k$, represent the output generated by process i—i.e., the "level at which the ith process is operated."

The linear production processes can be represented graphically if we let $m = 2$, thus restricting the technology to two inputs. In figure 10.4, the input quantities are graphed along the vertical and horizontal axes. Two processes, labeled 1 and 2, are also exhibited.

Also indicated in figure 10.4 are two levels of operation of the two processes, λ_1 and λ_2, each of which produces $\bar{q}$ units of output. Process 1 requires input bundle $\hat{v}$ and process 2 requires input bundle v' to produce $\bar{q}$. (Note that points in this space represent input bundles, not output or process-operation levels; hence, values of λ_1, λ_2, and q are entered parenthetically to remind the reader that the indicated point—input bundle—generates the indicated level of output or process operation.)

Output $\bar{q}$ can also be produced by combining the two processes. For example, operating the processes at levels $.5\lambda_1$ and $.5\lambda_2$ produces $.5\bar{q} + .5\bar{q} = \bar{q}$ units of output. The input requirement is $.5\hat{v} + .5v'$, a convex combination of $\hat{v}$ and v', which must therefore lie on the straight line joining $\hat{v}$ and v'. More generally, $\bar{q}$ can be produced by operating process 1 at level $\alpha\lambda_1$ and process 2

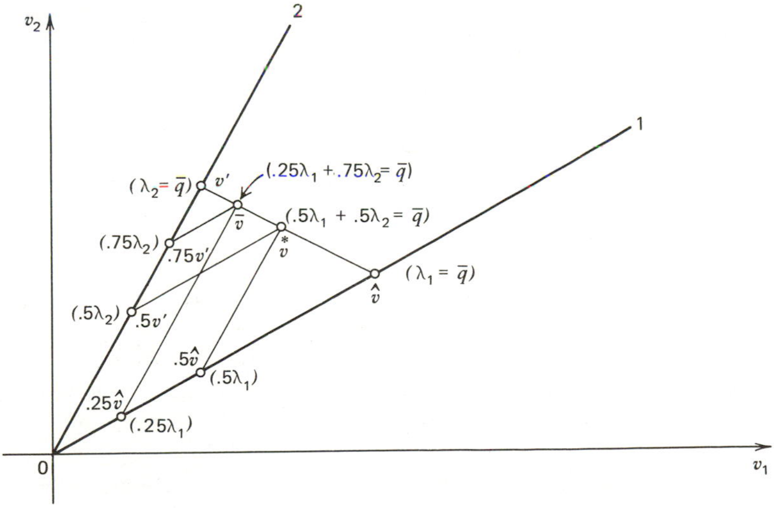

Figure 10.4

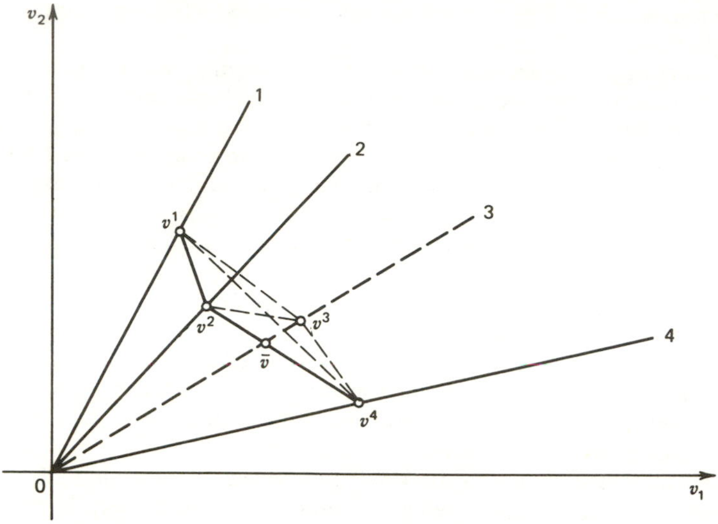

Figure 10.5

at level $(1-\alpha)\lambda_2$ where $0 \leq \alpha \leq 1$. The resultant input requirement is $\alpha\hat{v} + (1-\alpha)v'$. Thus, the set of input combinations that can produce $\bar{q}$ is represented by the set of points on the straight line connecting $\hat{v}$ and v'. If 1 and 2 are the only two basic processes, this straight line segment is the $\bar{q}$ isoquant.

Figure 10.5 illustrates a possible case of four basic processes, where it is supposed that the utilization of bundles v^1, v^2, v^3, and v^4 in the four respective processes produces a common output level, say $\bar{q}$. From the foregoing analysis, we know that input bundles represented by points on lines connecting any two of the above input bundles can also be used to produce $\bar{q}$.[2] For illustrative purposes, all of these line segments are drawn in figure 10.5. Note, however, that only two of the line segments (the solid ones) represent technologically efficient input bundles. All other line segments lie above these two and hence represent more of both inputs relative to some bundle represented by a point on one of the two solid line segments. Thus, the efficient activities in producing $\bar{q}$ use only basic processes 1, 2, or 4, or some combination of two of them. Because of the constant-returns-to-scale assumption (10.2), this is true for all output levels. Note, in particular, that process 3 in figure 10.5 is technologically inefficient. Combining processes 2 and 4, $\bar{q}$ can be produced with input bundle $\bar{v}$, which is strictly smaller than v^3 (both input quantities are lower). Thus, process 3 would never be used.

Figure 10.5 illustrates the fact that isoquants in two-space are composed of connected line segments and are convex (but not strictly convex) to the origin. In three-space, isoquants are composed of a set of "faces" or "facets" (flat

[2] Of course any input bundle represented by a point in the polygon with vertices $\{v^1, v^2, v^3, v^4\}$ can be used to produce $\bar{q}$ by combining perhaps more than two of the four processes.

surfaces). Each facet represents efficient input bundles used in the joint operation of the same production processes but differing in the level of operation of the processes. The substitution of inputs is achieved by varying the levels of operation of the processes.

The contrast between the isoquant maps in the neoclassical and linear theories of production underscores the difference between the two sets of assumptions. The isoquants of a neoclassical production technology are characterized by a continuously falling rate of technological substitution of input 1 for input 2 as v_1 is increased and v_2 decreased, holding output constant. The isoquants of a linear production technology, on the other hand, are characterized by constancy of the rate of technological substitution as v is moved along a facet and discontinuous changes in the rate of technological substitution as v moves from one facet to another.[3] Convexity of the isoquants means that the rate of technological substitution of input 1 for input 2 is nonincreasing everywhere and discontinuously decreasing at vertices as input 1 is substituted for input 2 along an isoquant.

Total-, Average-, and Marginal-Product Curves

Taking into account the discontinuity of the rate of technological substitution and the constant returns to scale, it is possible to carry out much of the analysis of chapter 8 with the linear production technology. Some of the parallel analyses are developed in the exercises at the end of this chapter, but it is perhaps instructive to close this section by drawing the total-, average-, and marginal-product curves generated by a linear production technology.

The top panel of figure 10.6 depicts four (efficient) basic processes utilizing two inputs. Fixing v_2 at, say, $\bar{v}_2$, we can construct a total-product curve for input 1. For values of v_1 between 0 and $\bar{v}_1$, only process 1 is used. Because of the constant-returns-to-scale assumption (10.2), output increases proportionately from 0 to $\bar{q}$ as v_1 increases from 0 to $\bar{v}_1$.

For values of v_1 between $\bar{v}_1$ and $\hat{v}_1$, processes 1 and 2 are combined in varying proportions (process 1 is gradually—linearly—phased out as v_1 increases). The isoquant segments between the rays 1 and 2 are parallel linear segments; this together with constant returns to scale implies that the total-product curve is linear over the interval $(\bar{v}_1, \hat{v}_1)$ with a slope less than that over the interval $(0, \bar{v}_1)$.

The easiest way to see this is by the use of geometry. Thus, in figure 10.7, are drawn two process rays, 1 and 2. We consider the increase in output as v_1 is increased from $\bar{v}_1$ to $\hat{v}_1$, holding v_2 fixed at $\bar{v}_2$. The outputs produced by $(\bar{v}_1, \bar{v}_2)$ and $(\hat{v}_1, \bar{v}_2)$ are denoted $\bar{q}$ and $\hat{q}$, respectively. Consider the parallel linear isoquant segments corresponding to $\bar{q}$, $(\bar{q} + \hat{q})/2$, and $\hat{q}$; by assumption 10.2 the intermediate isoquant segment is exactly half-way between the other

[3] Of course, at the points where facets are joined, the rate of technical substitution is undefined. Note also that, as the number of basic processes increases to infinity, the linear production technology approaches a constant-returns-to-scale neoclassical production technology, with continuous variation of the rate of technological substitution in the interior of the domain of the production function.

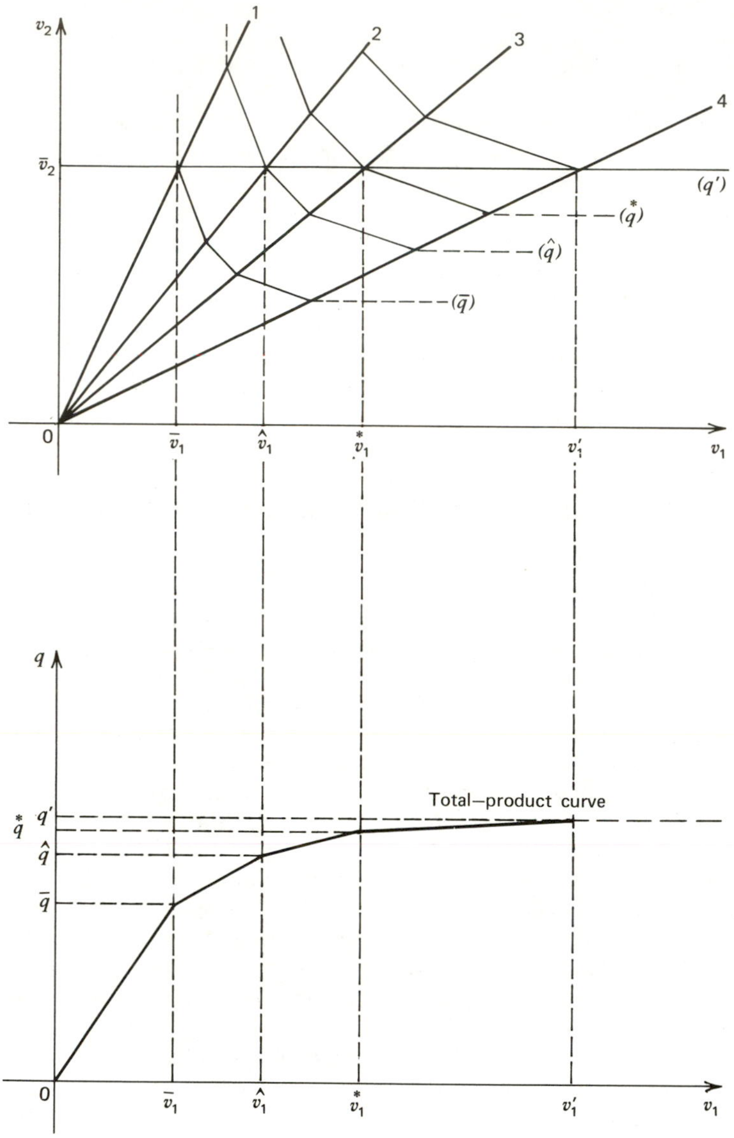

Figure 10.6

two, as depicted in figure 10.7. Consider the angle with vertex $(\bar{q})$ formed by the ray 1 and the horizontal line. The two arms of this angle are divided into equiproportional parts by the two parallel straight lines given by the $(\bar{q} + \hat{q})/2$-isoquant and the $\hat{q}$-isoquant. Hence the horizontal line segment $((\bar{q}), (\hat{q}))$ is divided into two equal parts and, therefore, the intersection of this horizontal line and the $(\hat{q} + \bar{q})/2$-isoquant corresponds to a value of $(\bar{v}_1 + \hat{v}_1)/2$ on the

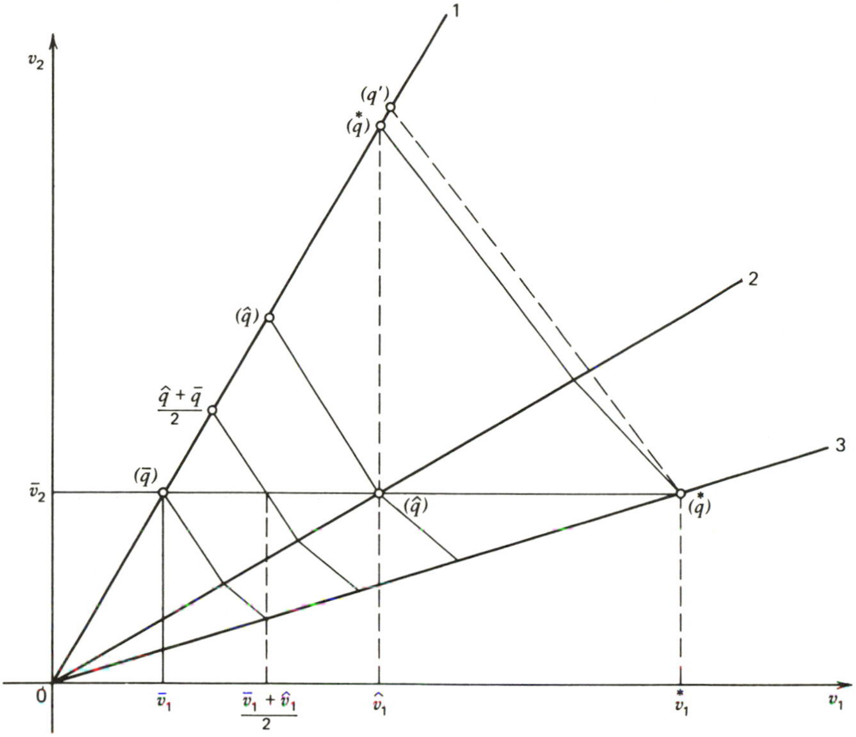

Figure 10.7

horizontal axis. Thus, $(\bar{v}_1 + \hat{v}_1)/2$ units of input 1 produces $(\bar{q} + \hat{q})/2$ units of output when $v_2 = \bar{v}_2$. This similarly holds for any proportional subdivision of the appropriate line segment so that, with $v_2 = \bar{v}_2$, $(\bar{v}_1 + \hat{v}_1)/\alpha$ produces $(\bar{q} + \hat{q})/\alpha$ for all α between zero and one. Thus output increases linearly with respect to increases in v_1 from $\bar{v}_1$ to $\hat{v}_1$.

To see that the (linear) rate of increase of q with respect to changes in v_1 is lower than the rate of increase over the interval $(0, \bar{v}_1)$, recall that over this latter interval output expands along the ray 1. If this expansion were extended as v_1 increases from $\bar{v}_1$ to $\hat{v}_1$, output would increase to $\overset{*}{q} > \hat{q}$, as indicated in figure 10.7. However, as v_2 is restricted to $\bar{v}_2$, output increases only to $\hat{q}$; thus, the rate of change of q with respect to changes in v_1 is smaller over the range $(\bar{v}_1, \hat{v}_1)$ than over the range $(0, \bar{v}_1)$. This fact is depicted in the lower panel of figure 10.6.

The total-product curve over the range $(\hat{v}_1, \overset{*}{v}_1)$ is another linear segment with a slope that is smaller than that of the linear segment over the range $(\bar{v}_1, \hat{v}_1)$. To see this, refer again to figure 10.7, in which the parallel linear isoquant segments between rays 2 and 3 have a smaller slope than those between rays 1 and 2. It is this fact which reduces the marginal product of input 1 as v_1 passes $\hat{v}_1$. Note that, if the isoquant segments between rays 2 and 3 had the same

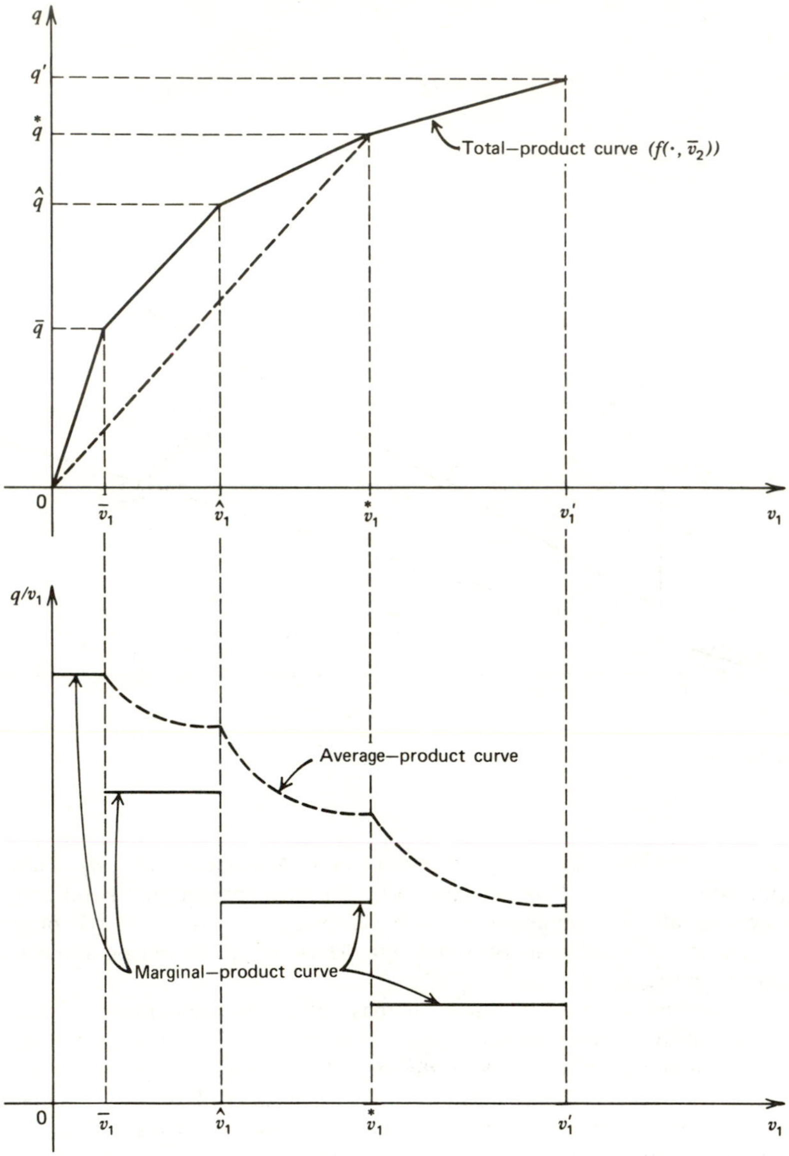

Figure 10.8

slope as those between rays 1 and 2, output at $(\overset{*}{v}_1, \bar{v}_2)$ would be equal to $q' > \overset{*}{q}$, as indicated by the dotted extension of the q' isoquant segment between rays 1 and 2.

To summarize, the total-product curve is a piecewise-linear curve with the number of linear segments equal to the number of (nonredundant) basic processes.

In figure 10.8, marginal- and average-product curves are derived from a total-product curve like that depicted in figure 10.6. (The method of derivation is described in detail in section 8.3.) The marginal-product curve is a set of four horizontal line segments with the discontinuities occurring at values of v_1 where a single process is used (inducing a kink in the total-product curve). The average-product curve is continuous and nonlinear with kinks at values of v_1 that generate discontinuities in the marginal-product curve.

10.4 LINEAR PROGRAMMING

Due to the development of an efficient class of computational algorithms—called the *simplex* technique[4]—to solve certain types of optimization problems employing linear production technologies, the production model described in the previous section has found widespread use in solving practical economic problems. The class of optimization problems is characterized loosely as the maximization of a linear function subject to a set of linear inequality constraints. A problem of this type is called a *linear programming problem* and the method of solution is called *linear programming.*

The function might be a sum of outputs from different processes weighted by their respective market prices and the inequality constraints might reflect the existence of fixed amounts of all inputs. Linear programming techniques have been applied to a wide variety of allocation problems including, for example, the determination of minimum-cost diets that satisfy certain nutrition constraints and the determination of least-cost transportation (routing) programs subject to vehicle-availability constraints (see the suggested readings following part II). Although we develop the theory of linear programming in the context of production theory, the more general applicability should be kept in mind.

The Linear Programming Problem

In order to set up a linear programming problem, we generalize the model of production presented in section 10.3 in one respect and particularize it in another. First, suppose that the different basic processes produce (possibly) different commodities which can be sold for different prices. Assume further that the m inputs are available in fixed quantities, say $\bar{v}_j$, $j = 1, \ldots, m$. The three basic assumptions (10.1–10.3) of section 10.2, which axiomatize the linear production technology, are retained. Thus, recalling that λ_i is the level of operation of the ith process—hence, the output of the ith commodity from that process—and that a_{ji} is the (nonnegative) quantity of input j required to operate process i at unit level, $a_{ji}\lambda_i$ is the (nonnegative) quantity of the jth input required to operate the ith process at level λ_i. The required quantity of input j to operate the k processes at levels $[\lambda_1, \ldots, \lambda_k]$ is therefore given by $\sum_{i=1}^{k} a_{ji}\lambda_i$.

[4] As this algorithm itself is not economics, we do not describe it in this book. The interested reader is referred to the suggested readings following part II.

The formal optimization problem—the linear programming problem—is as follows:

$$\max_{\lambda_1, \ldots, \lambda_k} \sum_{i=1}^{k} p_i \lambda_i = p_1\lambda_1 + p_2\lambda_2 + \cdots + p_k\lambda_k$$

$$\text{s.t. } \lambda_1 \geq 0, \ldots, \lambda_k \geq 0,$$

$$\sum_{i=1}^{k} a_{1i}\lambda_i = a_{11}\lambda_1 + a_{12}\lambda_2 + \cdots + a_{1k}\lambda_k \leq \bar{v}_1 \tag{10.1}$$

$$\vdots$$

$$\sum_{i=1}^{k} a_{mi}\lambda_i = a_{m1}\lambda_1 + a_{m2}\lambda_2 + \cdots + a_{mk}\lambda_k \leq \bar{v}_m.$$

The objective function in (10.1) is the total revenue from the operation of all k processes. The last m inequalities reflect the linear technology (embodied in the technological coefficients, a_{ji}, $i = 1, \ldots, k$, $j = 1, \ldots, m$) and the available resources. The solution to the linear programming problem requires the choice of nonnegative basic-process levels that maximize revenue while not exceeding in use the available amount of any input.

The linear programming problem can be illustrated graphically if we restrict our analysis to two inputs ($m = 2$). Given that the available amounts of the two inputs are $\bar{v}_1$ and $\bar{v}_2$, the feasible input combinations are defined by the rectangular set of points A in figure 10.9. Three basic linear production processes are also exhibited.

Iso-Revenue Curves

Since the different processes produce perhaps different commodities with different prices, the relevant technology cannot be represented by an "isoquant map." Rather, curves that indicate combinations of inputs that generate equal *revenue* are relevant to the graphical solution of the two-input revenue-maximization problem. To construct these curves—called *iso-revenue curves*—first note that since a_{ji} units of input j are required to produce one unit of output from the ith process, a_{ji}/p_i units are required to generate one dollar of revenue from process i. The unit iso-revenue curve (the combinations of inputs that generate one dollar of revenue) is therefore given by the piecewise linear curve connecting the points $(a_{11}/p_1, a_{21}/p_1)$, $(a_{12}/p_2, a_{22}/p_2)$, and $(a_{13}/p_3, a_{23}/p_3)$ on the three respective rays 1, 2, and 3 in figure 10.9. Because of constant returns to scale (e.g., α dollars of revenue from operating process i requires $\alpha a_{ji}/p_i$ units of input j), the complete map of iso-revenue curves is generated by radial projections of the unit iso-revenue curve.

The solution of the linear programming problem is characterized as choosing the input combination in A which attains the highest iso-revenue curve. This optimum is clearly obtained at input combination $\overset{*}{v}$ in figure 10.9. It is apparent that all of both inputs are used and only processes 1 and 2 are utilized at the optimum. It is also apparent that, if the quantity of input 2 were constrained to $\hat{v}_2$, only processes 2 and 3 would be utilized. Figure 10.10

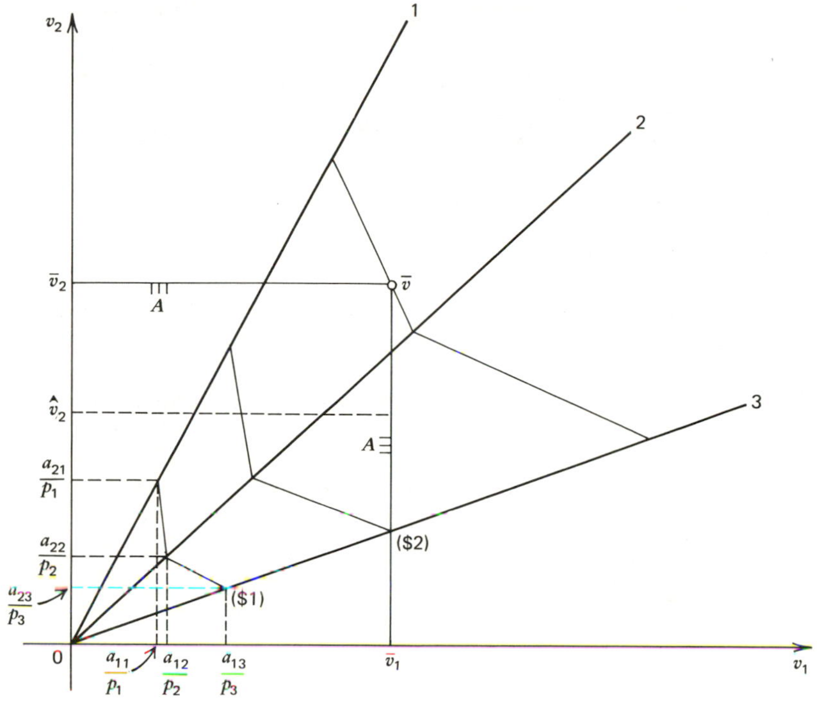

Figure 10.9

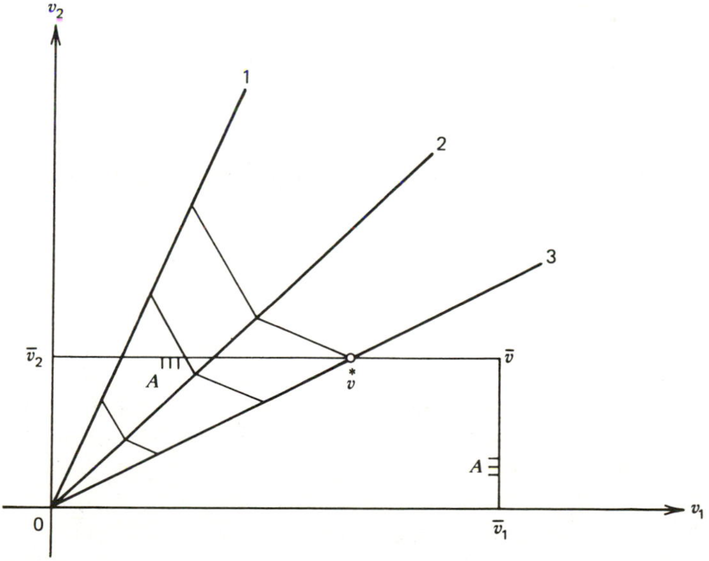

Figure 10.10

illustrates an alternative circumstance in which only one of the two inputs is fully utilized. In this case, only process 3 is employed.[5]

10.5 DUALITY AND LINEAR PROGRAMMING

The Dual Linear Program

The linear programming problem presented in the previous section assumed given amounts of the inputs utilized in the linear production processes. As it turns out, the theory of linear programming also has something to say about the purchase of additional amounts of the inputs. In particular, another linear programming problem, which is dual to the problem examined in section 10.4, can be used to calculate the value (in terms of revenue) to the producer of an additional unit of an input. This evaluation of a marginal unit is called a *shadow price*.

The linear programming *dual* to the *primal* problem of section 10.4 is as follows:

$$\underset{w_1,\ldots,w_m}{\text{Min}} \quad \sum_{j=1}^{m} w_j \bar{v}_j = w_1\bar{v}_1 + w_2\bar{v}_2 + \cdots + w_m\bar{v}_m$$

$$\text{s.t. } w_1 \geq 0, \ldots, w_m \geq 0$$

$$\sum_{j=1}^{m} a_{j1}w_j = a_{11}w_1 + a_{21}w_2 + \cdots + a_{m1}w_m \geq p_1 \tag{10.2}$$

$$\sum_{j=1}^{m} a_{jk}w_j = a_{1k}w_1 + a_{2k}w_2 + \cdots + a_{mk}w_m \geq p_k.$$

Conversely, corresponding to every minimization problem (10.2) is a dual maximization problem (10.1).

The dual problem has the following interpretations. The objective function is the *imputed value* of the stock of inputs, each evaluated at the appropriate *shadow price*, w_j. In the inequality constraints, $w_j a_{ji}$ is the imputed value of the quantity of the jth input required to operate the ith process at unit level. Thus, $\sum_{j=1}^{m} a_{ji} w_j$ is the imputed value of all inputs required to operate the ith process at unit level. The k inequality constraints therefore require that the imputed value of the inputs required to operate each process at unit level be no less than the revenue obtained from operating that process at unit level. Multiplying both sides of the ith constraint by the level of operation λ_i, we see that these constraints are equivalent to a nonpositive imputed-profit restriction; that is, no process can earn a positive imputed profit (revenue, $p_i\lambda_i$, minus imputed cost, $\lambda_i \sum_{j=1}^{m} a_{ji} w_j$). The dual linear-programming problem can thus be characterized

[5] There is a theorem in linear programming that states that a solution need never operate more processes than the number of scarce inputs. This theorem is reflected in the above illustrations.

as that of choosing the m shadow prices to minimize the imputed value of the inputs subject to the constraints that all shadow prices are positive and no process yield a positive profit (i.e., all revenues be imputed to the inputs).

Graphical Illustration of the Dual Problem

If we restrict the analysis to two imputs ($m = 2$), we can illustrate graphically the dual minimization problem. In figure 10.11, the horizontal and vertical axes plot the shadow prices of the two inputs, w_1 and w_2, respectively. Suppose that there are three basic processes. In order to represent the inequality constraints graphically, we first plot the equality parts of the three constraints:

$$a_{11}w_1 + a_{21}w_2 = p_1,$$

$$a_{12}w_1 + a_{22}w_2 = p_2,$$

$$a_{13}w_1 + a_{23}w_2 = p_3.$$

Solution of the first constraint for w_2 yields

$$w_2 = \frac{p_1}{a_{21}} - \frac{a_{11}}{a_{21}} w_1. \tag{10.3}$$

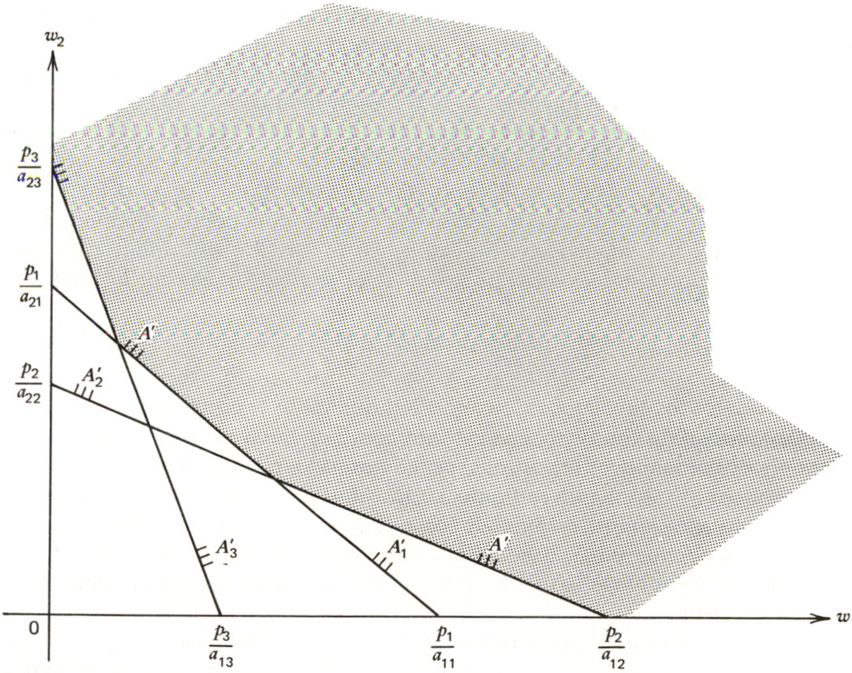

Figure 10.11

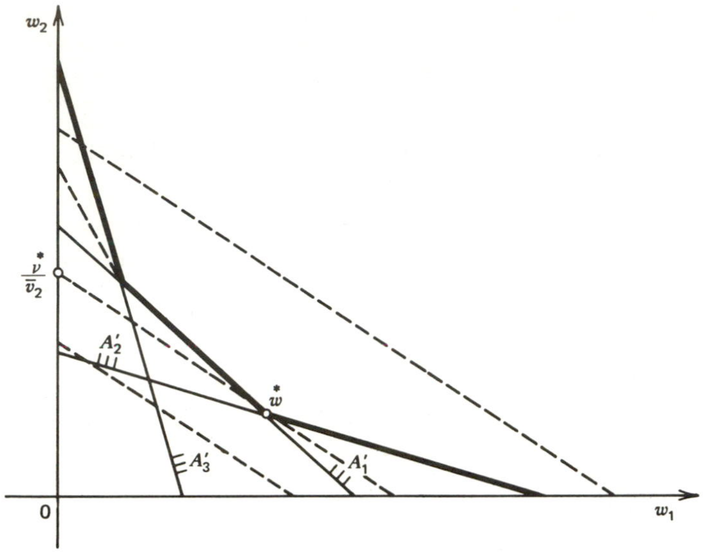

Figure 10.12

This constraint is represented in figure 10.11 by a straight line with a slope equal to $-a_{11}/a_{21}$ and vertical intercept of p_1/a_{21}. Solving for w_1 yields the horizontal intercept, p_1/a_{11}. In a similar manner, the second equality is illustrated in figure 10.11 with vertical intercept, p_2/a_{22}, and the third equality is represented by the straight line with vertical intercept p_3/a_{23}. Each inequality constraint is represented by the set of points on or above the respective straight line drawn in figure 10.11. For example, the set of points satisfying $a_{11}w_1 + a_{21}w_2 \geq p_1$ is given by the set A'_1. The sets A'_2 and A'_3 represent the other two inequality constraints. The set of points that satisfy *all three* constraints, denoted A', is represented by the shaded area in figure 10.11. In the two-input case, the objective function is represented by $v = w_1\bar{v}_1 + w_2\bar{v}_2$. Solving for w_2 yields

$$w_2 = \frac{v}{\bar{v}_2} - \frac{\bar{v}_1}{\bar{v}_2} w_1. \tag{10.4}$$

For each value of the imputation, v, this equality is represented in $w_1 - w_2$ space by a straight line with vertical intercept $v/\bar{v}_2$ and slope $-\bar{v}_1/\bar{v}_2$. A few members of the family of these lines, called equal-value lines, together with the constraint set A', are drawn in figure 10.12 (the equal-value lines are dotted). Each equal-value line represents all combinations of shadow prices that yield the same total value when used to evaluate the available amounts of the two inputs. Equal-value lines farther from the origin of course represent higher total imputation values.

The shadow-price combination that minimizes the cost of inputs while exhausting the profit from production is the point in the attainable set A' that is on the lowest equal-value line. In figure 10.12 this shadow-price vector is given by $\overset{*}{w}$. In this example, both inputs have positive shadow prices. An alternative combination of the available amounts of the two inputs can result in one input having a zero shadow price. Figure 10.13 represents a situation in which, as compared to figure 10.12, more of input 1 is available relative to the available amount of input 2. The solution to the minimization problem is $\overset{*}{w}$, with a zero shadow price for the relatively more abundant input 1.

The Fundamental Linear Programming Duality Theorem

A fundamental relationship between the primal and dual linear programs is summarized in the following proposition.

Fundamental Duality Theorem *If λ^* solves the primal problem* (10.1) *and $\overset{*}{w}$ solves the dual problem* (10.2),

$$\sum_{i=1}^{K} p_i \overset{*}{\lambda}_i = \sum_{j=1}^{m} \overset{*}{w}_j \bar{v}_j. \tag{10.5}$$

Thus, the optimal values of the primal and dual objective expressions are equal.[6]

A number of interesting implications can be extracted from this fundamental duality relationship. First note that, given the technology, the producer's revenue is a function of $\bar{v}$ and (because p affects $\overset{*}{w}$) of p:

$$R(p, \bar{v}) = \sum_{j=1}^{m} \overset{*}{w}_j \bar{v}_j.$$

Differentiation with respect to the jth input yields the value of the marginal product of this input (see section 8.4): $VMP_j(p, \bar{v}) = w_j$. Thus, the shadow price is equivalent to the value of the marginal product.

The foregoing interpretation of the shadow prices generated by the minimization problem suggests another dual relationship. Suppose that the jth constraint in the primal problem (10.1) is not binding; i.e., the jth constraint holds with strict inequality at the optimum:

$$\sum_{i=1}^{n} a_{ji} \overset{*}{\lambda}_i < \bar{v}_j.$$

This situation is illustrated for the two-imput case in figure 10.10 (where input 1 is redundant). In this case, the jth input is not fully utilized at the optimum and an increase in $\bar{v}_j$ would therefore have no effect on maximal revenue. Hence $VMP_j(p, \bar{v}) = \overset{*}{w}_j = 0$. If the jth constraint in the primal problem (10.1) is nonbinding, the jth shadow price is zero. Thus, figure 10.13 is the dual of figure 10.10.

[6] See Gale [1960, Chapter 3] for proof of this proposition. Assumptions 10.1–10.3 do not assure the existence of a solution to the optimization problems. A sufficient, but not necessary, condition for a solution to exist is that each a_{ij} be positive.

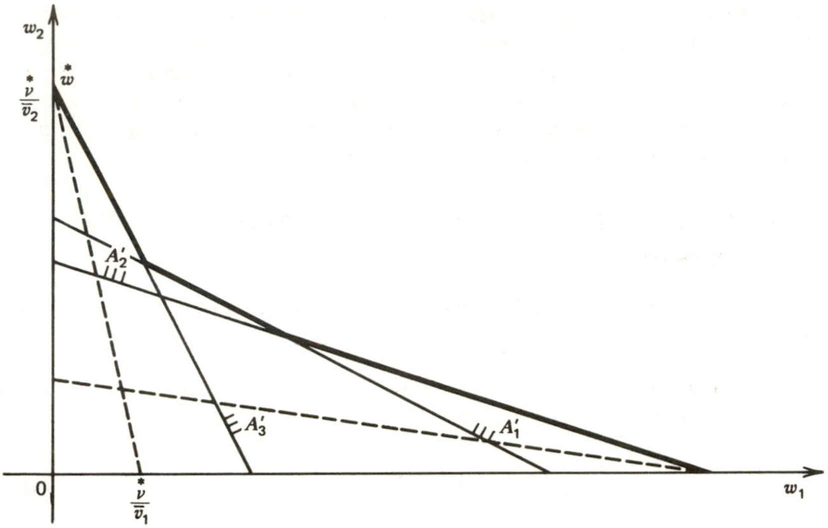

Figure 10.13

Suppose now that the ith constraint in the dual problem (10.2) is nonbinding:

$$\sum_{j=1}^{m} a_{ji} w_j > p_i .$$

Then the imputed "payments" to inputs used in the ith process exceed the revenue generated by that process. This imputed loss cannot be compensated for by positive imputed profit generated by other processes because all processes are constrained to nonpositive imputed profit. The dual relationship (10.3) thus requires that $\overset{*}{\lambda}_i = 0$. Thus, if the ith constraint in the dual problem (10.2) is nonbinding, the ith process is not utilized.

For example, in figure 10.12, it can be seen that the third constraint is not binding since relaxing this constraint by decreasing p_3 and hence shifting the boundary of A_3' downward would have no effect on the optimal w. On the other hand, decreasing p_1 or p_2 and hence shifting the boundary of A_1' or A_2' downward would change $\overset{*}{w}$. Thus, figure 10.12 corresponds to the dual figure 10.9, where only processes 1 and 2 are employed. Similarly, in figure 10.13, the third constraint is the only binding constraint; hence this situation corresponds to that in figure 10.10, where only process 3 is used.

To summarize, if a constraint in the maximization or minimization problem satisfies the strict inequality at the optimum, then the optimal value of the corresponding dual variable is zero. It should be noted that the converse is not true; a zero optimal value of a choice variable does not imply a corresponding strict inequality in the dual. The reason for this fact is illustrated in figures 10.14 and 10.15, which represent two anomalous situations referred to as *degenerate solutions*. In the top panel of figure 10.14, both inputs are fully utilized at the

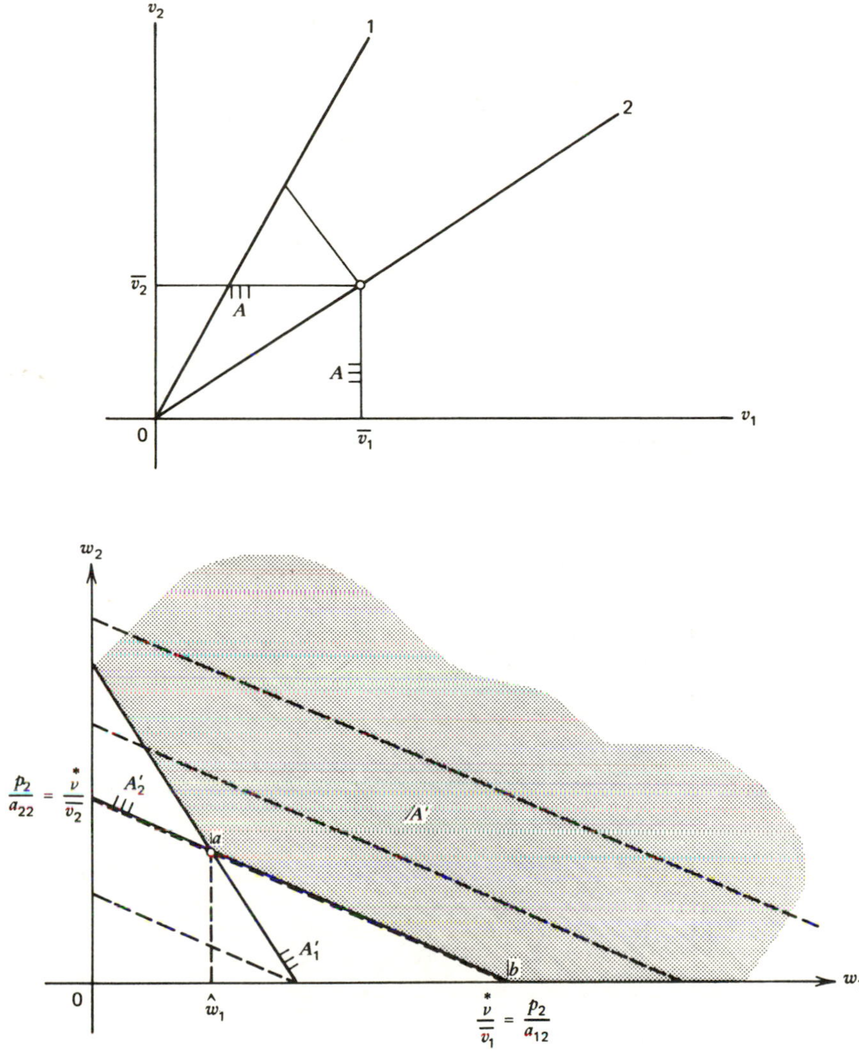

Figure 10.14

optimum $\bar{v}$ but only process 2 is used. In this case, $\overset{*}{\lambda}_2 = a_{12}\bar{v}_1$ and $\overset{*}{\lambda}_2 = a_{22}\bar{v}_2$ so that $a_{12}/a_{22} = \bar{v}_1/\bar{v}_2$. But, referring back to equations (10.3) and (10.4), we see that the slopes of the boundary of A_2' and of the equal-value lines are equal, as depicted in the bottom panel of figure 10.14. In this case every point on the line segment *ab* solves the dual minimization problem. This includes the possibility of $\overset{*}{w}_1 = 0$ even though the first constraint in the dual is satisfied with an equality rather than an inequality. The reason for the indeterminacy in the dual minimization problem is apparent. Increasing $\bar{v}_1$ would not increase revenue but decreasing $\bar{v}_1$ would decrease revenue. Hence the value of the marginal

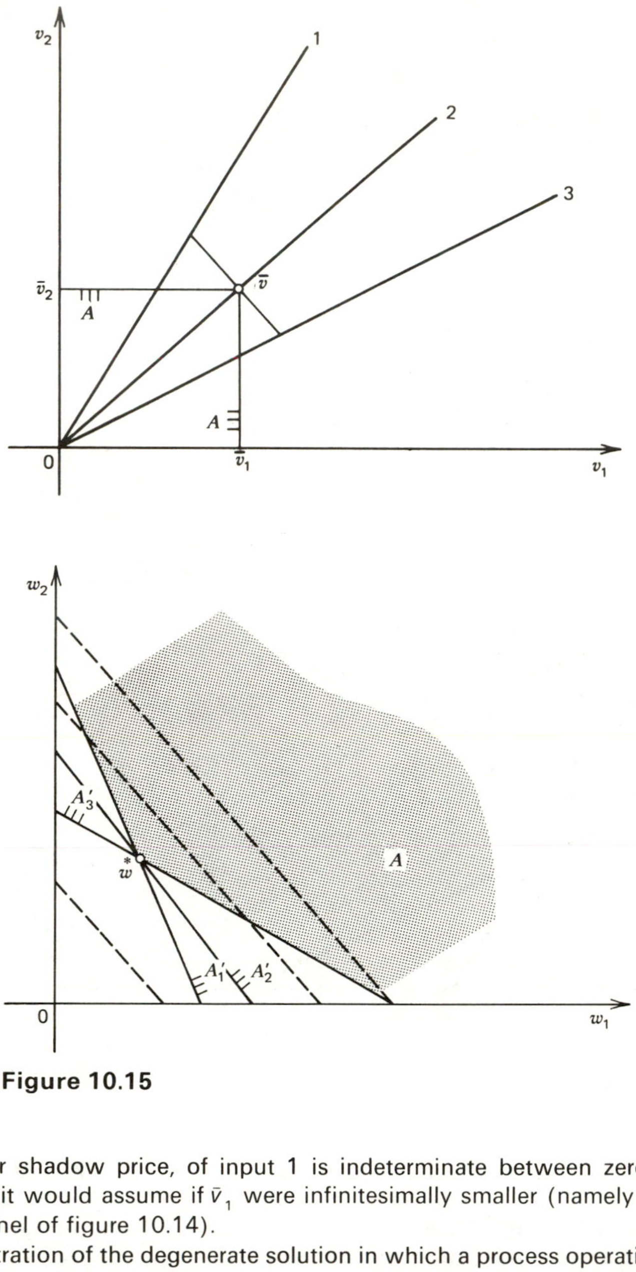

Figure 10.15

product, or shadow price, of input 1 is indeterminate between zero and the value that it would assume if $\bar{v}_1$ were infinitesimally smaller (namely $\hat{w}_1$ in the bottom panel of figure 10.14).

Illustration of the degenerate solution in which a process operation level is zero even though the corresponding constraint is satisfied as an equality requires the inclusion of a redundant process—process 2 in figure 10.15. In addition, the ratio of available input quantities $\bar{v}_1/\bar{v}_2$ is just equal to the slope of ray 2, a_{12}/a_{22}. The solution to the primal revenue-maximization problem employs either process 2 only or an appropriate combination of processes 1 and 3. Thus, it is possible to have $\overset{*}{\lambda}_2 = 0$ even though the second constraint in the dual is satisfied as an equality.

The dual linear-programming relationships described in this section undoubtedly appear at first to be quite complicated. The best way to become comfortable with these notions is by working large numbers of exercises whose solutions require that these dual relations be exploited. To facilitate this task, we close this chapter with a simple numerical example and provide a number of exercises at the end of the chapter.

10.6 AN EXAMPLE OF A LINEAR PROGRAMMING PROBLEM

Consider a technology in which four commodities can be produced by four basic processes, each of which utilizes two inputs as given by the following array of coefficients:

INPUTS	PROCESSES			
	1	2	3	4
1	.25	3.00	.75	5.00
2	1.00	3.00	1.50	4.00
Prices:	1	4	2	8

Thus, process 1 requires .25 units of input 1 and 1 unit of input 2 to produce one unit of output which sells for \$1, etc.

The primal problem is to find nonnegative numbers, $\lambda_1, \ldots, \lambda_4$, that maximize

$$\sum_{i=1}^{4} p_i \lambda_i = 1\lambda_1 + 4\lambda_2 + 2\lambda_3 + 8\lambda_4 \tag{10.6}$$

subject to the inequality constraints,

$$\begin{aligned} .25\lambda_1 + 3.00\lambda_2 + .75\lambda_3 + 5.00\lambda_4 &\leq \bar{v}_1 \\ 1.00\lambda_1 + 3.00\lambda_2 + 1.50\lambda_3 + 4.00\lambda_4 &\leq \bar{v}_2. \end{aligned} \tag{10.7}$$

The dual problem is to find nonnegative numbers, w_1 and w_2, that minimize

$$\sum_{j=1}^{2} w_j \bar{v}_j = w_1 \bar{v}_1 + w_2 \bar{v}_2, \tag{10.6$'$}$$

subject to the inequality constraints,

$$\begin{aligned} .25w_1 + 1.00w_2 &\geq 1 \\ 3.00w_1 + 3.00w_2 &\geq 4 \\ .75w_1 + 1.50w_2 &\geq 2 \\ 5.00w_1 + 4.00w_2 &\geq 8. \end{aligned} \tag{10.7)'$$

The Solution

In order to construct the linear-programming iso-revenue curves, standardize the production coefficients by multiplying each technology coefficient and each price by $p_2/p_i = 4/p_i$:

INPUTS	PROCESSES			
	1	2	3	4
1	1	3	1.5	2.5
2	4	3	3	2
Normalized Prices	4	4	4	4

Figure 10.16 exhibits the standardized coefficents (each indicated point yields \$4 in revenue). Clearly, commodity 2 would never be produced since an

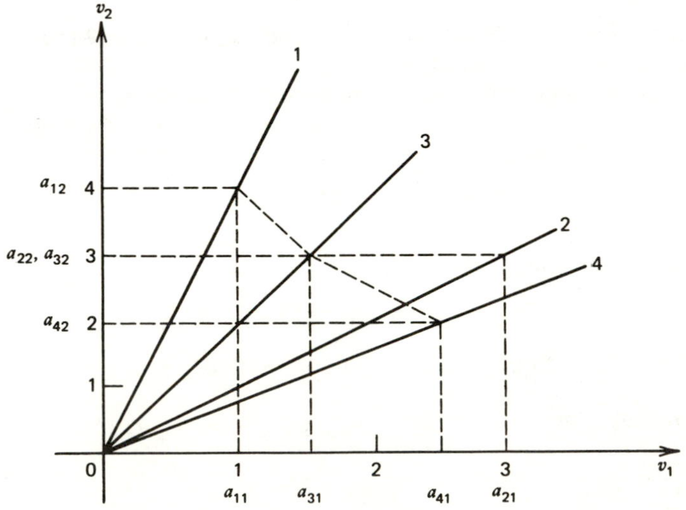

Figure 10.16

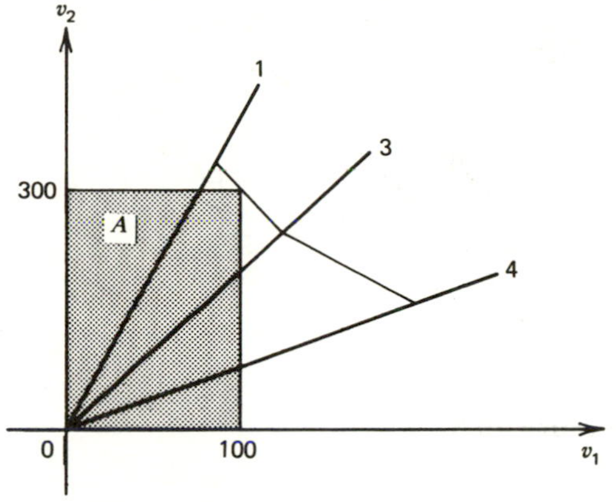

Figure 10.17

appropriate combination of process 3 and 4 generates the same revenue with less of both inputs. Hence, process 2 can be eliminated from consideration.

Given the amounts of the two inputs, $\bar{v}_1$ and $\bar{v}_2$, available for production, the linear programming problem is easily solved by drawing the feasible region and choosing that combination of processes that attains the highest iso-revenue curve. For example, if $\bar{v}_2 = 300$ and $\bar{v}_1 = 100$, the solution is to use a combination of processes 1 and 3, as indicated in figure 10.17. As both inputs are fully utilized, the two constraints (10.7) are satisfied as equalities. Hence, the optimal production of the two commodities (1 and 3) can be determined by setting $\overset{*}{\lambda}_2 = \overset{*}{\lambda}_4 = 0$ and solving the equalities:

$$.25\lambda_1 + .75\lambda_3 = 100$$

$$1.00\lambda_1 + 1.50\lambda_3 = 300.$$

The solutions are $\overset{*}{\lambda}_1 = 200.1$ and $\overset{*}{\lambda}_3 = 66.6$.

As $\overset{*}{\lambda}_1$ and $\overset{*}{\lambda}_3$ are both positive, the first and third constraints in the dual (10.7)′ are satisfied as equalities:

$$.25\overset{*}{w}_1 + 1.00\overset{*}{w}_2 = 1$$

$$.75\overset{*}{w}_1 + 1.50\overset{*}{w}_2 = 2.$$

Solution of these two equalities yields $\overset{*}{w}_1 = 1.333$ and $\overset{*}{w}_2 = .667$.

Evaluating the objective functions for the primal and dual by substituting in $\overset{*}{\lambda}_1$, $\overset{*}{\lambda}_2$, $\overset{*}{w}_1$, and $\overset{*}{w}_2$, we obtain

$$\sum_{i=1}^{4} p_i \overset{*}{\lambda}_i = 1(200.1) + 2(66.6) = 333.3$$

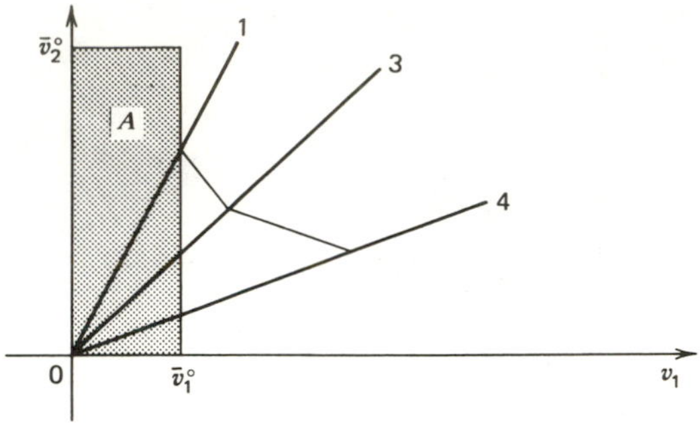

Figure 10.18

and

$$\sum_{j=1}^{2} \overset{*}{w}_j v_j = 1.333(100) + .667(300) = 333.3.$$

Hence,

$$\sum_i p_i \overset{*}{\lambda}_i = \sum_j \overset{*}{w}_j v_j,$$

as required by the fundamental duality theorem.

Should the feasible region be such that only one commodity is produced and only one input is fully utilized (see figure 10.18), the optimal production level is determined from the one binding constraint with all activity levels but one set equal to zero.

Derivation of the Total-Revenue and Value-of-Marginal-Product Curves

Let us now derive the total-revenue curve and the value-of-marginal-product curves from the above model. Assume that a fixed amount of input 2 is available, say 200 units, and that input 1 is the variable input. This situation is depicted in figure 10.19.

For $v_1 \leq 50$, only process 1 is utilized; hence, $\overset{*}{\lambda}_2 = \overset{*}{\lambda}_3 = \overset{*}{\lambda}_4 = 0$. As input 1 is fully utilized, the first constraint in (10.7) is an equality; hence, $.25\overset{*}{\lambda}_1 = v_1$ or $\overset{*}{\lambda}_1 = v_1/.25$. Hence total revenue over this range of v_1 is $p_1 v_1/.25 = v_1/.25$. The value of the marginal product of input 1 for $v_1 < 50$ is therefore $1/.25 = 4$. This value could be obtained alternatively by noting that, since $\overset{*}{\lambda}_1 > 0$, the first constraint in (10.7)′ is an equality. Moreover, since input 2 is redundant for $v_1 < 50$, $\overset{*}{w}_2 = 0$ and, hence, the first constraint in (10.7)′ is $.25\overset{*}{w}_1 = 1$.

When $v_1 = 100$, only process 3 is used and both inputs are fully utilized; hence, the constraints (10.7) are equalities with $\overset{*}{\lambda}_1 = \overset{*}{\lambda}_2 = \overset{*}{\lambda}_4 = 0$: $.75\overset{*}{\lambda}_3 = 100$

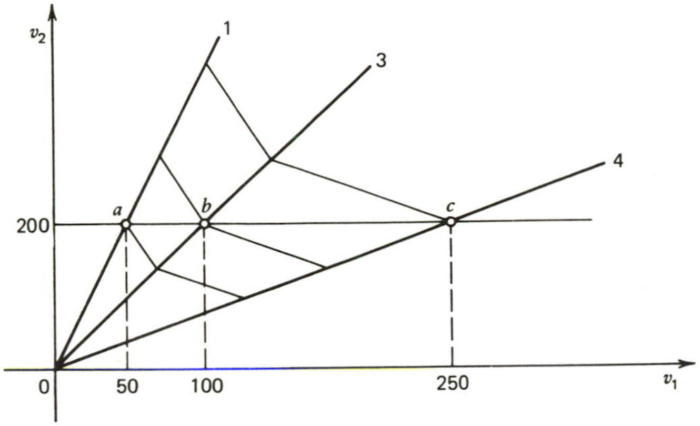

Figure 10.19

and $1.50\overset{*}{\lambda}_3 = 200$. Thus, $\overset{*}{\lambda}_3 = 133.3$ and revenue is $p_3(133.3) = 2(133.3) = 266.6$. The total-revenue curve for $50 \leq v_1 \leq 100$ is therefore a straight line segment connecting 200 to 266.6.

To compute the value of the marginal product over this range of v_1, we note that, since processes 1 and 3 are the only ones that are used, the first and third constraints in the dual are satisfied as equalities. Thus, $.25\overset{*}{w}_1 + 1\overset{*}{w}_2 = 1$ and $.75\overset{*}{w}_1 + 1.5\overset{*}{w}_2 = 2$. The solution values are $\overset{*}{w}_1 = 1.333$ and $\overset{*}{w}_2 = .667$.

The calculations for $v_1 > 100$ are quite analogous to the above and are therefore not repeated. The resultant total-revenue and value-of-marginal-product curves are plotted in figures 10.20 and 10.21.

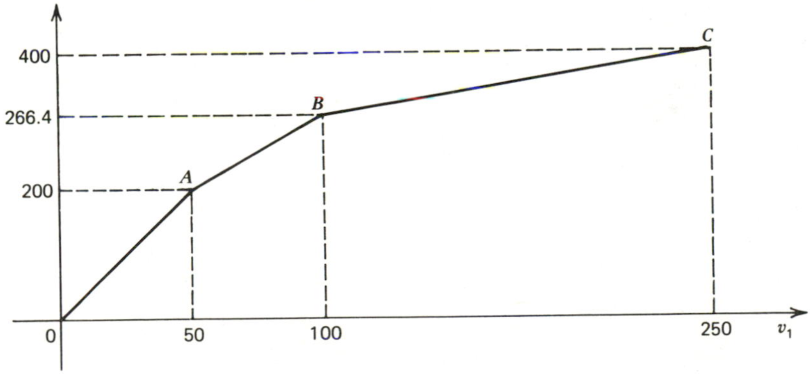

Figure 10.20

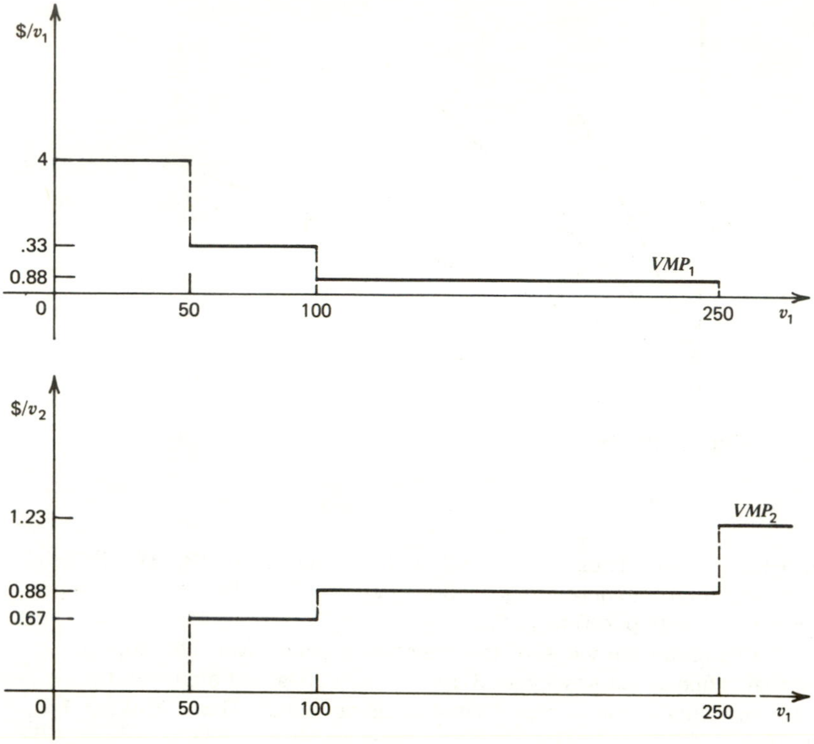

Figure 10.21

EXERCISES

10.1 Assume that the state of technological development in the rubber industry allows for synthetic and natural rubber to be combined in the following five mixtures for producing tires:

	POUNDS OF RUBBER INPUT PER TIRE	
TIRE TYPE	NATURAL	SYNTHETIC
1	8	6
2	2	12
3	4	10
4	6	8
5	10	4

The tires sell for the following prices.

Tire:	1	2	3	4	5
Price:	\$10	\$20	\$10	\$15	\$20

If the producer has on hand 2,240 pounds of natural rubber and the same amount of synthetic rubber, which tires should be manufactured in order to maximize profit?

10.2 Because of an oil shortage, the rationing authorities allocate total energy deliveries to coal manufacturers and require them to purchase coal and oil in the ratio of 5 to 3. The oil and coal requirements and the prices for five types of commodities are as follows:

ENERGY PER COMMODITY		
OIL	COAL	PRICE PER COMMODITY
6	2	$50
5	3	$50
4	4	$48
3	5	$35
2	6	$28

a. A manufacturer has been allocated a total energy ration of 80 units (i.e., 50 units of coal and 30 units of oil). The manufacturer's cost per commodity for inputs other than energy are $20. How many units of the commodity should be produced and what oil-coal mixes should be chosen in order to maximize profit?

b. You will find that the manufacturer utilizes less than its whole ration of energy. Could a change in the price schedule induce the manufacturer to exhaust the energy ration? Could an increase or decrease in the weekly ration induce the manufacturer to exhaust it?

10.3 A producer with a fixed supply of three inputs has three possible activities, each of which produces a different commodity selling for a different price. The input requirements, input supplies, and product prices are given in the following table. Find the levels of the three activities which maximize revenue. (Note: in the solution of the dual, only input 1 turns out to have a positive shadow price.)

	ACTIVITIES			
INPUT	1	2	3	FIXED INPUT QUANTITIES
1	6	1	2	12
2	2	2	1	10
3	1	5	20	200
Prices:	15	3	8	

10.4 Two methods can be used to produce a commodity with three inputs. The input requirements of the two methods and the fixed quantities of the two inputs are as follows:

INPUT	METHOD 1	METHOD 2	INPUT QUANTITIES
1	1	0	4
2	0	1	8
3	1	1	9

a. Calculate the maximal output.
b. How many units of each input are used?
c. If the output price is $1, what are the shadow prices of the three inputs?

10.5 Three processes employing labor and capital can be used to produce a commodity. The input requirements and revenues generated by operating these processes at unit level are as follows:

	PROCESSES		
INPUTS	1	2	3
Labor	2	3	3
Capital	4	2	3
Revenue	$3	$2	$4

The producer has 400 units of labor and 200 units of capital. If he does not use all of his capital he can dispose of the remainder at no cost. However, if he does not use all of his labor, it costs $1 per unit to get rid of the residual.

a. Determine the profit-maximizing activity levels, the imputed prices of the inputs, and the profit.
b. Rework (a) assuming that a new process, with labor and capital coefficients of 3 and 4, is developed.

10.6 A country produces two commodities, making use of two inputs, labor and capital. Two technologies are available for the production of each commodity, one more "labor intensive," the other more "capital intensive." The input requirements per unit of output are as follows:

	COMMODITY 1		COMMODITY 2	
	TECH. (1)	TECH. (2)	TECH. (1)	TECH. (2)
Capital	2	4	1.5	3
Labor	5	3	2	1

The (international) price of commodity 1 is twice that of commodity 2. The country maximizes the value of its output. Assuming that the total labor input is fixed at 150 units, derive (and graph) the relationship between the quantity of capital and

a. the quantity produced of commodity 1,

b. the quantity produced of commodity 2, and

c. the shadow prices of capital and labor.

10.7 A producer manufactures a commodity which is sold in a competitive market for $10 per unit. There are two possible methods of production. Input requirements per unit of output by each method are as follows:

	METHOD 1	METHOD 2
Input 1:	2	3
Input 2:	4	2

The price of input 1 is $2, but the producer cannot employ more than 60 units of this input. Derive the demand curve for input 2.

10.8 A producer is equipped to produce two types of commodities, making use of two inputs. Two technologies are available for producing each commodity. The input requirements per unit of output are as follows:

	COMMODITY 1		COMMODITY 2	
	TECH. (1)	TECH. (2)	TECH. (1)	TECH. (2)
Capital	1	3	3	5
Labor	2	1	4	3

Commodity 2 sells at $20 per unit, whereas commodity 1 sells at $10 per unit. The producer has 30 units of capital and can purchase labor at a fixed price.

a. Derive the demand curve for labor.

b. If the price of labor is $5 per unit, what is the optimal value of labor input and the optimal outputs of the two commodities?

c. Suppose that the producer develops a new technology for producing commodity 1 with capital and labor input requirements of .4 and .2, respectively. What does the isoquant map look like when this new technique is combined with the old? Derive the new labor demand curve.

10.9 Suppose that a commodity can be produced, using two inputs, with a technology described by a Cobb–Douglas production function (see exercise 8.5, equation (8.19)) or a linear process, or any combination of the two. Suppose further that the linear process is efficient (relative to the Cobb–Douglas technology) for some input combinations.

a. Construct the isoquant map that combines these two technologies.

b. Draw the marginal-product curve for one of the inputs.

PART II
HISTORICAL NOTES AND SUGGESTED READING

The classic presentations of the *theory of the producer* are **Hicks** [1939, chaps. 6–8 and associated appendices] and **Samuelson** [1947a, chap. 4].

The concept of the (two-input) *elasticity of substitution* was introduced by **Hicks** [1932, pp. 117 and 245] and **Robinson** [1933, pp. 256 and 330]. Two generalizations for production technologies with more than two inputs (now referred to as the "Allen elasticity of substitution" and the "direct elasticity of substitution") were formulated by **Hicks** and **Allen** [1934]. The Allen elasticity was analyzed by **Uzawa** [1962] and the direct elasticity was analyzed by **McFadden** [1963]. An alternative generalization has recently been proposed by **Morishima** (in Japanese) and analyzed by **Blackorby** and **Russell** [1976].

The question of the *divisibility* of commodities and the implications for returns to scale have been explored by **Chamberlin** [1948, 1949], **Hahn** [1949], and **Menger** [1954].

The functional forms that have traditionally been employed in empirical studies of production are the *Cobb–Douglas* function (**Douglas** [1948]) and the *constant-elasticity-of-substitution* function (**Arrow**, **Chenery**, **Minhas**, and **Solow** [1961]). Recent studies have employed the *flexible functional forms* cited in the part I suggested reading.

For the *duality* between cost and production functions and between profit and production functions, the reader is referred to the part I suggested reading.

Linear production technologies have a long history in economics literature. **Koopmans** [1957, pp. 37–39, 67 and 99–105; 1977] discusses the development of this body of theory and its utilization in economic analysis. **Koopmans** [1951, chap. 3] is a rigorous development of the linear activity analysis of production. **Gale** [1960] is a good reference for proofs of the duality theorems of linear programming. The survey article of **Hicks** [1960] and the book by **Dorfman**, **Samuelson**, and **Solow** [1958] contain extensive discussions and analyses of the applications of linear programming to the theory of the producer, input-output analysis, general equilibrium and welfare theory, and game theory. **Allen** [1950, pp. 618–32] contains a set of excellent linear programming exercises.

Nonlinear programming (i.e., maximization of a nonlinear objective function subject to nonlinear constraints) is not only applicable to production theory, but also to the theory of the consumer when one does not wish to assume away corner solutions (see section 3.5). The basic references are **Kuhn** and **Tucker** [1951] and **Arrow**, **Hurwicz**, and **Uzawa** [1961].

Dynamic or intertemporal profit maximization and *capital theory* begins with the classic treatises by **Fisher** [1930], **Wicksell** (translation [1934]), **Bohm–Bawerk** (translation [1930]), and **Clark** [1923]. **Hirschleiffer** [1970] provides an elementary introduction to the modern literature. The theory of optimal capital policy has been developed by **Arrow** [1962, 1964b, 1968].

Dynamic models of investment which incorporate the costs of adjusting capital are presented in **Eisner** and **Strotz** [1963] and **Lucas** [1967]. **Taubman** and **Wilkinson** [1970a; 1970b] analyze the relation between capital utilization and investment theory. **Arzac** [1976] compares the implications of expected utility maximisation and the safety-first criterion (preferences based upon expected profits and the probability of loss) for producer behavior under uncertainties. **Leland** [1974] and **Ekern** and **Wilson** [1974] analyze profit maximization in the context of *financial markets*.

The theory of the *nonclassical firm* which incorporates sales maximization, satisficing, and other corporate goals is developed by **Cyert** and **March** [1963], **Simon** [1959], **Ward** [1958], **Marris** [1964], and **Williamson** [1964].

PART III
THE THEORY OF MARKET STRUCTURES

Parts I and II analyze the behavior of the microcosms of the economic system—the consumer and the producer. The consumer is assumed to maximize utility subject to the budget constraint with fixed prices and income (or just fixed prices in the labor/leisure model of section 6.3). The producer is similarly assumed to maximize profit subject to fixed prices of outputs and inputs and the technological constraint embodied in the production function. Optimal output and input quantities of the producer and optimal consumption quantities (and labor supply) of the consumer are derived on the basis of fixed commodity prices. It is, however, the interaction of the many consumers and producers, all pursuing their own interests on the presumption that the prices they face are fixed, which determines commodity prices. In principle, quantity and price should be determined simultaneously. In part III, the theories of the consumer and the producer are brought together to determine the equilibrium price and quantity for a single commodity.

The theory of simultaneous determination of (commodity) price and quantity is called (commodity) *market theory*. A *commodity market* is defined loosely as a collection of agents engaged in transactions regarding the (current or future)[1] exchange of commodities (one of which is typically money). The commodity might be a *produced consumer commodity* (one, such as beer, that is produced by producers and consumed by consumers), an *intermediate commodity* (one, such as steel, that is produced by producers and used as inputs by other producers), or a *primary commodity* (one, such as labor, with which consumers are endowed and which is sold to other consumers or to producers).[2] Although most of the analysis in this part focuses on produced

[1] See the discussion of commodities in section 1.2. Markets in which agreements to deliver commodities in the future are transacted are called "futures markets."

[2] In addition to commodity markets, there are bond markets, stock markets, and many other types of markets. Although much of what is said below can be applied to these noncommodity markets, the (static) theory of consumer and producer behavior, developed in parts I and II and used in part III, is inadequate for the study of these markets. See the part III suggested reading.

consumer commodities, most of the basic principles that are derived from the analysis are equally applicable to the latter two types of markets.

It is important to note that the equilibrium examined in this part is "partial"; that is, the equilibrium price of a single commodity is derived under the assumption that all other commodity prices in the economy are fixed. From the perspective of the economy as a whole, however, the prices of other commodities do not in general remain unchanged when the price of a single commodity is adjusted to bring about equilibrium in the market for that commodity. We know from chapter 5 that, in general, an increase in the price of one consumer commodity either increases (in the case of gross substitutability) or decreases (in the case of gross complementarity) demand for other commodities. Furthermore, a change in the price of an input (such as labor) supplied by consumers affects the real income of consumers and hence the demand for the produced commodities by the consumers. A completely general determination of the equilibrium price and quantity in any one market would therefore require that we determine the equilibria in all commodity markets—output and input— simultaneously. This conceptual task is taken up in part IV. Meanwhile, a number of the important problems of resource allocation and price determination can be studied in the context of a single market—that is, using *partial-equilibrium* analysis. That is the task of this part.

Chapter 11 discusses equilibrium in a perfectly competitive market, characterized by the fact that all agents are price takers (as in parts I and II). This is the simplest and most tractable of market theories and is therefore the most commonly employed in applied economic analysis. In addition, many of the concepts developed in chapter 11 are fundamental to the general-equilibrium analysis of part IV. Chapter 11 also provides a first treatment and solution to the problem of resource allocation (and the dual problem of price determination) in an economic system. Chapter 12 analyzes the method of comparative statics and the problem of stability of equilibrium of perfectly competitive markets. Attention is focused on such dynamic phenomena as the time paths of price and quantity as they move from one equilibrium to another.

The model of perfect competition is useful for the study of markets (such as those for most agricultural commodities) in which there are a large number of buyers and sellers, but it does not provide a satisfactory framework for the study of markets (such as the automobile market) where there are few sellers or buyers, in which case the price-taking assumption is dubious. Chapter 13 develops models of markets with a single seller (monopolistic markets) and markets with a single buyer (monopsonistic markets). Chapter 14 develops models of markets with "few" sellers or buyers (oligopolistic and oligopsonistic markets).

CHAPTER 11 EQUILIBRIUM OF PERFECTLY COMPETITIVE MARKETS

11.1 INTRODUCTION

In this chapter the theories of the consumer and the producer are brought together to provide a theory of the determination of the price and quantity exchanged in a single perfectly competitive market for a produced consumer commodity.

The theory of the equilibrium of a perfectly competitive market assumes away the influence over price by a single agent or by coalitions of agents. Nevertheless, the equilibrium of a perfectly competitive market is fundamental to a great deal of applied economic analysis. In addition, the theory of general economic equilibrium, together with the propositions of modern welfare theory presented in part IV, draws heavily upon the partial (single-market) competitive-equilibrium theory developed in this chapter.

The following section discusses the assumptions that underlie the analysis of a perfectly competitive market for a produced consumer commodity. Section 11.3 derives the market supply function in a "short-run situation"—defined as a time period "short enough" so that some input quantities are fixed and producers cannot enter or leave the market—from the supply functions of the individual producers. Section 11.4 analyzes the market supply function in the "long run" when producers can both enter and exit the market and are free to vary the rate of utilization of all inputs. Finally, section 11.5 summarizes the major findings of the chapter.

11.2 THE ASSUMPTIONS OF PERFECT COMPETITION

We continue to assume that the economic environment is as described in section 1.2 and that consumers and producers behave according to the assumptions discussed in parts I and II. In particular, they choose consumption and production bundles subject to fixed positive prices (assumptions 2.4 and 7.1). That is, they behave as price takers in the perfectly competitive market.

In addition, we introduce the following three assumptions in order to guarantee that the equilibrium of a perfectly competitive market is characterized by the existence of a single commodity price for all consumers and producers and all transactions:

Assumption 11.1 (Identical Commodities) All producers sell commodities that are identical with respect to physical characteristics, location, and time of availability.

Assumption 11.2 (Free Exchange, Entry, and Exit) There is no cost involved in exchanging commodities, and there is free entry and exit from the market.

Assumption 11.3 (Perfect Information) Producers and consumers possess perfect information concerning the price, physical characteristics, and availability of each commodity.

These additional three assumptions, taken together, suffice to guarantee that a *single* price is taken as *given* by all producers and all consumers. The first assumption is obviously important since heterogeneous commodities would obviously result, in general, in a different price for each type or quality of the commodity. In the special case in which each producer is producing a slightly differentiated commodity, each producer in effect is the only supplier of the commodity, narrowly defined. In this case, the price of the narrowly differentiated commodity is not independent of the quantity supplied of the individual producer; the producer faces a downward-sloping demand curve.[1]

The second and third assumptions preclude the possibility of a single homogeneous commodity being supplied at different prices by different producers. So long as consumers possess perfect information about the prices of products supplied by the various producers and incur no exchange costs, price disparities cannot persist because consumers would shift their demand away from the high-price producers to the low-price producers. Perfect information and free exchange are similarly required on the part of the producers to guarantee that the prices of inputs are the same to all producers.

A special aspect of assumption 11.2 is the free entry and exit of producers into and out of the market. While the assumption that there are no barriers to the entry or exit of producers into or out of the market is not required in order to guarantee that a single price exists in equilibrium, we shall see that this assumption does have important implications for the optimality properties of general economic equilibrium analyzed in part IV (chapters 17–18).

The first two assumptions of perfect competition can be found in a somewhat different form in the literature:

[1] It is, at least in theory, possible to *define* a market according to the degree of homogeneity of the commodity. This, however, is not an empirically operational concept since it is difficult, if not impossible, to measure the degree of homogeneity of commodities. It has instead been suggested that the empirical *implications* of the degree of homogeneity—most notably the sizes of cross elasticities of demand—be used to delineate "markets."

Assumption 11.1′ All producers sell commodities that have identical physical characteristics.

Assumption 11.2′ There is perfectly free mobility of all consumers, producers, and resources (both within the market and into and out of the market.)

Assumption 11.1′ allows a commodity supplied and demanded in a market to differ in location and time of availability. In order to guarantee the existence of a single commodity price in equilibrium, assumption 11.2′ then assumes that consumers, producers and commodities can be moved, with respect to both time and place without incurring any costs. Thus consumers and producers incur no exchange costs regardless of the location or time that commodities are made available. Note also that the free entry and exit of producers into or out of the market is also guaranteed by assumption 11.2′. Assumptions 11.1′ and 11.2′, in combination with assumption 11.3, thus alternatively suffice to guarantee that a single commodity price exists in equilibrium for all producers, consumers, and transactions.

11.3 SHORT-RUN MARKET EQUILIBRIUM

The Market Demand Function

The market demand function for the ith commodity can be derived from the individual consumer demand functions, with images

$$x_i^c = d_i^c(p, y^c), \qquad i = 1, \ldots, n, \quad c = 1, \ldots, m, \tag{11.1}$$

where x_i^c is the amount demanded of the ith commodity by the cth consumer, $p = [p_1, \ldots, p_n]$ is the vector of commodity prices, and y^c is the income of the cth consumer. As this chapter (and those that follow in part III) deal with a single market (holding consumer incomes and prices in all other markets fixed), no confusion should result if we simplify the notation by employing the "restricted" demand function $\hat{d}_i^c$, defined by

$$x_i^c = \hat{d}_i^c(p_i) = d_i^c(p_i, \bar{p}^{-i}, \bar{y}^c), \tag{11.2}$$

where $\bar{p}^{-i}$ is the vector of fixed values of prices other than the ith. For the same reasons, we also drop the subscript i in this chapter:

$$x^c = \hat{d}^c(p). \tag{11.3}$$

The market demand for the commodity is obtained by aggregating the demand functions over the m consumers:

$$\sum_{c=1}^{m} x^c = \sum_{c=1}^{m} \hat{d}^c(p). \tag{11.4}$$

Define the *market demand function, D,* by

$$D(p) = \sum_{c=1}^{m} \hat{d}^c(p). \tag{11.5}$$

Letting

$$x = \sum_{c=1}^{m} x^c, \tag{11.6}$$

we have the market demand for the commodity as a function of the price:

$$x = D(p). \tag{11.7}$$

It should be emphasized, however, that the summation of the consumer demand functions in (11.4) is legitimate only if there is no interdependence between the utility functions of the consumers. This excludes such phenomena as the "demonstration effect" (keeping up with the Joneses) and philanthropic impulses.

Finally, while it is possible that $dd^c(p)/dp > 0$ for some consumers (see section 4.5), it is less likely that $dD(p)/dp > 0$. Consequently, we assume throughout this chapter that the market demand for the commodity is inversely related to its own price.

The Short-Run Market Supply Function

We first examine the determination of market equilibrium when producers are constrained by fixed input quantities. As pointed out in section 9.6., such constraints may be due to contractual obligations incurred by producers. The short run is also characterized by the assumption that the number of producers is fixed; this last assumption considerably simplifies the analysis of market equilibrium. In section 11.4, we consider a long-run situation where the market equilibrium is influenced by the possibility of entry and exit of producers.

Section 9.6 above derives the short-run supply function for the ith commodity of a producer with fixed inputs. The images are as follows:

$$q_i^\nu = \bar{s}_i^\nu(p, w, \bar{v}^f), \tag{11.8}$$

where q_i^ν is the output of the νth firm. Analogously to our simplified notation for demand functions, denote the restricted short-run supply function $\hat{\bar{s}}^\nu$, with image

$$q_i^\nu = \hat{\bar{s}}_i^\nu(p) = \bar{s}_i^\nu(p, \bar{w}, \bar{v}^f). \tag{11.9}$$

As with demand functions, no ambiguity results if we drop the subscripts:

$$q^\nu = \hat{\bar{s}}^\nu(p). \tag{11.10}$$

The short-run market supply of the commodity is obtained by aggregating the supply functions over the ℓ producers:

$$\sum_{\nu=1}^{\ell} q^\nu = \sum_{\nu=1}^{\ell} \hat{\bar{s}}^\nu(p). \tag{11.11}$$

Define the short-run market supply function $\bar{S}$, by

$$\bar{S}(p) = \sum_{v=1}^{\ell} \hat{\hat{s}}^{v}(p). \tag{11.12}$$

Letting

$$q = \sum_{v=1}^{\ell} q^{v}, \tag{11.13}$$

we have the market supply,

$$q = \bar{S}(p). \tag{11.14}$$

Section 7.5 demonstrated that the amount supplied of the ith commodity by a producer is directly related to the price of that commodity, i.e., $\partial \bar{s}_i^{v}(p, w, v^f)/\partial p_i > 0$. Thus, the market supply function is characterized by $d\bar{S}(p)/dp > 0$.

The aggregation of individual-producer supply curves to obtain the market supply curve can be illustrated by an (over simplified) example in which the market has only three producers. (Bear in mind that this example is merely illustrative of the relationship between the supply curve of the producer and of the market when there are a "large number" of producers; a market with only three producers is unlikely to satisfy the price-taking assumption of perfect competition.) The first three panels of figure 11.1 depict three producers with identical cost curves. As concluded in section 9.6, the producers cease to produce if the price falls below the minimum average variable cost ($\bar{p}$ in figure 11.1). The individual short-run supply curves are therefore equivalent to the marginal-cost curves truncated at the minimum points of the average-variable-cost curves. The short-run market supply curve is simply the horizontal summation of these individual supply curves, and is drawn in the right-hand panel of the diagram. Because of the "shut-down" criterion for the individual producers, the market supply curve is discontinuous at $\bar{p}$. With identical units on all four horizontal axes, the market supply curve has a much smaller slope than the supply curves of the individual producers (see exercise 11.1a–11.1b).

The derivation of the market supply curve is slightly more complicated when the individual producers are not constrained by identical cost curves (perhaps because of different quantities of the fixed inputs). In figure 11.2, as price falls below $\hat{p}$, the third producer discontinues production since the price is too low to cover variable costs. There is consequently a sharp drop in market supply from q' to $\hat{q}$, an amount equal to $\bar{q}^3$, the output of the third producer at the minimum point of his average-variable-cost curve. Another discontinuity in the market supply curve takes place at price $\bar{p}$, which is equal to the minimum point of the average-variable-cost curve of the second producer. Similarly, as price falls below $\tilde{p}$, market supply vanishes. These discontinuities are similar to one another and, indeed, similar to the single discontinuity in figure 11.1 at price $\bar{p}$ where market supply falls to zero. There are as many discontinuities in the market supply curve as there are distinct cost curves of the individual producers. If the market is composed of, say, 2,000 producers, each with slightly different average-variable-cost curves, there are 2,000 discontinuities. It is likely, however, that the larger the number of producers

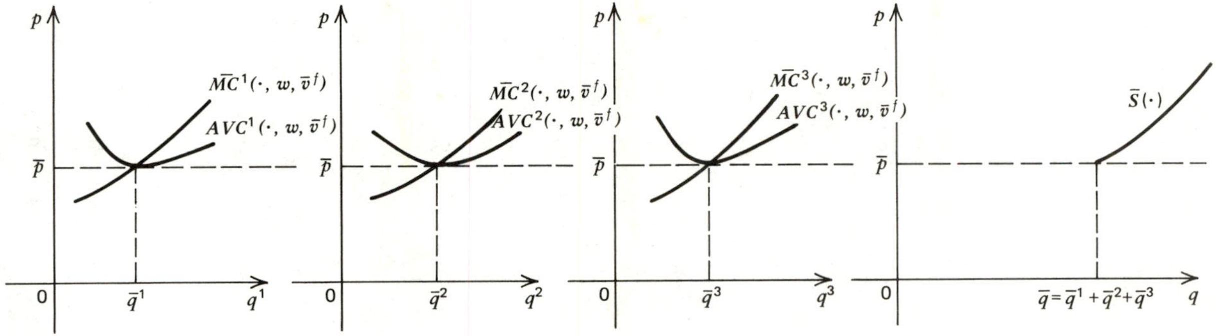
p
p
p
p
$\bar{MC}^1(\cdot, w, \bar{v}^f)$
$AVC^1(\cdot, w, \bar{v}^f)$
$\bar{MC}^2(\cdot, w, \bar{v}^f)$
$AVC^2(\cdot, w, \bar{v}^f)$
$\bar{MC}^3(\cdot, w, \bar{v}^f)$
$AVC^3(\cdot, w, \bar{v}^f)$
$\bar{S}(\cdot)$
$\bar{p}$
$\bar{p}$
$\bar{p}$
$\bar{p}$
0
$\bar{q}^1$
q^1
0
$\bar{q}^2$
q^2
0
$\bar{q}^3$
q^3
0
$\bar{q} = \bar{q}^1 + \bar{q}^2 + \bar{q}^3$
q

Figure 11.1

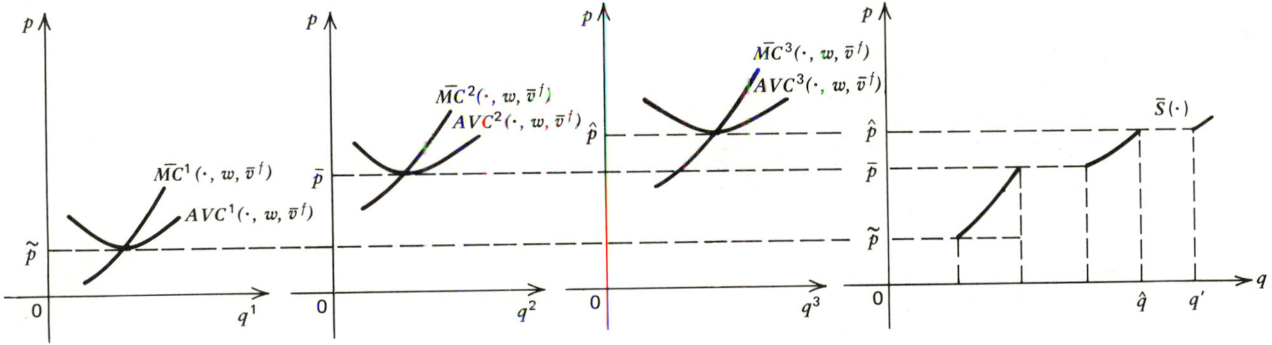

p
0
q¹
M̄C¹(·, w, v̄ᶠ)
AVC¹(·, w, v̄ᶠ)
p̃
p̄
q²
M̄C²(·, w, v̄ᶠ)
AVC²(·, w, v̄ᶠ)
p̂
q³
M̄C³(·, w, v̄ᶠ)
AVC³(·, w, v̄ᶠ)
S̄(·)
q̂
q′
q

Figure 11.2

the smaller is the change in output associated with each discontinuity relative to the output of the entire market. Hence, on any reasonable scale of the quantity axis, the discontinuities are imperceptible and we can approximate the discontinuous market supply curve by a continuous one.

Short-Run Equilibrium

Market equilibrium is established when, at the prevailing price, all producers and all consumers are satisfied with the amount they are producing or consuming, and market demand x and market supply q are equal. The equilibrium amount consumed and produced and equilibrium price is given by the solution to (11.7), (11.14) and

$$x = q. \tag{11.15}$$

Market equilibrium is illustrated in figure 11.3. Figure 11.3a shows the cost curves of a "typical producer." In figure 11.3b, the market supply curve, obtained by summing the supply curves of all producers, is shown. (Its slope should not, of course, be compared to the slope of the *MC* curve of the typical producer since the units on the horizontal axis are much different. If we were to employ the same units in figure 11.3b as in figure 11.3a, the market supply curve would be indistinguishable from a horizontal line.) If there are 1,000 producers in the market with *identical* cost functions, $\bar{q} = 1000\bar{q}^v$. Equilibrium is established at price $\overset{*}{p}$, which equates quantities supplied and demanded. Furthermore, each producer is in short-run equilibrium since he is equating short-run marginal cost and price, and producing $\bar{q}^v$ (see exercises 11.1c–11.1e).

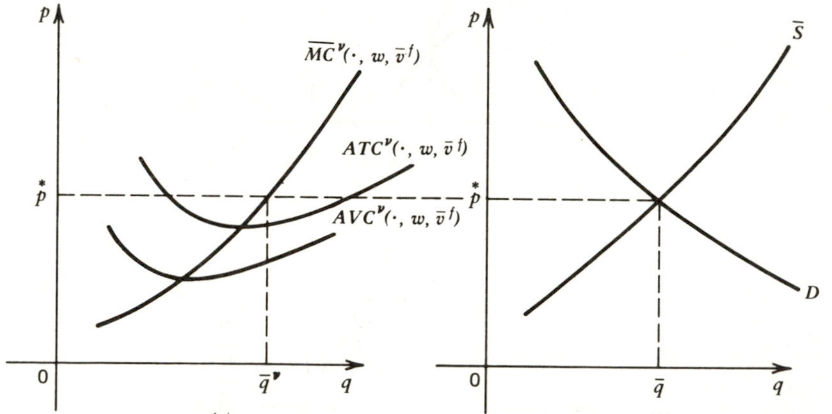

Figure 11.3

11.4 LONG-RUN MARKET EQUILIBRIUM

The Long-Run Market Supply Function

The derivation of the market supply function for the ith commodity is more complicated for the long run than for the short run. Two new problems are introduced because in the long run all inputs are assumed to be variable and producers can enter and leave the market. Both of these factors affect market supply.

Section 9.5 derives the supply function of a producer when all inputs are variable. The problem of choosing the profit-maximizing level of output for the νth producer can be restated as follows:

$$\underset{q^\nu}{\text{Max}}(R^\nu(p, q^\nu) - C^\nu(q^\nu, w))$$

where $C^\nu(q^\nu, w)$ is the long-run cost function with all inputs variable and $R(p, q^\nu)$ is the revenue function. The first-order condition for this problem can be restated as $p = MC^\nu(q^\nu, w)$. The long-run function is obtained by solving the first-order condition for q^ν and recalling that the producer ceases operation if price falls below the minimum point of the average-cost curve. Thus,

$$q^\nu = s^\nu(p, w), \tag{11.16}$$

where q^ν is the amount produced by the νth producer and $s^\nu(p, w) = 0$ if $p < \hat{p}$ where $\hat{p}$ is equal to the lowest value of avarage cost.

In the derivation of the long-run market supply function, we assume that the producers have identical cost functions. In the light of assumptions 11.2–11.3, this condition makes sense. Perfect information can be interpreted as meaning that each producer has access to the same technology. Given perfect mobility and identical prices of all inputs, and identical technologies, cost functions would be identical for all producers. Moreover, there is an unlimited number of "potential" producers with equivalent cost functions. Thus all producers—extant and potential—have identical cost functions.

Identical cost functions implies that supply functions are identical so that the superscript ν in (11.16) can be eliminated and market supply is

$$q = \ell \cdot s(p, w) = \tilde{S}(p, \ell),$$

where the given input prices, w, have been surpressed in $\tilde{S}(p, \ell)$.

Equating aggregate demand and supply,

$$D(p) = \tilde{S}(p, \ell),$$

we can solve for the equilibrium price for a given ℓ. Hence, the equilibrium price is a function of the number of producers:

$$\bar{p} = \bar{p}(\ell). \tag{11.17}$$

Long-Run Equilibrium

Given that all producers (extant and potential) operate subject to the same cost function, new producers enter the market when each producer's gross revenue exceeds gross costs (that is, profits are positive.) Likewise, producers leave the market when revenue is less than the cost of production. *Long-run market equilibrium* is defined as the situation in which (1) all producers and consumers are producing and consuming the optimal amounts of the commodity, (2) market demand and supply are equal, and (3) no producers have any motivation to enter or leave the market. The latter condition requires that the profits of producers be zero.

The profit of the νth producer π^ν can be expressed as a function of equilibrium price (see section 7.4):

$$\pi^\nu = \Pi^\nu(\bar{p}).$$

But substitution from (11.17) yields

$$\pi^\nu = \Pi^\nu(\bar{p}(\ell)). \tag{11.18}$$

Thus, the profit of each producer is a function of the number of producers in the market. Under the assumption that all producers have identical cost functions, the function Π^ν is the same for all producers and we can therefore write (11.18) without the superscript:

$$\pi = \Pi(\bar{p}(\ell)).$$

Long-run market equilibrium requires that $\pi = 0$; that is,

$$\Pi(\bar{p}(\ell)) = 0. \tag{11.19}$$

The solution of this equation for ℓ in terms of the parameters of the system determines the number of producers which generates zero profits. Substituting the solution for ℓ into (11.17) yields the long-run equilibrium price $\bar{p}$. These values can in turn be substituted into $\tilde{S}(p, \ell)$ to determine market output and into $s(p, w)$ to determine the output of each producer. Put differently, equations

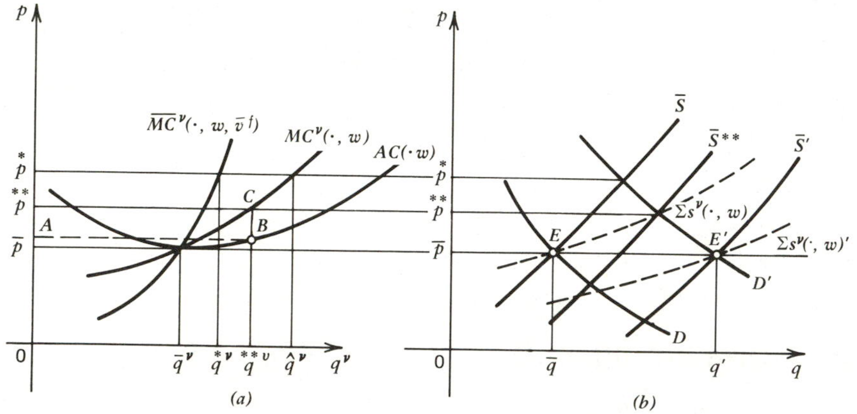

Figure 11.4

(11.17) and (11.19) constitute a system of two equations in two unknowns, $\bar{p}$ and ℓ. Thus, the long-run equilibrium price and the number of producers in the market are simultaneously determined. The locus of such equilibrium points as the market demand curve shifts is the long-run supply curve of the market.

The shape of the long-run market supply curve, thus determined, is best shown graphically. Figure 11.4a shows the long-run cost curves (assumed to be identical for all producers). Suppose that the equilibrium price is $\bar{p}$, so that each producer is producing output $\bar{q}$ and earning no profit, and consider a rise in demand. It needs to be emphasized that the following steps in the analysis of the changes in p and q are only logical, not chronological—the ordering of the steps is not intended to represent the path of p and q over time. We are dealing with comparative-static analysis, broken up into logical parts; to determine the chronological path of price and quantity would require a dynamic theory (see chapter 12).

With this caveat in mind, the rise in the market demand curve from D to D' might be thought of first as raising the price from $\bar{p}$ to $\overset{*}{p}$, which is determined by the intersection of the market demand curve and the short-run market supply curve—the summation of the individual-producer short-run supply curves. Each producer would then be selling output $\overset{*}{q}{}^v$. But, if the producers consider the price hike as a permanent one, they will adjust fixed input quantities to their optimal utilization rate. Indeed, at price $\overset{*}{p}$ the producers would maximize profits in the long run by producing output $\hat{q}^v$. As the producers increase their utilization of previously fixed inputs, however, the short-run market supply curve shifts to the right, since the producers' short-run marginal-cost curves are shifted. This, in turn, causes the price to fall. In the absence of new producers, a new equilibrium would be achieved when the increase in input utilization had shifted the short-run market supply curve to $\bar{S}^{**}$, where, at price $\overset{**}{p}$ each producer is producing $\overset{**}{q}$ with price equal to long-run marginal cost. This new equilibrium at $\overset{**}{p}$ is determined by the intersection of the market demand curve and the sum of the producers' long-run supply curves, $\sum_{v=1}^{\ell} s^v(\cdot, w)$, (which, as we learned above, would be the market supply curve in the absence of free entry and exit of producers.)

At price $\overset{**}{p}$, however, all producers earn positive profits equal to the area of the rectangle $ABC\overset{**}{p}$. With no barriers to entry, an influx of new producers to reap some profits ensues. But, as new producers enter the market, the short-run market supply curve and the horizontal summation of the individual producers' long-run supply curves shift to the right, lowering the price. The lower prices, in turn, induce all the producers to reduce output and their utilization of inputs. The new long-run equilibrium is achieved when each producer is equating price to long-run and short-run marginal cost and there are no excess profits and, hence, no incentive for producers to either enter or leave the market. This occurs only when the influx of producers (and the adaptation of fixed inputs) has shifted the short-run aggregate supply curve to $\bar{S}'$ (and the sum of producers' long-run marginal-cost curves to $\sum_{v=1}^{\ell} s^v(\cdot, w)'$) so that price is back to $\bar{p}$, where each producer is just covering costs and supplies output $\bar{q}^v$ again.

Thus, after all adjustments to the rise in demand are made, the price falls to the level which prevailed before the demand increase and each producer is selling the same output as before. Market output, however, has expanded from

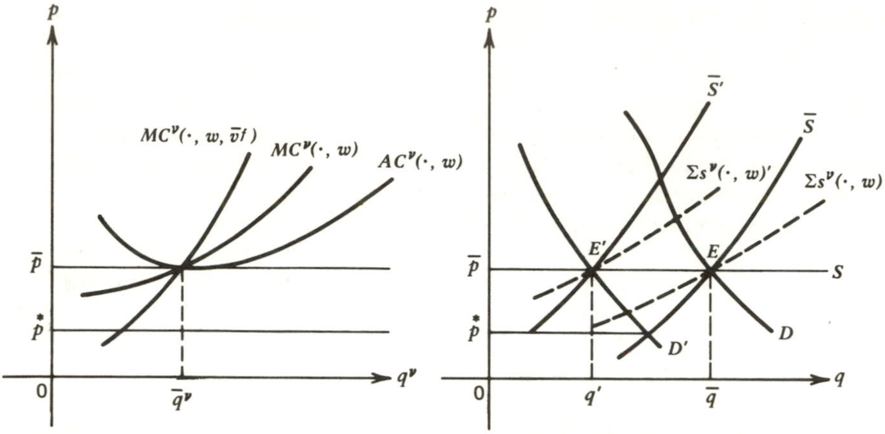

Figure 11.5

$\bar{q}$ to q' due to the increased number of producers in the market. By connecting equilibrium points such as E and E', we trace out the long-run market supply curve. Under the above assumptions—identical cost curves for all producers (extant and potential) and free entry and exit of producers—the long-run market supply curve is seen to be horizontal. This makes sense; no price other than $\bar{p}$ can be permanent since this is the only price that precludes (positive or negative) profits and hence discourages the entry or exit of producers.

It should be reemphasized that the sequence of (p, q) from $(\bar{p}, \bar{q})$ to $(\overset{*}{p}, \overset{*}{q})$ to $(\overset{**}{p}, \overset{**}{q})$ to $(\bar{p}, q')$ is entirely arbitrary. It is logical and not chronological. A dynamic model of the type discussed in chapter 12 would be required to analyze the time paths of price and quantity.

The horizontal long-run market supply curve can be similarly traced out by considering a *fall* in demand. This is illustrated in figure 11.5. The initial market equilibrium is displaced by a decline in demand from D to D'. In the short run, the price falls from $\bar{p}$ to $\overset{*}{p}$. At price $\overset{*}{p}$, however, all producers suffer losses and the result is an exodus of producers. It might be noted that in this case there is no adjustment of the fixed inputs of each producer. At price $\overset{*}{p}$, there is no output which can erase the losses. Hence, as soon as producers can liquidate their fixed costs, they leave the market.

The exodus of producers, however, shifts the short-run market supply curve and the horizontal summation of the individual producers' long-run supply curves to the left, raising the price. When the reduction in the number of producers shifts the short-run market supply curve to $\bar{S}'$ (and $\sum_{\nu=1}^{\ell} s^\nu(\cdot, w)$ to $\sum_{\nu=1}^{\ell} s^\nu(\cdot, w)'$), the price returns to $\bar{p}$ and each producer once again just covers costs. The exodus halts, and equilibrium is restored at price $\bar{p}$. Each firm is again producing $\bar{q}^\nu$, but there are now fewer producers in the market so that market output has fallen from $\bar{q}$ to q'.

11.5 SUMMARY AND CONCLUSION

In this chapter, we have derived the market demand and supply functions for a produced consumer commodity from the individual consumer and producer demand and supply functions. The market demand and supply functions are then utilized to determine the partial-equilibrium price of a single commodity. This is a partial-equilibrium price since we assume that the prices of all other commodities remain unchanged. The analysis of general-equilibrium prices is undertaken in part IV.

We have shown that the short-run market supply curve is simply the quantity summation of the supply curves of all producers in the market and is necessarily positively sloped. The long-run aggregate supply curve is more complicated because of the possible entry and exit of producers. If the cost curves of producers are identical (or at least are characterized by identical long-run average-cost minima) the supply curve is horizontal.

Equilibrium in the short run is defined as that state of affairs in which each producer is equating price to short-run marginal cost and the market supply is equal to the market demand so that the market is cleared. Long-run market equilibrium exists when each producer is equating price to long-run and short-run marginal cost, producers are earning zero profits (so that there is no tendency for producers to enter or leave the market), and the market supply equals the market demand. In each case, equilibrium can be characterized as a situation in which there is no tendency for any outputs or input utilization rates to change; i.e., all decision makers are satisfied with their choice of those variables over which they have control, given the output and input prices.

An important point to note here is the role played by output and input prices (and hence profits) in directing the allocation of scarce resources into and out of the market for the ith commodity (i.e., the consumption and production of the ith commodity).

Although the long-run market supply curve derived in section 11.4 is horizontal, this is in large part attributable to our partial-equilibrium analysis. That is, by assuming that all but the ith commodity prices are fixed, we abstract from developments elsewhere in the economy. If prices of inputs rise when the aggregate output of the ith commodity increases (thus increasing the demand for inputs) the cost curves (both short-run and long-run) of extant and potential producers of the ith commodity would not remain unaffected. These cost curves would shift upward. The result would be that the long-run market supply curve would be upward sloping. Analogously, if input prices fall when the aggregate output of the ith commodity increases, the supply curve is downward sloping. The institutional and technological phenomenon underlying an upward-(downward-) sloping long-run supply curve is referred to in much of the economics literature as an "increasing (decreasing) cost industry."

The supply curve for a primary commodity, such as labor, with which consumers are endowed, is obtained by aggregating the (labor) supply functions (6.21) over consumers. Demand curves are obtained by aggregating over the individual demand curves of consumers and/or producers, depending upon whether the primary commodity is a consumer commodity or a producer input (or both).

Finally, market theory for intermediate commodities and for primary commodities is analogous. The (short-run or long-run) supply curve for an intermediate commodity is derived exactly as in sections 11.2–11.4 above. The short-run or long-run demand curve for an intermediate commodity is obtained by summing the individual input demand functions (8.15) over all producers that employ the commodity as an input.[2]

EXERCISES

11.1 A perfectly competitive market is comprised of 1,000 producers, each with the variable cost function defined by $VC(q, w, \bar{v}^f) = 20q + \frac{1}{2}(q)^2$. The market demand function is defined by $q = D(p) = 105{,}000 - 500p$.

- **a.** Derive the short-run supply function of a producer.
- **b.** Derive the short-run market supply functions.
- **c.** What is the equilibrium price and quantity?
- **d.** What is the output of each producer?
- **e.** If each producer has fixed costs of $200, what is the profit of each producer?

11.2 What is the effect on equilibrium price and quantity of

- **a.** a minimum wage in a market for labor;
- **b.** a maximum price in a market for natural gas.

11.3 Why did the government agricultural price support programs result in huge stockpiles of agricultural commodities?

[2] This approach to long-run input demand abstracts from entry-and-exit phenomena in all of the industries that employ the commodity, a consideration that, if attempted, would push partial-equilibrium analysis far beyond its coherence threshold.

CHAPTER 12 COMPARATIVE STATICS AND THE STABILITY OF EQUILIBRIUM

12.1 INTRODUCTION

The previous chapter explicates the determination of equilibrium values of price and quantity in a single market. It is of paramount importance (particularly for the formulation of microeconomic policy) that we be able to predict the effect of a shift in either the supply or demand function upon these equilibrium values. For example, the imposition of an excise tax on the consumers of a particular commodity shifts the demand curve to the left. It would certainly be useful to be able to predict the impact of such a tax upon quantity and price (if only because this impact affects the total tax revenue) (see exercises 12.3–12.5).

The technique of determining the direction, and sometimes the magnitude, of changes in endogeneous variables, such as price and quantity, which result from exogenous shifts in one of the functions is known as comparative-static analysis; "comparative" because we are comparing values of the variables in different points of equilibrium and "static" because we are not examining the *time path* of the variables as they move from one equilibrium to the next. Strictly speaking, comparative-static analysis per se does not address the questions of "how" or indeed "whether" the variables approach the new equilibrium or of how long it takes to reach the new equilibrium. These questions fall into the domain of "dynamic" analysis—i.e., analysis involving "time" in an "essential" way. It is clear, however, that comparative-static analysis would be meaningless if the dynamic behavior of the market (or, more accurately, the dynamic behavior of the model) were such that the new equilibrium would never be achieved (or if the time required to achieve the new equilibrium were inordinately long).

Section 12.2 develops the method of comparative-static analysis. Section 12.3 discusses the distinction between static and dynamic models and sections 12.4–12.6 deal with the stability of equilibrium. The bulk of this chapter owes much to chapters 9–11 of Samuelson's classic *Foundations of Economic Analysis*, which greatly furthered dynamic economics.

12.2 THE METHOD OF COMPARATIVE STATICS

For the simple model of supply and demand in a single market analyzed in the previous chapter, the method of comparative statics might be set out as follows. The market demand and supply functions are given by

$$x = D(p) \qquad \text{and} \qquad q = S(p). \tag{12.1}$$

We now introduce a parameter, α, which represents an exogenous factor (such as consumer income, an excise tax, or the price of a related commodity) that shifts the market demand curve:

$$x = \hat{D}(p, \alpha). \tag{12.2}$$

The following analysis could be just as easily formulated by putting the shift parameter into the supply function instead of the demand function (see exercise 12.1).

The equilibrium price, $\bar{p}$, is defined by the market-equilibrium equation:

$$\hat{D}(\bar{p}, \alpha) = S(\bar{p}). \tag{12.3}$$

Furthermore, note that the equilibrium price is also a function of the parameter α:

$$\bar{p} = \bar{p}(\alpha). \tag{12.4}$$

Substitution of (12.4) into (12.3) yields the following identity:

$$\hat{D}(\bar{p}(\alpha), \alpha) = S(\bar{p}(\alpha)). \tag{12.5}$$

We are interested in determining the differential effect on the equilibrium values of x and p of an exogenous change or "shock" represented by a change in the value of α. Differentiate both sides of (12.5) with respect to α:

$$\frac{\partial \hat{D}(\bar{p}(\alpha), \alpha)}{\partial \bar{p}(\alpha)} \bar{p}'(\alpha) + \frac{\partial \hat{D}(\bar{p}(\alpha), \alpha)}{\partial \alpha} = S'(\bar{p}(\alpha))\bar{p}'(\alpha) \tag{12.6}$$

where $\bar{p}'(\alpha)$ and $S'(\bar{p}(\alpha))$ are the derivatives of the respective functions evaluated at α and $\bar{p}(\alpha)$. The solution for $\bar{p}'(\alpha)$ yields the differential effect of a change in α upon the equilibrium price:

$$\bar{p}'(\alpha) = \frac{\partial \hat{D}(\bar{p}(\alpha), \alpha)/\partial \alpha}{S'(\bar{p}(\alpha)) - \partial \hat{D}(\bar{p}(\alpha), \alpha)/\partial \bar{p}(\alpha)}. \tag{12.7}$$

Finally, denoting the equilibrium quantity supplied as $\bar{x}(\alpha)$, we have the identity

$$\bar{x}(\alpha) = S(\bar{p}(\alpha)). \tag{12.8}$$

Differentiation of both sides of (12.8) with respect to α yields the differential effect of a change in α upon the equilibrium quantity:

$$\bar{x}'(\alpha) = S'(\bar{p}(\alpha)) \cdot \bar{p}'(\alpha), \tag{12.9}$$

or, by substitution from (12.7),

$$\bar{x}'(\alpha) = \frac{S'(\bar{p}(\alpha)) \cdot \partial \hat{D}(\bar{p}(\alpha), \alpha)/\partial \alpha}{S'(\bar{p}(\alpha)) - \partial \hat{D}(\bar{p}(\alpha), \alpha)/\partial \bar{p}(\alpha)}. \tag{12.10}$$

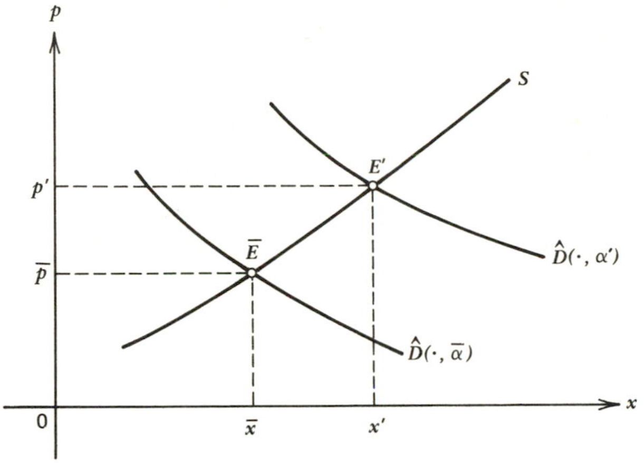

Figure 12.1

If the values of the slopes of the demand and supply functions and the derivative of the demand function with respect to a change in α are known, the effect on the equilibrium values, $\bar{p}$ and $\bar{x}$, can be computed. Economists, however, often work with models that specify only the *signs*, but not the values, of derivative functions. For example, assume that $\partial\hat{D}(\bar{p}(\alpha), \alpha)/\partial\alpha > 0$, as would be the case if α represented consumer income (and if the commodity were not inferior for the market as a whole) or if α represented the price of a substitute commodity. Furthermore, invoke the "Law of Demand," which implies $\partial\hat{D}(\bar{p}(\alpha), \alpha)/\partial\bar{p}(\alpha) < 0$, and assume that the market supply function satisfies $S'(\bar{p}(\alpha)) > 0$. Utilizing this information about the signs of the derivatives of the demand and supply functions in the comparative static equations (12.7) and (12.10), we see that $\bar{p}'(\alpha) > 0$ and $\bar{x}'(\alpha) > 0$. Hence, if the supply curve is upward sloping and the demand curve is downward sloping, an outward shift in the demand curve raises the equilibrium values of both quantity and price. This situation is illustrated (for a discrete increase in α from $\bar{\alpha}$ to α') in figure 12.1.

Suppose that the demand curve has a negative slope, as above, but that, unlike the above example, the supply curve also has a negative slope, $S'(\bar{p}(\alpha)) < 0$ (i.e., assume a decreasing-cost industry). Under these assumptions about the slopes of the demand and supply curves, it is not possible to determine the values of $\bar{p}'(\alpha)$ and $\bar{x}'(\alpha)$ since the signs of the denominators of the right-hand sides of the comparative-static equations are ambiguous. Additional information is required. In particular, it is necessary to know the relative absolute values of the derivatives of the demand and supply functions; i.e., it is necessary to know the sign of

$$\left|\frac{\partial\hat{D}(\bar{p}(\alpha), \alpha)}{\partial\bar{p}(\alpha)}\right| - |S'(\bar{p}(\alpha))|.$$

If the difference is positive, $\bar{p}'(\alpha) < 0$ and $\bar{x}'(\alpha) > 0$ and, if the difference is negative, $p'(\alpha) > 0$ and $x'(\alpha) < 0$.

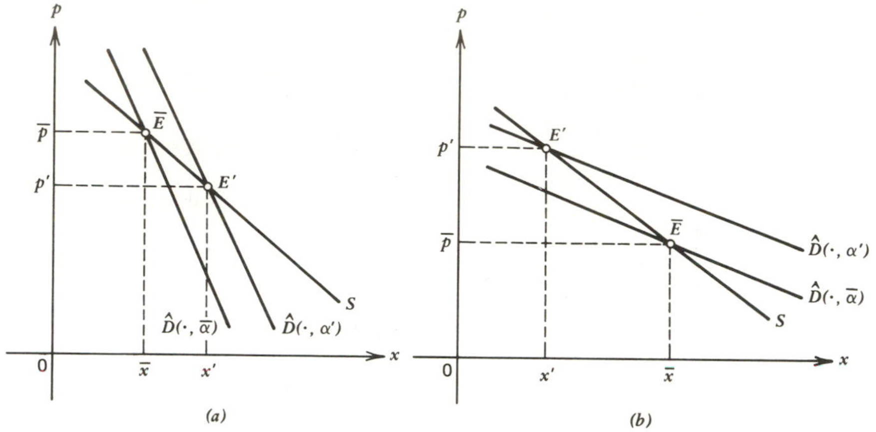

Figure 12.2

This situation is illustrated in figure 12.2. The exogenous shock is represented by a rise in the value of α from $\bar{\alpha}$ to α'. This, in turn, shifts the demand curve upward and to the right. In panel A, where the demand curve is steeper, the shift in demand lowers the equilibrium price from $\bar{p}$ to p' and raises the equilibrium quantity from $\bar{x}$ to x'. In panel B, where the supply curve is steeper, the shift in demand *raises* the equilibrium price from $\bar{p}$ to p' and *lowers* equilibrium output from $\bar{x}$ to x'.

12.3 DYNAMICS AND THE STABILITY OF EQUILIBRIUM

Dynamic Analysis

The comparative-static analysis of the previous section simply compares equilibrium points before and after a shift in the demand function. No attempt is made to explain the mechanism by which price and output move from $\bar{E}$ to E' in figures 12.1 and 12.2. Without an explicit specification of the mechanism, however, it cannot be unequivocally stated (within the context of the model) that the new equilibrium is ever reached. While comparative static analysis per se can *sometimes* tell us the direction of change of the *equilibrium* values of p and x, it cannot tell us the direction of change of the *actual* values of p and x. Thus, the comparative-static model is not complete enough to determine whether in, say, panel a of figure 12.2, p will, in fact, fall toward the new equilibrium after the shift in demand. Price could rise, in which case the new equilibrium would never be attained. In order to determine what happens to *actual* prices—whether the new equilibrium will ever be achieved—it is necessary to spell out a model showing how price and/or quantity behave *out of equilibrium*. That is, it is necessary to specify a *dynamic* model of disequilibrium price and quantity adjustment. This model will tell us how p and x behave out of equilibrium and, hence, whether the new equilibrium will be achieved.[1]

Following Samuelson [1947a] (who, in turn, followed Ragnar Frisch [1936]), we define a *dynamic system* as one in which the *behavior of variables over time is determined by a set of equations in which variables at different points in time are involved in an "essential" way*. A truly dynamic system is, then, one in which an (infinite) sequence of values of the variables over time is generated.

The two most common forms of equations which satisfy the requirements of dynamism are *difference equations* and *differential equations*. The simplest form of difference equation is

$$x(t) = ax(t-1), \tag{12.11}$$

where $x(t)$ is the value of x at time t and a is a parameter. Given any initial value of x, say $x(0)$, this single-equation system generates an infinite series of values of x. These values are given by the solution,

$$x(t) = x(0)a^t. \tag{12.12}$$

That this is the solution to (12.11) can be seen by substituting $x(0)a^t$ for $x(t)$ and $x(0)a^{t-1}$ for $x(t-1)$ in (12.11), yielding

$$x(0)a^t = x(0)a \cdot a^{t-1} = x(0)a^t.$$

Thus, (12.12) generates the same dynamic path as (12.11). Note that the value of x is determined by the initial value, $x(0)$, and the elapsed time, t.

The simplest type of differential equation is

$$\frac{dx(t)}{dt} = x'(t) = ax(t). \tag{12.13}$$

By relating the time rate of change of x to its value, an intertemporal relationship is implied. A stream of values of x over time is generated by the solution to (12.13):

$$x(t) = x(0)e^{at}. \tag{12.14}$$

That this is the solution to (12.13) can be seen by differentiating (12.14) with respect to t to obtain $x'(t) = ax(0)e^{at}$. Substitution from (12.14) yields $x'(t) = ax(t)$, which is identical to (12.13). Thus, as in the difference-equation example, the differential equation (12.13) yields a value of x in each period which depends upon the initial value, $x(0)$, and the elapsed time, t.

[1] This correspondence between statics and dynamics is part of what Samuelson [1947a] calls the *correspondence principle*. This principle is stated most generally as follows: ". . . the problem of stability of equilibrium is intimately tied up with the problem of deriving fruitful theorems in comparative statics" (Samuelson [1947a, p. 258]).

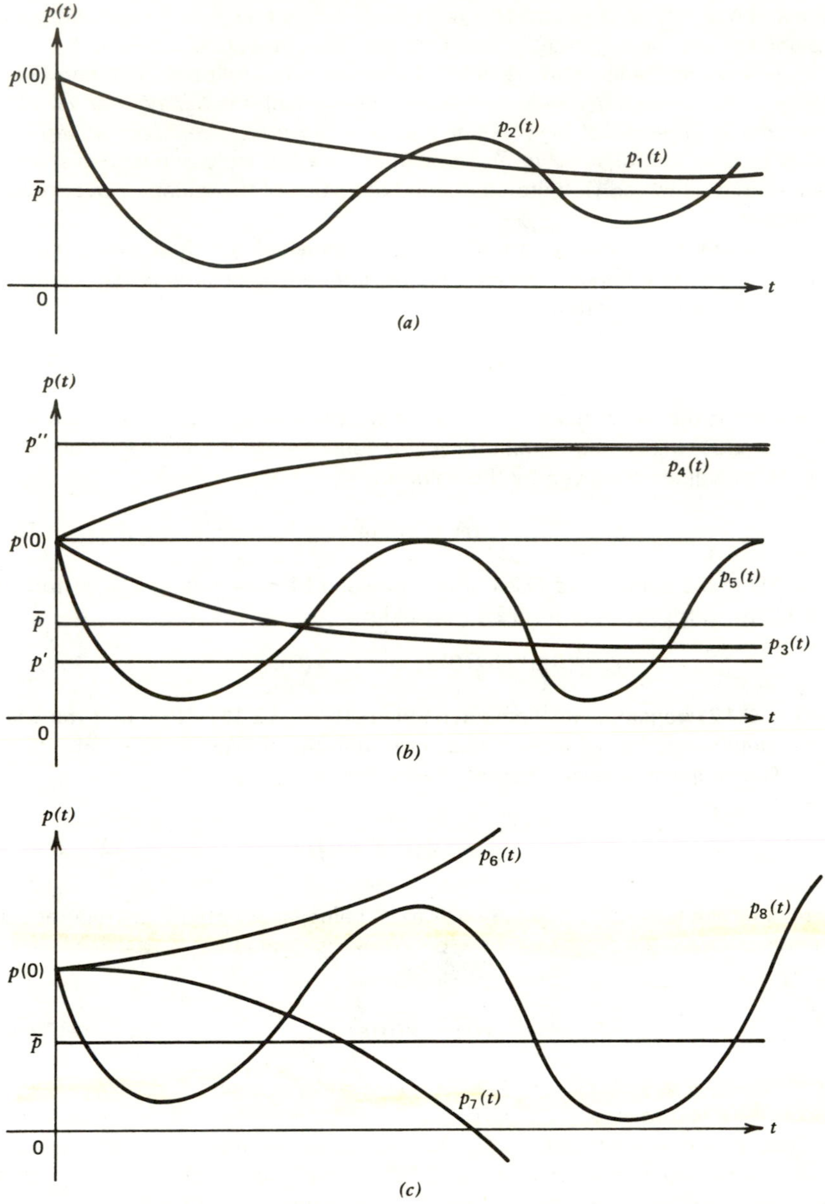
p(t)
p(0)
$p_2(t)$
$p_1(t)$
$\bar{p}$
0
t
(a)
p(t)
p''
$p_4(t)$
p(0)
$p_5(t)$
$\bar{p}$
$p_3(t)$
p'
0
t
(b)
p(t)
$p_6(t)$
$p_8(t)$
p(0)
$\bar{p}$
$p_7(t)$
0
t
(c)

Figure 12.3

Stability

If a displacement from equilibrium sets forces in motion which bring the variables back to equilibrium, the equilibrium is said to be *stable*. The shifts in the demand curve illustrated in figures 12.1 and 12.2 can be thought of as a displacement from equilibrium. Hence, if the equilibrium, E', is stable, p and x approach the new equilibrium when the demand curve is shifted.

An equilibrium is *stable* if

$$\lim_{t \to \infty} p(t) = \bar{p}. \tag{12.15}$$

If this equation holds for *any* initial value, $p(0)$, no matter how far from the equilibrium value, $\bar{p}$, we say that the equilibrium is *globally stable*. If, on the other hand, (12.15) holds only for "small" displacements from equilibrium—that is, only for cases where $p(0)$ is in a "neighborhood" of the equilibrium—we say that the equilibrium is only *locally stable*. Conversely, an equilibrium is defined as unstable if $p(t)$ explodes, that is, goes toward plus or minus infinity over time.

It may be that while $p(t)$ does not converge to $\bar{p}$ as time passes, neither does it "explode." The price might, for example, oscillate indefinitely about the equilibrium price with cycles of constant amplitude, or it might approach some *finite* value of p, but not $\bar{p}$, as time passes.[2]

Figure 12.3 illustrates several cases. Time is on the horizontal axis and the value of $p(t)$ is on the vertical axis. Panel a depicts two types of stability. The series $p_1(t)$, beginning at the initial price, $p(0)$, approaches the equilibrium price, $\bar{p}$, monotonically. The series $p_2(t)$, oscillates about $\bar{p}$, but the oscillations are "damped"; i.e., $p_2(t)$ converges to the equilibrium, $\bar{p}$, nonmonotonically.

Panel b illustrates three possible cases. Series $p_3(t)$ and $p_4(t)$ approach nonequilibrium values, p' and p'', respectively. Series $p_5(t)$ oscillates about the equilibrium with cycles of constant amplitude so that while price does not fully converge to $\bar{p}$, neither does it diverge without limit.

Panel c illustrates three cases of instability: $p_6(t)$ and $p_7(t)$ diverge toward plus and minus infinity, respectively, and $p_8(t)$ is characterized by explosive cycles about the equilibrium.

12.4 A PRICE-ADJUSTMENT MODEL

Walras's Disequilibrium Hypothesis

The time path corresponding to $p(t)$ depends upon the exact specification of the dynamic hypothesis about disequilibrium behavior. The most common adjustment mechanism dates back to Walras's *Elements of Pure Economics*, first published in 1874. Walras assumed that the price rises when quantity

[2] Samuelson [1947a, pp. 261–62] characterizes this as "stability of the second kind while (12.15) is called "stability of the first kind." Arrow and Hahn [1971, Chapter 11] present a modern treatment of stability. See also section 16.6, below.

demanded exceeds quantity supplied and falls when quantity supplied exceeds quantity demanded. This hypothesis can be represented by the differential equation,

$$p'(t) = H(D(p(t)) - S(p(t))) \tag{12.16}$$

where $H'(D(p(t)) - S(p(t))) > 0$ for all $p(t)$ and $H(0) = 0$. This formulation says that the greater the excess demand, $D(p) - S(p)$, the faster price rises; conversely, the larger the excess supply, the faster price falls. When demand and supply are equal, price does not change.

Despite its apparent plausibility, this dynamic model is not firmly grounded in the microeconomic theory of the producer and the consumer under conditions of disequilibrium.[3] Indeed, it is normally assumed that the buyers and the sellers operating in a perfectly competitive market take the price as given—beyond their control. Who then changes prices?[4] One way out of this quandary is to assume that, out of equilibrium, producers cease to act as perfect competitors. That is, when they see their stocks being prematurely depleted, so that some potential customers are left unsatisfied, producers reason that they can raise prices and still sell their entire stock of goods. Similarly, when sellers fail to sell their entire stock at the market price, they are tempted to lower the price. While one might argue that we cannot be too fastidious in our analysis of perfect competition when the market is out of equilibrium—that perfect competitors temporarily become monopolists until equilibrium is restored—the fact remains that the existing theories of disequilibrium price adjustment are fundamentally incompatible with the traditional assumptions of perfect competition. There is much need for a theory of disequilibrium price adjustment which is more firmly grounded in the behavior postulates of the perfectly competitive model.

Stability Property

In order to examine the stability property of the Walrasian price-adjustment model, we simplify matters by assuming that the demand and supply functions, D and S, and the speed-of-adjustment function, H, are linear:[5]

$$D(p) = a + bp, \tag{12.17}$$

$$S(p) = \alpha + \beta p, \tag{12.18}$$

[3] As Tjalling Koopmans [1957, p. 179] points out, equation (12.16) is more firmly grounded in the physical than in the behavioral sciences.

[4] Walras conveniently posited the existence of an "auctioneer" or "referee," who, upon examining the bids of buyers and sellers and determining the level of excess demand or supply, announces ("cries out") a new price. This, however, is clearly little more than an ingenious artifact.

[5] This simplification is only for the purpose of pedagogical convenience. In fact, local stability of the general system (12.16) can be examined by taking a first-order Taylor's-series approximation of equation (12.16) about the equilibrium price $\bar{p}$ (see exercise 12.7). Stability of the first-order approximation to (12.16) is sufficient (but not necessary) for stability of the nonlinear system (12.16) (see Samuelson [1947a, p. 291]). It is, however, necessary (as well as sufficient) for quasistability of the nonlinear system (see exercise 12.8).

and

$$H(D(p) - S(p)) = \gamma(D(p) - S(p)), \qquad \gamma > 0, \tag{12.19}$$

where a, b, α, β, and γ are parameters. Thus,

$$\begin{aligned} p'(t) &= H(D(p(t)) - S(p(t))) = \gamma(a + bp(t) - \alpha - \beta p(t)) \\ &= \gamma(a - \alpha) + \gamma(b - \beta)p(t). \end{aligned}$$

Moreover, the equilibrium price $\bar{p}$ is given by $\bar{p} = (a - \alpha)/(\beta - b)$, so that

$$p'(t) = \gamma(\beta - b)\bar{p} + \gamma(b - \beta)p(t) = \gamma(b - \beta)(p(t) - \bar{p}). \tag{12.20}$$

Define the new variable $z(t)$ by

$$z(t) = p(t) - \bar{p}. \tag{12.21}$$

Note that

$$z'(t) = p'(t) \tag{12.22}$$

and substitute (12.21) and (12.22) into (12.20):

$$z'(t) = \gamma(b - \beta)z(t). \tag{12.23}$$

This equation is the simplest type of first-order differential equation and has the solution $z(t) = z(0)e^{\gamma(b-\beta)t}$ see equations (12.13) and (12.14)). Substitution of (12.21) into this equation yields the solution to (12.20): $p(t) - \bar{p} = (p(0) - \bar{p})e^{\gamma(b-\beta)t}$ or

$$p(t) = \bar{p} + (p(0) - \bar{p})e^{\gamma(b-\beta)t}. \tag{12.24}$$

Recalling the definition of stability (12.15), we have to determine the conditions under which $\lim_{t\to\infty} p(t) = \bar{p}$. This limit condition holds if and only if the second term of equation (12.24) goes to zero as t goes to infinity. Since t enters this term exponentially, it can be seen that $\lim_{t\to\infty} p(t) = \bar{p}$ if and only if $\gamma(b - \beta) < 0$. However, as $\gamma > 0$ by assumption, this inequality implies $b - \beta < 0$. Thus, stability is equivalent to $b < \beta$; the Walrasian dynamic-adjustment process (12.19) is stable if and only if the derivative of the demand function is less than the derivative of the supply function.

In the "normal" event where the supply and demand curves are positively and negatively sloped, respectively, $\beta > 0$ and $b < 0$; hence, equilibrium is necessarily stable. If, however, both curves have negative slopes, the equilibrium is stable if and only if $|b| > |\beta|$; i.e., the demand curve is steeper (referred to the price axis) than the supply curve. Merely for the sake of completeness, it might be pointed out that in the highly unlikely case in which both curves are positively sloped (i.e., the Giffen paradox holds for the market as a whole), stability requires that the demand curve be steeper than the supply curve. In the even less likely event that the supply curve has a negative slope while the demand curve has a positive slope, equilibrium is necessarily unstable.

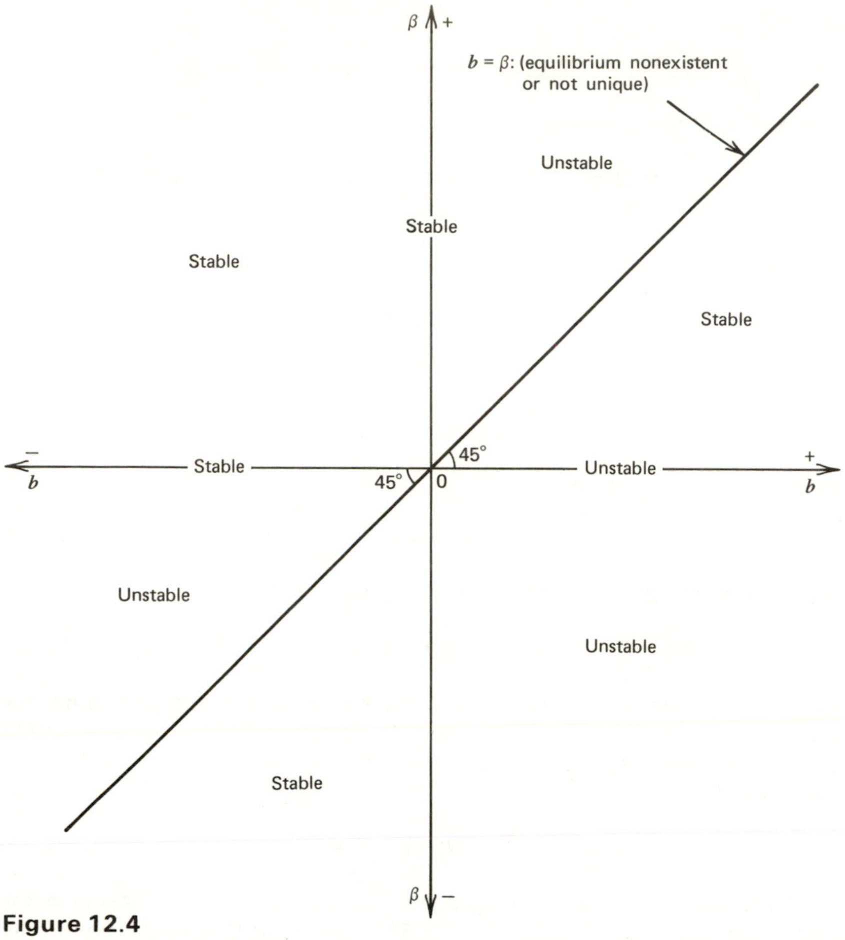

Figure 12.4

Figure 12.4a illustrates the set of values of the derivatives of the demand and supply functions that yield stability.

Graphical Illustration

These combinations of possibilities are illustrated in figure 12.5. In figure 12.5a, the demand and supply curves have negative and positive slopes, respectively. If the system is initially at equilibrium E' and the demand curve shifts from $\hat{D}(\cdot, \alpha')$ to $\hat{D}(\cdot, \bar{\alpha})$, excess demand equal to $\hat{x} - x'$ is created since the amount demanded at price p' is now $\hat{x}$ while the amount supplied remains at x'. Positive excess demand, according to Walras's adjustment mechanism (12.16), causes the price to rise. As the price rises from p', excess demand diminishes until equilibrium is restored at the higher price, $\bar{p}$, where the excess demand vanishes. Similarly, if the system is initially at the equilibrium $\bar{E}$ and

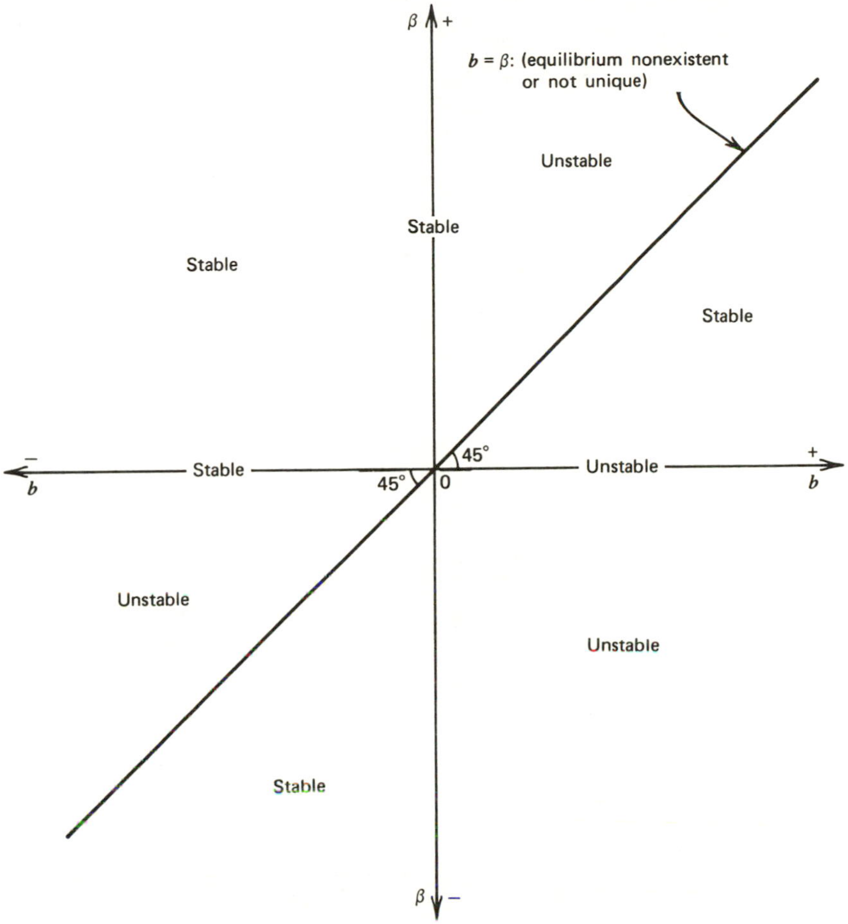

demand falls from $\hat{D}(\cdot, \bar{\alpha})$ to $\hat{D}(\cdot, \alpha')$, excess supply equal to $\bar{x} - \tilde{x}$ arises. As a result, the price falls and continues to fall until the excess supply is eliminated at price p'.

In figure 12.5b, the supply curve is negatively sloped but is not as steep as the demand function. A shift in the demand curve which changes the equilibrium from E' to $\bar{E}$ creates excess demand equal to $\hat{x} - x'$. Hence, the price rises. But the new equilibrium price, $\bar{p}$, is *lower* than p'. Furthermore, as the price rises, excess demand is increased, causing the rise in p to accelerate. A displacement which shifts equilibrium from $\bar{E}$ to E' similarly creates excess supply equal to $\bar{x} - \tilde{x}$, which, in turn, causes the price to *fall* away from the new equilibrium price, p'. Equilibrium is therefore unstable.

In figure 12.5c, the supply curve is again downward sloping but in this case has a steeper slope than does the demand curve. An outward shift in demand creates excess demand equal to $\hat{x} - x'$ and the price rises toward the new

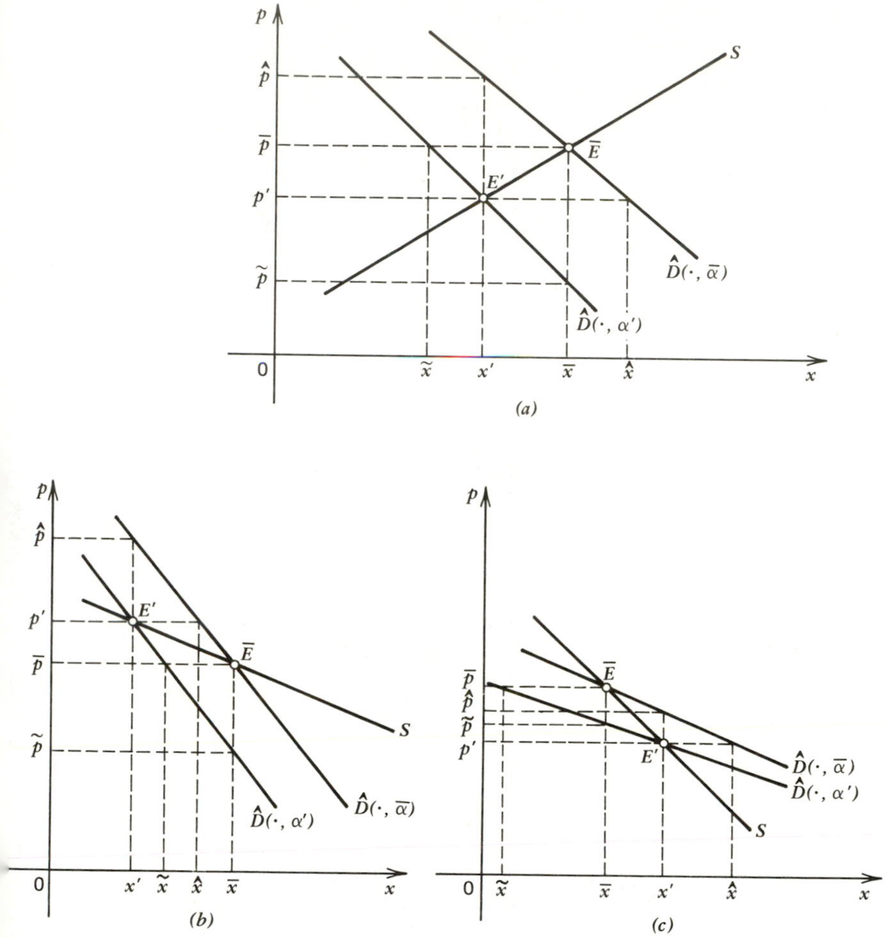

Figure 12.5

equilibrium price $\bar{p}$. A downward shift in demand similarly creates excess supply, causing the price to fall toward the new equilibrium price. Hence, equilibrium is stable.

Graphical illustration of the cases in which the demand and supply curves are positively and negatively sloped, respectively, and the case in which both curves have positive slopes is left to the reader (exercise 12.2).

12.5 A QUANTITY-ADJUSTMENT MODEL

Marshall's Disequilibrium Hypothesis

The dynamic price-adjustment model of Walras (12.16) is not the only possible disequilibrium model. Alfred Marshall conceived of price as the dependent variable in the demand and supply functions. That is, the demand price, $P_d(x)$, is the maximum price which the buyer is willing to pay for a given quantity and the supply price, $P_s(x)$, is the minimum price which the seller requires in order to supply a given output. The Marshallian, or "inverse," market demand and supply functions are therefore obtained by solving the "direct" market demand and supply functions (12.1) for p[6]. Thus, $P_d(x) = D^{-1}(x)$ and $P_s(x) = S^{-1}(x)$.

It is natural, therefore, that Marshall's disequilibrium model should be different from Walras's. Marshall assumed that if the demand price exceeds the supply price, in which case buyers are willing to pay a higher price than sellers are asking, the sellers respond by expanding supply and, if the supply price exceeds the demand price, sellers respond by reducing the quantity supplied. This adjustment mechanism is in the spirit of Marshall's period analysis. In Marshall's "very short run" or "market period," supply is fixed—that is, completely inelastic. The quantity-adjustment mechanism, then, represents shifts in this inelastic market-supply curve over time in response to disparities between supply price and demand price.

This model can be formulated analogously to (12.16) as follows:

$$x'(t) = G(P_d(x(t)) - P_s(x(t))) \tag{12.25}$$

where $G'(P_d(x(t)) - P_s(x(t)) > 0$ for all $x(t)$ and $G(0) = 0$. Hence, the greater is the disparity between demand price and supply price, the faster sellers change output.

Solving the linear demand and supply equations (12.17) and (12.18) for prices,[7]

$$P_d(x) = -\frac{a}{b} + \frac{1}{b}x \tag{12.26}$$

and

$$P_s(x) = -\frac{\alpha}{\beta} + \frac{1}{\beta}x. \tag{12.27}$$

Suppose further that

$$G(P_d(x(t)) - P_s(x(t))) = \theta(P_d(x(t)) - P_s(x(t))),$$

where θ is a positive parameter. Then

$$x'(t) = \theta\left(-\frac{a}{b} + \frac{1}{b}x(t) + \frac{\alpha}{\beta} - \frac{1}{\beta}x(t)\right) = \theta\left(\frac{\alpha}{\beta} - \frac{a}{b}\right) + \theta\left(\frac{1}{b} - \frac{1}{\beta}\right)x(t).$$

[6] This is possible so long as the demand and supply functions are strictly monotonic.

[7] As in the case of the Walrasian price-adjustment model, (local) stability of the nonlinear system can be examined by approximating (12.25) with a first-order Taylor's-series approximation.

The equilibrium quantity is

$$\bar{x} = \frac{\alpha/\beta - a/b}{1/\beta - 1/b}$$

so that

$$x'(t) = \theta\left(\frac{1}{\beta} - \frac{1}{b}\right)\bar{x} + \theta\left(\frac{1}{b} - \frac{1}{\beta}\right)x(t) = \theta\left(\frac{1}{b} - \frac{1}{\beta}\right)(x(t) - \bar{x}). \quad (12.28)$$

Define a new variable $z(t)$ by

$$z(t) = x(t) - \bar{x} \quad (12.29)$$

and note that

$$z'(t) = x'(t). \quad (12.30)$$

Substitution of (12.29) and (12.30) into (12.28) yields

$$z'(t) = \theta\left(\frac{1}{b} - \frac{1}{\beta}\right)z(t). \quad (12.31)$$

The solution to (12.31) is

$$z(t) = z(0)e^{\theta(1/b - 1/\beta)t}.$$

Substituting from (12.29), we obtain

$$x(t) = \bar{x} + (x(t) - x(0))e^{\theta(1/b - 1/\beta)t}.$$

Stability, $\lim_{t\to\infty} x(t) = \bar{x}$, holds if and only if $\theta(1/b - 1/\beta) < 0$ or, as $\theta > 0$,

$$\frac{1}{b} < \frac{1}{\beta}. \quad (12.32)$$

Thus, stability of the Marshallian quantity-adjustment process is equivalent to the condition that the value of the derivative of the demand-price function be less than the value of the derivative of the supply-price function.

If the demand curve is negatively sloped and the supply curve has a positive slope, (12.32) is satisfied and, as in the Walrasian model, the equilibrium is stable. If, however, the supply curve (as well as the demand curve) has a negative slope, stability requires $|1/b| > |1/\beta|$ or $\beta > b$.

It will be recalled that Walrasian stability under these conditions requires just the opposite: $b > \beta$. As in the Walrasian model, however, negatively sloped supply and positively sloped demand curves imply instability. These results are summarized in figure 12.4b.

These processes are illustrated graphically in figure 12.5. The increase in demand in figure 12.5a raises the price which buyers are willing to pay for quantity x' (the demand price) to $\hat{p}$, but the minimum price which sellers will accept for output x' (the supply price) is only p'. As demand price exceeds supply price, suppliers respond, according to Marshall, by increasing quantity. As quantity is increased, the disparity between demand price and supply price declines until, when output $\bar{x}$ is reached, the gap disappears, quantity stops increasing, and the new equilibrium, $\bar{E}$, is achieved.

A displacement from equilibrium $\bar{E}$ by a downward shift in demand similarly creates a gap in which the supply price, $\bar{p}$, exceeds the demand price, $\tilde{p}$, and output declines to x', which equates demand price and supply price at p'. Hence, equilibrium is stable.

In figure 12.5b the negatively sloped supply curve is not as steep as the negatively sloped demand curve. A displacement of equilibrium from E' to $\bar{E}$ increases the demand price to $\hat{p}$ and output rises until $\bar{E}$ is reached. Thus, the equilibrium in figure 12.5b is *stable* under a *Marshallian* adjustment process but *unstable* under a *Walrasian* adjustment process.

The displacement of equilibrium from E' to $\bar{E}$ due to the rise in demand in figure 12.5c results in a demand price $\hat{p}$ which exceeds the supply price p'. Consequently, output *rises*. But the new *equilibrium* output, $\bar{x}$, is *less* than x'. The system is thus moving away from equilibrium. Furthermore, as output rises, the gap between demand price and supply price widens and output moves away from the new equilibrium at an accelerating pace. Thus, the equilibrium in figure 12.5c is *unstable* under a *Marshallian* adjustment process although it is *stable* under the *Walrasian* adjustment process (see also exercise 12.2).

The moral of the foregoing analysis is that the stability of equilibrium cannot be gauged from slopes alone; it can only be discussed in the context of an explicit dynamic model of disequilibrium. Equilibrium is a *static* concept, but the stability of equilibrium is necessarily a *dynamic* concept. Different dynamic models can lead to different conclusions about the stability of a given equilibrium. This is the crux of Samuelson's correspondence principle.[8]

12.6 THE COBWEB MODEL

Before closing this chapter on the stability of equilibrium, let us consider a different type of dynamic model. Divide time into periods and assume that within each period the supply is fixed and price adjusts to equate demand and supply. Further assume that the sellers have to produce the commodity for sale in the previous period (i.e., there is a one-period lag in production) and that they base this supply on the price which prevails in that period. This means that the quantity supplied in period t is a function of the price in period $t-1$: $S(p(t-1))$. This type of supply function might characterize markets in which the period of

[8] Another facet of Samuelson's correspondence principle is that "... definite *operationally meaningful* theorems can be derived from the assumption that equilibrium is stable" (Samuelson [1947a, p. 5]). For example, it was shown above that if the supply curve is negatively sloped, $\bar{p}'(\alpha)$ and $\bar{x}'(\alpha)$ are unsigned. If, however, a Walrasian or Marshallian model of disequilibrium is posited and stability is *assumed*, the signs of $\bar{p}'(\alpha)$ and $\bar{x}'(\alpha)$ are determined. (The reader can easily verify that with a Walrasian adjustment model stability implies that $\bar{p}'(\alpha) > 0$ and $\bar{x}'(\alpha) < 0$ and that the opposite is true for a Marshallian adjustment model.)

Arrow and Hahn [1971, p. 321] point out, however, that while Samuelson's stability conditions are sufficient, they are not necessary in the general nonlinear case and this is why this facet of the correspondence principle "isn't."

production (the length of time needed to produce the commodity) is long relative to the length of time that it takes to clear the market. It has been found, for example, that the supply of hogs is closely related to the price of hogs months earlier, and the supply of engineers is related to the salary of engineers four years earlier.

Assuming that there is no lag in demand, the demand-function image is $D(p(t))$. Since the price adjusts to clear the market within each period,

$$D(p(t)) = S(p(t-1)). \tag{12.33}$$

Letting the demand and supply functions be linear as above (12.17–18)[9], we can rewrite equation (12.33) as $a + bp(t) = \alpha + \beta p(t-1)$, or

$$p(t) = \frac{\alpha - a}{b} + \frac{\beta}{b} p(t-1). \tag{12.34}$$

Recalling that the equilibrium price is

$$\bar{p} = \frac{\alpha - a}{b - \beta},$$

we can rewrite (12.34) as

$$p(t) = \frac{b - \beta}{b} \bar{p} + \frac{\beta}{b} p(t-1) = \bar{p} - \frac{\beta}{b} \bar{p} + \frac{\beta}{b} p(t-1).$$

Hence $p(t) - \bar{p} = (\beta/b)\,(p(t-1) - \bar{p})$.

Defining the new variable,

$$z(t) = p(t) - \bar{p}, \tag{12.35}$$

we obtain

$$z(t) = \frac{\beta}{b} z(t-1). \tag{12.36}$$

Equation (12.36) is the simplest type of difference equation with the solution $z(t) = z(0)\,(\beta/b)^t$ (see equations (12.11)–(12.12)). Substitution from (12.35) yields $p(t) - \bar{p} = (\bar{p}(0) - \bar{p})\,(\beta/b)^t$, or

$$p(t) = \bar{p} + (p(0) - \bar{p}))\left(\frac{\beta}{b}\right)^t. \tag{12.37}$$

Stability requires $|\beta/b| < 1$ or $|\beta| < |b|$. That is, the absolute value of the demand-function derivative must be greater than the absolute value of the supply-function derivative. (The model is quasistable if $|\beta| = |b|$.)

If $b < 0$ and $\beta > 0$, $\beta/b < 0$ and $(\beta/b)^t$ alternates in sign as t increases. From (12.37) it can be seen that this means that the price oscillates about the equilibrium price, $\bar{p}$. If $|\beta/b| < 1$ the oscillations are damped; if $|\beta/b| = 1$, the

[9] Again, local stability of the more general model can be carried out by taking a first-order Taylor's-series approximation.

$(p(t) - p(0))\,(\beta/b)^t$, or

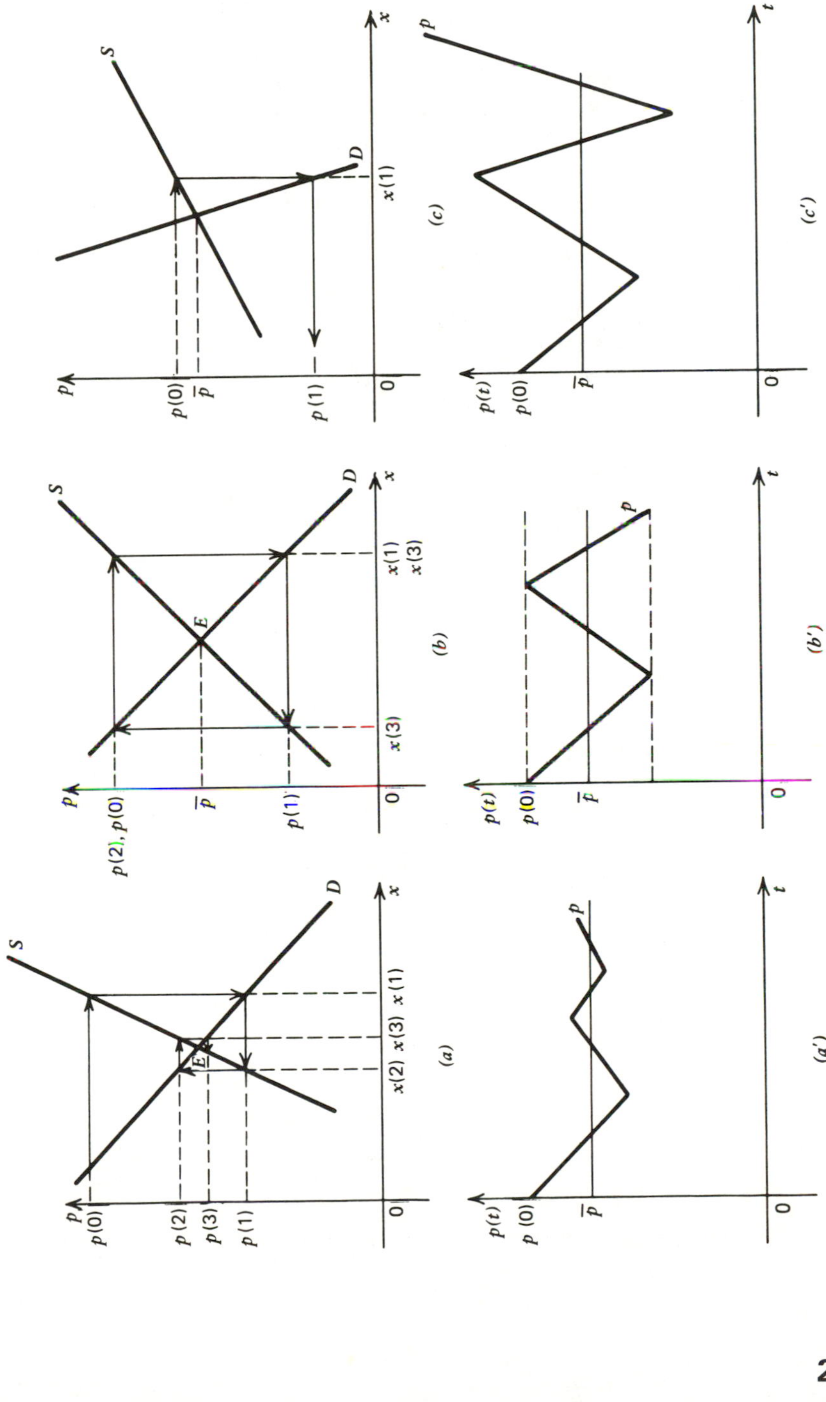

Figure 12.6

oscillations have constant amplitude, neither converging nor diverging; if $|\beta/b| > 1$, oscillations explode.

If both derivatives are negative, $\beta/b > 0$ and the sign of $(\beta/b)^t$ does not vary with respect to t. Thus, if $|\beta| < |b|$ $(\beta > b)$, the price moves monotonically toward equilibrium and if $|\beta| > |b|$ $(\beta < b)$, the price explodes monotonically.

These different possibilities are represented in figures 12.6 and 12.7. In figure 12.6, the supply curve has a positive slope and the demand curve has a negative slope. In figure 12.6a, the supply curve is steeper. Given price $p(0)$ in the initial period, sellers bring $x(1)$ to the market in period 1. In order to clear the market, the price must fall to $p(1)$. Cognizant of the lower price $p(1)$, the sellers contract production and bring only $x(2)$ to the market in period 2. The market is then cleared at price $p(2)$, which is again above $\bar{p}$, but lower than $p(0)$. The supply in period 3 is therefore $x(3)$, higher than $\bar{x}$, but less than $x(1)$. It can thus be seen from these few steps and from the succeeding path that the system is converging toward equilibrium. Figure 12.6a′ shows the corresponding path of price over time. Because of the pattern woven by the time path of price and quantity, this dynamic model has become known as the "cobweb model."

In figure 12.6b, the absolute slope is the same for both curves. In period 1 price falls to $p(1)$ but in period 2 it bounces back to $p(0)$, then to $p(1)$ again,

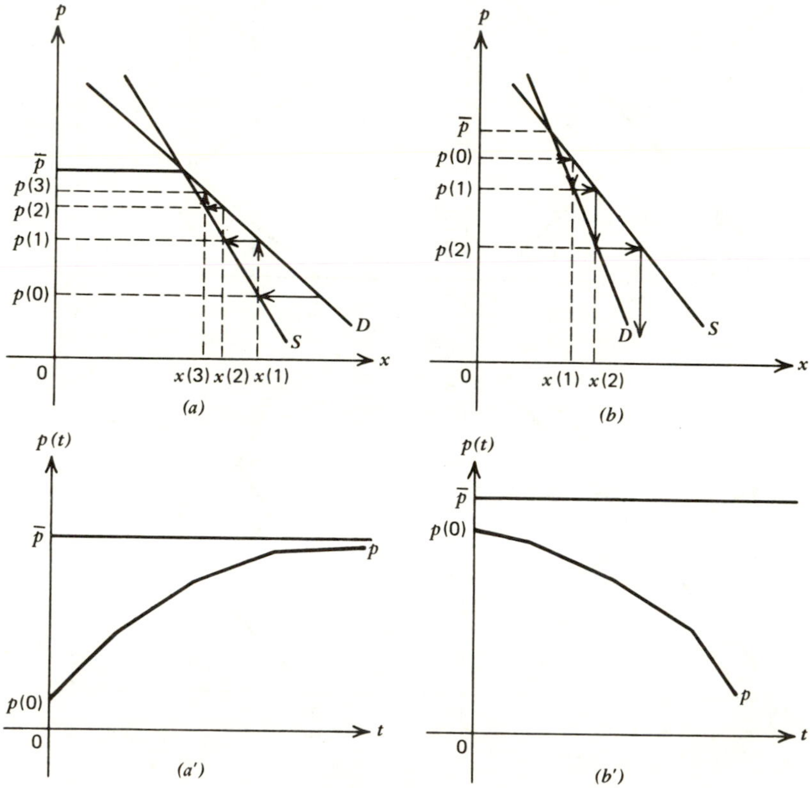

Figure 12.7

etc. Thus, the price does not converge to $\bar{p}$, but neither does it explode. Figure 12.6b′ illustrates this time path. In Figure 12.6c, the demand curve is more steeply sloped and the oscillations about equilibrium are seen to explode (see figure 12.6c′).

Figure 12.7 illustrates the case in which the supply curve, as well as the demand curve, is negatively sloped. In figure 12.7a, the supply curve is steeper. Initial price $p(0)$ solicits a supply of $x(1)$ in period 1. The price rises to $p(1)$ to clear the market and in period 2 output therefore falls to $x(2)$, raising price to $p(2)$. The price thus rises monotonically toward equilibrium (see figure 12.7a′). In figure 12.7b, the demand curve is steeper and the price diverges monotonically from equilibrium (see figure 12.7b′).

EXERCISES

Comparative Statics

12.1 Carry out the algebraic analysis of section 12.2, assuming, however, that the shift parameter, α, enters the supply function rather than the demand function.

12.2 Carry out the graphical analysis of section 12.4, where the demand and supply curves are (a) positively and negatively sloped, respectively, and (b) where both curves have positive slopes.
Repeat (a) and (b) for the quantity-adjustment model of section 12.5.

12.3 Prove that the relative incidence of an excise tax (i.e., the relative share of the tax [per unit sold] borne by (a) the buyers and (b) the sellers) is independent of whether the tax is imposed on the buyers or on the sellers of the commodity. (Hint: use the inverse demand and supply functions.)

12.4 Prove that the relative (differential) incidence of (a differential change in) an excise tax depends upon the relative slopes (hence the relative elasticities) of the demand and supply functions at the equilibrium point.

12.5 If the principal purpose of an excise tax is the procurement of government revenue, a given tax rate will be more effective as demand is *less* elastic. If the principle purpose of the tax is to reduce consumption of a "socially undesirable" commodity, a given tax rate is more effective as demand is *more* elastic. Illustrate these facts diagrammatically.

Stability

12.6 Suppose that the demand and supply functions are given by $D(p(t)) = a + bp(t)$, $b < 0$, and $S(p(t-1)) = c + dp(t-1)$, $d > 0$. Consider a "market-stabilization board" which enters the market to buy or sell if price falls below or above some "normal" price, $\hat{p}$. In particular, it follows the decision rule, $D^b(p(t-1)) = a(\hat{p} - p(t-1))$, $a > 0$, where $D^b(p(t-1))$ is its purchase in period t.

a. Is it possible for the board to stabilize an otherwise unstable market? Is it possible for the board to destabilize an otherwise stable market?

b. If the market (including the stabilization board activities) is stable, does the price approach $\bar{p}$? What is the implication of your answer for the viability of the stabilization board?

c. How would you modify the purchase rule of the stabilization board in order to reverse the answers to part (a)?

The next two exercises require some mathematical sophistication.

12.7 Examine the local stability of the general Walrasian disequilibrium model (12.16) by taking a first-order Taylor's-series approximation about the equilibrium price $\bar{p}$. (Hint: see Samuelson [1947, chap. 9].)

12.8 Construct a counterexample to the (false) assertion that stability of the general Walrasian dynamic system implies stability of the first-order system examined in exercise 12.7. (Hint: cogitate over the last sentence in footnote 5 and figure 12.4a.)

CHAPTER 13
THE THEORIES OF MONOPOLY AND MONOPOLISTIC COMPETITION

13.1 INTRODUCTION

Market Structure

In chapter 11, we consolidated the theories of the consumer and the producer in order to explain the determination of price and output in a single perfectly competitive market. The salient feature in the derivation of the demand and supply functions of this particular market structure is the assumption that individual buyers and sellers treat prices as parameters; that is, they act as if they have no control over the prevailing commodity prices. In many markets these assumptions approximate reality closely enough to yield accurate predictions. It is also true, however, that for a large number of commodities there are so few buyers or sellers that the decision of any one has a perceptible effect upon the commodity prices. In these markets, use of the perfectly competitive model might be inappropriate. Consequently, in this and the following chapter we drop the assumption that agents are price takers and consider markets where the number of buyers or sellers is too small to rationalize the price-taking assumption.

One type of market structure which has the same simplicity and tractability as the perfectly competitive model is that characterized by a single seller of a particular commodity. This market structure is called *monopoly*. A market with one buyer is called *monopsony*. These market structures, together with the perfectly competitive market structure, constitute the polar (or extreme) cases of market structures. In between these polar cases are markets characterized by more than one seller (or buyer) but not so many as to justify neglecting the influence of the actions of any one upon price. These intermediate market structures are referred to as *oligopolies*. Also intermediate between these polar cases is *monopolistic competition*, in which there are a large number of sellers of slightly differentiated commodities, so that each producer is a monopolist with respect to his own (narrowly defined) commodity but is subject to competitive pressures from producers of closely related commodities.

Sources of Monopoly

Monopolies may arise for a number of reasons, including: (1) exclusive control of essential resources needed to produce a given commodity, (2) cost and demand conditions which are such that no more than one supplier can earn nonnegative profits ("natural" monopolies), and (3) governmental exclusion of competitors.[1]

Important examples of the first type of monopoly are difficult to find, but the stylized notion of a single fresh-water spring in an otherwise parched community is a standby in the literature on monopoly.

Natural monopolies exist where the fixed costs of producing a particular commodity are so large relative to the size of the market that two firms could not survive. For example, the cost of constructing the complex network of lines and terminals in order to operate a telephone system is gargantuan. Hence, if two firms were to incur these costs with duplicate facilities and split the market for telephone services, it is unlikely that both could survive. Similarly, constructing a competitive dam and attendant facilities, transmission lines, etc., in order to service a particular area with competitive electricity would probably not be economically feasible.[2]

Many monopolies are legally sanctioned. One common type of legal monopoly is that which results from patents on inventions. The purpose of the patents is to encourage invention and innovation by bestowing legal monopolies on successful inventions for a period of 17 years. Patents may apply to a type of commodity or a type of production process.[3]

Other monopolies are constituted by exclusive licensed franchises. Most of these types of monopolies are referred to as public utilities (e.g., gas, light, and water companies; railroads and other public carriers; telephone, mail, and other communication services). Because the government grants these producers monopolistic market positions, government regulation of price and/or profit rates usually accompanies the legal franchise. Moreover, in many if not most of these cases the government franchising of monopoly does not create the monopolistic structure but is actually a de facto recognition of the existence of natural monopolies (described above).

Sections 13.2–13.5 develop the classical theory of monopoly for a produced commodity. Section 13.6 examines monopsonistic market structures, section 13.7 analyzes monopoly regulation, while section 13.8 considers monopolistic price discrimination. Finally, section 13.9 discusses the theory of monopolistic competition.

[1] Although these reasons for monopoly are formulated in the context of production, consumers may well be monopolists with regard to the supply of particular types of labor (e.g., professional athletes, entertainers, and surgeons).

[2] Intrinsically related to this source of monopoly are large capital costs of founding an airline, steel company, etc. The inability to raise such capital in financial markets may be explained by the inability of an additional producer to earn positive profits.

[3] Analogous to the patent is the copyright, which protects authors from plagiarism. The trademark is a more subtle economic phenomenon. If the trademark is one of the defining characteristics of a commodity, the trademark law bestows monopolies as well. (See the discussion of product differentiation in section 13.9 below.)

13.2 THE ASSUMPTIONS OF CLASSICAL MONOPOLY THEORY

In developing the theory of monopoly we retain the usual assumptions concerning the economic environment (section 1.2), and with one exception assume that consumers and producers satisfy all assumptions of parts I and II. The exception is the profit-maximization assumption for the producer (assumption 7.1) which will be replaced below in section 13.4. In addition we introduce the following four assumptions for the classical theory of monopoly.[4]

Assumption 13.1 The market consists of a single producer of a commodity for which there are no perfect substitutes.

Assumption 13.2 Buyers take prices as given while the single producer takes input prices as given.

Assumption 13.3 There is no cost of exchange.

Assumption 13.4 All buyers and the single producer possess perfect information concerning prices, availability, and physical characteristics of commodities.

The above four assumptions taken together guarantee that the entire market demand curve is the demand curve for the monopolist. The same price applies to all exchanges of the commodity, but the price depends upon the quantity sold.

Whatever the raison d'être of monopoly, the first assumption is that while a monopolist is the only producer of a given commodity, he is not immune from competitive pressures from close and distant substitutes for the commodity. Indeed, all consumer commodities are substitutes for one another in the sense that they all compete for the consumer's dollar. The critical difference between the monopolist and the perfect competitor is that there exist *perfect* substitutes for the perfect competitor's product whereas the substitutes for the monopolist's commodity are less than perfect. For example, while the telephone company may have a monopoly of a telephone service, the telegram is a (less than perfect) substitute. Hence, raising telephone rates will probably reduce the demand for telephone services as consumers shift their messages from the telephone medium to the telegram medium. A more distant substitute for telephone services is the mail. Similarly, although Alcoa enjoyed a monopolistic position in the aluminum market for years, it was still subject to competitive pressure from alternative metals such as steel, tin, and plastic. Thus, although the monopolist is the sole seller of a given commodity, he must take the availability of substitutes into account in his pricing policies. These competitive pressures are embodied in the form of the demand function, which for the monopolist is the entire market demand function.

[4] We refer to this theory as the classical monopoly model because it constitutes the simplest and most fundamental version upon which current extensions and elaborations are founded. See the suggestions for further reading at the end of part III.

Assumptions 13.2–13.4 guarantee that the same price applies to all exchanges of the commodity. The second assumption assures that each buyer believes he cannot influence price. In addition, there is no possibility of a number of buyers getting together (for example, in the form of a consumer cooperative) to influence price by bargaining with the monopolist. The third and fourth assumptions preclude multiple selling prices despite the large number of independent buyers. Given perfect information and no costs of exchange the monopolist is unable to charge different prices to different buyers since competitive bidding among the latter will eliminate any price differentials.[5] The third and fourth assumptions are the same as those made about buyers and sellers in perfectly competitive markets.

13.3 MONOPOLY DEMAND AND REVENUE FUNCTIONS

The Demand Curve for the Monopolist

The essential characteristic of a monopolistic market is that the demand curve for the monopolist is the entire market demand curve. This means that, unlike the producer operating in a perfectly competitive environment, the monopolist cannot construe the price as a parameter. As the monopolist changes production of the commodity, the price changes.

To formalize the variability of price, suppose that the produced commodity is a consumer commodity and recall that market demand is given by $D(p)$ where p is the price and D is the demand function (restricted by suppressing income and "other-price" variables and the commodity subscript). Thus, if the monopolist charges price $\bar{p}$, quantity demanded is $D(\bar{p})$. If quantity demanded varies monotonically with respect to price (e.g., the commodity is non-Giffen for the market as a whole), we can solve for (demand) price as a function of quantity (see section 12.5),

$$p = D^{-1}(q) = P_d(q).$$

Thus, if the monopolist wishes to sell $\bar{q}$ units, the price must be set no higher than $P_d(\bar{q})$.

Throughout this chapter, we assume that the commodity which is sold in the monopolistic market is not a Giffen commodity in the aggregate so that $D'(p) = dD(p)/dp < 0$, for all p and, therefore, $P_d'(q) = dP_d(q)/dq < 0$ for all q. That is, as the monopolist expands (contracts) output the price declines (rises). Conversely, as the monopolist increases (decreases) the price, the amount which is demanded falls (rises).

[5] We alter these assumptions in section 13.8 below, and consider the theory of price-discriminating monopoly.

The Revenue Function of the Monopolist

The revenue function of the monopolist is given by

$$R(q) = p \cdot q = P_d(q) \cdot q.$$

It is now convenient to define a new marginal concept. The *marginal revenue* is the rate at which revenue increases when output is expanded at the rate of one unit per time period. In the case where the demand function is differentiable, marginal revenue at a point is simply the derivative of the revenue function with respect to output,

$$MR(q) = R'(q) = p + qP_d'(q). \tag{13.1}$$

The demand curve for a producer operating in a perfectly competitive market is horizontal so that $P_d'(q) = 0$ and therefore $MR(q) = p$ for all q. On the other hand, the marginal-revenue function of a monopolist takes into the account the fact that as output is changed the output price changes. Thus, marginal revenue is the sum of two terms: the price plus the second term of equation (13.1) which adjusts for the fact that the price of all units sold changes as output changes. In the normal case where $P_d'(q) < 0$, this adjustment factor for the determination of marginal revenue of a monopolist is negative. Hence, in the normal case, marginal revenue is everywhere less than price. A demand curve, together with the corresponding marginal-revenue curve, is illustrated for the normal case in the top panel of figure 13.1. The bottom panel of figure 13.1 illustrates the corresponding revenue function. It will be noted that total revenue reaches a maximum where marginal revenue vanishes.

There is a simple and useful relationship between the own price elasticity of demand, marginal revenue, and price. This relationship can be derived by simple manipulation of (13.1), which can be written as

$$MR(q) = p\left(1 + \frac{q}{p} P_d'(q)\right)$$

or, noting that $P_d'(q)$ equals $1/D'(p)$,

$$MR(q) = p\left(1 + \frac{1}{D'(p)(p/q)}\right).$$

But, recalling the definition of the own-price elasticity of demand (Section 6.2), we have the desired relationship,

$$MR(q) = p\left(1 + \frac{1}{e_{ii}(p)}\right). \tag{13.2}$$

From this relationship it is apparent that when $e_{ii}(p) = -1$, marginal revenue is equal to zero; when $e_{ii}(p) < -1$, $MR(q) > 0$; and when $e_{ii}(p) > -1$, $MR(q) < 0$.

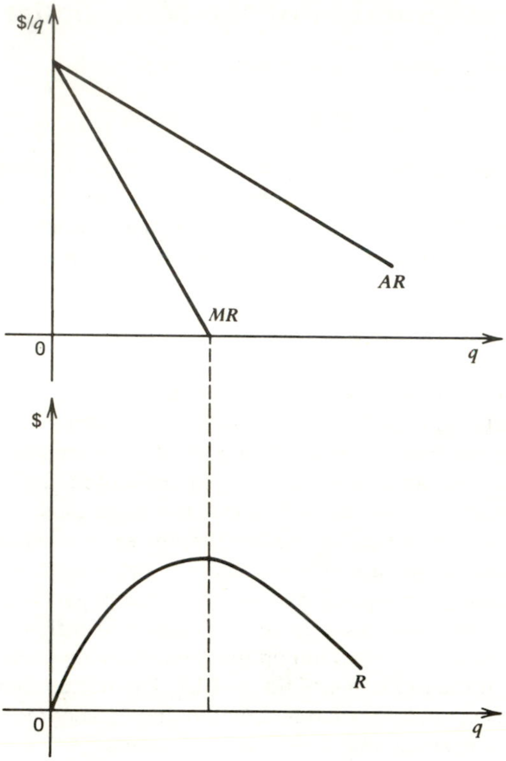

Figure 13.1

13.4 MONOPOLY EQUILIBRIUM

Profit Maximization

We now turn to the optimization problem for the monopolist.

Assumption 13.5 Given the market demand function, the monopolist chooses either quantity or price to maximize profit.

Thus, the optimization problem of the monopolist is

$$\max_{q} \Pi(q) = R(q) - C(q), \tag{13.3}$$

where C is the cost function (with input price variables suppressed). The first-order condition is

$$\frac{d\Pi(q)}{dq} = \frac{dR(q)}{dq} - \frac{dC(q)}{dq} = 0.$$

Recalling that the derivative of the revenue function is marginal revenue and that the derivative of the cost function is marginal cost, $MC(q)$, we have the profit-maximization condition,

$$MR(q) = MC(q). \tag{13.4}$$

Thus, at the optimum the monopolist produces an output that equates marginal revenue and marginal cost. This condition makes sense. For if marginal revenue were less than marginal cost, reducing output would decrease costs by more than it would decrease revenue so that total profit would increase. Similarly, profit cannot be maximized where $MR(q) > MC(q)$; an expansion in output would increase revenue by more than it would increase costs, thus raising the profit. Thus, the maximization of profit requires that marginal revenue and marginal cost be equated.

We might at this point note that this profit-maximization condition subsumes the perfectly competitive profit-maximization condition as a special case. It will be recalled from section 9.5 that a producer operating in a perfectly competitive market maximizes profits by equating price and marginal cost. However, for a producer operating in a perfectly competitive market, price and marginal revenue are equivalent so that (13.4) represents the profit-maximization condition for a producer operating in a perfectly competitive market as well as for a monopolist.

The second-order condition for q to solve (13.3) is

$$\frac{d^2\Pi(q)}{dq} = \frac{d^2R(q)}{dq^2} - \frac{d^2C(q)}{dq^2} < 0$$

or

$$\frac{dMR(q)}{dq} < \frac{dMC(q)}{dq}. \tag{13.5}$$

Thus, profit maximization requires that marginal revenue be equated to marginal cost *and* that the rate of change of marginal cost with respect to output be greater than the rate of change of marginal revenue with respect to output. Note that the second-order condition is satisfied if marginal cost is rising with respect to output and marginal revenue is falling. Rising marginal cost is not, however, necessary for an output to be optimal. If marginal cost is falling with respect to output but falling less rapidly than is marginal revenue, an output which equates marginal revenue and marginal cost yields an optimum.

Graphical Illustration of Profit Maximization

The optimality condition of the monopolist can be illustrated graphically. Merely for the purpose of illustration, let us assume that the production technology yields first decreasing, then increasing, marginal cost so that the total-variable-cost and total-cost curves take the form illustrated in figure 13.2. Also drawn in this figure is a revenue function with decreasing average and marginal revenue. Total profit in this diagram is given by the vertical difference between the revenue curve and the total-cost curve. It can be seen that at low outputs

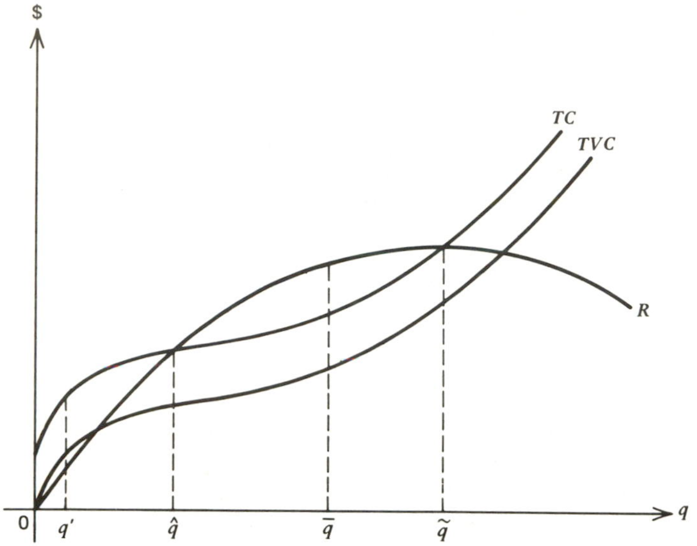

Figure 13.2

profit is negative since the total cost curve lies above the revenue curve. Profit becomes positive at output $\hat{q}$ and becomes negative again at output $\tilde{q}$. Maximum profits must therefore lie between $\hat{q}$ and $\tilde{q}$. It is clearly true that so long as the slope of the revenue curve is greater than the slope of the total-cost curve, the two curves are diverging (hence, profit is growing) as output is expanded in the interval $\hat{q} - \tilde{q}$. Moreover, when the slope of the revenue curve is less than the slope of the total-cost curve, the two curves are converging (hence, profit is falling) as output expands. It follows that the maximum vertical distance between the two curves occurs at that output at which the two slopes are equal. In the diagram, this equality occurs at output $\bar{q}$. But the slope of the revenue curve is simply marginal revenue and the slope of the total-cost curve is marginal cost. Hence, this diagrammatic analysis confirms the result derived mathematically above: profit is maximized at an output which equates marginal revenue and marginal cost.

It might be noted that the slopes of the revenue curve and the total-cost curve are also equal at the lower output, q'. Hence, at this output the first-order condition for a profit maximum, $MR(q') = MC(q')$, is satisfied. However, at this output the slope of the total-cost curve is falling at a faster rate than the slope of the total revenue curve; thus the second-order condition (13.5) is violated.

Profit maximization for the monopolist can also be illustrated using average-cost and marginal-cost curves. In figure 13.3, the marginal-cost, average-total-cost, average-variable-cost, and average-fixed-cost curves corresponding to the total-cost and total-variable-cost curves in figure 13.2 are drawn. We also superimpose on these cost curves the demand curve, or average-revenue curve, faced by the monopolist and the corresponding marginal-revenue curve. Profit is maximized at output $\bar{q}$ where the marginal-cost curve intersects the

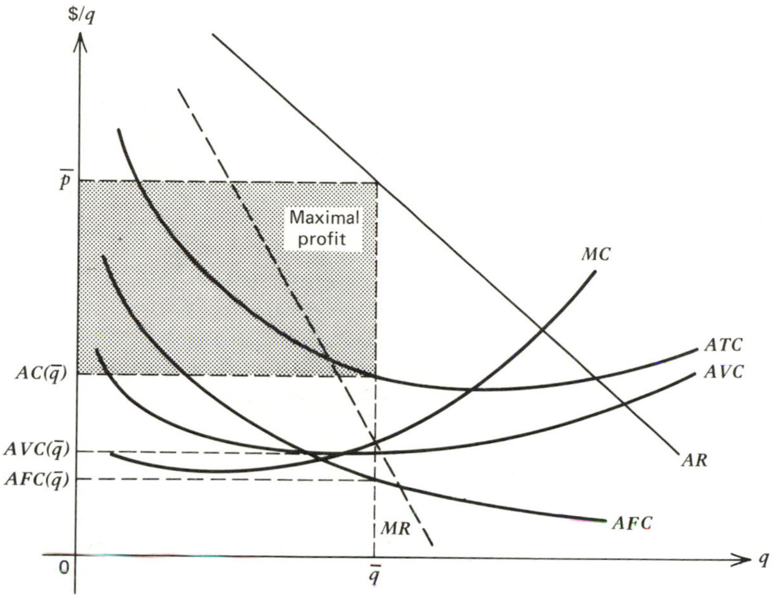

Figure 13.3

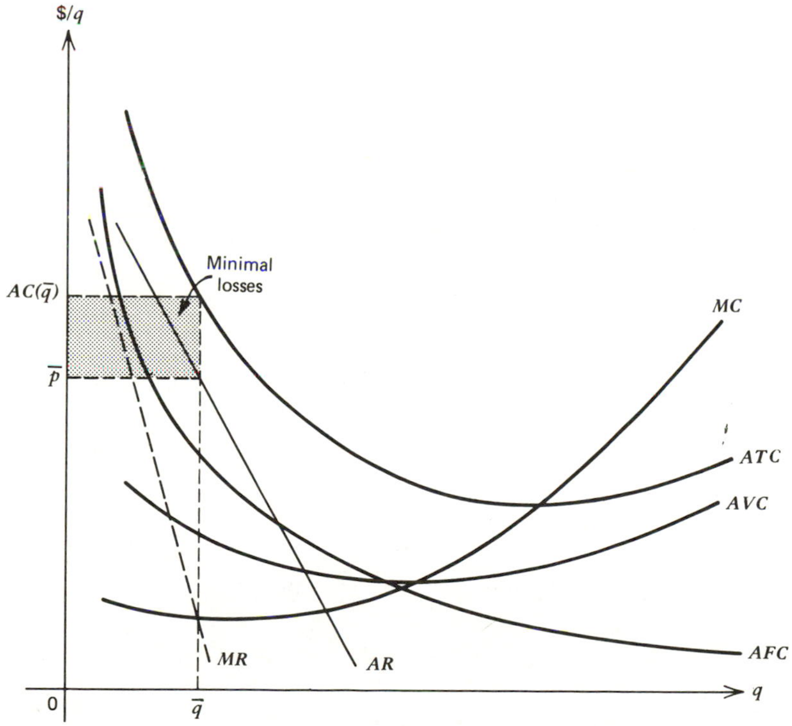

Figure 13.4

marginal-revenue curve. At this output, the price is $\bar{p}$ and average cost is $AC(\bar{q})$, the sum of average fixed cost AFC and average variable cost $AVC(\bar{q})$ of production. Hence, on each unit of output which is produced and sold, the monopolist earns a profit of $\bar{p} - AC(\bar{q})$. Total profit is therefore given by the shaded area in figure 13.3.

It is not a foregone conclusion that monopoly power yields positive profit. Figure 13.4 illustrates a cost structure and demand function which do not yield positive profit. At the profit-maximizing output, $\bar{q}$, the average cost of production $AC(\bar{q})$ is greater than the price $\bar{p}$. Thus, the monopolist suffers a loss equal to the shaded area in the diagram. A monopolistic producer in the position depicted in figure 13.4 will go out of business in the long run unless he can construct a more optimally sized plant which yields nonnegative profit. Finally, it is also possible to conceive of a situation in which a monopolist is unable to cover even variable cost of production. In this case, the monopolist ceases production even in the short run.

13.5 INPUT DEMAND OF THE MONOPOLIST

Profit Maximization

Even though a producer might be the only supplier of a particular commodity, he may be one of a large number of buyers of an input in his production process. We therefore first consider the problem of input demand of a monopolist who treats input prices as parameters (i.e., the monopolist has no market power in the input markets). Total outlay of the monopolist is then given by $\sum_{i=1}^{m} w_i v_i$, where w_i and v_i are the price and quantity of the ith input, respectively. Given a production function with image, $q = f(v_i, \ldots, v_m) = f(v)$, the monopolist's profit-maximization problem is

$$\max_{v}\left(p \cdot q - \sum_{i=1}^{m} w_i v_i\right) \qquad \text{s.t. } q = f(v) \text{ and } p = P_d(q).$$

Substituting the constraints into the objective function, we have

$$\max_{v} P_d f(v) \cdot f(v) - \sum_{i=1}^{m} w_i v_i.$$

The first-order conditions are

$$P_d'(f(v)) \cdot \frac{\partial f(v)}{\partial v_i} \cdot f(v) + P_d(f(v)) \cdot \frac{\partial f(v)}{\partial v_i} - w_i = 0, \qquad i = 1, \ldots, m.$$

Rearranging terms and substituting q for $f(v)$, we obtain

$$\frac{\partial f(v)}{\partial v_i}\,(P_d(q) + qP_d'(q)) = w_i, \qquad i = 1, \ldots, m.$$

Note, however, that $\partial f(v)/\partial v_i$ is the marginal product of the ith input and (from (13.1) above) the term in parentheses is the marginal revenue; hence, the first-order profit-maximization conditions are

$$MP_i(v) \cdot MR(q) = w_i, \qquad i = 1, \ldots, m. \tag{13.6}$$

Thus, the profit-maximizing monopolist hires each variable input up to the point where the product of the marginal product and the marginal revenue are equated to the input price. The marginal product multiplied by the marginal revenue has a natural interpretation: it reflects the amount by which revenue rises when the employment of the ith input is increased by one unit. The marginal product reflects the rise in output when the level of utilization of the input is increased by one unit. When this rise in output is multiplied by the change in total revenue resulting from a one-unit change in output, the result is the rise in revenue brought about by a unit increase in the rate of utilization of the ith variable input. This increase in revenue when input utilization is increased by one unit is called the *marginal revenue product* (MRP_i) of the ith input. Thus, the optimality conditions (13.6) can be rewritten as

$$MRP_i(v) = w_i, \qquad i = 1, \ldots, m. \tag{13.7}$$

This optimality condition makes sense. If the marginal revenue product of the ith input were, say, less than the ith input price, reducing the amount of the input employed would reduce revenue by less than it would reduce costs, thus raising profits. Conversely, if the marginal revenue product were greater than input price, raising the level of utilization of the input would increase revenue by more than it would increase costs, thus increasing profits. Consequently, profit maximization requires that the marginal revenue product and input price be equated.

This equilibrium condition is analogous to the input demand condition for the producer operating in a perfectly competitive market. It will be recalled from section 8.4 that a producer operating in a competitive market hires an input up to the point where the value of the marginal product (price of the product times marginal product) is equated to the price of the input. For the monopolist, however, the price of the product does not reflect the contribution to revenue of hiring additional units of the variable input and selling the resulting output in the market. The appropriate concept in this situation is the marginal revenue.

It can also be shown that the second-order conditions for solving the monopoly profit-maximization problem imply that the marginal revenue product be declining with respect to input quantity changes.

Graphical Illustration of Input Demand

The above optimality conditions are illustrated in figure 13.5 where a marginal-revenue-product curve reflecting first increasing, then decreasing, returns to the variable input (first rising, then falling, marginal product) is illustrated. At price $\overset{*}{w}_i$, the optimal employment of the ith variable input is given at output level $\overset{*}{v}_i$, where the horizontal line determined by the input price intersects the marginal-revenue-product curve. It will be noted that the horizontal

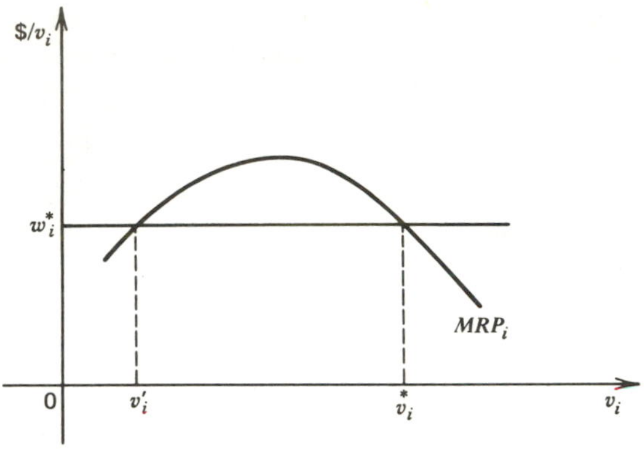

Figure 13.5

input-price line intersects the MRP curve in two places. At the first of these two intersections (at utilization rate v_i'), however, the *MRP* curve is rising. Consequently, the second-order condition for profit maximization is not satisfied and this represents a point of minimal rather than maximal profit.

The Input Demand Function

Finally, the monopolist's input demand functions can be obtained by solving the m first-order conditions (13.7) for the m values of v_i:

$$v_i = \delta_i(w), \qquad i = 1, \ldots, m. \tag{13.8}$$

Note that the input demands depend upon the m input prices—the only prices that are parametric to the monopolist who purchases inputs in competitive markets.[6] This contrasts with the input demands of producers who also sell in competitive markets—they depend upon all input prices *and* the output price.

13.6 MONOPSONY

The Input Supply Functions

In analyzing input demand, we have thus far assumed that the producer, although a monopolist in the product market, has no market power in input markets. We now consider the situation in which the monopolist is also dominant in the input markets. Under these circumstances, as the monopolist changes his demand for an input, the price which he pays for the input is altered. If the monopolist is the only buyer of an input, the price which he must pay for the input is determined by the input supply curve. This type of imperfectly competitive input market is called *monopsony*.

[6] If there is only one variable input, the input demand curve is equivalent to the downward-sloping portion of the marginal-revenue-product curve.

We assume that the input markets of the monopsonist are composed of large numbers of price-taking sellers. The input supply functions are therefore obtained by aggregating over the supply functions of individual producers (see section 11.3) or, in the case of labor markets, over the supply functions of individual consumers (see section 6.3).

We assume throughout the analysis of monopsonistic markets that the input supply functions, S_i, $i = 1, \ldots, m$, satisfy

$$\frac{dS_i(w_i)}{dw_i} > 0.^7 \tag{13.9}$$

For example, if the input is labor services, the above assumption precludes a backward-bending portion of the labor supply function. The constraint (13.9) allows us to invert the input supply function to obtain an input price function; i.e.,

$$w_i = S^{-1}(v_i) = W_i(v_i), \tag{13.10}$$

where W_i satisfies

$$\frac{dW_i(v_i)}{dv_i} > 0.$$

Marginal Input Cost

As the price of all units of the inputs employed by the monopsonist increases when employment increases, it is no longer true that the input price reflects the effect that hiring additional amounts of the input has upon costs. The change in total cost resulting from increasing the employment of the *i*th input by one unit is called the *marginal input cost* of the *i*th input and is denoted MIC_i. Marginal input cost at a point is determined by differentiating the expression for total expenditure on the *i*th input, $W_i(v_i) \cdot v_i$, with respect to v_i, yielding

$$MIC_i(v_i) = w_i + \frac{dW_i(v_i)}{dv_i} v_i. \tag{13.11}$$

This expression indicates that marginal input cost is the sum of two components. The first of these is the input price, w_i, and the second term is an adjustment factor which incorporates the effect upon cost of changing the input price of all units of the input employed by the monopsonist. Because of the assumption that $dW_i(v_i)/dv_i > 0$, it is clear that this adjustment factor is everywhere positive and hence marginal input cost exceeds the input price for all levels of utilization of the input. An input-price curve together with the corresponding marginal-input-cost curve is illustrated in figure 13.6.

The preceding discussion is summarized in the following substitute for assumption 13.2:

Assumption 13.2′ Suppliers of inputs to the monopolist and buyers of the output are price takers. Given the market demand and input supply functions,

[7] Note that, as in chapters 11 and 12, we suppress the other prices in the supply functions.

the monopolist-monopsonist chooses either the quantities of inputs or input prices to maximize profit.

Profit Maximization

Recalling that $p = P_d(q)$ and incorporating (13.10), we can write the profit of the monopolist-monopsonist as

$$P_d(q) \cdot q - \sum_{i=1}^{m} W_i(v_i) \cdot v_i.$$

Substitution of $f(v)$ for q and differentiation yields the first-order profit-maximization conditions:

$$\frac{\partial f(v)}{\partial v_i}(P_d(q) + f(v)P_d'f(v)) - W_i(v_i) - W_i'(v_i) \cdot v_i = 0, \qquad i = 1, \ldots, m.$$

Recalling the definitions of marginal revenue product and marginal input cost (13.10), we can rewrite these conditions as follows:

$$MRP_i(v) = MIC_i(v_i), \qquad i = 1, \ldots, m. \tag{13.12}$$

This equilibrium condition indicates that the monopolist-monopsonist should hire inputs up to the point where the marginal contributions to revenue are exactly equal to the marginal contributions to cost. If $MRP_i(v)$ and $MIC_i(v_i)$ were unequal, it would be possible to increase profit by either increasing or reducing the employment of the input (depending upon the direction of inequality between the two).

Graphical Illustration

Monopsony equilibrium is illustrated in figure 13.6. The optimal level of input employment is $\overset{*}{v}_i$, where the marginal-input-cost curve intersects the

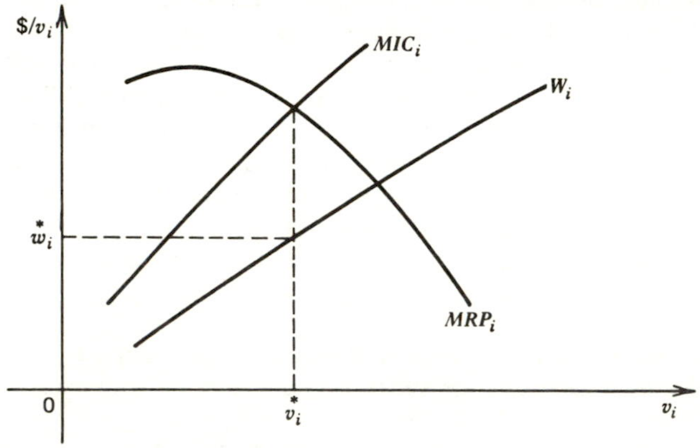

Figure 13.6

marginal-revenue-product curve. To employ this amount of the ith input, the monopsonist must pay the input price $\overset{*}{w}_i$.

Note that (13.12) is also the set of profit-maximization conditions for a monopsonist who sells his output in a perfectly competitive market. In this case, the output price is parametric so that marginal revenue and price are equivalent, hence marginal revenue product and value of marginal product are equivalent. The system of first-order profit-maximization conditions (13.12) can then be written as follows: $VMP_i(v) = MIC_i(v_i)$, $i = 1, \ldots, m$.

Finally, note that a producer could be a monopsonist in some input markets and a perfect competitor in others. In this case, an appropriate combination of the equations (13.7) and (13.12) constitutes the set of first-order profit-maximization conditions.

13.7 MONOPOLY REGULATION

A Rationale for Monopoly Regulation

The preceding analysis of monopoly equilibrium has been positive rather than normative. That is, we have simply examined the nature of monopoly and monopsony equilibrium without addressing the question of what ought to be. In chapter 17, we compare alternative market structures from a normative point of view. We might anticipate that discussion by noting that monopolistic market structures result in an inefficient allocation of resources. The argument may be partially appreciated by observing the profit-maximization condition for a monopolist, exhibited in figure 13.3. At the output which maximizes profit for the monopolist, $\bar{q}$, the price charged by the monopolist, $\bar{p}$, is greater than the marginal cost of production. Under a reasonable set of assumptions, discussed in chapter 17, the price which is paid by the consumer represents the value placed by society on one unit of the commodity and the marginal cost of production reflects the value of the best alternative use of the resources used in the production of one unit of the commodity. Consequently, by expanding production in the monopolistic market, more output can be produced at a price which the consumer is willing to pay and which more than covers the cost of the resources in their best alternative use. Hence, monopoly output is "too low" and monopoly price is "too high." This is one motivation for monopoly regulation.

Regulation of Output Price

One obvious form of regulation of a monopoly is to restrict the price below some maximal level. In figure 13.7, we illustrate the effect upon the demand conditions of imposing a price ceiling on a monopolist. In this diagram, $\bar{p}$ is the price ceiling. Because of the imposition of this price ceiling, the portion of the demand curve above point a is not relevant. In fact, the "effective" demand curve for the monopolist is given by the "kinked" curve formed by the horizontal line $\bar{p}a$ and the ordinary demand curve below point a. For outputs less than $\bar{q}$, although the market would bear a price above $\bar{p}$, the regulation restricts the price to this level. For output levels above $\bar{q}$, however, the buyers are willing to

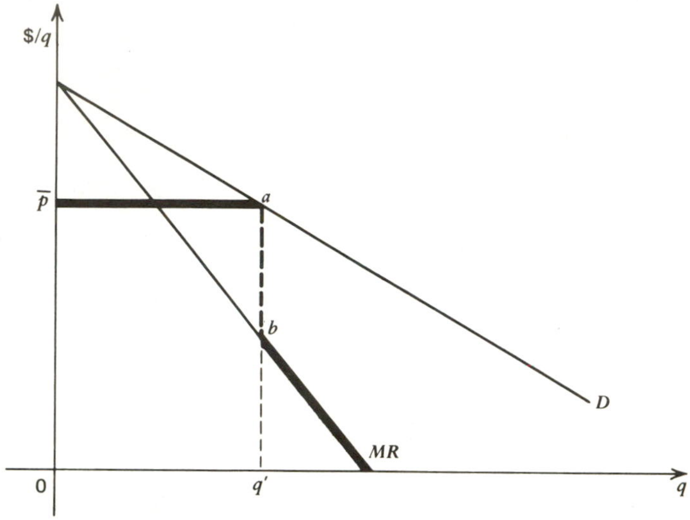

Figure 13.7

pay prices no more than that indicated by the demand curve and therefore the price ceiling is ineffective. The effective marginal-revenue curve corresponding to this kinked effective demand curve is in two parts. For output levels between 0 and $\bar{q}$, the effective demand curve is horizontal, price and marginal revenue are therefore equivalent, and hence the marginal-revenue curve is coincident with the horizontal segment of the effective demand curve. For output levels above $\bar{q}$, the appropriate marginal-revenue curve is that corresponding to the original demand curve. There is therefore a discontinuity at $\bar{q}$, where marginal revenue falls from *a* to *b*. At $\bar{q}$, marginal revenue, strictly speaking, is undefined but for reductions in output marginal revenue is equal to $\bar{p}$ and for increases in output marginal revenue is given by the segment of the original marginal-revenue curve on and below point *b*.

In figure 13.8, the unregulated monopoly optimum occurs at output $\overset{*}{q}$ and price $\overset{*}{p}$. It is apparent that, unless the price ceiling is less than $\overset{*}{p}$, the monopolist is unaffected by price regulation. On the other hand, if the maximum price that the monopolist may charge is below $\overset{*}{p}$, the profit-maximizing output is altered. For example, if the monopolist is required to charge a price of p' or less, the effective demand curve is $p'aD$ and the effective marginal-revenue curve is $p'abMR$. The marginal-cost curve "intersects"—more accurately "passes through"—the discontinuous range of the marginal-revenue curve, indicating that the profit-maximizing output is q'. Should quantity be less than q', it would be possible to increase profits by additional sales since, to the left of q', marginal revenue is greater than marginal cost. Similarly, the monopolist could sell more than this only by reducing price, and additional units of output would add more to cost than to revenue since the marginal-cost curve lies above the effective marginal-revenue curve.

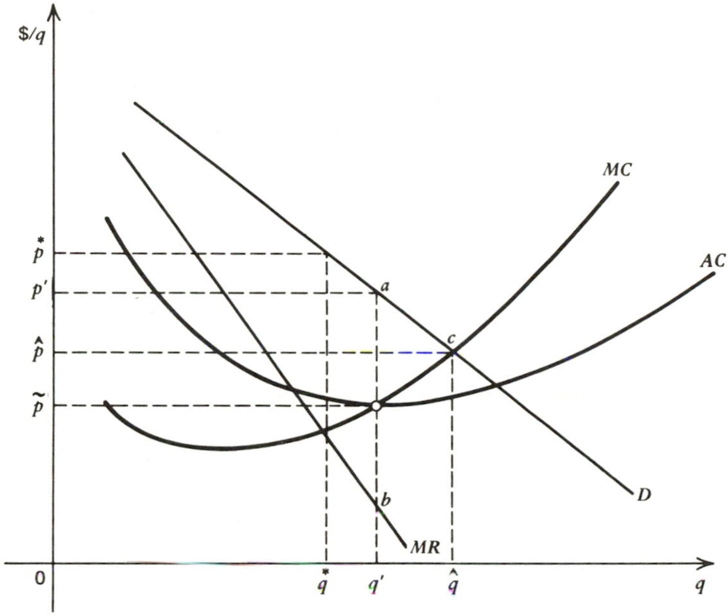

Figure 13.8

Other price ceilings below $\overset{*}{p}$ would result in alternative equilibrium output levels. It is easy to verify that the maximal level of output which the monopolist can be induced to produce by imposing price ceilings is $\hat{q}$. This output is brought about by setting a price ceiling equal to $\hat{p}$, in which case the intersection of the marginal-cost and effective marginal-revenue curves occurs at point *c*. Thus, the price ceiling which maximizes monopoly output is determined by the intersection of the marginal-cost curve and the demand curve. Given the price ceiling $\hat{p}$, the monopolist produces at a point where price equals marginal cost (a characteristic of perfectly competitive equilibrium) and the regulatory agency might claim that an optimum is achieved.

The lowest price ceiling which can be imposed upon the monopolist without driving him out of business is $\tilde{p}$, determined by the minimum point of the average-cost curve. Given this price ceiling, the monopolist just covers the cost of production and any lower price ceiling would cause him to withdraw (eventually) from the market.

Regulation of Input Price

The problem of input-price control in a monopsonistic market can be analyzed analogously. In this case, price control takes the form of a minimum price (e.g., a minimum wage rate) imposed by the government or, perhaps, by a collective bargaining unit (e.g., a labor union). Analysis of the profit-maximizing position for the monopsonistic firm under these conditions proceeds along lines similar to the above (see exercise 13.4).[8]

13.8 THE PRICE-DISCRIMINATING MONOPOLY

Conditions for Price Discrimination

In this section we modify assumptions 13.3 (exchange cost) or 13.4 (perfect information) to consider the situation in which it is possible for a monopolist to separate his market into two or more segments and charge a different price in each market, thus realizing higher profits than if he charged a single price in all of the separable markets.[9] The practice of charging different prices for the same commodity in different market segments is referred to as *price discrimination*. The two essential ingredients of price discrimination are (1) the ability to segment the market and (2) the existence of different demand functions in the market segments. If it is not possible to maintain the market segmentation, arbitrage will eliminate price discrepancies by making it impossible for the monopolist to sell the commodity in the higher-priced market segment. That is, arbitragers can make a profit by purchasing the commodity in the lower-priced market segment and reselling it in the higher-priced market segment. The profits of the arbitragers will eventually be forced to zero as competition equalizes the prices in the two segments. If the demand functions were not different in the segments of the market, there would be no reason to charge different prices; price discrimination would not enhance the monopolist's profits.

Market segmentation can be made possible by any of a number of factors. For example, it is frequently possible for producers to take advantage of foreign-trade restrictions in order to sell commodities abroad at a different price than in the domestic market (see exercise 13.3). It is also often possible to segment the market by requiring identification of the buyer. Examples of such price discrimination are special student rates (requiring the buyer to possess a student-body card), special faculty rates, special "stand-by" airfares for travelers under a given age (requiring proof of the age of the traveler), and special business

[8] Most forms of monopoly regulation are more sophisticated than simple price control. A more common type of monopoly regulation is the imposition of limitations on the rate of return on assets. That is, the regulatory agency assesses the value of the assets of a firm and places a limit on the profit/assets ratio. The firm is then free to choose its output or pricing policy so long as it does not result in a rate of return which exceeds the maximum. One possible result of this type of regulation, however, is an uneconomical substitution of capital for other inputs. This follows from the fact that capital is included in the assets of the firm. Hence, the accumulation of additional capital raises the value of the assets of the firm, thus allowing a higher level of profits for a given rate of return on assets. Consequently, the monopoly does not choose the least-cost combination of the factors of production. See the part III suggested readings for appropriate references.

[9] Another type of price discrimination sometimes practiced by monopolists is the charging of different prices—even to the same buyer—for different units sold (see exercise 13.6).

rates at hotels, car rental companies, and many other types of business. Thus we could alter assumption 13.3 as follows:

Assumption 13.3′ Buyers can be segmented into K groups such that no exchange between the groups is possible.

Alternatively, monopolists might also capitalize on consumer ignorance in order to segment the market. It has been claimed that some distilleries place the same liquor in bottles with different labels and succeed in charging different prices for the same spirits. Thus we could alter assumption 13.4 to the following:

Assumption 13.4′ Buyers possess imperfect information while the single producer possesses perfect information concerning prices, availability, and physical characteristics of commodities.

The Revenue Function and Profit Maximization

Whatever the conditions which make it possible for a monopolist to segment the market into two or more parts, the result is that the monopolist takes advantage of the fact that he faces more than one revenue function, each corresponding to a market segment. Letting P_d^k be the demand price function in the kth market segment, we can express revenue in this market segment by $R^k(q_k) = P_d^k(q_k) \cdot q_k$ where q_k is the quantity sold in the kth market segment. If there are K separated markets, total revenue is given by $R(q_1, \ldots, q_K) = \sum_{k=1}^K R^k(q_k)$.

Letting $C(q) = C(\sum_{k=1}^K q_k)$ be the cost of production, we write the profit-maximization problem as

$$\underset{q_1, \ldots, q_K}{\text{Max}} \ \Pi(q_1, \ldots, q_K) = \sum_{k=1}^{K} R^k(q_k) - C\left(\sum_{k=1}^{K} q_k\right).$$

Partial differentiation yields the first-order conditions,

$$\frac{dR^k(q_k)}{dq_k} - \frac{dC(\sum_{k=1}^K q_k)}{d\sum_{k=1}^K q_k} \frac{\partial \sum_{k=1}^K q_k}{\partial q_k} = 0, \qquad k = 1, \ldots, K,$$

or

$$\frac{dR^k(q_k)}{dq_k} = \frac{dC(q)}{dq}, \qquad k = 1, \ldots, K.$$

Recalling the definition of marginal revenue (section 13.3) and of marginal cost (section 9.3), we can rewrite these conditions as $MR^k(q_k) = MC(q)$, $k = 1, \ldots, K$. Thus, in order to maximize profit, the common marginal cost of production should be equated to marginal revenue in each of the K market segments. This, of course, implies that the marginal revenues in the separate markets should be equal to one another: $MR^k(q_k) = MR^{k'}(q_{k'})$, k', $k = 1, \ldots, K$. Unless this condition is fulfilled, it is possible to reallocate sales among the individual markets in order to increase total revenue. The reallocation would, of course, involve shifting sales from those markets with low marginal revenues to those markets with high marginal revenues, thus increasing total revenue without affecting cost.

Relation of Prices in the Separate Markets

Utilizing equation (13.2), we can relate the prices charged in the separate markets to the own-price elasticities of demand in each of these markets. The condition that the marginal revenues in the separate markets be equated implies, using (13.2), that $p_k(1 + 1/e_k(p_k)) = p_{k'}(1 + 1/e_{k'}(p_{k'}))$, $k, k' = 1, \ldots, K$, where $e_k(P_k)$ is the own-price elasticity of demand in the kth market. Thus,

$$\frac{p_k}{p_{k'}} = \frac{(1 + 1/e_{k'}(p_{k'}))}{(1 + 1/e_k(p_k))}, \qquad k, k' = 1, \ldots, K.$$

It is apparent from this relationship that the prices in any two markets are equal to one another if and only if the own-price elasticities of demand are equal. Moreover, note that, if $|e_{k'}(p_{k'})| > |e_k(p_k)|$,[10] then $1 + 1/|e_{k'}(p_{k'})| < 1 + 1/|e_k(p_k)|$, which in turn implies that $p_k/p_{k'} > 1$ or $p_{k'} < p_k$. Thus, the price should be higher in the market with the least elastic demand.

Graphical Illustration

Price discrimination where the market is separated into two parts is illustrated in figure 13.9. The first panel of the diagram shows the demand and marginal-revenue curves for the two market segments. To illustrate the optimality condition, we first concentrate on the equality of marginal revenues in the two market segments. Consider a particular value of marginal revenue, say $\overset{*}{mr}$ in the diagram. This value of marginal revenue is attained in both markets if and only if quantities sold in the two market segments are $\overset{*}{q}_1$ and $\overset{*}{q}_2$. Consequantity, the marginal revenue equals $\overset{*}{mr}$ in both market segments only if total output is $\overset{*}{q} = \overset{*}{q}_1 + \overset{*}{q}_2$; hence the coordinates $(\overset{*}{q}, \overset{*}{mr})$ in the second panel of the diagram represent an output level and a marginal revenue that are consistent with the profit-maximization condition that the marginal revenues in the two market segments be equated. Output levels that generate other equal marginal revenues in both markets are obtained by the horizontal summation of the two marginal revenue curves. $\sum MR$ in figure 13.9 represents the set of pairs (q, mr) that are consistent with equality of marginal revenue in the two market segments.

The remaining first-order profit-maximization condition is that the common marginal revenue in the two market segments be equated to marginal cost; this determines the optimal (q, mr) combination. This condition is given by the intersection of the marginal cost and $\sum MR$ curves in the diagram. As drawn, this intersection occurs at output $\overset{*}{q}$. The optimal quantities and prices in the two markets are therefore $\overset{*}{q}_1$, $\overset{*}{q}_2$, $\overset{*}{p}_1$, and $\overset{*}{p}_2$. It will be noted that the price is highest in the market segment with the more steeply sloped demand function (i.e., the market with the least elastic demand).

[10] Recall that we are assuming that demand curves slope downward so that $e_k(p_k) < 0$.

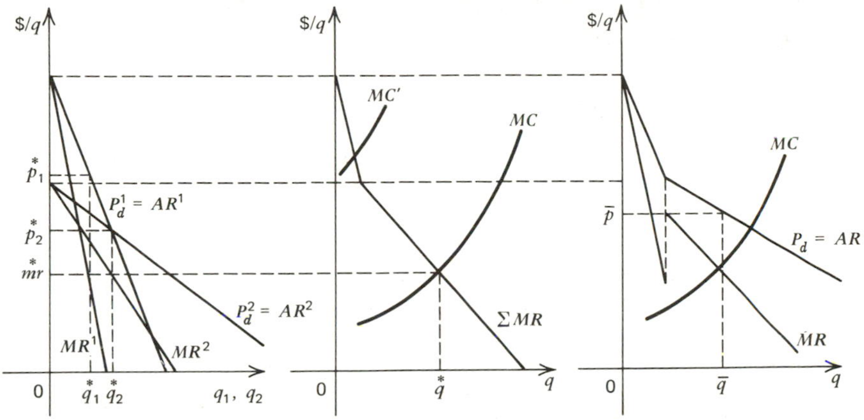

Figure 13.9

The demand and marginal-cost curves in figure 13.9 are drawn so that at the optimum sales are undertaken in both market segments. This does not have to be the case. If the marginal-cost curve were given by *MC′* in figure 13.9, the intersection of the marginal-cost and aggregate marginal-revenue curves would occur at an output to the left of the kink in the $\sum$ *MR* curve and the result would be that the entire output would be sold in the first market segment.

Relation of Ordinary Monopoly to Price Discrimination

It is of some interest to illustrate the equilibrium under identical market conditions when the monopolist does not practice price discrimination. In this case, we simply determine the ordinary monopoly equilibrium in the face of the aggregate demand curve illustrated in the third panel of figure 13.9. $P_d = AR$ is the price-demand (average-revenue) curve for the entire market (obtained by horizontal summation of the demand-price curves in the two market segments). The marginal-revenue curve corresponding to the market-demand curve has a discontinuity at that output where there is a kink in the market-demand curve. Thus, the marginal-revenue curve which the monopolist faces when he makes no attempt to segment his market is very different from the aggregate marginal-revenue curve, $\sum$ *MR*, which is predicated on the practice of price discrimination (equating marginal revenues rather than price in the two market segments). The optimal output is determined by the intersection of the marginal-cost and marginal-revenue curves at output $\bar{q}$. It will be noted that this optimality condition yields a common price, $\bar{p}$, which is inbetween the prices charged in the two market segments when price discrimination is practiced. Note also that charging this common price in the two markets implies that the marginal revenue in the first market segment is higher than the marginal revenue in the second market segment. This simply underscores the fact that the monopolist could increase profits by practicing price discrimination instead of treating the market as a unified whole, charging a single price to all buyers.

13.9 THE THEORY OF MONOPOLISTIC COMPETITION

Basic Assumptions

The Theory of Monopolistic Competition by Edward H. Chamberlin [1960] is an attempt to formulate a more general model embodying important elements of the perfectly competitive and monopoly models. This model is based upon the observation that many markets, while being neither perfectly competitive nor simple monopolies, contain important elements of both. In the first place, the commodities produced and sold in these markets are differentiated in the minds of the buyers. The basis for this differentiation may be real or fancied. Patents and trademarks issued by government agencies tend to differentiate one commodity from another. In addition, the location of retail sales outlets constitutes an important source of product differentiation isofar as the buyer is concerned. Finally, advertising has as its main objective the differentiation of one commodity from another.

Since the commodities sold in many markets are considered by the consumer to be differentiated, each producer experiences some of the elements of a monopoly. At the same time, since the commodity differentiation is not complete, each producer also experiences some of the effects of competition from producers of close substitutes.

> *Monopolistic competition, then, concerns itself not only with the problem of an* individual *equilibrium (the ordinary theory of monopoly), but also with that of a* group *equilibrium (the adjustment of economic forces within a group of competing monopolists, ordinarily regarded merely as a group of competitors). In this it differs both from the theory of competition and from the theory of monopoly (Chamberlin* [1960, *p.* 69]).

Large-Group Equilibrium

Given the above institutional framework, let us analyze one of the most important cases considered by Chamberlin. This is the case of a large-group equilibrium. The latter is a market characterized by a large number of producers, each producing under identical cost situations a commodity which is slightly differentiated from the others. Furthermore, the preferences of the consumers of this commodity are such that the producers sell equal shares of the total output of the market if they all charge the same price. This implies that the preferences of consumers are distributed uniformly among the individual producers in the market.[11] Given this market structure, Chamberlin argues that it is quite likely that the producers will not recognize their interdependence with respect to output and price. This follows from the uniform distribution of sales among the producers. A change in the price of any one of the producers in this large group

[11] A similar characterization of uniformity is required if we are dealing with intermediate commodities or primary commodities.

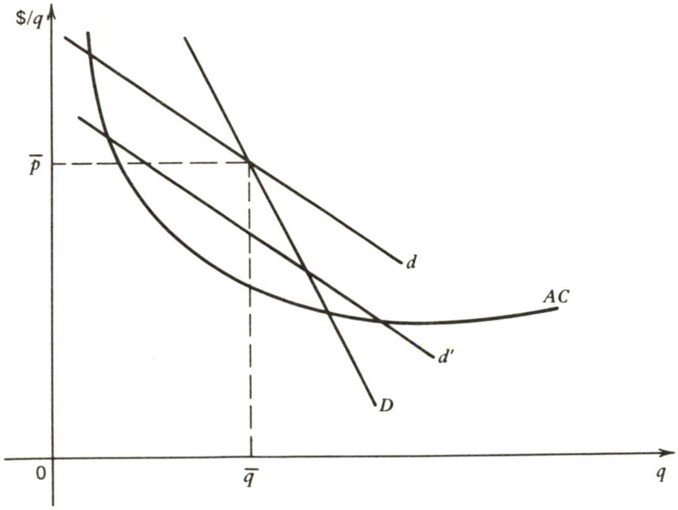

Figure 13.10

results in an equal impact upon all of the remaining producers in the group. Thus, Chamberlin argues, the change in their individual sales is likely to be so small as to be imperceptible and the interdependence of the producers will be ignored.

In figure 13.10, a typical member of this group of producers is represented. Let us assume that the producer is originally operating at the output and price combination ($\bar{q}$, $\bar{p}$). There are two demand curves in this diagram. The curve labeled *d* is the demand curve envisioned by the individual producer when his interdependence with other producers is ignored. It reflects the change in demand as this producer varies his price and the prices of all other producers in the group remain constant. The producer believes that he can alter his price and sell the resulting output indicated by this demand curve. The curve labeled *D* indicates the price and output which will be achieved by the producer when all the producers in the market follow a similar pattern of price reduction or increase.

If only a single producer seeks to increase sales and profits by reducing his price below $\bar{p}$, the other producers will not experience a sufficient change in sales to initiate a change in their pricing policy. This follows from the assumption concerning the uniform distribution of sales among the producers in the market. However, since all producers in the market face uniform profit opportunities, all producers reduce price in the same manner. If all producers reduce price, the sales of individual producers in the industry increase as the uniform reduction in price increases aggregate demand. However, the share of any individual producer does not change as the distribution of buyers among the producers remains the same. Thus, the result of all producers in the group changing price uniformly is to move down the demand curve *D* rather than the demand curve *d*. Should the individual producers continue to believe that they are able to act

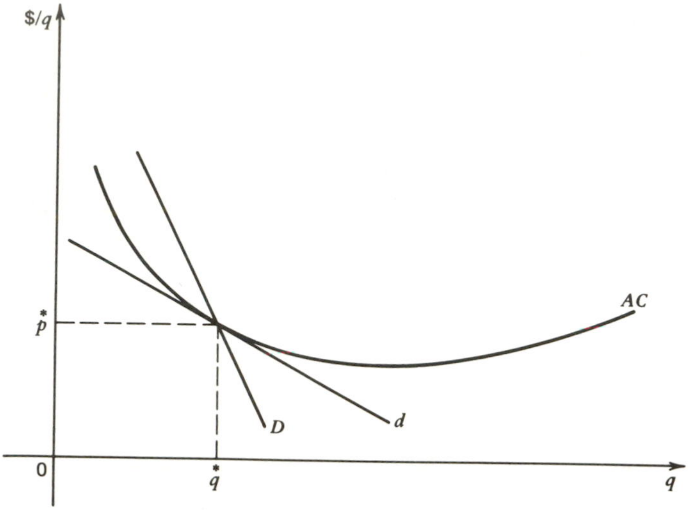

Figure 13.11

independently of other producers in the group, the demand curve labeled *d′* now represents the expectations of the individual producers concerning price and sales. In short, the old demand curve slides down demand curve *D*.

Market supply is also affected by the entry and exit of producers. Producers enter or leave the market depending upon the profits that are being earned. The demand curve *D* moves either to the left (with an increase in the number of producers in the group) or to the right (with a decrease in the number of producers in the group). The price and output, and thus the profit position, of the individual producers is thus affected by the entry and exit of producers as well as by their uniform changes in price.

Group equilibrium obtains when each member of the group is maximizing profit subject to the demand curve *d* and each member earns zero profit. This equilibrium is represented graphically by the tangency of the demand curve *d* and the average-cost curve at the point of intersection of the demand curve *D* and the average-cost curve (see figure 13.11). In this situation, there is no incentive for any producer to change his price (any other price would generate negative profit) and no incentive for entry into or exit out of the group (since maximal profit is zero).

Comparison with Perfectly Competitive Equilibrium

It is instructive to compare the Chamberlinian large-group equilibrium with the perfectly competitive equilibrium. A salient conclusion of the analysis of long-run perfectly competitive equilibrium in section 11.4 is that all producers operate at the minimum point of the average-cost curve. Using Chamberlin's notions of the demand curve *d* (reflecting the demand conception of the

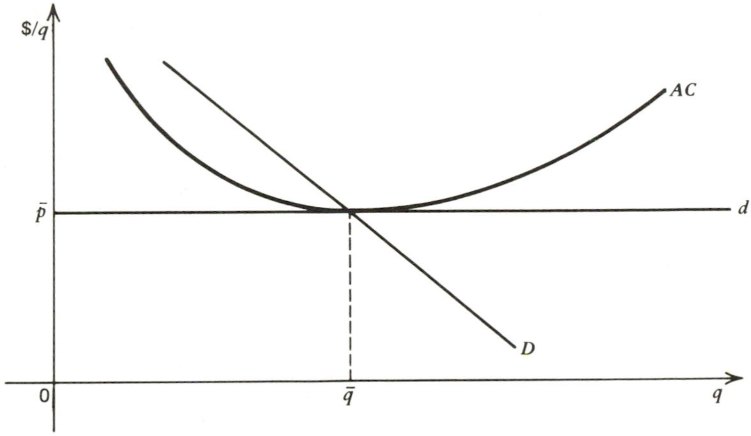

Figure 13.12

individual producer) and the demand curve D (reflecting equal market shares at common prices), the perfectly competitive equilibrium is depicted in figure 13.12. This equilibrium contrasts with the monopolistic-competition equilibrium depicted in figure 13.11; the monopolistic-competition equilibrium is characterized by a higher price, a lower output for each producer, and a larger number of producers (since the demand curve D in figure 13.11 is to the left of demand curve D in figure 13.12). All of these results follow from the differentiation of the product in the minds of the consumers. One might contend that the monopolistically competitive equilibrium has the wasteful property of excess capacity since increasing output would reduce the average cost of production. Chamberlin maintains that this excess capacity and the resulting higher price is the cost of variety, or product differentiation, which consumers desire and obtain in this type of market structure.

Criticisms of the Monopolistic Competition Model

The Theory of Monopolistic Competition, only one facet of which is considered above, has been criticized on two main grounds.[12] First, it is operationally very difficult to specify which set of producers constitute a group in the sense that their products are close substitutes for one another but not perfect substitutes. While the model emphasizes the interdependence among producers within the group, no attempt is made to consider the interdependence with producers outside the group. Presumably, the cross-price elasticities of demand among the producers in the group is larger than the cross-price elasticities of producers who are excluded from the group.

A second and more important criticism of the Chamberlin model concerns its predictive content. Is it possible to analyze such questions as what effect placing a tax upon the products sold in the market will have on the equilibrium

[12] See Shubik [1959a], Archibald [1961], and the part III suggested reading.

of the group and the individual producers? The reader can easily ascertain that unless the theory deals explicitly with entry conditions, financial structure of producers, and other institutional features one does not know the relationship between the two demand curves (d and D) and it is not possible to predict the effect on price and output and the number of producers in the group when an ad valorem or unit tax is imposed upon the sale of the commodities. Note that this is not the case with the perfectly competitive equilibrium depicted in figure 13.12.

13.10 CONCLUDING REMARKS

The examination of monopoly equilibrium in sections 13.2–13.5 abstracts from extant or potential competition for the monopolist's market. In fact, monopoly power might be preserved only by a pricing policy that impedes entrants into the market. Thus, a more elaborate theory of monopoly behavior might take into account the possibility of emerging competitors (see the part III suggested readings).

Moreover, monopolists might be subject to competitive pressures from close substitutes. The theory of monopolistic competition, analyzed in section 13.9, deals with this situation when the interdependence between producers is not recognized by them. Chapter 14 develops the analysis of markets in which interdependence is the principal feature.

EXERCISES

13.1 A profit-maximizing monopolist never produces an output at which the price elasticity of demand is less than one (in absolute value). Why?

13.2 A monopolist sells in two separated markets with demand functions given by $D^1(p_1) = 160 - p_1$ and $D^2(p_2) = 160 - 2p_1$. The monopolist's cost function (restricted to output space) has the image $C(q) = 5q + \frac{1}{2}q^2$.

a. Determine the profit-maximizing quantities and prices in the two markets.

b. Suppose now that the monopolist is legally restrained from practicing price discrimination (i.e., forced to charge the same price in both markets). Calculate the new profit-maximizing quantities and prices and compare the profit to that attained in part (a).

13.3 Because of international-trade restrictions, a manufacturer enjoys a monopolistic position in the domestic market but faces perfect competition in the world market. What effect does the imposition of an excise tax (on all sales—foreign and domestic) have on the domestic price?

13.4 Consider a profit-maximizing, monopsonistic purchaser in a labor market characterized by an upward-sloping labor supply curve. Assess the effect that a minimum wage has upon the quantity of labor employed. (Consider all possible minimum wages, ranging from one which is ineffectively low to one which is prohibitively high.)

13.5 A supply function is defined as a one-to-one relationship between price and quantity (associated with each price is a unique quantity supplied). Use a diagram to illustrate that it makes no sense to speak of the "supply function of a monopolist."

13.6 In the diagram, $\bar{q}$ is, of course, the profit-maximizing output of a single monopolist and $\bar{p}$ is the equilibrium price.

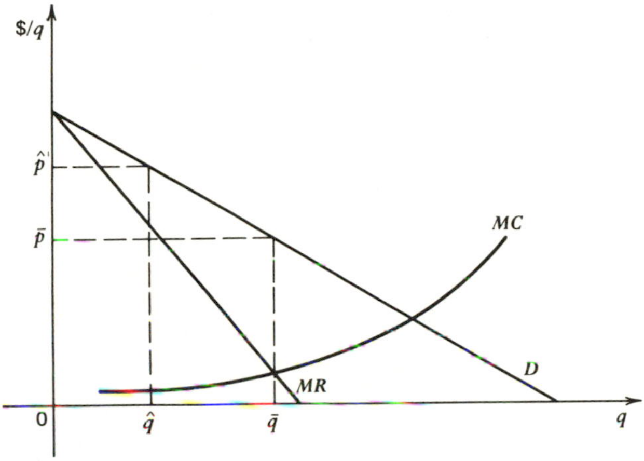

a. Suppose that instead of charging a single price, $\bar{p}$, for all units sold, the monopolist sells the first $\hat{q}$ units at price $\hat{p}$ and (assuming the demand curve is unaffected by this sale) sells the next $\bar{q} - \hat{q}$ units at the lower price $\bar{p}$. Compare the revenue obtained by the sale of $\bar{q}$ units under this "unit-price-discrimination" scheme to the revenue obtained by charging the single price $\bar{p}$.

b. Show that the monopolist can increase revenue above that obtained in the two-price "bulk discount" scheme in part (a) by charging *three* different prices.

c. What is the revenue obtained for output $\bar{q}$ by practicing "perfect price discrimination"—charging a different price for every infinitesimally small unit that is sold?

d. What is the profit-maximizing output of the perfect-price-discriminating monopolist?

e. Is the parenthetic proviso in part (a) sensible?

13.7 Assume that the Chamberlinian group is not sufficiently large to justify the assumption that the interdependence of the producers in the industry goes unrecognized. Make the further behavioral assumption that each producer in the industry assumes that other producers will follow any price decrease (in order to preserve their "market shares") but will not follow a price increase (instead capitalizing on the shifts in demand to increase their market shares).

a. Draw the demand and marginal revenue curves for a producer in this group. (Hint: the demand curve will exhibit a kink at the existing quantity and the marginal revenue curve will be discontinuous at this point; see section 13.8.)

b. Show how this model can explain price rigidity in the face of large changes in the cost conditions of the producer.

13.8 Show that Chamberlin's monopolistic-competition assumptions are insufficient to yield qualitative comparative-static results for price, output, and number of producers of the effect of, say, imposing (or increasing) an excise tax on the sale of commodities.

CHAPTER 14
GAME THEORY AND MODELS OF OLIGOPOLISTIC INTERDEPENDENCE

14.1 INTRODUCTION

In the model of perfect competition (for a produced commodity), producers are assumed to be price takers who choose profit-maximizing input and output quantities independently of the actions of other producers (or buyers). In the pure monopoly model, on the other hand, the interdependence between price and quantity sold is taken into account but the monopolist still acts independently of producers of other (perhaps closely related) commodities. Chamberlin's group equilibrium takes explicit account of this interdependence (as does the perfectly competitive equilibrium), but the producers are still assumed to ignore it.

In this chapter, we examine market structures in which the producers are cognizant of their interdependence. As the "large-members" assumption is commonly cited as the intuitive rationale for the independent decision making of both perfect and monopolistic competitors, "fewness" of the number of sellers is the salient characteristic of markets in which the interdependence is recognized by the agents. The market structure with a few sellers is called *oligopoly*.

The analysis of oligopolistic markets and the notion of equilibrium in these markets is not nearly as simple as the analysis of equilibrium in the perfectly competitive and monopolistic (competition) market structures. The complications in analyzing oligopolistic equilibrium result from the need to take into account the exact nature of the interdependence between the producers in the market. Indeed, there is no single theory of oligopolistic equilibrium. The equilibrium (if it exists) depends crucially upon the particular behavioral assumption which is made regarding the producers' attitudes toward interdependence. There are as many market solutions to oligopoly problems as there are assumptions regarding the behavior of producers in such markets.

While there is no single theoretical solution for oligopoly markets, there is a valuable analytical framework within which such markets can be analyzed. The *theory of games* provides a unifying conceptual and analytical structure with which to illustrate the salient principles of price and output determination under oligopolistic market conditions. Many of the oligopoly models that appear in the literature and that have achieved a reasonably wide use in applied research can be analyzed in the context of game theory. Accordingly, in this chapter we utilize some of the concepts from the theory of games to deal with a few of the more important models that have been developed for oligopolistic markets.

No attempt will be made to deal with all of the voluminous literature on oligopolistic equilibrium. The bulk of this analysis is better left to the applied field of industrial organization, in which the institutional and empirical features of oligopolistic interdependence are treated in some detail.

Section 14.2 discusses one of the oldest models of oligopolistic price determination: the duopoly (two-seller) model of Cournot [1838]. Section 14.3 takes into account the possibility of interdependent behavior that is more sophisticated than the (naive) decision rule of the Cournot duopolist. Section 14.4 discusses the rudiments of game theory and its application to models of oligopolistic interdependence. Finally, section 14.5 closes the chapter with a few concluding remarks.

14.2 THE COURNOT DUOPOLY MODEL

Duopoly

The essence of interdependent decision making is perhaps best illuminated by examination of one of the oldest problems of oligopolistic interdependence—the duopoly problem. A *duopoly* is a market that contains two sellers of a single commodity or of two slightly differentiated commodities.

One of the first models of a duopoly market was provided by Cournot in 1838. He considered the situation in which two producers face a linear demand-price function:

$$P_d(q) = a - bq, \tag{14.1}$$

where a and b are positive parameters and all producers have the identical marginal-cost functions, defined by $MC(q) = c$, where c is a positive constant.[1] Thus, both producers employ a production technology characterized by constant marginal cost. If the demand-price function in (14.1) were a market-demand function for a perfectly competitive market, the output in that market could be obtained by setting the market-supply function (the sum of the individual producers' supply functions) equal to the market-demand function for the commodity. Thus, for the case of constant costs, we have $P_d(q^c) = MC(q^c)$ or $a - bq^c = c$. The perfectly competitive equilibrium quantity is therefore given by $q^c = (a - c)/b$.

In a similar manner, if the industry were monopolistic, the amount supplied by the monopolist could be determined by setting marginal revenue equal to marginal cost, $MR(q) = MC(q^m)$ or $a - 2bq^m = c$. Solving for q^m, we see that monopoly output is equal to one-half of that of the competitive output, $q^m = (a - c)/2b = 1/2q^c$.

[1] In this chapter, as in other chapters of part III, in the interest of notational simplicity, we suppress the input-price variables in the marginal-cost-function image.

Cournot's Assumption

In the case of a duopoly model, the market output is the sum of the amounts produced by the two producers in the market: $q = q^1 + q^2$. The market-equilibrium solution for this problem now depends crucially upon the assumption that is made regarding the behavior of each of the two producers with respect to one another's actions. Cournot assumed that each of the producers assumes that the amount currently being produced by the other producer is not changed if his own output is altered. With this behavioral assumption, the optimization problem for one of the duopolists (say the first) is

$$\max_{q^1} \Pi^1(q^1, q^2) = R^1(q^1, q^2) - C^1(q^1) \tag{14.2}$$

where

$$R^1(q^1, q^2) = P_d(q^1, q^2) \cdot q^1 = [a - b(q^1 + q^2)]q^1 \tag{14.3}$$

and

$$C^1(q^1) = cq^1.$$

The first-order condition for solving (14.2) is

$$\frac{\partial \Pi^1(q^1, q^2)}{\partial q^1} = a - 2bq^1 - bq^2 - c = 0. \tag{14.4}$$

Solving (14.4) for the output of duopolist 1, given the output of the second duopolist, we obtain

$$q^1 = \frac{a - c}{2b} - \frac{1}{2} q^2 = r^1(q^2). \tag{14.5}$$

The output of the second duopolist, given that of the first, is derived similarly:

$$q^2 = \frac{a - c}{2b} - \frac{1}{2} q^1 = r^2(q^1). \tag{14.6}$$

The functions r^1 and r^2 are termed *reaction functions* since they indicate the amount by which one of the duopolists will change his output in reaction to a change in the amount produced by the other.

The Cournot Equilibrium

Equilibrium in the Cournot market is defined as a pair of outputs $(\overset{*}{q}{}^1, \overset{*}{q}{}^2)$ that are mutually consistent in terms of the two reaction functions; i.e., $(\overset{*}{q}{}^1, \overset{*}{q}{}^2)$ is a Cournot equilibrium if $\overset{*}{q}{}^1 = r^1(\overset{*}{q}{}^2)$ and $\overset{*}{q}{}^2 = r^2(\overset{*}{q}{}^1)$, in which case $\overset{*}{q}{}^1$ maximizes the profit of the first duopolist, given $\overset{*}{q}{}^2$, and $\overset{*}{q}{}^2$ maximizes the profit of the second duopolist, given $\overset{*}{q}{}^1$.

It is instructive to calculate the Cournot-equilibrium quantities. Solving (14.5) and (14.6) for $\overset{*}{q}{}^1$ and $\overset{*}{q}{}^2$, we obtain $\overset{*}{q}{}^1 = (a - c)/3b$ and $\overset{*}{q}{}^2 = (a - c)/3b$. Cournot's solution to the duopoly problem thus indicates that in equilibrium each of the duopolists produces an amount equal to one-third of the

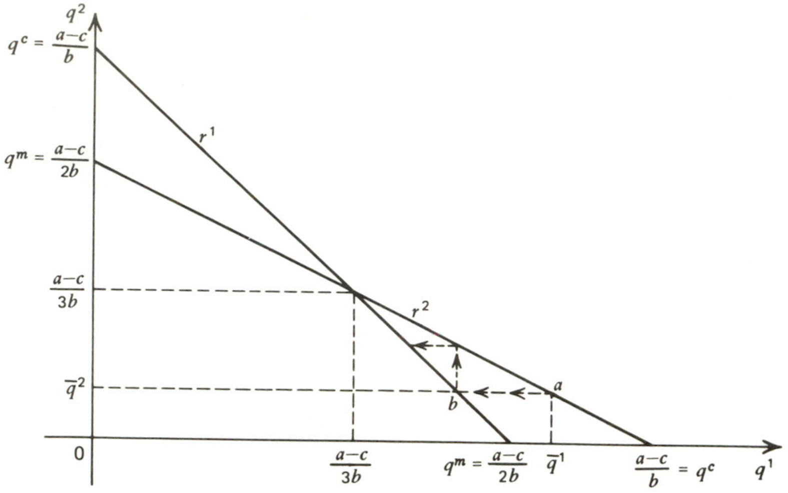

Figure 14.1

perfectly competitive equilibrium output. Thus, the total amount that is produced in the Cournot duopoly equilibrium is two-thirds of the competitive market equilibrium: $\overset{*}{q}^1 + \overset{*}{q}^2 = \overset{*}{q} = 2(a - c)/3b = \frac{2}{3}q^c$.

The Cournot equilibrium is illustrated in figure 14.1. The two reaction curves, r^1 and r^2, are obtained by plotting equations (14.5) and (14.6). Note that the intercepts of these reaction curves make sense. For example, the horizontal intercept of r^1 is the optimal monopoly output, reflecting the fact that, if duopolist 2 discontinues operation, duopolist 1 will supply the monopoly output. On the other hand, the vertical intercept of r^1 is equal to the competitive-equilibrium output, indicating that, if duopolist 2 supplies the competitive-equilibrium output, duopolist 1 will discontinue operation; this is true because supplying the competitive-equilibrium output drives the price down to the (constant) marginal cost, in which case an additional unit of output can only be sold at a price below marginal (equals average) cost.

The Cournot equilibrium is represented in figure 14.1 by the intersection of the two reaction curves, where each duopolist is supplying one-third of the competitive-equilibrium output. The nature of this intersection point can perhaps be explicated somewhat by some pseudodisequilibrium dynamics.[2] Suppose that the first duopolist is initially producing the amount $\bar{q}^1$. If duopolist 2 believes that this output would not be changed regardless of his own actions, then the profit-maximizing output for this duopolist is indicated by point a on duopolist 2's reaction curve and the profit-maximizing output of duopolist 2 is

[2] Strictly speaking, stability of the Cournot-equilibrium solution to the duopoly problem cannot be analyzed unless the above static model is transformed into a dynamic model where the quantity adjustment of each of the duopolists is explicitly spelled out. See the discussion of the relationship between comparative statics and dynamics in chapter 12 and the part III suggested reading.

$\bar{q}^2$. If duopolist 1 follows the same behavioral pattern, then his profit-maximizing output falls to an output less than $\bar{q}^1$; in particular, his output is reduced to that corresponding to point b on his reaction curve. As long as both duopolists retain the same assumptions regarding each other's actions, the solution to the duopoly problem is given by the intersection point of the reaction curves. The path of adjustment of the respective outputs is indicated by the arrows in figure 14.1.

Generalization to an Oligopoly Market

Cournot's solution to the duopoly problem is easily generalized to an oligopoly market consisting of ℓ producers, each operating under Cournot's behavioral assumption regarding the interdependence between them. The total output of the oligopoly market is the sum of the outputs of the ℓ individual producers, $q = \sum_{r=1}^{\ell} q^r$. Given the assumption that each of the oligopolists believes that the output of the remaining oligopolists is fixed, the profit of the rth producer is given by $\Pi^r(q^r, q) = P_d(q) \cdot q^r - cq^r$, and the first-order condition for profit maximization

$$\frac{\partial \Pi^r(q^r, q)}{\partial q^r} = P_d(q) + P_d'(q) \cdot q^r - c = 0. \tag{14.7}$$

Summation of (14.7) over the ℓ producers in the market yields

$$\ell P_d(q) + P_d'(q) \cdot \sum_{r=1}^{\ell} q^r - \ell c = 0. \tag{14.8}$$

Substituting the image of the linear demand-price function (14.1) into (14.8) and taking the indicated derivatives, we arrive at the following equation: $\ell(a - bq) - bq - \ell c = 0$. Solving this equation, we obtain the equilibrium output of the Cournot oligopoly market consisting of ℓ producers:

$$q^{(\ell)} = \frac{\ell(a-c)}{b(1+\ell)} = \frac{\ell}{\ell+1}\, q^c.$$

Setting $\ell = 1$ yields the monopoly solution, $q^{(1)} = \frac{1}{2}q^c$, and setting $\ell = 2$ yields the duopoly solution, $q^{(2)} = \frac{2}{3}q^c$. As ℓ gets very large, $\ell/(\ell + 1)$ approaches 1 and the market output approaches the perfectly competitive output; i.e.,

$$\lim_{\ell \to \infty} q^{(\ell)} = \lim_{\ell \to \infty} \left(\frac{\ell}{\ell+1}\, q^c \right) = q^c.$$

Thus, the Cournot behavioral assumption is consistent with perfectly competitive behavior in the sense that the Cournot equilibrium approaches the perfectly competitive equilibrium as the number of producers in the market gets very large.

14.3 QUANTITY AND PRICE LEADERSHIP AND COLLUSION

The principle flaw—as well as the principle attraction—of the Cournot model of duopoly and oligopoly is its simplicity. In particular, the naiveté of the decision makers is unrealistic. Each oligopolist assumes, quite naively, that the other oligopolists will leave their outputs unchanged whatever he chooses to do. Moreover, out of equilibrium, each Cournot oligopolist continues to believe that other oligopolists will not react to his own output changes, although this assumption is repeatedly refuted. In this section, we elaborate on the basic Cournot model by incorporating slightly more sophisticated strategies for dealing with the interdependence in oligopolistic markets. In particular, we consider models of quantity and price leadership (where only one of the oligopolists adopts a more sophisticated strategy) and collusion (where the oligopolists collude to maximize joint profits).

Although these models incorporate more sophisticated attitudes toward oligopolistic interdependence, it should not be contended that they are realistic descriptions of oligopolistic markets. Perhaps the main purpose of presenting these additional models is to underscore the sensitivity that the solution to the oligopoly problem has to the assumption that is made about the strategies for dealing with market interdependence. In addition, some additional concepts, with somewhat more widespread applicability, are developed.

Quantity Leadership

In some oligopolistic markets, one producer attains dominance over the others in that the other oligopolists react passively to each other's output decisions, but the dominant producer capitalizes on this naive behavior to extract a larger share of the market. In particular, the dominant producer is assumed to possess complete information regarding the reaction functions of the other oligopolists and maximizes his profit subject to these reaction functions (rather than the outputs of his competitors). In the context of the Cournot duopoly problem, if the first duopolist is the dominant producer, his optimization problem is obtained by substituting the reaction function of the second duopolist (14.6) for q^2 in his profit function:

$$\operatorname*{Max}_{q^1}(P_d(q^1 + r^2(q^1)) \cdot q^1 - cq^1) = \operatorname*{Max}_{q^1}\left(a - b\left(q^1 + \frac{a-c}{2b} - \frac{1}{2}q^1\right)q^1 - cq^1\right).$$

The first-order condition is

$$-2bq^1 - b\frac{a-c}{2b} + bq^1 - c = 0$$

or

$$q^1 = \frac{a-c}{2b} = \frac{1}{2}q^c. \tag{14.9}$$

Thus, the optimal output of the dominant producer is the equilibrium monopoly output. Substitution of (14.9) into the reaction function of the second duopolist yields $\overset{*}{q}{}^2 = (a-c)/4b$. Straightforward calculations indicate that, relative to the Cournot equilibrium, the dominant producer earns a higher profit and the other producer earns a lower profit.[3]

[3] The profit of the dominant producer is, however, lower than that of the monopolist because the equilibrium price is lower.

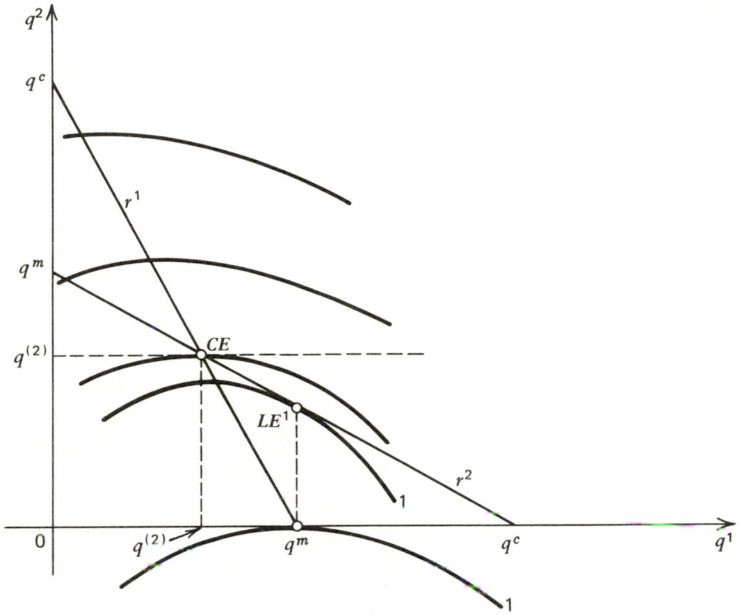

Figure 14.2

The quantity-leadership solution to the duopoly problem can be illustrated using Stackelberg indifference curves, named after the German economist who conceived them. Recall from (14.2) that the profit of duopolist 1 is given by

$$\Pi^1(q^1, q^2) = [a - b(q^1 + q^2)]q^1. \tag{14.10}$$

The Stackelberg indifference curve for duopolist 1 is obtained by setting profits, $\Pi^1(q^1, q^2)$, equal to a constant, say $\bar{\pi}^1$, in equation (14.10) and solving for q^2 as a function of q^1. Thus, a Stackelberg indifference curve is simply an iso-profit curve in $q^1 - q^2$ space. A Stackelberg indifference map is generated by varying the level of profits in equation (14.10).

Given the structure of the duopoly problem as developed in this chapter, the Stackelberg indifference map for duopolist 1 has the characteristics depicted in figure 14.2. In particular, the iso-profit curves are convex from above (see exercise 14.1). In addition, lower iso-profit curves represent higher levels of profit for duopolist 1 since they correspond to lower levels of output for duopolist 2. Moreover, the iso-profit curves are horizontal at the points of intersection with the reaction curve, r^1. This latter property follows from the way in which the reaction curve is constructed. In particular, the reaction curve indicates the output of duopolist 1, who maximizes profit subject to a given level of output of duopolist 2. Thus, for example, if the output of duopolist 2 is given by the Cournot-equilibrium output $q^{(2)}$, the profit-maximization problem for duopolist 1 can be characterized as that of choosing the lowest iso-profit curve (i.e., the highest level of profit) subject to the constraint that the iso-profit curve intersect (or touch) the horizontal line through q^2. This point of tangency must occur at output $q^{(2)}$ of duopolist 1. Thus, as each iso-profit curve of duopolist 1 is tangent to a horizontal line at the point of intersection with the reaction curve r^1, the iso-profit line must be horizontal at this point of intersection. One particularly relevant example of this characteristic of the Stackelberg indifference map of duopolist 1 is the iso-profit curve that is tangent to the horizontal axis at the intercept of the reaction curve r^1. The profit level associated with this iso-profit curve is, of course, the monopoly-equilibrium profit level, obtained by maximizing profit subject only to the demand function as a constraint.

The quantity-leadership equilibrium can now be illustrated using the Stackelberg indifference curves. The optimization problem for the quantity leader, duopolist 1, is to maximize profit subject to the reaction curve of duopolist 2 as a constraint. That is, the problem of the quantity leader is to obtain the lowest possible iso-profit curve (i.e., the highest level of π^1) that intersects (or touches) the reaction curve of duopolist 2, r^2. Thus, the quantity-leadership equilibrium is reflected in this diagram by the point of tangency between an iso-profit curve of the quantity leader and the reaction curve of the quantity follower. This point of tangency is labeled LE^1 in figure 14.2.

Figure 14.3 superimposes the Stackelberg indifference maps of the two duopolists. LE^1 and LE^2 represent the quantity-leadership equilibria for the cases where duopolists 1 and 2, respectively, are the leaders. As one might

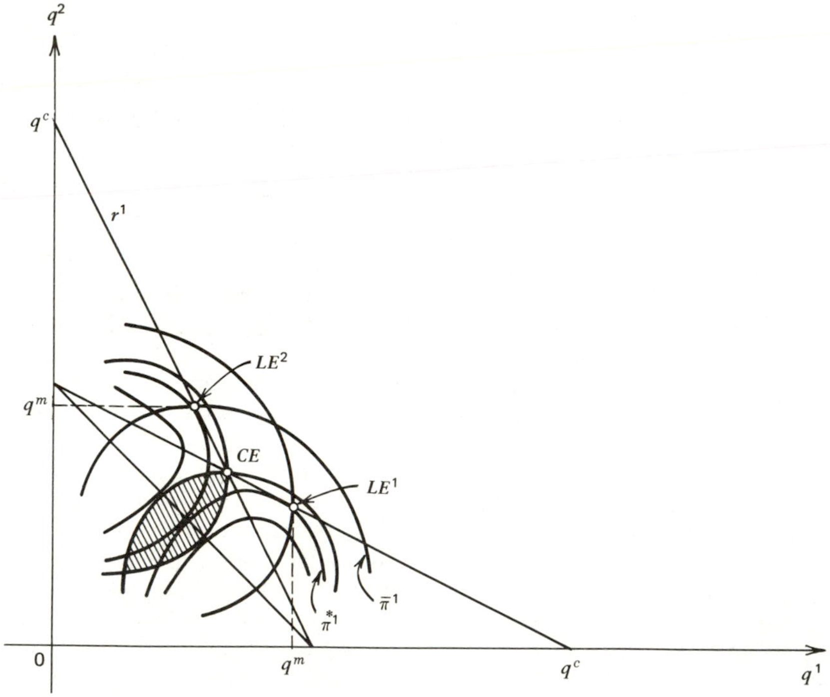

Figure 14.3

perhaps expect, each duopolist is better off as a leader than as a follower. For example, in the LE^1 equilibrium the profit of duopolist 1 is represented by the iso-profit curve labeled $\overset{*}{\pi}{}^1$, whereas the profit of duopolist 1 in the LE^2 equilibrium is represented by the higher iso-profit line, with the concomitantly lower profit level, $\bar{\pi}^1$. A situation in which each duopolist is better off being a leader rather than a follower is called a "Stackelberg disequilibrium." In a situation characterized by Stackelberg disequilibrium in which each of the duopolists also has equal information about the reaction curve of the other, the outcome of the interdependent decision making is indeterminate. Only by assuming that at least one of the duopolists plays a more sophisticated game (or that both adopt the naive behavior of the Cournot duopolist), is it possible to describe the outcome of the interdependent decision making.[4]

The Stackelberg indifference maps are interesting because they can, at least in principle, be used to analyze interdependent decision making with respect to very diverse types of variables. For example, the variables on the two axes of the Stackelberg diagram might be advertising expenditures, or some other type of promotional activity. In this case, one would expect that the profits of each duopolist would be inversely related to the advertising expenditure of his competitor. One would also expect that increased advertising expenditure by one duopolist would induce additional advertising expenditure by the other, so that the reaction curves of the two duopolists would have positive rather than negative slopes as in figures 14.2 and 14.3. There is a wide variety of configurations of Stackelberg indifference curves and reaction curves that can be generated by considering alternative choice variables for the interdependent decision makers. The interested reader is referred to the classic treatise of Fellner [1949], who introduced the Stackelberg concepts to the English-speaking subset of the economics profession. We complete this section by considering two more examples of oligopolistic decision making: price leadership and collusion.

Price Leadership

A natural alternative to the Cournot assumption which is as deeply rooted in the history of economic thought (Bertrand [1883]) is the assumption that each oligopolist presumes that the others will hold their *prices* fixed regardless of his own action. The analysis of this model depends crucially upon whether it is assumed that the commodities sold by the oligopolists are identical or slightly differentiated. If the oligopolists sell an identical commodity, the inevitable immediate outcome of the pricing behavior implied by the Bertrand assumption is indiscriminate price war. Assuming that competitors keep their prices fixed, the optimal (profit-maximizing) strategy (if the extant price is high enough) is to undercut these competitors by a small amount, thus capturing some (or all) of their market shares. However, as in the Cournot model, the presumption of the Bertrand oligopolist regarding his competitors' pricing behavior is specious; the others are just as busily undercutting *his* own price. The result is a downward spiral of prices. Where this spiral terminates is impossible to say without making

[4] The more sophisticated game might be one in which the duopolists choose, or "announce," reaction curves.

additional assumptions. If one oligopolist has lower costs of production than the others, he might be able to drive the others out of business, thus establishing a monopolistic position, by cutting the price below their minimum average costs.[5]

If the oligopolists have identical cost functions, will the outcome be such that price stabilizes at the (common) minimum average cost, thus simulating the perfectly competitive equilibrium? This is unlikely, as this solution would entail zero profit for all of the producers, thus opening up the possibility of charging a higher price, selling a reduced quantity, but making positive profit.[6]

As the Bertrand model with undifferentiated commodities has no equilibrium, it is difficult to analyze. Moreover, the Bertrand assumption is especially naive in the case of undifferentiated commodities. This assumption makes more sense, however, if the commodities being sold by the oligopolists are slightly differentiated. We examine the Bertrand model with differentiated commodities graphically, leaving the algebra to the reader (exercise 14.3).

If the two commodities are (gross) substitutes, an increase in the price by one duopolist will increase the demand for the commodity of the other duopolist, thus increasing his profit-maximizing price.[7] Consequently, the reaction curves of the duopolists have positive slopes. Moreover, each duopolist would charge a positive price even if the other were (quite implausibly) to charge a zero price; therefore, the reaction curve of each duopolist intersects his own price axis. Thus, the reaction curves of the Bertrand duopolists might look something like those in figure 14.4. Also drawn in figure 14.4 are two of the Stackelberg indifference curves for each of the two duopolists. If each of the duopolists' demand curves is linear in the two prices, p^1 and p^2, the reaction curves will be linear and the Stackelberg indifference curves will be convex from below as in figure 14.4. Moreover, higher indifference curves are associated with higher profit levels for the two duopolists. As drawn, the Bertrand equilibrium is at prices $(\overset{*}{p}{}^1, \overset{*}{p}{}^2)$.

As in the case of the Cournot model, the Bertrand assumption entails very naive behavior on the part of the duopolist. In particular, out of equilibrium each duopolist continues to assume that the other duopolist will hold his price fixed no matter what the first duopolist does, although this assumption is repeatedly refuted. Only in equilibrium is the assumption rationalized. A more sophisticated strategy on the part of either one of the duopolists is to recognize the reactions of the other duopolists and maximize his own profit subject to the reaction curve of the other duopolist. This results in a price-leadership equilibrium. For example, if the first duopolist behaves as a leader and the second duopolist behaves as a follower, the leadership equilibrium is given by the point labeled LE^1 in figure 14.4. On the other hand, the leadership equilibrium in which duopolist 2 is the leader and duopolist 1 is the follower is indicated by the point LE^2 in figure 14.4.

[5] Of course, the monopolist would then have to keep his price low enough to prevent reentry of producers.

[6] This is, of course, not inevitable. Whether it is possible depends upon the cost functions of the oligopolist and the nature of the Chamberlin demand curve d (see section 13.9).

[7] Actually, one could concoct a situation in which a rise in demand *lowers* the profit-maximizing price (by lowering marginal revenue in the relevant region). We ignore this perverse situation in what follows.

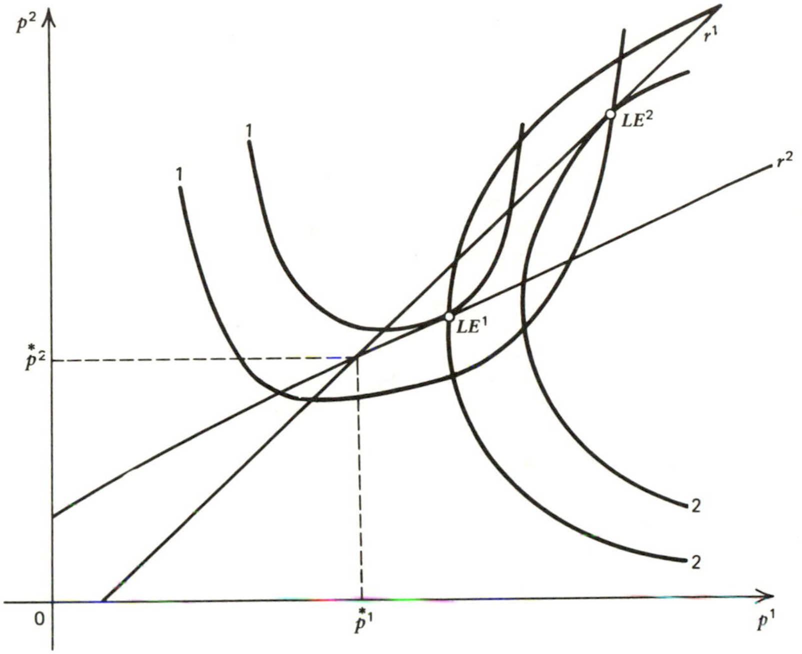

Figure 14.4

Given the indifference map in figure 14.4, each of the duopolists is better off being price leader than being a price follower. Thus, figure 14.4 depicts a situation of Stackelberg disequilibrium. This is not, however, the necessary outcome of the Bertrand pricing process; figure 14.5 illustrates an asymmetric situation in which duopolist 1 prefers to lead and duopolist 2 prefers to follow. Thus, figure 14.5 reflects the case of Stackelberg equilibrium. One can, of course, construct other cases. For example, it is possible to draw a Stackelberg diagram in which each of the duopolists would prefer to follow (see exercise 14.2).[8]

Collusion

An important characteristic of the quantity- and price-leadership equilibria as well as the simple Cournot and Bertrand equilibria is the fact that cooperation between the competitors could increase the profits of both. The real-world counterpart of this characteristic is the fact that competitive "dumping" policies and aggressive price cutting are mutually detrimental. It is for this reason, perhaps, that quantity competition and price wars frequently terminate in a

[8] Fellner [1949, p. 108] refers to the case where each would like to follow as "intersection-point equilibrium." However, it is apparent that if both duopolists are sophisticated enough to ascertain the relative merits of the two leadership equilibria, they will not typically settle for the intersection-point equilibrium, which is necessarily inferior to both of the leadership equilibria.

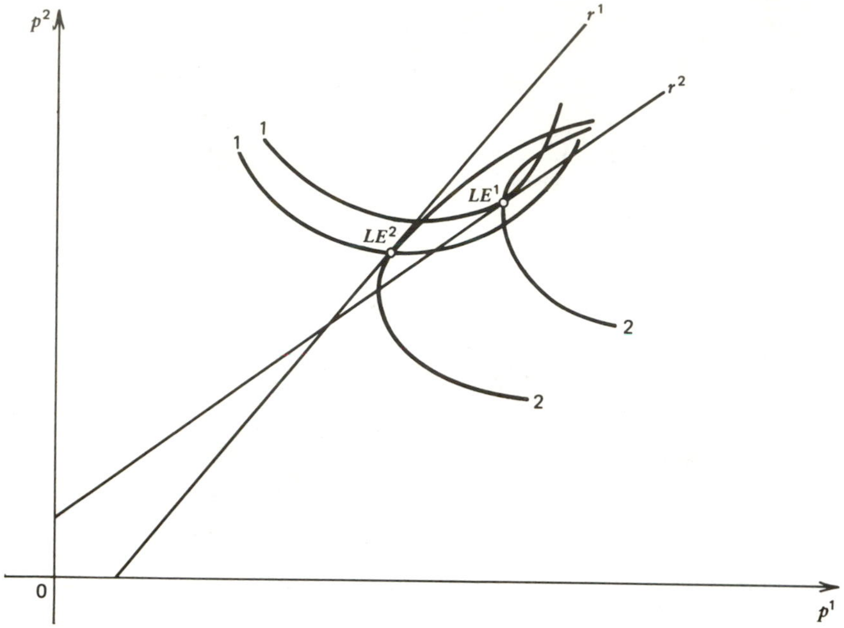

Figure 14.5

tacit agreement to restrict quantity or to eschew undercutting competitors' prices.[9]

The cooperative solution to the duopoly problem is most easily illustrated in the context of the Cournot quantity-competition model. The obvious objective of the cooperative arrangement is to maximize joint profit; this is accomplished, of course, by selling the monopoly output, q^m. As the marginal costs of the two duopolists are assumed to be identically constant, it does not matter in this particular model how the production is distributed between the two. Thus, any point on the straight line connecting the coordinate values of q^m on the horizontal and vertical axes in figure 14.3 would maximize joint profit.

It might be noted that the straight line representing output levels that maximize joint profit is also characterized by the fact that the iso-profit curves of the two duopolists are tangent to one another along this line. This is no accident; were the iso-profit curves not tangent to one another, it would be possible to increase the profit level of both duopolists by changing the output level to the interior of the lens area formed by the intersecting iso-profit curves. For example, at the Cournot equilibrium *CE* in figure 14.3, the iso-profit curves of the two duopolists intersect. Moving to any output combination in the interior of the shaded area would put both duopolists on iso-profit curves corresponding to higher levels of profit.

[9] Explicit agreement—collusion—is typically prohibited by antitrust legislation in the United States.

The foregoing discussion leaves unanswered the question of how the maximal joint profit is distributed among the members of the collusion. If the producers have identical cost functions, it seems natural (though by no means inevitable) that the profit be evenly distributed. If, however, the producers have different cost functions, there is no natural distribution of the profit.[10] In such situations the ultimate distribution depends upon the bargaining power of the participants. Little that is definitive can be said about this bargaining process.[11]

Nevertheless, the theory of games, alluded to in the introduction to this chapter, has been employed to analyze bargaining situations of this type. Although a thorough treatment of game theory is beyond the scope of this book, in the next section we introduce the fundamental features of game theory and relate them to the models of oligopolistic interdependence that were developed in the foregoing pages.

14.4 GAME THEORY

Framework

The theory of games is the modern mathematical approach to the conflict of interest between separate decision-making units. *The Theory of Games and Economic Behavior* by John von Neumann and Oskar Morgenstern [1944] (inspired by some earlier papers by von Neumann) is the classic treatise for this rich conceptual approach to the analysis of individuals engaged in competitive situations such as military conflict, poker, or production in an oligopoly market. The decision-making units are defined as the players in the game. The players could constitute individual consumers, producers, nation-states, etc. The competitive situation in which the players are involved is called the game. The rules of the game completely describe each player's feasible strategies, the information available to him prior to the selection of a strategy, and his payoff function. A solution to a game is a set of strategies chosen by the players in which no player can increase his payoff by changing his strategy, assuming that the strategies of the other players remain fixed. That is, a set of strategies is a solution to the game if there is no incentive for any player to change his strategy.

The models of oligopolistic interdependence described in the preceding pages can be fitted into the framework of game theory. For example, in the

[10] In the von Neumann-Morgenstern game-theoretic approach to this problem (see section 14.4), joint-profit maximization would require that the inefficient producers restrict output, for which they would receive a side payment from the more efficient producers. The amount of the side payment is not uniquely determined in the von Neumann–Morgenstern solution, but is limited by the profit that each producer could obtain by unilateral action.

[11] Nash [1953] has analyzed the use of "threats" by oligopolists to arrange a division of profits. For example, inefficient producers might seek to increase the side payments by threatening to ruin the joint-profit maximum by increasing their outputs. Nash has developed the concept of an optimal threat in terms of the damage that can be inflicted upon opponents while also considering the cost incurred by the threatener. The selection of an optimal threat strategy leads to a bargaining model as the basis for a division of profits.

Cournot model, a strategy is a choice of an output and the payoff function is the duopolist's profits expressed as a function of the outputs of the two duopolists.

Two-Person, Constant-Sum Games

If the total payoff to the players of the game is a constant, the game is referred to as *constant-sum*. A two-person, constant-sum game is completely described by a two-dimensional array (a matrix) of payoffs to one of the two players (since the payoff to the other player is uniquely determined by the elements of this matrix: the constant value of the game minus the payoff to the other player).

By way of illustration, let us consider the simplest possible two-person, constant-sum game in which there are only two strategies. To make the example somewhat concrete, let us suppose that the two players are duopolists and that the payoffs are market shares (in which case the constant value of the game is 100 percent). Thus, for example, the game might be described by the following two-by-two array, where the entries are the shares of the market captured by player 1 given the strategies adopted by the two players:

		Player 2		
	Strategy	1	2	Row Minima
Player 1	1	60%	50%	50%
	2	55%	45%	45%
Column Maxima		60%	50%	50 = maximin; 50% = minimax

Thus, for example, if both players chose strategy 1, player 1 receives 60 percent of the market, leaving 40 percent of the market to player 2.

It is easily ascertained that the unique equilibrium of this game is attained when player 1 chooses strategy 1 and player 2 chooses strategy 2, in which case the two duopolists split the market evenly. No other pair of strategies yields a situation in which one of the two players cannot do better by changing his strategy, given the strategy choice of the other player.

There exists an interesting algorithm for finding solutions to a constant-sum game. Also listed in the above table are the column maxima and the row minima. For example, the column 1 maximum, 60 percent, represents the largest share of the market that can be captured by player 1 if player 2 chooses strategy 1. The column maxima therefore indicate the worst that can happen to player 2 for any given strategy choice. Similarly, the row minima indicate the smallest share of the market that player 1 can receive for any given strategy choice. If we compare the two column maxima, we see that the smallest of these is 50 percent, indicating that the worst that can happen to player 2 if he chooses strategy 2 is not as bad as the worst that can happen if he chooses strategy 1. This minimum of the column maxima, referred to as the "minimax," is entered in the last row and column. Similarly, the maximum of the row minima, the "maximin," is entered in this last row and column as well. It will be noted that the maximin is equal to the minimax and identifies the solution to the game: namely, the pair of strategies which yield this minimax-maximin payoff.

This particular way of characterizing the solution to a constant-sum game has given rise to an alternative interpretation of the solution concept. Suppose that we view the game as one in which the players choose their strategies simultaneously without knowing the strategy chosen by the opponents. In this case, we cannot interpret the choice problem as that of choosing a strategy given the strategy chosen by the opponent. An alternative approach is to assume that the players are very conservative (or risk averse) and adopt that strategy which minimizes the worst that can happen to them. Thus, for example, player 1 chooses strategy 1 because the worst that can happen if he chooses this strategy is that he gets 50 percent of the market whereas the worst that can happen if he chooses strategy 2 is that he gets 45 percent of the market. Player 2 chooses strategy 2 according to this criterion because the worst that can happen if he chooses this strategy is that he receives 50 percent of the market, whereas the worst that can happen if he chooses strategy 1 is that he receives only 40 percent of the market. Thus, the unique "minimax solution" is where player 1 chooses strategy 1 and player 2 chooses strategy 2.[12]

Not every game has a solution. This is easily demonstrated by the following two-person, constant-sum game:

		Player 2		Row Minima
	Strategy	1	2	
Player 1	1	55%	50%	50%
	2	45%	60%	45%
Column Maxima		55%	60%	50% = maximin; 55% = minimax

The reader can verify by examination that there is no pair of strategies which constitutes a solution in the sense that neither player has an incentive to change his strategy given the strategy of the other.

[12] Of course, in this particular example, strategy 1 dominates strategy 2 for player 1 and strategy 2 dominates strategy 1 for player 2 because a choice of the alternative strategy *cannot* yield a better outcome for the respective player. However, in games with a larger number of strategies, this is not necessarily the case (see exercise 14.5).

Another way to verify that the above game has no solution is to note that the minimax is not equal to the maximin; hence, there is no minimax solution to the game.

As a way around the problem that many (simple) games have no solution, von Neumann and Morgenstern suggested the notion of an "extensive form of the game" in which the players choose "mixed strategies" rather than the "pure strategies" listed in the above array. A mixed strategy is essentially a lottery in which the player decides not upon one of the two pure strategies in the above array but rather chooses a pair of probabilities (which sum to unity) with which he will choose each of the two pure strategies. Thus, for example, a player might adopt a mixed strategy in which he will choose pure strategy 1 30 percent of the time (i.e., with probability .3) and strategy 2 70 percent of the time (i.e., with probability .7). The motivation for a player to adopt a mixed strategy is to conceal his choice of strategy from his opponent. Von Neumann and Morgenstern go on to show that every two-person, constant-sum game in extended form has a solution (given certain restrictions on the utility functions defined over payoffs and probabilities). The reader who is interested in pursuing the ideas of mixed strategies and extended-form games is referred to the part III suggested reading.

Another (minor) problem with the von Neumann–Morgenstern solution concept is that the equilibrium is not necessarily unique, as demonstrated by the following game:

		Player 2		Row Minima
	Strategy	1	2	
Player 1	1	60%	30%	30%
	2	80%	20%	20%
	3	60%	30%	30%
Column Maxima		80%	30%	30% = maximin 30% = minimax

It is easily ascertained that there are two solutions to this game: one in which players 1 and 2 choose strategies 1 and 2, respectively, and one in which players 1 and 2 choose strategies 3 and 2, respectively.

When the solution is not unique, the outcome of the game is indeterminate. This is not a matter of great concern, however, as the payoffs in the different equilibria of constant-sum games must be identical (see exercise 14.6).

Two-Person Nonconstant-Sum Games

A salient feature of a constant-sum game is that it is strictly competitive in the sense that there is no possibility of collusion—the choice of a joint strategy—that can improve the positions of both players. Virtually all economic situations are not constant-sum. Thus, in most economic situations, there is a possibility of cooperation or collusion. For example, in the Cournot duopoly problem, the profits of both duopolists can be increased by the adoption of a joint strategy in which the two duopolists jointly produce the monopoly output and split the maximal joint profit.

Games in which the losses to one side are not offset by gains to the other are termed *nonconstant-sum*. A classic example of a nonconstant-sum game is the so-called Prisoner's Dilemma, attributable to A. W. Tucker (see Luce and Raiffa [1957, p. 94]). The setting is as follows. Two prisoners are accused of a crime for which the district attorney does not have sufficient evidence for conviction. If, however, one of the two prisoners were to turn state's evidence, conviction would be a certainty. The district attorney therefore separately offers each of the prisoners a deal. If one turns state's evidence and confesses while his accomplice remains silent, the talkative prisoner will receive only one year in prison, whereas his partner will be sent up for the maximum of ten years. If neither confesses, both will be prosecuted on a lesser offense with a two-year jail sentence for both of them. Finally, if both confess, in which case the testimony of neither is essential to the prosecution, both will be convicted of the major offense and sent up for five years.

The payoff matrix for this game, where the first figure in each entry is the number of years in jail for prisoner A and the second figure is the number of years in jail for prisoner B, is as follows:

		Prisoner B	
		not confess	confess
Prisoner A:	not confess	(2, 2)	(10, 1)
	confess	(1, 10)	(5, 5)

It is apparent that the unique equilibrium to the prisoner's dilemma game is where each prisoner confesses and each is sentenced to five years in jail. No other pair of strategies is in equilibrium because if either prisoner confesses (or is expected to confess) the best strategy of the other prisoner is to confess as well and if one of the prisoners does not confess (or is not expected to confess) it is still in the interest of the other prisoner to turn state's evidence. The salient feature of the prisoner's dilemma equilibrium is that the equilibrium outcome is dominated by a joint strategy in which both agree not to confess. Thus, this game illustrates the situation, common in economics, where cooperation can improve the welfare of all players. If the two prisoners can find a way to agree upon this joint strategy and, just as important, a way to enforce this agreement, both will be better off than when they play the game independently. This last aspect of any joint strategy—enforcement—is important because, even if the two prisoners agree upon the joint strategy, it is still in the interest of both prisoners to secretly break the agreement.

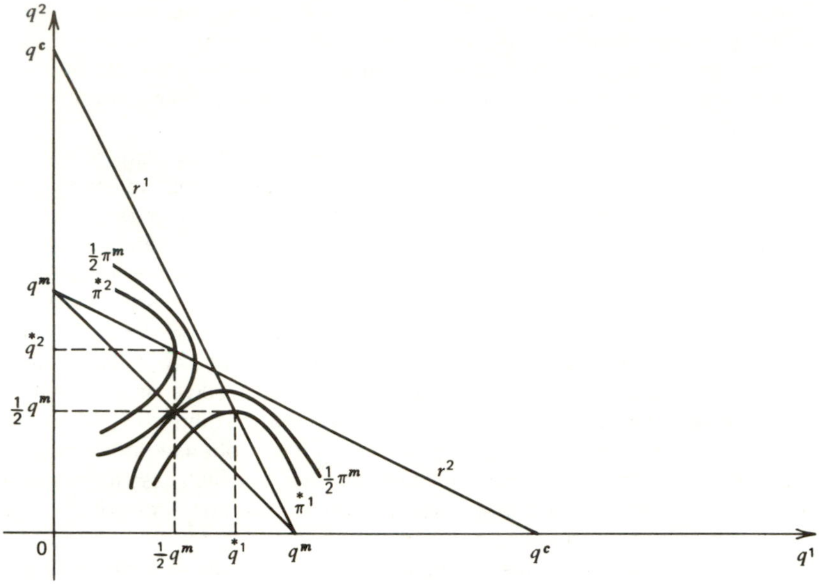

Figure 14.6

The Cournot duopoly problem has the characteristics of the Prisoner's Dilemma game. We have already noted that a collusive agreement to maximize joint profit can result in a higher profit level than is obtained in the solution to the Cournot game for both duopolists.

The incentive to cheat is illustrated in figure 14.6. Suppose that the collusive arrangement entails each of the duopolists producing one-half of the monopoly output. The collusive profit of the participants is, of course, given by the values attached to the two iso-profit curves that are tangent to each other at the point $(\frac{1}{2}q^m, \frac{1}{2}q^m)$, namely (if they have identical cost curves), one-half of the monopoly profit, $\frac{1}{2}\pi^m$. However, given that duopolist 2 sticks to the agreement, it is in the interest of duopolist 1 to cheat and expand his output to $\overset{*}{q}{}^1$, determined by the tangency of an iso-profit curve of duopolist 1 to the horizontal line through the coordinate value $\frac{1}{2}q^m$. This point of tangency must, by construction, occur on the reaction curve of duopolist 1. It is similarly in the interest of duopolist 2 to cheat on the collusive agreement by expanding his output to $\overset{*}{q}{}^2$, given by the intersection of the vertical line through the point $(\frac{1}{2}q^m, \frac{1}{2}q^m)$ and the reaction curve of duopolist 2. Thus, the collusive arrangement is inherently unstable.

The Bertrand duopoly model, in which price is the choice variable, also has the characteristics of the Prisoner's Dilemma game. The profits of both duopolists can be increased by a collusive arrangement whereby each agrees to maintain a price above that which results in the Bertrand equilibrium. However, having agreed upon a collusive pricing practice, it is in the interest of either duopolist to cheat on the collusive arrangement by secretly offering slightly lower prices to customers in order to bid away customers from the other duopolist. The diagrammatic illustration of this point is analogous to the illustration for the Cournot model and is left to the reader.

The upshot of this discussion of collusive production or pricing ageements is that there is generally an incentive for the members of a collusive arrangement, or cartel, to cheat on the agreement. For this reason, it is generally thought that cartels are inherently unstable and hence not very viable in the absence of some binding constraints on the participants. Many economists believe that the purpose of many government regulatory agencies and minimum-price laws (such as "fair-trade" pricing) is to institutionalize cartelizations in order to prevent cheating on the part of the members of the cartel.

n-Person Games and the Core Solution Concept

Two-person game theory, developed by von Neumann and Morgenstern, was extended to incorporate any finite number of persons by Nash [1950b]. The fundamental solution concept for an n-person game is essentially the same as that for a two-person game. We say that a set of strategies for all of the players of the game is a *Nash equilibrium* if the strategy of each player maximizes the payoff to that player, given the strategies of all of the players. Note that the Cournot and Bertrand equilibria are Nash equilibria.

One problem with the Nash concept for n-person games is that it does not allow for the possibility that subsets of players will form coalitions in order to further their own cause at the expense of players left out of the coalition. That is, the Nash solution concept precludes the possibility of cooperation. Games in which cooperation is allowed are called cooperative games. The most common solution concept for a cooperative n-person game is that of the *core*. In order to define the core, let $s = \{s^1, \ldots, s^n\}$ be a set of strategies for the n players and let $\pi^k(s)$ be the payoff to player k when s is the set of strategies adopted by the n players. We say that a set of strategies $\hat{s}$ is *blocked* by a coalition (a subset of the players) if there exists an alternative set of strategies for the members of the coalition, say $\mathring{s}^c$, such that $\pi^k(\mathring{s}^c, s^{\bar{c}}) > \pi^k(\hat{s}^c, s^{\bar{c}})$ for all (feasible) values of the strategies of the players who are not in the coalition, $s^{\bar{c}}$, for all k in the coalition. That is, a set of strategies is blocked by a coalition if it is possible for that coalition to agree on a set of alternative strategies which makes every member of the coalition better off no matter what strategies the other players adopt. Note that a blocking coalition need not be a proper subset of the set of players; that is, a set of strategies is blocked if it is possible for *all* players to agree upon an alternative set of strategies which makes all players better off.[13]

The set of strategies that cannot be blocked by some coalition is called the *core* of the game. The core is therefore the set of solutions to n-person games in which cooperation is allowed. It is apparent that a set of strategies that is not in the core is not viable if cooperation is allowed because there is an incentive for some coalition to undermine that set of strategies.

Not all games have a nonempty core; that is, using the core as a solution concept, there exist games with no solution. The notion of the core and its nonexistence can be explicated by using an example due to Luce and Raiffa

[13] A subset is proper if it excludes some players.

[1957]. Suppose that a rich, elderly citizen will bequeath his entire estate of \$3 million to three squabbling heirs if they can agree unanimously on a way of dividing this sum of money among them. If only two of the heirs can agree, the elderly citizen will give them a smaller amount. We consider the two cooperative games that arise from two such smaller amounts: (i) \$$1\frac{1}{2}$ million and (ii) \$$2\frac{1}{2}$ million.

In this game a coalition is a (not necessarily proper) subset of the three players (heirs) who agree on a way of dividing the sum of money which they inherit. In order to describe this game, let $\pi(C)$ be the total payoff to the members of the coalition. Then the payoffs to alternative coalitions, $\pi(s)$, in games (i) and (ii) corresponding to the \$$1\frac{1}{2}$ million- and \$$2\frac{1}{2}$-million inheritance for two-member coalitions, respectively, are as follows:

GAME (i)	GAME (ii)
$\pi(\{1\}) = \pi(\{2\}) = \pi(\{3\}) = 0$	$\pi(\{1\}) = \pi(\{2\}) = \pi(\{3\}) = 0$
$\pi(\{1, 2\}) = \pi(\{1, 3\}) = \pi(\{2, 3\}) = 1\frac{1}{2}$	$\pi(\{1, 2\}) = \pi(\{1, 3\}) = \pi(\{2, 3\}) = 2\frac{1}{2}$
$\pi(\{1, 2, 3\}) = 3$	$\pi(\{1, 2, 3\}) = 3$

Thus, in both games one-person coalitions receive no payoff at all since at least two persons must agree on a division in order to receive money from the benefactor. Similarly, in both games, if all three persons agree on a way to divide the dividends, the payoff to the coalition is \$3 million. On the other hand, in games (i) and (ii) the payoffs to two-person coalitions are \$$1\frac{1}{2}$ million and \$$2\frac{1}{2}$ million, respectively.

Consider the first game. The allocations resulting from complete disagreement (from "one-person coalitions") are trivially blocked by both two-person and three-person coalitions. The allocations generated by two-person coalitions are blocked because the excluded third person can offer each of the two members of the coalition a quantity of money slightly above his share of the \$$1\frac{1}{2}$-million payoff, thus increasing his payoff from zero to a little less than \$$1\frac{1}{2}$ million. Consequently, such allocations are blocked by three-person coalitions.

However, allocations generated by three-person coalitions are not necessarily blocked because there are many ways to divide \$3 million among three persons in such a way that any two persons receive a total of at least \$$1\frac{1}{2}$ million, so that no two-person coalition can block the allocation. Thus, the core to game (i) is nonempty and a solution exists.

However, the core is empty in game (ii). To see this, note that allocations resulting from noncooperation are quite trivially blocked by either two-person or three-person coalitions and that allocations generated by two-person coalitions are blocked by three-person coalitions because the excluded third person can offer the coalition pair a sum of money slightly in excess of \$$2\frac{1}{2}$ million, thus increasing his share in the new coalition from zero to a little less than \$$\frac{1}{2}$ million. To show that any allocation generated by the three-person coalition is blocked, we have to show that there is no way of dividing \$3 million among three people in such a way that any two receive at least $2\frac{1}{2}$ million, the value of a two-person coalition. Suppose that there were such a way of dividing \$3 million. Then the following three inequalities, where $\pi^k(\{1, 2, 3\})$ is the payoff to player k of the three-person coalition, would hold:

$$\begin{aligned}
\pi^1(\{1, 2, 3\}) + \pi^2(\{1, 2, 3\}) \qquad\qquad\qquad\qquad &\geq 2\tfrac{1}{2}.\\
\pi^1(\{1, 2, 3\}) \qquad\qquad\qquad\qquad + \pi^3(\{1, 2, 3\}) &\geq 2\tfrac{1}{2}.\\
\pi^2(\{1, 2, 3\}) + \pi^3(\{1, 2, 3\}) &\geq 2\tfrac{1}{2}.
\end{aligned}$$

Summing both sides of these inequalities, we have

$$2\pi^1(\{1, 2, 3\}) + 2\pi^2(\{1, 2, 3\}) + 2\pi^3(\{1, 2, 3\}) \geq 7\tfrac{1}{2}$$

or

$$\pi^1(\{1, 2, 3\}) + \pi^2(\{1, 2, 3\}) + \pi^3(\{1, 2, 3\}) \geq 3\tfrac{3}{4}.$$

But this implies that the value of the coalition is $\$3\frac{3}{4}$ million, violating the constraint that there is only \$3 million to divide among the three members of the coalition. Thus, any allocation generated by a three-person coalition is blocked by two-person coalitions and the core of game (ii) is empty.

14.5 CONCLUSION

In this chapter we have dealt rather briefly with several models of oligopolistic interdependence. The objective has not been to present a comprehensive survey, but rather to introduce the reader to the salient features of oligopolistic market structures.

The essential characteristic of these market structures is the concept of producer interdependence with respect to decisions concerning price, output, input demand, etc. The equilibrium solution to oligopolistic models depends crucially upon the assumptions that are made concerning the behavior of each producer with respect to competitors. The actual way in which individual producers perceive and react to interdependence probably varies considerably from market to market. For this reason, there is no general theory of oligopolistic market structures. Empirical work often requires different models for different oligopolistic markets.

At the same time, the theory of games offers an attractive conceptual and analytical framework within which to consider not only oligopolistic interdependence but also other problems of conflict of interest in economics (and in many other disciplines such as political science, sociology, and moral philosophy).

EXERCISES

14.1 Setting profit equal to $\bar{\pi}^1$, derive the iso-profit curve—showing q^2 as a function of q^1—for duopolist 1 from equation (14.10). Show that the iso-profit curve is convex from above; i.e., the second-order derivative with respect to q^1 is negative.

14.2 Draw a Stackelberg diagram for the price-leadership duopoly model when each duopolist prefers to be a follower.

14.3 Duopolists selling slightly differentiated commodities have demand functions defined by $D^1(p_1, p_2) = a - bp_1 + cp_2$ and $D^2(p_1, p_2) = \alpha - \beta p_2 + \gamma p_1$ where p_1 and p_2 are the prices of duopolists 1 and 2, respectively, and a, b, c, α, β, and γ are positive parameters. For computational convenience, assume zero marginal costs.

a. Find the Bertrand equilibrium (i.e., assuming that each duopolist maximizes profit subject to the price of the other, calculate the equilibrium prices in terms of the parameters).

b. Find the leadership equilibrium (i.e., suppose that duopolist 1 wises up and maximizes profit subject to the reaction function of duopolist 2). Compare the equilibrium prices to the Bertrand equilibrium prices.

c. Compare the joint-profit-maximization prices to the Bertrand-equilibrium prices and to the leadership-equilibrium prices.

14.4 Assume that the buyers of a commodity are distributed uniformly along a line of finite length (Main Street, say) and purchase one unit of a commodity from the closest seller (street vendor, say). (If two sellers occupy the same location, purchases from them are divided evenly between the two.) Assuming that sellers can change locations (strategies) costlessly, identify the equilibrium (if it exists) (i) when there are two sellers and (ii) when there are three sellers.

14.5 Find the solutions to the constant-sum games described by the following payoff matrices (for the player with strategies corresponding to rows of the matrix):

$$\begin{bmatrix} 4 & 3 \\ 6 & 0 \end{bmatrix} \quad \text{and} \quad \begin{bmatrix} 6 & 3 & 2 & 5 \\ 5 & 4 & 6 & 8 \\ 8 & 1 & 9 & 4 \\ 1 & 0 & 1 & 9 \end{bmatrix}$$

14.6 Prove that two equilibria of a constant-sum game must have identical payoffs. (Hint: proceed by way of contradiction.)

14.7 Find the solutions to the nonconstant-sum games described by the following payoff matrices:

$$\begin{bmatrix} (4, 3) & (1, 2) \\ (3, 4) & (5, 2) \end{bmatrix} \quad \text{and} \quad \begin{bmatrix} (0, 0) & (3, 1) & (4, 2) & (6, 4) \\ (2, 2) & (3, 6) & (0, 7) & (5, 1) \\ (4, 3) & (1, 0) & (5, 4) & (0, 2) \\ (7, 3) & (6, 1) & (3, 1) & (5, 5) \end{bmatrix}$$

14.8 Construct a nonconstant-sum game with two equilibria that have different payoffs.

14.9 Prove that any constant-sum game can be converted into a zero-sum game with the same equilibrium.

14.10* Consider a neighborhood with three persons, each with a lawn and a bag of garbage. All garbage must be dumped on somebody's lawn. The utility (payoff) of having b bags of garbage dumped on one's lawn is $-b$. Garbage can be transferred costlessly among coalition members. Prove that the core of this game is empty. (Hint: use the inequalities generated by possible coalitions and the feasibility constraint, $b_1 + b_2 + b_3$ equals a constant, to obtain a contradiction).

PART III
HISTORICAL NOTES AND SUGGESTED READING

Marshall [1920, Book V] is a classic work on the *equilibrium of a single market*. **Frisch** [1936] contains a good discussion of the concepts of equilibrium and disequilibrium. **Samuelson** [1947a, chaps 9–11] is the seminal work on the method of *comparative statics* and the *stability* of equilibrium.

Cournot [1838] first analyzed a *duopoly market*. **Bertrand** [1883] provided an alternative solution to the **Cournot** duopoly problem. **von Stackelberg** [1934] explored the implications of alternative behavioral assumptions for the duopoly model. **Fellner** [1949] is a good diagrammatic analysis of duopoly and oligopoly models, including the contributions of **Cournot**, **Bertrand**, and **Stackelberg**. The *stability properties of oligopoly models* have been analyzed by **Fisher** [1961], **Hahn** [1962] and **Quandt** [1967].

Chamberlin [1960], first published in 1933, is the seminal work on the theory of *monopolistic competition*. (A related treatise was published independently by **Robinson** [1933].) **Shubik** [1959a] and **Archibald** [1961] analyze the criticisms of this approach to economic interdependence. Recently the framework of monopolistic competition has been used to examine the problem of the optimal number of differentiated commodities (**Dixit** and **Stiglitz** [1977] and **Spence** [1976]).

The *theory of economic regulation* attempts to analyze the response of producers (and other economic agents) to various types of economic regulation. **Baumol** and **Klevorick** [1970] review the literature on rate-of-return regulation. Also see **Baumol** and **Bradford** [1970] and **Bailey** [1973]. **Scherer** [1973] is an excellent introduction to the *industrial organization* literature.

The seminal work on *game theory* and economics is **von Neumann** and **Morgenstern** [1944]. **Nash** [1950a, 1950b] extended the two-person game theory of **von Neumann** and **Morgenstern** to incorporate any finite number of players. These papers also develop the important concept of a Nash equilibrium. **Luce** and **Raiffa** [1957] and **Shubik** [1959a] are good introductions to the theory of games.

PART IV THE THEORY OF GENERAL EQUILIBRIUM AND ECONOMIC WELFARE

Economics is defined succinctly in the introductory chapter as the study of the allocation of scarce resources. Part I examines the way in which a consumer allocates scarce resources (wealth or income) among the commodities that are available for consumption. It is assumed that the consumer takes prices as given. Part I also derives a labor supply function which, with a given wage rate, can be used to determine the income of the consumer. Part II develops the theory of production and derives the net supply functions of the individual producer. Part III examines, among other things, the derivation of the supply function in a perfectly competitive market where the commodity price is taken as a parameter by all producers. The consumer demand functions of part I are combined with the supply functions to show how equilibrium is achieved, and hence price determined, in a single market.

This study of single-market equilibrium takes all other commodity prices as given. If the equilibrium price is determined in this way in each market independently of what happens in all other markets, there is surely no reason to believe that the resultant set of prices would be consistent with each other. All markets—commodity and input—are *interdependent*. This interdependence derives from the relationships (of substitutability and complementarity) between commodities in the utility functions and production functions and from the fact that all commodities compete for the consumer's dollar. Consequently, equilibrium in the multitude of markets—and, indeed, the equilibrium of every producer and every consumer in the economy—must be determined simultaneously.

It is the purpose of chapters 15 and 16 to describe and analyze such a *general*, as opposed to *partial*, equilibrium. Chapter 15 examines general equilibrium for a pure "exchange economy" in which there is no production and each consumer is endowed with initial allotments of the commodities. Many important general-equilibrium (and welfare economic) concepts can be adequately illustrated in this simple economy. Chapter 16 examines the general competitive equilibrium in a production and exchange economy.

General competitive equilibrium is not a sterile scientific concept. That is, it is not just a condition under which all markets are cleared. As it turns out, competitive equilibrium has certain important optimality properties (which generally cannot be ascribed to equilibrium under alternative market structures). Chapters 17–18 examine the nexus between competitive equilibrium and the social optimality (in a certain sense to be defined later) of the allocation of resources. While all of the other chapters of this book deal with positive economic problems, the last four concentrate on normative economic problems. That is, while the first sixteen chapters purport to describe "what is," chapters 17–20 examine the question of "what ought to be." The latter issue raises the problem of defining what we mean by a "socially optimal allocation of resources." Welfare economics is directed toward the problem of constructing and evaluating rules for making social decisions about alternative uses of the scarce resources of the economy and about the distribution of final goods and services.

Chapters 17 and 18 explore the implications of the "unanimity rule." In particular, chapter 17 describes the nexus between general competitive equilibrium and optimality under this unanimity rule. Chapter 18 examines the circumstances under which this nexus breaks down. Chapters 19 and 20 conclude with a discussion of alternative social decision rules, making the case that the "values" of society must be explicitly incorporated into the construction of such rules. Our conclusion therefore carries us to boundaries of other intellectual disciplines—most notably the philosophy of ethics and social justice. It is a fitting point on which to conclude.

CHAPTER 15 GENERAL COMPETITIVE EQUILIBRIUM IN AN EXCHANGE ECONOMY

15.1 INTRODUCTION

The introduction to part IV points out that it is in principle impossible to determine the equilibrium price and output in a single market in isolation from the rest of the economy. This is because of the interdependence that exists between commodities in the consumers' utility functions and the technological interdependence between commodities in the production functions. The amount demanded of any commodity by any individual consumer in general depends not just upon the price of that commodity but upon the prices of all other commodities as well. Similarly, the amount supplied or demanded of any commodity by an individual producer depends not just upon the price of that commodity but upon the prices of all other commodities in his production function. Thus, all prices and amounts of all commodities demanded and supplied must be determined simultaneously rather than in isolation.

Because of this interdependence in supply and demand, when an equilibrium in a specific market is displaced (for example, by the imposition of an excise tax), the resultant change in the price sets off a chain reaction which generally displaces equilibrium in all other markets. This displacement of equilibrium in other markets results in price changes which, in turn, affect the ultimate equilibrium in the market that experienced the initial displacement. That is, the induced price changes in other markets feed back into the market in which the displacement occurs. It is because of these "feedback" effects that we should consider all markets simultaneously in assessing the effect of a displacement of equilibrium in a single market.

It should be clear at the outset that the determination of equilibrium in all markets simultaneously is a gargantuan task. It is primarily for this reason that the great bulk of applied economics takes place in the context of partial- rather than general-equilibrium analysis. In many cases, partial-equilibrium analysis is perfectly appropriate; this would be the case when the secondary or feedback effects of displacements of equilibrium in a single market are insignificant relative to the direct effect within the market, which is determined holding all other prices in the economy constant. In many other cases, however, ignoring the interdependence between markets leads to serious miscalculation. But the principal reason for studying general-equilibrium theory is not because it is more appropriate for applied economics but because there are a number of important theoretical principles to be learned from general-equilibrium analysis. This theory is especially useful in normative economics, studied in chapters 17–20.

Most of the salient principles of general-equilibrium theory can be analyzed in a highly simplified economy where no production takes place. This chapter therefore first considers a world in which each of the consumers in the society is endowed with a positive amount of at least one commodity. This endowment is an abstraction and we therefore do not try to justify it with any reference to a realistic example. (Patinkin [1965] has referred to this endowment as "manna from heaven.")

Each consumer could simply consume his endowment each period. However, since the different members of the society may be blessed with different endowments of the various commodities and in general have different tastes, it is generally true that the members of the society can improve their welfare by entering into exchanges of commodities in order to consume bundles of commodities that are preferred to the initial endowments. It is the purpose of this chapter to analyze the set of exchanges that take place. Section 15.2 begins with the highly simplified case of bilateral exchange, where there are only two commodities in the economy and only two consumers. This section contains some tedious algebra, but a graphical illustration of bilateral exchange equilibrium is presented in section 15.3. Finally, section 15.4 examines the general exchange equilibrium when there are m consumers and n commodities.

15.2 BILATERAL EXCHANGE

Assumptions

The economy to be examined in this section is described in part by the following assumption:

Assumption 15.1 The economy consists of two commodities and two consumers. The consumers' preference orderings over the two-dimensional nonnegative quadrant satisfy assumptions 3.1 (nonsatiation with at least one commodity) and 3.2 (strict convexity) and are representable by continuous utility functions. Each consumer is endowed with nonnegative quantities of the two commodities.

The utility functions are denoted U^1 and U^2 with images $U^1(x_1^1, x_2^1)$ and $U^2(x_1^2, x_2^2)$ where $[x_1^1, x_2^1]$ and $[x_1^2, x_2^2]$ are the consumption bundles of consumers 1 and 2, respectively. Under our assumptions, these utility functions can be represented graphically by convex indifference maps with no point of satiation (with both commodities).

The following exchange assumptions (analogous to the partial-competitive-equilibrium assumptions of chapter 11) are also posited:

Assumption 15.2 There is no cost of exchange.

Assumption 15.3 There is perfect information about the rate at which one commodity can be exchanged for the other.

Exchange Rates and Consumer Constraints

Let us denote the rate of exchange of commodity 2 for commodity 1 (the price of commodity 2 in units of commodity 1) by p_{21}. Thus, p_{21} is the amount of commodity 1 which must be given up to obtain one unit of commodity 2. The amount of commodity 1 which must be given up in exchange for x_2 units of commodity 2 is therefore $p_{21}x_2$. Similarly, letting p_{12} be the price of commodity 1 in units of commodity 2, the quantity of commodity 2 which must be given up in exchange for x_1 units of commodity 2 is $p_{12}x_1$. However, the rate at which commodity 2 can be traded for commodity 1 is the inverse of the rate at which commodity 1 can be traded for commodity 2. That is, the fact that two apples exchange for one orange is equivalent to the fact that one orange exchanges for two apples. Thus,

$$p_{12} = \frac{1}{p_{21}}. \tag{15.1}$$

The consumption of each commodity by each consumer must be no greater than his endowment of that commodity plus the net amount that he acquires through exchange. For example,

$$x_1^1 \leq \bar{x}_1^1 + p_{21}(\bar{x}_2^1 - x_2^1) \tag{15.2}$$

where $\bar{x}_1^1$ and $\bar{x}_2^1$ are the first consumer's endowments of commodities 1 and 2, respectively. In this constraint, $\bar{x}_2^1 - x_2^1$ is the net amount of commodity 2 traded by the first consumer for commodity 1; hence, as p_{21} is the price of commodity 2 in units of commodity 1, $p_{21}(\bar{x}_2^1 - x_2^1)$ is the net quantity acquired of commodity 1 though exchange. Of course, $\bar{x}_2^1 - x_2^1$ can be positive, negative, or zero.

The similar constraint for commodity 2 is $x_2^1 \leq \bar{x}_2^1 + p_{12}(\bar{x}_1^1 - x_1^1)$ or, because of the identity (15.1),

$$x_2^1 \leq \bar{x}_2^1 + \frac{1}{p_{21}}(\bar{x}_1^1 - x_1^1). \tag{15.3}$$

Multiplying through (15.3) by p_{21} converts the units of all variables to those of commodity 1:

$$p_{21}x_2^1 \leq p_{21}\bar{x}_2^1 + \bar{x}_1^1 - x_1^1. \tag{15.4}$$

Equations (15.4) and (15.2) can be added to obtain a single constraint:

$$x_1^1 + p_{21}x_2^1 \leq 2\bar{x}_1^1 + 2p_{21}\bar{x}_2^1 - p_{21}x_2^1 - x_1^1.$$

Addition of $p_{21}x_2^1 + x_1^1$ to both sides and division by 2 yields

$$x_1^1 + p_{21}x_2^1 \leq \bar{x}_1^1 + p_{21}\bar{x}_2^1. \tag{15.5}$$

This constraint says that total consumption expressed in units of commodity 1 must be no greater than the total endowment expressed in units of commodity 1. The analogous constraint for consumer 2 is

$$x_1^2 + p_{21}x_2^2 \leq \bar{x}_1^2 + p_{21}\bar{x}_2^2. \tag{15.6}$$

A utility-maximization hypothesis, which corresponds to assumptions 2.4 (fixed prices and income) and 2.5 (consumer choice), is now added.

Assumption 15.4 The consumers maximize utility subject to the (respective) constraints (15.5) and (15.6).[1]

In fact, because of the nonsatiation assumption, the two constraints (15.5) and (15.6) can be written as equalities:

$$x_1^1 + p_{21}x_2^1 = \bar{x}_1^1 + p_{21}\bar{x}_2^1 \tag{15.7}$$

and

$$x_1^2 + p_{21}x_2^2 = \bar{x}_1^2 + p_{21}\bar{x}_2^2. \tag{15.8}$$

So long as p_{21} is strictly positive and finite, solutions to the two maximization problems exist. As the "givens" to the consumers are endowments and the exchange rate, the optimal consumption bundles depend on these variables:*

• •

**Note* If the utility functions are differentiable and both solutions are interior, these demand functions are derived by solving the first-order conditions, given by the two constraints, (15.7) and (15.8), and the conditions,

$$\frac{\partial U^1(x_1^1, x_2^1)}{\partial x_1^1} = \lambda^1$$

$$\frac{\partial U^1(x_1^1, x_2^1)}{\partial x_2^1} = \lambda^1 p_{21},$$

$$\frac{\partial U^2(x_1^2, x_2^2)}{\partial x_1^2} = \lambda^2,$$

[1] Implicit in this assumption is the hypothesis that the consumers are price takers. As the "large-numbers" rationalization is blatently false in the two-consumer exchange economy, this is, to say the least, a dubious postulate. It is possible to construct a rationalizing scenario in which there are a large number of consumers of each of the two "types" (characterized by the two preference orderings and the two endowments), but a more forthright rationalization is that the price-taker assumption is a notion we adopt in this simple economy in order to explicate more clearly the nature of general competitive equilibrium in more complex economies.

and

$$\frac{\partial U^2(x_1^2, x_2^2)}{\partial x_2^2} = \lambda^2 p_{21},$$

where λ^1 and λ^2 are the Lagrange multipliers.

• •

$$x_1^1 = d_1^1(p_{21}, \bar{x}_1^1, \bar{x}_2^1), \quad (15.9)$$

$$x_2^1 = d_2^1(p_{21}, \bar{x}_1^1, \bar{x}_2^1), \quad (15.10)$$

$$x_1^2 = d_1^2(p_{21}, \bar{x}_1^2, \bar{x}_2^2), \quad (15.11)$$

and

$$x_2^2 = d_2^2(p_{21}, \bar{x}_1^2, \bar{x}_2^2). \quad (15.12)$$

Competitive Equilibrium and Walras's Law

Competitive equilibrium requires that the demands for the two commodities be compatible with the total endowments; that is, that the total amount demanded of each commodity by the two consumers be equal to the total endowment. Algebraically, these market-equilibrium conditions are

$$\bar{x}_1^1 + \bar{x}_1^2 = x_1^1 + x_1^2 \quad (15.13)$$

and

$$\bar{x}_2^1 + \bar{x}_2^2 = x_2^1 + x_2^2. \quad (15.14)$$

The competitive equilibrium is generated by solving the demand equations (15.9)–(15.12) and the market-equilibrium equations (15.13) and (15.14) for the consumption quantities x_1^1, x_2^1, x_1^2, and x_2^2, and the exchange rate p_{21}. Superficially, this system of equations might appear to be overdetermined since there are six equations in only five unknowns. However, these six equations are not independent—if five are satisfied, so is the sixth. To see this, note that the individual demand equations (15.9)–(15.12) must be consistent with the consumer budget identities (15.7) and (15.8). Next add these two budget constraints to obtain the aggregate budget identity.

$$\bar{x}_1^1 + \bar{x}_1^2 + p_{21}(\bar{x}_2^1 + \bar{x}_2^2) = x_1^1 + x_1^2 + p_{21}(x_2^1 + x_2^2). \quad (15.15)$$

Now subtract the first market-equilibrium equation (15.13) from this equation to obtain

$$p_{21}(\bar{x}_2^1 + \bar{x}_2^2) = p_{21}(x_2^1 + x_2^2). \quad (15.16)$$

Division by p_{21} yields

$$\bar{x}_2^1 + \bar{x}_2^2 = x_2^1 + x_2^2, \quad (15.17)$$

which is equivalent to the second market-equilibrium condition (15.14).

Thus, the second market-equilibrium equation has been derived as a linear combination of the two budget identities and the first market-equilibrium equation. The *first* market-equilibrium equation could just as easily have been derived as a linear combination of the budget identities and the *second* market-equilibrium equation.

What this means in terms of the economics is that if the market for one commodity is in equilibrium then the market for the other commodity *must* be in equilibrium also. That is, if supply and demand are equal for one of the two commodities, they must be equal for the other. This makes sense because there is really only *one* market in which the two commodities exchange for one another. The act of supplying commodity 1 is equivalent to the act of demanding commodity 2 and vice versa.

Indeed, the *net* demand for commodity 1, $(x_1^1 + x_1^2) - (\bar{x}_1^1 + \bar{x}_1^2)$ is identically equal to the net *supply* of commodity 2 in units of commodity 1, $p_{21}(\bar{x}_2^1 + \bar{x}_2^2) - p_{21}(x_2^1 + x_2^2)$. This follows directly from the aggregate budget identity (15.15), which can be rewritten as

$$(x_1^1 + x_1^2) - (\bar{x}_1^1 + \bar{x}_1^2) = p_{21}(\bar{x}_2^1 + \bar{x}_2^2) - p_{21}(x_2^1 + x_2^2). \qquad (15.15')$$

Similarly, multiplying through (15.15′) by −1, we see that the net *supply* of commodity 1 is identically equal to the net *demand* for commodity 2. Consequently, if supply and demand for commodity 1 are equal (i.e., the net demand for, or supply of, commodity 1 is zero), supply and demand for commodity 2 are necessarily equal also.

The fact that equilibrium for commodity 1 implies equilibrium for commodity 2 is the two-commodity version of *Walras's Law*, named after the French economist who is the intellectual father of general-equilibrium analysis.

15.3 BILATERAL EXCHANGE: A GRAPHICAL EXPOSITION

The Consumption Box Diagram

Bilateral exchange can be illustrated by using a construct referred to as the *consumption box diagram*.[2] To see how this box is constructed, refer to figure 15.1 where units of commodity 1 are plotted on the horizontal axis and units of commodity 2 are plotted on the vertical axis. The total endowment of the economy can be represented by a point in this space; e.g., $(\bar{x}_1, \bar{x}_2)$. The endowment of consumer 1 can also be represented by a point in this space; e.g., $(\bar{x}_1^1, \bar{x}_2^1)$. As the total resources of the economy are divided between the two consumers, specification of the first consumer's endowment uniquely determines the endowment of the second consumer. The point $(\bar{x}_1^1, \bar{x}_2^1)$ therefore identifies the endowment of the second consumer. In fact, the endowment of the second consumer is represented by the lengths of the two line segments *ab* and *ac*, corresponding to $\bar{x}_1^2$ and $\bar{x}_2^2$, respectively. Thus, the point $(\bar{x}_1^1, \bar{x}_2^1)$ represents the endowment of consumer 2 if point *a* is interpreted as the origin.

[2] This diagram is commonly called an "Edgeworth box diagram;" we, however, choose to eschew this terminology because Edgeworth [1881] only popularized the concept, which is originally attributable to Pareto (see Weatherby [1976]).

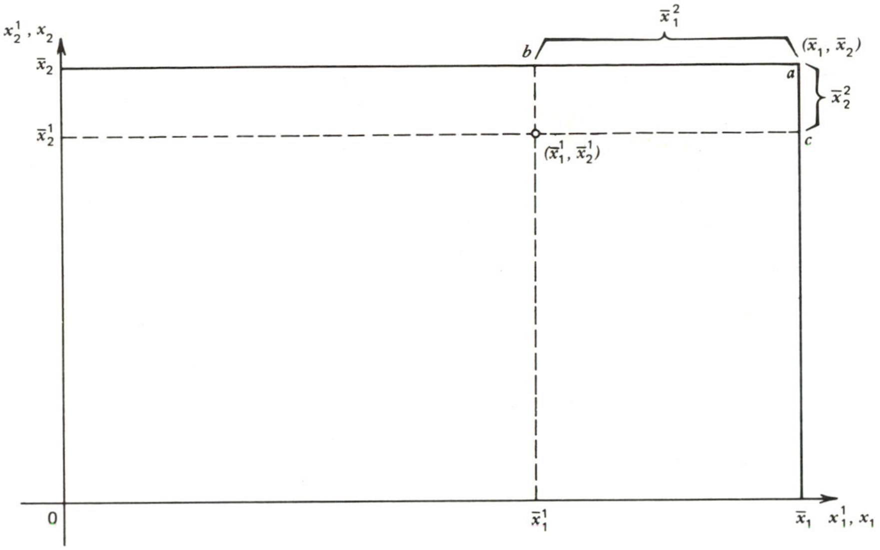

Figure 15.1

That is, the endowment of consumer 2 is given by the vector from $(\bar{x}_1, \bar{x}_2)$ to $(\bar{x}_1^1, \bar{x}_2^1)$. Thus, the bottom and left-hand sides of the box constitute the axes along which the first consumer's endowments of the two commodities are measured, and the top and right-hand sides of the box constitute the axes along which the second consumer's endowments of the two commodities are measured (in a direction opposite to that of the first consumer).

Since the total *consumption* of the two consumers must be equal to the total endowment, the consumption bundles of the two consumers can also be represented by a point in this box referred to the lower left-hand corner and the upper right-hand corner as origins for the first and second consumer, respectively. It is therefore also possible to represent the preference orderings of the two consumers by indifference maps drawn with respect to these two origins. Some of these indifference curves are illustrated in figure 15.2. The indifference curves of consumer 1 are drawn convex to the origin O^1 and the indifference curves of consumer 2 are drawn convex to the origin O^2.

Exchange and the Contract Curve

Let the endowment of the two consumers be represented by the point $\bar{x}$ in figure 15.2. The corresponding endowment of each commodity for each consumer is projected onto the respective axes.

If both of the consumers simply consume their initial endowments, they attain utility of $\bar{u}^1$ and $\bar{u}^2$, respectively. However, the two can engage in trades that would move them anywhere within the box. Many feasible trades would reduce their utility but there may be a large number of exchanges that would increase the utility of both or of one without reducing the utility of the other.

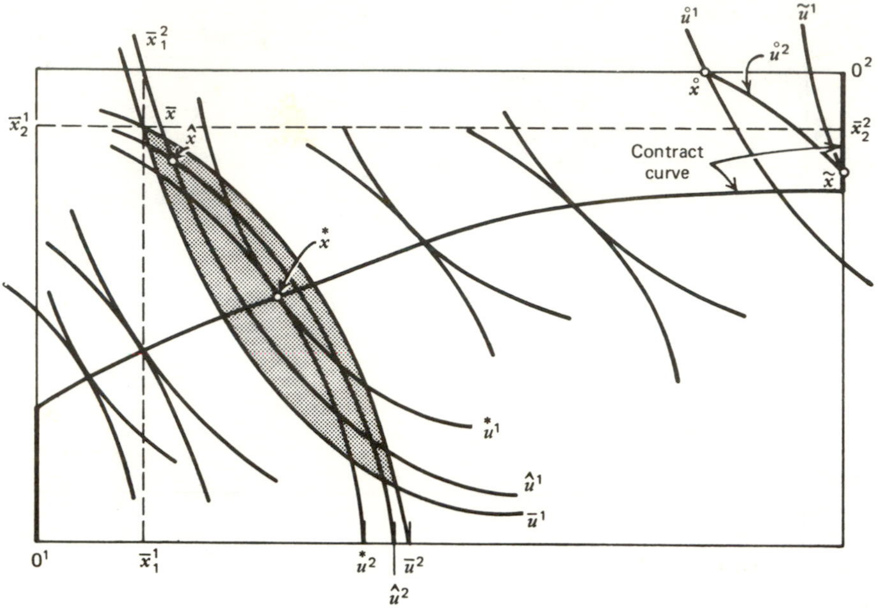

Figure 15.2

In fact, it is easily seen that the utility of at least one of the two consumers is increased without decreasing the utility of the other by any exchange that results in a new allocation inside the shaded area, which has the two indifference curves passing through $\bar{x}$ as its boundaries. Any exchange that places the new allocation in the interior of this area with respect to the two indifference curves increases the welfare of *both* consumers. An exchange that moves along one of the indifference curves increases the utility level of one while leaving the utility of the other unchanged. For example, an exchange that results in the new allocation $\hat{x}$ would raise the utility of both consumers—to $\hat{u}^1$ and $\hat{u}^2$, respectively. However, at this new allocation it remains possible to improve the welfare of both consumers by an appropriate exchange. Any exchange which places the new allocation in the area with the two indifference curves passing through $\hat{x}$ as its boundaries increases the utility of at least one of the two consumers without lowering the utility of the other.

If trade resulted in the allocation $\overset{*}{x}$, which is a point of tangency between indifference curves of the two consumers, no additional exchange could enhance one consumer's utility without lowering the utility of the other. The set of all allocations that make mutually beneficial exchange impossible is called the *contract curve*. It is apparent that all *interior* allocations on the contract curve are characterized by tangency of the indifference curves. This is not necessarily true for allocations that are on the contract curve and the boundary of the consumption box (where $x_i^c = 0$ for some i and c). For example, the boundary allocation $\tilde{x}$ in figure 15.2 is on the contract curve but the slopes of the $\tilde{u}^1$ and $\tilde{u}^2$ indifference curves at this point are unequal.

The reader should note the distinction between boundary points such as $\hat{x}$ in figure 15.2 that are on the contract curve and boundary points such as $\mathring{x}$ that are not on the contract curve. An appropriate exchange from the allocation $\mathring{x}$ into the interior of the consumption box would enhance the utility of both trades. Note also that if the indifference curves of the consumers approach asymptotically but do not intersect the boundaries, the only boundary points on the contract curve are the two origins, O^1 and O^2.

Exchange Rates and the Offer Curve

The exchanges that appear to be feasible to a single consumer for a given exchange rate are represented graphically by a straight line which passes through the initial endowment. The slope of the line represents the rate at which one commodity can be exchanged for the other. Figure 15.3 illustrates one such possible exchange line. Letting $\bar{x}$ represent the initial allocation, this exchange line indicates that by giving up $\bar{x}_2^1 - \hat{x}_2^1$ units of commodity 2, consumer 1 can obtain $\hat{x}_1^1 - \bar{x}_1^1$ units of commodity 1, arriving at the allocation $\hat{x}$. Thus, the rate of exchange of commodity 1 for commodity 2 (the price of commodity 1 in units of commodity 2) is $(\bar{x}_2^1 - \hat{x}_2^1)/(\hat{x}_1^1 - \bar{x}_1^1) = p_{12}$. Thus, the slope of this exchange line is p_{12}. Alternatively, the slope of this line can be represented as

$$\frac{1}{(\hat{x}_1^1 - \bar{x}_1^1)/(\bar{x}_2^1 - \hat{x}_2^1)} = \frac{1}{p_{21}}.$$

Thus, the slope of this line is also equivalent to the inverse of the price of commodity 2 in units of commodity 1. It is left to the reader to show that consistent definitions of the exchange rate in terms of the slope of the exchange line

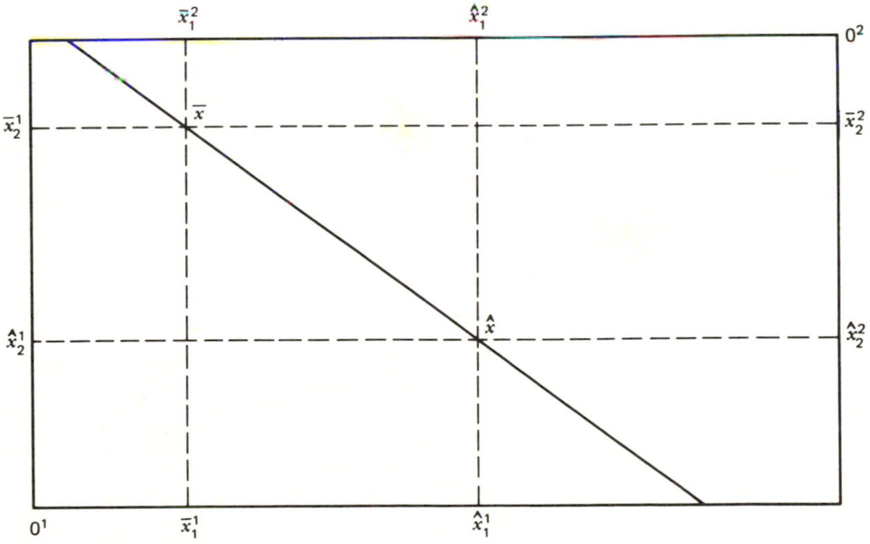

Figure 15.3

can be obtained by reference to the other origin, O^2. The only difference is that in moving from $\bar{x}$ to $\hat{x}$, consumer 2 gives up units of the first commodity to obtain additional units of the second commodity. Thus, in moving from $\bar{x}$ to $\hat{x}$ along the exchange line, consumer 1 is trading commodity 2 for commodity 1 and consumer 2 is trading commodity 1 for commodity 2.

Given our assumptions about the preference orderings, there is an optimal exchange on the part of each consumer for any given rate of exchange. In general, altering the exchange rate alters the optimal exchange. Figure 15.4 illustrates three optimal exchanges from the standpoint of consumer 1 corresponding to three different rates of exchange. Given an initial allocation at $\bar{x}^1$ and an exchange rate of $\hat{p}_{12}$, consumer 1 would like to give up $\bar{x}_1^1 - \hat{x}_1^1$ units of commodity 1 to attain $\hat{x}_2^1 - \bar{x}_2^1$ units of commodity 2 to move him to allocation $\hat{x}^1$. This is the point of tangency between an indifference curve and the exchange line corresponding to exchange rate $\hat{p}_{12}$ and is therefore the most preferred bundle of commodities on the exchange line.

Alternatively, if the rate of exchange of commodity 1 for commodity 2 were much lower, say $\tilde{p}_{12}$, the first consumer would like to give up some of the second commodity to enhance his consumption of commodity 1. The optimal bundle of commodities at this exchange rate is given by $\tilde{x}$, where the consumer's indifference curve is tangent to the exchange line representing exchange rate $\tilde{p}_{12}$. Finally, at a very high rate of exchange of commodity 1 for commodity 2 (i.e., a low rate of exchange of commodity 2 for commodity 1, p_{21}), say $\overset{*}{p}_{12}$, the first consumer would like to give up some of commodity 1 to attain more of commodity 2, moving to allocation $\overset{*}{x}^1$, which is a corner solution on the boundary of the box.

Any number of such optimal bundles can be generated corresponding to

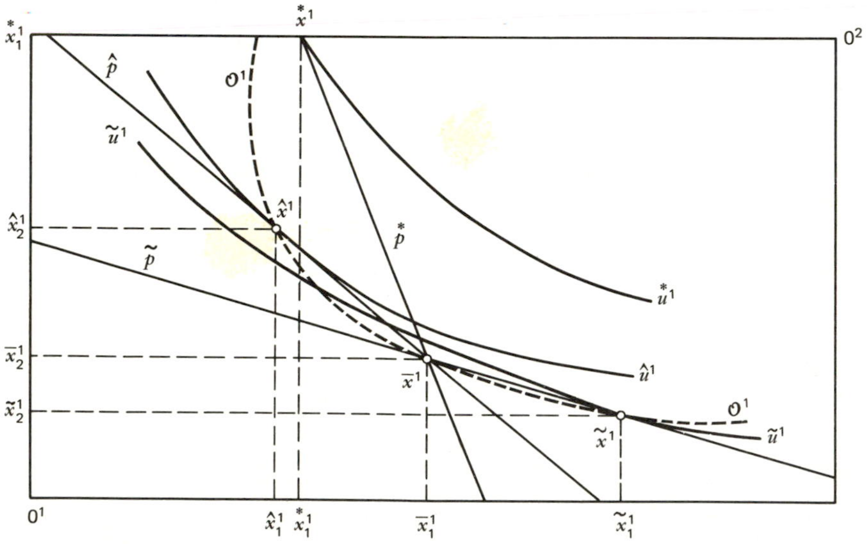

Figure 15.4

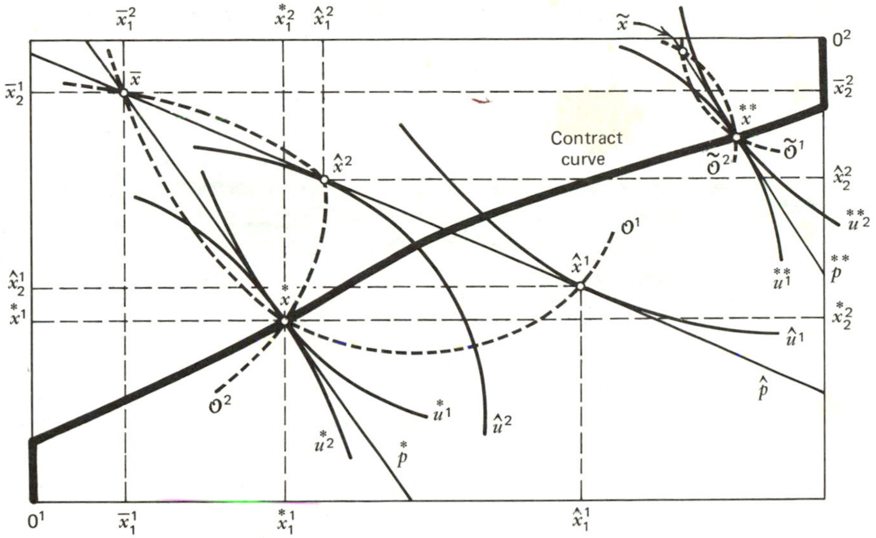

Figure 15.5

alternative rates of exchange. The locus of such points is called an *offer curve* and is denoted $\mathcal{O}^1$ in figure 15.4. This curve is analogous to the price-consumption curve derived in section 4.5.

The offer curve clearly must pass through the initial allocation $\bar{x}^1$. This follows from the fact that there exists an exchange line that is tangent to the indifference curve passing through $\bar{x}^1$. The corresponding exchange rate, which is exactly equal to the slope of the indifference curve passing through $\bar{x}^1$, would leave the first consumer with no incentive to enter into an exchange since the original endowment is the most preferred bundle of commodities on that particular exchange line.

An offer curve can be constructed similarly for the second consumer. This offer curve must also pass through the initial endowment. Two possible offer curves for the two consumers are drawn in figure 15.5. By construction, the exchange offers that would be made by the two consumers is given by the intersection of the exchange line (drawn through the initial endowment) with the two offer curves. For example, at the exchange rate $\hat{p}_{12}$ reflected in the exchange line in figure 15.5, consumer 1 would like to move to $\hat{x}^1$ and consumer 2 would like to move to $\hat{x}^2$. That is, at this exchange rate, consumer 1 would like to give up $\bar{x}_2^1 - \hat{x}_2^1$ of commodity 2 in exchange for $\hat{x}_1^1 - \bar{x}_1^1$ of commodity 1 and the second consumer would like to give up $\bar{x}_1^2 - \hat{x}_1^2$ units of the first commodity in exchange for $\hat{x}_2^2 - \bar{x}_2^2$ of the second commodity.

Competitive Equilibrium

Competitive equilibrium requires that the choices of consumption bundles on the part of the two consumers be compatible with the total resources available to the economy; i.e., competitive equilibrium requires that supply be equal to demand. It is clear that $\hat{p}_{12}$ is not an equilibrium exchange rate since the first consumer wishes to supply $\bar{x}_1^2 - \hat{x}_1^2$ of commodity 2, whereas the second consumer has a net demand of only $\hat{x}_2^2 - \bar{x}_2^2$ for this commodity. Similarly, while the first consumer demands $\hat{x}_1^1 - \bar{x}_1^1$ of the first commodity, the second consumer wishes to supply only $\bar{x}_1^2 - \hat{x}_1^2$. Thus, there is an excess supply of commodity 2 and (equivalently) an excess demand for commodity 1.

It is clear from the construction that the supply of and demand for the two commodities are equal only if the exchange rate is given by the slope of an exchange line drawn through the initial endowment and through a point of intersection of the two offer curves. Only at this point of intersection are the two optimal consumption bundles compatible with one another. In figure 15.5, this intersection occurs at the allocation $\overset{*}{x}$. At the corresponding exchange rate, $\overset{*}{p}_{12}$, the first consumer wishes to exchange $\bar{x}_2^1 - \overset{*}{x}_2^1$ of commodity 2 for $\overset{*}{x}_1^1 - \bar{x}_1^1$ units of commodity 2 and consumer 2 wishes to supply an equal amount of the first commodity in exchange for an equal amount of the second commodity.

The exchange rate $\overset{*}{p}_{12}$ is an equilibrium exchange rate and $\overset{*}{x}$ is an equilibrium allocation *relative to the particular initial endowment*, $\bar{x}$. The equilibrium allocation and exchange rate relative to the alternative initial endowment $\tilde{x}$ in figure 15.5 are represented by the point $\overset{**}{x}$ and the exchange line labeled $\overset{**}{p}$.

The intersection of the offer curves, and hence the competitive-equilibrium allocation, is necessarily on the contract curve. This is easy to see for the case of interior equilibria. Interior allocations on the contract curve are characterized by the tangency condition. Moreover, as the offer-curve intersection point reflects an optimum for both consumers, the exchange line is tangent to the indifference curves of both consumers. But if each indifference curve is

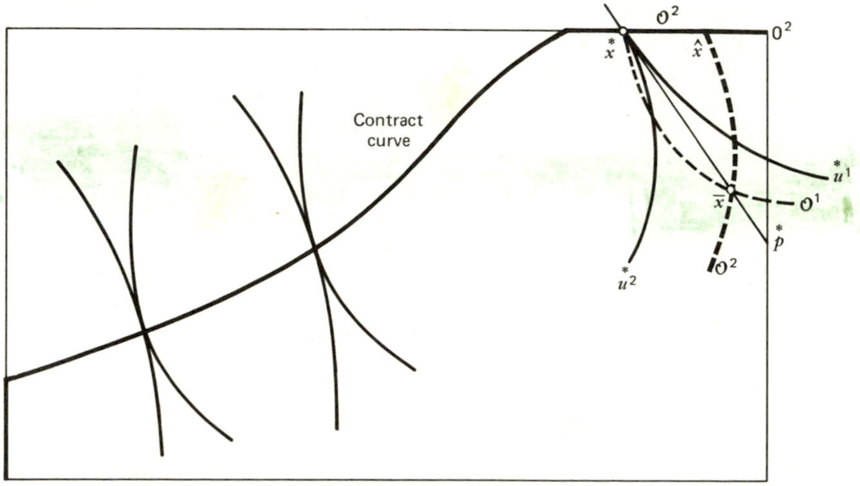

Figure 15.6

tangent to a common exchange line, they must of course be tangent to one another. Therefore, interior offer-curve intersections are on the contract curve, as shown in figure 15.5.

Competitive-equilibrium allocations on the boundary of the consumption box are also on the contract curve. This fact is illustrated in figure 15.6. The second consumer's offer curve $\mathcal{O}^2$ is coincident with the x_1^2 axis to the left of $\hat{x}$ and intersects $\mathcal{O}^1$ at the point $\overset{*}{x}$. The equilibrium allocation relative to the initial endowment $\bar{x}$ is therefore generated by a tangency condition for consumer 1 and a corner solution for consumer 2. It will be noted that the point $\overset{*}{x}$ is a boundary point on the contract curve.

15.4 GENERAL EXCHANGE EQUILIBRIUM

The general exchange economy is described by the following assumption:

Assumption 15.1′ The economy consists of m consumers and n commodities. The consumers' preferences satisfy assumptions 3.1 (nonsatiation) and 3.2 (strict convexity) and are represented by continuous utility functions, U^c, $c = 1, \ldots, m$. Each consumer is endowed with a nonnegative (but not necessarily positive) bundle of the n commodities,

$$\bar{x}^c = [\bar{x}_1^c, \ldots, \bar{x}_n^c],\ c = 1, \ldots, m.$$

Assumptions 15.2 and 15.3, regarding the possibility of fully informed and costless exchange of commodities among consumers, are retained.

Arbitrage and the Choice of a Numeraire

In the case of bilateral exchange, there is essentially a single market where the two commodities can be exchanged for one another. In the n-commodity market, there are as many markets as there are distinct pairs of commodities; namely, $(n^2 - n)/2$. We associate with each market an exchange rate; for example in the $i - j$ market where the ith and jth commodities are exchanged, we let p_{ij} be the rate of exchange of commodity i for commodity j (the price of commodity i in units of commodity j). Superficially, there is therefore an $n \times n$ array of such exchange rates which can be displayed as

$$\begin{bmatrix} p_{11} & p_{12} & \cdots & p_{1n} \\ p_{21} & & \cdots & p_{2n} \\ \vdots & & & \vdots \\ p_{n1} & & \cdots & p_{nn} \end{bmatrix}.$$

Of course, the rate at which a commodity can be exchanged for itself is identically equal to one; hence, $p_{ii} = 1$, $i = 1, \ldots, n$. Moreover, the rate of exchange of commodity i for the commodity j is equal to the inverse of the rate of exchange of commodity j for commodity i,

$$p_{ij} = \frac{1}{p_{ji}}, \qquad i, j = 1, \ldots, n. \tag{15.18}$$

Hence, the array of exchange rates is reduced to

$$\begin{bmatrix} 1 & p_{12} & & \cdots & p_{1n} \\ \dfrac{1}{p_{12}} & 1 & p_{23} & \cdots & p_{2n} \\ \vdots & & & & \vdots \\ \dfrac{1}{p_{1n}} & \dfrac{1}{p_{2n}} & & \cdots & 1 \end{bmatrix}$$

There are $(n^2 - n)/2$ independent exchange rates in this array (equal to the number of markets). However, the potential for free and costless exchange in all markets by any consumer (implied by assumptions 15.2 and 15.3) rationalizes a further reduction in the number of independent exchange rates. To see this, note that $p_{kj}p_{ik} = p_{ik}/p_{jk}$ constitutes an *indirect* rate of exchange of commodity i for commodity j; p_{ik} is the rate at which commodity i can be converted into commodity k and p_{kj} is the rate at which commodity k can be converted into commodity j. Consequently, if this indirect exchange rate were not equal to the direct exchange rate p_{ij}, a shrewd trader could costlessly increase the size of his holdings by opportunistic exchange. To see this, suppose that

$$p_{ij} < \frac{p_{ik}}{p_{jk}} \tag{15.19}$$

and note that $\hat{x}_i$ units of commodity i can be exchanged for

$$\hat{x}_k = p_{ik}\hat{x}_i \tag{15.20}$$

units of commodity k. This quantity of commodity k can in turn be exchanged for $\hat{x}_j = p_{kj}\hat{x}_k = (1/p_{jk})\hat{x}_k$ units of commodity j. Substitution from (15.20) yields $\hat{x}_j = (p_{ik}/p_{jk})\hat{x}_i$. Finally, the $\hat{x}_j$ units of commodity j can be converted into

$$\hat{\hat{x}}_i = p_{ji}\hat{x}_j = \frac{1}{p_{ij}}\hat{x}_j = \frac{1}{p_{ij}}\frac{p_{ik}}{p_{jk}}\hat{x}_i$$

units of commodity i. However, because of (15.19), which implies $1 < (1/p_{ij})(p_{ik}/p_{jk})$, we have $\hat{\hat{x}}_i > \hat{x}_i$. Hence, a shrewd trader, taking advantage of the fact that $p_{ij} < p_{ik}/p_{jk}$, has converted a certain amount of commodity i into a larger amount of the same commodity by engaging in judicious exchange in the three markets: $i - k$, $j - k$, and $i - j$. This type of opportunistic exchange is called *arbitrage*. Arbitrage is possible whenever an indirect exchange ratio among any three commodities (e.g., p_{ik}/p_{jk}) is not equal to the direct exchange rate (p_{ij}). If the inequality (15.19) were reversed, the reverse set of trades using successively markets $j - k$, $i - k$, and $i - j$ would convert a given quantity of commodity j into more of the same commodity.

The process of arbitrage described in the previous pages would tend to equalize direct and indirect exchange rates. Trading commodity i for commodity k tends to drive p_{ik} down, trading commodity k for commodity j tends to drive

p_{jk} up, and trading commodity j for commodity i tends to drive p_{ij} up. All of these forces diminish the disparity between p_{ij} and p_{ik}/p_{jk}. Thus, given costless exchange, we expect that $p_{ij} = p_{ik}/p_{jk}$, $i, j, k = 1, \ldots, n$.

This interdependence between the exchange rates allows all rates to be expressed in terms of a single commodity. For example, all prices can be expressed in units of commodity 1 using the following relationships: $p_{1j} = 1/p_{j1}$, $j = 1, \ldots, n$, and $p_{ij} = p_{i1}/p_{j1}$, $i, j = 1, \ldots, n$. Then, without ambiguity the prices can be relabeled as follows: $p_{i1} = p_i$, $i = 2, \ldots, n$, and $p_{11} = 1$.

Expressing all prices in units of commodity 1 effectively normalizes the price of commodity 1 to be unity. In this case, it is said that we have normalized on the first commodity; that is, commodity 1 is chosen as the *numeraire*. We could, of course, just as easily normalize on any other commodity since the above relationships between the prices are symmetrical.

Thus, the choice of a particular commodity as a numeraire is of no particular significance. It does not, for example, imply that the numeraire commodity is traded in every market. That is, it does not mean that the numeraire commodity is a medium of exchange; it is in fact nothing more than a unit of account, and this choice is entirely arbitrary. Hence the choice of a particular commodity as numeraire should not be interpreted as making that commodity "money."

The message of the above exercise is that the expression of all prices in terms of a common numeraire implicitly requires "arbitrage equilibrium."

Competitive Equilibrium and Walras's Law

A feasible exchange involving commodities i and j satisfies

$$p_{ij} = \frac{\bar{x}_j^c - \hat{x}_j^c}{\hat{x}_i^c - \bar{x}_i^c} \tag{15.21}$$

where $\bar{x}_j^c - \hat{x}_j^c$ is the quantity of the jth commodity given up in exchange for $\hat{x}_i^c - \bar{x}_i^c$ units of the ith commodity. (Of course, an exchange of commodity i for commodity j is reflected by negative values of these differences.) In fact, (15.21) defines p_{ij} if $\bar{x}_j^c - \hat{x}_j^c$ and $\hat{x}_i^c - \bar{x}_i^c$ constitute a feasible trade.

Equation (15.21) can be rewritten as $p_{ij}(\hat{x}_i^c - \bar{x}_i^c) + (\bar{x}_j^c - \hat{x}_j^c) = 0$ or, because $p_{ij} = p_{i1}/p_{j1} = p_i/p_j$, it follows that $p_i(\hat{x}_i^c - \bar{x}_i^c) + p_j(\bar{x}_j^c - \hat{x}_j^c) = 0$. This says that feasible trades do not change the value of the consumer's holdings, evaluated in terms of the numeraire good. As this constraint holds for all feasible trades, it follows that

$$\sum_{i=1}^{n} p_i(\hat{x}_i^c - \bar{x}_i^c) = 0, \qquad c = 1, \ldots, m. \tag{15.22}$$

Rewriting (15.22), we obtain

$$\sum_{i=1}^{n} p_i \hat{x}_i^c = \sum_{i=1}^{n} p_i \bar{x}_i^c, \qquad c = 1, \ldots, m;$$

i.e., the value of each consumer's commodity bundle attained by trade at normalized prices $[p_2, \ldots, p_n]$ must be equal to the value of the initial endowment.

It follows that each consumer's consumption bundle $[x_1^c, \ldots, x_n^c]$ must satisfy

$$\sum_{i=1}^{n} p_i(x_i^c - \bar{x}_i^c) \leq 0, \qquad c = 1, \ldots, m.$$

These are the m consumer budget constraints.

The following utility-maximization hypothesis is now introduced:

Assumption 15.4 Each consumer chooses a consumption bundle x^c that solves

$$\operatorname*{Max}_{x^c} U^c(x^c) \qquad \text{s.t.} \sum_{i=1}^{n} p_i(x_i^c - \bar{x}_i^c) = 0.$$

The optimal consumption bundle depends upon the $n - 1$ normalized prices and the initial endowment. Hence, the demand functions can be written as*

$$x_i^c = d_i^c(p_2, \ldots, p_n, \bar{x}_1^c, \ldots, \bar{x}_n^c), \qquad i = 1, \ldots, \mathrm{n}, \quad c = 1, \ldots, m. \tag{15.23}$$

General equilibrium requires that the demands be consistent with the resource endowment of the economy; i.e., that the total amount demanded of each commodity equal the total endowment,

$$\sum_{c=1}^{m} x_i^c = \sum_{c=1}^{m} \bar{x}_i^c, \qquad i = 1, \ldots, n. \tag{15.24}$$

The task of finding general equilibrium is therefore one of finding a set of prices that generates demands through equations (15.23) that satisfy the market-equilibrium conditions (15.24). That is, the general exchange equilibrium is simply a solution of (15.23) and (15.24) for $n - 1$ prices $[\overset{*}{p}_2, \ldots, \overset{*}{p}_n]$ and m consumption bundles, $[\overset{*}{x}{}_1^1, \ldots, \overset{*}{x}{}_n^1], \ldots, [\overset{*}{x}{}_1^m, \ldots, \overset{*}{x}{}_n^m]$. (The endowments, of course, are fixed.)

• •

* *Note* If the utility functions are differentiable and if all solutions are interior, the demand system of each consumer is a solution of the first-order conditions:

$$\frac{\partial U^c(x^c)/\partial x_i^c}{\partial U^c(x^c)/\partial x_1^c} = p_i, \qquad i = 2, \ldots, n.$$

and

$$\sum_{i=1}^{n} p_i(x_i^c - \bar{x}_i^c) = 0.$$

(Recall that $p_i = p_i/p_1$ for all i since $p_1 = 1$.)

• •

This problem can be simplified conceptually by aggregating the demand functions over the m consumers for each commodity:

$$\sum_{c=1}^{m} x_i^c = \sum_{c=1}^{m} d_i^c(p_2, \ldots, p_n; \bar{x}_1^c, \ldots, \bar{x}_n^c), \qquad i = 1, \ldots, n,$$

and substituting into the market-equilibrium equation (15.24),

$$\sum_{c=1}^{m} d_i^c(p_2, \ldots, p_n; \bar{x}_1^c, \ldots, \bar{x}_n^c) = \sum_{c=1}^{m} \bar{x}_i^c.$$

Next define aggregate demands,

$$D_i(p_2, \ldots, p_n) \equiv \sum_{c=1}^{m} d_i^c(p_2, \ldots, p_n; \bar{x}_1^c, \ldots, \bar{x}_n^c), \qquad i = 1, \ldots, n, \tag{15.25}$$

where, for simplicity, we do not explicitly include the endowments in the aggregate demand function since they are parametric (though it should be kept in mind that aggregate demands do depend upon the individual endowments). Noting that aggregate endowments satisfy

$$\bar{x}_i \equiv \sum_{c=1}^{m} \bar{x}_i^c, \qquad i = 1, \ldots, n, \tag{15.26}$$

and substituting (15.25) and (15.26) into (15.24), we can write the market-equilibrium conditions as follows:

$$D_i(p_2, \ldots, p_n) = \bar{x}_i, \qquad i = 1, \ldots, n. \tag{15.27}$$

The determination of general exchange equilibrium is thus reduced to finding a set of prices that satisfy (15.27). It will be noted that there are n market-equilibrium equations to be solved for only $n - 1$ normalized prices, $[\overset{*}{p}_2, \ldots, \overset{*}{p}_n]$. Similarly, the individual demand functions (15.23) together with the market-equilibrium conditions (15.24) constitute $mn + n$ equations to be solved for $mn + n - 1$ variables (namely, mn amounts consumed and $n - 1$ prices).

However, as in the simpler bilateral exchange economy examined in sections 15.2 and 15.3, there is a redundant equation in this model. To see this interdependence, note that the demand equations (15.23) must be consistent with the consumer budget constraints. Aggregating (15.22) across consumers, we obtain

$$\sum_{c=1}^{m} \sum_{i=1}^{m} p_i x_i^c - \sum_{c=1}^{m} \sum_{i=1}^{m} p_i \bar{x}_i^c = 0. \tag{15.28}$$

But, since the prices do not have c superscripts, interchanging the order of summation yields

$$\sum_{i=1}^{n} p_i \sum_{c=1}^{m} x_i^c - \sum_{i=1}^{n} p_i \sum_{c=1}^{m} \bar{x}_i^c = 0. \tag{15.29}$$

Next, multiply the market-equilibrium conditions (15.24) by the respective prices,

$$p_i \sum_{c=1}^{m} x_i^c = p_i \sum_{c=1}^{m} \bar{x}_i^c, \qquad i = 1, \ldots, n,$$

and, summing over the first $n - 1$ commodities, we have

$$\sum_{i=1}^{n-1} p_i \sum_{c=1}^{m} x_i^c = \sum_{i=1}^{n-1} p_i \sum_{c=1}^{m} \bar{x}_i^c. \tag{15.30}$$

Noting that (15.29) and (15.30) are identical except for the fact that (15.29) contains the nth term whereas (15.30) doesn't, and subtracting (15.30) from (15.29), we obtain

$$p_n \sum_{c=1}^{m} x_n^c = p_n \sum_{c=1}^{m} \bar{x}_n^c,$$

or

$$\sum_{c=1}^{m} x_n^c = \sum_{c=1}^{m} \bar{x}_n^c.$$

But this is the nth market-equilibrium condition. Hence, we have derived the nth market-equilibrium equation as a linear combination of the m budget identities and the first $n - 1$ market-equilibrium equations. There are therefore only (at most) $nm + n - 1$ *independent* equations in the system (15.22) and (15.24) and, equivalently, only $n - 1$ *independent* equations in the system (15.27). This matches the number of variables in the system: $n - 1$ normalized prices and the nm amounts consumed of each commodity by each consumer.

The economics of this result is the following general statement of Walras's Law: if supply and demand are equal for $n - 1$ of the n commodities, then supply and demand are equal for the remaining commodity as well. This follows directly from the aggregate budget constraint (15.28), also sometimes referred to as Walras's Law, which, rewritten as

$$\sum_{c=1}^{m} \sum_{\substack{i=1 \\ i \neq j}}^{m} p_i (x_i^c - \bar{x}_i^c) = \sum_{c=1}^{m} p_j (x_j^c - \bar{x}_j^c),$$

says that the net demand for any one commodity (the jth in the above expression) is identically equal to the net supply of the other $n - 1$ commodities, both measured in units of the numeraire commodity. Therefore, if the net demands vanish for $n - 1$ of the commodities, net demand must vanish for the remaining commodity as well. (Note that Walras's Law is an identity in prices; that is, (15.28) holds for all prices, not just equilibrium prices.)

EXERCISE

15.1 Consider a two-person, two-commodity exchange economy with initial endowments, $(\bar{x}_1^1, \bar{x}_2^1, \bar{x}_2^2, \bar{x}_2^2) = (100, 350, 100, 50)$, and utility-function images $U^1(x^1) = x_1^1 \cdot x_2^1$ and $U^2(x^2) = x_1^2 \cdot x_2^2$.

a. Derive the equation defining the contract curve.

b. Derive the offer-curve equations.

c. Solve for the competitive-equilibrium allocation and prices.

CHAPTER 16
GENERAL COMPETITIVE EQUILIBRIUM IN A PRODUCTION ECONOMY

16.1 INTRODUCTION

While many important principles of general-equilibrium theory can be examined in the context of the fictional economy of chapter 15, in which all commodities simply appear as manna from heaven, it is nevertheless important to describe general competitive equilibrium in a production economy as well. Recall that an essential aspect of general competitive equilibrium is the notion of the consistency of the decisions of a multitude of agents acting independently of one another. In an exchange economy, consistency means that the independent consumption choices of the m consumers do not require more of any commodity than the aggregate endowment. In a production economy, the consistency problem is more complicated. The consumption choices of the consumers and the production choices of the producers must be jointly consistent with the aggregate endowments. In particular, the aggregate amount consumed of each commodity must be no greater than the total initial endowment of the economy plus the aggregate net amount of the commodity produced. In competitive equilibrium, this consistency of the myriad of consumer and producer decisions is brought about by the establishment of equilibrium commodity prices which consumers and producers take as given.

Another complication that arises in dealing with a production economy is the distribution of producer profits. In the institutional framework of this chapter, all profits are distributed to the consumers. This distribution can be effected by private ownership of the production units ("capitalism") with no retained earnings. Alternatively, the production units might be owned by the government ("socialism"), which balances its budget by distributing all profits to individual consumers. Either institutional setting is consistent with the economy that is described in this chapter.

Finally, as will be seen in chapters 17 and 18, the introduction of production into the economy also has important implications for the social optimality of competitive equilibrium. The possibility of production adds to the list of conditions that are sufficient for competitive equilibrium to be socially optimal (in a sense to be defined precisely in succeeding chapters).

The following section provides an algebraic description of general competitive equilibrium for a production-and-exchange economy and demonstrates that Walras's Law also holds for such an economy so long as all producers' profits are distributed to consumers. Sections 16.3 and 16.4 examine the consistency of consumption and production allocations in a competitive equilibrium.

As the graphical illustration of competitive equilibrium with consumption and production is rather complicated, section 16.3 first introduces the basic notions of competitive equilibrium for a very simple economy with one consumer, one producer, and two commodities. Section 16.4 examines the more complicated case of two consumers, two producers, and four commodities (two of which are produced while the other two are necessarily net inputs in production). The different economies examined in sections 16.3 and 16.4 are also utilized in chapters 17 and 18 (and, to a lesser extent, in chapter 20) to illustrate the optimality of competitive equilibrium (and certain aspects of social choice theory).

Section 16.5 uses the concept of the core, introduced in section 14.4, to examine the "viability" of a general competitive equilibrium—immunity to the destabilizing effect of cartel formation. Finally, Section 16.6 concludes the chapter with a brief discussion of the existence, uniqueness, and stability of competitive equilibrium.

16.2 GENERAL EQUILIBRIUM FOR A PRODUCTION-AND-EXCHANGE ECONOMY

The Assumptions

The economy to be considered in this chapter is characterized by consumers and producers who satisfy the assumptions of chapters 2, 3, and 7. In particular, the following assumptions are made:

Assumption 16.1 The economy consists of m consumers, ℓ producers, and n commodities, and has at its disposal certain original resources (and possibly capital equipment which is inherited from the past).

Assumption 16.2 The producers satisfy assumption 7.1 (profit maximization). The technology sets of the producers satisfy assumptions 7.2 (boundedness), 7.3 (regularity), and 7.5 (strict convexity) and are represented by net production functions, F^r, $r = 1, \ldots, \ell$.

Assumption 16.3 The consumers receive a share of the profits of each of the ℓ producers, $s^c = [s^c_1, \ldots, s^c_\ell]$, $c = 1, \ldots, m$. All profits are distributed to the consumers.

Assumption 16.3 is consistent with a wide range of institutional arrangements that determine the distribution of profits. These arrangements could include Western "capitalism" (a mixture of publicly and privately owned producers) and Soviet communism. If, for example, s_r^c is independent of r for all c, each consumer receives (or pays) a given share, s^c, of aggregate profits (or losses), which, in a socialist economy is the government budget surplus (or loss).

Assumption 16.4 The consumer's preferences satisfy assumptions 3.1 (nonsatiation) and 3.2 (strict convexity) and are represented by continuous utility functions, U^c, $c = 1, \ldots, m$. Each consumer is endowed with a nonnegative (but not necessarily positive) bundle of the n commodities, $\bar{x}^c = [\bar{x}_1^c, \ldots, \bar{x}_n^c]$, $c = 1, \ldots, m$.

Assumption 16.5 There is no cost of exchange.

Assumption 16.6 There is perfect information about the rate at which one commodity can be exchanged for any other.

As assumptions 16.5 and 16.6 imply that direct and indirect exchange ratios are equated by the possibility of arbitrage (see section 15.4), we normalize on commodity 1 so that the set of prices to be determined can be represented by an $n - 1$ dimensional vector, $[p_2, \ldots, p_n]$. The profit of the rth producer is denoted π^r. The cth consumer therefore receives $s_r^c \pi^r$ in profit income from the rth firm. Assumption 16.3 guarantees that all profits are distributed to the consumers (i.e., there are no retained earnings) so that,

$$\sum_{c=1}^{m} s_r^c = 1, \qquad r = 1, \ldots, \ell. \tag{16.1}$$

The cth consumer's wealth, expressed in units of the numeraire commodity 1, is

$$\omega_c = \sum_{i=1}^{n} p_i \bar{x}_i^c + \sum_{r=1}^{\ell} s_r^c \pi^r,$$

where the first term is the value of his commodity endowment and the second term is his share of aggregate profits. The consumer's total consumption, expressed in units of commodity 1, equals his wealth:

$$\sum_{i=1}^{n} p_i x_i^c = \sum_{i=1}^{n} p_i \bar{x}_i^c + \sum_{r=1}^{\ell} s_r^c \pi^r. \tag{16.2}$$

The following utility-maximization hypothesis is now posited:

Assumption 16.7 Each consumer chooses a consumption bundle x^c that solves

$$\underset{x^c}{\text{Max}}\ U^c(x^c) \qquad \text{s.t.} \sum_{i=1}^{n} p_i(x_i^c - \bar{x}_i^c) - \sum_{r=1}^{\ell} s_r^c \pi^r = 0.$$

The optimal consumption bundle depends upon the $n - 1$ normalized prices, the commodity endowment, and the profit income. Hence the consumer demand function images can be written as

$$x_i^c = d_i^c\left(p_2, \ldots, p_n, \bar{x}_1^c, \ldots, \bar{x}_n^c, \sum_{r=1}^{\ell} s_r^c \pi^r\right), \qquad \begin{array}{l} i = 1, \ldots, n, \\ c = 1, \ldots, m. \end{array} \tag{16.3}$$

Let z_i^r represent the net amount of the ith commodity produced by the rth producer. It will be recalled from section 7.2 that a positive value of z_i^r indicates that the rth producer is a net producer of the ith commodity and a negative value of z_i^r indicates that the ith commodity serves as a net input to the rth producer. The profit of the rth producer can be expressed as

$$\pi^r(z^r) = \sum_{i=1}^{n} p_i z_i^r. \tag{16.4}$$

Assumption 16.2 allows the optimization problem of the producer to be written as

$$\underset{z^r}{\text{Max}}\ \pi^r(z^r) \qquad \text{s.t. } F^r(z^r) = 0.$$

The optimal production bundle depends upon the $n - 1$ normalized prices. Hence the net-output-supply and net-input-demand function images can be written as

$$z_i^r = \phi_i^r(p_2, \ldots, p_n), \qquad i = 1, \ldots, n, \quad r = 1, \ldots, \ell. \tag{16.5}$$

Walras's Law

Market equilibrium requires that the aggregate amount consumed of each commodity be equal to the total initial endowment of the commodity plus the *net* amount of the commodity produced (which may be positive or negative); that is,

$$\sum_{c=1}^{m} x_i^c - \sum_{c=1}^{m} \bar{x}_i^c - \sum_{r=1}^{\ell} z_i^r = 0, \qquad i = 1, \ldots, n. \tag{16.6}$$

(16.3)–(16.6) constitute a system of $n(\ell + m + 1) + \ell$ equations, classified as follows:

Type of Equation	Number of Equations
Consumers' demand functions	nm
Producers' profit and net supply functions	$(1 + n)\ell$
Market-equilibrium conditions	n
Total	$n(\ell + m + 1) + \ell$

On the other hand, the number of variables in this system is only $n(\ell + m + 1) + \ell - 1$, classified as follows:

Variables	Number
(x_i^c)	nm
(z_i^r)	$n\ell$
(π^r)	ℓ
(p_i)	$n - 1$
	$n(\ell + m + 1) + \ell - 1$

The alert reader is, however, not fooled by this arithmetic. Walras's Law, equally applicable to a production economy, indicates that the number of independent equations is equal to the number of variables. To see this, sum over all of the consumers' budget identities (16.2),

$$\sum_{c=1}^{m} \sum_{i=1}^{n} p_i x_i^c - \sum_{c=1}^{m} \sum_{i=1}^{n} p_i \bar{x}_i^c - \sum_{c=1}^{m} \sum_{r=1}^{\ell} s_r^c \pi^r = 0.$$

Reversing the order of summation, we obtain

$$\sum_{i=1}^{n} p_i \sum_{c=1}^{m} x_i^c - \sum_{i=1}^{n} p_i \sum_{c=1}^{m} \bar{x}_i^c - \sum_{r=1}^{\ell} \pi^r \sum_{c=1}^{m} s_r^c = 0.$$

But, recalling the "no undistributed-profit" condition (16.1), we have

$$\sum_{i=1}^{n} p_i \sum_{c=1}^{m} x_i^c - \sum_{i=1}^{n} p_i \sum_{c=1}^{m} \bar{x}_i^c - \sum_{r=1}^{\ell} \pi^r = 0. \tag{16.7}$$

Addition over the profit functions (16.4) yields

$$\sum_{r=1}^{\ell} \pi^r = \sum_{r=1}^{\ell} \sum_{i=1}^{n} p_i z_i^r = \sum_{i=1}^{n} p_i \sum_{r=1}^{\ell} z_i^r.$$

Substitution of the result into (16.7) yields

$$\sum_{i=1}^{n} p_i \sum_{c=1}^{m} x_i^c - \sum_{i=1}^{n} p_i \sum_{c=1}^{m} \bar{x}_i^c - \sum_{i=1}^{n} p_i \sum_{r=1}^{\ell} z_i^r = 0. \tag{16.8}$$

Next multiply the market-equilibrium conditions (16.6) by their respective prices,

$$p_i \sum_{c=1}^{n} x_i^c - p_i \sum_{c=1}^{m} \bar{x}_i^c - p_i \sum_{r=1}^{\ell} z_i^r = 0, \quad i = 1, \ldots, n,$$

and sum over the first $n - 1$ of the resulting equations,

$$\sum_{i=1}^{n-1} p_i \sum_{c=1}^{m} x_i^c - \sum_{i=1}^{n-1} p_i \sum_{c=1}^{m} \bar{x}_i^c - \sum_{i=1}^{n-1} p_i \sum_{r=1}^{\ell} z_i^r = 0. \tag{16.9}$$

(16.9) is identical to (16.8) except for the fact that the nth set of terms is omitted from the summations in (16.9). Therefore, subtracting (16.9) from (16.8) leaves the nth set of terms,

$$p_n \sum_{c=1}^{m} x_n^c - p_n \sum_{c=1}^{m} \bar{x}_n^c - p_n \sum_{r=1}^{\ell} z_n^r = 0. \qquad (16.10)$$

Division through (16.10) by p_n leaves the nth market-equilibrium equation,

$$\sum_{c=1}^{m} x_n^c - \sum_{c=1}^{m} \bar{x}_n^c - \sum_{r=1}^{\ell} z_n^r = 0.$$

Thus, we have shown that in a production economy, as well as an exchange economy, if all but one of the markets are in equilibrium this one market must also be in equilibrium. Walras's Law is as applicable to a production economy as it is to a pure exchange economy.

General Competitive Equilibrium

An allocation of commodities among consumers, $x = [x^1, \ldots, x^m]$, is termed the *consumption allocation* while an allocation of commodities among producers, $z = [z^1, \ldots, z^r]$, is termed the *production allocation*.[1] A consumption allocation, $\overset{*}{x}$, and a production allocation, $\overset{*}{z}$, constitute a competitive equilibrium relative to the price vector $[\overset{*}{p}_2, \ldots, \overset{*}{p}_n]$ if

(a) $\overset{*}{x}{}^c$ maximizes $U^c(x^c)$ s.t. $\sum_{i=1}^{n} \overset{*}{p}_i(x_i^c - \bar{x}_i^c) - \sum_{r=1}^{\ell} s_r^c \sum_{i=1}^{n} \overset{*}{p}_i \overset{*}{z}{}_i^r = 0,$

$c = 1, \ldots, m,$

(b) $\overset{*}{z}{}^r$ maximizes $\sum_{i=1}^{n} \overset{*}{p}_i z_i^r$ s.t. $F^r(z^r) = 0, \qquad r = 1, \ldots, \ell,$

and

(c) $$\sum_{c=1}^{m} \overset{*}{x}{}_i^c - \sum_{c=1}^{m} \bar{x}_i^c - \sum_{r=1}^{\ell} \overset{*}{z}{}_i^r = 0, \qquad i = 1, \ldots, n.$$

A competitive equilibrium is thus a set of prices and a consumption and production allocation such that (a) each consumer maximizes utility at the given prices and with the income generated by those prices in combination with initial endowment and profit shares; (b) each producer maximizes profit at the given prices; and (c) aggregate consumption of any commodity equals the sum of the aggregate net production and initial endowment of that commodity.

In the next section, we examine a simple economy to see how equilibrium prices lead to a consumption and production allocation that satisfies conditions (a)–(c).

[1] The consumption and production allocations are thus points in Euclidean nm-space and $n\ell$-space, respectively.

16.3 GRAPHICAL ILLUSTRATION OF COMPETITIVE EQUILIBRIUM WITH ONE CONSUMER, ONE PRODUCER, AND TWO COMMODITIES

The Economy

The economy consists of one consumer, one producer, and two commodities (say leisure, or labor time, and food). The producer utilizes the labor supplied by the consumer to produce food. The consumer is endowed with γ hours of leisure/labor time and receives all the profit of the producer.

The structure of this simple economy can be modified to accommodate a wide range of institutional arrangements concerning the control of resources. For example, Koopmans [1957] introduces a third economic agent—the resource holder—who controls nonlabor commodities. As Koopmans [1957, p.44] puts it, ". . . the resource holders are separated from other decision makers not out of logical necessity, but because the function or control of resources is in principle distinct from those of production and consumption." We adopt assumption 16.3 simply to facilitate the graphical presentation.

The consumer chooses a consumption bundle composed of food and leisure that solves

$$\max_{x,\ell} U(x, \ell) \qquad \text{s.t. } px - w(\gamma - \ell) - \pi \leq 0 \quad \text{and} \quad \ell \leq \gamma,$$

where x represents units of food, ℓ is hours of leisure, p is the price of food, w is the hourly wage rate which the consumer can earn by selling labor services to the producer, and π is the profit of the producer (see section 6.3 for a detailed discussion of the work-leisure choice).[2] The labor services supplied by the consumer to the producer, L, are equal to $\gamma - \ell$.

The optimization problem of the producer is

$$\max_{x,L} \Pi(x, L) \qquad \text{s.t. } (x, L) \quad \text{in} \quad Z$$

where Z is the technology set and

$$\pi = \Pi(x, L) = px - wL. \tag{16.11}$$

The problem of consumer choice is illustrated in figure 16.1, where hours of leisure are plotted on the horizontal axis and units of food on the vertical axis. The consumer's utility function is represented by a family of indifference curves that are convex to the origin. The consumer's budget constraint can be solved for x:

$$x = \frac{w(\gamma - \ell)}{p} + \frac{\pi}{p}. \tag{16.12}$$

[2] Invoking Walras's Law, we could normalize the prices so that $p = 1$ or $w = 1$; instead it will be seen below that in equilibrium only the ratio, w/p, is determined.

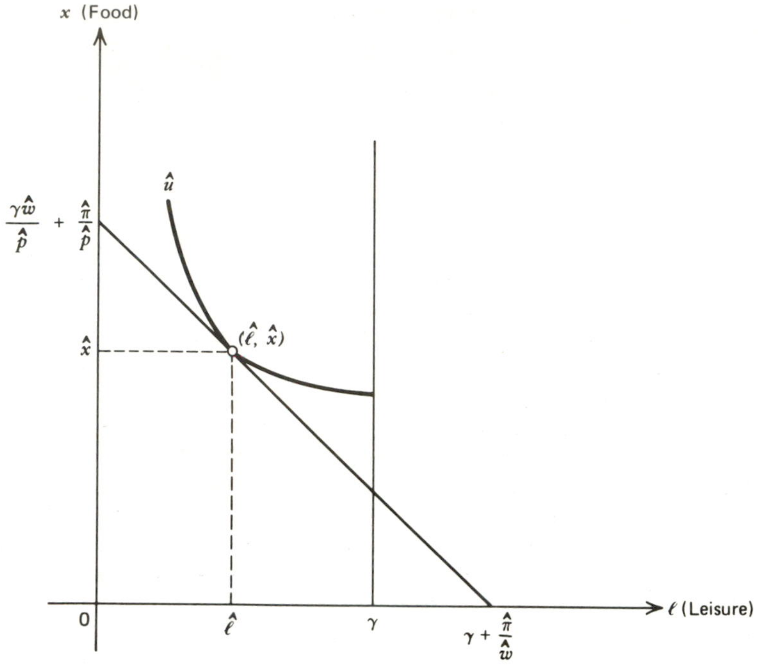

Figure 16.1

The budget constraint is therefore represented in $x - \ell$ space by a line with a slope equal to $-w/p$ and a vertical intercept of $\gamma w/p + \pi/p$. Similarly, the horizontal intercept can be shown to be $\gamma + \pi/w$. A particular budget constraint, for given prices and profits, $\hat{p}$, $\hat{w}$, and $\hat{\pi}$ is illustrated in figure 16.1.

The consumer's problem can be described graphically as choosing a commodity bundle represented by a point on the budget constraint to the left of the vertical line through γ that is on the highest possible indifference curve. In figure 16.1 $(\hat{\ell}, \hat{x})$ represents such an optimal consumption bundle.

The production technology is represented by a convex technology set in which labor is restricted to be an input and food is restricted to be an output. The set Z in figure 16.2 satisfies these restrictions. Of course, the upper boundary of this set is simply a total-product curve (with labor input measured by negative values) (see sections 7.3 and 8.2). In order to examine the consistency of producer and consumer choice, it is convenient to redraw this technology set, and the attendant total-product curve in leisure-food space.[3] This is accomplished by a simple translation; as $L = 0$ implies zero output, $\ell = \gamma$ implies zero output. Thus, the total-product curve has its origin at $\ell = \gamma$, as drawn in figure 16.2. The translated technology set is labeled $\hat{Z}$.

[3] Alternatively, we could redraw the consumer's indifference curve in labor-food space (see Koopmans [1957]).

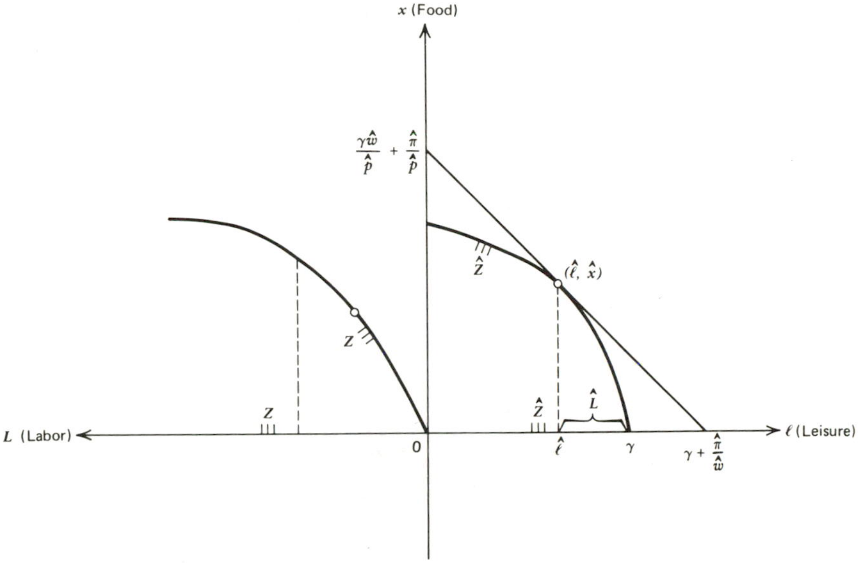

Figure 16.2

In order to represent the profit equation (16.11) of the producer in $\ell - x$ space, first solve it for x: $x = (\hat{\pi}/\hat{p}) + (\hat{w}/\hat{p})L$, and substitute $\gamma - \ell$ for L,

$$x = \frac{\hat{\pi}}{\hat{p}} + \frac{\hat{w}}{\hat{p}}\gamma - \frac{\hat{w}}{\hat{p}}\ell. \tag{16.13}$$

Thus, the slope of the equal-profit line in figure 16.2 is $-(\hat{w}/\hat{p})$ and the vertical intercept is $(\hat{\pi}/\hat{p}) + (\hat{w}/\hat{p})\gamma$. The horizontal intercept can similarly be shown to be $\gamma + \hat{\pi}/\hat{w}$. The vertical intercept gives the value of profit in units of food whereas the horizontal intercept gives profit in units of leisure. The important thing to note about this equal-profit line is that, for given values of the prices, p and w, and the profit, π, the equal-profit line, defined by (16.13) and the consumer's budget line, defined by (16.12), have the same slope and intercept and hence are equivalent. Note also that the slope of the equal-profit line, like the slope of the budget line, depends only on the price ratio, w/p.

It is apparent from equation (16.13) that, for a given price ratio, w/p, higher profit lines are associated with higher profits. Hence, production bundles on higher profit lines generate higher profit. Thus, the profit-maximization problem of the producer is to choose a production bundle in the translated technology set $\hat{Z}$ that is on the highest possible equal-profit line (see section 7.4 for a detailed analysis of profit maximization on a technology set). In figure 16.2 $(\hat{\ell}, \hat{x})$ is the production bundle that maximizes profit, given the values of p and w.

The Competitive Equilibrium

Figure 16.3 combines the consumer and producer choice problems in a single graph. Suppose that the commodity price ratio is $\hat{w}/\hat{p}$. In this case,

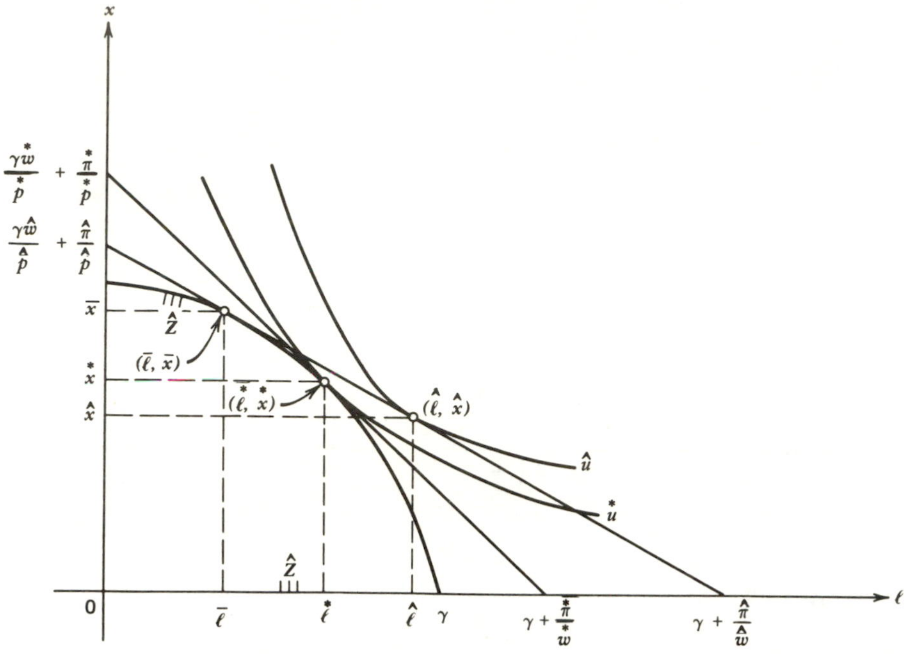

Figure 16.3

the producer would choose the production bundle $(\bar{\ell}, \bar{x})$, thereby producing $\bar{x}$ units of food and demanding $\gamma - \bar{\ell}$ hours of labor. This production bundle generates a maximum profit of $\hat{\pi}$. The consumer receives $\hat{\pi}$ and faces prices of $\hat{p}$ and $\hat{w}$. With the budget line thus defined, and equivalent to the maximal equal-profit line, the utility-maximizing consumption bundle is $(\hat{\ell}, \hat{x})$. The consumer offers the producer $\gamma - \hat{\ell}$ hours of labor and demands $\hat{x}$ units of food. Thus, at the price ratio, $\hat{w}/\hat{p}$, the producer and consumer choices are inconsistent; there is an excess supply of food and an excess demand for leisure. It follows that $\hat{w}/\hat{p}$ is not an equilibrium price ratio.

Consider the higher price ratio $\overset{*}{w}/\overset{*}{p}$ and the corresponding profit-maximizing bundle $(\overset{*}{\ell}, \overset{*}{x})$ in figure 16.3. The producer demands $\gamma - \overset{*}{\ell}$ hours of labor to produce $\overset{*}{x}$ units of food. The consumer receives the profit, $\overset{*}{\pi}$, and with prices of $\overset{*}{p}$ and $\overset{*}{w}$ chooses the consumption bundle $(\overset{*}{\ell}, \overset{*}{x})$. Thus, the consumer demands $\overset{*}{x}$ units of food and offers the producer $\gamma - \overset{*}{\ell}$ hours of labor, and the production and consumption choices are consistent. Thus, the consumption allocation $(\overset{*}{x}, \overset{*}{\ell})$, the production allocation $(\overset{*}{x}, \gamma - \overset{*}{\ell})$, and the price ratio $\overset{*}{w}/\overset{*}{p}$ constitute a general competitive equilibrium. The consumption allocation solves the consumer choice problem, the production allocation solves the producer choice problem, and the aggregate demand for each commodity is equal to the sum of the initial endowment of the commodity plus the net production of the commodity.

16.4 GRAPHICAL ILLUSTRATION OF COMPETITIVE EQUILIBRIUM WITH TWO CONSUMERS, TWO PRODUCERS, TWO INPUTS, AND TWO OUTPUTS

The Economy

In this section, we expand the economy of section 16.3 to include two consumers, two producers, two inputs, and two outputs. This expansion allows us to examine more generally the interdependence between the input and output markets. Of the four commodities, only two are consumed, while the other two are inputs in the production processes. Each of the two producers uses both inputs to produce one of the two consumption commodities. The two consumers own the endowments of the two inputs and also share ownership of the two producing units.

As in sections 16.2 and 16.3, the institutional structure could be modified to incorporate alternative ownership arrangements without affecting the formal analysis that follows.

Denote the resources owned by the first and second consumers, respectively, by $[\bar{v}_1^1, \bar{v}_2^1]$ and $[\bar{v}_1^2, \bar{v}_2^2]$. Let $[x_1^1, x_2^1]$ and $[x_1^2, x_2^2]$ represent the consumption bundles of the two consumers. Assume that producer 1 produces only commodity 1 and producer 2 produces only commodity 2, and denote the amounts produced by q_1 and q_2, respectively. Finally, represent the amounts of the first and second inputs used by producer 1 by $[v_1^1, v_2^1] = v^1$ and represent the amounts of the two inputs used by producer 2 by $[v_1^2, v_2^2] = v^2$.

The Production Box Diagrams

The production technologies of the two producers are represented by production functions (see section 8.2) with images $q_1 = f^1(v_1^1, v_2^1) = f^1(v^1)$ and $q_2 = f^2(v_1^2, v_2^2) = f^2(v^2)$. The two production functions, along with the total-resource endowment of the economy, can be represented graphically by a production box diagram. This diagram, which is analogous to the consumption box diagram described in section 15.3, is constructed as follows. In figure 16.4, units of the first and second input are plotted on the horizontal and vertical axes, respectively. In this space, the total-resource endowment $[\bar{v}_1, \bar{v}_2]$ is represented by a point, denoted O^2 in figure 16.4. The amounts used of the two inputs by producer 1 can be represented by a point in this space referred to the original origin. For example, the point $\overset{*}{v}$ in figure 16.4 indicates that producer 1 uses $\overset{*}{v}{}_1^1$ of input 1 and $\overset{*}{v}{}_2^1$ of input 2. This, of course, leaves $\bar{v}_1 - \overset{*}{v}{}_1^1$ of input 1 and $\bar{v}_2 - \overset{*}{v}{}_2^1$ of input 2 for use by producer 2. These amounts of the two inputs used by producer 2 can be represented by the point $\overset{*}{v}$, referred to the point O^2 as its origin. Thus, the horizontal and the vertical lines through the aggregate resource endowment point, O^2, constitute the axes, referred to O^2 as the origin, along which the respective amounts of input 1 and input 2 used by producer 2 are measured.

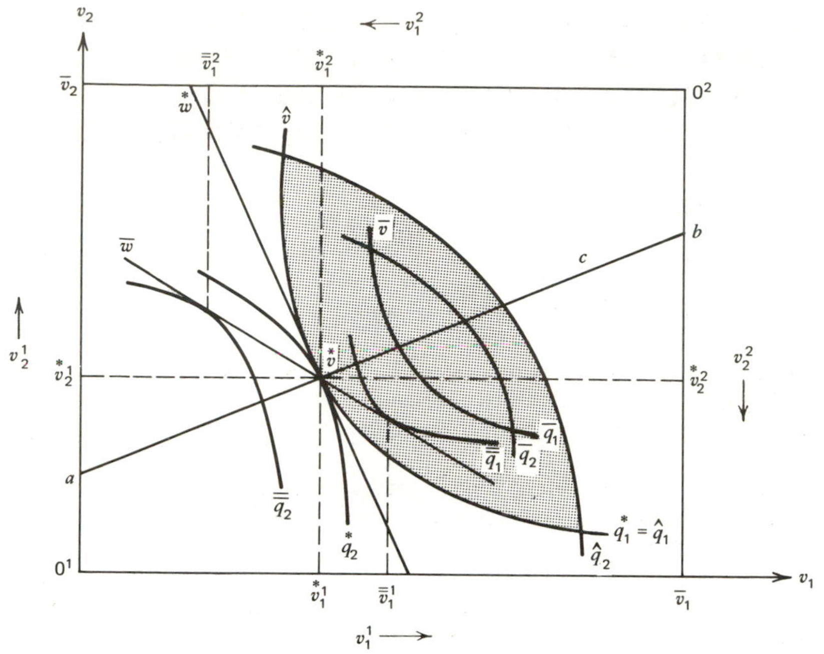

Figure 16.4

It will be recalled from section 8.2 that a production function with one output and two inputs can be represented in input space by an isoquant map. Thus, just as the utility functions of two consumers are represented by two indifference maps in the consumption box in figure 15.2, the production functions of the two producers can be represented by isoquant maps referred to the two origins in the production box in figure 16.4. The isoquants of producer 2 are strictly convex to the origin O^2 and the isoquants of producer 1 are strictly convex to the origin O^1.

Consider the point $\hat{v}$ in figure 16.4, at which the corresponding utilization of each input by each producer may be projected onto the respective axes. These input bundles allow the two producers to produce outputs of $\hat{q}_1$ and $\hat{q}_2$. The output of at least one of the two commodities is increased without decreasing the output of the other by any reallocation that results in a new utilization of inputs inside the (shaded) lens area with the two isoquants passing through $\hat{v}$ as its boundaries. Any reallocation into the interior of this lens area increases the output of *both* commodities. For example, a reallocation to $\bar{v}$ increases the outputs to $\bar{q}_1$ and $\bar{q}_2$, respectively. At $\bar{v}$, it is still possible to increase the output of both commodities by a reallocation of inputs to a point inside the lens area with the two isoquants passing through $\bar{v}$ as its boundaries.

The set of all input allocations which make mutually beneficial reallocations impossible is called the *production contract curve*. It is apparent that all allocations on the production contract curve in the interior of the box are characterized

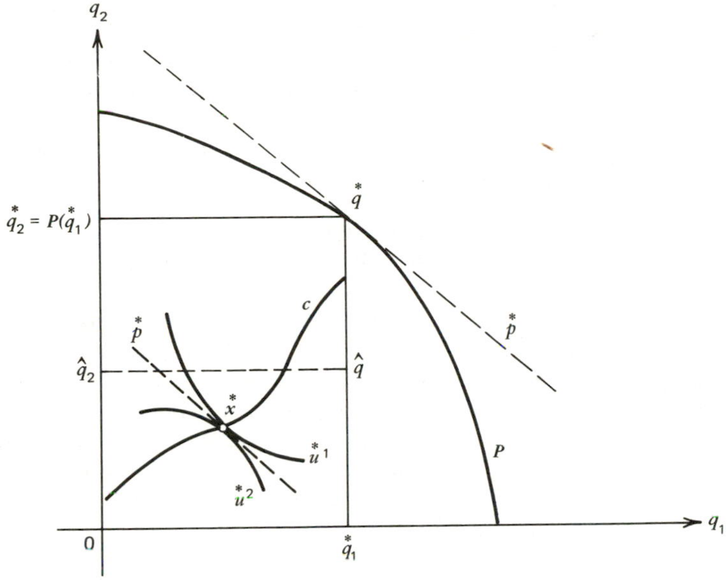

Figure 16.5

by tangency of the isoquants. One such allocation is $\overset{*}{v}$. Points on the production contract curve are efficient in the same sense that points on the consumption contract curve are efficient. Given an input allocation on the production contract curve, the output of one producer can only be increased by reducing the output of the other producer.

The Production-Possibility Curve

Reallocation of the inputs along the production contract curve results in increasing output of one commodity and decreasing output of the other. The relationship between the production of commodities 1 and 2 as the input allocation is shifted along the contract curve can be represented by a curve in $q_1 - q_2$ space. This relationship, referred to as the *production-possibility curve*, is represented by the curve labeled P in figure 16.5. This curve reflects the production possibilities for the entire (two-producer) economy.[4]

Given strict convexity (relative to the origins) of the isoquant maps, there is a one-to-one correspondence between the production-possibility curve and the production contract curve; i.e., each point on the production-possibility curve in figure 16.5 (each output combination) corresponds to a single point on the contract curve in figure 16.4 (an input combination) and conversely each point on the production contract curve corresponds to a single point on the transformation curve.

[4] The concept can be generalized to economies with more than two producers.

The output combinations represented by points on the production-possibility curve do not exhaust the collection of possible combinations of outputs of the two commodities. Production would be represented by a point below this curve if the input allocation were represented by a point in figure 16.4 which is not on the contract curve. For example, the input combination v^* in figure 16.4 might correspond to output combination q^* in figure 16.5. This point is on the production-possibility curve. But the input combination $\hat{v}$ in figure 16.4, which is off the contract curve, results in the same output of commodity 1 but a lesser amount, say, $\hat{q}_2$, of commodity 2. This might be represented by the point $\hat{q}$ in figure 16.5, which is below the production-possibility curve. If we permit some or all of the inputs to go unused, every point in the nonnegative quadrant bounded by the production-possibility curve represents a feasible output combination. For example, by simply disposing of all of both inputs, the resultant output combination is given by the origin in figure 16.5. While all of the points in the area beneath the production-possibility curve represent feasible output combinations, only points on the production-possibility curve represent *efficient* output combinations. Points below the production-possibility curve correspond to inefficient input allocations represented by points off the production contract curve in figure 16.4.

Properties of the Production-Possibility Curve

It will be noted that the production-possibility curve in figure 16.5. is strictly concave to the origin. This property of the curve follows from strict convexity of the individual technology sets (assumption 7.5),[5] but an heuristic explanation can be obtained by calculating the derivative of the function relating q_1 and q_2. The function P can be defined by solving the maximization problem,

$$\max_{v_1^2, v_2^2} f^2(v_1^2, v_2^2) \qquad \text{s.t. } q_1 = f^1(\bar{v}_1 - v_1^2, \bar{v}_2 - v_2^2). \tag{16.14}$$

That is, maximize the output of commodity 2 with respect to the input allocation to producer 2 subject to the constraint that $\bar{v}_1 - v_1^2$ and $\bar{v}_2 - v_2^2$ (the remaining input quantities) be sufficient to produce output q_1. Given $\bar{v}_1$ and $\bar{v}_2$, the maximizing values of v_1^2 and v_2^2 depend upon the specified value of q_1:

$$\overset{*}{v}{}_1^2 = \phi_1(q_1), \tag{16.15}$$

and

$$\overset{*}{v}{}_2^2 = \phi_2(q_1). \tag{16.16}$$

[5] The aggregate technology set for the economy is the sum of the individual technology sets. As the sum of (strictly) convex sets are (strictly) convex (Rockafellar [1970, Theorem 3.1]), the aggregate technology set is convex. The set of feasible outputs, given fixed quantities of inputs, is simply a projection of the aggregate technology set onto output space. As projections of convex sets are convex (Rockafellar [1970, Corollary 3.4.1]), the set of feasible outputs is convex. The production-possibility curve, as an appropriate segment of the boundary of this set, is therefore concave to the origin.

Substitution into $f^2(v_1^2, v_2^2)$ yields the image of the production-possibility function:

$$P(q_1) = f^2(\phi_1(q_1), \phi_2(q_1)). \tag{16.17}$$

That is, $P(q_1)$ is the most that can be produced of commodity 2, given output q_1 of commodity 1. For example, in figure 16.5, given commodity $\mathring{q}_1$ of commodity 1, $\mathring{q}_2 = P(\mathring{q}_1)$ is the maximal output of commodity 2. Thus, the derivative $P'(q_1)$ is the slope of the production-possibility curve. In order to evaluate this slope, differentiate the identity (16.17):

$$P'(q_1) = \frac{\partial f^2(\phi_1(q_1), \phi_2(q_1))}{\partial \phi_1(q_1)} \phi_1'(q_1) + \frac{\partial f^2(\phi_1(q_1), \phi_2(q_1))}{\partial \phi_2(q_1)} \phi_2'(q_1)$$

$$= \frac{\partial f^2(\mathring{v}^2)}{\partial v_1^2} \phi_1'(q_1) + \frac{\partial f^2(\mathring{v}^2)}{\partial v_2^2} \phi_2'(q_1), \tag{16.18}$$

where

$$\mathring{v}^2 = [\mathring{v}_1^2, \mathring{v}_2^2].$$

Next substitute the maximizing values from (16.15) and (16.16) into the constraint in (16.14), $q_1 = f^1(\bar{v}_1 - \phi_1(q_1), \bar{v}_2 - \phi_2(q_1))$, and differentiate both sides with respect to q_1:

$$1 = \frac{\partial f^1(\bar{v}_1 - \phi_1(q_1), \bar{v}_2 - \phi_2(q_1))}{\partial(\bar{v}_1 - \phi_1(q_1))} (-\phi_1'(q_1))$$

$$+ \frac{\partial f^1(\bar{v}_1 - \phi_1(q_1), \bar{v}_2 - \phi_2(q_1))}{\partial(\bar{v}_2 - \phi_2(q_1))} (-\phi_2'(q_1)). \tag{16.19}$$

Solving this expression for $\phi_1'(q_1)$ and letting $\mathring{v}^1 = [1 - \phi_1(q_1), 1 - \phi_2(q_1)]$, we obtain

$$\phi_1'(q_1) = -\frac{(\partial f^1(\mathring{v}^1)/\partial v_2^1)\phi_2'(q_1) + 1}{\partial f^1(\mathring{v}^1)/\partial v_1^1}.$$

Substituting this expression into (16.18) and collecting terms, we obtain

$$P'(q_1) = \left(\frac{\partial f^2(\mathring{v}^2)}{\partial v_2^2} - \frac{(\partial f^2(\mathring{v}^2)/\partial v_1^2)\,(\partial f^1(\mathring{v}^1)/\partial v_2^1)}{\partial f^1(\mathring{v}^1)/\partial v_1^1}\right) \phi_2'(q_1)$$

$$- \frac{\partial f^2(\mathring{v}^2)/\partial v_1^2}{\partial f^1(\mathring{v}^1)/\partial v_1^1}. \tag{16.20}$$

It will now be shown that the first term in this expression vanishes. The first-order conditions for $\mathring{v}^2$ to solve (16.14) require that

$$\frac{\partial f^2(\mathring{v}^2)}{\partial v_1^2} - \lambda \frac{\partial f^1(\mathring{v}^1)}{\partial v_1^1} = 0, \tag{16.21}$$

and

$$\frac{\partial f^2(\mathring{v}^2)}{\partial v_2^2} - \lambda \frac{\partial f^1(\mathring{v}^1)}{\partial v_2^1} = 0, \tag{16.22}$$

where λ is the Lagrange multiplier. Rearrangement and division of (16.21) by (16.22) yields

$$\frac{\partial f^2(\overset{*}{v}^2)/\partial v_1^2}{\partial f^2(\overset{*}{v}^2)/\partial v_2^2} = \frac{\partial f^1(\overset{*}{v}^1)/\partial v_1^1}{\partial f^1(\overset{*}{v}^1)/\partial v_2^1}.$$

This condition says that the rate of technological substitution between inputs 1 and 2 must be equal in the production of the two commodities. This is, of course, the condition defining the contract curve (in the interior of the production box diagram). Note, however, that this tangency condition implies that the term in parentheses in (16.20) vanishes so that

$$P'(q_1) = -\frac{\partial f^2(\overset{*}{v}^2)/\partial v_1^2}{\partial f^1(\overset{*}{v}^1)/\partial v_1^1} = -\frac{MP_1^2(\overset{*}{v}^2)}{MP_1^1(\overset{*}{v}^1)}. \tag{16.23}$$

That is, the absolute value of the slope of the production-possibility curve is equal to the ratio of the marginal product of input 1 in producing commodity 2 to the marginal product of the same input in producing commodity 1. Moreover, had (16.19) been solved for $\phi'_2(q_2)$ instead of $\phi'_1(q_1)$, the above algebra would have led to

$$P'(q_1) = -\frac{MP_2^2(\overset{*}{v}^2)}{MP_2^1(\overset{*}{v}^1)}.$$

Thus, the slope of the production-possibility curve, or the rate at which output of commodity 2 can be transformed into output of commodity 1 is equal to the ratio of marginal products of each input in the two uses to which it can be put. This makes sense. The higher the marginal products of inputs in producing commodity 1 are relative to the marginal products in producing commodity 2, the lesser is the reduction of output of commodity 2 required to increase the output of commodity 1 by a given amount per time period (i.e., the lower is the absolute value of $P'(q_1)$).

Concavity of the production-possibility curve reflects the fact that, as q_1 is increased and q_2 decreased, the marginal products of inputs used by producer 1 fall and the marginal products of inputs used by producer 2 rise.

General Equilibrium

We are now ready to examine graphically the properties of competitive equilibrium in an economy with four commodities, two consumers, and two producers. Let us first consider the competitive-equilibrium input allocation. The first-order conditions for producer profit maximization can be written as follows (see section 8.4):

$$p_1 \frac{\partial f^1(v^1)}{\partial v_1^1} = w_1, \tag{16.24}$$

$$p_1 \frac{\partial f^1(v^1)}{\partial v_2^1} = w_2, \tag{16.25}$$

$$p_2 \frac{\partial f^2(v^2)}{\partial v_1^2} = w_1, \tag{16.26}$$

and

$$p_2 \frac{\partial f^2(v^2)}{\partial v_2^2} = w_2, \tag{16.27}$$

where p_1 and p_2 are the (unnormalized) prices of the two outputs and w_1 and w_2 are the (unnormalized) prices of the two inputs.

Division of (16.24) by (16.25) and of (16.26) by (16.27) indicates that the rates of technological substitution between the two inputs in the production of each of the two commodities are equal to a *common* input price ratio, w_1/w_2:

$$\frac{\partial f^1(v^1)/\partial v_1^1}{\partial f^1(v^1)/\partial v_2^1} = \frac{w_1}{w_2} = \frac{\partial f^2(v^2)/\partial v_1^2}{\partial f^2(v^2)/\partial v_2^2} \tag{16.28}$$

This implies that the competitive-equilibrium input allocation is necessarily on the production contract curve.

The graphical representation of (16.28) is analogous to the graphical analysis in section 9.2 of the maximization of output subject to an outlay constraint (or the dual problem of minimizing outlay subject to an output constraint). It will be recalled that this optimum is achieved where the equal-outlay line is tangent to an isoquant. But a straight line in the production box constitutes an equal-outlay line for *both* producers. Consider, for example, the straight line labeled $\overset{*}{w}$ in figure 16.4, which is assumed to have a slope of $\overset{*}{w}_1/\overset{*}{w}_2$. This is an equal-outlay line for each of the two producers where the total outlay is given by the value of any input allocation on the line at prices $\overset{*}{w}_1$ and $\overset{*}{w}_2$. Thus, the total outlay corresponding to this equal-outlay line is $\overset{*}{\delta}^1 = \overset{*}{w}_1 v_1^1 + \overset{*}{w}_2 v_2^1$ for the first producer and $\overset{*}{\delta}^2 = \overset{*}{w}_1 v_1^2 + \overset{*}{w}_2 v_2^2$ for the second producer.

For the input prices to be equilibrium prices, it is necessary that the corresponding price line be tangent to isoquants of both producers and that the points of tangency imply that both of the inputs are exactly used up. For example, the input price ratio yielding price line $\bar{w}$ in figure 16.4 is not an equilibrium price ratio since it implies that the second producer uses the first input at the rate $\bar{v}_1^2$ and that the first producer utilizes this input at the rate $\bar{\bar{v}}_1^1$. But these two input utilization rates add up to much more than the aggregate endowment of input 1. This input price ratio therefore cannot be an equilibrium price ratio. It is clear that the optimality conditions and the resource-constraint conditions are both satisfied only if the point of tangency of the price line for the two producers is at the same point in the box. But if the isoquants of the two producers are tangent to a common price line at the same point, they must be tangent to each other. Therefore, the equilibrium allocation of the two inputs is necessarily on the production contract curve. For example, the input price ratio yielding price line $\overset{*}{w}$ in figure 16.4 is clearly an equilibrium price ratio since this price line is tangent to both isoquants at the point $\overset{*}{v}$ on the contract curve.

While we now know that the equilibrium input combination must lie on the contract curve, this does not actually identify the equilibrium amounts of the two inputs utilized by each producer—nor therefore the output of each producer—since there is an infinite number of points on the contract curve. In order to determine the amounts of the two commodities produced, and hence the amounts of each input utilized by each producer, we must refer to output space in figure 16.5. It will be recalled that there is a one-to-one correspondence between points on the production-possibility curve in figure 16.5 and points on the contract curve in figure 16.4. Hence the identification of an equilibrium point on the production-possibility curve necessarily determines a unique equilibrium point on the contract curve. We know that the equilibrium output combination must lie on the production-possibility curve since points below the product-possibility curve correspond to points that are not on the contract curve in figure 16.4.

The equilibrium output combination in figure 16.5 must satisfy the profit-maximization conditions of the two producers. The latter can be directly related to the slope of the production-possibility curve. Solve (16.26) and (16.24) for $\partial f^2(v^2)/\partial v_1^2$ and $\partial f^1(v^1)/\partial v_1^1$ and substitute into the equation for the slope of the production-possibility curve (16.23) to obtain $P'(q_1) = -(w_1/p_2)/(w_1/p_1)$ or

$$-P'(q_1) = \frac{p_1}{p_2}. \tag{16.29}$$

Thus, an equilibrium output combination must satisfy (16.29), which states that the rate at which one output can be transformed into the other is equal to their price ratio.

This equilibrium condition (16.29) can be clarified by recalling from section 9.5 that profit maximization for the competitive producer implies that

$$MC_1(\overset{*}{q}_1) = p_1, \tag{16.30}$$

and

$$MC_2(\overset{*}{q}_2) = p_2, \tag{16.31}$$

where $MC_1(\overset{*}{q}_1)$ and $MC_2(\overset{*}{q}_2)$ are the marginal costs of producing commodities 1 and 2, respectively. Substitution of (16.30) and (16.31) into (16.29) yields

$$-P'(q_1) = \frac{MC_1(\overset{*}{q}_1)}{MC_2(\overset{*}{q}_2)}.$$

Thus, in equilibrium the slope of the production-possibility curve is equated to the ratio of the marginal costs of producing the two goods. This makes sense. The negative of the slope of the production-possibility curve tells us how much the production of commodity 2 must be reduced in order to produce one additional unit of commodity 1. But the value of the resources used in the production of one additional unit of commodity 1 is simply the marginal cost of commodity 1. Moreover, the required decrease in the output of commodity 2 is given by the total increase in outlay on commodity 1 divided by the marginal cost of producing commodity 2. Since the total increase in outlay on commodity 1 when its production is raised by one unit is $MC_1(\overset{*}{q}_1)$, the number of units by which the production of commodity 2 must be reduced when the output of commodity 1 is increased by one unit is equal to the ratio of the marginal costs, $MC_1(\overset{*}{q}_1)/MC_2(\overset{*}{q}_2)$.

The output and input price ratios, $\overset{*}{p}_1/\overset{*}{p}_2$ and $\overset{*}{w}_1/\overset{*}{w}_2$, and the associated output and input bundles, $\overset{*}{q}$ and $\overset{*}{v}_1$ together constitute production equilibrium for the economy. General equilibrium requires, in addition, that the two consumers maximize utility subject to the budget constraint generated by the same price ratio, $\overset{*}{p}_1/\overset{*}{p}_2$. Since the two commodities produced are the only commodities consumed, consumption of commodities 1 and 2 can also be measured along the two axes of figure 16.5. Thus, the point $\overset{*}{q}$ represents not only the aggregate output combination of the two commodities but also the maximal aggregate consumption bundle of the society. A *consumption* box with the original origin in fig. 16.5 as the origin of the consumption space of consumer 1 and the point $\overset{*}{q}$ as the origin of the consumption space of consumer 2 can be constructed. Thus, a point inside this consumption box reflects a given distribution of the total output of the two commodities between the two consumers in the economy. The indifference maps for the two consumers can also be drawn in this box. The consumption contract curve is labeled C in figure 16.5.

As in the case of pure exchange, the equilibrium distribution of any output combination among the two consumers must lie on the contract curve in the consumption box formed by the point $\overset{*}{q}$ in figure 16.5. Point $\overset{*}{x}$ is one such point.

The input allocation represented by the point $\overset{*}{v}$ in figure 16.4, the output combination represented by point $\overset{*}{q}$ in figure 16.5, the consumption bundles represented by the point $\overset{*}{x}$ in figure 16.5, and the nonnormalized price vector $(\overset{*}{p}_1, \overset{*}{p}_2, \overset{*}{w}_1, \overset{*}{w}_2)$ constitute a general competitive equilibrium in the case of two outputs, two inputs, and two consumers *for a particular distribution of the wealth of the economy among the two consumers*. That is, in order for this set of outputs, consumption bundles, and prices to be a competitive equilibrium the distribution of the wealth among the two individuals must be such that

$$p_1\overset{*}{x}{}_1^1 + p_2\overset{*}{x}{}_2^1 = w_1\bar{v}_1^1 + w_2\bar{v}_2^1 + s_1^1\pi^1 + s_2^1\pi^2 = \omega_1 \tag{16.32}$$

and

$$p_1\overset{*}{x}{}_1^2 + p_2\overset{*}{x}{}_2^2 = w_1\bar{v}_1^2 + w_2\bar{v}_2^2 + s_1^2\pi^1 + s_2^2\pi^2 = \omega_2. \tag{16.33}$$

That is, the above combination of prices, outputs, inputs, and consumption bundles constitutes an equilibrium for any set of profit shares (s_1^1, s_2^1, s_1^2, and s_2^2) and resource endowments ($\bar{v}_1^1$, $\bar{v}_2^1$, $\bar{v}_1^2$, and $\bar{v}_2^2$) which satisfy the above two equations.

It only remains to show that the wealth of the two consumers adds up to the value of the total output of the economy. To see this, add the wealth of the two consumers, using equations (16.32) and (16.33),

$$\begin{aligned}\omega_1 + \omega_2 = {} & w_1(\bar{v}_1^1 + \bar{v}_1^2) + w_2(\bar{v}_2^1 + \bar{v}_2^2) + (s_1^1 + s_1^2)(p_1x_1 - w_1v_1^1 - w_2v_2^1) \\ & + (s_2^1 + s_2^2)(p_2x_2 - w_1v_1^2 - w_2v_2^2).\end{aligned}$$

But, recalling that $s_1^1 + s_1^2 = s_2^1 + s_2^2 = 1$ and rearranging terms, we find that

$$\begin{aligned}\omega_1 + \omega_2 = {} & w_1(\bar{v}_1^1 + \bar{v}_1^2 - v_1^1 - v_1^2) + w_2(\bar{v}_2^1 + \bar{v}_2^2 - v_2^1 - v_2^2) \\ & + p_1x_1 + p_2x_2.\end{aligned}$$

As the aggregate resource constraints are satisfied in competitive equilibrium, the first two terms in parentheses vanish. Finally, as total consumption and total production are equal, we arrive at the desired result: $\omega_1 + \omega_2 = p_1q_1 + p_2q_2$. Thus, the total value of the wealth of the two consumers exactly equals the value of the total output of the economy. This means that the budget lines of the two consumers exactly coincide in the consumption box in figure 16.5.

This graphical illustration of competitive equilibrium in the case in which there are only two inputs, two outputs, two producers, and two consumers displays an equilibrium for a particular distribution of the wealth. If, however, we were to begin the analysis with arbitrary profit shares and resource endowments, the equilibrium might be very different. The algebraic analysis of the previous section shows the way in which such an equilibrium might be found, but to analyze this equilibrium for arbitrary profit shares and initial resource endowments from a graphical viewpoint would be too complicated to make it worthwhile.

16.5 COMPETITIVE EQUILIBRIUM AND THE CORE*

The treatment of general competitive equilibrium thus far in part IV has been entirely descriptive. The important content of general-equilibrium theory, however, has to do with the properties of competitive equilibrium. These properties are discussed in the final two sections of this chapter and in chapters 17 and 18.

One important property of general competitive equilibrium is that it is *viable*. Given a competitive-equilibrium allocation, there is no gain to be made by the formation of coalitions of agents (excluding other agents in the economy) in order to reallocate resources. The notion of the viability of competitive equilibrium, in this sense of the term, is closely related to the game-theoretic concept of the core, analyzed in section 14.4. The use of this concept in the context of general competitive equilibrium is effected by interpreting trades as strategies.

As long ago as 1881, Edgeworth showed that the set of competitive equilibria of an exchange economy are (under very reasonable regularity conditions regarding consumer preferences) contained in the core of the economy; thus, competitive-equilibrium allocations are viable. The converse is not generally true however; many viable allocations are not competitive equilibria (i.e., the core is not a subset of the set of competitive equilibria). Debreu and Scarf [1963] recently have shown, however, that as the economy gets very large (more particularly as the number of agents goes to infinity in a very particular replicative way), the core shrinks to the set of competitive equilibria. Hence, in the limit all competitive equilibria are viable and all viable allocations are competitive equilibria.

Edgeworth called the game that he constructed to describe the attainment of allocations that are in the core *recontracting*. The idea is that agents enter freely into tentative contracts to trade with other agents. These trades are actually consummated, however, only if every agent is completely satisfied with the contracts that he has negotiated in the sense that he cannot, through recontracting with other agents, increase his utility. As long as it is possible for

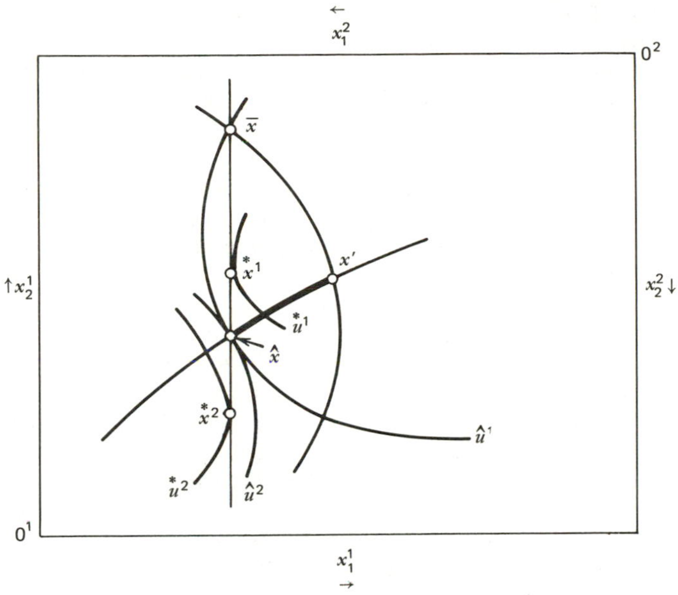

Figure 16.6

some subset (coalition) of the agents to increase the utility of every member of the subset by recontracting, this negotiation process continues. Thus, in an Edgeworth recontracting equilibrium it is not possible for any coalition of traders to enter into a new set of trades, thus abrogating the old contracts, and increase the utility of every member of the coalition. The formal equivalence of the Edgeworth recontracting equilibrium to the game-theoretic equilibrium concept of the core should be obvious.

To illustrate the results of Edgeworth and of Debreu and Scarf, it is convenient to return to the bilateral exchange economy developed in sections 15.2 and 15.3. Thus, in the consumption box diagram in figure 16.6, suppose that the initial endowments of the two agents are represented by the point $\bar{x}$. The set of competitive equilibria must lie on the darkened portion of the contract curve, i.e., the portion of the contract curve bounded by the two indifference curves intersecting at the initial endowment $\bar{x}$. (It is easy to show that the competitive equilibrium need not be unique; see exercise 16.3.)

Let us now identify the core of the exchange economy represented by the consumption box in figure 16.6 and the initial endowment $\bar{x}$. Any allocation that is not on the contract curve is clearly not in the core; this is so because the two agents can form a two-person coalition to shift the allocations to the contract curve in such a way as to increase the utility of both. Also, points on the contract curve that are not on the darkened line are not elements of the core because such allocations involve a lower utility for one of the two consumers than the utility of the initial endowment. Thus, it would pay one of the two consumers to form a one-person coalition that refuses to trade at all from the point $\bar{x}$. Thus, all trades that move the allocation from $\bar{x}$ to points that are not on the darkened portion of the contract curve in figure 16.6 are blocked by some coalition. In the language of Edgeworth, the recontracting will not terminate until the contracted trade places both consumers on this darkened portion of the contract curve. Thus, it is apparent that the set of competitive equilibria is a subset of the core in this two-person exchange economy.

Let us now increase the number of agents in a very particular replicative way. In particular, consider the four-person exchange economy in which there are two agents with the preferences of consumer 1 and two agents with the preferences of consumer 2 in figure 16.6. Similarly, the two consumers of type 1 are assumed to have identical endowments, as are the two consumers of type 2. Thus, the initial endowments of the four consumers can again be represented by the point $\bar{x}$ in figure 16.6. Thus, this four-person exchange economy is a simple replication of the two-person exchange economy discussed above. This replication makes it clear that the set of competitive-equilibrium allocations must be represented by points on the darkened portion of the contract curve in figure 16.6. Indeed, it is easy to see that the set of competitive-equilibrium allocations in this replicated economy must be formally identical to those in the two-person exchange economy. This is true because the competitive-equilibrium allocation must occur at a point where a price line through the initial endowment $\bar{x}$ is tangent to the *identical* indifference curves of consumers of type 1 and the *identical* indifference curves of consumers of type 2. Thus, diagrammatically, the competitive equilibria look exactly as they did in the two-person exchange economy.

It is now shown, however, that the core is smaller in this four-person economy. To see this, first note that points represented by allocations that are not on the darkened portion of the contract curve are not in the core for reasons identical to those described above for the two-person economy. If therefore suffices to show that the two end points of the darkened portion of the contract curve, $\hat{x}$ and x', are blocked by three-person coalitions.

To see this, consider a three-person coalition composed of the two consumers of type 1 and one of the two consumers of type 2. Trading down the exchange line through $\bar{x}$ and $\hat{x}$, each unit of commodity 2 given up by *both* consumers of type 1 results in an increase of *two* units of commodity 2 consumed by the *one* consumer of type 2. A similar two-to-one relationship holds for the units of commodity 1 attained by the two consumers of type 1 and given up by the one consumer of type 2. Thus, allocations attained by such trades between the members of this three-person coalition must be represented by two points on the exchange line through $\bar{x}$ and $\hat{x}$. In particular, a given trade will move the endowment of the one consumer of type 2 twice as far down the exchange line as it moves the two consumers of type 1. One such feasible trade yields the allocations $\overset{*}{x}{}^1$ (two-thirds of the distance from $\bar{x}$ to $\hat{x}$) for the two consumers of type 1 and an allocation of $\overset{*}{x}{}^2$ (four-thirds of the distance from $\bar{x}$ to $\hat{x}$) for the one type-2 member of the three-person coalition. The important thing to notice about this trade is that it places all three members of the coalition on higher indifference curves than those which pass through the allocation $\hat{x}$. Thus, the new three-person coalition increases the utility of each of its members. Consequently, the end-point $\hat{x}$ is not in the core of the four-person (replicated)

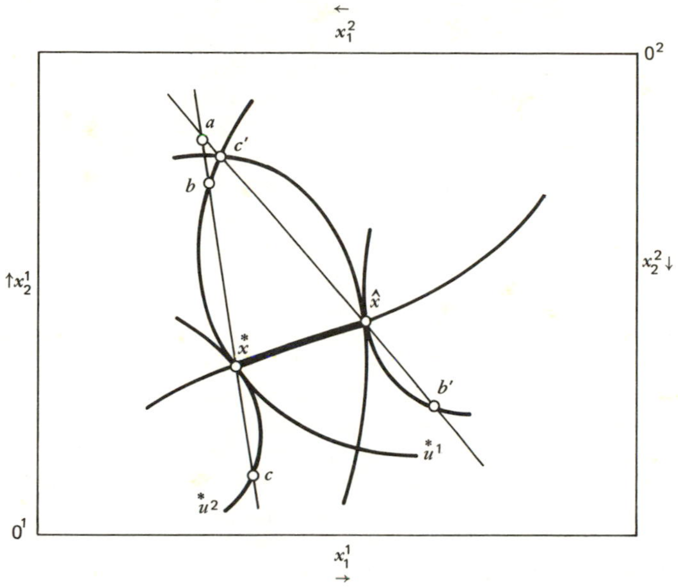

Figure 16.7

economy. It is left to the reader to show that the allocation x' is similarly excluded from the core in this four-person exchange economy.

We have thus shown that the two end points of the darkened portion of the contract curve, $\hat{x}$ and x', are not in the core of the four-person exchange economy although they are in the core of the two-person exchange economy. Moreover, no allocations that are not on the darkened portion of the contract curve can belong to the core. It is therefore apparent that increasing the size of the economy by replication from two to four persons causes the core to shrink.

Let us now characterize the set of points on the contract curve which represent allocations in the core. To facilitate this characterization, consider figure 16.7 with slightly different notation than that in figure 16.6. Thus, the point, a, represents the initial endowment and the points $\overset{*}{x}$ and $\hat{x}$ are in the interior of the darkened portion of the contract curve. The latter is true because the initial endowment, a, lies below (relative to the appropriate origin) the indifference curves passing through $\overset{*}{x}$ and $\hat{x}$.

The allocation $\overset{*}{x}$ is blocked by a coalition of two persons of type 1 and one person of type 2 if trading down the exchange line through a and $\overset{*}{x}$ can move all three members of the coalition to a higher indifference curve. This is true if the consumers of type 1 reach the intersection point b, thus obtaining the utility level $\overset{*}{u}{}^1$, *before* the one consumer of type 2 is pushed beyond the intersection point c, beyond which the utility of the type 2 consumer is lower than $\overset{*}{u}{}^2$. In other words, $\overset{*}{x}$ is blocked if and only if $2ab < ac$, where ab and ac are the lengths of the indicated line segments. Thus, $\overset{*}{x}$ is in the core of the two-person economy if and only if $2ab \geq ac$. Similarly, the allocation $\hat{x}$ is blocked by a coalition of two persons of type 2 and one person of type 1 if and only if $2ac' < ab'$; thus, $\hat{x}$ is in the core of the two-person economy if and only if $2ac' \geq ab'$.

More generally, let b be the (nontangency) intersection of the $\overset{*}{u}^1$-indifference curve with the straight line through a and $\overset{*}{x}$ (also let $b = \overset{*}{x}$ if there does not exist such an intersection point). Similarly, let c be the (nontangency) intersection of the $\overset{*}{u}^2$-indifference curve with the straight line through a and $\overset{*}{x}$ (and $c = \overset{*}{x}$ if there does not exist such an intersection point). Thus, in this simplified notation, the allocation $\overset{*}{x}$ is blocked if and only if $2ab < ac$ or $2ac < ab$. Therefore, $\overset{*}{x}$ is in the core of the four-person economy if and only if

$$2ab \geq ac \quad \text{and} \quad 2ac \geq ab. \tag{16.34}$$

Note that, if $\overset{*}{x}$ is a competitive-equilibrium allocation, then the straight line through a and $\overset{*}{x}$ is tangent to the indifference curves of the type 1 and type 2 consumers and therefore $ab = ac$ and $\overset{*}{x}$ is in the core. Moreover, for allocations very close to the equilibrium, it is true that ab is approximately equal to ac and therefore that $2ab \geq ac$ and $2ac \geq ab$. Therefore, as the size of the economy is expanded by replication from two to four persons, the core shrinks but it is still in general larger than the set of competitive equilibria.

Let us now further expand the economy, again by replication, to six persons, three of each type. It is again apparent that allocations represented by points that are not on the darkened portion of the contract curve are again not in the core. Allocations that are off the contract curve are blocked by six-person (also two-person and four-person) coalitions. Moreover, points on the contract curve but not on the darkened portion of the curve are blocked by one-person coalitions.

There remains the possibility of three-, four-, and five-person coalitions. As before, an allocation $\overset{*}{x}$ is blocked by a three-person coalition if $2ab < ac$ or $2ac < ab$. By analogous reasoning, $\overset{*}{x}$ is blocked by a four-person coalition (three persons of one type and one person of the other type) if $3ab < ac$ or $3ac < ab$. This is true because a trade along an exchange line among the members of this coalition moves the person with the unique preferences three times as far as it moves the three persons of the same type. Finally, $\overset{*}{x}$ is blocked by a five-person coalition (three of one type and two of the other) if and only if $\frac{3}{2}ab < ac$ or $\frac{3}{2}ac < ab$. This last relationship holds because a trade among the five members of this coalition moves the two persons of one type three-halves of the distance moved by the three persons of the other type.

It is apparent from the above inequalities that if $\overset{*}{x}$ is blocked by a four-person coalition, it is blocked by a three-person coalition, and if $\overset{*}{x}$ is blocked by a three-person coalition, it is blocked by a five-person coalition. Therefore, for an allocation to be in the core, it is necessary and sufficient that it cannot be blocked by a five-person coalition.[6] Thus, the allocation $\overset{*}{x}$ is in the core of the three-person economy if and only if

$$\tfrac{3}{2}ab \geq ac \tag{16.35}$$

[6] It is easy to see that if an allocation is blocked by a five-person coalition with four agents of one type and one of the other, it is also blocked by any of the above coalitions as well. This is because a coalition of this type blocks $\overset{*}{x}$ if and only if $4ab < ac$ or $4ac < ab$.

and

$$\tfrac{3}{2}ac \geq ab.$$

Since the pair of inequalities (16.35) implies the pair of inequalities (16.34), it is apparent that the core of the six-person economy is a subset of the core of the four-person economy (which, as was noted above, is in turn a subset of the core of the two-person economy). Also, as before, $\overset{*}{x}$ is a competitive-equilibrium allocation if and only if $ab = ac$ so that the set of competitive equilibria is a subset of the core of the six-person economy.

By induction of the above argument, it can be seen that the allocation $\overset{*}{x}$ belongs to the core of the $2n$-person economy if and only if the following inequalities hold: $(n/(n-1))ab \geq ac$ and $(n/(n-1))ac \geq ab$, $n > 1$. As the number of agents goes to infinity, the ratio $n/(n-1)$ goes to 1. Consequently, letting the number of agents go to infinity, we obtain the following conditions for $\overset{*}{x}$ to be in the core: $ab \geq ac$ and $ac \geq ab$. This implies, however, that $ab = ac$; i.e., that the exchange line through a and $\overset{*}{x}$ be tangent to the indifference curves of the two types of consumers. That is, the allocation $\overset{*}{x}$ is a competitive-equilibrium allocation. Thus, in the limit, the core and the set of competitive equilibria coincide.

16.6 CONCLUDING REMARKS: EXISTENCE, UNIQUENESS, AND STABILITY*

The algebraic and diagrammatic analyses of this chapter are designed to be illustrative of the mechanism by which resources are allocated in a competitive economy. Logically, competitive equilibrium is equivalent to the consistency of decentralized decision making with an appropriate set of prices. The theoretical and practical importance of this model has been the subject of searching inquiry for decades. In addition to the question of viability discussed in the previous section, these analyses revolve primarily around the issues of the existence, uniqueness, stability, and optimality of general competitive equilibrium.

The foregoing illustrations are relevant only if an equilibrium price vector exists. It is, however, possible to construct economies in which competitive equilibrium does not exist (see section 17.4). Sufficient conditions for the existence of a competitive equilibrium have been established by Arrow and Debreu [1954], Debreu [1959, 1962], and other modern theorists. In particular, the assumptions listed in section 16.2, together with a certain restriction regarding the endowments of consumers,[7] suffice to prove that competitive equilibrium exists. The existence issue is not pursued in this book (see the part IV suggested reading for references). However, a closely related, and perhaps more interesting, problem is examined in section 17.4. This section examines the conditions under which a "social optimum" (to be defined more carefully there) can be attained by a competitive pricing mechanism—put differently, the

[7] This restriction, which essentially puts the consumers' endowments in the interiors of their consumption sets, is necessary in order to eliminate the "Arrow exceptional case" (see footnote 7 in section 17.4).

conditions under which a centralized optimization problem can be decentralized, using prices.

Assuming that competitive equilibrium exists, it might not be unique (for a given allocation of initial endowments). If, for example, an indifference curve of the consumer and the boundary of the technology set of the producer in the economy analyzed in section 16.3 had coincident flat segments, the equilibrium allocation would not be unique although the equilibrium price ratio might be unique. If the point of "tangency" occurs at a cusp (or corner) of both the technology set and the indifference curve, the equilibrium price is not unique, although the equilibrium allocation is unique (see exercise 16.2). Finally, even if indifference curves are strictly convex without cusps, it is possible to construct a consumption box diagram with multiple equilibria for some initial endowment (see exercise 16.3). If competitive equilibrium is not unique, the outcome of the competitive mechanism is in some sense indeterminate. This is probably not a matter of great importance, however, as the general-equilibrium model—in its most general formulation—has no comparative-static content.[8]

Even if competitive equilibrium exists, there remains the important question of how (or indeed whether) the equilibrium price is established. This is the issue that is addressed by the extensive literature on the stability of general competitive equilibrium (see the part IV suggested reading). Analysis of the stability of general equilibrium requires that a general dynamic disequilibrium model be developed, just as the analysis of the stability of partial equilibrium in chapter 12 requires the specification of a partial disequilibrium model. The dynamic model that has been most commonly employed in the literature is a (Walrasian) price-adjustment model, in which the rate of exchange of the ith price is an increasing function of the aggregate excess demand for the ith commodity ($i = 2, \ldots, n$) (see section 12.4). That is, the ith price rises if aggregate demand exceeds aggregate supply and falls if aggregate supply exceeds aggregate demand. This model can therefore be described as a system of (interdependent) differential equations (each rate of change depends upon the levels of *all* $n - 1$ normalized prices), and the mathematical conditions for stability are well known. However, the usual economic assumptions (such as those posited in section 16.2) do not suffice for the Walrasian price-adjustment model to be stable (see Arrow and Hahn [1971, pp. 297–99]). Hence, there is no a priori reason to believe that price-adjustment mechanisms of this type are stable.[9] The stability literature has established, however, that asymmetries in cross-price derivatives of demand functions (in an exchange economy) are responsible for the lack of stability in some economies. Thus, if there are no income effects, in which case cross-price derivatives are symmetric (see section 5.3), general competitive equilibrium in an exchange economy is stable. Moreover, equilibrium is stable so long as the income effects are, in some sense, "small" (see Arrow and Hahn [1971, p. 298]).

The final property of general competitive equilibrium that has been a matter of considerable attention is its optimality. This is undoubtedly the most

[8] Very highly structured general-equilibrium models, such as the input-output model of Leontief [1949, 1966] have proved useful in quantitative comparative-static applications.

[9] This contrasts with the case of partial-equilibrium stability (see section 12.4).

important aspect of competitive equilibrium and is the subject matter of the next two chapters.

EXERCISES

16.1 An economy is endowed with fixed quantities of two inputs: $\bar{v}_1 = 108$ and $\bar{v}_2 = 64$. The production functions for two commodities are $q_1 = 3(v_1^1)^{1/3}(v_2^1)^{2/3}$ and $q_2 = v_1^2$. The two outputs are consumed by consumers with identical utility functions given by

$$U^c(x_1^c, x_2^c) = (x_1^c)^{1/2}(x_2^c)^{1/2}, \; c = 1, \ldots, m.$$

a. Derive the equation defining the production-possibility curve: $q_1 = P(q_2)$.

b. Calculate the competitive-equilibrium

i. output quantities, $\overset{*}{q}_1$ and $\overset{*}{q}_2$,

ii. output price ratio, $\overset{*}{p}_1/\overset{*}{p}_2$,

iii. input allocation, $\overset{*}{v}_1^1$ and $\overset{*}{v}_1^2$,

iv. input-output price ratios, $\overset{*}{w}_1/\overset{*}{p}_1$, $\overset{*}{w}_1/\overset{*}{p}_2$, $\overset{*}{w}_2/\overset{*}{p}_1$, and $\overset{*}{w}_2/\overset{*}{p}_2$, and

v. shares of national income going to the two inputs.

(Hint: use the fact that all consumers allocate their "income," or wealth, equally between the two commodities.)

c. Assuming that there are only two consumers, derive the equation for the consumption contract curve in competitive equilibrium.

16.2 Show that, if the boundary of the technology set and the tangent indifference curve have coincident flat segments, the equilibrium allocation is not unique. Show that the equilibrium price is not unique if the point of "tangency" occurs at a cusp of both the technology set and the indifference curve.

16.3 Show that, even if preferences are strictly convex, equilibrium is not necessarily unique in the two-person exchange economy.

CHAPTER 17 PARETO OPTIMALITY AND COMPETITIVE EQUILIBRIUM

17.1 INTRODUCTION

The previous two chapters analyze in some detail the way in which the final goods and services of an economy are allocated among the consumers when a competitive price system balances supplies and demands of all commodities. The natural question to ask is: so what? Surely there are many other institutional mechanisms for determining what is produced and what is consumed. Therefore, we might wish to determine whether or not the allocation mechanism described in the previous chapters is in any sense optimal; that is, is there a sense in which this allocation mechanism is "better" than certain alternatives? In particular, in this chapter the allocation of resources under perfect competition is compared with the allocation that results when some agents have monopolistic power over prices.

It is also clear from the description of general competitive equilibrium that the ultimate allocation of consumption bundles among the consumers of the economy depends upon the initial distribution of commodities (wealth) among these agents. The initial allocation of each consumer is taken as a given in the analysis of competitive equilibrium. But it is these initial endowments (relative to the endowments of others) that determine the distribution of income. Thus, the theory outlined in chapters 15 and 16 has little to say about the very important issue of income distribution. It merely describes, given the particular initial endowment, how much of each commodity is produced and how much of each commodity is consumed by each consumer. Surely, changing the initial distribution of wealth among the consumers (perhaps by a lump-sum tax devised by a government as an income-redistributive measure) changes the ultimate competitive equilibrium. The following question then arises: how do we evaluate the competitive equilibria associated with alternative distributions of wealth?

Any attempt to evaluate alternative distributions of the initial endowments among individuals in a society, and, more broadly, to evaluate alternative mechanisms for the distribution of primary resources to the production of consumption goods, thrusts the economist into the realm of normative economics. The issue of "what ought to be," as opposed to "what is," is one that has been deliberately eschewed in the preceding chapters of this book. The remaining four chapters are devoted to this issue—i.e., to normative economics.

In order to compare alternative systems and alternative wealth distributions, it is necessary to devise a social decision rule. This rule necessarily involves value judgments. As there is no compelling reason to believe that the values of an economist are superior to the values of other members of a society, the task of the economist in analyzing normative issues surely ought not to be one of specifying values. It is not the economist's role to shape the values of society; rather, the appropriate role of the economist in the formulation of normative economics is to incorporate the values of society explicitly into a program for the formulation of economic policy. The revelation of social values—a very difficult problem—is not an intrinsically economic issue. In fact, most of the propositions of welfare economics explore the implications of alternative value systems which may or may not be held by the economist.

Because of the many problems involved in the determination of social values, much of the research on the formulation of consistent welfare criteria and their implications for the formulation of economic policy has relied on an apparently innocuous value judgment: the so-called unanimity rule. This rule, usually referred to as the Pareto criterion after its original promulgator, stipulates that one state of the economy is "Pareto preferred" to another if no individual is worse off and at least one person is better off than in the latter state. Similarly, if some state of the economy has the property that no alternative state is Pareto preferred to it, it is said to be "Pareto optimal."

As it turns out, there is in general no "most preferred state" under the Pareto ordering of states of the economy. It is nevertheless true that some interesting propositions can be derived from this welfare criterion, the most important of which deal with the relationship between Pareto optimality and competitive equilibrium. In section 17.2, we examine this nexus in the context of an exchange economy. In particular, it is shown that the general competitive equilibrium described above is optimal from the standpoint of this criterion. This is often referred to as the "first fundamental proposition of welfare economics." The "second fundamental proposition of welfare economics" is that any Pareto-optimal state of the economy can be generated by a competitive pricing mechanism with some specification of initial endowments.

As is the case with general competitive equilibrium, most of the important propositions of welfare economics can be demonstrated and illustrated quite adequately in the context of an exchange economy. Nevertheless, for the sake of completeness, we examine the relationship between Pareto optimality and perfectly competitive equilibria in a production economy in section 17.3.

It is unfortunately true that the close relationship between Pareto optimality and competitive equilibrium has been erroneously treated as an identity by some economists and has been artificially sublimated to the status of an almost religious doctrine. There are a large number of circumstances—most notably when externalities (such as air pollution) exist—under which the relationship between Pareto optimality and competitive equilibrium breaks down. These circumstances are discussed in chapter 18.

The fundamental inadequacy of the Pareto welfare criterion is that it does not lead to a complete ranking of the states of the economy and is therefore a useless criterion in the context of many policy propositions. One of the principal messages of modern welfare theory is that, if policy recommendations are to be made, it is necessary to indulge in interpersonal utility comparisons and therefore in value judgments. The important thing is that these value judgments be treated explicitly and systematically in the economic analysis. That is, the value judgments, whatever their source, must be clearly apparent in the recommendation of alternative economic policies.

In chapter 20, we develop and analyze the concept of a social welfare function, which is nothing more than a representation of the values of society regarding states of the economy. Once an explicit social welfare function is formulated, it is in principle possible to identify the social optima. The theme of chapter 19, however, is the famous "impossibility theorem" of Nobel Laureate Kenneth Arrow, which asserts that it is impossible to construct a consistent social decision rule which does not embody assumptions that most classical economists find objectionable (e.g., interpersonal utility comparisons or dictatorship).

17.2 PARETO OPTIMALITY AND COMPETITIVE EQUILIBRIUM IN AN EXCHANGE ECONOMY

The Pareto Criterion

The most convenient way to examine the notion of Pareto optimality in an exchange economy is in the two-person, two-commodity case so that we can use the consumption box diagram introduced in section 15.3. We retain all the assumptions of chapter 15. The two consumers have strictly convex preferences so that the indifference curves drawn in the box diagram in figure 17.1 are convex to the appropriate origin. Recall that the Pareto criterion stipulates that one state of the economy is *Pareto preferred* to another if no individual is worse off and at least one person is better off than in the former state. Similarly, if some state of the economy has the property that no alternative state is Pareto preferred to it, it is said to be *Pareto optimal.*

To illustrate this concept, consider the allocation $\bar{x}$ in figure 17.1. All of the allocations in the adjacent lightly shaded area, including all of those on the boundary except $\bar{x}$ and $\hat{x}$, are Pareto preferred to the allocation $\bar{x}$ since all of these allocations place at least one of the two consumers on a higher indifference curve than the indifference curve passing through $\bar{x}$ and neither on a lower indifference curve. Also, the allocations in the darkly shaded area, including all allocations on the boundary except $\bar{x}$ and $\hat{x}$, are Pareto inferior to $\bar{x}$ since each of these allocations places at least one of the two consumers on a lower indifference curve and neither on a higher indifference curve. Finally, the allocation $\hat{x}$ is *Pareto indifferent* to $\bar{x}$ since both consumers are on the same indifference curves at these two points.

The allocations in the adjacent lightly shaded and adjacent darkly shaded areas are the only states of the exchange economy that can be compared under

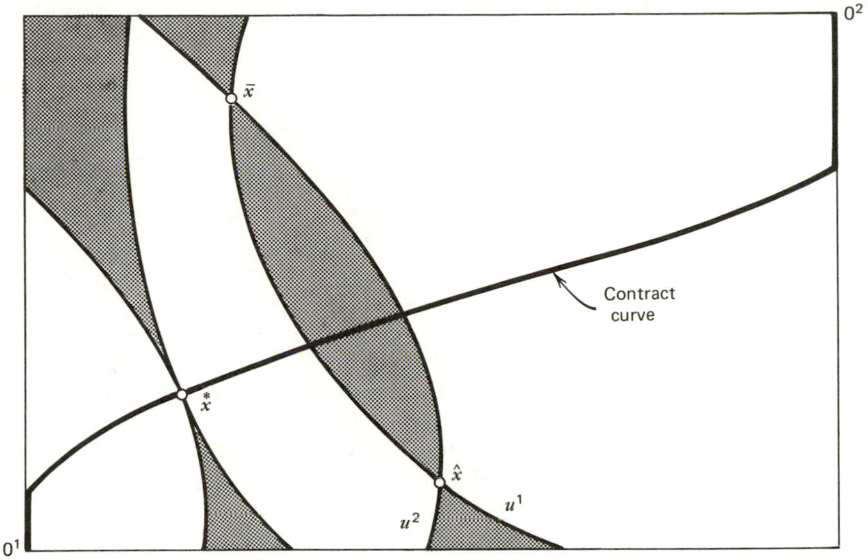

Figure 17.1

the Pareto criterion to the allocation $\bar{x}$. All other allocations in the box yield a higher utility for one of the consumers but a lower utility for the other relative to the utility levels corresponding to $\bar{x}$, and are therefore noncomparable.

Consider the allocation $\overset{*}{x}$ on the contract curve in figure 17.1. This allocation is clearly Pareto preferred to all of the allocations in the adjacent darkly shaded area, including the boundaries, except, of course, for $\overset{*}{x}$ itself. Moreover, there is no allocation in the box which is Pareto preferred to $\overset{*}{x}$, since all alternative allocations entail a lower utility for at least one of the two consumers. Thus, the state of the economy $\overset{*}{x}$ is Pareto optimal. This is, in fact, characteristic of all of the points on the contract curve. Moreover, *only* points on the contract curve are Pareto optimal. Thus, the set of Pareto optima of this exchange economy is represented by all of the allocations on the contract curve. Note that there are an infinite number of such Pareto optima. Moreover, these Pareto optima cannot be compared to one another under the Pareto criterion since alternative points on the contract curve entail a higher level of utility for one of the two consumers, but a lower level of utility for the other. Note also that, although $\bar{x}$ in figure 17.1 is *not* Pareto optimal and $\overset{*}{x}$ *is* Pareto optimal, it is not possible to say that $\overset{*}{x}$ is preferred to $\bar{x}$ under the Pareto criterion. Thus, a Pareto optimum is noncomparable not only to other Pareto optima but also to many allocations that are not Pareto optimal.

The First Fundamental Optimality Principle

Interior Pareto-optimal allocations are characterized by equality of the marginal rates of substitution of the two consumers (since this equality is a property of the contract curve in the interior of the consumption box). This equality similarly characterizes (interior) Pareto optimality in an m-consumer, n-commodity exchange economy:

$$MRS^{c}_{ij}(\overset{*}{x}^{c}) = MRS^{c'}_{ij}(\overset{*}{x}^{c'}), \qquad i, j = 1, \ldots, n, \quad c, c' = 1, \ldots, m. \tag{17.1}$$

If these equalities did not hold, it would be possible to reallocate consumption between two consumers, making both better off. For example, if $MRS^{c}_{ij}(\overset{*}{x}^{c}) > MRS^{c'}_{ij}(\overset{*}{x}^{c'})$ for some i, j, c, c', transferring an appropriate amount of commodity j from consumer c to consumer c' and an appropriate amount of commodity i from consumer c' to consumer c would increase the utility of both.

In section 15.3 it was demonstrated that a general competitive equilibrium in the two-commodity, two-person exchange economy results in an allocation which is on the contract curve. Thus, a competitive equilibrium—given our assumptions—is necessarily Pareto optimal. This important property of competitive equilibrium, often called the "first fundamental optimality principle of welfare economics," generalizes to the m-consumer, n-commodity economy. To see this, note that if the competitive-equilibrium allocation is interior,[1] all consumers equate *common* (equilibrium) price ratios to respective marginal rates of substitution; hence marginal rates of substitutions are equated for each commodity pair and (17.1) holds.

The above discussion emphasizes the important allocative role that prices play in a perfectly competitive economic system. Guided by (equilibrium) prices, the self-interested decisions of individual agents lead to a social optimum according to the Pareto criterion. This is a paraphrase of Adam Smith's principle of the "invisible hand."

The Second Fundamental Optimality Principle

A second important property of competitive equilibrium, often called "the second fundamental optimality principle of welfare economics," is that, given our assumptions, any Pareto-optimal allocation is a competitive equilibrium for some initial endowment. Consider the arbitrary Pareto optimum $\overset{*}{x}$ (located, of course, on the contract curve) in figure 17.2. Since $\overset{*}{x}$ is an interior allocation on the contract curve, the indifference curves of the two consumers are tangent at the allocation $\overset{*}{x}$. Consider a line drawn through $\overset{*}{x}$ with a slope equal to the common slope of the indifference curves of the two consumers at $\overset{*}{x}$. Given any initial endowment represented by a point on this line, the competitive-equilibrium price ratio is given by the slope of this line and a competitive-equilibrium exchange between the two consumers results in the allocation $\overset{*}{x}$. Thus, there is an infinite number of initial endowments (all represented by points on the line through $\overset{*}{x}$) that yield the competitive-equilibrium allocation $\overset{*}{x}$. Hence the Pareto-optimal allocation $\overset{*}{x}$ is a competitive-equilibrium allocation.

This result can be extended to Pareto-optimal allocations on the boundary of the consumption box. In figure 17.3 the boundary allocation $\overset{*}{x}$ is a Pareto optimum, again located on the contract curve. The two exchange lines labeled $\overset{*}{p}$ and $\hat{p}$ are competitive-equilibrium prices that result in the competitive-equilibrium

[1] A tedious, but straightforward version of the following argument goes through if some optimal consumption bundles are corner solutions.

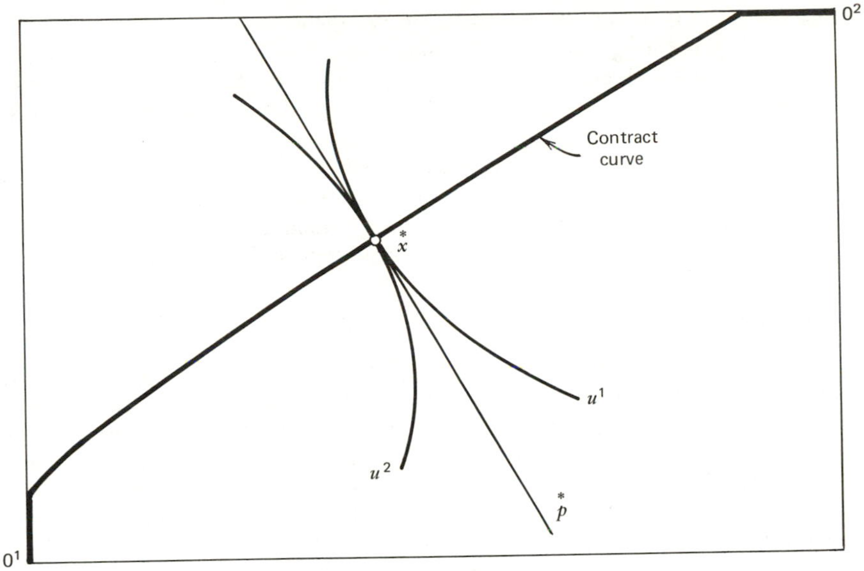

Figure 17.2

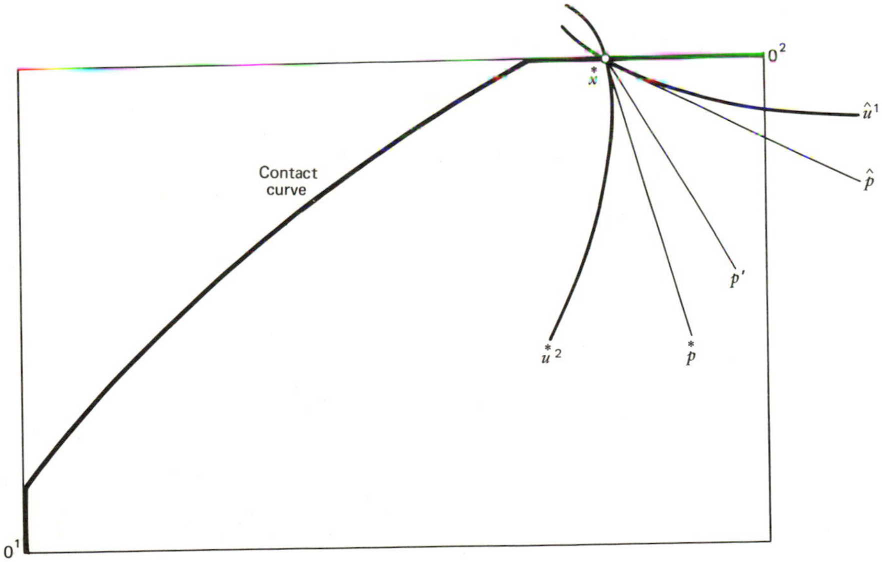

Figure 17.3

allocation $\overset{*}{x}$ if the initial endowment is on the respective exchange line. The $\overset{*}{p}$ exchange line is tangent to $\overset{*}{u}^2$ at the allocation $\overset{*}{x}$ and the $\hat{p}$ exchange line is tangent to $\hat{u}^1$ at $\overset{*}{x}$. In fact, any exchange rate represented by an exchange line in between $\overset{*}{p}$ and $\hat{p}$—e.g., p^1—is an equilibrium exchange rate that results in allocation $\overset{*}{x}$.

The significance of the second fundamental optimality principle is that, given our assumptions, any Pareto-optimal allocation can be achieved by the decentralized decision making of consumers pursuing their own self-interest in competitive markets. Centralized planning is unnecessary.

Monopoly and Pareto Optimality

Of course, if alternative market structures also generate Pareto-optimal equilibria, the two fundamental optimality principles establishing a nexus between competitive equilibrium and Pareto optimality would be of less interest. It is therefore instructive to demonstrate that the existence of monopolistic power over prices does not result in a Pareto-optimal allocation. The inefficiency of monopoly can be demonstrated in the simple two-commodity, two-consumer model using the consumption box diagram. Assume that consumer 1 has monopoly power over prices, whereas consumer 2 behaves as a perfect competitor (i.e., takes the prices as given).

Given the initial endowment $\hat{x}$ in figure 17.4, the trade offers of the competitor, consumer 2, at various prices set by the monopolist are represented by the offer curve, $\mathcal{O}^2$. Consumer 1 exploits his monopolistic power by setting the price to maximize utility subject to the constraint that the trade at any price generates a new allocation on the offer curve of consumer 2. It is apparent therefore that the maximum utility for the monopolist is obtained at allocation x',

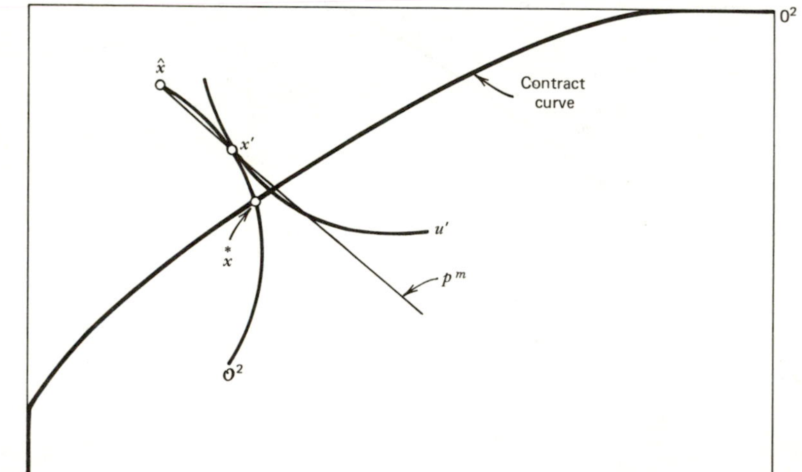

Figure 17.4

which can be effected by setting the exchange rate equal to the slope of the line through $\hat{x}$ and x'. Due to the strict convexity of the indifference curves, the monopoly equilibrium always lies on the offer curve, $\mathcal{O}^2$, between the initial allocation and a point on the contract curve, $\overset{*}{x}$ in Figure 17.4. Thus, the monopoly equilibrium cannot lie on the contract curve. It is possible to reallocate consumption bundles in such a way as to improve the welfare of both consumers.

It is tempting to conclude from the fact that monopoly equilibrium is not Pareto optimal that it is socially optimal to "break up" the monopoly, thus generating a competitive equilibrium, which unlike the monopoly equilibrium, is Pareto optimal. This simplistic conclusion, however, is not supported by the Pareto welfare criterion. Although the competitive-equilibrium allocation $\overset{*}{x}$ is Pareto optimal, it is *not* Pareto preferred to the monopoly equilibrium x'. Thus, antitrust action per se is not an obvious policy prescription, using the Pareto criterion, for dealing with monopolistic market power.

The reason the Pareto criterion does not support a simplistic antitrust policy is, of course, because the monopolist at whom the antitrust policy is directed suffers from this policy. Consequently, without adopting an explicit value judgment regarding the interpersonal comparison of the loss of utility of the monopolist vis à vis the gain in utility to the competitor, it is not possible to recommend such a policy.

The nature of the problem, however, suggests a solution. The solution is embodied in the so-called "compensation principle." The idea is that the welfare of both consumers can be improved if the monopoly is broken up and the monopolist is compensated for his losses. This policy prescription, which is very complicated and difficult to implement in practice, is easily illustrated in the simple two-commodity, two-consumer model. In figure 17.5, $\hat{x}$ is the initial endowment and x' is the monopoly allocation. The set of allocations that are Pareto preferred to x' are represented by the portion of the contract curve between

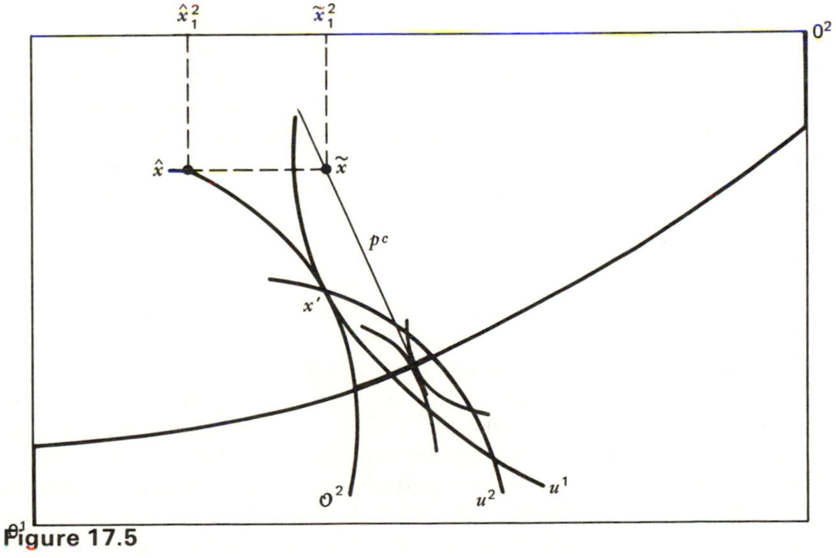

Figure 17.5

u^1 and u^2. The second optimality principle implies that each of these Pareto optima can be supported as a competitive equilibrium if the initial endowment can be redistributed. The redistribution of the initial endowment amounts to the compensation of the monopolist. For example, consider the Pareto-optimal allocation $\overset{*}{x}$. The price ratio represented by the slope of the line p^c tangent to both indifference curves at $\overset{*}{x}$ is the competitive-equilibrium price ratio and $\overset{*}{x}$ is the equilibrium allocation for any endowment on this line. For example, $\overset{*}{x}$ is a competitive-equilibrium allocation corresponding to the endowment $\tilde{x}$. Moreover, $\tilde{x}$ can be achieved by transferring $\hat{x}_1^2 - \tilde{x}_1^2$ of the initial endowment of commodity 1 from consumer 2 to consumer 1. This transfer constitutes the compensation of the monopolist for the utility loss attributable to the breaking up of his monopoly power.

The combination of antitrust policy and compensation for the monopolist results in the competitive equilibrium $\overset{*}{x}$, which is Pareto preferred to the monopoly equilibrium x'. The moral of this exercise is that the welfare of every consumer can be improved by forcing the monopolist to adopt a competitive pricing rule and compensating him for the resultant loss by a lump-sum transfer from those consumers who gain by the imposed competitive market structure.

17.3 PARETO OPTIMALITY AND COMPETITIVE EQUILIBRIUM IN A PRODUCTION ECONOMY

Pareto Optimality in a Production Economy

The essence of the relationship between competitive equilibrium and Pareto optimality was conveyed in the previous section in the context of a pure exchange economy. Thus, this analysis of Pareto optimality in a production economy is rather brief.

In an exchange economy, Pareto optimality requires that the consumption allocation lie on the contract curve of the consumption box diagram. This condition is necessary for Pareto optimality because an allocation off the contract curve means that mutually beneficial trades can be effected. On the other hand, if the allocation is on the contract curve, no consumer can be made better off without impairing the welfare of another consumer. Hence, this condition is sufficient as well as necessary for Pareto optimality.

When commodities are produced, Pareto optimality again requires that these commodities be distributed among consumers in such a way as to make mutually beneficial trades impossible. The reasoning is exactly analogous to that employed in the analysis of Pareto optimality in an exchange economy. The possibility of production, however, necessitates additional conditions that must be satisfied in order for a state of the economy to be Pareto optimal. Most immediately, it is easy to see that it must not be possible to increase the output of one commodity without reducing the output of any other by reallocating inputs among producers. Consider the two-consumer, two-producer, two-output, two-input model introduced in section 16.4. Figure 17.6 depicts the production box diagram for the two producers with isoquants convex to the appropriate

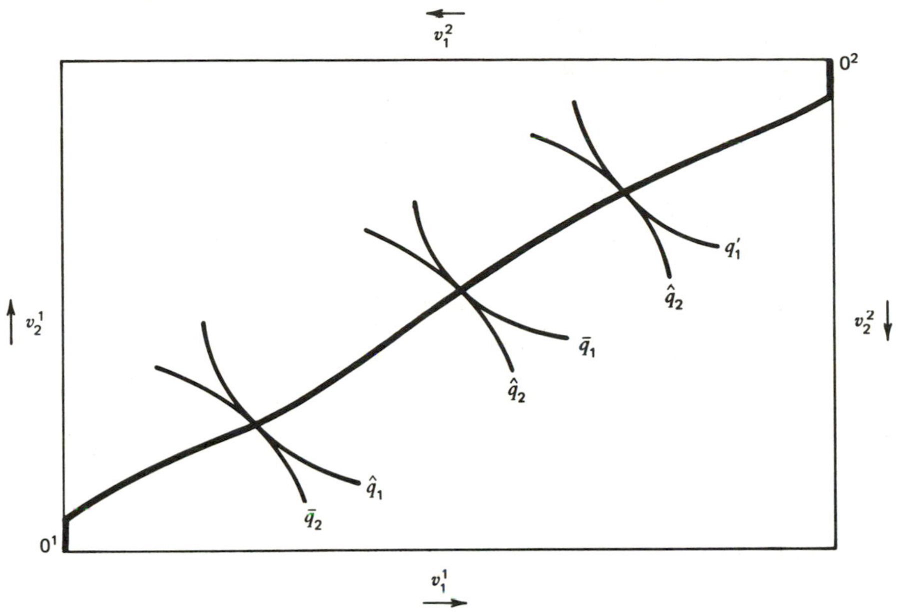

Figure 17.6

origins. Only production bundles on the contract curve represent efficient allocations, at which it is impossible to increase the output of one commodity without reducing the amount produced of the second.

As long as some consumer is not sated with all commodities, the possibility of producing more of some commodity without reducing the production of any other means that it is possible to enhance the welfare of at least one consumer without lowering the welfare of any other. Consequently, production efficiency is necessary for Pareto optimality in a production economy.

Interior efficient allocations are characterized by tangency of the isoquants or equality of the rates of technological substitution of the two producers (since this equality is a property of the contract curve in the interior of the production box diagram):

$$RTS_{12}^{1}(\overset{*}{v}^{1}) = RTS_{12}^{2}(\overset{*}{v}^{2}). \tag{17.2}$$

Recall from section 16.4 that the production contract curve can be represented in output space by the production-possibility curve, P. Figure 17.7 exhibits a production-possibility curve which satisfies the concavity condition discussed in section 16.4. An inefficient allocation of the inputs generates an output combination that is below the production-possibility curve. Pareto optimality thus requires that inputs be allocated in such a way as to generate an output combination on the production-possibility curve.

Corresponding to any point on the production-possibility curve, a consumption box diagram can be constructed. One such box diagram is included in

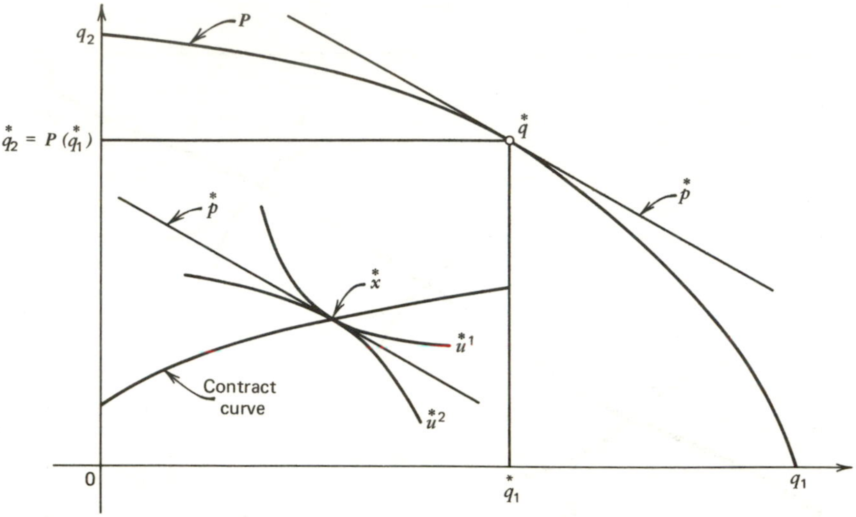

Figure 17.7

figure 17.7. A Pareto-optimal allocation requires that the output combination be on the production-possibility curve and that the allocation of the two commodities among the two consumers be on the contract curve of the corresponding consumption box diagram. These conditions are not, however, sufficient for Pareto optimality. If the slope of the production-possibility curve, $P'(q_1)$, is different from the rate at which the two consumers exchange the two commodities, it is possible to improve the welfare of both consumers by a change in the output combination. This follows from the fact that an inequality between the rate of exchange and $P'(q_1)$ means that the rate at which the consumers are willing to exchange one commodity for another differs from the rate at which the two commodities can be substituted for one another in production. For example, if the marginal rate of substitution of commodity 1 for commodity 2 exceeds $P'(q_1)$, the consumers are willing to give up more of commodity 2 for additional unit of commodity 1 than is required. Consequently, both consumers can be made better off by substituting commodity 1 for commodity 2 in production and allocating the new output combination between the two consumers in an appropriate manner. Thus, Pareto optimality requires that

$$MRS^1_{12}(\overset{*}{x}^1) = MRS^2_{12}(\overset{*}{x}^2) = -P'(\overset{*}{q}_1). \tag{17.3}$$

In figure 17.7, $\overset{*}{q}$ and $\overset{*}{x}$ are an output combination and consumption allocation which satisfy this condition.

For reasons that should be apparent from the above discussion, the interior Pareto-optimality conditions, (17.2) and (17.3), generalize straightforwardly to an economy with an arbitrary number of consumers, producers, produced commodities, and inputs. The rate of technological substitution between any two inputs must be the same in the production of one commodity as in the production of any other. The marginal rates of substitution between any two commodities must be equal, for all consumers, to the rate at which the production of one commodity can be converted into the production of the other. If these conditions are satisfied, there is no possibility of mutually beneficial trades between consumers, no possibility of reallocating inputs among producers so as to increase the output of at least one commodity without reducing the output of any other commodity, and no possibility of substituting one efficient output combination for another so as to change the consumption allocation to make at least one consumer better off without reducing the welfare of any other consumer.

The First Fundamental Optimality Principle

The graphical analysis of section 16.4 demonstrated that a competitive equilibrium results in an allocation of the two inputs that is on the contract curve of the production box diagram and hence an output combination on the production-possibility curve. Moreover, the outputs are allocated between the two consumers in a way that equates their marginal rates of substitution to the negative of the slope of the production-possibility curve and hence to one another. The latter relationships hold because the consumers equate a *common* price ratio to their marginal rates of substitution,

$$MRS^1_{12}(\overset{*}{x}{}^1) = \frac{p_1}{p_2} = MRS^2_{12}(\overset{*}{x}{}^2), \tag{17.4}$$

and the producers equate respective prices to marginal costs so that, recalling that $-P'(\overset{*}{q}_1) = MC_1(\overset{*}{q}_1)/MC_2(\overset{*}{q}_2)$, we obtain

$$-P'(\overset{*}{q}_1) = \frac{p_1}{p_2}. \tag{17.5}$$

Combining (17.4) and (17.5) yields the (interior) Pareto-optimality condition (17.3). Thus, the foregoing graphical analysis illustrates an important optimality principle: a competitive equilibrium is Pareto optimal.

This property of competitive equilibrium generalizes to economies with more than two producers, consumers, outputs, and inputs. Producers equate rates of technological substitution to a common input-price ratio and consumers equate marginal rates of substitution to a common output-price ratio. These marginal rates of substitution are in turn equated to the respective rates at which they can be converted into one another—ratios of marginal costs—since producers equate output prices to marginal costs.

The Second Fundamental Optimality Principle

For a production economy that satisfies our assumptions (strictly convex isoquants, and a strictly concave transformation function), the second fundamental optimality principle of welfare theory also holds: any Pareto-optimal state of the economy is a competitive equilibrium for some initial endowment. That is, given a Pareto-optimal state of the economy, there exists a price vector which has the property that, if each consumer maximizes utility and each producer maximizes profit given these prices, the resultant quantities demanded and supplied of all commodities are balanced and generate the Pareto-optimal allocation.

The supporting price system of a Pareto optimum is illustrated in figure 17.7. The output combination $\overset{*}{q}$ on the production-possibility curve and the consumption allocation $\overset{*}{x}$ constitute a Pareto-optimal allocation. The supporting output-price ratio is represented by the slope of the line through $\overset{*}{x}$. By the characterization of Pareto-optimal allocations in section 17.2, the slope of this line is equal to the slope of a line drawn tangent to the production-possibility curve at $\overset{*}{q}$. The equilibrium input-price ratio is similarly constructed in the production box diagram (not drawn here) by drawing a line through the (unique) input combination that can produce the output combination $\overset{*}{q}$. Of course, this input combination must be on the contract curve since $\overset{*}{q}$ lies on the production-possibility curve.

The significance of the second fundamental optimality principle of welfare economics is that a Pareto-optimal state of the economy can be arrived at through a competitive pricing mechanism in which each consumer and producer independently pursues his own welfare given what he perceives to be fixed prices. As an alternative to the use of the price system, a central planner with the authority to dictate production quotas, input allocations among firms and income distribution among consumers, could, in principle, generate a Pareto-optimal state of the economy by knowing the production function of every firm, the total availability of each input, and the utility function of each consumer. It is clear that the informational requirements of a central planner are gargantuan. The virtue of a price system is that the allocation decisions are decentralized in such a way that the informational requirements of each decision maker are minimal. In particular, each consumer need know only his own utility function, initial endowment, and prices, and each producer need know only his own production function and prices.

17.4 THE FUNDAMENTAL OPTIMALITY PRINCIPLES REEXAMINED*

Introduction

The previous section examined the nexus between general competitive equilibrium and Pareto-optimal states of the economy, stated in terms of the two fundamental optimality principles of welfare theory. These principles, of course, require certain assumptions (some of which have been more implicit than explicit in our discussion). If these assumptions do not hold, a price system might fail to allocate resources optimally. This section first investigates the consequences for the first optimality principle of relaxing the assumptions of nonsatiation of consumer preferences and perfect divisibility of commodities. Secondly, the role of the convexity assumptions in the decentralization of Pareto-optimal allocations (the second optimality principle) is analyzed.

The Optimality of Competitive Equilibrium

Recall from section 16.2 that the price vector is denoted by p, the initial endowment by $\bar{x}$, the consumption allocation by x, the production allocation by z, and a state of the economy by $s = [x, z]$. We say that $\overset{*}{x}^c$ is a point of local satiation if there exists a neighborhood about $\overset{*}{x}^c$ such that no bundle in that neighborhood is preferred by consumer c to $\overset{*}{x}^c$.[2] The first fundamental optimality principle can be rigorously stated as follows: A competitive-equilibrium allocation $\overset{*}{s} = [\overset{*}{x}, \overset{*}{z}]$ relative to an initial endowment $\bar{x}$, where, for all c, $\overset{*}{x}^c$ is *not* a point of local satiation, is Pareto optimal.

The first optimality principle can easily be proved, by way of contradiction, as follows: Suppose that $\overset{*}{s}$ is not Pareto optimal. Then there exists an alternative state of the economy, say $\hat{s} = [\hat{x}, \hat{z}]$, such that $\hat{z}^r$ is feasible for all r and $U^c(\hat{x}^c) \geq U^c(\overset{*}{x}^c)$ for all c, with strict inequality for at least one consumer, say (without loss of generality) the first. From the definition of competitive equilibrium (section 16.2), $\overset{*}{x}^c$ maximizes $U^c(x^c)$ subject to the cth wealth constraint at the equilibrium price vector $\overset{*}{p}$, for all c. Consequently, $\hat{x}^1$ is not feasible at these prices; i.e.,

$$\sum_{i=1}^{n} \overset{*}{p}_i \hat{x}_i^1 > \sum_{i=1}^{n} \overset{*}{p}_i \overset{*}{x}_i^1. \tag{17.6}$$

As $\overset{*}{x}^c$ is not a point of local satiation for all c,

$$\sum_{i=1}^{n} \overset{*}{p}_i \hat{x}_i^c \geq \sum_{i=1}^{n} \overset{*}{p}_i \overset{*}{x}_i^c, \qquad c = 2, \ldots, m \tag{17.7}$$

(see exercise 3.2). Combining (17.6) and (17.7), we have

$$\sum_{c=1}^{m} \sum_{i=1}^{n} \overset{*}{p}_i \hat{x}_i^c > \sum_{c=1}^{m} \sum_{i=1}^{n} \overset{*}{p}_i \overset{*}{x}_i^c. \tag{17.8}$$

On the other hand, the definition of competitive equilibrium requires that

$$\sum_{i=1}^{n} \overset{*}{p}_i \overset{*}{z}_i^r \geq \sum_{i=1}^{n} \overset{*}{p}_i \hat{z}_i^r, \qquad r = 1, \ldots, \ell, \tag{17.9}$$

since $\overset{*}{z}^r$ maximizes profit and $\hat{z}^r$ is feasible for each r. The competitive equilibrium balance condition (supply equals demand) requires that

$$\sum_{c=1}^{m} x_i^c = \sum_{c=1}^{m} \bar{x}_i^c + \sum_{r=1}^{\ell} z_i^r, \qquad i = 1, \ldots, n.$$

Substituting this condition in (17.9), we obtain

$$\sum_{i=1}^{n} p_i \left(\sum_{c=1}^{m} \sum_{i=1}^{n} (\overset{*}{x}_i^c - \bar{x}_i^c) \right) \geq \sum_{i=1}^{n} p_i \left(\sum_{c=1}^{m} \sum_{i=1}^{n} (\hat{x}_i^c - \bar{x}_i^c) \right),$$

[2] An ε-neighborhood of $\overset{*}{x}$ is defined rigorously as the set of x in X such that $|x - \overset{*}{x}| < \varepsilon$.

which simplifies to

$$\sum_{c=1}^{m} \sum_{i=1}^{n} \overset{*}{p}_i \overset{*}{x}_i^c \geq \sum_{c=1}^{m} \sum_{i=1}^{n} \overset{*}{p}_i \hat{x}_i^c \tag{17.10}$$

But (17.10) contradicts (17.8). Hence $\overset{*}{s}$ is Pareto optimal

Thus, in the absence of points of local satiation for consumers, every competitive equilibrium is a Pareto-optimal state of the economy. In other to appreciate the necessity of excluding points of local satiation, consider the example of bilateral exchange in figure 17.8. The preference ordering of the first consumer exhibits no points of local satiation. However, all of the commodity bundles represented by points on the "thick" indifference curve labeled $\overset{*}{u}_2$ (the shaded area excluding the upper boundary) are points of local satiation. The consumption allocation $\hat{x}$ is a competitive-equilibrium allocation relative to the price vector $\hat{p}$. This competitive equilibrium is not a Pareto-optimal allocation, however, since, for example both $\bar{x}$ and $\overset{*}{x}$ are consumption allocations that make consumer 1 better off without making consumer 2 worse off.

Implicit in the above statement of the first fundamental principle of optimality is the assumption of perfect divisibility of the commodities (assumption 2.1), maintained throughout the entire preceding discussion. If, however, the perfect-divisibility assumption is violated, the first principle of optimality collapses. The problem caused by indivisibility is illustrated in figure 17.9. The feasible consumption allocations for this economy with two indivisible commodities are represented by the dots. Thus, the economy is endowed with four units of commodity 1 and two units of commodity 2 and these commodities

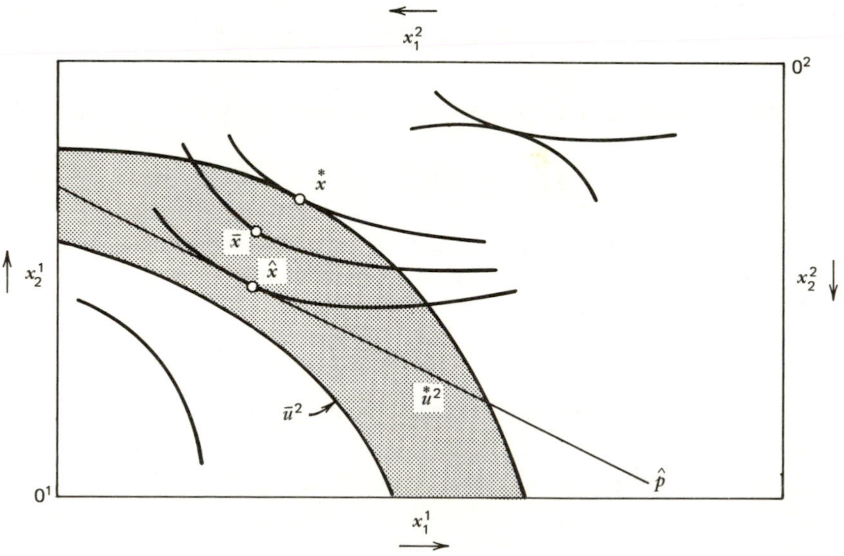

Figure 17.8

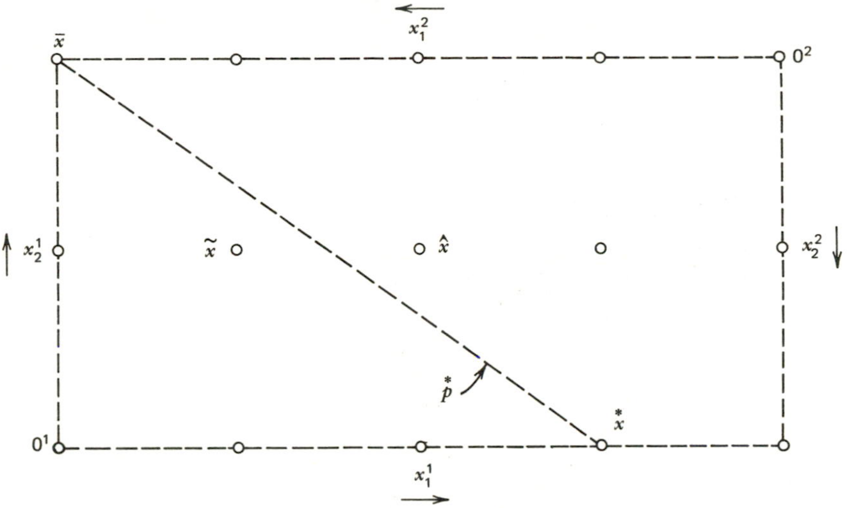

Figure 17.9

cannot be divided into fractions for the purpose of consumption. Suppose that the initial endowment is given by $\bar{x}$ (i.e., consumer 1 is endowed with both units of commodity 2 and consumer 2 is endowed with all four units of commodity 1). Suppose further that consumer 1 prefers $\overset{*}{x}^1$ to $\bar{x}^1$, to $\tilde{x}^1$, and to all other commodity bundles below the dotted line. He prefers $\hat{x}^1$ to $\overset{*}{x}^1$, however. Suppose that consumer 2 is indifferent between $\overset{*}{x}^2$ and $\hat{x}^2$ and prefers $\overset{*}{x}^2$ to $\bar{x}^2$ and to all bundles except $\hat{x}^2$ above (relative to O^1) the dotted line connecting $\bar{x}$ and $\overset{*}{x}$. It follows that $\overset{*}{x}$ is a competitive-equilibrium allocation and that $\overset{*}{p}$, represented by the dotted line, is an equilibrium price since $\overset{*}{x}$ maximizes the utility of each consumer subject to the budget constraint. However, $\overset{*}{x}$ is not Pareto optimal since consumer 1 prefers $\hat{x}$ to $\overset{*}{x}$ while consumer 2 is indifferent between them.

Convexity and the Decentralization of Pareto Optimal States

The second fundamental principle of welfare theory states that, given suitable convexity conditions for consumers' preferences and producers' technology sets, a Pareto-optimal state of the economy is realizable as a competitive equilibrium. That is, given a Pareto-optimal state of the economy, $\overset{*}{s} = [\overset{*}{x}, \overset{*}{z}]$, there exists a price vector $\overset{*}{p}$ and an initial endowment $\bar{x}$ such that $\overset{*}{s} = [\overset{*}{x}, \overset{*}{z}]$ is a competitive equilibrium and $\overset{*}{p}$ is an equilibrium price relative to $\bar{x}$ if (a) each consumer's preference ordering satisfies assumption 3.2 (strict convexity) and (b) each producers' technology set satisfies assumption 7.5 (strict convexity).

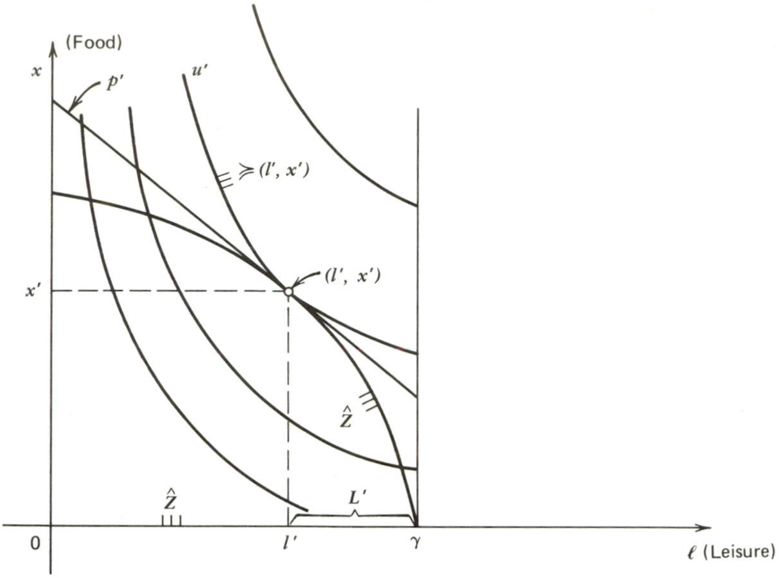

Figure 17.10

Note that the convexity assumptions are fundamental to the proof of the second optimality principle, whereas the first principle holds without any convexity assumption.

In order to illustrate the need for the convexity assumptions in the second optimality principle, consider the one-consumer, one-producer, two-commodity economy introduced in section 16.3. Figure 17.10 illustrates, in leisure-food space, the convex technology set, $\hat{Z}$, of the one producer and the convex indifference map of the one consumer. As there is only one consumer in this economy, Pareto optimality is equivalent to maximal utility of this consumer, given the technology set of the economy (i.e., of the one producer). Thus, (ℓ', x') is the unique Pareto optimum in figure 17.10. A central planner would therefore choose (ℓ', x') as the unique Pareto-optimal allocation. The planner would give the producer an allotment of $L' = \gamma - \ell'$ units of labor and impose on the producer a quota of x' units of food output. The planner would also require the consumer to work $L' = \gamma - \ell'$ hours and give him a consumption allotment of x' units of food.

The point of the second fundamental optimality principle is that, given convexity of the technology set and the consumer preferences, this same Pareto-optimal allocation can be arrived at, using the price mechanism, by the decentralized decision making of the (two) individual economic agents. More fundamentally, this decentralization of the Pareto optimal allocation (ℓ', x') is possible if the set of consumption bundles that are no worse than (ℓ', x'), $\succcurlyeq(\ell', x')$, is separated from the technology set, $\hat{Z}$, by a straight line that has only the one point, (ℓ', x'), in common with $\hat{Z}$ and $\succcurlyeq(\ell', x')$. The straight line labeled

p' in figure 17.10 fulfills this requirement. It is called a *separating line* and it defines the set of prices that decentralize the Pareto optimum (ℓ', x'). In particular, any pair of prices for labor and food, w and p, whose ratio, w/p, is equal to the absolute value of the slope of the separating line is a decentralizing price system.

Given the price system defined by the separating line, the equal-profit lines for the producer are parallel to the separating line since they have slopes equal to $-w/p$. Consequently, the producer maximizes profit by choosing the point (ℓ', x'). Distribution of the profit to the consumer results in a budget line that is coincident with the separating line (see section 16.3). The consumer then maximizes utility by choosing (ℓ', x').

Although this example is simplistic and artificial, it illustrates a principle that holds in much more general economies: if a separating line exists,[3] it defines a price system that makes possible the decentralization of a Pareto-optimal allocation. Moreover, the critical condition that must be posited to assure the existence of a separating line is convexity of technology sets and preferences.[4] Thus, Koopmans [1957, p. 35] has summarized the matter succinctly by noting that the convexity assumptions "are in some sense minimum assumptions ensuring the existence of a price system that permits or sustains compatible and efficient decentralized decision making." We now turn to an illustration of the importance of the convexity assumptions.

Relaxing the Convexity Assumptions

In figure 17.11, the technology set of the producer is not convex. As a result, there does not exist a line through the Pareto-optimal allocation (ℓ', x') that separates Z and $\succcurlyeq (\ell', x')$. The nonexistence of a separating line implies that there is no price ratio for food and leisure that will induce the profit-maximizing producer to choose the Pareto-optimal allocation (ℓ', x'). At the price ratio

[3] In a more general economy, a separating hyperplane defines the price vector. The existence of a separating hyperplane is guaranteed by the convexity assumptions.

[4] Although we assume strict convexity, ordinary convexity would suffice for the existence of a separating hyperplane. However, relaxing the strict-convexity assumption to ordinary convexity would raise additional problems. One of these is that, without strict convexity, the separating hyperplane might have more than one point in common with the technology set or the no-worse-than-(ℓ', x') set, in which case the profit-maximizing production bundle and/or the utility-maximizing consumption bundle need not be unique. In this case, decentralizing the Pareto optimum requires the conveyance of information (additional to prices) to the decision-making agents (see the discussion below). In addition, if the strict-convexity assumption for consumer preferences were relaxed to ordinary convexity, we would have to add the regularity assumption (assumption 2.6) in order to guarantee that a Pareto optimum can be decentralized. Illustration of the need for this assumption in the absence of strict convexity, which is quite tricky, is left to the reader since this is a technical problem without much practical importance. We might also note that, by letting the consumption set be equal to the entire nonnegative quadrant, we have avoided another problem (referred to as the "Arrow exceptional case") in which the existence of a separating hyperplane does not imply decentralizability of the Pareto optimum. For additional discussion of these issues, the reader is referred to the excellent exposition by Koopmans [1957].

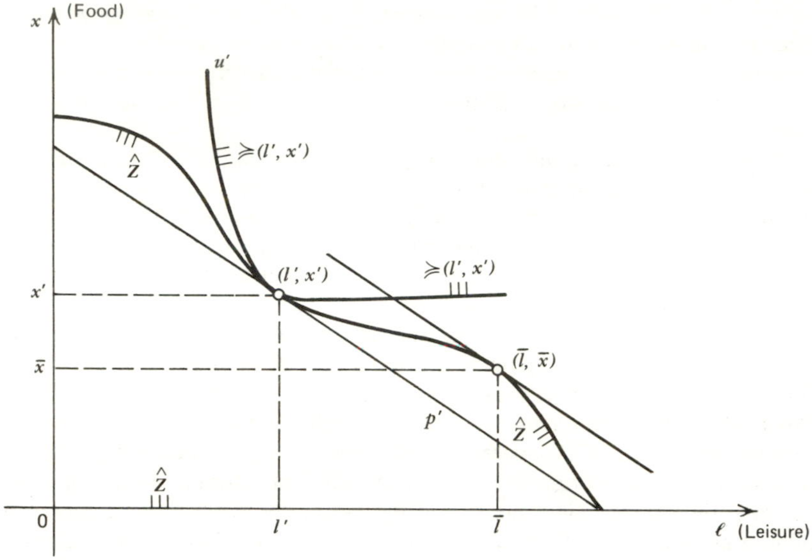

Figure 17.11

defined by the slope of the separating line that is tangent to the u' indifference curve at (ℓ', x'), labelled, p', the producer would choose $(\bar{\ell}, x)$ rather than (ℓ', x'). Thus, the Pareto optimum (ℓ', x') cannot be decentralized by a price system.

In figure 17.12, the preference ordering of the consumer is not convex and once again there is no separating line and there does not exist a price system that decentralizes the Pareto-optimal allocation (ℓ', x'). At the price ratio defined by the straight line in figure 17.14, the producer chooses (ℓ', x') but the consumer chooses $(\bar{\ell}, \bar{x})$. The market-clearing condition is not fulfilled and the Pareto optimum (ℓ', x') cannot be achieved as a competitive equilibrium.

Figures 17.13 and 17.14 illustrate situations in which the technology set and preference ordering, respectively, are convex but not strictly convex since they contain flat segments. In each case, a separating line exists, but the Pareto-optimal allocation (ℓ', x') is not necessarily achieved by means of the price system defined by the separating line. In figure 17.13, while the consumer chooses (ℓ', x'), the producer is not necessarily led to choose this bundle by the existing prices since all points on the line segment connecting $(\bar{\ell}, \bar{x})$ and $(\hat{\ell}, \hat{x})$ yield maximal profits. The producer must be instructed to choose (ℓ', x') by means of nonprice information; i.e., quantity information for food and leisure. Similarly, in figure 17.14 the producer chooses (ℓ', x') but the consumer is indifferent between the points on the line segment between $(\bar{\ell}, \bar{x})$ and $(\hat{\ell}, \hat{x})$. The Pareto-optimal allocation can only be achieved by supplying quantity information to the consumer.

To summarize, if each producer has a strictly convex technology set and if each consumer has a strictly convex ordering, every Pareto-optimal allocation

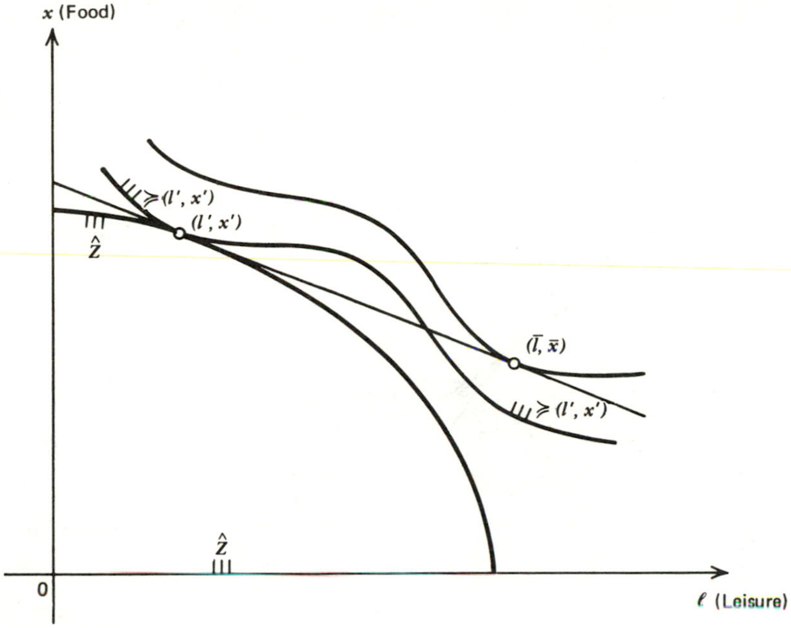

Figure 17.12

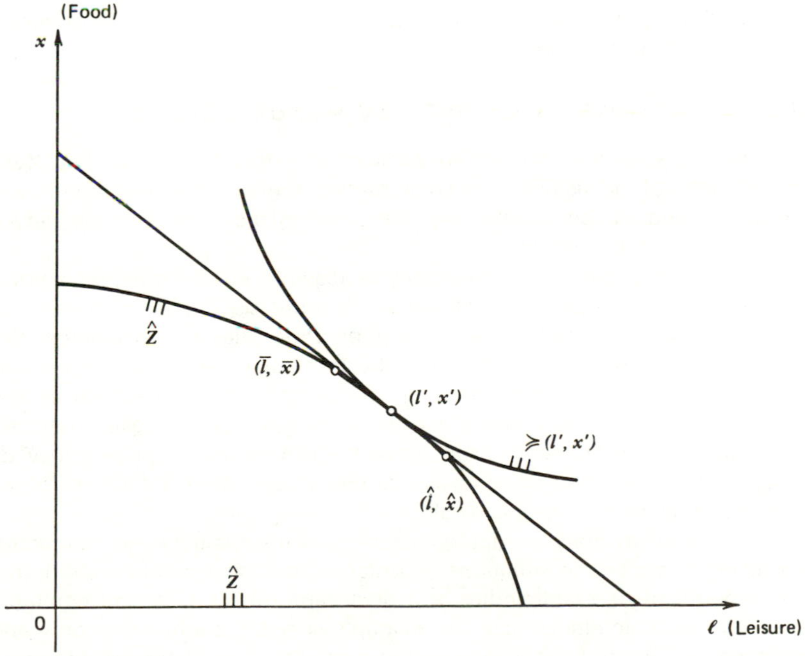

Figure 17.13

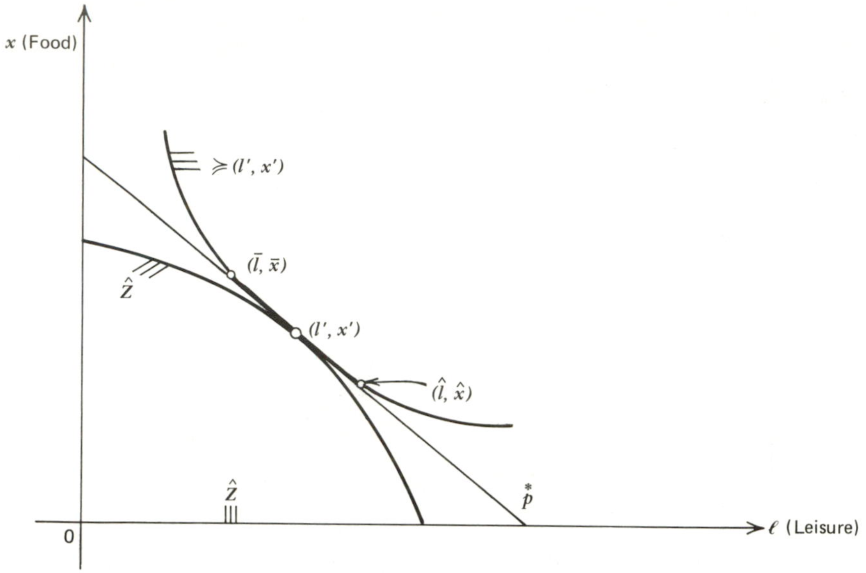

Figure 17.14

can be achieved as a competitive equilibrium. Decentralized decision making by means of the price system can be utilized to secure the economies of information that characterize a market system.

Restrictiveness of Convexity Assumptions

The convexity assumptions are somewhat restrictive because they assume away all types of indivisibilities in commodities, regions of increasing returns in production, and anticomplementary (or antagonistic) relationships between commodities in consumption.

If the net output of a commodity is feasible in two different amounts, convexity (or strict convexity) of the technology set implies that *any* intermediate amount is feasible. The assumption thus rules out production technologies that incorporate resources in the form of large pieces of indivisible capital equipment (steel mills, etc.). Convexity of a technology set excludes increasing returns to scale and strict convexity implies decreasing returns to scale (see section 9.4). Insofar as increasing returns to scale can be achieved by means of large indivisible units of capital equipment, the justification for strict convexity of technology sets is weak.

Anticomplementary (or antagonistic) relationships between commodities in consumption refers to situations in which a consumer would prefer either a given amount of one commodity *or* a given amount of a second commodity rather than both simultaneously. For example, a hostess who cares only about the largest number of people she can serve on *matching* plates would consider

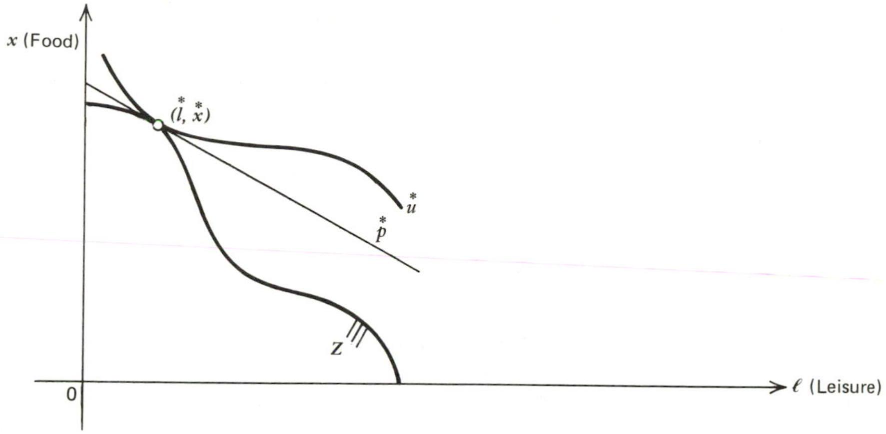

Figure 17.15

plates with alternative patterns to be anticomplements. Insofar as such phenomena exist, nonconvexities in the preference ordering result.

It should be noted that strict convexity of preference orderings and technology sets is not a necessary condition for the conclusion of the second optimality principle—it is only sufficient. That is, it is possible to have Pareto optima which can be decentralized by price systems even if the strict convexity assumptions are not satisfied. Figure 17.15 illustrates the decentralization of a Pareto optimum when neither the technology set nor the preference ordering is convex.

17.5 CONCLUDING REMARKS

The above characterization of the role of a price system in decentralizing a Pareto-optimal allocation is overly glib. For a number of reasons, the price system is not as omnipotent as the above discussion would indicate. In the first place, nothing has been said about how the equilibrium price vector is arrived at. We have only discussed efficient decentralization of decision making given the existence of such a price vector. The information that a central authority would need in order to announce the equilibrium prices to attain a specific Pareto optimum are equivalent to the informational requirements for the dictation of input, output, and consumption quotas. Faith in the competitive price system's efficacy in generating Pareto-optimal states of the economy must therefore rest on the belief that there are equilibrating forces which tend to cause the prices in a competitive system to converge to the equilibrium vector (see section 16.6).

There are other important reasons why a price system might fail to allocate resources optimally. The previous section demonstrates that nonconvexities in consumption or in production breach the nexus between competitive equilibrium and Pareto optimality.[5] Chapter 18 examines the problem of the failure of competitive markets to allocate resources optimally when externalities (such as pollution) and public commodities (such as many government services) exist.

EXERCISES

17.1 The non-Pareto optimality of monopoly equilibrium in an exchange economy was illustrated in section 17.2. Suppose that the monopolist, instead of simply setting a price and letting the price taker choose a consumption bundle, were to exercise his market power by making a take-it-or-leave-it offer of *both* price and quantity—i.e., a take-it-or-leave-it offer of a trade. Suppose further that the price taker accepts any offer that does not lower his utility.

a. Illustrate the optimal take-it-or-leave-it offer of the monopolist.

b. Explain the Pareto-optimality characteristics of the resultant allocation.

c. This solution to the resource-allocation problem is sometimes referred to as the "perfect-price-discrimination" solution (see exercise 13.6). Why?

17.2 Use the consumption box diagram to illustrate that

a. Pareto-optimal allocations are not necessarily decentralizable if one (or both) of the preference orderings is not convex, and

b. convexity of preferences is not *necessary* for decentralizability of a Pareto optimum.

17.3* A state of the (exchange) economy $\overset{*}{x}$ is *weakly Pareto optimal* if there is no alternative state $\hat{x}$ satisfying $\hat{x}^c \succ \overset{*}{x}^c$ for *all* c. Prove that, so long as the preferences satisfy the regularity (2.6) and nonsatiation (3.1) assumptions, weak Pareto optimality and Pareto optimality are equivalent.

[5] This chapter treats the nexus between competitive equilibrium and Pareto optimality dichotomously—that is, we have only considered the two possibilities of competitive equilibrium being Pareto optimal or not Pareto optimal and the two possibilities of a Pareto optimum being decentralizable or not decentralizable. An alternative approach is to examine how "close" a competitive equilibrium is to being Pareto optimal and how "close" a price system comes to decentralizing a Pareto optimum. For example, Starr [1969] has shown that the second optimality principle remains approximately true if the nonconvexity is "small" relative to the size of the economy. Similarly, Emmerson [1972] has shown that the distance between a competitive-equilibrium allocation and the closest Pareto optimum can be bounded in a way that is related to the size of the indivisibilities in consumption.

* Starred exercises are relatively more difficult.

CHAPTER 18
THE THEORY OF ECONOMIC EXTERNALITIES AND PUBLIC COMMODITIES

18.1 INTRODUCTION

The previous chapter examines the nexus between general competitive equilibrium and Pareto-optimal states of the economy. Arrow states this nexus in terms of the fundamental principles of welfare economics:

> *When the assumptions of* [*the first optimality principle*] *are valid, then the case for the competitive price system is strongest. Any complaints about its operation can be reduced to complaints about the distribution of income, which should then be rectified by lump-sum transfers. Of course, as Pareto already emphasized, the proposition provides no basis for accepting the results of the market in the absence of accepted levels of income equality* (*Arrow* [1971]).

At the same time, it is important to realize that the economy we have been dealing with is an abstract representation of a real economic and social system. Many important economic and social phenomena are not considered within the context of this abstract model of general competitive equilibrium. This chapter considers some important economic phenomena that are excluded from the competitive-equilibrium model developed in the preceding three chapters.

All commodities that have been analyzed in the previous chapters share two properties. First the consumption or use in production by one economic agent of a particular unit of that commodity precludes the simultaneous consumption or use in production by other agents of the identical unit. Two consumers cannot both consume the identical unit of bread and two producers cannot simultaneously utilize in production the identical unit of labor. A commodity with this property is called *a rival commodity*. Commodities that do not have this property are *nonrival* commodities. For example, two or more consumers can simultaneously consume the same unit of "national defense."

A second property of the commodities analyzed in previous chapters is *excludability*; it is possible to prevent any consumer or producer from consuming or using in production a given unit of a commodity. The excludability property of a commodity makes it possible for consumers and producers to engage in mutually beneficial exchanges. If consumer 1 can exclude consumer 2 from consuming a unit of bread, and consumer 2 can do the same with respect to beer, the exchange of bread for beer may be the only way in which both consumers can achieve preferred commodity bundles. A commodity which is both rival and excludable is called a *private commodity*. There are, however, commodities that do not share the excludability property. Air and water pollution are commodities which are nonexcludable in consumption and production. Consumers cannot exclude pollution from the air that they must consume.

In this chapter we analyze the consequences for the nexus between competitive equilibrium and Pareto-optimal allocations of commodities that are nonrival and those that are nonexcludable. These commodities are known in the literature as *public commodities* and *externalities*, respectively.

Thus, an *externality* is said to exist when a decision variable of one consumer or producer cannot be excluded from entering directly into the utility or production function of some other consumer or producer. A common example is air or water pollution that is an output of one producer and enters into the utility or production functions of other consumers or producers. This example is a *negative externality* since the consumption of pollution might be presumed to reduce the utilities or profits of consumers or producers. An example of a *positive externality* is the often-cited case of bees and nectar. Bees raised by a producer of honey pollinate the trees of nearby producers of fruit. In this way, the profits of fruit producers are directly related to the number of bees kept by the honey producer. Similarly, a display of flowers in a garden is a positive externality to consumers who pass by.

Externalities and public commodities are not mutually exclusive concepts. An externality can be either rival or nonrival and a public commodity can be either excludable or nonexcludable. Pollution, for example, is a substantially nonrival externality since my suffering from poor air quality does not diminish your discomfort. On the other hand, my appreciation of someone's flower garden might be substantially diminished by the crowding effect of large numbers of sightseers.

Similarly, public commodities like national defense and public health programs (such as mosquito eradication programs and vaccination programs) redound, nonexcludably, to the benefit of all in the commodity. On the other hand, public parks are excludable since individuals can be excluded or charged an entry fee.

Nonrival, nonexcludable commodities are called *public externalities*.

The foregoing classification is summarized as follows:[1]

[1] In actual practice the distinctions between these concepts can be very fuzzy. For example, consumers can exclude air pollution by moving to a location with cleaner air. For the discussion of the theoretical issues in this chapter, however, clear-cut distinctions between the four types of commodities are quite helpful. We might mention, however, that a commodity which completely satisfies the property of nonrivalness (*each* consumer consumes the *total* amount available) is sometimes called a *pure* public commodity.

	Excludable	Nonexcludable
Rival	Private Commodity	Private Externality
Nonrival	Public Commodity	Public Externality

The remainder of this chapter demonstrates that the relationships between competitive equilibrium and Pareto optimality break down if externalities or public commodities exist, and goes on to examine possible solutions to the problems created by these phenomena. Externalities and public commodities are taken up respectively in sections 18.2 and 18.3. Section 18.4 discusses the problem of implementing procedures that correct for the resource misallocation caused by the existence of externalities and/or public commodities. Section 18.5 concludes with some remarks on the implications of uncertainty for the link between Pareto optimality and competitive equilibrium.

18.2 ECONOMIC EXTERNALITIES

Pareto Optimality and Economic Externalities

The breach of the nexus between competitive equilibrium and Pareto optimality in the presence of economic externalities can be illustrated adequately in a highly simplified economy with a single consumer, two producers, two produced commodities, and one primary commodity (labor/leisure time). The consumer is endowed with γ units of leisure, consumes ℓ units, and supplies the difference, $\gamma - \ell$, to the two producers in exchange for the two produced commodities. The single consumer owns both production units. Finally, we assume that the externality takes place in the production technology in the sense that the output of producer 1 depends upon the output of producer 2 (as well as labor input).

The production functions of the two producers have images,

$$q_1 = f^1(L^1, q_2) \tag{18.1a}$$

and

$$q_2 = f^2(L^2), \tag{18.1b}$$

where $L^r (r = 1, 2)$ is the quantity of labor used by the rth producer. The economic externality is reflected by the nonexcludable presence of q_2 in the production function f^1. If f^1 is increasing (decreasing) in q_2, equation (18.1a) reflects a positive (negative) externality.

The equilibrium, or market-clearing, condition for labor/leisure time is

$$L^1 + L^2 + \ell = \gamma. \tag{18.2}$$

The state of the economy $(q_1, q_2, \ell, L^1, L^2)$ must satisfy equations (18.1) and (18.2).

A state of the economy is Pareto optimal if it maximizes the consumer's utility, $U(q_1, q_2, \ell)$, subject to (18.1) and (18.2). The (interior) solution to this optimization problem is obtained by setting the first derivatives of the Lagrange expression,

$$L(q_1, q_2, \ell, L^1, L^2, \lambda_1, \lambda_2, \lambda_3) = U(q_1, q_2, \ell) + \lambda_1(q_1 - f^1(L^1, q_2)) + \lambda_2(q_2 - f^2(L^2)) + \lambda_3(\gamma - L^1 - L^2 - \ell),$$

equal to zero. Carrying out the required differentiation and taking ratios, we obtain

$$\frac{\partial U(q_1, q_2, \ell)/\partial q_1}{\partial U(q_1, q_2, \ell)/\partial \ell} = \frac{1}{\partial f^1(L^1, q_2)/\partial L^1} \tag{18.3a}$$

and

$$\frac{\partial U(q_1, q_2, \ell)/\partial q_2}{\partial U(q_1, q_2, \ell)/\partial \ell} = \frac{1}{df^2(L^2)/dL^2} - \frac{\partial f^1(L^1, q_2)/\partial q_2}{\partial f^1(L^1, q_2)/\partial L^1} \tag{18.3b}$$

Conditions (18.3) characterize Pareto optimality. In order to characterize the competitive equilibrium, let p_1, p_2, and w represent the prices of the two produced commodities and labor/leisure time, respectively. The consumer maximizes his utility subject to the constraint $p_1 q_1 + p_2 q_2 = w(\gamma - \ell)$. Assuming that the solution to this utility-maximization problem is interior, the following conditions must be satisfied:

$$\frac{\partial U(q_1, q_2, \ell)/\partial q_1}{\partial U(q_1, q_2, \ell)/\partial \ell} = \frac{p_1}{w} \tag{18.4a}$$

and

$$\frac{\partial U(q_1, q_2, \ell)/\partial q_2}{\partial U(q_1, q_2, \ell)/\partial \ell} = \frac{p_2}{w}. \tag{18.4b}$$

The two producers maximize profit, $\pi^r = p_r q_r - wL^r$, $r = 1, 2$, subject to their respective production functions. First-order conditions for interior solutions to these profit-maximization problems are as follows:

$$p_1 \frac{\partial f^1(L^1, q_2)}{\partial L^1} = w \tag{18.5a}$$

and

$$p_2 \frac{df^2(L^2)}{\partial L^2} = w. \tag{18.5b}$$

We can now show that the competitive equilibrium, characterized by equations (18.4)–(18.5), does not satisfy the necessary conditions, (18.3), for the competitive-equilibrium allocation to be Pareto optimal. Solving (18.5) for p_1/w and p_2/w and substituting into (18.4), we obtain

$$\frac{\partial U(q_1, q_2, \ell)/\partial q_2}{\partial U(q_1, q_2, \ell)/\partial \ell} = \frac{1}{\partial f^1(L^1, q_2)/\partial L^1} \tag{18.6a}$$

and

$$\frac{\partial U(q_1, q_2, \ell)/\partial q_2}{\partial U(q_1, q_2, \ell)/\partial \ell} = \frac{1}{df^2(L^2)/dL^2}. \tag{18.6b}$$

Comparison of the conditions (18.6), which are implied by the competitive-equilibrium conditions, with the Pareto-optimality conditions (18.3), reveals that they differ by the second term on the right-hand side of (18.3b). Note that this term vanishes if

$$\frac{\partial f^1(L^1, q_2)}{\partial q_2} = 0; \tag{18.7}$$

that is, if the externality vanishes. Moreover, the sign of this partial derivative, and hence of the second term in equation (18.3b), depends upon whether the technology is characterized by a positive or a negative externality. In the former case, the partial derivative is positive, and in the latter it is negative. Thus, if we are dealing with a positive externality, the marginal rate of substitution of the second produced commodity for leisure in the competitive equilibrium is too high (relative to the Pareto optimum), indicating that the consumer can be made better off by substituting commodity 2 for leisure. Similarly, if we are dealing with a negative externality, this marginal rate of substitution is too *low* in the competitive equilibrium, indicating that the consumer could be made better off by substituting leisure for commodity 2. The upshot of this discussion, therefore, is that if there is a positive (negative) externality, not enough (too much) of the second commodity is produced.

The breach between Pareto optimality and competitive equilibrium in the presence of this externality in production can be further explicated by examining the producers' profit-maximization conditions. Substitution of (18.4) into (18.3) and rearrangement yields the following characterization of a Pareto-optimal allocation:

$$p_1 \frac{\partial f^1(L^1, q_2)}{\partial L^1} = w \tag{18.8a}$$

and

$$p_2 \frac{df^2(L^2)}{dL^2} = w - w \frac{\partial f^1(L^1, q_2)}{\partial q_2} \frac{df^2(L^2)/dL^2}{\partial f^1(L^1, q_2)/\partial L^1}. \tag{18.8b}$$

It will be noted that (18.8a) corresponds to the profit-maximization condition, (18.5a), for the first producer. However, equation (18.8b) differs from the profit-maximization condition (18.5b) by the second term on the right-hand side. Again, this term would vanish in the absence of economic externalities. Note, in particular, that if we are dealing with a positive externality, in which case the sign of the derivative in (18.7) is positive, the adjustment factor in (18.8b) is negative, indicating that the competitive-equilibrium value of the marginal product of labor in producing commodity 2 is too high (relative to the value required for Pareto optimality). Since the value of the marginal product must be falling with respect to output increases (in order for second-order conditions to be satisfied), it follows that too little labor is utilized in producing commodity 2 and hence that not enough of this commodity is produced. The reason for this, of course, is that producer 2 does not take into account the salutary effect that his production has on the production possibilities of producer 1. Similarly, if the sign of the derivative in (18.7) is negative, reflecting a negative externality, the competitive-equilibrium value of the marginal product of labor in producing commodity 2 is too *low*, indicating that *too much* labor is utilized in producing this commodity. Again, the reason why this is true of the competitive equilibrium is that producer 2 does not take into account in his profit-maximization decision the detrimental effect that his production has on the production possibilities of producer 1.

Although somewhat complicated, the adjustment factor in (18.8b) can be interpreted. The direct externality effect, multiplied by the marginal product of labor in producing commodity 1,

$$\frac{\partial f^1(L^1, q_2)}{\partial q_2}\frac{df^2(L^2)}{dL^2},$$

measures (differentially) the increase (or decrease) in the output of commodity 1 attributable to the external effect of producer 2 utilizing an additional increment of labor. The inverse of the marginal product of labor in producing commodity 1,

$$\frac{1}{\partial f^1(L^1, q_2)/\partial L^1},$$

measures the reduction in labor input of producer 1 that is made possible by reducing the output of commodity 1 by one unit. Consequently, the product of these two, as the term in (18.8b),

$$\frac{\partial f^1(L^1, q_2)}{\partial q_2}\frac{df^2(L^2)/dL^2}{\partial f^1(L^1, q_2)/\partial L^1},$$

measures the external effect that changes in the output of producer 2 have upon the amount of labor required by producer 1 to produce a given output. Multiplication by w converts this measure into units of dollars per unit of labor. The direction of this effect, of course, depends upon whether we are dealing with a positive or a negative externality.

The breach between Pareto optimality and competitive equilibrium illustrated for the simple case where the output of producer 2 affects the production of producer 1 can as easily be illustrated for the case in which *each* producer generates an externality that affects the other producer's production. Moreover, by distinguishing between consumption and production, the effect of an externality in which the production of one or both producers affects directly the consumer's utility can be worked out in the same manner as above. Finally, by considering the case where there is more than one consumer, one can illustrate the breach between competitive equilibrium and Pareto optimality caused by *consumption* externalities (i.e., the consumption of one consumer cannot be excluded from affecting the utility of others). In each case the algebra is similar to the above; we therefore leave these calculations to exercises 18.1 and 18.2.

The above analysis demonstrates that a competitive-equilibrium allocation is not Pareto optimal since the second producer does not take the economic externality into account in his decision making. If an agreement could be reached by the two producers so that they maximize profits while taking into account the economic externality, a Pareto-optimal production allocation could be achieved. For example, with only two producers and an easily identifiable externality, an incentive exists for merger and joint-profit maximization. With a larger number of producers there is an incentive for an arrangement whereby each producer pays for the externality rendered by other producers. If the externalities are priced correctly, the production decisions satisfy the marginal conditions for a Pareto-optimal allocation. In short, economic externalities do not pose an insurmountable problem for the definition of prices that correctly specify the marginal rates of substitution in consumption and rates of technical substitution in production. Commodity prices can be corrected to reflect external effects. The problem is to find an institutional mechanism that decentralizes the production allocation. This problem is primarily attributable to the very nature of externalities: nonexcludability. The producer of a positive externality cannot exclude consumers or other producers from benefiting; consequently, it is impossible for him to sell the positive externality and the appropriate market fails to come into being. This scenario suggests another way of characterizing externalities; namely, as the lack of a "property right," which in turn explains the nonexistence of a market that is needed for Pareto optimality. The next subsection discusses the absence of property rights.

Absence of Property Rights

In the absence of a property right that allows agents to exclude themselves from the effects of a negative externality, or to preclude others from enjoying a positive externality that they generate, no market for the externality can be formed.

In order to illustrate this point, consider a community in which there are no property rights over the use of land and no institutional arrangements for the disposal of garbage. In the absence of such property rights, individuals might dump their garbage in the vicinities of other households. If, however, the amount of money that some persons would be willing to pay to dispose of their garbage in the vicinity of someone else's house exceeded the amount of monetary compensation that would entice some households to endure garbage in their neighborhood, the potential would exist for a mutually beneficial exchange. However, given that property rights are not assigned to the members of the community, no market would arise. If, however, a property right that held each individual responsible for his own garbage were established, the (private) externality would be transformed into a private commodity and a market would be established. In the absence of other imperfections, the outcome should be a Pareto-optimal allocation of resources (including the waste-disposal capacity of the environment).

A second example of the effect of the absence of a property right on the optimality of competitive equilibrium is furnished by commodities produced from "common-property" replenishable resources such as ocean fisheries, hunting grounds, grazing land for livestock, and groundwater supplies. The management of fisheries has long been beset by difficulties traceable to the common-property feature of this resource (see the part IV suggested reading). The externality in this market appears as the effect of the fishing effort of one producer upon the technology of other producers. There is a direct relation between the amount of fish that can be caught with a given amount of inputs (capital and labor) and the biomass of fish in a free-access fishery. The production technology can be defined over the amount of fish, the amount of capital and labor, and the biomass. By increasing the catch of fish, a producer reduces the fish population and increases the amount of capital and labor required to produce a given quantity of fish. Due to the absence of a property right (common-property status), producers consider the biomass to be a free resource beyond their control. Thus, the competitive equilibrium results in each producer utilizing more labor and capital than is necessary to produce a given amount of fish (year after year). The production allocation might not be Pareto optimal since the same annual output might be produced with less capital and labor if a property right to the biomass were established.

The close relationship between the absence of a market and the existence of an externality can be illustrated in the context of the simple algebraic example of an externality developed above. The competitive-equilibrium solution to the resource allocation problem in that example is not Pareto optimal due to the fact that the production of commodity 2 has a direct side effect on the technology set of producer 1 (e.g., pollution of the environment or pollination of fruit trees). This side effect can be viewed as a commodity for which there is no market. More specifically, we could let $\gamma(q_2)$ be the quantity of this nonmarketed commodity. However, as this quantity is a function of q_2, the production technology of producer 1 is a function of q_2, as in equation (18.1a). Consequently, no essentials are lost if we presume that q_2 and $\gamma(q_2)$ are identical.[2]

Suppose that a market for the externality arises. This might happen because the producer is given property rights over the environment, or the bee keeper is given property rights over the pollination. Alternatively, producer 1 might find a mechanism for paying producer 2 to restrict his polluting production process (thus repairing the damaged environment), or to produce more honey (thus generating greater pollination of producer 1's fruit trees). In any case, the emergence of a market results in the establishment of a market price for the externality; this price is negative in the case of a negative externality and positive in the case of a positive externality.

[2] Formally, it would suffice in what follows to suppose that $\gamma(q_2) = a + bq_2$ where a and b are parameters.

Letting p_{12} be the price paid by producer 1 to producer 2 for the externality, the profit-maximization problems become

$$\max_{L^1, q_2} \; p_1 f^1(L^1, q_2) - wL^1 - p_{12} q_2$$

and

$$\max_{L^2} \; p_2 f^2(L^2) - wL^2 + p_{12} f^2(L^2).$$

(Remember that $p_{12} > 0$ in the case of a positive externality and $p_{12} < 0$ in the case of a negative externality; i.e., producer 1 pays for the positive externality or is compensated for the negative externality.)[3]

The first-order profit-maximization conditions are as follows:

$$p_1 \frac{\partial f^1(L^1, q_2)}{\partial L^1} - w = 0, \tag{18.9a}$$

$$p_1 \frac{\partial f^1(L^1, q_2)}{\partial q_2} - p_{12} = 0, \tag{18.9b}$$

and

$$p_2 \frac{df^2(L^2)}{dL^2} - w + p_{12} \frac{df^2(L^2)}{dL^2} = 0. \tag{18.9c}$$

Substituting (18.9b) into (18.9c) and solving for p_1/w and p_2/w, we obtain

$$\frac{p_1}{w} = \frac{1}{\partial f^1(L^1, q_2)/\partial L^1} \tag{18.10a}$$

and

$$\frac{p_2}{w} = \frac{1}{df^2(L^2)/dL^2} - \frac{\partial f^1(L^1, q_2)/\partial q_2}{\partial f^1(L^1, q_2)/\partial L^1}. \tag{18.10b}$$

Substitution of (18.10) into (18.4) yields the Pareto-optimality conditions (18.3).

The foregoing calculations illustrate the fact that, if a market for the externality exists, the resultant equilibrium is Pareto optimal. This suggests that the establishment of property rights is a panacea for the problems caused by the existence of externalities. There are, however, several reasons why the establishment of a property right might fail to solve those problems. In the remainder of this section, we discuss three of them: (1) the possibility that nonconvexities of preferences or technologies (which, it will be recalled, breach

[3] If, alternatively, producer 1 pays producer 2 p_{12} for each unit that he reduces his output below the (competitive-equilibrium) level $\bar{q}_2$, say, the optimization problems become $\max_{L^1, q_2} p_1 f^1(L^1, q_2) - wL^1 - p_{12}(\bar{q}_2 - q_2)$ and $\max_{L^2} p_2 f^2(L^2) - wL^2 + p_{12}(\bar{q}_2 - q_2)$. It is left to the reader to show that the following conclusions are unchanged by this alternative formulation.

the nexus between competitive equilibrium and Pareto optimality) are *fundamental* to markets for externalities; (2) the possibility that the transaction costs of establishing and operating a market for externalities exceed the potential gains to the market participants; and (3) the possibility that the number of agents that are affected by the externality or that generate the externality is so small that competitive markets cannot operate. (A fourth reason why the externality market might fail to work is that it is often impossible or undesirable to exclude nonpaying individuals from benefiting from the reduction of a negative externality or the generation of a positive externality; i.e., many, indeed most, externalities have the nonrivalry property of a public commodity. The public-commodity problem is discussed in detail in section 18.3.)

Nonconvexities in the Production and Consumption of Externalities

One reason a market may fail to function properly is the existence of fundamental nonconvexities in the production and/or consumption of externalities. Consider the example of a farmer who produces food and whose crops are subject to damage by wandering cattle kept by a local herdsman. Figure 18.1 illustrates a "pseudotechnology" set of the farmer, in which the level of the externality (the number of units of cattle on the farmer's land) is measured along the horizontal axis and the profit along the vertical axis. As the level of the externality increases, profit from the production of food falls at an increasing rate. Consequently, the psuedotechnology set is convex for levels of the externality less than or equal to $\hat{E}$, where the profits vanish. However, as

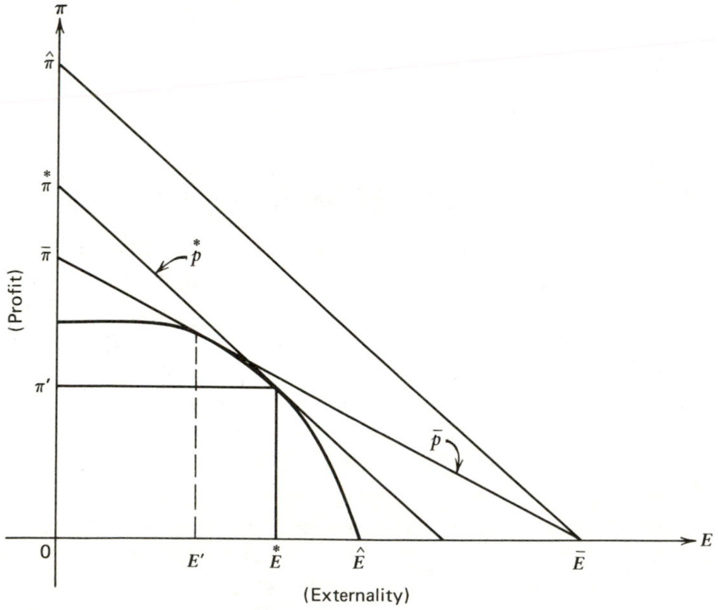

Figure 18.1

the farmland can absorb additional cattle beyond the point $\hat{E}$, the technology set includes a segment of the horizontal axis beyond $\hat{E}$. In particular, suppose that the farmland can absorb additional units of cattle up to the point $\bar{E}$. The pseudotechnology set of the farmer is therefore given by the convex set for externalities less than or equal to $\hat{E}$ *plus* the spike from $\hat{E}$ to $\bar{E}$. It is apparent therefore that the pseudotechnology set of the farmer is nonconvex, since a straight line drawn from a point on the spike $\hat{E}\bar{E}$ to any point in the technology set that is not on the horizontal axis is not entirely contained in the psuedotechnology set.

Assume that the farmer has the property right to the externality; that is, he can collect a price from the herdsman for the destruction of his crops by wandering cattle. The slope of the straight lines in figure 18.1 reflect two possible prices of the externality. If a market for the externality comes into existence and the price $\overset{*}{p}$ is established, the farmer could absorb $\overset{*}{E}$ of the externality and earn a profit of π' from the production of food. The total profit of the farmer resulting from the production of food and sale of externalities would then be equal to $\overset{*}{\pi} = \pi' + \overset{*}{p}\overset{*}{E}$. This price, however, could not be a market-equilibrium price since the profit of the farmer is not maximized at $(\pi', \overset{*}{E})$. At the price $\overset{*}{p}$, the farmer could increase his profit to $\hat{\pi}$ by ceasing the production of food and accepting the maximum number of cattle wandering upon his land, $\bar{E}$. In fact, at any price greater than $\bar{p}$, the farmer would always maximize profit by ceasing the production of food and selling $\bar{E}$ externality rights.

The externality supply curve of the farmer, derived from figure 18.1, is illustrated in figure 18.2. For externality prices below $\bar{p}$, the supply curve is continuous and upward sloping. However, at $\bar{p}$ the farmer's supply of externality rights jumps to $\bar{E}$; the result is a discontinuity in the supply curve.

Given the nonconvexity in the production of externalities and the resulting discontinuity in the externality-right supply function, an equilibrium might not

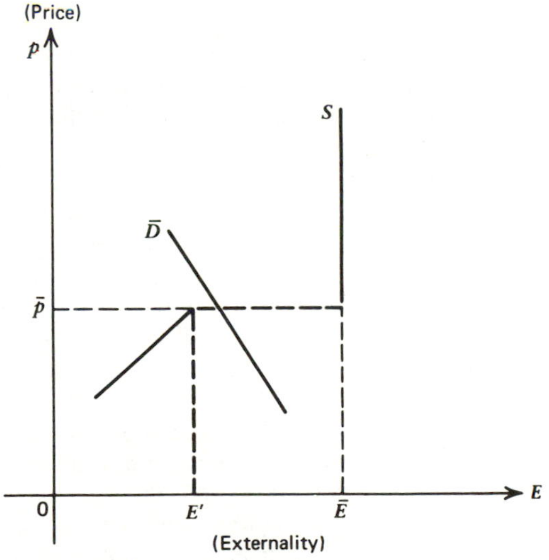

Figure 18.2

exist for this market. If the demand curve of the herdsman passes through the gap of the supply-curve discontinuity (e.g., $\bar{D}$ in figure 18.2), there is no market equilibrium; at every price below $\bar{p}$, quantity demanded exceeds quantity supplied and at every price equal to or greater than $\bar{p}$, quantity supplied exceeds quantity demanded. Thus, in the presence of fundamental nonconvexities in production externalities, the establishment of property rights might not solve the externality problem.

The problem of fundamental nonconvexities is equally applicable to a consumer who swims in a river into which producers dump their effluents. Beyond a particular level of pollution, the consumer will cease swimming in the river altogether. Suppose that the consumer's preference ordering is defined over swimming, pollution, and all other commodities. Assume that it is possible to compensate the consumer by a sufficiently large amount of other commodities to induce him to give up swimming entirely. If the consumer is endowed with the property right for pollution and the market comes into existence, the price of pollution will be negative. That is, those economic agents generating pollution will have to pay the consumer for absorbing their output. With a negative price for pollution, the consumer could offer to sell an arbitrarily large amount of pollution rights and attain a commodity bundle with zero swimming and an arbitrarily large amount of all other commodities. Thus, with the consumer as the recipient of an externality, the same nonconvexity problem arises and there is no assurance that a market that has an equilibrium will come into existence.

In short, both production and consumption externalities may well involve fundamental nonconvexities that would render the usual analysis of general economic equilibrium irrelevant since there may be no equilibrium that involves an efficient allocation of resources.

Transaction Costs

Transaction costs are explicitly assumed to be absent in the theory of general competitive equilibrium considered above (see assumption 15.2). However, in the establishment of markets for externalities, transaction costs appear to be fundamental. Consider the example of garbage allocation introduced above. With the establishment of a property right in garbage, a market might come into existence if the price that economic agents are willing to pay to get rid of garbage exceeds the price that other economic agents are willing to accept to absorb garbage. If, however, the transaction cost incurred to run this market (i.e., to negotiate and to transfer the garbage from one group of economic agents to another) exceeds the potential profit, no garbage will be exchanged and the market will remain inactive. However, as the property right requires each agent to be responsible for his or her own garbage, no externality will appear. Furthermore, as long as the transaction technology sets are convex, the general competitive equilibrium will be efficient with regard to that transaction technology. That is, the introduction of transaction costs into the general competitive model will not change the relationship between competitive equilibrium and Pareto-optimal allocations so long as the transaction technologies satisfy the convexity assumptions.

It seems more likely, however, that transaction technologies will involve substantial fixed costs and are, therefore, not likely to satisfy the convexity assumptions. That is, the amount of resources required to exchange one unit of garbage might not be significantly less than the resources required to carry out the exchange of a greater number of units. The marginal transaction cost is therefore diminishing, violating the convexity assumptions required for the second optimality principle. Thus, even with the existence of property rights, so long as a market is characterized by transaction costs that violate the convexity assumptions, the market may be inactive *and* fail to achieve an optimal allocation of resources.

Small Number of Buyers and Sellers

The principal rationale for the assumption of price-taking behavior which underlies the competitive-equilibrium model is the existence of large numbers of buyers and sellers. Unfortunately, small numbers of buyers and sellers would appear to be endemic to markets for private externalities. This characteristic of externality markets can be characterized by recalling our original definition of a private externality as the presence of a decision variable of one economic agent—in particular, a rival commodity—in a utility or production function of another. Thus, a private externality variable, in principle, requires *three* identification subscripts; e.g., x_{ijk} can represent the amount of the kth commodity consumed by individual j that enters into the ith individual's utility function. Clearly, each commodity has exactly one buyer and one seller. Consequently, there is little reason to believe that the establishment of property rights will result in a competitive equilibrium that achieves a Pareto-optimal allocation of resources.[4]

Externality Taxes and Subsidies

Much of the foregoing discussion is predicated on the intrinsic relationship between externalities and the absence of property rights, and therefore concentrates on the establishment of property rights and the resultant emergence of a market as a possible remedy for dealing with externalities. Markets that are established by the conferral of property rights are sometimes referred to as "artificial" markets. An alternative remedy, first suggested in 1920 by Pigou, is the use of externality taxes and subsidies by the government (or other central authority). This remedy avoids such problems as small numbers of participants and transaction costs that may prevent artificial markets from correctly pricing an externality commodity. The government taxes beneficiaries of positive externalities or generators of negative externalities and subsidizes generators of positive externalities or victims of negative externalities. For example, in the case of a positive externality, the government chooses a per-unit tax equal to the loss to the victims for a marginal unit of the externality. The herdsmen in the cattle example are taxed, for each unit of cattle that they allow on the farmer's land, an

[4] Nonrival, or public, externalities are another matter (large numbers of individuals generate and are affected by air pollution); however, nonrivalness creates additional problems, which are discussed in section 18.3.

amount determined by the marginal damage to the farmer's crop yield. Similarly, producers are taxed per unit of pollution according to the marginal loss to swimmers of an additional unit of pollution.

The government may transfer the tax revenues to the externality victims—also referred to as the parties with externality rights—in accordance with the marginal losses attributable to the externality. Such transfers are not, however, required to achieve a Pareto-optimal allocation. When the budget of the tax agency is balanced, equilibrium is established if there are no nonconvexities in production. It should be apparent that the resulting allocation is identical to that established by the emergence of an (artificial) externality market and is therefore Pareto optimal. To see this, return to the algebraic example of section 18.2 above. The marginal (monetary) damage to producer 1 of the externality generated by producer 2 is $p_1\, \partial f^1(L^1, q_2)/\partial q_2 < 0$. Thus, the externality tax is equal to the negative of this value, evaluated at the optimal values of L^1 and q_2. Recall, however, from equation (18.9b) that the externality price in the artificial-market equilibrium is also equal to this expression. Moreover, (18.9c) represents the first-order profit-maximization condition for producer 2 regardless of whether p_{12} is an externality price (paid to producer 1) or a government tax. Finally, in either case, $p_{12}q_2$ is transferred from producer 2 to producer 1. Thus, given full convexity and many buyers and sellers, the establishment of either artificial markets or taxation schemes generates the identical (Pareto-optimal) allocation of resources (see exercise 18.3).

Either solution requires a clear definition of which economic agents have the rights to the externality. The optimality of the resulting allocation is not affected by whether the rights are given to the economic agent responsible for the externality or to the economic agent affected by the externality. On the other hand, the endowment of the rights to the externality obviously affects the resulting distribution of income. Note, however, that it is not sufficient merely to subsidize (tax) the economic agent affected by the external diseconomy (economy) without taxing (subsidizing) the agent responsible for the external diseconomy (economy). Pareto optimality requires that the agent responsible for the externality take this into account in his decision making.

It was pointed out earlier in this section that in the absence of full convexity, an artificial market scheme might fail to lead to an equilibrium that is Pareto optimal. Can a taxation scheme be successfully utilized to remedy the externality? Figure 18.1 suggests that there are two possible tax/subsidy equilibria. Suppose that the government informs the farmer that there are to be $\overset{*}{E}$ head of cattle on his land. The farmer announces his marginal loss, and when that tax $\overset{*}{p}$ is imposed on the herdsman, he wants to keep $\overset{*}{E}$ head of cattle. Thus, equilibrium is established. On the other hand, there is a second possible equilibrium at $\bar{E}$ with the farmer no longer producing food, no marginal losses and hence no taxes, and the herdsmen maintaining $\bar{E}$ cows.

The only way in which to choose between the two equilibria is to calculate whether society is a net gainer or loser from having the farmer remain in operation. That is, the government must engage in an overall analysis of social benefits and costs. If market prices measure social benefits and costs (a dubious assumption), the optimal equilibrium is that which maximizes the sum of the profits of the farmer and herdsmen. The required cost-benefit analysis would be enormously complicated and expensive in terms of the resources required for its administration.[5]

The above discussion also assumes that the consumer or producer with the property rights correctly informs the government of his marginal loss, rather than overstating it. This problem is discussed in more detail in the next section in the form of consumers attempting to get a "free ride" for public commodities. That is, consumers might attempt to conceal their true preferences for public commodities if they believe that they can thereby reduce their share of the cost of producing the commodity.

In short, in the presence of nonconvexities in the production (or consumption) of externalities, a taxation scheme, like artificial markets, is not necessarily a remedy for the externality.

18.3 THE THEORY OF PUBLIC COMMODITIES

It is perhaps the case that most important externalities also have the property—nonrivalness—of a public commodity. My discomfort caused by cigarette smokers fouling the air of an enclosed seminar room does not reduce the suffering of other nonsmokers. The interruption of my solitude by low-flying airplanes does not reduce the noise that my neighbors must suffer. My lost time due to severe road congestion does not save time for others.[6] The public nature of many externalities is important because the mechanisms for attaining Pareto optimality (artificial markets and tax-subsidy schemes) described in the previous section do not work if the externality is nonrival. Indeed, the existence of an *excludable* public commodity is itself sufficient to destroy the Pareto optimality of competitive equilibrium. Demonstration of this fact is contained in the next subsection. We then go on to discuss a possible mechanism for attaining Pareto optimality and the difficulties with that mechanism.

Pareto Optimality and Competitive Equilibrium with Public Commodities

With respect to the consumers' preferences and the producers' technology sets, public commodities are just like private commodities. The consumer has a preference ordering over consumption bundles consisting of public and private commodities; or the production of public commodities requires private (and perhaps public) commodities as inputs and is constrained by the existing technology available to the producer. It is the market-equilibrium conditions for public commodities that differ, since the sum of individual consumer and

[5] This paragraph summarizes the "practical" approach (which isn't all that practical). The formal resolution to this problem is the construction of a social decision rule, or a social welfare function, for choosing between alternative Pareto optima (see chapters 19 and 20).

[6] Road congestion is an externality because my decision to enter a congested freeway exacerbates the congestion problem, thus decreasing the utility of others by increasing the time required to traverse a section of the freeway.

producer demands for public commodities do not add up to the sum of the amounts produced plus the initial endowment of public commodities.

The relationship between competitive equilibrium and Pareto optimality in an economy with public commodities can be examined adequately in the context of a highly simplified economy in which there are m consumers but only one producer and three commodities. The first commodity is a public commodity, which is produced (but not used as an input)[7] by the one producer and consumed by the m consumers. The two private commodities can be either produced or utilized as inputs by the producer. Following the notation of chapter 7, we therefore represent the total amount produced of the public commodity with the notation q_1 and the *net* quantities produced of the two private commodities by z_2 and z_3. The production technology of the producer can be represented by the net-production-function identity: $F(q_1, z_2, z_3) = 0$.

As the first commodity is a public commodity, each consumer consumes the total amount available, x_1. The utility functions of the consumers therefore have images $u^c = U^c(x_1, x_2^c, x_3^c)$, $c = 1, \ldots, m$. The initial endowments of the two private commodities are owned by the consumers, who also share ownership of the production unit. Denote these endowments $\bar{x}_i^c$, $i = 2, 3$, $c = 1, \ldots, m$. The endowment of the public commodity, $\bar{x}_1$, is collectively owned (i.e., owned by the "government"). The balance conditions for the three commodities are

$$x_1^c = q_1 + \bar{x}_1, \qquad c = 1, \ldots, m,$$

and

$$\sum_{c=1}^{m} x_i^c = \sum_{c=1}^{m} \bar{x}_i^c + z_i, \qquad i = 2, 3.$$

That is, the quantity of the public commodity consumed by *each* consumer is equal to the quantity produced plus the initial endowment and the total quantities of the private commodities consumed by *all* consumers are equal to the total endowments plus the net outputs of the producer.

The necessary conditions for an allocation to be Pareto optimal can be derived by maximizing $U^1(x_1, x_2^1, x_3^1)$ subject to the technology and endowment

[7] It is, of course, quite possible for a public commodity to be public in production as well as in consumption. Indeed, the simple general-equilibrium model introduced in section 18.2 to analyze Pareto optimality and competitive equilibrium in an economy with externalities can be formally reinterpreted as a model with a public commodity. In this interpretation, the commodity produced by producer 2 is a public commodity in that the *entire* amount produced is consumed by the one consumer *and* used by producer 1 in production. (The consumer pays the entire bill for the production of the public commodity.) Thus, the formal analysis of section 18.2 demonstrates that competitive equilibrium in an economy with a public commodity (as well as in an economy with an externality) is not necessarily Pareto optimal. (The foregoing remarks underscore the intimate formal similarity between economies with externalities and those with public commodities.) Additional features of economies with public commodities are explicated in the following m-consumer model.

constraints and subject to the constraints that all other consumers have a specified level of utility:

$$\max_{x_1, x_2^1, x_3^1} U^1(x_1, x_2^1, x_3^1)$$

$$\text{s.t. } U^c(x_1, x_2^c, x_3^c) = \bar{u}^c, \qquad c = 2, \ldots, m,$$

$$F(q_1, z_2, z_3) = 0,$$

$$x_1 = q_1 + \bar{x}_1,$$

and

$$\sum_{c=1}^{m} x_i^c - \sum_{c=1}^{m} \bar{x}_i^c - z_i = 0, \qquad i = 2, 3.$$

The (interior) solution to this optimization problem is derived by calculating the critical values of the choice variables in the Lagrange expression,

$$\begin{aligned} L(x_1, x_2^c, x_3^c, q_1, z_2, z_3, \lambda_1, \ldots, \lambda_{m+3}) = {} & U^1(x_1, x_2^1, x_3^1) + \lambda_1 F(q_1, z_2, z_3) \\ & + \sum_{c=2}^{m} \lambda_c (U^c(x_1, x_2^c, x_3^c) - \bar{u}^c) \\ & + \lambda_{m+1}(x_1 - q_1 - \bar{x}_1) \\ & + \sum_{i=2}^{3} \lambda_{m+i}\left(\sum_{c=1}^{m} x_i^c - \sum_{c=1}^{m} \bar{x}_i^c - z_i\right). \end{aligned}$$

The critical values are found by solving the necessary first-order conditions, which, after elimination of the Lagrange multipliers, can be written as follows:

$$\frac{\partial U^c(x_1, x_2^c, x_3^c)/\partial x_i^c}{\partial U^c(x_1, x_2^c, x_3^c)/\partial x_j^c} = \frac{\partial F(q_1, z_2, z_3)/\partial z_i}{\partial F(q_1, z_2, z_3)/\partial z_j}, \qquad \begin{array}{l} c = 1, \ldots, m, \\ i, j = 2, 3, \end{array} \tag{18.11}$$

and

$$\sum_{c=1}^{m} \frac{\partial U^c(x_1, x_2^c, x_3^c)/\partial x_1}{\partial U^c(x_1, x_2^c, x_3^c)/\partial x_i} = \frac{\partial F(q_1, z_2, z_3)/\partial q_1}{\partial F(q_1, z_2, z_3)/\partial z_i}, \qquad \begin{array}{l} c = 1, \ldots, m, \\ i = 2, 3. \end{array} \tag{18.12}$$

The marginal conditions (18.9) involving only private commodities are identical to those derived in section 17.3 (equation (17.3)) for a completely private economy. The conditions involving the public commodity, (18.10), are fundamentally different. These conditions require that the sum of the marginal rates of substitution of the public commodity for (either) private commodity be equal to the corresponding rate of commodity transformation:

$$\sum_{c=1}^{m} MRS_{1i}^c(x_1, x_2^c, x_3^c) = RCT_{1i}(q_1, z_2, z_3), \qquad i = 2, 3. \tag{18.13}$$

On the other hand, competitive equilibrium requires (see section 17.3)

$$MRS^c_{1i}(x_1, x^c_2, x^c_3) = \frac{p_1}{p_i} = RCT_{1i}(q_1, z_2, z_3), \qquad i = 2, 3, \; c = 1, \ldots, m,$$

in sharp contrast to the Pareto-optimality condition (18.13).

Thus, competitive equilibrium is not Pareto optimal in an economy with a public commodity. The "solution" to this problem emanates from the insight (originally attributable to Lindahl) that, as in the case of externalities, the Walrasian equilibrium is characterized by too few prices to decentralize a Pareto optimum. Consequently, Lindahl [1919] suggested the construct of "personalized prices" of public commodities—different prices for different agents for the same commodity. An economy with personalized prices is a fictional one which, however, provides insight into the appropriate role of a government in engineering an optimal allocation of resources in an economy with public commodities. Because of the importance of the "pseudoeconomy" with personalized prices, we describe its formal structure in the next subsection. The reader who is uninterested in the formal development of these concepts can omit this subsection; the basic notions are illustrated in the subsection after this in the context of a simple economy with m consumers, one producer, and one public commodity.

The Public-Commodity Economy with Personalized Prices

The public-commodity economy with personalized prices is described formally by the following assumptions.

Assumption 18.1 The economy consists of m consumers, ℓ producers, and n commodities, of which the first d are public commodities and the remainder are private commodities. The economy has at its disposal certain original resources (and possibly capital equipment which is inherited from the past).

Assumption 18.2 The producers satisfy assumption 7.1 (profit maximization). The technology sets of the producers satisfy assumptions 7.2 (boundedness), 7.3 (regularity), and 7.5 (convexity) and are represented by net production functions, F^r, $r = 1, \ldots, \ell$.

Assumption 18.3 The consumers receive a share of the profits of each of the ℓ producers, $s^c = [s^c_1, \ldots, s^c_\ell]$, $c = 1, \ldots, m$. All profits are distributed to the consumers and there are no retained earnings by the producers.

Assumption 18.4 The consumers' preferences satisfy assumptions 3.1 (nonsatiation) and 3.2 (strict convexity) and are represented by continuous utility functions, U^c, $c = 1, \ldots, m$. Each consumer is endowed with a non-negative (but not necessarily positive) bundle of the $n - d$ private commodities, $\bar{x}^c = [\bar{x}^c_{d+1}, \ldots, \bar{x}^c_n]$, $c = 1, \ldots, m$.

Assumption 18.5 There is no cost of exchange.

Assumption 18.6 There is perfect information about the rate at which one commodity can be exchanged for any other.

The economy with public commodities has a price system consisting of a vector of private commodity prices, $p = [p_{d+1}, \ldots, p_n]$, and vectors of personalized prices for each public commodity and for all consumers $p^c = [p_1^c, \ldots, p_d^c]$, $c = 1, \ldots, m$, and all producers, $\rho^r = [\rho_1^r, \ldots, \rho_d^r]$, $r = 1, \ldots, \ell$. The interpretation of these personalized prices will become clearer as we proceed.

While the initial endowment of private commodities is owned by consumers, the initial endowment of public commodities is assumed to be held collectively by consumers and producers:

Assumption 18.7 The initial endowment of public commodities, $\bar{x}_i$, $i = 1, \ldots, d$, is owned collectively by consumers and producers with the value of individual shares determined by the personalized prices for public commodities, p^c, $c = 1, \ldots, m$, and ρ^r, $r = 1, \ldots, \ell$.

Producers can produce both public and private commodities and can utilize both as inputs in production. The net output of the *i*th private commodity by the *r*th producer is denoted (as in chapter 16) z_i^r. For public commodities, q_i^r is the gross output of the *i*th public commodity by the *r*th producer and v_i^r is the input of the *i*th public commodity utilized by the *r*th producer. Also let $q^r = [q_1^r, \ldots, q_d^r]$ and $v^r = [v_1^r, \ldots, v_d^r]$, $r = 1, \ldots, \ell$.

The profit of the *r*th producer is determined by the net revenue from the production of private commodities,

$$\sum_{i=d+1}^{n} p_i z_i^r,$$

the gross revenue from the sale of public commodities to consumers,

$$\sum_{c=1}^{m} \sum_{i=1}^{d} p_i^c q_i^r,$$

and to producers,

$$\sum_{r'=1}^{\ell} \sum_{i=1}^{d} \rho_i^{r'} q_i^r,$$

and the algebraic difference between the payments for public commodities used in production and the producer's share of the initial endowments of public commodities,

$$\sum_{i=1}^{d} \rho_i^r (v_i^r - \bar{x}_i^r).$$

The interpretation of these expressions is that, in this fictional economy, each producer is compensated (in accordance with the personalized prices) by all consumers and all producers for each unit of the public commodity he produces and he must pay (in accordance with his personalized price) for use of each public commodity in excess of the economy's endowment. The total profit of the rth producer can therefore be written as

$$\Pi^r(z^r, q^r, v^r) = \sum_{i=d+1}^{n} p_i z_i^r + \sum_{c=1}^{m} \sum_{i=1}^{d} p_i^c q_i^r + \sum_{r'=1}^{\ell} \sum_{i=1}^{d} \rho_i^{r'} q_i^r - \sum_{i=1}^{d} \rho_i^r (v_i^r - \bar{x}_i).$$

Assumption 18.2 allows the optimization problem of the rth producer to be written as

$$\underset{z^r,\, q^r,\, v^r}{\text{Max}}\ \Pi^r(z^r, q^r, v^r) \qquad \text{s.t. } F^r(z^r, q^r, v^r) = 0.$$

The supplies and input demands for private and public commodities clearly depend upon the vector of private commodity prices, $p = [p_{d+1}, \ldots, p_n]$, and the vectors of personalized consumer and producer prices for public commodities,

$$z_i^r = \phi_i^r(p, p^1, \ldots, p^m, \rho^1, \ldots, \rho^\ell), \qquad i = d+1, \ldots, n, \quad r = 1, \ldots, \ell,$$

$$q_i^r = \theta_i^r(p, p^1, \ldots, p^m, \rho^1, \ldots, \rho^\ell), \qquad i = 1, \ldots, d, \quad r = 1, \ldots, \ell,$$

$$v_i^r = s_i^r(p, p^1, \ldots, p^m, \rho^1, \ldots, \rho^\ell), \qquad i = 1, \ldots, d, \quad r = 1, \ldots, \ell.$$

The cth consumer's wealth is defined by

$$\omega_c = \sum_{i=d+1}^{n} p_i \bar{x}_i^c + \sum_{i=1}^{d} p_i^c \bar{x}_i + \sum_{r=1}^{\ell} s_r^c \pi^r,$$

where the first term is the value of his private-commodity endowment, the second term is the value of his share of the public-commodity endowment, and the last term is his share of aggregate profits. The consumer's total consumption cannot exceed his wealth. The nonsatiation assumption allows this constraint to be written as an equality:

$$\sum_{i=d+1}^{n} p_i x_i^c + \sum_{i=1}^{d} p_i^c x_i^c = \omega_c.$$

The following utility-maximization assumption is now posited:

Assumption 18.8 Each consumer chooses a consumption bundle x^c, consisting of private and public commodities, that solves

$$\underset{x^c}{\text{Max}}\ U^c(x^c) \qquad \text{s.t. } \sum_{i=d+1}^{n} p_i x_i^c + \sum_{i=1}^{d} p_i^c x_i^c - \omega_c = 0.$$

The optimal consumption bundle depends upon the vectors of private commodity prices and personalized consumer prices for public commodities, the endowments of private and public commodities, and the profit income. Hence the consumer-demand function images for private and public commodities can be written as

$$x_i^c = d_i^c\left(p, p^c, \bar{x}^c, \sum_{r=1}^{\ell} s_r^c \pi^r\right), \qquad i = 1, \ldots, n, \quad c = 1, \ldots, m.$$

Market equilibrium requires that the following conditions be fulfilled:

$$\sum_{c=1}^{m} x_i^c = \sum_{r=1}^{\ell} z_i^r + \sum_{c=1}^{m} \bar{x}_i^c, \qquad i = d+1, \ldots, n,$$

$$x_i^c = \sum_{r=1}^{\ell} q_i^r + \bar{x}_i, \qquad i = 1, \ldots, d, \quad c = 1, \ldots, m,$$

$$v_i^r = \sum_{r'=1}^{\ell} q_i^{r'} + \bar{x}_i, \qquad i = 1, \ldots, d, \quad r = 1, \ldots, \ell.$$

The market-equilibrium conditions for private commodities require that the aggregate amount consumed of each private commodity be equal to the sum of the total initial endowment plus the net amount produced. The market-equilibrium conditions for public commodities require that the amount consumed of each public commodity by each consumer be equal to the aggregate output of the commodity plus the total initial endowment of the commodity, and that the aggregate amount of each public commodity used as an input in production by each producer be equal to the aggregate output of the commodity plus the total initial endowment.

The principal analytical distinction between public and private commodities is contained in the market-equilibrium conditions and in the collective ownership of the initial endowment of public commodities.

The extension of the Walrasian concept of equilibrium to an economy with public commodities and personalized prices for public commodities for each consumer and producer is often referred to as a *Lindahl equilibrium*. Because of the role played by the personalized prices, a Lindahl equilibrium is not a pure market equilibrium corresponding to that discussed in chapters 15–17. It is often referred to as a quasiequilibrium or pseudoequilibrium since we must go beyond the market equilibrium to inquire how the personalized prices are determined.[8]

Interest in this pseudoequilibrium centers on the fact that, unlike the Walrasian equilibrium, it is Pareto optimal. The reader is referred to the suggested readings following part IV for a formal proof of this proposition. The principle is illustrated in the next subsections using the simple model developed earlier in this section. The next subsection interprets the equilibrium personalized prices

[8] There actually are several related concepts of equilibrium for economies with public commodities. These concepts essentially differ according to the maximizing assumptions that are made concerning the economic agents or collection of agents. See the conclusion of this section and the suggestions for further reading following part IV.

in terms of the marginal conditions for an interior optimum allocation. The subsection after that analyzes the characterizations of personalized prices as taxes used to finance the production of public commodities.

Pareto Optimality and Pseudoequilibrium

The simplified economy described earlier in this section contains one public commodity (1) and two private commodities (2, 3). Thus, the Lindahl price system is comprised of ordinary prices for the public commodity for each consumer, p_1^c, $c = 1, \ldots, m$. (There is no personalized price for the producer since he does not use the public commodity as an input in this simplified version of the public-commodity economy.)

The m utility-maximization problems,

$$\max_{x^c} U^c(X^c) \quad \text{s.t.} \quad p_1^c x_1^c + p_2 x_2^c + p_3 x_3^c = p_1^c \bar{x}_1^c + p_2 \bar{x}_2^c + p_3 \bar{x}_3 + s^c \Pi, \quad c = 1, \ldots, m,$$

imply the following first-order conditions:

$$MRS_{1i}^c(\overset{*}{x}{}^c) = \frac{p_1^c}{p_i}, \qquad i = 2, 3, \quad c = 1, \ldots, m. \tag{18.14}$$

Profit maximization of the one producer,

$$\max_{q_1, z_2, z_3} \sum_{c=1}^{m} p_1^c q_1 + p_2 z_2 + p_3 z_3 \qquad \text{s.t. } F(q_1, z_2, z_3) = 0,$$

implies the following first-order conditions:

$$RCT_{1i}(\overset{*}{q}_1, \overset{*}{z}_2, \overset{*}{z}_3) = \frac{\sum_{c=1}^{m} p_1^c}{p_i}, \qquad i = 2, 3. \tag{18.15}$$

Summing over c in (18.12) and combining the result with (18.13), we obtain

$$RCT_{1i}(\overset{*}{q}_1, \overset{*}{z}_2, \overset{*}{z}_3) = \sum_{c=1}^{m} MRS_{1i}^c(\overset{*}{x}{}^c), \qquad i = 2, 3.$$

This is equivalent to the Pareto-optimality condition (18.13). Thus, this example illustrates the way in which a personalized price system can decentralize a Pareto optimum. In this example, the personalized prices represent consumers' contributions to the cost of producing the public commodity.[9] The equilibrium is

[9] Recalling from an earlier footnote that the externality model discussed in section 18.2 can be formally reinterpreted as a public-commodity model, we can use that model to illustrate the Pareto optimality of a pseudoequilibrium in which the personalized prices are p_1 for the consumer and p_{12} for producer 1. Thus, p_{12} can be interpreted either as the price of an ("artificial") externality commodity or as a personalized public-commodity price for the first producer. These alternative interpretations of that model underscore again the close relationship between the externality problem and the public-commodity problem.

called a pseudoequilibrium because there is no rational reason for such prices to arise in an economy with price-taking agents. Indeed, if the public commodity is also nonexcludable, as is the case for most important examples (individual members of a society cannot be excluded from the benefits of national defense or public health programs), there is no mechanism available to the producer for imposing the personalized prices on the consumers. It is this feature of an economy with public commodities that rationalizes the intervention of the government in order to assess the consumers for their shares of the cost of producing the public commodity. Thus, one could reinterpret the personalized prices as per-unit assessments imposed on each of the consumers by the government, which then pays the producer $p_1 = \sum_{c=1}^{m} p_1^c$ for each unit produced.

The importance of the foregoing analysis is that if the government chooses the set of personalized commodity-specific tax rates and the public-commodity prices appropriately, decentralized decision making on the part of producers and consumers results in a Pareto-optimal allocation even in the presence of public commodities. It is not possible to demonstrate that this result holds for more general tax systems. That is, unless taxes are differentiated by each public commodity and each economic agent, equilibrium cannot be shown to be Pareto optimal.

18.4 DECENTRALIZED PLANNING AND INCENTIVE COMPATIBILITY

The existence of externalities and public commodities perhaps constitute the most compelling case for government intervention in competitive markets.[10] Fundamentally, this is because there is no natural reason for the appropriate markets (those needed to generate Pareto-optimal allocations) to arise. This explains the terminology "artificial markets" (for externalities) and "pseudo-equilibrium" (of a public-commodity economy). Even if the government creates externality markets by assigning property rights, such markets are unlikely to decentralize Pareto optima because of the existence of fundamental non-convexities. Thus, the analysis of externalities points toward tax/subsidy schemes as the solutions and the analysis of public commodities points toward personalized prices, or taxes, as the solution. Unfortunately, these proposed solutions are not panaceas; two fundamental problems must be addressed: (1) determining the equilibrium taxes/subsidies and (2) providing incentives for producers and consumers to reveal truthfully their technological rates of transformation and marginal rates of substitution, respectively.

Decentralized Planning

The determination of taxes/subsidies or personalized prices that decentralize a Pareto optimum is a problem in decentralized planning. Suggested procedures for finding the optimal taxes/subsidies are typically dynamic systems

[10] As noted in section 17.2, market imperfections (monopoly power) also justify government intervention (see also section 18.5).

describing the exchange of price or quantity information (or both) between the government and the private economic agents (consumers and producers).[11] The economic agents respond to the information offered by the government by providing information about their preferences and technology sets. The latter information in turn is used by the government to revise the price or quantity information supplied to consumers and producers, and so forth. Such dynamic processes can be shown, under certain conditions, to converge to an optimal state of the economy.

The most commonly cited decentralized planning procedure for an economy with public commodities was first presented by Malinvaud [1971].[12] In this procedure the planning board (government) chooses an initial set of prices for the private commodities and a set of personalized prices for the public commodities. An initial endowment of commodities and a specification of profit shares is assumed. Consumers respond by proposing commodity bundles that solve their utility-maximization problems, given the prices proposed by the planning board. Producers take the commodity prices proposed by the government as given and choose production bundles that solve their profit-maximization problems. The planning board examines the market-clearing equations for each commodity, revises its prices and imposes income transfers between consumers. The price adjustments are made in order to increase (decrease) the price of a commodity whose demand is greater (smaller) than the amount available. The income transfer is designed to compensate individual consumers for the changes in their personalized prices for public commodities. The purpose of the income transfers is to prevent the initial income distribution from being completely altered by the changing commodity prices. Under certain restrictive assumptions, Malinvaud is able to show that this procedure converges to a Pareto-optimal state of the economy (see also Milleron [1972, 472–474]).

Additional decentralized planning procedures have been proposed and analyzed. The planning board might instead propose commodity and production bundles to the economic agents. The latter would respond with marginal rates of substitution and technical rates of substitution. Finally, mixed procedures, in which the planning board proposes some of the prices and some of the commodity and production bundles, have also been formulated.

Incentive Compatibility

The decentralized planning procedures discussed above require that private economic agents provide correct information to the center about their preferences and technologies. However, private agents have an incentive to

[11] The mathematical structure of these procedures is similar to the dynamic models of a single competitive market analyzed in chapter 12. The analysis of the latter, however, is far simpler than the procedures under discussion in this section.

[12] As early as 1919, Lindahl analyzed a procedure for determining the optimal amount of government expenditure on public commodities. The procedure draws upon the market-adjustment processes of Walras and Marshall (chapter 12). Samuelson [1969] discusses "the pseudo-demand algorithm" utilizing "pseudo-tax prices" for public commodities. No formal mathematical analysis is presented.

misrepresent their preferences or technologies. For example, a producer, by exaggerating the damage to his productive capacity of a negative externality ($\partial f^1(L^1, q_2)/\partial q_2$ in equation (18.9b)), increases the externality tax ($-p_{12}$) and hence increases the subsidy paid to him by the government. The outcome of this misrepresentation by the producer of his technology is an externality tax that is too high and hence a quantity of commodity 2 (and the associated externality) that is too low.

Similarly, if a consumer understates his marginal rate of substitution between a public commodity and a private commodity, his personalized price, p_1^c, will be reduced by the government, which seeks to satisfy the condition in equation (18.14). That is, it is advantageous to understate one's willingness to pay for a public commodity, thus enjoying a "free ride" at the expense of others (this is called the "free-rider problem"). The result is that the production of public commodities is too low.

The problem of designing a resource-allocation mechanism that is individual-agent incentive compatible has been analyzed in several recent papers (see the part IV suggested readings). The seminal contribution in this literature is the Groves mechanism (Groves [1973] and Groves and Ledyard [1977]), which unhorses the free rider. (See also Clarke [1971] and Vickrey [1961].)

18.5 UNCERTAINTY AND THE PARETO OPTIMALITY OF COMPETITIVE EQUILIBRIUM

This chapter has discussed some important economic phenomena that appear to break the nexus between general competitive equilibrium and Pareto optimality. Lack of property rights, nonconvexities in the production and consumption of externalities and in transaction technologies, noncompetitive behavior in artificial markets, and the existence of public commodities all generate violations of the fundamental optimality principles. A characteristic of economic systems not discussed above that may also account for the failure of markets to achieve an efficient allocation of resources is uncertainty. Uncertainty, or imperfect information, which is ruled out by assumption 18.6, may be due to a number of factors. For example, resource availability, production technologies, or consumer preferences might be, in part, determined by a set of factors that are independent of the decisions of individual agents and are partially unknown. In production, the outputs of farmers depend, in part, upon weather conditions. Preferences of consumers for certain commodities such as ice cream might also depend upon the state of the weather. Finally, the feasible production set of some producers might depend upon the remaining reserves in mines and oil wells that might not be known with certainty.

We alluded in the introductory chapter to the possibility that the markets being examined could include future commodities, i.e., commodities that will not be delivered until some future date. This interpretation is a viable one for all of the preceding discussions of market mechanisms. However, perfect information on the part of the economic agents in the case of these intertemporal markets is not credible. To assume perfect information about the present is heroic; to assume perfect information about the future is nonsense. Thus, we might expect that the optimality principles would be violated because of the presence of uncertainty in intertemporal markets. Indeed, it is apparent that in real economies markets do not exist for all future commodities.

There is, however, a strong profit incentive for some economic agent to set up a market for such commodities if individual economic agents expect different future outcomes. Arrow and others have shown that the nexus between competitive equilibrium and Pareto optimality can be maintained under uncertainty by a simple redefinition of the consumption space to include "contingent commodities." A contingent commodity is specified not only by its physical characteristics, time, and location of availability, but also by the circumstances under which it would become available (i.e., weather, resource availability, etc.). For each Pareto-optimal state of the economy, there is associated a price system that specifies the price for every commodity in every possible state of the environment or state of nature. Such an economic system under uncertainty is formally analogous to competitive equilibrium under certainty and has an equilibrium under the same conditions as those that have been discussed in chapters 15–17.

Such a theory of competitive equilibrium under uncertainty, however, does not appear to provide an adequate description of economic systems that lack markets for contingent commodities. Our discussion of uncertainty or incomplete information as a basis for the failure of a market to internalize an externality thus reduces to the absence of another market—in this case markets for contingent commodities. Furthermore, it seems likely that the reasons for the failure of such markets to come into existence might be traced to some of the factors we have discussed above. For example, markets for contingent commodities might involve nonconvex transaction technologies. Fixed costs or set-up costs in security and insurance markets would imply nonconvexities that could account for the nonexistence of equilibria in these markets. Alternatively, economic agents might perceive futures contracts as being quite risky and there might be a lack of buyers for such commodities. In this case, futures markets would be characterized by the problems of "thinness" (small numbers of buyers and sellers) and noncompetitive results would hold.

These issues and problems are the object of intensive current research and are beyond the scope of this book. References to this literature may be found in the suggestions for further reading at the end of part IV.

EXERCISES

18.1 Consider a highly simplified economy with two consumers, two producers, two produced commodities, and one primary commodity (labor/leisure time). Each consumer is endowed with a given amount of leisure, $\gamma^c (c = 1, 2)$, consumes ℓ^c units, and supplies the difference, $\gamma^c - \ell^c$, to the two producers in exchange for the two produced commodities. The consumers share ownership of the two production units. Both the consumers' preferences and the producers' technology sets satisfy the respective convexity assumptions. Assume that the utility of consumer 1 depends upon the output of producer 2 (as well as his consumption of the two commodities). Demonstrate that the competitive equilibrium is not Pareto optimal and explain the reason why.

18.2 Assume that in the economy described in exercise 18.1 the utility of consumer 1 depends upon the amount consumed of commodity 1 by consumer 2 (as well as his own consumption of both commodities). Demonstrate that the equilibrium is not Pareto optimal and explain why.

18.3 Assume that in the economy described in exercise 18.2 consumer 1 receives a property right to the externality such that he pays consumer 2 for the externality (the price is positive for a positive exernality and negative for a negative externality). Demonstrate that the equilibrium might be Pareto optimal. Why might a market for the externality fail to come into operation? Why might the equilibrium not be Pareto optimal even if the market for the externality comes into operation?

18.4 Repeat the analysis undertaken in exercise 18.3 for the economy described in exercise 18.1. Assume that consumer 1 receives the property right.

18.5 Assume that in the economy described in exercise 18.1 the commodity produced by producer 2 is a public commodity in that both consumers consume the *entire* amount produced while producer 1 uses only the primary commodity. Why is the equilibrium not necessarily Pareto optimal? Demonstrate that the government could choose personalized prices (taxes) for each consumer and pay producer 1 to produce commodity 1 such that the equilibrium would be Pareto optimal.

18.6 Consider the following situations:

a. A consumer owns a home and on a neighboring plot of land a smelly factory is erected. The odor it emits makes the home less pleasant, therefore lowering its market value.

b. A consumer owns a home and on a neighboring plot of land other homes are erected. These homes, by increasing the supply of housing, lower the market value of the house.

Demonstrate which of these situations are economic externalities that could result in the equilibrium not being optimal.

CHAPTER 19
THE THEORY OF SOCIAL CHOICE

19.1 INTRODUCTION

The classical welfare economics of chapters 16–17, relating competitive equilibrium to social optimality, is predicted upon the eminently conservative Pareto rule. The Pareto criterion can be interpreted as a *social decision rule* for making choices between pairs of states of the economy. In particular, one state of the economy is socially preferred to another if at least one member of the society prefers the former to the latter and no member prefers the latter. This rule for social decision making has played a steadfast role in normative economic analysis ever since it was formulated by Pareto in 1897. The apparent reason for its longevity is that it purports to eschew value judgments—particularly those required to compare the well-being of two members of the society with conflicting interests. The Pareto criterion grew out of an attempt to separate economic efficiency considerations (about which economists have much to say) from comparisons or evaluations of the distribution of income (about which economists have much less to say).

However, the Pareto criterion is *not* devoid of value judgment. The fundamental value implicit in the Pareto criterion is the "welfarist" value that social decisions be based exclusively upon individual preferences. While this is a value that might be held by most of us, it is nevertheless a value judgment. Moreover, many would be offended by the value judgment implicit in the Pareto criterion that *all* preferences (including those of the immoral, the criminal, and the insane) should count (and count *equally* if it is the exclusive criterion).[1]

The principal problem with the Pareto criterion (and the welfare economics based exclusively upon it) is that it is of limited usefulness because most social choice problems *require* value judgments that are not implicit in the Pareto criterion. If one member of the society prefers $\hat{s}$ to s and another member prefers s to $\hat{s}$, the Pareto criterion does not allow us to choose one of these two social alternatives, regardless of the preferences of all other members of the society.

[1] Sen [1977a] objects to "welfarism" on the grounds that it is too restrictive in that it fails to make use of "nonwelfare" information: information about the identity and personal characteristics of the individuals and information about the states of the economy being compared. A social decision rule that does not use information about the social states is called "neutral." Sen notes that "any neutral framework cannot properly accommodate the principles of liberty" (Sen [1977a, p. 1559]). Essentially this is because neutrality implies that the social rule for making decisions or evaluations about my own private actions (in the secret cloisters of my own house) is no different from the rule for making decisions about who should be president.

As it turns out, few practical economic policies can be evaluated on the exclusive basis of the Pareto criterion because virtually all of them work to the benefit of some and to the detriment of others. There is therefore a danger in exclusive concentration on the Pareto criterion. Perhaps Sen [1970a, p. 22] puts it best:

> *An economy can be optimal in this [Pareto] sense, even when some people are rolling in luxury and others are near starvation as long as the starvers cannot be made better off without cutting into the pleasures of the rich. If preventing the burning of Rome would have made Emperor Nero feel worse off, then letting him burn Rome would have been Pareto optimal. In short, a society or an economy can be Pareto optimal and still be perfectly disgusting.*

The obvious inadequacies of the Pareto criterion for a theory of social choice have provided the motivation for much inquiry in recent years into the rudiments of social choice. This literature examines the question of how alternative states of an economy (or any social organization for that matter) might be ordered so that choices can be made in a manner that is both rational and in some sense equitable. The essential characteristic of the economics literature on this social choice issue is that it concentrates on working out the implications of alternative properties (e.g., transitivity, nondictatorship, the Pareto criterion) of social choice rules. In particular, this literature has especially elucidated the issue of whether or not particular conditions which we might want a social choice rule to satisfy are mutually compatible.

The literature on social choice theory, stimulated by the pioneering treatise of Nobel Laureate Kenneth Arrow [1951b], is by now voluminous. It is nevertheless true that many of the fundamental issues of social choice are as yet unresolved. Indeed, even the issue of what questions economists ought to be asking about social choice is itself a matter of considerable professional contention. For this reason it might be argued that social choice theory remains too inchoate to justify a textbook treatment of these complicated issues. One thing that is not a matter of contention, however, is that the seminal piece by Arrow, cited above, remains the touchstone of virtually all research on social choice theory. This chapter is therefore constructed around Arrow's "impossibility theorem." In particular, section 19.2 lays out the formal setting in which the issues of social choice are analyzed. Section 19.3 discusses the Arrow theorem and section 19.4 provides a proof for a simplified version of it. Arrow's result indicates that a certain set of restrictions on social choice (more precisely, on the aggregation rule, or "social welfare function," that maps individual preference orderings into social orderings), which many might consider to be eminently reasonable and desirable restrictions, are in fact logically incompatible with one another. This means that any social choice function actually employed by society must violate one of Arrow's "reasonable conditions."

The remainder of this chapter and chapter 20 discuss some possible ways of weakening Arrow's conditions to permit the existence of social choice rules. Section 19.5 weakens the requirement that social choice be transitive. Chapter 20 weakens the "informational constraints" that are implicit in Arrow's formal framework by explicitly allowing for the use of interpersonal comparability.

19.2 SOCIAL ORDERINGS AND SOCIAL CHOICE

Social States

The choice space of the social choice problem, denoted S, is the set of all *conceivable* social states. The list of elements of a social state depends of course upon the particular society under study. If the society is an economy similar to those examined in the previous few chapters, a social state is a list of all of the relevant economic variables such as the quantities of all commodities consumed by every consumer, the amounts produced of each commodity by each producer, etc.

More relevant than the set of all conceivable social states is the set of *feasible* social states—i.e., social states that can in fact be attained given the constraints faced by the society. The set of feasible social states, which we will usually denote $\hat{S}$, is typically smaller than the set of conceivable social states because of the existence of various constraints faced by society. For example, the economy analyzed in the previous chapters faces certain technological constraints which are embodied in the technology sets of the producers. In addition to technological constraints, a decision-making body may be faced by social or political constraints. A governing body is generally constrained by its constitution and the collection of laws and other decisions that elaborate the constitution.

Some technical complications will be avoided by assuming, in most of what follows, that the feasible set of social states has a finite number of elements.

Social Choice Function

It will be recalled from part I that the rudimentary or primitive notion underlying the theory of consumer choice is the notion of consumer preference regarding alternative bundles of commodities in the consumer's consumption space. Analogously, the theory of social choice is predicated on the primitive notion of individual preferences regarding alternative social states. We let $\succcurlyeq_c$ be the weak-preference relation of the cth consumer over the set of social states S. Thus, $s \succcurlyeq_c \bar{s}$ means that the cth consumer considers social state s to be at least as good as social state $\bar{s}$. The critical distinction between this preference relation and the preference relation of consumer choice theory in part I is that the relation $\succcurlyeq_c$ reflects the consumer's preferences for the consumption of others as well as himself. One might refer to the preference relation of part I as reflecting individual tastes and the preference relation of social choice theory as reflecting individual "values." It may well be, of course, that the cth consumer doesn't care at all about the lot of others and that his ranking of social states is therefore completely determined by his own consumption bundle. These types of values are perfectly consistent with the preference relation $\succcurlyeq_c$, but this relation is also general enough to incorporate altruism and/or malevolence (and others types of consumption externalities).

It is assumed that $\succcurlyeq_c$ is a complete ordering (a complete, reflexive, and transitive relation) for all c.[2] Thus, all members of the society are able to rank social states.

[2] See section 2.2 for a discussion of these concepts.

The essential ingredient of a theory of social choice is a rule for aggregating the values of the m members of society into a social decision rule or a social ordering of social states. Formally, a *social choice function* associates with every possible set of individual orderings, $\{\succcurlyeq_1, \ldots, \succcurlyeq_m\}$ and every subset of the social-state space, $\hat{S}$, a "chosen" subset of $\hat{S}$. That is, the social-choice-function image is written as

$$C(\hat{S}, \succcurlyeq_1, \ldots, \succcurlyeq_m) \tag{19.1}$$

where m is the number of members of the society.

Several aspects of this social choice function should be emphasized. First, the image, or choice set, must be a subset of the given set of feasible social states, $\hat{S}$. Second, the choice-function image must be defined and be nonempty for *all* possible profiles of individual orderings, $\{\succcurlyeq_1, \ldots, \succcurlyeq_m\}$. That is, the social choice rule must generate a choice for any given set of individual values on the part of the members of the society. This property is known as the condition of "unrestricted domain" (Sen [1970a, p. 41]), and, because of its importance, we state it as a formal assumption:

(UD) $C(\hat{S}, \succcurlyeq_1, \ldots, \succcurlyeq_m)$ is defined for all preference profiles $\{\succcurlyeq_1, \ldots, \succcurlyeq_m\}$.

Although the choice set must be nonempty, it need not be a singleton; that is, the social decision rule might generate more than one optimal social state.

Although it is important to remember that the social choice depends upon the preference profile of the society, where no confusion will result we simplify the notation by writing (19.1) as $C(\hat{S})$. Also, in what follows, it is convenient to introduce the shorthand notation, $s \in C(\hat{S})$, which means that the social state s is in the social choice set when the feasible social-state subset is $\hat{S}$. Similarly, $\bar{S} \subseteq C(\hat{S})$ means that the set of social states $\bar{S}$ is a subset of the social choice set when $\hat{S}$ is the feasible set of social states. Thus $\bar{S} \subseteq C(\hat{S})$ if and only if $s \in C(\hat{S})$ for all $s \in \bar{S}$.

It is important to note that the definition of a social choice function requires that choice be made out of every possible set of feasible social states; that is, $C(\hat{S})$ must be nonempty for all nonempty subsets $\hat{S}$ of the social-state space. Thus, the Pareto criterion does not generate a social choice function; $C(\{\overset{*}{s}, \hat{s}\})$ is nonempty only if every member of the community ranks $\overset{*}{s}$ as highly as $\hat{s}$ or every member ranks $\hat{s}$ at least as highly as $\overset{*}{s}$ (i.e., $\overset{*}{s} \succcurlyeq_c \hat{s}$ for all c or $\hat{s} \succcurlyeq_c \overset{*}{s}$ for all c, or both). When the community is not unanimous social choice is not defined.

Social Preference Ordering

An alternative to the construction of social choice functions is a procedure for aggregating individual preferences into a *social preference ordering*. A mapping from individual preference orderings into a social preference ordering is usually referred to as the *Arrow social welfare function*. This social preference ordering can then be used to generate social choice functions just as individual preference orderings are used to generate consumer demand functions. That is, given a (weak) social preference relation, $\succcurlyeq$, the social choice function is generated by the following rule: $\overset{*}{s} \in C(\hat{S})$ if and only if $\overset{*}{s} \succcurlyeq s$ for all $s \in \hat{S}$.

It is similarly possible to associate with any social choice function a social preference relation as follows: $\overset{*}{s} \succcurlyeq s$ if and only if $s \in C(\{\overset{*}{s}, s\})$. That is, social state $\overset{*}{s}$ is at least as good as s if and only if $\overset{*}{s}$ is in the choice set when the only alternatives are $\overset{*}{s}$ and s. Similarly, strict social preference can be derived from the social choice function by $\overset{*}{s} \succ s$ if and only if $\{\overset{*}{s}\} = C(\{\overset{*}{s}, s\})$, and social indifference can be defined by $\overset{*}{s} \sim s$ if and only if $\{\overset{*}{s}, s\} = C(\{\overset{*}{s}, s\})$.

19.3 THE IMPOSSIBILITY THEOREM

This section examines a number of conditions that we might want a social choice function to satisfy. The reasonableness and desirability of these conditions is established by examining the shortcomings of several well-known social choice rules—simple majority rule, extension of majority rule, and rank-order voting (the "Borda [1781] rule"). The final part of this section discusses Arrow's "impossibility theorem" which indicates that certain of these desirable restrictions on social choice are logically incompatible with one another.

Transitivity of the Social Choice Rule

The construction of social choice functions and social preference orderings are alternative approaches to social choice. These two approaches to social choice are not equivalent. There is no immediate reason why a social choice rule must be "rationalized" by a social preference ordering (i.e., a reflexive, complete, transitive preference relation). Although the associated social preference relation must be complete (since $C(\{\bar{s}, \hat{s}\})$ cannot be empty for any pair of social states), it need not be transitive. For example, a social choice rule might yield $\overset{*}{s} \in C(\{\overset{*}{s}, \bar{s}\})$, $\bar{s} \in C(\{\bar{s}, \hat{s}\})$, and $\overset{*}{s} \notin C(\{\overset{*}{s}, \hat{s}\})$. This implies that $\overset{*}{s} \succcurlyeq \bar{s}$, $\bar{s} \succcurlyeq \hat{s}$, and $\hat{s} \succ \overset{*}{s}$ so that social choice and the associated social preference relation do not satisfy the transitivity condition:

(T) $\quad \overset{*}{s} \in C(\{\overset{*}{s}, \bar{s}\})$ and $\bar{s} \in C(\{\bar{s}, s'\})$ implies $\overset{*}{s} \in C(\{\overset{*}{s}, s'\})$.

Some well-known social choice rules are not transitive. Consider for example, the method of majority rule.[3] Suppose that $\hat{S} = \{\overset{*}{s}, \bar{s}, \hat{s}\}$ and that the three members of the voting community have the following rankings of the social states:

	$c =$ 1	2	3
Rank = 1	$\overset{*}{s}$	$\bar{s}$	$\hat{s}$
2	$\bar{s}$	$\hat{s}$	$\overset{*}{s}$
3	$\hat{s}$	$\overset{*}{s}$	$\bar{s}$

In a pairwise choice over $\{\overset{*}{s}, \bar{s}\}$, $\overset{*}{s}$ wins two votes to one; i.e., $\{\overset{*}{s}\} = C(\{\overset{*}{s}, \bar{s}\})$ and $\overset{*}{s} \succ \bar{s}$. Similarly, $\{\bar{s}\} = C(\{\bar{s}, \hat{s}\})$ so that $\bar{s} \succ \hat{s}$ and $\{\hat{s}\} = C(\{\hat{s}, \overset{*}{s}\})$ so that $\hat{s} \succ \overset{*}{s}$; consequently, $\succ$ (and hence $\succcurlyeq$) is intransitive.

[3] Intransitivity of majority rule has been known for almost two centuries. This property was first noted by Condorcet in 1785.

We have already indicated that the Pareto criterion fails as a definitive social choice rule because the implied social preference relation is incomplete (hence, some choice sets are empty). Majority rule is flawed because the implied social preference relation is not transitive. This means that the outcome of majority rule processes can depend upon the agenda—that is, upon the order in which votes are taken. In the three-person, three-alternative example described above, any of the three alternative social states can be enacted by appropriate manipulation of the agenda. For example, if the agenda entails first a vote between $\bar{s}$ and $\hat{s}$ and then a vote between $\overset{*}{s}$ and the winner of the first vote (viz., $\bar{s}$), $\overset{*}{s}$ is adopted. But an agenda in which $\overset{*}{s}$ and $\bar{s}$ are first voted upon and then $\hat{s}$ is matched against the winner of the first vote (viz., $\overset{*}{s}$) generates $\hat{s}$ as the outcome.

These two agendas and outcomes and the third possible agenda and outcome are illustrated below. In each case, the social state that receives a "bye"

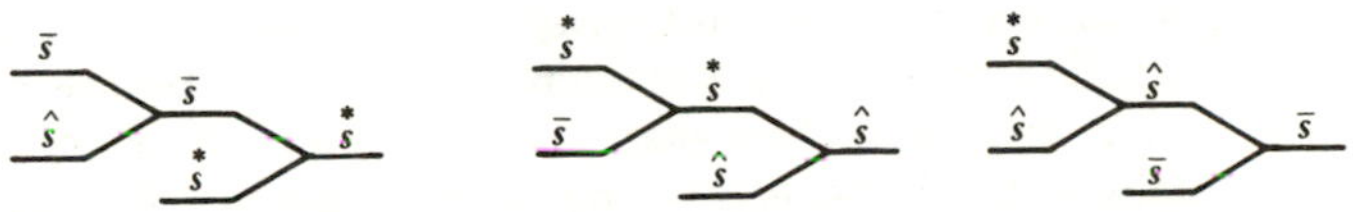

in the first round is the ultimate winner. Thus, intransitivity in the social preference relation makes the social decision procedure vulnerable to the (possibly sinister) manipulation of the agenda. One might therefore argue that a social preference relation should satisfy the transitivity condition. As Arrow [1951b, p. 120] puts it, transitivity will insure the ". . . independence of the final choice from the path to it . . . an intransitive social choice mechanism may . . . produce decisions that are clearly unsatisfactory."

One possible escape from the dilemma posed by the intransitivity of majority rule is to acknowledge the preference cycles and simply treat the elements of such cycles as members of an indifference class. That is, since in the above example $\{\overset{*}{s}, \bar{s}, \hat{s}\}$ forms a preference cycle, $\overset{*}{s} \succ \bar{s} \succ \hat{s} \succ \overset{*}{s}$, it might make sense to say that society is indifferent between these alternatives. This idea is formalized as follows. Let $\succcurlyeq^m$ be the preference relation induced by simple majority rule; i.e., $\overset{*}{s} \succ^m \bar{s}$ if and only if $N(\overset{*}{s}, \bar{s}) \geq N(\bar{s}, \overset{*}{s})$ where $N(\overset{*}{s}, \bar{s})$ is the number of individuals who prefer $\overset{*}{s}$ to $\bar{s}$. We know from the above example that $\succcurlyeq^m$ is intransitive. Define a new preference relation $\succcurlyeq$ by $\overset{*}{s} \succcurlyeq \bar{s}$ if and only if there exists a "chain" $\{s^1, \ldots, s^k\}$in S such that $\overset{*}{s} \succcurlyeq^m s^1, s^1 \succcurlyeq^m s^2, \ldots, s^{k-1} \succcurlyeq^m s^k, s^k \succcurlyeq \bar{s}$. Also, $\overset{*}{s} \sim \bar{s}$ if and only if $\overset{*}{s} \succcurlyeq \bar{s}$ and $\bar{s} \succcurlyeq \overset{*}{s}$, and $\overset{*}{s} \succ \bar{s}$ if and only if $\overset{*}{s} \succcurlyeq \bar{s}$ and not $\bar{s} \succcurlyeq \overset{*}{s}$. Finally, the choice function is defined by $\overset{*}{s} \in C(S)$ if and only if $\overset{*}{s} \succcurlyeq s$ for all $s \in S$.

The relation $\succcurlyeq$ is called the "transitive closure" of $\succcurlyeq^m$ since it eliminates the intransitivities of majority rule. To see this, suppose that we have an intransitivity cycle, $\overset{*}{s} \succ^m s^1$, $s^1 \succ^m s^2, \ldots, s^{k-1} \succ^m s^k, s^k \succ^m \bar{s}, \bar{s} \succ^m \overset{*}{s}$. Then, according to the above definition, $\overset{*}{s} \succcurlyeq \bar{s}$ since the chain $\{s^1, \ldots, s^k\}$ connects $\overset{*}{s}$ to $\bar{s}$. Moreover $\bar{s} \succ^m \overset{*}{s}$ trivially implies $\bar{s} \succcurlyeq^m \bar{s}$ and $\bar{s} \succcurlyeq^m \overset{*}{s}$ so that $\bar{s} \succcurlyeq \overset{*}{s}$ ($\{\bar{s}\}$ is the "chain"). Hence $\bar{s} \sim \overset{*}{s}$, eliminating the intransitivity. In the three-person, three-alternative example above, the cycle $\overset{*}{s} \succ \bar{s}$, $\bar{s} \succ \hat{s}$, and $\hat{s} \succ \overset{*}{s}$ implies that $\overset{*}{s} \sim \bar{s}$, $\overset{*}{s} \sim \hat{s}$, and $\bar{s} \sim \hat{s}$. Thus, $C(\{\overset{*}{s}, \bar{s}, \hat{s}\}) = \{\overset{*}{s}, \bar{s}, \hat{s}\}$, $C(\{\overset{*}{s}, \bar{s}\}) = \{\overset{*}{s}, \bar{s}\}$, etc.

The Weak Pareto Condition

Does the transitive-closure operation salvage majority rule as a satisfactory social decision rule? Not really. Suppose that we expand to four the number of alternatives and consider the following set of preferences:

c =	1	2	3
Rank = 1:	s^1	s^2	s^3
2:	s^2	s^3	s^4
3:	s^3	s^4	s^1
4:	s^4	s^1	s^2

Clearly, $N(s^1 \succ_c s^2) > N(s^2 \succ_c s^1)$, $N(s^2 \succ_c s^3) > N(s^3 \succ_c s^2)$, $N(s^3 \succ_c s^4) > N(s^4 \succ_c s^3)$, and $N(s^4 \succ_c s^1) > N(s^1 \succ_c s^4)$ so that $s^1 \succ^m s^2$, $s^2 \succ^m s^3$, $s^3 \succ^m s^4$, and $s^4 \succ^m s^1$. It follows that $\{s^1, s^2, s^3, s^4\}$ constitutes a social indifference class; society is indifferent between the four alternatives according to the transitive closure of the simple majority-rule relation. Hence, $C(\{s^1, s^2, s^3, s^4\}) = \{s^1, s^2, s^3, s^4\}$. Note, however, that all three members of the community strictly prefer s^3 to s^4; that is, s^4 is in the choice set out of $\{s^1, s^2, s^3, s^4\}$ even though it is Pareto inferior to s^3! Worse yet, $\{s^3, s^4\} = C(\{s^3, s^4\})$, since society is indifferent between s^3 and s^4; hence even in a pairwise choice s^3 is not adopted over the Pareto-dominated social state s^4. Thus, this extension of majority rule suggests the need for the "(weak) Pareto principle"

(P) $\overset{*}{s} \succ_c \bar{s}$ for all c implies $\{\overset{*}{s}\} = C(\{\overset{*}{s}, \bar{s}\})$.[4]

This condition states that Pareto-dominated social states should never be adopted in pairwise choices. This is certainly a reasonable condition to require of a social decision procedure. It would be a perverse social choice rule that did not adopt $\overset{*}{s}$ over $\hat{s}$ if *every* member of the community preferred $\overset{*}{s}$ to $\hat{s}$. Such a social choice function would appear to be unacceptably *unresponsive* to the preferences of the members of the society. Another obvious example of a social choice rule that violates the Pareto principle—and focuses on unresponsitivity—is one that is *imposed* from outside the community (by, e.g., foreign imperialists, God, or an "absolute" moral code).

The Nonimposition and Nonnegative Responsiveness Conditions

In fact, rather than the weak Pareto condition (P), Arrow required the closely related conditions of nonimposition (NI) and nonnegative responsiveness (R), defined as follows:

[4] (P) is a "weak" Pareto restriction because (a) it only requires that society choose $\overset{*}{s}$ if every member of the community strictly prefers $\overset{*}{s}$ to $\bar{s}$ (rather than requiring that $\overset{*}{s}$ be adopted if $\overset{*}{s}$ is at least as good as $\bar{s}$ in each individual ordering and strictly better than $\bar{s}$ in some ordering) and (b) it only applies to pairwise choices.

(NI) For each pair of social states $\{s, \bar{s}\}$ in S, there is some collection of individual preferences $\{\succcurlyeq_1, \ldots, \succcurlyeq_m\}$ such that $\overset{*}{s} \in C(\{\overset{*}{s}, \bar{s}\}, \succcurlyeq_1, \ldots, \succcurlyeq_m)$.

(R) Consider two collections of individual orderings, $\{\succcurlyeq_1, \ldots, \succcurlyeq_m\}$ and $\{\succcurlyeq'_1, \ldots, \succcurlyeq'_m\}$, satisfying, for all c and for any $\{\overset{*}{s}, s\}$, each of the following conditions:

(a) $\overset{*}{s} \succcurlyeq_c s$ implies $\overset{*}{s} \succcurlyeq'_c s$;

(b) $\overset{*}{s} \succ_c s$ implies $\overset{*}{s} \succ'_c s$; and

(c) $\bar{s} \succcurlyeq_c \hat{s}$ if and only if $\bar{s} \succcurlyeq'_c \hat{s}$ for all $\{\bar{s}, \hat{s}\} \subseteq S - \{\overset{*}{s}, s\}$.[5]

If $\{\overset{*}{s}\} = C(\{\overset{*}{s}, s\}, \succcurlyeq_1, \ldots, \succcurlyeq_m)$, then $\{\overset{*}{s}\} = C(\{\overset{*}{s}, s\}, \succcurlyeq'_1, \ldots, \succcurlyeq'_m)$.

Nonimposition (NI) requires that there exist some preference profile such that $\overset{*}{s}$ is adopted in a pairwise choice. This condition clearly precludes "choice" that is extraneously imposed. It is also obviously weaker than the Pareto condition (P) since, if (P) is satisfied, the set of preferences that will do the trick in (NI) is one that satisfies $\overset{*}{s} \succ_c \bar{s}$ for all c.

Nonnegative responsiveness requires the following. Suppose that, given a set of individual preferences $\{\succcurlyeq_1, \ldots, \succcurlyeq_m\}$, society adopts $\overset{*}{s}$ over $\hat{s}$. Suppose further that some individual changes his preferences more favorably toward $\overset{*}{s}$. Perhaps his preferences change from $\hat{s} \succ_c \overset{*}{s}$ to $\overset{*}{s} \sim'_c \hat{s}$ or from $\overset{*}{s} \sim_c s$ to $\overset{*}{s} \succ'_c \hat{s}$. Also suppose that his preferences regarding all other pairs of social states remain unchanged. Then it must remain true that society still chooses $\overset{*}{s}$ over $\hat{s}$. Thus, if (some) individual preferences change favorably regarding $\overset{*}{s}$ vis-à-vis any other social state, say $\hat{s}$, and everything else remains the same, social choice cannot change adversely regarding social state $\overset{*}{s}$. Thus, social choice cannot be perversely responsive to individual preferences.

Nonnegative responsiveness is neither weaker nor stronger than the Pareto principle (P). However, it is easy to show that nonnegative responsiveness together with nonimposition implies the weak Pareto principle (see exercise 19.2). On the other hand, (P) does not imply (R); hence the conjunction of (NI) and (R) is stronger than (P).

The Independence-of-Irrelevant-Alternatives Condition

We have found that simple majority rule violates the transitivity condition (T) and the obvious extension of majority rule to eliminate preference cycles violates the Pareto condition (P) (and therefore the conjunction of (NI) and (R)). An alternative voting rule which might offer some salvation from this dilemma is the method of rank-order voting or, as it is often called, the "Borda rule" (after its promulgator, Borda [1781]). We distinguish between the "broad Borda rule" and the "narrow Borda rule." Each of these procedures assigns numbers to social states according to their ranking in each individual's preference ordering. That is, a certain number is assigned to a social state for being first in an individual's ordering, a smaller number for being second, etc. Given a set of individual preference orderings, we can then associate with each social alternative in any feasible subset of S the total number of points received

[5] $S - \{\overset{*}{s}, s\}$ is the set S with the two elements $\{\overset{*}{s}, s\}$ deleted.

by adding across individuals. The alternative with the most points wins. The difference between the broad Borda rule and the narrow Borda rule is that the former procedure assigns numbers to social states according to their rank in the complete social state space S, whereas the latter assigns numbers according to their rank in the relevant feasible subset $\hat{S}$.

It is apparent that the narrow Borda rule is plagued by intransitivity. Consider again the three-person, three-alternative example with preferences:

	c = 1	2	3
Rank = 1:	$\overset{*}{s}$	$\bar{s}$	$\hat{s}$
2:	$\bar{s}$	$\hat{s}$	$\overset{*}{s}$
3:	$\hat{s}$	$\overset{*}{s}$	$\bar{s}$

If we assign two and one points for first and second ranks, respectively, in binary choices and three, two, and one points in trinary choices, the scores are given by the following:

$\hat{S}$	$\overset{*}{s}$	$\bar{s}$	$\hat{s}$
$\{\overset{*}{s}, \bar{s}\}$	5	4	
$\{\bar{s}, \hat{s}\}$		5	4
$\{\overset{*}{s}, \hat{s}\}$	4		5
$\{\overset{*}{s}, \bar{s}, \hat{s}\}$	6	6	6

Thus, $\{\overset{*}{s}\} = C(\{\overset{*}{s}, \bar{s}\})$, $\{\bar{s}\} = C(\{\bar{s}, \hat{s}\})$, and $\{\hat{s}\} = C(\{\overset{*}{s}, \hat{s}\})$, violating condition (T).

What about the broad Borda count? Employing the "three-two-one" scoring rule for $S = \{\overset{*}{s}, \bar{s}, \hat{s}\}$ yields:

$\hat{S}$	$\overset{*}{s}$	$\bar{s}$	$\hat{s}$
$\{\overset{*}{s}, \bar{s}\}$	6	6	
$\{\bar{s}, \hat{s}\}$		6	6
$\{\overset{*}{s}, \hat{s}\}$	6		6
$\{\overset{*}{s}, \bar{s}, \hat{s}\}$	6	6	6

Thus, $\{\overset{*}{s}, \bar{s}\} = C(\{\overset{*}{s}, \bar{s}\})$, etc. That is, the social preference relation generated by the broad Borda rule generates indifference between all three pairs of alternatives. Moreover, the transitivity condition is clearly satisfied since the total scores provide a complete preference ordering. Finally, the broad Borda rule satisfies the Pareto criterion (P) (if every member ranks $\overset{*}{s}$ higher than $\bar{s}$, $\overset{*}{s}$ receives more points), and, in fact, the stronger nonimposition (NI) and nonnegative responsiveness (R) conditions.

So is the broad Borda rule a "reasonable" social decision rule? There is, unfortunately, a problem with it. Suppose that the third individual reversed the order of $\overset{*}{s}$ and $\bar{s}$ in his preference ordering. This would lower the total points assigned to $\overset{*}{s}$ from 6 to 5 so that $\hat{s}$ now wins in a social choice over the pair $\{\overset{*}{s}, \hat{s}\}$. This change in the social choice over $\{\overset{*}{s}, \hat{s}\}$ occurs even though the ranking of this pair is unchanged in each individual preference ordering. Thus, the relation between $\overset{*}{s}$ and the *irrelevant* alternative $\bar{s}$ has affected the choice over

$\{\overset{*}{s}, \hat{s}\}$. This dependence upon preferences over irrelevant alternatives might be viewed as an unsatisfactory characteristic of a social choice rule. It is as if the choice between Ford and Carter depended on individual preferences between Nixon and Ford or between Churchill and Stalin.

The mischievous nature of this dependence upon preferences over irrelevant alternatives led Arrow to posit the "independence of irrelevant alternatives" condition:

(I) Let $\{\succcurlyeq_1, \ldots, \succcurlyeq_m\}$ and $\{\succcurlyeq'_1, \ldots, \succcurlyeq'_m\}$ be two sets of individual orderings. If, for all pairs of alternatives, $\{\overset{*}{s}, \hat{s}\}$, in a subset $\hat{S}$ of S, $\overset{*}{s} \succcurlyeq_c \hat{s}$ if and only if $\overset{*}{s} \succcurlyeq'_c \hat{s}$ for all c, then $C(\hat{S}, \succcurlyeq_1, \ldots, \succcurlyeq_m) = C(\hat{S}, \succcurlyeq'_1, \ldots, \succcurlyeq'_m)$.

Condition (I) says the following: If we consider two alternative sets of individual orderings that, however, agree on a subset $\hat{S}$ of S, the social choice out of $\hat{S}$ must be identical for the two sets of individual values. In particular, the social choice out of $\hat{S}$ depends exclusively on the individual orderings over $\hat{S}$; it does not depend upon the individual orderings over the social states that are not in $\hat{S}$.

The Impossibility Theorem

We have provided examples of social choice rules, each of which violates one of the "reasonable" conditions: unrestricted domain (UD), transitivity (T), the Pareto principle (P), and the independence of irrelevant alternatives (I). The question that now arises is the following: What is an example of a social choice rule that satisfies all of these restrictions? The startling answer to this question is that any social choice function that satisfies (UD), (T), (P), and (I) when there are more than two social states[6] must be dictatorial—i.e., there must be a dictator, say individual d, such that, for all pairs $\{\overset{*}{s}, \bar{s}\}$ and all possible profiles of individual social orderings, $\overset{*}{s} \succ_d \bar{s}$ implies $\overset{*}{s} = C(\{\overset{*}{s}, \bar{s}\})$. That is, some member of the community must be a dictator in the sense that society adopts $\overset{*}{s}$ over $\bar{s}$ whenever $\overset{*}{s}$ is preferred by this dictator to $\bar{s}$ regardless of the preferences of the other members of the community. In a word, the only type of social organization that satisfies the four "reasonable" conditions—unrestricted domain, transitivity, the Pareto principle, and independence of irrelevant alternatives—is the particularly obnoxious antidemocratic form of government characterized by dictatorship. Social choice must be dictated by the preferences of one individual.

Arrow's discovery, which has had profound ramifications in political science, sociology, and philosophy as well as in economics, can be reformulated by adding a weak democracy condition; namely, "nondictatorship":

(ND) There is no individual d such that for all $\{\overset{*}{s}, \bar{s}\}$ in S and all possible profiles of individual social orderings, $\overset{*}{s} \succ_d \bar{s}$ implies $\{\overset{*}{s}\} = C(\{\overset{*}{s}, \bar{s}\})$.

[6] If S has only two elements, the method of majority rule satisfies all of the foregoing conditions.

Arrow's result, as modified in subsequent research, is as follows:

The Impossibility Theorem *If there are more than two social states, there does not exist a social choice function satisfying* (*UD*), (*T*), (*P*), (*I*), *and* (*ND*).

The result originally proved by Arrow is slightly weaker:[7]

The Arrow Impossibility Theorem *If there are more than two social states, there does not exist a social choice function satisfying* (*UD*), (*T*), (*NI*), (*R*), (*I*), *and* (*ND*).

The importance of this striking result, referred to both as the "Arrow impossibility theorem" and the "Arrow possibility theorem,"[8] is that it avoids a fruitless search for a social decision rule that satisfies all of Arrow's conditions. The construction of a social choice procedure must take cognizance of the fact that one of Arrow's conditions *must* be relaxed. The rapidly proliferating literature on social choice theory, all inspired by the seminal work of Arrow, has branched out into (at least) two distinct lines of research, each of which relaxes an alternative condition of Arrow's theorem. One branch of the social-choice literature concentrates on relaxation of the transitivity condition. It is suggested that transitivity of both social preference and social indifference is much too strong to be hoped for and unnecessary for a theory of rational social choice. This literature, which works out the implications of weaker forms of "collective rationality," is discussed briefly in section 19.5.

An alternative branch of the post-Arrow research on social choice modifies Arrow's framework to relax the implicit condition regarding the type of information that is admissible in the making of social decisions. Arrow's framework requires that only information about individual preference orderings be used in social choice procedures. In particular, information regarding interpersonal welfare comparisons—comparing the welfare of one (perhaps impoverished) individual with the welfare of another (perhaps wealthy) person—is precluded from consideration. One might argue that in practice all important social decisions require such information. Chapter 20 explores the implications of relaxing Arrow's informational constraints.

Given the importance of Arrow's result, a proof would seem to be called for here. Thus, before proceeding to a discussion of the post-Arrow research on social choice theory, we provide a proof in the next section.

[7] The result is slightly weaker because (NI) and (R) imply (P) whereas (P) does not imply (NI) and (R); hence there exist social choice functions satisfying (P) but not (NI) and (R), but no social choice function can satisfy (NI) and (R) but not (P).

[8] It is sometimes called the Arrow *possibility* theorem because of his original formulation: "if the social choice function satisfies (T), (NI), (R), (I), and (UD), then it is dictatorial."

19.4 PROOF OF THE IMPOSSIBILITY THEOREM*

In this section, we prove a slightly weakened form of Arrow's theorem, in which it is assumed that there are at least five alternatives in the social-state space (which is true of most economic models). The proof is attributable to Blau [1972], who also proves the theorem under the weakened (Arrow) hypothesis of three or more alternatives.

The logic of the proof is illuminated by proving a succession of lemmata. We assume throughout that the unrestricted domain (UD), independence-of-irrelevant-alternatives (I), Pareto (P), and transitivity (T) conditions are satisfied. The first lemma uses the notion of a decisive coalition. Let $M = \{1, \ldots, m\}$ be the set of individuals and let E be a subset of M. Also let E' be the individuals who are in M, but not in E (i.e., the complement of E in M). We say that E is *decisive* over $\{\overset{*}{s}, \bar{s}\}$ if $\overset{*}{s} \succ_c \bar{s}$ for all $c \in E$ and $\bar{s} \succ_c s^*$ for all c in E' implies $\{\overset{*}{s}\} = C(\{\overset{*}{s}, \bar{s}\})$, or $\overset{*}{s} \succ \bar{s}$. I.e., E is a *winning coalition* with respect to social choice over the pair $\{\overset{*}{s}, \bar{s}\}$ since unanimity of the members of E allows this group to prevail when members of E' unanimously disagree with E.

Lemma 1 *If s_1, s_2, s_3, and s_4 are distinct and if E is decisive over $\{s_1, s_2\}$, then E is also decisive over $\{s_3, s_4\}$.*

PROOF By (UD) and (I), $\{s_1\} = C(\{s_1, s_2\})$, or $s_1 \succ s_2$, so long as $s_1 \succ_c s_2$ for all $c \in E$ and $s_2 \succ_c s_1$ for all $c \in E'$ regardless of the preferences of these groups with respect to s_3 and s_4. Let the orderings over these four alternatives for all members of each group be as follows:

E	E'
s_3	s_2
s_1	s_4
s_2	s_3
s_4	s_1

Because of (P), $s_3 \succ s_1$ and $s_2 \succ s_4$. As E is decisive over $\{s_1, s_2\}$, $s_1 \succ s_2$. Applying (T) twice, we obtain $s_3 \succ s_2$ and then $s_3 \succ s_4$, as was to be shown. ‖

Lemma 2 *If S has at least five elements, $s_3 \neq s_4$, and E is decisive over $\{s_1, s_2\}$, then E is also decisive over $\{s_3, s_4\}$.*

PROOF If s_1, s_2, s_3, and s_4 are distinct, lemma 1 applies. If they are not distinct, there are at most three distinct elements among them. In that case, as S has at least five elements, there are s_5 and s_6 distinct from s_1, s_2, s_3, and s_4, and from each other. Then E decisive over $\{s_1, s_2\}$ implies that E is decisive over $\{s_5, s_6\}$ by lemma 1. But, again invoking lemma 1, decisiveness of E over $\{s_5, s_6\}$ implies decisiveness of E over $\{s_3, s_4\}$. ‖

Lemma 2 says that if E is decisive over a pair $\{\overset{*}{s}, \bar{s}\}$, it is decisive over *every* distinct pair of social states; i.e., whether E prevails against E' depends solely upon E and not upon the "issues." Independently of the pair of social states being considered, we can therefore say that if E prevails against E', it is a *winning coalition*. *Losing sets* are sets of individuals that do not win. (Note that a losing set is *never* decisive, for if it were so once, it would be so always by lemma 2.)

Decisiveness is defined only for the case where all members of E strictly prefer one social state to another and all members of E' have opposite strict preferences. The next lemma shows that if E is decisive over a pair of alternatives, it gets its way regardless of the preferences of E .

Lemma 3 *If E is a winning coalition and if $\overset{*}{s} \succ_c \bar{s}$ for all $c \in E$, then $\overset{*}{s} \succ \bar{s}$.*

PROOF Regardless of the preferences of E' over $\{\overset{*}{s}, \bar{s}\}$, by (UD) and (I), we can place a third alternative (since S has at least five), say $\hat{s}$, between $\overset{*}{s}$ and $\bar{s}$ in the preferences of the members of E and above $\overset{*}{s}$ and $\bar{s}$ in the preferences of all $c \in E'$. Then $\overset{*}{s} \succ \hat{s}$ because E is decisive and $\hat{s} \succ \bar{s}$ by (P). Hence, $\overset{*}{s} \succ \bar{s}$ by (T). ‖

Because of lemma 3, if a singleton $\{c\}$ is a winning coalition, then c is a dictator. To exploit this fact, we need one more lemma.

Lemma 4 *Let E and F be two losing sets with no common members. Then the set of individuals in either E or F, denoted $E \cup F$, is a losing set.*

PROOF Let G be the individuals in M but not in E or F. Invoking (UD) and (I), we can consider the following preferences over $\{\overset{*}{s}, \hat{s}, \bar{s}\}$ of the members of each of the three groups:

E	F	G
$\overset{*}{s}$	$\bar{s}$	$\hat{s}$
$\hat{s}$	$\overset{*}{s}$	$\bar{s}$
$\bar{s}$	$\hat{s}$	$\overset{*}{s}$

As E and F are losing sets, $\bar{s} \succ \overset{*}{s}$ and $\hat{s} \succ \bar{s}$. This implies $\hat{s} \succ \overset{*}{s}$ by (T). As $\overset{*}{s} \succcurlyeq_c \hat{s}$ for all $c \in E \cup F$, $\hat{s} \succ \overset{*}{s}$ implies that $E \cup F$ is a losing set. ‖

We are now prepared to prove the impossibility theorem for five or more social alternatives.

Impossibility Theorem for Five or More Alternatives *If there are more than four social states, there does not exist a social choice function satisfying (T), (P), (I), (ND), and (UD).*

PROOF The nondictatorship condition (ND) implies that each singleton $\{c\}$ is a losing set (otherwise, by lemmas 2 and 3, c would be a dictator). Invoking lemma 4, this implies that any pair $\{c, c'\}$, being the union of two singletons, is a losing set. Proceeding by induction, we arrive at the conclusion that the entire community M is a losing set; i.e., $\overset{*}{s} \succ_c \bar{s}$ for all $c \in M$ implies $\bar{s} \succ \overset{*}{s}$. But this contradicts the Pareto condition (P). ‖

19.5 COLLECTIVE RATIONALITY*

Quasitransitivity

To many, the most obvious candidate for relaxation among Arrow's restrictions of a social choice function is the transitivity condition. It can be argued that there is little reason to require that social preference and social indifference *both* be transitive. One suggestion, first made by Sen [1970a, p. 49], is that we require transitive strict social preference but not transitive social indifference. That is, we require that, for all possible sets of individual preference orderings, $\overset{*}{s} \succ \bar{s}$ and $\bar{s} \succ \hat{s}$ implies $\overset{*}{s} \succ \hat{s}$ but $\overset{*}{s} \sim \bar{s}$ and $\bar{s} \sim \hat{s}$ does not necessarily imply $\overset{*}{s} \sim \hat{s}$. Transitive strict preference but not necessarily transitive indifference is referred to as *quasitransitivity*. A principal attraction of quasitransitivity is that transitive strict preference assures the existence of optimal social states for any (appropriate) feasible set of social states. That is, given any feasible subset $\hat{S}$ of the social-state space, there exists at least one element $\overset{*}{s}$ that satisfies $\overset{*}{s} \succcurlyeq \hat{s}$ for all $\hat{s}$ in $\hat{S}$. Thus, intransitive indifference does not preclude the existence of a best element. It is only intransitive strict preference that generates cycles in the social preferences (such as illustrated in the majority rule example above) and it is these cycles that make social choice impossible.

The Extended Pareto Criterion

Weakening transitivity to quasitransitivity obviates the Arrow impossibility conclusion. That is, there do exist social choice functions that satisfy the quasitransitivity, responsiveness, nondictatorship, independence-of-irrelevant-alternatives, and unrestricted domain conditions. An example of a social choice function that satisfies these conditions has been suggested by Sen [1970a, pp. 27 and 69]. This social choice function is a straightforward extension of the Pareto criterion, in which Pareto-incomparable alternatives are redefined to be equivalent in the social preference ordering. That is, $\overset{*}{s} \succ \bar{s}$ if and only if $\overset{*}{s} \succcurlyeq_c \bar{s}$ for all c and $\overset{*}{s} \succ_c \bar{s}$ for some c and $\bar{s} \succcurlyeq \overset{*}{s}$ otherwise. Thus, s is socially preferred to $\bar{s}$ if every member of the community ranks $\overset{*}{s}$ at least as high as $\bar{s}$ and at least one member ranks it higher, and society is indifferent between $\overset{*}{s}$ and $\bar{s}$ if all members of the community are indifferent between these two alternatives *or* there is disagreement about them (some member prefer $\overset{*}{s}$ and others prefer $\bar{s}$).

It is easy to see that this extension completes the social weak preference relation and that the social choice set is nonempty for all possible individual orderings and for all feasible subsets of the social-state space.

It is also easy to see that this extended Pareto criterion is quasitransitive. Suppose that $\overset{*}{s} \succ \bar{s}$ and $\bar{s} \succ \hat{s}$. It follows that $\overset{*}{s} \succcurlyeq_c \bar{s}$ and $\bar{s} \succcurlyeq_c \hat{s}$ for all c and $\overset{*}{s} \succ_c \bar{s}$ for some c, say $\bar{c}$. Transitivity of the individual preference orderings therefore implies that $\overset{*}{s} \succcurlyeq_c \hat{s}$ for all c and $\overset{*}{s} \succ_{\bar{c}} \hat{s}$ so that $\overset{*}{s} \succ \hat{s}$.

The extended Pareto criterion also satisfies the nondictatorship condition (in fact, all agents are treated equally, or at least "anonymously"), the Pareto condition (trivially) and, indeed, the stronger responsiveness and nonimposition conditions, and the independence-of-irrelevant-alternatives condition (since choice is based entirely upon comparison of relevant alternatives).

If quasitransitivity is accepted as a reasonable criterion for collective rationality, one might be tempted to conclude that the extended Pareto criterion constitutes a reasonable basis for social choice. It requires little thought, however, to see that the extended Pareto criterion is plagued by serious deficiencies; in fact, redefining incomparable Pareto alternatives to be characterized by social indifference simply sweeps the important problems with the Pareto criterion under the rug. If *any* member of the community (no matter how perverse or diabolical his preferences may be) prefers social state $\overset{*}{s}$ to social state $\hat{s}$, $\overset{*}{s}$ must be in the social choice set even if every other member of the community prefers $\hat{s}$. Thus, *every* member of the community has veto power. If Nero wants to burn down Rome, we cannot say that not burning down Rome is socially preferred to burning it down. An individual with veto power certainly has some dictatorial power.

We refer to an individual with veto power as a "weak dictator." Formally, individual w is a weak dictator if, for all $\{\overset{*}{s}, \hat{s}\}$ in S and for all possible preference profiles, $\overset{*}{s} \succ_w \hat{s}$ implies that $\overset{*}{s} \in C(\{\overset{*}{s}, \hat{s}\})$ (i.e., $\overset{*}{s} \succcurlyeq \hat{s}$). The difference between a weak dictator and a dictator, then, is that the latter is able to impose his will on society, whereas the former is in a sense able to block social programs. If the weak dictator prefers $\overset{*}{s}$ to $\hat{s}$, the extended Pareto criterion never allows us to infer that $\hat{s}$ is preferred to $\overset{*}{s}$ even if every other member of the community prefers $\hat{s}$ to $\overset{*}{s}$.

The extended Pareto criterion is, of course, just one example of a quasi-transitive social choice rule. The question arises as to whether there are other quasitransitive social choice rules that are not plagued by the implication that a weak dictator exists. That such is not the case has been shown by Gibbard [1969] (see also Mas-Colell and Sonnenschein [1972]). Thus, we have another impossibility theorem: if a social choice rule satisfies the conditions of quasitransitivity, the Pareto principle, and the independence of irrelevant alternatives, it must be weakly dictatorial, meaning that some member of the community has veto power in the sense described above.

Gibbard actually established the stronger condition of the existence of an "oligarchy"—i.e., a *group* of weak dictators with the additional characteristic that if $\overset{*}{s} \succ_c \hat{s}$ for all c in the group, $\{\overset{*}{s}\} = C(\{\overset{*}{s}, \hat{s}\})$; i.e., "the oligarchy is decisive if united and furthermore everyone in the oligarchy has a veto" (Sen [1975, p. 7]). Thus, while it is true that weakening Arrow's transitivity requirement obviates his conclusion regarding the existence of a social choice function, the collective rationality requirement of quasitransitivity implies that the social choice rule must be almost as undemocratic as the dictatorial social choice rule required by transitivity.

The Acyclicity Condition

If quasitransitivity of the social preference relation and democracy (described here as implying the absence of a weak dictator) are fundamentally incompatible (given, of course, the conditions: (UD), (P), and (I)), the question that now arises is whether or not a further weakening of the collective rationality requirement would make possible the formulation of a social choice rule that is significantly more democratic. There does exist a natural weakening of the quasitransitivity restriction. Recall that quasitransitivity means that *strict* social preference is transitive and that the appeal of this condition is that it precludes cycles in society's preferences such as can be evinced by the method of majority rule. Formally, transitivity of strict preference says that $\overset{*}{s} \succ \hat{s}$ and $\hat{s} \succ \bar{s}$ implies $\overset{*}{s} \succ \bar{s}$. This condition is equivalent to the following condition (see exercise 2.4):

(TSP) For all finite chains $\{s^1, \ldots, s^m\}$, $s^1 \succ s^2, s^2 \succ s^3, \ldots, s^{m-1} \succ s^m$ implies $s^1 \succ s^m$.

Given asymmetry of $\succ$, this condition, in turn, obviously implies the following:

(A) For all finite chains $\{s^1, \ldots, s^m\}$, $s^1 \succ s^2, s^2 \succ s^3, \ldots, s^{m-1} \succ s^m$ implies "*not* $s^m \succ s^1$."

Thus, (A), referred to as "acyclicity," says that strict preference cannot cycle. Note, however, that the transitivity condition (TSP) is logically stronger than the acyclicity condition (A). Acyclicity—but *not* transitivity—is consistent with $s^1 \succ s^2, s^2 \succ s^3, \ldots, s^{m-1} \succ s^m$, and $s^1 \sim s^m$.[9]

The appeal of acyclicity of a social preference relation is that, given that the social preference relation is complete, acyclicity is necessary and sufficient for the existence of a social choice function. That is, given completeness, acyclicity is necessary and sufficient for the social choice set $C(\hat{S})$ to be nonempty for all finite subsets of the social-state space.

Does weakening the quasitransitivity condition to acyclicity resolve the conflict between collective rationality, the Pareto condition, and the independence of irrelevant alternatives? Not really. Brown [1975] has shown that if (A), (P), and (I) are satisfied, there exists a group of individuals—called a "collegial polity"—such that $\{\overset{*}{s}\} = C(\{\overset{*}{s}, \hat{s}\})$ only if $\overset{*}{s} \succ_c \hat{s}$ for all c in the group. Thus, the collegial polity has a veto even though it can't dictate choice. In other words, a collegial polity is collectively a "weak dictator" much as an oligarchy is collectively a "dictator."

The Path-Independence Concept

The social choice dilemma posed by the preceding discussion has been very clearly summarized by Ferejohn and Grether [1975]:

> *Essentially the results of Arrow, Mas-Colell and Sonnenschein, and Brown indicate that when a collective rationality requirement is combined with* [*the Pareto principle and the independence-of-irrelevant-alternatives condition*], *the "distribution of power" in society is required to be quite asymmetric or social choice must be indecisive. Requiring* [*transitivity*] *implies the existence of a dictator, quasitransitivity yields an oligarchy, and acyclic social choice implies the existence of what Brown has called a "collegial polity."*

[9] Although the transitivity condition defined on triples extends to any finite chain, the condition that strict preference does not cycle on triples cannot similarly be extended to any finite chain. If we wish to preclude cycles in strict preferences, therefore, we must posit the assumption (A) directly.

Ferejohn and Grether go on to argue that, consistent with the spirit of Arrow's discussion, the social-rationality condition can be weakened even further (beyond acyclicity) in such a way as to allow for a symmetric distribution of power, thus precluding the existence of a powerful coalition (and therefore precluding the existence of an oligarchy and, a fortiori, a dictator).[10] It is obvious that acyclicity (and, a fortiori, quasitransitivity and transitivity) of social preferences is sufficient to preclude the possibility of producing decisions that are clearly unsatisfactory because it insures the "independence of the final choice from the path to it" (Arrow [1963, p. 120]). Ferejohn and Grether argue, however, that while acyclicity is sufficient for this property, it is not necessary. They therefore suggest an alternative collective rationality axiom that is essentially a formalization of Arrow's verbal notion of path independence.

In order to formalize the Ferejohn–Grether path-independence concept, it is convenient to introduce some additional set theoretic notation. Consider two sets of social states, denoted S^1 and S^2. The *union* of these two sets, denoted $S^1 \cup S^2$ is defined as the collection of all social states that are in either S^1 or S^2 (or both). This concept is easily generalized to a larger collection of sets, say $\{S^1, \ldots, S^k\}$. The union of this collection of sets, denoted $\bigcup_{i=1}^{k} S^i$, is the collection of social states that are members of at least one of the sets, $S^i, i = 1, \ldots, k$.

The Ferejohn–Grether path-independence assumption can now be stated formally as follows:

(PI) For all $\hat{S} \subseteq S$, $C(\bigcup_{i=1}^{k} C(S^i)) \subseteq C(\hat{S})$ for any collection of sets $\{S^1, \ldots, S^k\}$ such that $S^i \subseteq \hat{S}$, $i = 1, \ldots, k$, and $\bigcup_{i=1}^{k} S^i = \hat{S}$.

In words, this condition says that "if the problem of choosing over S is broken up into choosing over subsets and then choosing over the remaining elements, the final choice from this procedure should still be in the choice set from S. That is, we do not want to end up in an unsatisfactory position because of the way the agenda was manipulated or because of the way the institutions we are dealing with work. As we read Arrow, the principle reason that society should choose transitivity is to insure that [(PI)] will be satisfied" (Ferejohn and Grether [1975, p. 4]).[11]

Ferejohn and Grether go on to show that it is possible to construct a social choice function that satisfies path independence, the Pareto condition, and independence of irrelevant alternatives, but does not require the existence of a powerful coalition. They show this by constructing a social decision rule with the required properties. This social choice function is essentially an extension of the method of majority rule. In fact, the Ferejohn–Grether social decision rule

[10] Note that although acyclicity is necessary for $\succcurlyeq$ to generate a choice out of every feasible set (i.e., for $\succcurlyeq$ to yield a C such that $C(\hat{S})$ is nonempty for all $\hat{S} \subseteq S$) it is *not* a necessary property of a social choice function since a given C need not be generated by any social ordering $\succcurlyeq$.

[11] Ferejohn and Grether actually call this condition "weak path independence" in order to differentiate it from a stronger path-independence concept, attributable to Plott [1973], in which the set inclusion in (PI) is strengthened to equality: $C(\bigcup_{i=1}^{k} C(S^i)) = C(\hat{S})$.

is a modification of the extended majority-rule procedure described above. Recall that $\overset{*}{s} \succ^m \hat{s}$ if and only if $N(\overset{*}{s} \succ_c \hat{s}) > N(\hat{s} \succ_c \overset{*}{s})$—i.e., the number of individuals who prefer $\overset{*}{s}$ to $\hat{s}$ is greater than the number who prefer $\hat{s}$ to $\overset{*}{s}$. We say that $\overset{*}{s} \succ_{\hat{S}} \hat{s}$ if there exists a chain $\{s^1, \ldots, s^k\}$ in $\hat{S}$ such that $\overset{*}{s} \succ^m s^1$, $s^1 \succ^m s^2, \ldots, s^{k-1} \succ^m s^k$, and $s^k \succ^m \hat{s}$. Now define $C^{fg}(\hat{S})$ as the set of $\hat{s} \in \hat{S}$ such that $\hat{s} \succ_{\hat{S}} s$ for all $s \in \hat{S}$, for all $\hat{S}$. The difference between this social choice function and that induced by the extended majority rule ordering is that the connecting chain defining $\hat{S}$ must be in the feasible set $\hat{S}$ rather than in the universal set S. It is this restriction that forces the Ferejohn–Grether social choice function to satisfy the weak Pareto condition (P). Consider, in particular, the three-person, four-alternative example:

	c = 1	2	3
Rank = 1:	s^1	s^2	s^3
2:	s^2	s^3	s^4
3:	s^3	s^4	s^1
4:	s^4	s^1	s^2

It will be recalled that the simple extension of majority rule induces a social preference relation characterized by indifference between all pairs. Hence $\{s^3, s^4\} = C(\{s^3, s^4\})$ even though every member of the community strictly prefers s^3 to s^4. The Ferejohn–Grether extension of majority rule, however, implies that $\{s^3\} = C^{fg}(\{s^3, s^4\})$ since there is no preference chain in $\{s^3, s^4\}$ connecting s^4 to s^3. The Ferejohn–Grether social choice function does not satisfy acyclicity (since $\{s^1\} = C^{fg}(\{s^1, s^2\})$, $\{s^2\} = C^{fg}(\{s^2, s^3\})$, $\{s^3\} = C^{fg}(\{s^3, s^4\})$, and $\{s^4\} = C^{fg}(\{s^4, s^1\})$) but it does satisfy path independence (PI) since, for example,[12] $C^{fg}(\{s^1, s^2\}) = \{s^1\} \subseteq C^{fg}(\{s^1, s^2, s^3\}) = \{s^1, s^2, s^3\} \subseteq C^{fg}(\{s^1, s^2, s^3, s^4\}) = \{s^1, s^2, s^3, s^4\}$.

It also satisfies the weak Pareto condition ($\overset{*}{s} \succ_c \hat{s}$ for all c implies $m = N(\overset{*}{s} \succ_c \hat{s}) > N(\hat{s} \succ_c \overset{*}{s}) = 0$ which in turn implies $\{\overset{*}{s}\} = C^{fg}(\{\overset{*}{s}, \hat{s}\})$) and the independence-of-irrelevant-alternatives condition ($\succ_{\hat{S}}$ is constructed using elements in $\hat{S}$ only), yet is clearly quite democratic. In fact, the constructed social decision rule actually satisfies a democratic property that is stronger than the mere absence of a powerful coalition. In order to formalize this concept, let $\sigma(1), \sigma(2), \ldots, \sigma(m)$ be any permutation (reordering) of the consumer indices, $1, \ldots, m$. That is, $\sigma(1), \ldots, \sigma(m)$ is a renumbering (or relabeling, or renaming) of the members of the society. Mathematically, σ is a mapping that maps each of the original indices, $1, \ldots, m$, into a possibly different integer that is between 1 and m. The condition that we wish to formalize, called "anonymity," is given by the following:

(A) $C(\hat{S}, \succcurlyeq_1, \ldots, \succcurlyeq_m) = C(\hat{S}, \succcurlyeq_{\sigma(1)}, \ldots, \succcurlyeq_{\sigma(m)})$ for all $\hat{S} \subseteq S$ and for all preference profiles.

In words, the anonymity condition says that the social choice out of a feasible $\hat{S}$ depends only on the collection of preference orderings of society

[12] For a formal proof, see Ferejohn and Grether [1975].

without regard to the ownership of these preferences. If the president of General Motors and an automobile assembly line worker were to trade preferences, the outcome of a particular social decision would not be changed. It is as if the social decision procedure required that all members of the community submit their preferences over social states by secret ballot, thus preserving the anonymity of the voter. It is obvious that the anonymity condition is strongly democratic. Power is symmetrically distributed among members of the community. In particular, powerful coalitions are inconsistent with anonymity. The Ferejohn–Grether social decision rule is very egalitarian in terms of preferences, since everybody's preferences count equally in the social decision process.

The particular construction used by Ferejohn and Grether in their proof of the possibility of a social decision rule that satisfies both anonymity and path independence (as well as the Pareto criterion and independence of irrelevant alternatives) also serves to underscore the democratic feature of the anonymity assumption. It will be recalled that the choice procedure proposed by Ferejohn and Grether is a natural extension of majority rule in the sense that on two-element sets the procedure simply chooses the majority winner. Does this mean that (given (I)) "democracy," collective rationality (formalized by path independence), and the Pareto principle are compatible properties of a social decision procedure? Of course, the Ferejohn–Grether possibility theorem means that the answer to this question is in the affirmative so long as we are willing to accept the foregoing formalizations of each of these three concepts.

However, the Pareto principle (P) is actually a rather weak notion of the unanimity rule since it is stated in terms of choice over pairs only. As it turns out, the Ferejohn–Grether social decision procedure does not satisfy the Pareto criterion with respect to choices over sets with more than two elements. To see this, consider again the three-voter, four-alternative example, which yields $C^{fg}(\{s^1, s^2, s^3, s^4\}) = \{s^1, s^2, s^3, s^4\}$. However, every member of the community prefers s^3 to s^4. Thus, s^4 is one of the chosen social states even though it is Pareto dominated by s^3. This is a disturbing characteristic of the Ferejohn–Grether social choice function.

The natural question that arises is whether there is any extension of majority rule that satisfies the Pareto criterion for choices over sets with more than two elements. Ferejohn and Grether show that the answer to this question is in the negative. In order to state this result, we formalize the notions of the *strong Pareto criterion* and *simple majority rule* as follows:

($\bar{\mathrm{P}}$) If $\overset{*}{s} \succ_c \bar{s}$ for all c, then $\overset{*}{s} \in \hat{S}$ implies $\bar{s} \notin C(\hat{S})$

and

(SM) $\{\overset{*}{s}\} = C(\{\overset{*}{s}, \bar{s}\})$ if and only if $N(\overset{*}{s} \succ_c \bar{s}) > N(\bar{s} \succ_c \overset{*}{s})$.

Thus, the strong Pareto criterion says that if every member of the community prefers $\overset{*}{s}$ to $\bar{s}$, and if $\overset{*}{s}$ is one of the feasible social states, then the Pareto-dominated social state $\bar{s}$ must not be in the social choice set. The principle of simple majority rule says that, in a pairwise choice between $\overset{*}{s}$ and $\bar{s}$, $\overset{*}{s}$ is the unique choice if and only if more individuals strictly prefer $\overset{*}{s}$ to $\bar{s}$ than prefer

$\bar{s}$ to $\overset{*}{s}$. Ferejohn and Grether prove that if the number of individuals in a society exceeds four and if the number of alternative social states exceeds three, there does not exist a social choice function which satisfies (SM), (IP), and ($\bar{\text{P}}$). This striking result suggests a fundamental incompatibility between the desirable properties of unanimous choice (the strong Pareto principle), democracy (the simple majority-rule principle), and collective rationality (path independence).

19.6 CONCLUSIONS

Relaxing any one of Arrow's conditions obviates the impossibility theorem. "Does this mean that the Arrow problem is not really serious for social choice? I am afraid it does not. What all this really shows is how *economic* Arrow's impossibility theorem is. Release any of his restrictions and his result collapses" (Sen [1970a, p. 49]). What this means is that the assumptions employed by Arrow in order to arrive at his impossibility result are not redundant; it is a very tightly constructed result. Note also that, as pointed out by Sen [1969, p. 388], Arrow's conditions "were thought by Arrow to be *necessary* for a reasonable social choice mechanism; he did not claim the set to be *sufficent* for it." That is, a social decision rule which satisfies all but one of Arrow's conditions is not necessarily an acceptable one, as many of the foregoing examples illustrate.

Section 19.5 traces one particular strand of research emanating from the classic impossibility theorem of Arrow [1951b]. This strand of research tells the following story. Weakening the strong Arrow collective-rationality assumption of transitivity of the social preference ordering obviates his conclusion regarding the impossibility of a social decision rule. In fact, the method of majority rule, which violates transitivity, satisfies the other Arrow assumptions. However, strengthening nondictatorship (to nonweak dictatorship and nonoligarchical structures successively) and weakening transitivity (to quasitransitivity and acyclicity successively) generates similar impossibility results. The particular chain of research sketched in this section culminates in the impossibility theorem of Ferejohn and Grether, in which collective rationality is weakened to path independence while the Pareto condition is strengthened to hold over subsets of social states with more than two elements and the nondictatorship condition is strengthened to a simple majority-rule condition.

This particular strand of research is, however, only one of many that have emanated from the classic treatise of Arrow. The literature is by now replete with possibility theorems and impossibility theorems, all of which are variations on Arrow's theme. In the course of generating these possibility and impossibility theorems, researchers have formalized many additional concepts that one might want a social decision rule to satisfy. Footnote 1, for example, introduces the notion of neutrality with respect to alternative social states; for some purposes it might be desirable to treat social states "anonymously." An example of a social decision rule that is not neutral between alternatives is one that requires, say, a two-thirds vote to override the status quo.

Another important concept is that of *positive responsiveness.* This means that if $\overset{*}{s}$ is no worse that $\bar{s}$ in the social preference ordering and if one individual, say $\bar{c}$, were to change his preferences from $\bar{s} \succcurlyeq_{\bar{c}} \overset{*}{s}$ to $\overset{*}{s} \succ_{\bar{c}} \bar{s}$, then society should change its ordering to strict preference of $\overset{*}{s}$ over $\bar{s}$. For example, if the social decision process resulted in a tie between $\overset{*}{s}$ and $\bar{s}$ under one set of preferences, and if one member of the community were to change his vote to favor $\overset{*}{s}$, society then uniquely adopts $\overset{*}{s}$. An example of a social decision process that does not satisfy positive responsiveness is a bicameral legislature in which $\overset{*}{s}$ is chosen over $\bar{s}$ if both branches of the legislature choose $\overset{*}{s}$ over $\bar{s}$. In this case, a vote change by members of one of the two branches of the legislature need not resolve a tie in the legislature as a whole. Adding neutrality or positive responsiveness to a list of conditions that must be satisfied by a social choice function of course restricts the class of admissible social choice functions and proliferates impossibility results.

Another interesting property of a social decision rule that has been introduced by Sen is the notion of *liberalism*. Sen describes this concept as follows: "Liberal values seem to require that there are choices that are personal and the relevant person should be free to do what he likes. It would be socially better, in these cases, to permit him to do what he wants, everything else remaining the same" (Sen [1970b, p. 87]). Sen formalizes this concept and shows that there does not exist a social choice function that satisfies both liberalism and the (weak) Pareto criterion; hence the apt title of his paper: "The Impossibility of a Paretian Liberal."

As the above discussion indicates, there is an extensive and interesting literature on the problems of social choice discussed in this section. Although our discussion could, therefore, be substantially extended, we turn instead in chapter 20 to a discussion of the rather different body of research concerned with interpersonal comparability. The reader interested in learning more about the problems of voting and social choice discussed in this section is referred to the part IV suggested reading.

EXERCISES

19.1 Consider the social preference relation derived from a social choice function as described in section 19.2. Is this relation

a. complete?

b. transitive?

19.2 Prove that nonnegative responsiveness (R) and nonimposition (NI) imply the weak Pareto principle (P).

CHAPTER 20 INTERPERSONAL COMPARABILITY AND SOCIAL OPTIMALITY

20.1 INTRODUCTION

The framework of social choice formulated by Arrow explicitly precludes the use of specific types of information in social welfare evaluations. This is because the social choice function is defined as a mapping from the collection of individual preference orderings over social states into the space of social choice sets. Thus, the only information that is admissible in the social choice procedure is the constraint set (the set of feasible social states) and the collection of individual *orderings* over the social states. Of course, it is always possible to represent these individual orderings by individual welfare functions,[1] but the social choice must be independent of the particular representation of the preference orderings that are chosen; i.e., monotonic transformations of these representations do not affect the social decision. In particular, Arrow's framework precludes specific information concerning the *measurability* of individual welfare and *interpersonal comparability* (e.g., comparing the welfare of a beggar with the welfare of a corporate president). As we shall see, the latter class of information is the more essential for social choice. An impossibility result still holds even allowing for cardinal individual welfare measures.

Given that interpersonal welfare comparisons are essential for social choice, what types of comparisons (information) are needed? Section 20.2 introduces the concept of a social welfare function and different types of measurability and comparability frameworks. These concepts are used to reexamine Arrow's "impossibility theorem" and the central role played by the condition that individual welfare be noncomparable. Section 20.3 weakens the noncomparability condition to allow for information concerning interpersonal welfare comparisons. In this framework, the utilitarian and Rawlsian approaches are particularly interesting examples of rules for aggregating over individual

[1] See section 3.2 for a discussion of the representation of the preference ordering by a real-valued function. It might be noted that since we have assumed that the number of social states is finite, it is unnecessary to posit a regularity condition (assumption 2.5) in order to guarantee the existence of such a representation.

social welfare functions. Section 20.4 discusses the Bergson-Samuelson "social welfare function" and social optimality and section 20.5 concludes the chapter.

20.2 MEASURABILITY AND COMPARABILITY

Let W^c, $c = 1, \ldots, m$, be the individual social welfare functions; that is, W^c is the representation of the cth individual's ordering over social states $\succcurlyeq_c$. The social welfare functional,[2] $\mathscr{W}$, maps individual social welfare functions into social preference orderings $\succcurlyeq$; that is, $\mathscr{W}$ is a rule for aggregating individual welfare functions into social orderings, $\mathscr{W}(W^1, \ldots, W^m)$.

The social welfare functional is to be contrasted with the Arrow social welfare function which maps individual *orderings* into social preference orderings. The social welfare functional provides us with a much richer structure for characterizing social decision procedures. This is because a monotonic transformation of an individual welfare function (which does *not* change the underlying ordering $\succcurlyeq_c$) in general changes the social ordering $\mathscr{W}(W^1, \ldots, W^m)$. If we restrict $\mathscr{W}(W^1, \ldots, W^m)$ to be invariant with respect to arbitrary strictly monotonic transformations of any of the individual welfare functions, we are back in Arrow's framework where only individual orderings matter in generating social preference orderings. This point underscores the restrictiveness of Arrow's framework.

Weaker restrictions on the invariance of $\mathscr{W}(W^1, \ldots, W^m)$ with respect to transformations of the individual welfare functions allow for the possibility of incorporating information about measurability and interpersonal comparability into the social decision-making procedure. Information about the measurability of individual welfare is introduced by requiring that $\mathscr{W}(W^1, \ldots, W^m)$ be invariant with respect to a more restrictive class of strictly monotonic transformations (e.g., affine transformations); this is a *weakening* of the invariance restrictions on $\mathscr{W}$.

Information about interpersonal comparability is introduced by requiring that $\mathscr{W}(W^1, \ldots, W^m)$ be invariant with respect to monotonic transformations that are restricted to be identical (in some respect) across individuals. Again, this weakens the invariance restriction that is required to generate Arrow's framework.

Following Sen [1977a], we make these notions more rigorous, and clearer, by defining the following classes of invariance of $\mathscr{W}$.

Cardinal full comparability $\mathscr{W}(W^1, \ldots, W^m)$ is invariant with respect to identical affine transformations, $\overset{*}{W}{}^c = a + bW^c$, $b > 0$, for all c.

Ordinal level comparability $\mathscr{W}(W^1, \ldots, W^m)$ is invariant with respect to identical strictly monotonic transformations, $\overset{*}{W}{}^c = \psi(W^c)$, for all c.

[2] A "functional" is characterized by the property that some of the arguments of its image are functions. The concept of a social welfare functional is attributable to Sen [1970a].

Cardinal unit comparability $\mathscr{W}(W^1, \ldots, W^m)$ is invariant with respect to transformations of the type, $\overset{*}{W}{}^c = a_c + bW^c$, $b > 0$, for all c.

Cardinal noncomparability $\mathscr{W}(W^1, \ldots, W^m)$ is invariant with respect to possibly different affine transformations, $\overset{*}{W}{}^c = a_c + b_c W^c$, $b_c > 0$, for all c.

Ordinal noncomparability $\mathscr{W}(W^1, \ldots, W^m)$ is invariant with respect to possibly different strictly monotonic transformations, $\overset{*}{W}{}^c = \psi^c(W^c)$, for all c.

Of the above, the *most* demanding in terms of informational requirements (the *weakest* invariance assumption) is cardinal full comparability. This framework requires classical cardinal measurability—measurability up to an arbitrary origin and unit of measurement (see section 3.6)—and comparability across individuals of both the origin and the unit of measurement (neither the origin nor the unit of measurement of any individual welfare function can be changed without making identical changes for every other individual).[3]

Of the above, the framework with the *least* demanding informational requirements (the *most* restrictive invariance assumption) is ordinal noncomparability. As noted earlier, this is the Arrow framework.

In between these two extremes are three intermediate cases.[4] Ordinal level comparability and cardinal noncomparability make it abundantly clear that interpersonal comparability and welfare (or utility) measurability are entirely distinct concepts; full comparability is possible without (cardinal) measurability and measurability does not imply comparability.

Cardinal unit comparability requires (as does cardinal full comparability) that a commensurate "welfare unit" be defined for the purpose of interpersonal comparison but does not require comparable origins.

Arrow's conditions can be restated in terms of the social welfare functional. In the following definitions, it will be understood that $\succcurlyeq = \mathscr{W}(W^1, \ldots, W^m)$ and $\overset{*}{s} \succ \hat{s}$ means $\overset{*}{s} \succcurlyeq \hat{s}$ and not $\hat{s} \succcurlyeq \overset{*}{s}$.

Unrestricted domain (UD) $\mathscr{W}(W^1, \ldots, W_m)$ is defined for all logically possible sets of individual welfare functions, $\{W^1, \ldots, W^m\}$.

Weak Pareto principle (P) For any pair $\{\overset{*}{s}, \hat{s}\}$, if $W^c(\overset{*}{s}) > W^c(\hat{s})$ for all c, then $\overset{*}{s} \succ \hat{s}$.

Independence of irrelevant alternatives (I) Let $\{W^1, \ldots, W^m\}$ and $\{\hat{W}^1, \ldots, \hat{W}^m\}$ be two sets of individual welfare functions. If, for any pair $\{\overset{*}{s}, \hat{s}\}$, $W^c(\overset{*}{s}) = \hat{W}^c(\overset{*}{s})$ and $W^c(\hat{s}) = \hat{W}^c(\hat{s})$ for all c, then $\overset{*}{s} \succcurlyeq \hat{s}$ if and only if $\overset{*}{s} \mathrel{\hat{\succcurlyeq}} \hat{s}$ (where, of course, $\hat{\succcurlyeq} = \mathscr{W}(\hat{W}^1, \ldots, \hat{W}^m)$).

[3] One could define an even more demanding informational setup (a weaker invariance restriction) by requiring invariance with respect to identical linear transformations, $\overset{*}{W} = bW^c$, $b > 0$, for all c. This makes the origin nonarbitrary (see section 3.6), a useful restriction for some types of welfare analysis (see, e.g., Sen [1973]).

[4] Of course, many other intermediate cases could be specified since there are any number of strictly monotonic transformations that are more general than affine transformations.

Nondictatorship (ND) There is no individual, d, such that, for all pairs $\{\overset{*}{s}, \hat{s}\}$ and for all sets of individual welfare functions, $W^d(\overset{*}{s}) > W^d(\hat{s})$ implies $\overset{*}{s} \succ \hat{s}$.

Note that Arrow's transitivity condition (see section 19.3) is subsumed in the definition of the social welfare functional; in particular, $\mathscr{W}$ maps into social orderings, which by definition satisfy the transitivity condition.

Arrow's impossibility theorem (modified to incorporate the weak Pareto condition) can be restated in terms of the social welfare functional as follows:

Ordinal Impossibility Theorem *If there are more than two alternative social states, there is no social welfare functional satisfying* (*UD*), (*P*), (*I*), (*ND*), *and ordinal noncomparability.*

This restatement of Arrow's theorem makes explicit the fundamental role played by his implicit assumption regarding measurability and comparability. This, in turn, raises the possibility that Arrow's paradox can be resolved by weakening his very restrictive measurability/comparability condition. In fact, as the following theorem (due to Sen [1970a]) makes vividly clear, Arrow's implicit assumption regarding measurability is unnecessary for his conclusion:

Cardinal Impossibility Theorem *If there are more than two alternative social states, there is no social welfare functional satisfying* (*UD*), (*P*), (*I*), (*ND*), *and cardinal noncomparability.*

This theorem makes it clear that the search for a social decision-making procedure through the weakening of the restriction on informational requirements must concentrate on the noncomparability condition. In fact, it is apparent that, in the absence of interpersonal comparability, completeness of the social ordering requires that all Pareto noncomparable alternatives be indifferent (see exercise 20.2).

20.3 SOCIAL ORDERINGS AND QUASIORDERINGS

In this section, we consider some social orderings and "quasiorderings" (reflexive, transitive, symmetric relations that are not necessarily complete) that require relaxation of the noncomparability condition (and, in some cases, of the nonmeasurability condition) of Arrow.

The Bergson–Samuelson Social Welfare Function

We now restrict the social welfare functional by supposing that individuals' orderings of social states depend only on their own consumption bundles, x^c, $c = 1, \ldots, m$. Consequently, the social welfare functional maps individual *utility* functions, U^c, $c = 1, \ldots, m$, into social orderings, $\mathscr{U}(U^1, \ldots, U^m)$. For a fixed collection of utility functions, this social ordering can be represented by a real-valued function, W, that associates a level of "social welfare" with each social state. Let us, in particular, suppose that the social welfare depends upon the social state only through the individual utility functions; that is, social welfare is given by $W(U^1(x^1), \ldots, U^m(x^m))$. Thus, $W(U^1(\bar{x}^1), \ldots, U^m(\bar{x}^m)) \geq W(U^1(\hat{x}^1), \ldots, U^m(\hat{x}^m))$ if and only if $\bar{s} \succcurlyeq \hat{s}$ where $\succcurlyeq\ = \mathscr{W}(U^1, \ldots, U^m)$.

The function W, which maps individual utilities into a level of social welfare, is called the *Bergson–Samuelson social welfare function* (see Bergson [1938] and Samuelson [1947a, chap. 8]).

Note that the Bergson–Samuelson social welfare function is obtained from the more general Arrow–Sen framework by invoking three restrictions: (1) each individual's welfare evaluation depends only on his own utility, (2) individual orderings—and utility functions—are *fixed*, and (3) social welfare is a function of individual utilities.[5] The second of these restrictions is especially important; the social welfare of alternative social states can be assessed only for fixed welfare (in this case, utility) functions. This fact is important for the discussion of social optimality in the next section.

Fixing the preference profile circumvents the Arrow problem. However, Samuelson goes on to say the following:

> *But the W function is itself only ordinally determinable so that there are an infinity of equally good indicators of it which can be used. Thus, if one of these is written as $W = F(U^1, U^2, \ldots)$, and if we were to change from one set of cardinal indexes of individual utility to another set, $(V^1, V^2, \ldots)$, we should simply change the form of the function F so as to leave all social decisions invariant* (*Samuelson* [1947a, *p.* 228]).

Thus, Samuelson clearly views the Bergson–Samuelson approach to welfare economics as satisfying the ordinal-noncomparability invariance axiom of section 20.2. However, the Ordinal Impossibility Theorem of section 20.2 implies that, so long as Samuelson insists on this restrictive invariance condition, his approach *must* violate one of the other axioms: unrestricted domain (UD), the weak Pareto principle (P), independence of irrelevant alternatives (I), or nondictatorship (ND). It is clear, however, that the Bergson–Samuelson approach is intended to satisfy (UD) (see Samuelson [1967, p. 49], where it is noted that the preference profile "could be any one"), (P) (see section 20.4 and Samuelson [1967, p. 49]), and nondictatorship (otherwise the entire approach is trivial). This means that, viewed in the perspective of the Arrow impossibility theorem, the Bergson–Samuelson approach violates the independence-of-irrelevant-alternatives condition.

An alternative approach (which, it is argued in section 20.4, is more promising) is to relax the strong measurability/comparability invariance

[5] Another way to rationalize this restriction of the social welfare function is to invoke the libertarian value that information only about the utility derived from one's own consumption bundle is to be used in making social decisions. For example, the disutility that I get from somebody else reading pornography or the positive satisfaction that I get out of other motorcyclists being forced to wear a helmet are not to be taken into account in making social decisions. See Archibald and Donaldson [1976].

restriction of the Bergson–Samuelson framework. The succeeding subsections introduce some interesting examples of social welfare functions that do just that.

The Classical Utilitarian Social Welfare Function

The classical utilitarian school of welfare economics, associated primarily with the early writings of Bentham [1789], was predicated on the nineteenth-century notion of cardinally measurable individual utilities. The policy prescription of the classical utilitarian school was to simply maximize the general welfare, defined as the simple sum of individual utilities. That is, this school of welfare economics posited the existence of a Bergson–Samuelson social welfare function of the following form:

$$W(U^1(x^1), \ldots, U^m(x^m)) = \sum_{c=1}^{m} U^c(x^c). \tag{20.1}$$

Thus, according to the classical utilitarian criterion, $\overset{*}{s} \succcurlyeq \bar{s}$ if and only if

$$\sum_{c=1}^{m} U^c(\overset{*}{x}{}^c) \geq \sum_{c=1}^{m} U^c(\bar{x}^c).$$

The measurability/comparability information required in the utilitarian approach is cardinal unit comparability. To see that this informational basis suffices, suppose that (20.2) holds so that $s\,\mathscr{W}(U^1, \ldots, U^m)\bar{s}$, and consider the set of affine transformations, $\hat{U}^c(x^c) = a_c + bU^c(x^c)$, $b > 0$, for all c. Clearly, $\sum_{c=1}^{m} \hat{U}^c(\overset{*}{x}{}^c) \geq \sum_{c=1}^{m} \hat{U}^c(\bar{x}^c)$, as can be seen by multiplying both sides of (20.2) by b and then adding the $\sum_{c=1}^{m} a_c$ to both sides to obtain

$$\sum_{c=1}^{m} (a_c + bU^c(\overset{*}{x}{}^c)) \geq \sum_{c=1}^{m} (a_c + bU^c(\bar{x}^c)).$$

Thus, $\overset{*}{s}\,\mathscr{W}(\hat{U}^1, \ldots, \hat{U}^m)\bar{s}$, indicating that $\mathscr{W}(U^1, \ldots, U^m)$ is invariant with respect to affine transformations with a common positive slope.[6] To summarize, interpersonal comparisons of the units in which utility is measured are essential to

[6] Cardinal unit comparability is also *necessary* for the classical utilitarian approach. This is easy to show if we restrict the set of admissible transformations, ψ^c, $c = 1, \ldots, m$, to those that are differentiable. First note that

$$\text{(a)} \qquad \sum_{c=1}^{m} \overset{*}{u}{}^c \geq \sum_{c=1}^{m} \hat{u}^c \Leftrightarrow \sum_{c=1}^{m} \psi^c(\overset{*}{u}{}^c) \geq \sum_{c=1}^{m} \psi^c(\hat{u}^c)$$

implies that

$$\text{(b)} \qquad \sum_{c=1}^{m} \overset{*}{u}{}^c = \sum_{c=1}^{m} \hat{u}^c \Leftrightarrow \sum_{c=1}^{m} \psi^c(\overset{*}{u}{}^c) = \sum_{c=1}^{m} \psi^c(\hat{u}^c).$$

(Any combination of an equality and a strict inequality can easily be shown to violate (a).) Taking total differentials of the identities in (b), we obtain

$$\sum_{c=1}^{m} d\overset{*}{u}{}^c = \sum_{c=1}^{m} d\hat{u}^c \Leftrightarrow \sum_{c=1}^{m} \frac{d\psi^c(\overset{*}{u}{}^c)}{du^c}\,du^c = \sum_{c=1}^{m} \frac{d\psi^c(\hat{u}^c)}{du^c}\,du^c.$$

This equivalence holds for all values of $d\overset{*}{u}{}^c$ and $d\hat{u}^c$, for all c, only if $d\psi^c(\overset{*}{u}{}^c)/du^c = d\psi^c(\hat{u}^c)/du^c$ for all values of $\overset{*}{u}{}^c$ and $\hat{u}^c$ for all c. In other words $d\psi^c(u^c)/du^c = b$ for all c. Moreover, (a) holds only if $b > 0$.

classical utilitarian welfare economics. The choice of the origin in the individual utility functions is arbitrary and irrelevant but the choice of units in which utility is measured must be comparable across consumers.

The choice of particular cardinalizations of individual utilities for the purpose of making social decisions is unrelated to the notion of cardinality in utility and demand theory (see section 3.6). The fact that particular cardinalizations of individual orderings are used in order to make social welfare decisions or judgments does not imply that individual private decisions are based upon anything other than their preference orderings.

The Rawlsian Social Welfare Function

Interest in the choice of the form of a social welfare function has been reactivated by the recent writings of the philosopher John Rawls [1971]. Rawls's theory of social justice is based in part upon the postulate that the ethical way to organize society is one which the individuals would consider to be optimal if they did not know what role they would play in the society. Consider the hypothetical possibility that individuals are allowed to vote for alternative social structures not knowing which individual they would be in the hypothetical society. That is, the organizers of this ethically ideal society have an equal probability of being any particular individual in that society. Rawls goes on to argue that rational individuals would opt for the society which makes the worst person best off among all of the alternatives. The implied form of the Bergson–Samuelson social welfare function, referred to as the *Rawlsian social welfare function*, therefore has the following form:

$$W(U^1(x^1), \ldots, U^m(x^m)) = \text{Min}\{U^1(x^1), \ldots, U^m(x^m)\}. \qquad (20.3)$$

That is, social welfare is equal to the welfare of the worst-off member of society. As will be seen below, the Rawlsian welfare criterion leads to an extremely egalitarian society.

It is apparent that the Rawlsian welfare criterion, $\overset{*}{s} \succ \bar{s}$ if $\min\{U^1(\overset{*}{x}^1), \ldots, U^m(\overset{*}{x}^m)\} \geq \min\{U^1(\bar{x}^1), \ldots, U^m(\bar{x}^m)\}$, requires ordinal level comparability since the above inequality is equivalent to $\min\{\psi^1(U^1(\overset{*}{x}^1)), \ldots, \psi^m(U^m(\overset{*}{x}^m))\} \geq \min\{\psi^1(U^1(\bar{x}^1)), \ldots, \psi^m(U^m(\bar{x}^m))\}$ for all states if and only if $\psi^c = \psi$ for all c. Intuitively, to compare the "worst-off person" in two social states requires comparison of levels of utility. Note, however, that no cardinal measurability is required.

If we restrict ourselves to a community with only two individuals, the ethical postulates of the classical utilitarian and Rawlsian welfare economics can be contrasted diagrammatically. In this case, the Bergson–Samuelson social welfare function has the image $W(u^1, u^2)$, where u^1 and u^2 are the utility levels of the two individuals. A *social indifference curve* is defined as the locus of points in $u^1 - u^2$ space that generate a given level of social welfare. In figure 20.1, the set of utility levels that yield social welfare equal to $W(\bar{u}^1, \bar{u}^2)$ according to the Rawlsian criterion are given by the points on the right angle *cde*. This follows from the fact that $\min\{\bar{u}^1, \bar{u}^2\} = \bar{u}^2 = \hat{u}^1 < \bar{u}^1$. That is, increasing the utility of consumer 1 from $\hat{u}^1$ to $\bar{u}^1$ while maintaining the second consumer's utility level at $\bar{u}^2$ does not increase social welfare according to the Rawlsian criterion. It is

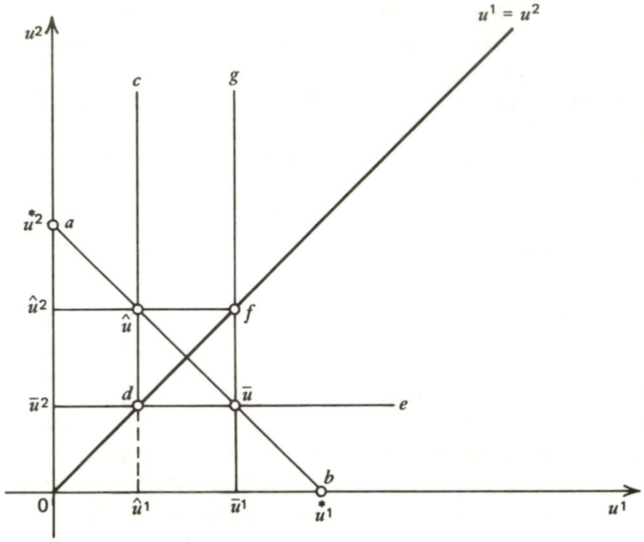

Figure 20.1

apparent that the Rawlsian social indifference map is given by the set of all right angles with cusps on the 45° line through the origin. Of course, points above the Rawlsian indifference curve through $\bar{u}$ represent utility levels that generate higher levels of social welfare. Similarly, points below this right angle represent utility levels that generate social welfare below $\bar{u}$. Figure 20.2a depicts the set of utility combinations that, according to the Rawlsian criterion, are socially at least as good as $\bar{u}$, $\succcurlyeq_R(\bar{u})$, and the set of utility combinations that are no better than $\bar{u}$, $\preccurlyeq_R(\bar{u})$.

On the other hand, the social indifference curve through $\bar{u}$ in figure 20.1 according to the classical utilitarian criterion is the straight line *ab*, with a slope equal to -1; all of the points on this line yield a sum of utilities equal to $\bar{u}^1 + \bar{u}^2 (= \hat{u}^1 + \hat{u}^2)$. Points above this straight line represent utility levels that generate higher levels of social welfare, and points below the line represent utility levels that generate lower levels of social welfare. The social no-worse-than-$\bar{u}$ set, $\succcurlyeq_U(\bar{u})$, and no-better-than-$\bar{u}$ set, $\preccurlyeq_U(\bar{u})$, according to the utilitarian criterion are depicted in figure 20.2b.

The classical utilitarian and Rawlsian social preference orderings can be viewed conceptually as polar extremes with respect to the trade-off between total utility on the one hand and equality, or "equity," on the other. Each of these social welfare criteria emphasizes one of these two desirable objectives to the exclusion of the other. The classical utilitarian criterion leads us to regard as socially indifferent the state of the economy that generates utility levels $\bar{u}^1$ and $\bar{u}^2$ and the state of the economy in which consumer 1 has utility level $\overset{*}{u}^1$ and consumer 2 has zero utility. On the other hand, according to the Rawlsian criterion, the utility combination $(\bar{u}^1, \bar{u}^2)$ is no better than the combination $(\hat{u}^1, \bar{u}^2)$ despite the fact that the former is Pareto superior to the latter.

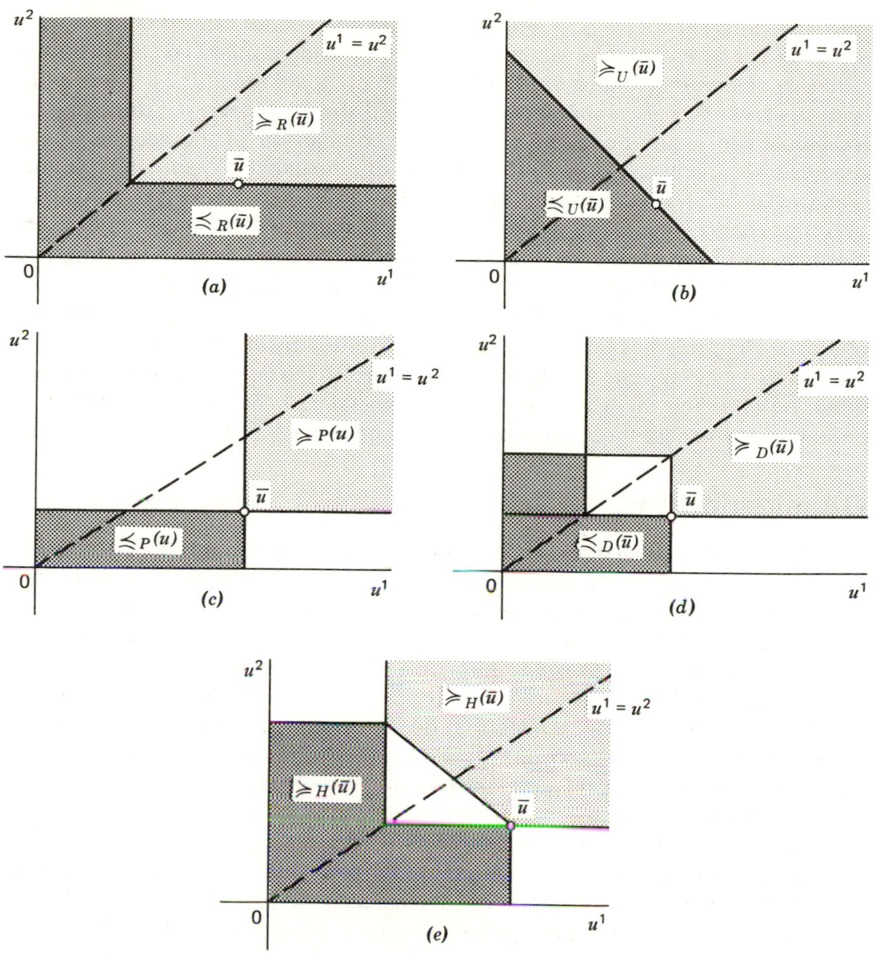

Figure 20.2 (a) Rawlsian ordering. (b) Classical utilitarian ordering. (c) Pareto quasiordering. (d) Dominance quasiordering. (e) Hull-of-dominance quasiordering.

In order to rectify this problem with the Rawlsian criterion, Sen [1975] has suggested a modification which allows us to rank (strictly) two alternative social states in which the utilities of the worst-off persons are equal. According to this criterion, in the two-person economy, a social state $\overset{*}{s}$ is strictly preferred to a social state $\bar{s}$ if *either* (a) the utility of the worst-off person is higher in the state $\overset{*}{s}$ *or* (b) the utilities of the worst-off persons in the two social states $\overset{*}{s}$ and $\bar{s}$ are equal and the utility of the other consumer is higher in state $\overset{*}{s}$. In other words, the utility levels of the best-off persons in the two social states are taken into consideration in ranking them only if the utilities of the worst-off persons in the two states are equal. Although we do not bother to state it formally, this modified

Rawlsian criterion is easily generalized to m-person economies. To compare two states of the economy, one simply orders the individual utility levels in the two states from lowest to highest and proceeds to compare the utility levels starting with the lowest levels of the two states. Only if the utility levels of the worst-off individuals are equal does one go on to a comparison of the second-lowest utility levels. Similarly, only if the utilities of the worst-off and the second-worst-off members of the society are equal does this criterion take into consideration the relative welfares of the third-worst-off members in the two states. The modified Rawlsian criterion is often referred to as the *leximin* social ordering (see the discussion of a lexigraphic preference ordering in section 2.4).

In figure 20.1, the set of utility combinations that are socially preferable to $\bar{u}$ according to the leximin criterion is represented by all of those points on or above the right angle *cde* except for those points on the portion of this right angle given by $\hat{u}d\bar{u}$. The utility combination $\bar{u}$ is socially preferred to all other utility combinations except those represented by the points $\hat{u}$ and, of course, $\bar{u}$ itself.

Quasiorderings

The classical utilitarian and Rawlsian social welfare criteria are based upon complete orderings of the social-state space; that is, under these criteria, any conceivable state can be compared to any other. For many purposes, the requirement that all social states be completely ordered—an explicit condition in the welfare-economic frameworks of Bergson and Samuelson and of Arrow—might well be stronger than needed for most purposes. This has led to the investigation of alternative social decision rules that do not require a complete ordering and are based instead upon a social quasiordering—a transitive and reflexive, but not necessarily complete, relation (see section 2.1 and exercises 2.2 for definitions of these terms).

We have already encountered one social decision criterion that is founded on a quasiordering: the Pareto criterion. According to the Pareto quasiordering, the set of utility combinations that are at least as good as $\bar{u}$ is represented by the set of points on or above the right angle $g\bar{u}e$ in Figure 20.1. The collection of utility combinations that are no better than $\bar{u}$ according to this criterion are represented by points on or below the right angle $\bar{u}^2\bar{u}\bar{u}^1$. All other utility combinations (i.e., those above the right angle $\bar{u}^2\bar{u}g$ and below the right angle $\bar{u}^1\bar{u}e$) are Pareto noncomparable to $\bar{u}$. The no-worse-than-$\bar{u}$ and no-better-than-$\bar{u}$ sets induced by the Pareto quasiorderings, $\succcurlyeq_p(\bar{u})$ and $\preccurlyeq_p(\bar{u})$, are depicted in figure 20.2c.

The problem with the Pareto quasiordering, as noted above, is that it allows for so much noncomparability as to render it virtually useless as a social decision rule. The inadequacy of the Pareto criterion and the stringent comparability requirements (across states) of the classical utilitarian criterion and the Rawlsian criterion (and its modification, leximin) have led some social choice theorists to suggest quasiorderings that entail more comparability than the Pareto criterion, and which are therefore much richer in terms of their implications for the ranking of alternative social states, but do not demand the complete comparability required by the classical utilitarian and Rawlsian approaches.

One quasiordering that is in fact inspired by the Pareto criterion is that generated by the so-called dominance criterion, first suggested by Suppes [1966] in a somewhat different context and further analyzed by Sen [1970c] and Barry and Rae [1975]. Essentially, the dominance criterion says that social state $\overset{*}{s}$ is at least as good as social state $\bar{s}$ if there is a way of reassigning the utilities of the members of the society in the two states to different individuals in a way that makes $\overset{*}{s}$ preferred in the sense of Pareto. This criterion is perhaps best understood by way of illustration. Recall that the utility combination $(\hat{u}^1, \hat{u}^2)$ represented by point $\hat{u}$ in figure 20.1 and the utility combination $(\bar{u}^1, \bar{u}^2)$ represented by the point $\bar{u}$ in figure 20.1 are Pareto noncomparable; although consumer 2 is better off at point $\hat{u}$ than at point $\bar{u}$, consumer 1 is worse off. Note, however, that the utilities of consumers 1 and 2 at $\hat{u}$ are equal to the utilities of consumers 2 and 1, respectively, at $\bar{u}$. That is, the only difference between these two states is that the utility levels of the two individuals have been interchanged. The dominance criterion then says that society is indifferent between these alternative social states, which are equivalent in utility space except for the names of the individuals. In addition, according to the dominance criterion, the points on or above the line segment, $c\hat{u}f$, except for the point $\hat{u}$, are preferred to $\bar{u}$, although they are noncomparable to $\bar{u}$ according to the Pareto criterion. The reason for this is that, for example, points on the line segment $c\hat{u}$ above $\hat{u}$ correspond to utility levels for consumer 2 that are *higher* than the utility level of consumer 1 at $\bar{u}$ and a utility level of consumer 1 (namely $\hat{u}^1$) which is *equal* to the utility level of consumer 2 at $\bar{u}$. Thus, reassigning the utility levels of the two consumers would result in a Pareto improvement. Thus, according to the dominance criterion, the set of points that represent utility combinations that are no worse than $\bar{u}$ are those on or above the line segment $c\hat{u}f\bar{u}e$. By similar reasoning, the collection of points that represent utility combinations that are no better than $\bar{u}$ are given by points on or below the line segment $\hat{u}^2\hat{u}d\bar{u}\bar{u}^1$.

The set of points that represent utility levels that are not comparable to $\bar{u}$ are given by those points above the line segment $\hat{u}^2\hat{u}c$, below the line segment $\bar{u}^1\bar{u}e$, and in the interior or the square $\hat{u}f\bar{u}d$. Utility combinations in these regions cannot be reassigned to members of the society in a way that makes both of them better off than at $\bar{u}$. Nevertheless, it is apparent that the dominance criterion extends considerably the Pareto quasiordering (adding to the region of points that represent utility levels that are comparable to $\bar{u}$ the regions $\hat{u}^2\hat{u}d\bar{u}^2$ and $c\hat{u}fg$). The no-worse-than-$\bar{u}$ and no-better-than-$\bar{u}$ sets implied by the dominance criterion, $\succcurlyeq_D(\bar{u})$ and $\preccurlyeq_D(\bar{u})$, are depicted in figure 20.2d.

It should be apparent that the measurability/comparability requirements of the dominance criterion exceed those of the Pareto criterion. The latter entails ordinal noncomparability whereas the former clearly requires ordinal comparability; reassigning utility levels to individuals requires ordinal comparabilty.

The dominance quasiordering has some attractive features with respect to the trade-off between total utility and equity. Unlike the utilitarian criterion, it does not treat as equivalent the alternative utility combinations represented by the points $\bar{u}$, where the consumers enjoy utility levels $\bar{u}^1$ and $\bar{u}^2$, and that represented by the point b where consumer 1 has utility $\overset{*}{u}^1$ and consumer 2 has zero utility. Moreover, unlike the Rawlsian criterion, the dominance criterion does not sacrifice total utility to achieve more equality by moving, say, from $\bar{u}$ to a point in the interior of the triangular area $\hat{u}d\bar{u}$.

On the other hand, unlike the Rawlsian and utilitarian criteria, the dominance criterion is unable to make social decisions regarding some alternatives. Blackorby and Donaldson [1977a] have noted that, with respect to the trade-off between total utility and equity, much of this noncomparability makes sense. For example, points in the interiors of the areas $a\hat{u}c$ and $b\bar{u}e$ represent utility combinations with more total utility but less equality than $\bar{u}$. Similarly, points in the interiors of the triangular areas, $a\hat{u}\hat{u}^2$, $b\bar{u}\bar{u}^1$, and $\hat{u}d\bar{u}$, represent utility combinations with less total utility but more equality than $\bar{u}$. It therefore makes sense that these utility combinations be noncomparable to $\bar{u}$ from the standpoint of considerations of total utility and equity. On the other hand, utility combinations represented by points in the interior of the triangular area $\hat{u}f\bar{u}$ generate more total utility *and* more equality than $\bar{u}$. It seems reasonable then that these utility combinations should be socially preferred to $\bar{u}$. Blackorby and Donaldson go on to suggest that the dominance quasiordering be extended to include these utility combinations in the set of combinations that are at least as good as $\bar{u}$. They call this the *hull-of-dominance* quasiordering because the set of points on or above $c\hat{u}\bar{u}e$ in figure 20.1 is referred to mathematically as the convex hull of the set of points on or above $c\hat{u}f\bar{u}e$.[7]

The sets of points that represent utility combinations no worse than $\bar{u}$, $\succcurlyeq_H(\bar{u})$, and of those that are no better than $\bar{u}$, $\preccurlyeq_H(\bar{u})$, according to the hull-of-dominance criterion, are depicted graphically in figure 20.2e.

20.4 SOCIAL OPTIMALITY

The social optimality problem can be described as that of choosing a best social state out of a feasible set $\hat{S}$. For a fixed set of individual welfare functions, this problem can be described formally as choosing a social state $\overset{*}{s}$ in the feasible subset $\hat{S}$ that satisfies $\overset{*}{s} \succcurlyeq s$ for all $s \in \hat{S}$, where $\succcurlyeq\, = \mathscr{W}(W^1, \ldots, W^m)$. If the conditions rationalizing the Bergson–Samuelson social welfare function are satisfied (see section 20.3), the social optimization problem can be reformulated as follows: $\text{Max}_s\ W(U^1(x^1), \ldots, U^m(x^m))$ s.t. $s \in \hat{S}$.

In order to make this optimization problem somewhat more concrete, let us recall the exchange economy described in some detail in chapters 15 and 17. In this economy, the social optimization problem is given by

$$\max_{x^1, \ldots, x^m} W(U^1(x^1), \ldots, U^m(x^m)) \qquad \text{s.t. } \sum_{c=1}^{m} x_i^c = \bar{x}_i,\ i = 1, \ldots, n, \tag{20.4}$$

where $\bar{x}_i$ is the aggregate endowment of the ith commodity.[8]

[7] Formally, the convex hull of a set A is the smallest convex set containing A.

[8] The principles developed below are equally applicable to a production economy. In order to analyze social optimality in such an economy, we need only replace the constraints $\sum_{c=1}^{m} x_i^c = \bar{x}_i$, $i = 1, \ldots, n$, with a constraint (or a set of constraints) that characterizes the production technology of the economy. The incorporation of the possibility of production into this social-optimization problem would considerably complicate the exposition below, but would leave the basic principles unchanged. We therefore abstract from production in this discussion.

Let us suppose that the Bergson–Samuelson social welfare function and the individual utility functions are differentiable and that the solution to (20.4) is interior. In this case the social optimum is a saddle point of the Lagrange function,

$$L(x^1, \ldots, x^m, \lambda_1, \ldots, \lambda_n) = W(U^1(x^1), \ldots, U^m(x^m)) + \sum_{i=1}^{n} \lambda_i \left(\bar{x}_i - \sum_{c=1}^{m} x_i^c \right),$$

where λ_i, $i = 1, \ldots, n$, are the Lagrange multipliers. The first-order conditions are therefore given by

$$\frac{\partial}{\partial x_i^c} L(x^1, \ldots, x^c, \lambda_1, \ldots, \lambda_n) = W_c(U^1(x^1), \ldots, U^m(x^m)) \cdot U_i^c(x^c)$$

$$- \lambda_i = 0, \quad c = 1, \ldots, m, \quad i = 1, \ldots, n, \tag{20.5a}$$

and

$$\bar{x}_i - \sum_{c=1}^{m} x_i^c = 0, \qquad i = 1, \ldots, n, \tag{20.5b}$$

where W_c is the derivative of W with respect to the cth consumer's utility value and U_i^c is the derivative of U^c with respect to the ith quantity. Taking the ratio of the two first-order-condition equations corresponding to a particular consumer and two commodities, say i and j, yields

$$\frac{W_c(U^1(x^1), \ldots, U^m(x^m)) \cdot U_i^c(x^c)}{W_c(U^1(x^1), \ldots, U^m(x^m)) \cdot U_j^c(x^c)} = \frac{U_i^c(x^c)}{U_j^c(x^c)} = \frac{\lambda_i}{\lambda_j}.$$

This condition says that the cth individual's marginal rate of substitution of the ith for the jth commodity is equal to λ_i/λ_j. Note, however, that λ_i and λ_j must be the same for all c; hence, the marginal rate of substitution of i for j must be the same for all consumers. Recall, however, that this is precisely the (interior solution) condition for Pareto optimality discussed in section 17.2. Thus, Pareto optimality is a necessary condition for social optimality.

Pareto optimality is not a sufficient condition for social optimality. Equating marginal rates of substitution across consumers for all pairs of commodities is not sufficient to satisfy the first-order optimality conditions (20.5). To further explicate these conditions, consider the first-order-condition equations corresponding to one commodity, say the ith, and two individuals, say the cth and the $\bar{c}$th. Combining these two equations, we obtain

$$W_c(U^1(x^1), \ldots, U^m(x^m))U_i^c(x^c) = W_{\bar{c}}(U^1(x^1), \ldots, U^m(x^m))U_i^{\bar{c}}(x^{\bar{c}}) \tag{20.6}$$

where, from above, we know that $W_c(U^1(x^1), \ldots, U^m(x^m))U_i^c(x^c)$ is the (differential) increase in social welfare that is generated by increasing the consumption of the ith commodity by the cth individual at the rate of one unit per time period; that is, this expression is the *marginal social welfare* of the ith commodity consumed by the cth individual. The equality (20.6) therefore says that the commodities in the exchange economy must be allocated to the individuals in such a way that the marginal social welfare of consumption of the ith commodity, say, is equal for all consumers. This, of course, makes sense. If this equality were not satisfied, social welfare could be increased by taking some of commodity i away from one member of the community and giving it to another. It is this rule that allows us to choose, among the large number of Pareto-optimal distributions, the socially optimal distribution. Thus, if a particular Bergson–Samuelson social welfare function, incorporating the values of society, is specified, a social optimum is generated by a straightforward optimization problem. Note, however, that the necessary social-optimality condition (20.6), which compares marginal utilities of different individuals, requires cardinal unit comparability. Thus, the foregoing analysis requires a strengthening of the (ordinal noncomparability) informational basis envisioned by Samuelson.

Graphical Illustration of Social Optimality

The foregoing ideas can be illustrated graphically by considering the case in which there are two commodities and two consumers. The preference orderings of the two consumers are represented by the indifference maps in the consumption box diagram in figure 20.3 (see section 15.3 for a discussion of this diagrammatic construction). The set of Pareto optima is represented by the contract curve in this box diagram. The construction of a social welfare function for this society requires that particular cardinalizations of the utility functions representing the two orderings be adopted. In terms of the graph, this is equivalent to choosing particular values to be attached to the indifference curves of the two

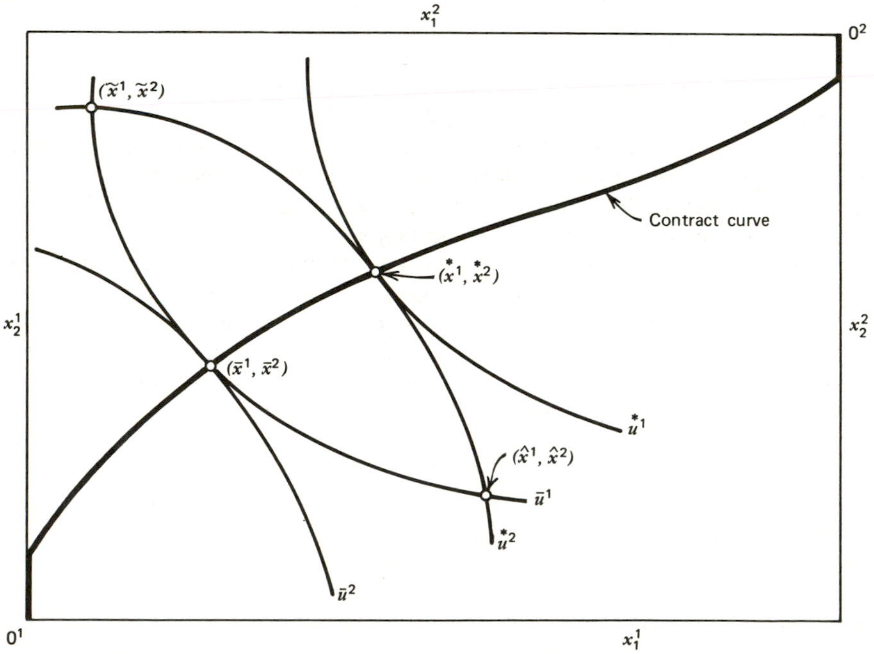

Figure 20.3

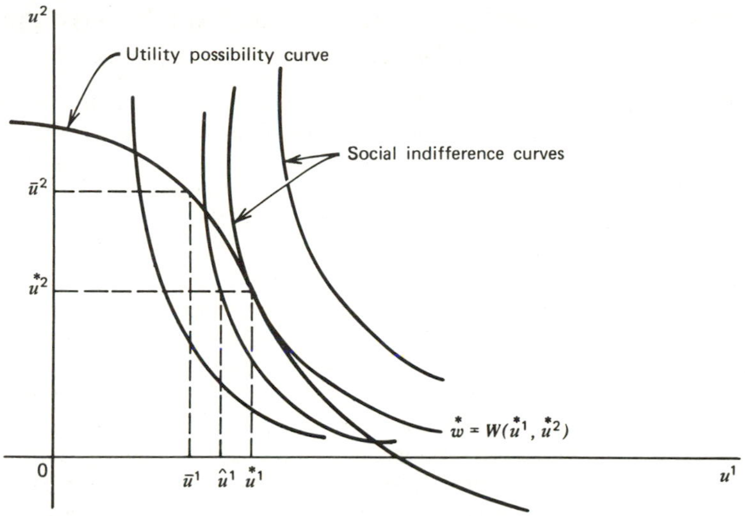

Figure 20.4

consumers. Given particular choices of the utility indicators for the two consumers, each point on the contract curve can be represented by a pair of utility values, one for each consumer. We can therefore represent the points on the contract curve by a locus of points in $u^1 - u^2$ space—i.e., in utility space. This construction, referred to as the *utility-possibility curve*, is represented in figure 20.4. Thus, each point on the utility-possibility curve corresponds to a unique point on the contract curve in the consumption box diagram. For example, the points $(\bar{u}^1, \bar{u}^2)$ and $(\overset{*}{u}^1, \overset{*}{u}^2)$ in figure 20.4 correspond to the points $(\bar{x}^1, \bar{x}^2)$ and $(\overset{*}{x}^1, \overset{*}{x}^2)$, respectively, in figure 20.3. Points below the utility-possibility curve correspond to points (not necessarily unique) off the contract curve in figure 20.3. For example, the point $(\bar{u}^1, \overset{*}{u}^2)$ corresponds to the points $(\hat{x}^1, \hat{x}^2)$ and $(\tilde{x}^1, \tilde{x}^2)$ in figure 20.3. Points below the utility-possibility curve are inefficient, or Pareto dominated, and points on the utility-possibility curve are efficient or Pareto optimal. The similarity between the utility-possibility curve in figure 20.4 and the production-possibility curve constructed in section 16.3 should be obvious.

The social welfare function is represented in figure 20.4 by a set of social indifference curves. Note that inefficient points may yield a higher level of social welfare than efficient points on the utility-possibility curve (e.g., $W(\hat{u}^1, \overset{*}{u}^2) > W(\bar{u}^1, \bar{u}^2)$). The social optimum is, of course, given by the point of tangency between the utility-possibility curve and a social indifference curve at $(\overset{*}{u}^1, \overset{*}{u}^2)$.[9]

[9] Of course, the social optimum need not be unique. If the utility-possibility frontier and the social indifference curves are, respectively, strictly concave and strictly convex to the origin, the social optimum will be unique, but there is no obvious reason why these strict convexity and concavity conditions should be satisfied. Whether the social indifference curve is convex depends, of course, upon whether or not the "law of diminishing social marginal rate of substitution is satisfied."

Graphical Illustration of Optimality with Utilitarian and Rawlsian Social Welfare Functions

It is perhaps illuminating to consider graphically the social optima generated by the two special Bergson–Samuelson social welfare functions discussed in section 20.3. The social indifference curves generated by the classical utilitarian social welfare function (20.1) are linear with slopes everywhere equal to −1. The social indifference map reflecting this characteristic and the resulting social optimum ($\overset{*}{u}^1$, $\overset{*}{u}^2$) are illustrated in figure 20.5. It is perhaps worth noting that this particular social welfare function is consistent with a distribution in which one consumer receives the entire aggregate endowment. This possibility is illustrated by the social optimum ($\hat{u}_1$, 0) with the utility-possibility curve represented by the dotted line.

The Rawlsian social welfare function (20.3) has very different implications for social optimality. The indifference curves corresponding to the Rawlsian social welfare function are right angles with the cusps located on a 45-degree line emanating from the origin. This social indifference map and the social optimum ($\overset{*}{u}^1$, $\overset{*}{u}^2$) are illustrated in figure 20.6. Note that the Rawlsian welfare criterion is apparently extremely "egalitarian" since the social optimum always yields equal utilities for the two members of the community. This follows quite obviously from the fact that social welfare is given by the utility of the worst-off member of the community. Note, however, that, as formulated, the Rawlsian criterion is egalitarian only in terms of utility. It is quite possible for

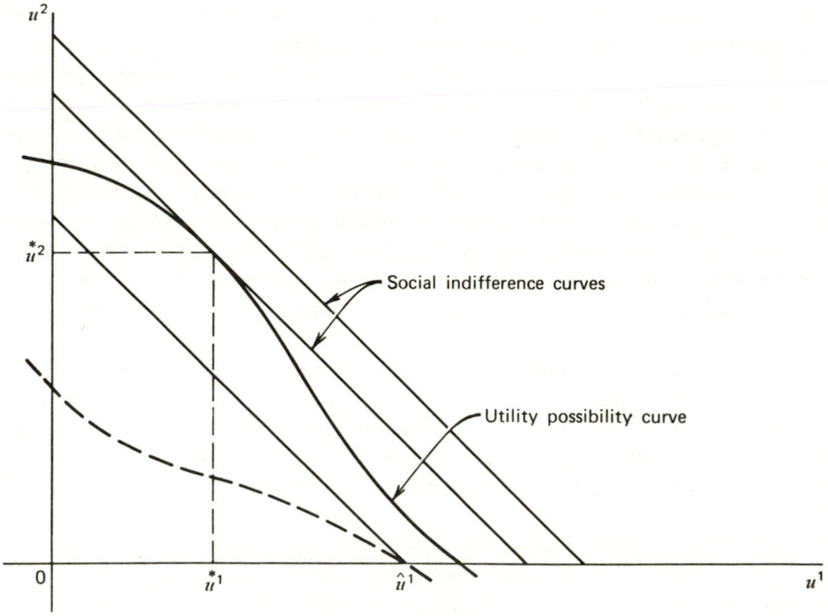

Figure 20.5

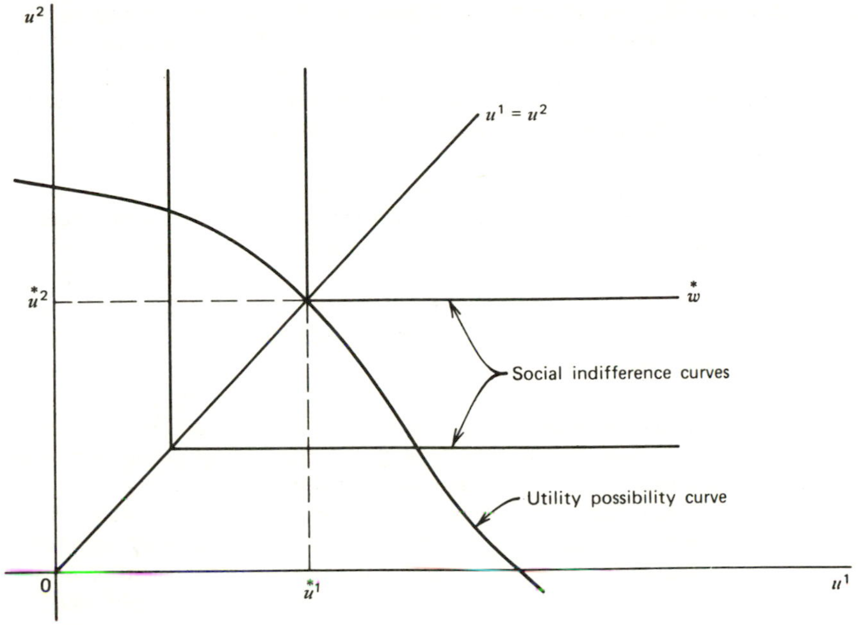

Figure 20.6

an egalitarian society in terms of utility to be very nonegalitarian in terms of some other criterion such as the distribution of income.

The Rawlsian criterion could, however, be reformulated in terms of income rather than utility levels; i.e., social state $\overset{*}{s}$ would be socially preferred to state $\hat{s}$ if $\min\{\overset{*}{y}_1, \ldots, \overset{*}{y}_m\} > \min\{\hat{y}_1, \ldots, \hat{y}_m\}$, where $\overset{*}{y}_1, \ldots, \overset{*}{y}_m$ and $\hat{y}_1, \ldots, \hat{y}_m$ are the income levels in the two social states. This criterion obviously puts a high premium on income equality. Along this line of thought, the classical utilitarian criterion, reformulated in terms of income levels, would prescribe the maximization of aggregate personal income as the social-optimization problem.

20.5 CONCLUDING REMARKS

Chapters 19 and 20 undoubtedly make it apparent that many of the ideas of social choice theory are in a very inchoate state. Although the field has a rich heritage in the philosophy of ethics, the political theory of voting, and the utilitarian theory of economics, and although the literature on social choice is now large and burgeoning, the answers to many important questions are not yet available or at least not widely recognized as such. Indeed, the issue of what questions social choice theorists ought to be asking is itself a matter of some contention. In a recent survey of social choice theory, Sen notes "that some of the difficulties in the general theory of social choice arise from a desire to fit essentially different classes of group aggregation problems into one uniform framework and from seeking excessive generality." Sen [1975, pp. 1–2] goes on to suggest three very different broad headings of interpersonal aggregation or social choice problems which, he contends, require different approaches:

(1) Committee Decision: *A committee has to choose among alternative proposals for action on the relative merits of which the members hold different views.*

(2) Social Welfare Judgment: *A person wants to make a judgment whether a certain change will be better for the society, some members of which will gain from the change while others will lose.*

(3) Normative Indication: *Measurement of "national income," "inequality," "poverty," "and other indicators" defined with normative motivation incorporating interpersonal weighting in some easily tractable way.*

The discussion in section 19.3 on collective rationality is perhaps most relevant to social choice problems of type (1). Transitivity is probably not an essential requirement of committee decision making. It is, however, perhaps reasonable to require that the outcome be as independent as possible from the agenda so that it is not susceptible to the machinations of possibly pernicious committee members. On the other hand, interpersonal comparisons of the intensity of individual committee members' feelings about the alternatives is probably not an important or even a legitimate concern in the construction of committee rules.

Conditions that might be considered reasonable to impose upon the making of social welfare judgments perhaps differ radically from those that might be imposed upon committee decision procedures. For example, weakening transitivity to path independence so that the outcome is independent of the agenda would appear to be relatively unimportant for the purpose of making social welfare judgments. On the other hand, one might argue that it is hopelessly impractical to attempt to make social welfare judgments (regarding, for example, the distribution of income) without being able to make any interpersonal utility comparisons. Thus, the theory of social choice based upon the relaxation of Arrow's (implicit) ordinal noncomparability condition is perhaps most relevant to problems of type (2).

Finally, it might appear that problems of type (3) are fairly closely related to problems of type (2). For example, it is often possible to associate with particular measures of inequality particular Bergson–Samuelson social welfare functions that rationalize it (see, for example, Blackorby and Donaldson [1977b]).

Thus, it might well be that the alternative approaches of chapters 19 and 20 are more complementary to one another than substitutable for one another. One might expect political scientists to be especially interested in ways of relaxing the transitivity condition and one might expect welfare economists to be most interested in expanding the informational basis to allow for (cardinal or ordinal) interpersonal utility comparisons.

Perhaps the most important impression that might be obtained from reading the last two chapters is that it is possible to discuss rigorously concepts such as "justice," "equity," and "fairness" in the context of economic problems.

EXERCISES

20.1 Consider the two-person, two-commodity exchange economy described in exercise 15.1.

a. Derive the equation for the utility-possibility curve.

b. Identify the socially optimal state of the economy if the Bergson–Samuelson social welfare function is

i. $W(u^1, u^2) = u^1 u^2$;

ii. $W(u^1, u^2) = (u^1)^2 u^2$;

iii. classical utilitarian;

iv. Rawlsian.

c. If U^1 is subjected to the strictly monotonic transformation, $\hat{U}^1(x^1) = [U^1(x^1)]^2$, what modification of the Bergson–Samuelson social welfare function (i) is required in order to make social choice invariant to this transformation?

20.2 Show that interpersonal noncomparability implies that the social preference ordering has the property that society is indifferent between all Pareto-noncomparable alternatives. (Hint: see Sen [1973].)

20.3 Draw the diagrams in figure 20.2 for the case where $\bar{u}$ is on the 45-degree line through the origin (i.e., $\bar{u}^1 = \bar{u}^2$).

20.4 Show that, in the exchange economy situation analyzed in section 20.4, the quasiorderings of section 20.3 do not generally allow us to solve the social-optimality problem.

20.5 Represent the utilitarian and Rawlsian social orderings by $\succsim_U$ and $\succsim_R$, respectively; that is, $\overset{*}{s} \succsim_U \hat{s}$ and $\overset{*}{s} \succsim_R \hat{s}$ mean that social state $\overset{*}{s}$ is no worse that $\hat{s}$ according to the utilitarian and Rawlsian criteria, respectively. Consider the social preference relation, $\succsim$, defined by $\overset{*}{s} \succsim \hat{s}$ if and only if $\overset{*}{s} \succsim_U \hat{s}$ *and* $\overset{*}{s} \succsim_R \hat{s}$.

a. Show that $\succsim$ is a quasi ordering.

b. Show that $\succsim$ is equivalent to the dominance relation (see Blackorby and Donaldson [1977]).

PART IV
HISTORICAL NOTES AND SUGGESTED READING

The founder of *general equilibrium theory* was **Walras** [1874] (English translation by **Jaffe** [1954]). **Arrow** and **Hahn** [1971, chap. 1 and end-of-chapter notes] briefly trace the development of the major results concerning the existence and uniqueness (Schlesinger, Wald, McKenzie, Arrow and Debreu), comparative statics and stability (Hicks, Hotelling, Samuelson, Allen, Mosak, and Metzler), and optimality (Edgeworth, Pareto, Arrow, Debreu, and Koopmans) of general competitive equilibrium. This major treatise is a superb exposition of many results in general-equilibrium theory (some exceptions being optimality of competitive equilibrium, economic externalities and public commodities, and markets with a continuum of traders). **Newman** [1965] is a very careful treatment of the theory of general exchange equilibrium. The concept (though not the terminology) of *the core* is due to **Edgeworth** [1881]. It was first applied in a game theoretic context to market economies by **Shubik** [1959b]. **Scarf** [1962] first proved Edgeworth's results for an exchange economy while **Debreu** and **Scarf** [1963] extended the results to an economy with production.

Arrow [1951a] is the original reexamination and extension of neoclassical *welfare theory* in terms of modern economic theory. **Debreu** [1954] is also a classic paper on the optimality of competitive equilibrium. **Koopmans** [1957, essay 1] is an excellent exposition of the nexus between Pareto optimality and competitive equilibrium.

The *existence of equilibrium* is not guaranteed in the presence of *nonconvexities* in preferences and technologies. Furthermore, it may not be possible to decentralize an optimal allocation in the presence of nonconvexities. **Arrow** and **Hahn** [1971, chap. 7] provide a good introduction to the problem of measuring and assessing the seriousness of nonconvexities in preferences and production. **Starr** [1969] provides a rigorous mathematical treatment and shows that the second optimality principle remains approximately true if the nonconvexity is "small" relative to the economy. **Emmerson** [1972] examines the optimality of competitive equilibrium in the presence of *indivisibilities in commodities* and shows how the distance between a competitive-equilibrium allocation and the nearest Pareto optimum can be related to the size of the indivisibility.

General equilibrium under monopolistic competition is briefly analyzed in **Arrow** and **Hahn** [1971, chap. 6, section 4]. **Negishi** [1960–61] presented a formal model and proved an existence theorem for an economy where each monopolist produces one commodity with a convex technology set.

The concept of *economic externalities*, and the narrower one of *public commodities*, has a long history in economics. The attempt to clarify these concepts has been conducted at quite different levels of abstraction and generalization and directed toward answering different questions. For example, the consequences of economic externalities for the existence and optimality of competitive equilibrium has been analyzed in a very rigorous and abstract manner. On the other hand, remedies for economic externalities (criteria for nonmarket allocation, "correcting" market prices, and the role of private property and other institutional settings in creating or allowing markets to form) have usually been analyzed in the context of specific, partial-equilibrium examples. **Arrow** [1969; reprinted in 1971] is a valuable essay which provides both commentary on the major contributions to this literature, and, more importantly, a conceptual framework within which the major questions can be organized. **Starrett** [1972] utilizes one model of economic externalities suggested by Arrow to show that economic externalities in production and consumption may involve fundamental nonconvexities that break the nexus between Pareto-optimal allocations and competitive equilibrium. **Heller** [1972] analyzes nonconvexities in transactions technologies. **Shapley** and **Shubik** [1969] examine the core of an economy with externality diseconomies in production and show that the core does not necessarily exist.

Coase [1960] is a discussion of *property rights* as a possible source of the failure of a market to emerge in order to allocate an economic externality. Many authors have suggested *remedies for externalities.* **Pigou** [1920] suggested correction by taxation. The conditions under which this remedy would achieve an optimal allocation of resources has recently been reexamined by **Starrett** [1972], **Diamond** [1973], and **Green** and **Sheshinski** [1976]. **Meade** [1952] suggested setting up "an artificial market" for the externality. **Heller** and **Starrett** [1976] review the possible ways in which economic externalities result in nonoptimal allocations and analyze under what conditions the various remedies might be effective.

Specific applications of the theory of economic externalities are **Gordon** [1954] and **Smith** [1969] for fisheries, and **Smith** [1968] for natural resources (fish, timber, petroleum, and minerals).

The seminal work on the *optimality* of equilibrium of an economy *with public commodities* is **Samuelson** [1954]. Samuelson attempted to provide a unifying theory for the economics of public expenditure and taxation (public finance). The finest presentation of this traditional area of economics is the text by **Musgrave** [1959] (see also the anthology by **Musgrave** and **Peacock** [1958]). **Lindahl** [1919] first used the concept of "personalized prices" in a partial-equilibrium analysis of the optimal supply of public commodities.

Foley [1967], inspired by Samuelson's contribution, utilized the analytical methods of modern economics (associated with Arrow, Debreu, Koopmans, et al.) to analyze the *existence and optimality of equilibrium with public commodities.* Foley also introduced government into the economy as an economic agent and attempted to analyze the relations between the tax structure, optimality, and social welfare functions. **Milleron** [1972] is a survey article on the existence and optimality of equilibrium with public commodities. Some of the European literature on the existence of equilibrium and the core of an economy with public commodities is also briefly discussed. **Foley** [1970] also analyzes the latter question.

Hurwicz [1972] [1974] analyzes *decentralized reasource allocation* mechanisms. *Planning procedures* for decentralizing an optimal allocation with public commodities have been analyzed by **Malinvaud** [1971] and **Drèze** and **Vallée Poussin** [1971]. **Groves** and **Ledyard** [1977] deal with the problem of devising a decentralized procedure for allocating public commodities that is compatible with the consumers' incentives to correctly reveal their preferences for public commodities (the "free rider" problem).

The seminal work on *general* (*exchange*) *equilibrium under uncertainty* is **Arrow** [1953; translation in 1964a]. **Debreu** [1959, chap. 7] extends the analysis to include production (the suggested readings to parts I and II of this book include additional literature on consumer and producer choice under uncertainty). **Diamond** [1967] analyzes the role of the stock market. **Radner** [1968] analyzes the concept of the information available to economic agents and the consequences of different "information structures" for equilibrium. **Radner** [1974] is a good review of market equilibrium under uncertainty and the important distinction between complete and incomplete markets.

A natural starting point for those interested in pursuing *social choice theory* is the excellent book by **Sen** [1970a]. Other treatises on social choice (which are, however, tougher going) are **Fishburn** [1973] and **Pattanaik** [1971]. Shorter surveys of social choice theory and of welfare economics in general can be found in **Sen** [1977b, 1975] and **Plott** [1976]. The first *impossibility theorem* can of course be found in the classic treatise of **Arrow** [1951b]. A simpler and modernized proof of Arrow's theorem can be found in **Blau** [1972]. Additional impossibility theorems generated by weakening Arrow's transitivity condition but by strengthening other conditions can be found in **Sen** [1969], **Mas-Colell** and **Sonnenschein** [1972], and **Ferejohn** and **Grether** [1974, 1975]. An alternative approach to the problem of cyclical majorities is "single-peaked preferences" (**Arrow** [1951b]).

The concept of fairness of outcomes of social decision rules has been analyzed by **Schmeidler** and **Vind** [1972], **Varian** [1974], **Pazner** and **Schmeidler** [1974], **Pažner** [1977], and **Crawford** [1977]. The possibility of liberal social decision rules satisfying the Arrow condition has been analyzed by **Sen** [1970b].

The concept of *strategy proofness* of a social decision rule, which in principle incorporates the concept of true demand revelation for public commodities analyzed by Groves and Ledyard in the paper cited above, is attributable to **Gibbard** [1973] and **Satterthwaite** [1975].

The notion of a *social welfare function* dates back at least to **Berg** (**Bergson**) [1938]. The concept was also discussed extensively by **Samuelson** [1947a, chap. 8].

The issues of *cardinality and interpersonal comparisons* have been examined by **Harsanyi** [1955], **Sen** [1970c], and **Blackorby** [1975]. Closely related to the concept of interpersonal comparisons is that of *equity*, examined by **Suppes** [1966], **Rawls** [1971], **Hammond** [1976], **Blackorby** and **Donaldson** [1977a], **d'Aspremont** and **Gevers** [1978], **Sen** [1977b], and **Atkinson** [1970].

REFERENCES

Allen, R. G. D. [1950], *Mathematical Economics*, Macmillan.

Apostle, T. [1974], *Mathematical Analysis*, Addison-Wesley.

Archibald, G. C. [1961], "Chamberlin and the Chicago School," *Review of Economic Studies* 29:1-28.

———. [1963], "Reply to Chicago," *Review of Economic Studies* 30:68–71.

Archibald, R. W., and D. Donaldson [1976], "Non-Paternalism and the Basic Theorems of Welfare Economics," *Canadian Journal of Economics* 9:492-507.

Arrow, K. J. [1951a], "An Extension of the Basic Theorems of Classical Welfare Economics," in *Proceedings of the Second Berkeley Symposium on Mathematical Statistics and Probability*, ed. J. Neyman, University of California Press.

———. [1951b], *Social Choice and Individual Values*, Wiley.

———. [1953], "Le Role des Valeurs Boursieres pour la Repartition la Meilleure des Risques," *Econometric*, Centre National de la Recherche Scientifique, 41–48.

———. [1959], "Rational Choice Functions and Orderings," *Economica* 26:121–127.

———. [1962], "Optimal Expansion of the Capacity of the Firm" in *Studies in the Theory of Inventory and Production*, ed. A. S. Manne, Stanford University Press.

———. [1964a], "The Role of Securities in the Optimal Allocation of Risk-Bearing," *Review of Economic Studies* 31:91–96.

———. [1964b], "Optimal Capital Policy, the Cost of Capital, and Myopic Decision Rules," *Annals of the Institute of Statistical Mathematics* 16:20–30.

———. [1965], *Aspects of the Theory of Risk-Bearing*, Academic Bookstore.

———. [1968], "Optimal Capital Policy with Irreversible Investment," in *Value, Capital and Growth*, ed. J. N. Wolfe, Aldine.

———. [1970], *Essays in the Theory of Risk-Bearing*, Markham; North Holland.

———. [1971], "Political and Economic Evaluation of Social Effects and Externalities," in *Frontiers of Quantitative Economics*, ed. M. J. Intriligator, North Holland.

Arrow, K. J., H. P. Chenery, B. S. Minhas, and R. M. Solow [1961], "Capital-Labor Substitution and Economic Efficiency," *Review of Economics and Statistics* 63:225–50.

Arrow, K. J., and G. Debreu [1954], "Existence of Equilibrium for a Competitive Economy," *Econometrica* 22:265–90.

Arrow, K. J., and F. H. Hahn [1971], *General Competitive Analysis*, Holden-Day.

Arrow, K, J., L. Hurwicz, and H. Uzawa [1961], "Constraint Qualifications in Non-Linear Programming," *Naval Research Logistics Quarterly* 8:175–91.

Arrow, K. J., and M. Kurz [1970], *Public Investment, the Rate of Return, and Optimal Fiscal Policy*, Johns Hopkins Press.

Arzac, E. [1976], "Profits and Safety in the Theory of the Firm Under Price Uncertainty," *International Economic Review* 17: 163–71.

Atkinson, A. B. [1970], "On the Measurement of Inequality," *Journal of Economic Theory* 2:244–63.

Bailey, E. [1973], *Economic Theory of Regulatory Constraint*, Lexington.

Barry, B. and D. W. Rae [1975], "Political Evaluation," in *The Handbook of Political Science*, Vol. 1, Addison-Wesley.

Baumol, W. J., and D. F. Bradford [1970], "Optimal Departures from Marginal Cost Pricing," *American Economic Review* 60:265–83.

Baumol, W. J. and A. K. Klevorick [1970], "Input choices and rate-of-return regulation," *The Bell Journal of Economics and Management Science* 1: 162–190.

Becker, G. [1965], "A Theory of the Allocation of Time," *The Economic Journal* 75:494–517.

Bentham, J. [1789], *An Introduction to the Principle of Morals and Legislation*, Oxford [1907].

Bergson [Berg], A. [1938], "A Reformulation of Certain Aspects of Welfare Economics," *Quarterly Journal of Economics* 52:310–34.

Bertrand, J. [1883], "Review of Cournot's Researches," *Journal des Savants*.

Blackorby, C. [1975], "Degrees of Cardinality and Aggregate Partial Orderings," *Econometrica* 45:845–53.

Blackorby, C., R. Boyce, and R. R. Russell [1978], "Estimation of Demand Systems Generated by the Gorman Polar Form; a Generalization of the S-Branch Utility Tree," *Econometrica* 46 : 345–65.

Blackorby, C., and D. Donaldson [1977a], "Utility vs. Equity: Some Plausible Quasi-Orderings," *Journal of Public Economics* 7:365–81.

———. [1977b], "Measures of Relative Equality and Their Meaning in Terms of Social Welfare," Discussion Paper 77–27, Department of Economics, University of British Columbia.

Blackorby, C., D. Primont, and R. R. Russell [1978], *Duality, Separability, and Functional Structure; Theory and Economic Applications*, Elsevier/ North Holland.

Blackorby, C., and R. R. Russell [1976], "Functional Structure and the Allen Partial Elasticities of Substitution: An Application of Duality Theory," *Review of Economic Studies* 43: 285–92.

Blau, J. H. [1972], "A Direct Proof of Arrow's Theorem," *Econometrica* 40:61–67.

Bohm-Bawerk, E. V. [1930], *The Positive Theory of Capital*, G. E. Stechert & Company.

Borda, J. C. [1781], "Memoire sur les Élections as Scrutin," *Mémoires de l'Acadèmie Royale des Sciences* (English translation by A. de Grazia [1953], *Isis* 44).

Brown, D. J. [1975] "Aggregation of Preferences," *Quarterly Journal of Economics* 89: 456–69.

Brown, M., and D. Heien [1972], "The S-Branch Utility Tree: A Generalization of the Linear Expenditure System," *Econometrica* 40:737–47.

Butters, G. R. [1977], "Equilibrium Distributions of Sales and Advertising Prices," *Review of Economic Studies* 44:465–93.

Chamberlin, E. H. [1948], "Proportionality, Divisibility, and Economies of Scale," *Quarterly Journal of Economics* 62:229–62.

———. [1949], "Proportionality, Divisibility, and Economies of Scale: Reply," *Quarterly Journal of Economics* 63:137–43.

———. [1960], *The Theory of Monopolistic Competition*, 7th ed., Harvard University Press.

Christensen, L. R., D. W. Jorgenson, and L. J. Lau [1975], "Transcendental Logarithmic Utility Functions," *American Economic Review* 65:367–83.

Clark, J. B. [1923], *The Distribution of Wealth*, Macmillan.

Clarke, E. H. [1971], "Multipart Pricing of Public Goods," *Public Choice* 11:17–33.

Coase, R. [1960], "The Problem of Social Cost," *Journal of Law and Economics* 3:1–44.

Courant, R., and H. Robbins [1941], *What is Mathematics?*, Oxford University Press.

Cournot, A. A. [1838], *Recherches sur les Principles Mathematiques de la Theorie des Richesses,* Librairie des Sciencies Politiques et Sociales, M. Riviere & cie. English translation, *Researches into the Mathematical Principles of the Theory of Wealth* (translated by N. T. Bacon, 2nd ed., 1927).

Crawford, V. P. [1977], "A Game of Fair Division," *Review of Economic Studies* 44:235–47.

Cyert, R. M. and J. G. March [1963], *A Behavioral Theory of the Firm,* Prentice-Hall.

d'Aspremont, C., and L. Gevers [1978], "Equity and the Informational Basis of Collective Choice," *Review of Economic Studies* 46:199–210.

Debreu, G. [1954], "Valuation Equilibrium and Pareto Optimum," in *Proceedings of the National Academy of Sciences of the USA* 40:588–92.

———. [1959], *Theory of Value*, Wiley.

———. [1962], "New Concepts and Techniques for Equilibrium Analysis," *International Economic Review* 3:257–73.

Debreu, G., and H. Scarf [1963], "A Limit Theorem on the Core of an Economy," *International Economic Review* 4:235–46.

Denny, M. [1974], "The Relationship Between Functional Forms for the Production System," *Canadian Journal of Economics* 7:21–31.

Diamond, P. [1967], "The Role of a Stock Market in a General Equilibrium Model with Technological Uncertainty," *American Economic Review* 57:759–76.

———. [1973], "Consumption Externalities and Imperfect Corrective Pricing," *Bell Journal of Economics and Management Science* 4:526–38.

Diewert, W. E. [1971], "An Application of the Shephard Duality Theorem: A Generalized Leontief Production Function," *Journal of Political Economy* 79: 481–507.

———. [1974], "Applications of Duality Theory," in *Frontiers of Quantitative Economics*, II, eds. M. Intriligator and D. Kendrick, North Holland.

Dixit, A. K., and J. E. Stiglitz [1977], "Monopolistic Competition and Optimum Product Diversity," *American Economic Review* 67:297–308.

Dorfman, R., P. Samuelson, and R. Solow [1958], *Linear Programming and Economic Analysis*, McGraw-Hill.

Douglas, P. H. [1948], "Are There Laws of Production?" *American Economic Review* 38 :1–41.

Drèze, J. H. [1974], "Axiomatic Theories of Choice, Cardinal Utility and Subjective Probability: A Review," in *Allocation Under Uncertainty: Equilibrium and Optimality*, ed. J. H. Drèze, Macmillan.

Drèze, J. H., and D. Vallée Poussin [1971], "A Tâtonnement Process for Public Goods," *Review of Economic Studies* 38:133–50.

Edgeworth, F. Y. [1881], *Mathematical Psychics*, C. Kegan Paul.

Eisner, R., and R. H. Strotz [1963], "Determinants of Business Investment," in *Impacts of Monetary Policy* (Commission on Money and Credit), Prentice-Hall.

Ekern, S., and R. Wilson [1974], "On the Theory of the Firm in an Economy with Incomplete Markets," *Bell Journal of Economics and Management Science* 5:71–80.

Emmerson, R. D. [1972], "Optima and Market Equilibria with Indivisible Commodities," *Journal of Economic Theory* 5:177–88.

Fellner, W. [1949], *Competition Among the Few*, Knopf.

Ferejohn, J. A., and D. M. Grether [1974], "On a Class of Rational Social Decision Procedures," *Journal of Economic Theory* 8:471–83.

———. [1975], "Weak Path Independence," *Journal of Economic Theory* 14:19–31.

Fishburn, P. D. [1973], *The Theory of Social Choice*, Princeton University Press.

Fisher, F. M. [1961], "Stability of the Cournot Oligopoly Solution: The Effects of Speeds of Adjustment and Increasing Marginal Cost," *Review of Economic Studies* 28:125–35.

———. [1976], "The Stability of General Equilibrium: Results and Problems," in *Essays in Economic Analysis*, eds. Artis and Nobay, Cambridge University Press.

Fisher, I. [1930], *The Theory of Interest*, Yale University Press.

Foley, D. K. [1967], "Resource Allocation and the Public Sector," *Yale Economic Essays* 7:45–98.

———. [1970], "Lindahl's Solution and the Core of Economy with Public Goods," *Econometrica* 38:66–72.

Friedman, M. [1953], "The Methodology of Positive Economics," *Essays in Positive Economics*, University of Chicago Press.

———. [1963], "More On Archibald Versus Chicago," *Review of Economic Studies* 30:65–67.

Friedman, M., and L. J. Savage [1948], "The Utility Analysis of Choices Involving Risk," *Journal of Political Economy* 56:279–304.

Frisch, R. [1936], "On the Notion of Equilibrium and Disequilibrium," *Review of Economic Studies* 3:100–105.

Gale, D. [1960], *The Theory of Linear Economic Models*, McGraw-Hill.

Gibbard, A. [1969], "Intransitive Social Indifference and the Arrow Dilemma," unpublished manuscript.

———. [1973], "Manipulation of Voting Schemes: A General Result," *Econometrica* 41:587–603.

———. [1974], "A Pareto-Consistent Libertarian Claim," *Journal of Economic Theory* 7:388–411.

Gordon, H. S. [1954], "The Economic Theory of a Common Property Resource: The Fishery," *Journal of Political Economy* 62:124–42.

Gorman, W. M. [1953], "Community Preference Fields," *Econometrica* 21:63–80.

———. [1959], "Separable Utility and Aggregation," *Econometrica* 27:469–81.

———. [1968], "Measuring the Quantities of Fixed Factors," in *Value, Capital, and Growth*, ed. J. N. Wolfe, Aldine.

Green, J., and E. Sheshinski [1976], "Direct vs. Indirect Remedies for Externalities," *Journal of Political Economy*, 84:797–808.

Groves, T. [1973], "Incentives in Teams," *Econometrica* 41:617–63.

Groves, T., and J. Ledyard [1977], "Optimal Allocation of Public Goods: A Solution to the Free-Rider Problem," *Econometrica* 45:783–810.

Hadley, G. [1961], *Linear Algebra*, Addison-Wesley.

Hahn, F. H. [1949], "Proportionality, Divisibility, and Economies of Scale: Comment," *Quarterly Journal of Economics* 63:131–37.

———. [1962], "The Stability of the Cournot Oligopoly Solution," *Review of Economic Studies* 29:329–31.

Hammond, P. [1976], "Equity, Arrow's Conditions and Rawls' Difference Principle," *Econometrica* 44:793–804.

Hansson, B. [1969], "Group Preferences," *Econometrica* 37:50–54.

Harsanyi, J. C. [1955], "Cardinal Welfare, Individualistic Ethics, and Interpersonal Comparisons of Utility," *Journal of Political Economy* 63:309–21.

Heller, W. P. [1972], "Transactions with Set-Up Cost," *Journal of Economic Theory* 4:465–78.

Heller, W. P., and D. Starrett [1976], "On the Nature of Externalities," in *Theory and Measurement of Economic Externalities*, ed. S. Lynn, Academic Press.

Hicks, J. R. [1932], *The Theory of Wages*, Macmillan.

———. [1939], *Value and Capital*, Clarendon Press.

———. [1943], "The Four Consumer's Surpluses," *Review of Economic Studies* 11:31–41.

———. [1956], *A Revision of Demand Theory*, Clarendon Press.

———. [1960], "Linear Theory," *The Economic Journal* 70:671–709.

Hicks, J. R., and R. G. D. Allen [1934], "A Reconsideration of the Theory of Value, I, II," *Economica* 1:52–75, 196–219.

Hirshleifer, J. [1966], "Investment Decision Under Uncertainty: Applications of the State-Preference Approach," *Quarterly Journal of Economics* 80:252–77.

———. [1970], *Investment, Interest and Capital*, Prentice-Hall.

Hotelling, H. [1931], "The Economics of Exhaustible Resources," *Journal of Political Economy* 39:137–75.

———. [1932], "Edgeworth's Taxation Paradox and the Nature of Supply and Demand Functions," *Journal of Political Economy* 40:557–616.

Houthakker, H. S. [1950], "Revealed Preference and the Utility Function," *Economica* 17:159–74.

———. [1960], "Additive Preferences," *Econometrica* 28:244–57.

———. [1963], "Some Problems in the International Comparison of Consumption Patterns," *L'évaluation et le Rôle des Besoins de Biens de Consommation dans les Divers Régimes Économiques*, Centre National de la Recherche Scientifique.

Hurwicz, L. [1963], "Mathematics in Economics: Language and Instrument in *Mathematics and the Social Sciences*, ed. J. D. Charlesworth, American Academy of Political Science.

———. [1972], "On Informationally Decentralized Systems," in *Decision and Organization*, eds. C. B. McGuire and R. Radner, North Holland.

———. [1974], "The Design of Mechanisms for Resource Allocation," in *Frontiers of Quantitative Economics*, II, eds. M. D. Intriligator and D. A. Kendrick, North Holland.

Hutchinson, T. W. [1938], *The Significance and Basic Postulates of Economic Theory*, A. Kelley.

Intriligator, M. [1978], "Mathematical Programming, with Applications to Microeconomic Theory," in *Handbook of Mathematical Economics*, eds. K. J. Arrow and M. D. Intriligator, North Holland.

Katzner, D. W. [1970], *Static Demand Theory*, Macmillan.

Keynes, J. N. [1891], *The Scope and Method of Political Economy*, Macmillan.

Klein, E. [1973], *Mathematical Methods in Theoretical Economics*, Academic Press.

Klein, L. R., and H. Rubin [1947], "A Constant-Utility Index of the Cost of Living," *Review of Economic Studies* 15:84–87.

Koopmans, T. C. [1947], "Measurement Without Theory," *Review of Economics and Statistics* 29:161–72.

———. [1951], *Activity Analysis of Production and Allocation*, Wiley.

———. [1957], *Three Essays on the State of Economic Science*, McGraw-Hill.

———. [1977], "Concepts of Optimality and Their Uses," *American Economic Review* 67:261–74.

———. [1949], "Discussion between Rutledge Vining and Tjalling Kropmans on Methodological Issues in Quantitative Economics," *Review of Economics and Statistics* 31: 77–94.

Kuhn, H. W., and A. W. Tucker [1951], "Non-Linear Programming," in *Proceedings of the Second Berkeley Symposium on Mathematical Statistics and Probability*, ed. J. Neyman, University of California Press.

Lancaster, K. [1966], "A New Approach to Consumer Theory," *Journal of Political Economy* 74:132–57.

———. [1971], *Consumer Demand, A New Approach*, Columbia University Press.

Leland, H. [1974], "Production Theory and the Stock Market," *Bell Journal of Economics and Management Science* 5:125–44.

Leontief, W. W. [1936], "Composite Commodities and the Problem of Index Numbers," *Econometrica* 4:39–59.

———. [1947a], "A Note on the Interrelation of Subsets of Independent Variables of a Continuous Function with Continuous First Derivatives," *Bulletin of the American Mathematical Society* 53:343–50.

———. [1947b], "Introduction to a Theory of the Internal Structure of Functional Relationships," *Econometrica* 15:361–73.

———. [1949], *The Structure of the American Economy*, 1919–1939, Oxford University Press, London and New York.

———. [1966], *Input-output Economics*, Oxford University Press, London and New York.

———. [1971], "Theoretical Assumptions and Nonobserved Facts," *American Economic Review* 61:1–7.

Lindahl, E. [1919], "Just Taxation: A Positive Solution," reprinted in Musgrave and Peacock [1958].

Lucas, R. E. [1967], "Adjustment Costs and the Theory of Supply," *Journal of Political Economy* 75:321–33.

Luce, R. D., and H. Raiffa [1957], *Games and Decisions*, Wiley.

McFadden, D. [1963], "Further Results on the CES Production Function," *Review of Economic Studies* 30: 78–83.

———. [1970], "Cost, Revenue, and Profit Functions," Working Paper, Department of Economics, University of California, Berkeley, (forthcoming in *Econometric Approach to Production Theory*, eds. M. Fuss and D. McFadden, North Holland).

Machlup, Fritz [1967], "Theories of the Firm: Marginalist, Behavioral, Managerial," *American Economic Review* 57:1–33.

Malinvaud, E. [1971], "A Planning Approach to the Public Good Problem," *Swedish Journal of Economics* 73:96–112.

Malmquist, S. [1953], "Index Numbers and Indifference Surfaces," *Trabajosde Estatistica* 4:209–42.

Markowitz, H. [1952], "Portfolio Selection," *Journal of Finance* 7:77–91.

Marris, R. [1964], *The Economic Theory of "Managerial" Capitalism*, Free Press.

Marshall, A. [1920], *Principles of Economics*, 8th ed., Macmillan.

Mas-Colell, A., and H. Sonnenschein [1972], "General Possibility Theorems for Group Decisions," *Review of Economic Studies* 39:185–92.

Meade, J. E. [1952], "External Economies and Diseconomies in a Competitive Situation," *Economic Journal* 62:54–67.

Menger, J. [1954], "The Laws of Return: A Study on Metaeconomics," in *Economic Activity Analysis*, ed. O. Morgenstern, Wiley, pp. 419–81.

Milleron, J. C. [1972], "Theory of Value with Public Goods: A Survey Article," *Journal of Economic Theory* 5:419–77.

Morgenstern, O. [1963], "Limits to the Use of Mathematics in Economics," in *Mathematics and the Social Sciences*, ed. J. C. Charlesworth, American Academy of Political Science.

———. [1972], "Thirteen Critical Points in Contemporary Economic Theory: An Interpretation," *Journal of Economic Literature* 10:1163–89.

Muellbauer, J. [1974], "Household Production Theory, Quality, and the 'Hedonic Technique'," *American Economic Review* 64:977–94.

Musgrave, R. A. [1959], *The Theory of Public Finance*, McGraw-Hill.

Musgrave, R. A., and A. T. Peacock, eds. [1958], *Classics in the Theory of Public Finance*, Macmillan.

Nagel, E. [1963], "Assumptions in Economic Theory," *American Economic Review* 53:211–19.

Nash, J. F. [1950a], "The Bargaining Problem," *Econometrica* 18:155–62.

———. [1950b], "Equilibrium in N-Person Games," in *Proceedings of the National Academy of Sciences* 36:48–49.

———. [1953], "Two-Person Cooperative Games," *Econometrica* 21:128–40.

Negishi, T. [1960–61], "Monopolistic Competition and General Equilibrium," *Review of Economic Studies* 28:196–201.

Newman, P. K. [1965], *The Theory of Exchange*, Prentice-Hall.

Pareto, M. [1909], *Manuel d'Economie Politique*, Girard and Briere.

Patinkin, D. [1965], *Money, Interest, and Prices*, 2nd edition, Harper and Row.

Pattanaik, P. K. [1971], *Voting and Collective Choice*, Cambridge University Press.

Pazner, E. [1977], "Pitfalls in the Theory of Fairness," *Journal of Economic Theory* 44:458–66.

Pazner, E. A., and D. Schmeidler [1974], "A Difficulty in the Concept of Fairness," *Review of Economic Studies* 41:441–43.

Phlips, L. [1974], *Applied Consumption Analysis*, North Holland.

Pigou, A. C. [1920], *The Economics of Welfare*, Macmillan.

Plott, C. [1973], "Path Independence, Rationality and Social Choice," *Econometrica* 41:1075–91.

———. [1976], "Axiomatic Social Choice Theory: An Overview and Interpretation," *American Journal of Political Science*, 511–96.

Pollak, R. A. [1968], "Consistent Planning," *Review of Economic Studies* 35:201–8.

Pollak, R. A., and M. Wachter [1975], "The Relevance of the Household Production Function and Its Implications for the Allocation of Time," *Journal of Political Economy* 83:255–78.

Quandt, R. E. [1967], "On the Stability of Price Adjusting Oligopoly," *Southern Economic Journal* 33:332–36.

Radner, R. [1968], "Competitive Equilibrium Under Uncertainty," *Econometrica* 36:31–58.

———. [1974], "Market Equilibrium and Uncertainty: Concepts and Problems," in *Frontiers of Quantitative Economics*, II, eds. M. D. Intriligator and D. A. Kendrick, North Holland.

Rawls, J. [1971], *A Theory of Justice*, Oxford.

Richter, M. K. [1966], "Revealed Preference Theory," *Econometrica* 34:635–45.

Robbins, L. [1932], *An Essay on the Nature and Significance of Economic Science*, Macmillan.

Robinson, J. [1933], *The Economics of Imperfect Competition*, Macmillan.

Rockafellar, R. T. [1970], *The Theory of Convex Structures*, Princeton University Press.

Roy, R. [1942], *De l'Utilite, Contribution à la Théorie des Choix*, Hermann.

Samuelson, P. A. [1938], "A Note on the Pure Theory of Consumer's Behavior," *Economica* 5:353–54.

———. [1947a], *Foundations of Economic Analysis*, Harvard University Press.

———. [1947b], "Some Implications of Linearity," *Review of Economic Studies* 15:88–90.

———. [1948], "Consumption Theory in Terms of Revealed Preference," *Economica* 15:243–53.

———. [1950], "The Problem of Integrability in Utility Theory," *Economica* 17:355–85.

———. [1953a], "Consumption Theorems in Terms of Over-Compensation Rather than Indifference Comparisons," *Economica* 20:1–9.

———.[1953b], "Prices of Factors and Goods in General Equilibrium," *Review of Economic Studies* 21:1–20.

———. [1954], "The Pure Theory of Public Expenditures," *Review of Economics and Statistics* 36:387–89.

———. [1956], "Social Indifference Curves," *Quarterly Journal of Economics* 70:1–22.

———. [1963], "Discussion of Problems of Methodology," *American Economic Review* 53:231–36.

———. [1967], "Arrow's Mathematical Politics," in *Human Values and Economic Policy*, ed. S. Hook, New York University Press.

———. [1969], "Pure Theory of Public Expenditure and Taxation," in *Public Economics*, eds. J. Margolis and H. Guitton, Macmillan.

———. [1972], "Maximum Principles in Analytical Economics," *American Economic Review*, 62:249–62.

Sandmo, A. [1974], "Two-Period Models of Consumption Decisions Under Uncertainty: A Survey," in *Allocation Under Uncertainty: Equilibrium and Optimality*, ed. J. H. Drèze, Macmillan.

Satterthwaite, M. A. [1975], "Strategy-Proofness and Arrow's Conditions," *Journal of Economic Theory* 10:187–217.

Scarf, H. [1962], "An Analysis of Markets with a Large Number of Participants," in *Recent Advances in Game Theory*, Princeton University Press.

Scherer, F. M. [1973], *Industrial Market Structure and Economic Performance*, Rand McNally.

Schmeidler, D., and K. Vind [1972], "Fair Net Trades," *Econometrica* 40:637–42.

Sen, A. K. [1969], "Quasi-Transitivity, Rational Choice and Collective Decisions," *Review of Economic Studies* 36:381–93.

———. [1970a], *Collective Choice and Social Welfare*, Holden-Day.

———. [1970b], "The Impossibility of a Paretian Liberal," *Journal of Political Economy* 78:152–57.

———. [1970c], "Interpersonal Aggregation and Partial Comparability," *Econometrica* 38:393–409.

———. [1973], *On Income Inequality*, Clarendon Press and Norton.

———. [1975], "Welfare Theory," in the *Encyclopedic Handbook of the Mathematical Economic Sciences*, forthcoming.

———. [1976], "Poverty: An Ordinal Approach to Measurement," *Econometrica* 44:219–33.

———. [1977a], "On Weights and Measures: Informational Constraints in Social Welfare Analysis," *Econometrica* 45:1539–72.

———. [1977b], "Social Choice Theory: A Reexamination," *Econometrica* 45:53–90.

Shapley, L. S., and M. Shubik [1969], "On the Core of an Economic System with Externalities," *American Economic Review* 59:678–84.

Shephard, R. W. [1953], *Cost and Production Functions*, Princeton University Press.

———. [1970], *Theory of Cost and Production Functions*, Princeton University Press.

Shubik, M. [1959a], *Strategy and Market Structure*, Wiley.

———. [1959b], "Edgeworth Market Games," in *Contributions to the Theory of Games*, IV, eds. A. W. Tucker and R. D. Luce, Princeton University Press.

Simon, H. [1959], "Theories of Decision Making in Economics and Behavioral Sciences," *American Economic Review* 49:253–83.

Slutsky, E. [1915], "Sulla teoria del bilancio del consumatore," *Giornale degli Economisti e Rivista di Statistica* 51:1–26. English translation: "On the Theory of the Budget of the Consumer," in *Readings in Price Theory*, eds. G. J. Stigler and K. E. Boulding, Richard D. Irwin, pp. 27–56.

Smith, V. L. [1968], "Economics of Production from Natural Resources," *American Economic Review* 58:409–31.

———. [1969], "On Models of Commercial Fishing," *The Journal of Political Economy* 77:181–98.

Sono, M. [1945], "The Effect of Price Changes on the Demand and Supply of Separable Goods," (in Japanese) *Kokumin Keisai Zasshi* 74:1–51.

———. [1961], "The Effects of Price Changes on the Demand and Supply of Separable Goods," *International Economic Review* 2:239–71.

Spence, A. M. [1976], "Product Selection, Fixed Costs, and Monopolistic Competition," *Review of Economic Studies* 43:217–35.

Starr, R. M. [1969], "Quasi-Equilibria in Markets with Non-Convex Preferences," *Econometrica* 37:25–38.

Starrett, D. [1972], "Fundamental Nonconvexities in the Theory of Externalities," *Journal of Economic Theory* 4:180–99.

Stigler, G. J. [1963], "Archibald Versus Chicago," *Review of Economic Studies* 30:63–64.

Stone, R. [1954], "Linear Expenditure Systems and Demand Analysis: An Application to the Pattern of British Demand," *The Economic Journal* 64: 511–27.

Strotz, R. H. [1955], "Myopia and Inconsistency in Dynamic Utility Maximization," *Review of Economic Studies* 23:165–80.

———. [1957], "The Empirical Implications of a Utility Tree," *Econometrica* 25:269–80.

Suppes, P. [1966], "Some Formal Models of Grading Principles," *Synthese* 6:284–306 (reprinted in P. Suppes, *Studies in the Methodology and Foundations of Science*, Reidel).

Taubman, P., and M. Wilkinson [1970a], "User Cost, Capital Utilization and Investment Theory," *International Economic Review* 11:209–15.

———. [1970b], "User Cost, Output, and Unexpected Price Changes," in *Microeconomic Foundations of Employment and Inflation Theory*, ed. E. S. Phelps, Norton.

Taylor, A. E., and W. R. Mann [1972], *Advanced Calculus*, Wiley.

Theil, H. [1975–76], *Theory and Measurement of Consumer Demand*, I & II, North Holland.

Tobin, J. [1958], "Liquidity Preference as Behavior Toward Risk," *Review of Economic Studies*, 25:65–86.

Uzawa, H. [1960], "Preference and Rational Choice in the Theory of Consumption," in *Mathematical Methods in the Social Sciences*, eds. K. J. Arrow, S. Karlin, and P. Suppes, Stanford University Press, pp. 129–48.

———. [1962], "Production Functions with Constant Elasticities of Substitution" *Review of Economic Studies* 29:291–99.

———. [1964], "Duality Principles in the Theory of Cost and Production," *International Economic Review* 5:216–20.

Varian, H. [1974], "Equity, Envy, and Efficiency," *Journal of Economic Theory* 9:63–91.

Vickrey, W. [1961], "Counterspeculations, Auctions, and Competitive Sealed Tenders," *Journal of Finance* 16:8–37.

Vining, R. [1949], "Koopmans on the Choice of Variables to be Studied and of Methods of Measurement," *Review of Economics and Statistics* 31:77–94.

von Neumann, J., and O. Morgenstern [1944], *Theory of Games and Economic Behavior*, Princeton University Press.

von Stackelberg, H. [1934], *Marktform und Gleichgewicht*.

Wales, T. W. [1972], "A Generalized Linear Expenditure Model of Demand for Nondurable Goods in Canada," *Canadian Journal of Economics* 4:471–84.

Walras, L. [1874, 1877], *Elements d'Economie Politique Pure*, L. Corbaz. English translation by William Jaffe [1954], *Elements of Pure Economics* Allen and Unwin.

Ward, B. [1958], "The Firm in Illyria: Market Syndicalism," *American Economic Review* 48: 566–589.

Weatherby, J. L., Jr. [1976], "Why Was It Called An Edgeworth-Bowley Box: A Possible Explanation," *Economic Inquiry* 14:294–96.

Wicksell, K. [1934], *Lectures on Political Economy*, vol. 1, Routledge and Kegan Paul.

Williamson, O. E. [1964], *The Economics of Discretionary Behavior: Managerial Objectives in a Theory of the Firm*, Prentice-Hall.

Willig, R. [1977], "Consumer Surplus Without Apology," *American Economic Review* 66:589–97.

Winter, S. G. [1969], "A Simple Remark on the Second Optimality Theorem of Welfare Economics," *Journal of Economic Theory* 1:99–103.

Wold, H. [1943–44], "A Synthesis of Pure Demand Analysis I–III," *Skandinavisk Aktuarietidskrift* 26:85–118, 220–263; 27:69–120.

Wold, H., in association with L. Jureen [1953], *Demand Analysis*, Wiley.

Yaari, M. [1971], *Linear Algebra for Social Scientists*, Prentice-Hall.

INDEX

Activity analysis, 183
Acyclicity, 25, 414
Anonymity and collective rationality, 417
Arbitrage, choice of numeraire, 317
Arrow exceptional case, 367n
Arrow's impossibility theorem, 409
  proof of, 411
Arrow social welfare function, 403, 421
Asymmetry, of preference relation, 14
Average-cost curve, 166
  with fixed inputs, 172
Average-product curve, 147
  for linear production technology, 189

Bilateral exchange, assumptions, 306
  and contract curve, 311
  graphical exposition, 310
  and offer curve, 313
Borda rule, 407
Budget constraint, 15
Budget set, 15

Capital theory, 213
Chain or composite function rule, 37n
Cobb-Douglas function, 138, 213
Cobwebb model, 245
Cofactor, 89n
Collective rationality, 413
Collegial polity, 415
Collusion, 289
Commodity, complements, gross and net, 93
  contingent, 398
  defined, 7
  excludability, 374
  Giffen, 64
  inferior, 61
  intermediate, 215
  luxury, 61
  nonrival, 373
  normal, 61
  primary, 215
  private and public, 374, 441
  produced consumer, 215
  rival, 373
  substitutes, gross and net, 93
Commodity bundle, 12
Comparative statics, of consumer, 86
  method, 232
  of producer, 134
Compensation principle, 357
Competitive equilibrium, 315, 324, 440
  and core, 342, 441
  existence, uniqueness, and stability, 347, 440
  graphical illustration, 329, 333
  optimality of, 363, 440
  and uncertainty, 397, 442
Complementarity, dominance of, in substitution, 94
Composite commodity theorem, 55
Cones, 185
Consistency of preferences, 14
Constant-elasticity-of-substitution production function, 158, 213
Constrained outlay minimization and the cost function, 159
Consumer, defined, 7
Consumer choice, defined, 17
Consumer surplus, 118
Consumption box diagram, 310
Consumption-characteristics model, 118
Consumption space, defined, 12
Contingent commodity, 398
Contract curve, 311
Convexity, and competitive equilibrium, 370
  and decentralization of Pareto optimal states, 365
  and economic externalities, 382
  of preferences, 30
  of technology sets, 131
Core, 297
  and competitive equilibrium, 342, 441
Correspondence principle, 235n, 245n
Cost function, 161
  with fixed inputs, 172
Cost-of-living indices, 84
  Laspeyres, 116
  Paasche, 116
  revealed preference theory, 113, 116
Cournot duopoly model, 302, 380
Cournot's assumption, 281
Cournot equilibrium, 281
  generalization to oligopoly market, 283
Cramer's rule, 89n

Decentralization, of Pareto optimal states, 365, 441
relaxing convexity, 367
Decentralized planning, 395, 441
Decreasing cost industry, 229
Demand, functions, 52
law of, 69
theory of, 51
Demand systems, addilog, 118
empirical, 117
generalized leontief, 118
linear expenditure, 117
translog, 118
Determinant of matrix, 89n
Dictatorship and social choice, 409
weak dictator, 414
Difference equations, 235
Differentiability of utility function, 33
Differential equations, 235
Dipsomaniac, 19
Divisibility of commodities, 213
and optimality of competitive equilibrium, 364, 440
Duality, 73
and consumer theory, 74
and producer theory, 134n, 159
and linear programming, 196
Dual linear program, 196
graphical illustration, 197
Duopoly, 302, 380
Dynamic analysis, 234

Economic environment, 6
Economic externalities and Pareto optimality, 375, 441
Economic regulation, 302
Economics, defined, 1
normative and positve, 1
Economic theory, defined, 2
evaluation and testing of, 5
role of, 3
structure of, 4
Elasticity of demand, 96
income, 97
luxury and necessity, defined, 98
normal and inferior commodities, 97
own- and cross-price, 97
Elasticity of substitution, 144, 213
Engel curve, 62
Equal-outlay line, 162
Equity, 442
Exchange rates, 307
Existence of competitive equilibrium, 347, 440
Expansion path, 162
Expected utility maximization, 214
Expenditure function, 81
Extended Pareto criterion, 413
Externality, private and public, 374, 441
consumption, 379
nonconvexities, 382
production, 375
property rights, 379
small number of buyers and sellers, 385
taxes and subsidies, 385
transaction costs, 384

Feasible process, 185
Financial markets, 214
First-order conditions for interior solutions to optimization problem, 36
Flexible functional forms for demand and production, 118
generalized Leontief, 118
quadratic mean of order *r*, 118
translog, 118
Free-rider problem, 396, 442
Functions, 27
Fundamental linear-programming duality theorem, 199
Fundamental optimality principles, 353, 441
in production economy, 361

Game theory, 291, 302
General competitive equilibrium, 328, 440
General exchange equilibrium, 317. 440
Giffen paradox, 64
Gorman's theorem, 134n

Homethetic function, 188
Homogeneity, of demand function, 54
of function, 53
of production function, 167
Homogeneous production functions, 167
Hotelling's theorem, 81
Household production, 118

Income-consumption curve, 61
Income effect, 59, 66
mathematical analysis of, 86
Increasing cost industry, 229
Impossibility theorem, 409
proof of, 411
Incentive compatibility, 396, 442
Independence-of-irrelevant-alternatives

condition of social choice, 407, 423
Indifference curves, 21
convexity, 30
indirect, 75
and marginal rate of substitution, 33
Indifference relation, 13
Industrial organization, 302
Input demand functions, 153
of monopolist, 260
Intertemporal theory, consumer, 118
producer, 213
Investment, 214
Isoquants, 141
for linear production technology, 186
strict convexity of, 142
Iso-revenue curve, 194

Labor supply, 101
Lagrange, method of, 41
Law of diminishing marginal rate of substitution, 36
Law of diminishing rate of technological substitution, 144
Law of variable proportions, 147
Liberalism, 420
Lindahl equilibrium, 393
Linear expenditure system, 117
Linear production technologies, 185, 213
Linear programming, 193
example of problem, 203

Macroeconomics, 1
Majority rule, simple, 418
Marginal-cost curve, 166
Marginal product, 141
Marginal-product curve, 147
for linear production technology, 189
Marginal rate of substitution, 32
defined, 33
relation to marginal utilities, 34
Marginal revenue, 255
Marginal revenue product, 261
Marginal social welfare, 433
Marginal utility, 33
Market, defined, 215
demand function, 219
equilibrium, long-run, 225
short-run, 219, 224
stabilization board, 249
supply function, 220, 255
Marshall's disequilibrium hypothesis, 242
graphical illustration, 244
stability property, 244
Matrix, 88n
Maximum principles, 4
Measurability of utility, 45
ordinal and cardinal, 48
Microeconomics, 2
Monopolistic competition, 272, 302
comparison with perfect competition, 274
criticisms of, 275
large-group equilibrium, 272
Monopoly, 251
assumptions, 253
demand curve, 254
equilibrium, 256
input demand, 260
and Pareto optimality, 356
regulation, 265, 302
revenue function, 255
sources of, 252
supply function, 277
Monopsony, 262
input supply functions, 262
marginal input cost, 263

Nash equilibrium, 297, 302
Net production function, 130
differentiability of, 131
Net supply functions, of producer, 134
Nonclassical firm, 214
bounded rationality, 214
corporate goals, 214
Nonimposition condition of social choice, 406
Nonlinear programming, 213
Nonnegative-responsiveness condition of social choice, 406
Nonsatiation, 29
global and local, 50

Offer curve, 313
Oligopoly, 279
stability of, 302
Optimal consumption bundle, 17
existence of, 18
Orderings, 15

Pareto criterion, 351, 352
extended, 413
strong, 418
weak, 406
Pareto optimality, 352, 441
and externalities, 375
of general competitive equilibrium, 363
and monopoly
in production economy, 358

and pseudoequilibrium, 394
and uncertainty, 397
Partial-equilibrium, 216
Path-independence concept, 415
Perfect-competition assumptions, 217
Perfect information, 218
Personalized prices for public commodities, 390, 441
Portfolio choice, 119
Postulate, 4
Preference relation, 13
representation of, 26
Preference theory, 11
Price, 7
normalized, 74
Price adjustment model, 237
Price discrimination, 268
conditions for, 269
relation of ordinary monopoly price to price discrimination, 271
relation of prices in separate markets, 270
revenue function and profit maximization, 270
Price effect, 62
Price leadership, 287
Private commodity, 374
Producer, 7, 123
Production box diagram, 333
Production bundle, 124
Production function, single-output, 140
Production-possibility curve, 335
properties of, 336
Profit, 125
Profit function, 134n
Profit maximization, 125, 151
and cost function, 169
dynamic or intertemporal, 213
with fixed inputs, 177
graphical illustration, 153, 170
Property rights and economic externalities, 379, 441
Pseudoeconomy with personalized prices, 390
Pareto optimality of, 394
Public commodity, defined, 374
and Pareto optimality, 387
and personalized prices, 390
theory of, 387, 441

Quantity-adjustment model, 242
Quantity leadership, 283
Quasiorderings, 424, 430
Quasitransitivity, 413

Rate of commodity transformation, 132
relation to first-order conditions for profit maximization, 133
Rate-of-return regulation, 302
Rate of technological substitution, 143
Reaction function, 281
Regularity of consumer preferences, 20
Regulation, of monopoly, 265, 302
input price, 267
output price, 265
rate-of-return, 268n, 302
Relations, mathematical, 15
Returns to outlay, 164
Revealed preference, 108
applications, 113
homogeneity of in income and price, 110
negativity of compensated price effect, 111
overcompensation, 111n
strong axiom, 113
theory of, 108
weak axiom, 109
Roy's theorem, 80

Safety-first criterion, 214
Scarcity, 1
Second fundamental optimality principle, 354
and convexity, 365, 441
Second-order conditions for constrained optimization, 45, 87
Separability, 117
Separating line, 367
hyperplane, 367n
Single-peaked preferences, 442
Slutsky equation, 92
Social-choice function, 402
transitivity of, 404
Social-choice theory, 401, 442
Social-indifference curve, 427
Social optimality, 432
graphical illustration, 434
Social orderings, 424
Social-preference ordering, 403
Social states, 402
Social-welfare function, 403, 442
Arrow, 403
Bergsan-Samuelson, 424
Rawls, 427
utilitarian, 426
Social welfare functional, 422
Stability, 237
of competitive equilibrium, 347, 440

defined, 237
of first and second kind, 237n
global, 237
local, 237
Stackelberg disequilibrium, 287
Stackelberg indifference curves, 285
Strategy proofness, 442
Strict convexity, of preferences, 30
Substitution and complements, in consumption, 93
in production, 137
Substitution effect, in consumption, 67
Supply function of producer, 170
with fixed inputs, 178

Taylor's-series approximation, 250
Technological efficiency, 129, 141
Technology set, 124
boundedness and regularity of, 131
strict convexity of, 131
Time period, 6
Total-cost curve, 164
Total-product curve, 145
for linear production technology, 189
Transactions costs, 218
and economic externalities, 384, 441
Transformations, mathematical, 46
affine, 48
linear, 48
strictly monotone, 46
Transitivity, 14
of preference relation, 14
of social choice, 404

Two-person constant-sum games, 292
Two-person nonconstant-sum games, 292

Uncertainty, 118
consumer theory, 118
and Pareto optimality of competitive equilibrium, 397, 442
producer behavior, 214
Uniqueness of competitive equilibrium, 347, 440
Utility function, 26
indirect, 74
Utility maximization, 36
Utility-possibility curve, 435
Uncertainty, producer behavior, 214
Unrestricted-domain condition of social choice, 403, 423

Value of marginal product, 153

Walras's disequilibrium hypothesis, 237
defined, 237
graphical illustration, 240
stability property, 238
Walras's law, 309
in exchange economy, 319
in production-and-exchange economy, 326
Weak dictator, 414
Weak Pareto criterion, 406
Welfare, measurability and interpersonal comparability, 421